Rick Steves'

AMSTERDAM

RUGES & BRUSSELS

D0054536

ISBN 978-1-61238-543-3   US $21.99

Rick Steves'

AMSTERDAM
BRUGES & BRUSSELS

Rick Steves & Gene Openshaw

CONTENTS

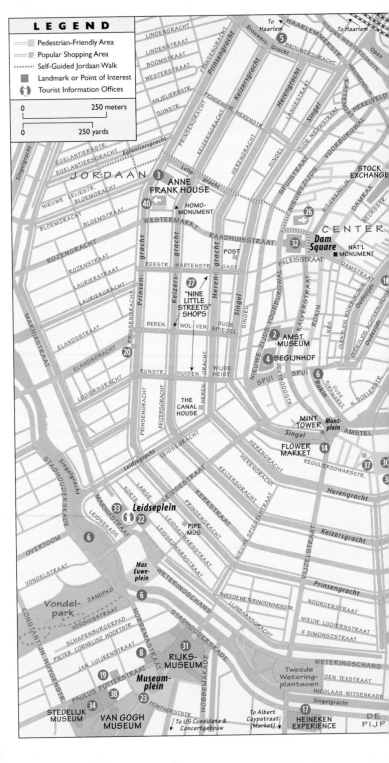

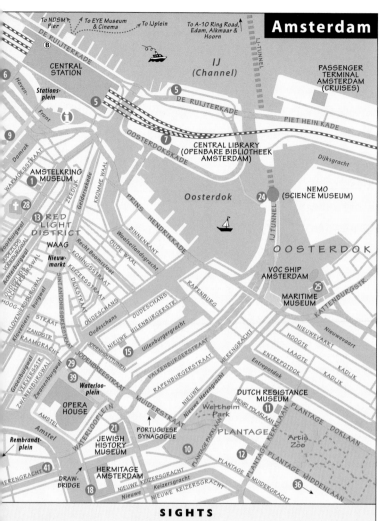

Amsterdam

Labels on map:

To NDSM Pier
To EYE Museum & Cinema
To IJplein
To A-10 Ring Road, Edam, Alkmaar & Hoorn

DE RUIJTERKADE
(B)
CENTRAL STATION
Stationsplein
Haven
Front
IJ (Channel)
PASSENGER TERMINAL AMSTERDAM (CRUISES)
DE RUIJTERKADE
PIET HEIN KADE
IJ TUNNEL
OOSTERDOKSKADE
CENTRAL LIBRARY (OPENBARE BIBLIOTHEEK AMSTERDAM)
Damrak
WARMOESSTRAAT
AMSTELKRING MUSEUM
ZEEDIJK
GELDERSEKADE
KROMME WAAL
PRINS HENDRIKKADE
Oosterdok
Dijksgracht
NEMO (SCIENCE MUSEUM)
RED LIGHT DISTRICT
WAAG
Nieuwmarkt
BINNENKANT
Waalseilandgracht
RECHT BOOMSSLOOT
OUDE WAAL
KONINGSSTRAAT
KEIZERSSTRAAT
DIJKSTRAAT
SINT ANTONIESBREESTRAAT
RAPENBURG
OOSTERDOK
VOC SHIP AMSTERDAM
MARITIME MUSEUM
KATTENBURGSTR.
Voorburgwal
JUDZDS
Achterburgwal
OUDEZIJDS ACHTERBURGWAL
OUDEZIJDS VOORBURGWAL
HOOG-
burgwal
KLOVENIERS-burgwal
STRAAT
Klovenier.
ZANDSTR.
RAAMGRACHT
Oudeschans
NIEUWE UILENBURGERSTR.
Uilenburgergracht
HERENGRACHT
NIEUWEVAART
Nieuwevaart
HOOGTE
LAAGTE
ENTREPOTDOK
KADIJK
KADIJK
Entrepotdok
Groenburgwal
VERVERSSTR.
ZWANENBURGWAL
Zwanenburgwal
JODENBREESTRAAT
JODENHOUTTUINEN
VALKENBURGERSTRAAT
RAPENBURGERSTRAAT
NIEUWE
Nieuwe Herengracht
HERENGRACHT
DUTCH RESISTANCE MUSEUM
HENRI POLAKLAAN
PLANTAGE
DOKLAAN
REMBRANDT'S HOUSE
Waterlooplein
OPERA HOUSE
AMSTEL
WATERLOOPLEIN
JEWISH HISTORY MUSEUM
MUIDERSTRAAT
PORTUGUESE SYNAGOGUE
Wertheim Park
PLANTAGE PARKLAAN
PLANTAGE
PLANTAGE KERKLAAN
Artis Zoo
PLANTAGE MIDDENLAAN
PLANTAGE MUIDERGRACHT
Rembrandtplein
HERMITAGE AMSTERDAM
HERENGRACHT
DRAWBRIDGE
NIEUWE KEIZERSGRACHT
Nieuwe KEIZERSGRACHT
NIEUWE KEIZERSGRACHT
Rembrandtplein
IJ TUNNEL

SIGHTS

1. Amstelkring Museum
2. Amsterdam Museum
3. Anne Frank House
4. Begijnhof
5. Bike Rentals (3)
6. Canal-Boat Tours (4)
7. Central Library
8. Coster Diamonds & Mus.
9. Damrak Sex Museum
10. De Hortus Botanical Garden
11. Dutch Resistance Museum
12. Dutch Theater Memorial
13. Erotic Museum
14. Flower Market
15. Gassan Diamonds
16. Hash, Marijuana & Hemp Museum
17. Heineken Experience
18. Hermitage Amsterdam
19. House of Bols
20. Houseboat Museum
21. Jewish Hist. Museum
22. Leidseplein
23. Museumplein
24. NEMO (Science Museum)
25. Netherlands Maritime Museum
26. New Church
27. "Nine Little Streets" Shopping District
28. Old Church
29. Rembrandt's House
30. Rembrandtplein
31. Rijksmuseum
32. Royal Palace
33. Stadsschouwburg Theater
34. Stedelijk Museum
35. Tassen Museum
36. To Tropical Museum
37. Tuschinski Theater
38. Van Gogh Museum
39. Waterlooplein Flea Market
40. Westerkerk
41. Willet-Holthuysen Mus.

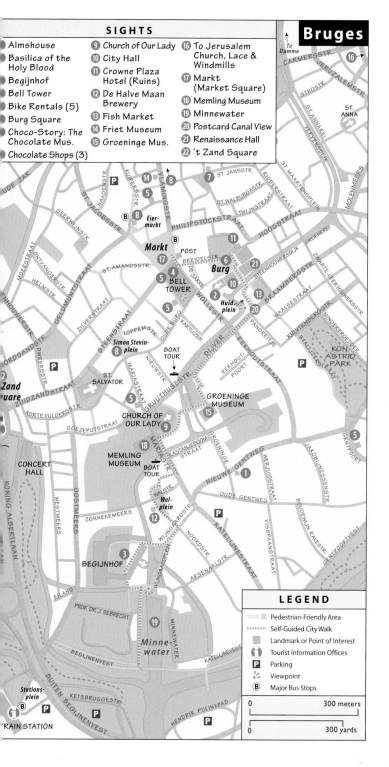

SIGHTS

Bruges

- Almshouse
- Basilica of the Holy Blood
- Begijnhof
- Bell Tower
- Bike Rentals (5)
- Burg Square
- Choco-Story: The Chocolate Mus.
- Chocolate Shops (3)
- ⑨ Church of Our Lady
- ⑩ City Hall
- ⑪ Crowne Plaza Hotel (Ruins)
- ⑫ De Halve Maan Brewery
- ⑬ Fish Market
- ⑭ Friet Museum
- ⑮ Groeninge Mus.
- ⑯ To Jerusalem Church, Lace & Windmills
- ⑰ Markt (Market Square)
- ⑱ Memling Museum
- ⑲ Minnewater
- ⑳ Postcard Canal View
- ㉑ Renaissance Hall
- ㉒ 't Zand Square

LEGEND

- ▬▬ Pedestrian-Friendly Area
- ••••••• Self-Guided City Walk
- ▬ Landmark or Point of Interest
- 👫 Tourist Information Offices
- 🅿 Parking
- 👟 Viewpoint
- Ⓑ Major Bus Stops

| 0 | 300 meters |
| 0 | 300 yards |

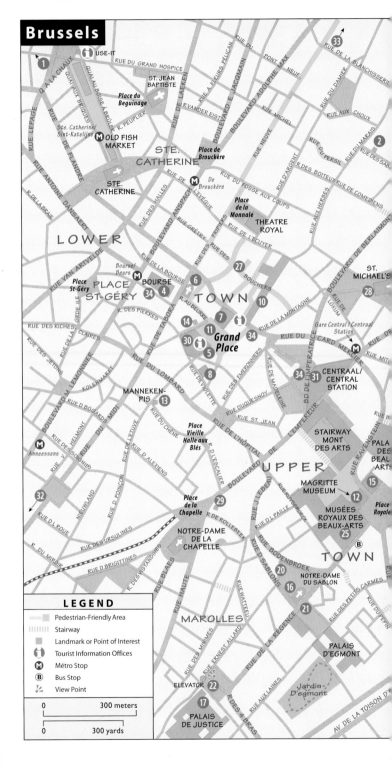

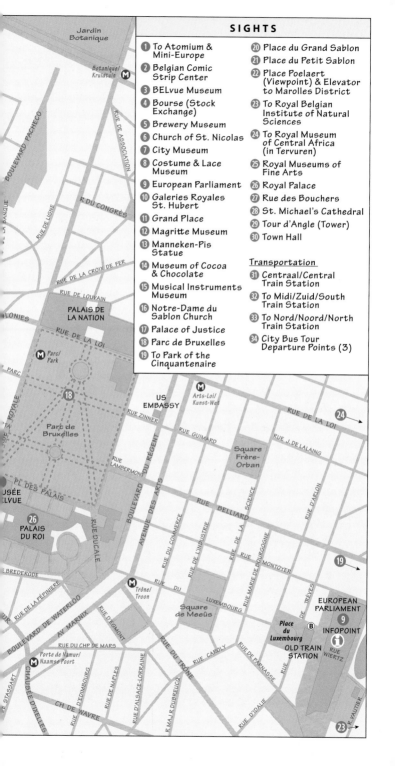

SIGHTS

1 To Atomium & Mini-Europe
2 Belgian Comic Strip Center
3 BELvue Museum
4 Bourse (Stock Exchange)
5 Brewery Museum
6 Church of St. Nicolas
7 City Museum
8 Costume & Lace Museum
9 European Parliament
10 Galeries Royales St. Hubert
11 Grand Place
12 Magritte Museum
13 Manneken-Pis Statue
14 Museum of Cocoa & Chocolate
15 Musical Instruments Museum
16 Notre-Dame du Sablon Church
17 Palace of Justice
18 Parc de Bruxelles
19 To Park of the Cinquantenaire
20 Place du Grand Sablon
21 Place du Petit Sablon
22 Place Poelaert (Viewpoint) & Elevator to Marolles District
23 To Royal Belgian Institute of Natural Sciences
24 To Royal Museum of Central Africa (in Tervuren)
25 Royal Museums of Fine Arts
26 Royal Palace
27 Rue des Bouchers
28 St. Michael's Cathedral
29 Tour d'Angle (Tower)
30 Town Hall

Transportation

31 Centraal/Central Train Station
32 To Midi/Zuid/South Train Station
33 To Nord/Noord/North Train Station
34 City Bus Tour Departure Points (3)

Belgium

Bruges

An Amsterdam canal

Guildhalls on the Grand Place, Brussels

Wooden clogs

A Bruges canal

Rick Steves'

AMSTERDAM
BRUGES & BRUSSELS

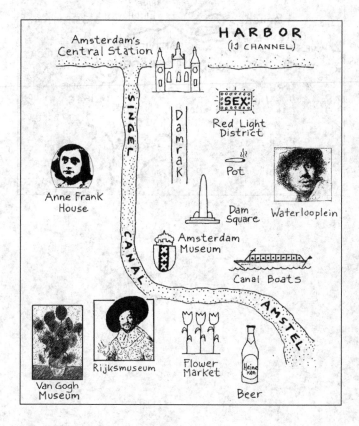

AVALON
TRAVEL

INTRODUCTION

Amsterdam, Bruges, and Brussels—the three greatest cities of the Low Countries—are a delight to experience. Rattling on your bike over the cobbles, savoring fresh pralines, lingering in flower-carpeted squares, you'll find a slow-down-and-smell-the-tulips world that enchants. Any time of year, you can enjoy the intimate charms of these cities.

Amsterdam is called "the Venice of the North," both for its canals and for its past position as an economic powerhouse. Bruges—once mighty, now mighty cute—comes with fancy beers in fancy glasses, lilting carillons, and lacy Gothic souvenirs of a long-gone greatness. Brussels—the de facto capital of Europe, with a low-rise Parisian ambience—exudes a joie de vivre, from its famous cuisine to its love of chocolate and comic strips.

Belgium and the Netherlands are called the Low Countries because nearly half their land is below sea level. Surrounded by mega-Europe, the Low Countries are easy to overlook. But travel here is a snap, the area is steeped in history, and all the charming icons of the region—whirring windmills, Dutch Masters, dike hikes, one-speed bikes, and ladies tossing bobbins to make fine lace—line up for you to enjoy. If ever an area were a travel cliché come true, it's the Low Countries.

This book covers the predictable biggies in and around Amsterdam, Bruges, and Brussels—and mixes in a healthy dose of Back Door intimacy. In Amsterdam you can see Vincent van Gogh's *Sunflowers*...and climb through Captain Vincent's tiny houseboat museum. You'll tour Brussels' ultramodern European Parliament and enjoy a Michelangelo statue in small-town Bruges. Beyond these three cities you'll discover the hidden charms of Haarlem, the funky, fashion-forward port of Antwerp, and the thriving urban scene of Ghent. And you'll meet intriguing people who will show you how to swallow pickled herring, paddle you in a canoe through the *polderland* to a stuck-in-the-mud (and stuck-in-the-past) village, and pop a taste of the latest chocolate into your mouth.

This book is selective, including only the top sights. The best is, of course, only my opinion. But after spending more than half of my adult life exploring and researching Europe, I've developed a sixth sense for what travelers enjoy.

About This Book

Rick Steves' Amsterdam, Bruges & Brussels is a personal tour guide in your pocket. Better yet, it's actually two tour guides in your pocket: The co-author of this book is Gene Openshaw. Since our first "Europe through the gutter" trip together as high-school buddies in the 1970s, Gene and I have been exploring the wonders of the Old World. An inquisitive historian and lover of European culture, Gene wrote most of this book's self-guided museum tours and neighborhood walks. Together, Gene and I keep this book up-to-date and accurate (though for simplicity, from this point "we" will shed our respective egos and become "I").

This book is organized by destination. Each recommended destination is a mini-vacation on its own, filled with exciting sights, strollable neighborhoods, affordable places to stay, and memorable places to eat.

You'll find the following sections in this book:

Orientation includes specifics on public transportation, helpful hints, local tour options, tourist information, and easy-to-read maps. "Planning Your Time" sections suggest schedules for how to best use your limited time.

Sights describes the top attractions and includes their cost and hours.

Self-Guided Walks and **Tours** take you through interesting neighborhoods and must-see sights. In Amsterdam, these include the Rijksmuseum, Van Gogh Museum, Anne Frank House, a city walk, the Jordaan neighborhood, the Red Light District, and more. In nearby Haarlem, tour the Grote Kerk and the Frans Hals Museum. In Bruges you'll find a city walk and tours of the Groeninge and Memling museums, and in Brussels, take a Grand Place walk, an Upper Town walk, and a tour of the Royal Museums of Fine Arts and the Magritte Museum.

Sleeping describes my favorite hotels, from good-value deals to cushy splurges.

Eating serves up a range of options, from inexpensive cafés to fancy restaurants.

Smoking covers Amsterdam's best "coffeeshops," which openly sell marijuana.

Key to This Book

Updates

This book is updated regularly, but things change. For the latest, visit www.ricksteves.com/update. For a valuable list of reports and experiences—good and bad—from fellow travelers, check www.ricksteves.com/feedback.

Abbreviations and Times

I use the following symbols and abbreviations in this book:

Sights are rated:

▲▲▲	**Don't miss**
▲▲	**Try hard to see**
▲	**Worthwhile if you can make it**
No rating	**Worth knowing about**

Tourist information offices are abbreviated as **TI,** and bathrooms are **WCs.** To categorize accommodations, I use a **Sleep Code** (described on page 17).

Like Europe, this book uses the **24-hour clock** for schedules. It's the same through 12:00 noon, then keep going: 13:00, 14:00, and so on. For anything over 12, subtract 12 and add p.m. (14:00 is 2:00 p.m.).

When giving **opening times,** I include both peak season and off-season hours if they differ. So, if a museum is listed as "May-Oct daily 9:00-16:00," it should be open from 9 a.m. until 4 p.m. from the first day of May until the last day of October (but expect exceptions).

If you see a ☉ symbol near a sight listing, it means that sight is described in far greater detail elsewhere—either with its own self-guided tour, or as part of a self-guided walk.

For **transit** or **tour departures,** I first list the frequency, then the duration. So a train connection listed as "2/hour, 1.5 hours" departs twice each hour, and the journey lasts an hour and a half.

Shopping gives you tips for shopping painlessly and enjoyably, without letting it overwhelm your vacation or ruin your budget.

Nightlife is your guide to evening fun, including music, comedy, movies, and other things to do after dark.

Chapters in the **Dutch Day Trips** section cover **Delft and The Hague, Near Arnhem,** and small towns and destinations (such as Dutch open-air folk museums) in the Netherlands. In addition to Bruges and Brussels, you'll find chapters on the major Belgian destinations of **Antwerp, Ghent,** and WWI sites at **Flanders Fields.**

Connections lays the groundwork for your smooth arrival and departure, covering transportation by train, bus, plane, and cruise ship (with detailed information on major airports).

The **History** chapter gives you a quick overview of Dutch and

Belgian history and a timeline of major events.

The **appendix** is a traveler's tool kit, with telephone tips, useful phone numbers, transportation basics (on trains, buses, car rentals, driving, and flights), recommended books and films, a festival list, climate chart, handy packing checklist, a hotel reservation form, and Dutch and French survival phrases.

Browse through this book and choose your favorite destinations, and link them up. Then have a *prachtig* trip! Traveling like a temporary local, you'll enjoy the absolute most out of every mile, minute, and dollar. As you visit places I know and love, I'm happy that you'll be meeting some of my favorite Dutch and Belgian people.

Planning

This section will help you get started on planning your trip—with advice on trip costs, when to go, and what you should know before you take off.

Travel Smart

Your trip to the Netherlands and Belgium is like a complex play—easier to follow and really appreciate on a second viewing. While no one does the same trip twice to gain that advantage, reading this book before your trip accomplishes much the same thing.

Design an itinerary that enables you to visit the various sights at the best possible times. Note festivals, holidays, specifics on sights, and days when sights are closed or most crowded (all covered in this book). For example, nearly all museums in Bruges are closed on Mondays. To get between destinations smoothly, read the tips in this book's appendix on taking trains and buses, and renting a car and driving. A smart trip is a puzzle—a fun, doable, and worthwhile challenge.

Be sure to mix intense and relaxed periods in your itinerary. To maximize rootedness, minimize one-night stands. It's worth taking a long drive after dinner (or a train ride with a dinner picnic) to get settled into a town for two nights. Every trip (and every traveler) needs slack time (picnics, laundry, people-watching, and so on). Pace yourself. Assume you will return.

Reread this book as you travel, and visit local tourist information offices (abbreviated as TI in this book). Upon arrival in a new town, lay the groundwork for a smooth departure; note the schedule for the train or bus that you'll take when you depart. Drivers can study the best route to their next destination.

Get online at Internet cafés or your hotel, and carry a mobile phone (or use a phone card) to make travel plans: You can find tourist information, learn the latest on sights (special events, tour schedule, etc.), book tickets and tours, make reservations, reconfirm hotels, research transportation connections, and keep in touch with your loved ones.

Enjoy the friendliness of the Dutch and Belgian people. Connect with the culture. Set up your own quest to find the best salted herring or canal boat ride. Slow down and be open to unexpected experiences. Ask questions—most locals are eager to point you in their idea of the right direction. Keep a notepad in your pocket for organizing your thoughts and confirming prices. Wear your money belt, learn the currency, and figure out how to estimate prices in dollars. Those who expect to travel smart, do.

Trip Costs

Five components make up your trip costs: airfare, surface transportation, room and board, sightseeing and entertainment, and shopping and miscellany.

Airfare: A basic, round-trip, US-to-Amsterdam flight can cost, on average, about $1,000-1,800 total, depending on where you fly from and when (cheaper in winter). You can often save time in Europe by flying into one city and out of another; if you're sticking to the Low Countries, you're never more than about three hours from Amsterdam's or Brussels' international airports.

Surface Transportation: If you're just touring Amsterdam, Bruges, Brussels, and nearby day-trip destinations, you're best off enjoying the region's excellent and affordable train system. Trains leave at least hourly between each of the cities. It costs about $50 for a ticket from Amsterdam to Brussels or to Bruges. If you plan to venture farther afield, you may want a rental car. Driving in the Low Countries is flat-out easy (figure $900 per person—based on two people sharing—for a three-week car rental, gas, and insurance). Leasing is worth considering for trips of three weeks or more. Car rentals and leases are cheapest if arranged from the US. Train passes normally must be purchased outside Europe but aren't necessarily your best option—you may save money by simply buying tickets as you go. For more on public transportation and car rental, see "Transportation" in the appendix.

Room and Board: You can thrive in the Low Countries on $125 a day per person for room and board (less for Bruges and Brussels, more for Amsterdam). That allows $20 for lunch, $30 for dinner, and $70 for lodging (based on two people splitting the cost of a $140 double room that includes breakfast). That leaves you $5 for *friet*s and chocolate. To live and sleep more elegantly, I'd propose a budget of $145 per day per person ($20 for lunch, $40 for dinner, and $80 each for a $160 hotel double with breakfast). Students and tightwads eat and sleep for as little as $60 a day ($30 per bed, $30 for meals and snacks).

Sightseeing and Entertainment: In big cities, figure $15-20 per major sight (Rijks, Memling, and Van Gogh museums); $6-10 for minor ones (climbing church towers or windmills); $10-18 for guided walks, boat tours, and bike rentals; and $30-60 for splurge experiences such as concerts, special art exhibits, big-bus tours, and guided canoe trips. An overall average of $25 a day works for most people. Don't skimp here. After all, this category is the driving force behind your trip—you came to sightsee, enjoy, and experience the Low Countries.

Shopping and Miscellany: Figure $1-2 per postcard, tea, or ice-cream cone, and $5 per beer. Shopping can vary in cost from nearly nothing to a small fortune. Good budget travelers find that this category has little to do with assembling a trip full of lifelong and wonderful memories.

Sightseeing Priorities

With affordable flights from the US, minimal culture shock, almost no language barrier, and a well-organized tourist trade, the Low Countries are a good place to start a European trip. Depending on the length of your trip, and taking geographic proximity into account, these are my recommended priorities:

2 days:	Amsterdam, Haarlem
4 days, add:	Bruges, more time in Amsterdam
5 days, add:	Brussels
6-7 days, add:	Antwerp and slow down
8-9 days, add:	Delft/The Hague and Ghent
10-14 days, add:	More time in Amsterdam, plus side-trips from Amsterdam (e.g., Edam/Waterland, Arnhem, the Historic Triangle, Alkmaar, and more)

When to Go

Although Bruges and Amsterdam can be plagued by crowds, the long days, lively festivals, and sunny weather make summer a great time to visit. It's rarely too hot for comfort. Brussels' fancy business-class hotels are also deeply discounted in the summer.

Peak Season: Amsterdam is surprisingly crowded—and hotel prices can be correspondingly high—in late March, April, and May, when the tulip fields are flowering in full glory. Seasonal conferences can also drive up prices in September in Amsterdam. July and August have typical summer crowds.

Shoulder Season: Late spring and fall are pleasant, with generally mild weather and lighter crowds (except during holiday weekends—see page 626).

Winter Season: Travel from late October through mid-March is cold and wet in this region, as coastal winds whip through these low, flat countries. It's fine for visiting Amsterdam,

Bruges, Antwerp, and Brussels, but smaller towns and country-side sights feel dreary and lifeless. Some sights close for lunch, TIs keep shorter hours, and some tourist activities (like English-language windmill tours) vanish altogether.

Know Before You Go

Your trip is more likely to go smoothly if you plan ahead. Check this list of things to arrange while you're still at home.

You need a **passport,** but no visa or shots, to travel in the Netherlands and Belgium. You may be denied entry into certain European countries if your passport is due to expire within three to six months of your ticketed date of return. Get it renewed if you'll be cutting it close. It can take up to six weeks to get or renew a passport (for more on passports, see www.travel.state.gov). Pack a photocopy of your passport in your luggage in case the original is lost or stolen.

Book your rooms in advance if you'll be traveling during peak season (late March-May and Sept) or any major holidays (see page 626).

Call your **debit- and credit-card companies** to let them know the countries you'll be visiting, to ask about fees, request your PIN code (it will be mailed to you), and more. See page 11 for details.

Do your homework if you want to buy **travel insurance.** Compare the cost of the insurance to the likelihood of your using it and your potential loss if something goes wrong. Also, check whether your existing insurance (health, homeowners, or renters) covers you and your possessions overseas. For more tips, see www.ricksteves.com/insurance.

If you're planning on **renting a car** in the Low Countries, bring your driver's license. Confirm pickup hours—many car-rental offices close Saturday afternoon and all day Sunday.

The big three **museums** in Amsterdam—Rijks, Van Gogh, and Anne Frank—can come with long lines during high season. Consider buying tickets online from home (for details, see page 42).

If you plan to hire a **local guide,** reserve ahead by email. Popular guides can get booked up.

If you're bringing a **mobile device,** download any apps you might want to use on the road, such as translators, maps, and transit schedules. Check out **Rick Steves Audio Europe,** featuring audio tours of major sights, hours of travel interviews on the Netherlands and Belgium, and more (via www.ricksteves.com/audioeurope, iTunes, Google Play, or the Rick Steves Audio Europe smartphone app; for details, see page 624).

Check the **Rick Steves guidebook updates** page for any recent changes to this book (www.ricksteves.com/update).

Because **airline carry-on restrictions** are always changing, visit the Transportation Security Administration's website (www .tsa.gov) for an up-to-date list of what you can bring on the plane with you...and what you must check.

Practicalities

Emergency and Medical Help: Dial 112 for police or medical emergencies in both the Netherlands and Belgium. If you get sick, do as the Dutch and Belgians do and go to a pharmacist for advice. Or ask at your hotel for help—they'll know the nearest medical and emergency services.

Theft or Loss: To replace a passport, you'll need to go in person to an embassy (see page 612). If your credit and debit cards disappear, cancel and replace them (see "Damage Control for Lost Cards" on page 12). File a police report, either on the spot or within a day or two; you'll need it to submit an insurance claim for lost or stolen railpasses or travel gear, and it can help with replacing your passport or credit and debit cards. For more information, see www .ricksteves.com/help. Precautionary measures can minimize the effects of loss—back up your photos and other files frequently.

Time Zones: The Low Countries, like most of continental Europe, are generally six/nine hours ahead of the East/West Coasts of the US. The exceptions are the beginning and end of Daylight Saving Time: Europe "springs forward" the last Sunday in March (two weeks after most of North America) and "falls back" the last Sunday in October (one week before North America). For a handy online time converter, try www.timeand date.com/worldclock.

Business Hours: Most stores throughout the Low Countries are open from about 9:00 until 18:00-20:00 on weekdays, but close early on Saturday (generally between 12:00 and 17:00, depending on whether you're in a town or a big city). In the Netherlands, the first Sunday of every month is "shopping Sunday" *(koopzondag),* when many stores are open. Otherwise, Sundays in the Low Countries come with the same pros and cons as they do for travelers in the US (special events, limited hours, banks and many shops closed, limited public transportation, no rush hours). Popular destinations are even more crowded on weekends. Rowdy evenings are rare on Sundays. Many museums and sights are closed on Monday.

Watt's Up? Europe's electrical system is 220 volts, instead of North America's 110 volts. Most newer electronics (such as laptops, battery chargers, and hair dryers) convert automatically, so you won't need a converter, but you will need an adapter plug with two round prongs, sold inexpensively at travel stores in the US.

INTRODUCTION

Avoid bringing older appliances that don't automatically convert voltage; instead, buy a cheap replacement in Europe.

Discounts: Discounts aren't listed in this book. However, many sights offer discounts for children under 18, seniors, groups of 10 or more, families, and students or teachers with proper identification cards (www.isic.org). Always ask. Some discounts are available only for citizens of the European Union (EU).

Online Translation Tip: You can use Google's Chrome browser (available free at www.google.com/chrome) to instantly translate websites. The browser automatically detects if a webpage is in a foreign language and offers to translate it for you; with one click, you can see the site with a (very rough) English translation. (If you prefer using other browsers, you can also go to www.google .com/translate, then paste the URL of the site into the translation window.)

Money

This section offers advice on how to pay for purchases on your trip (including getting cash from ATMs and paying with plastic), dealing with lost or stolen cards, VAT (sales tax) refunds, and tipping.

What to Bring

Bring both a credit card and a debit card. You'll use the debit card at cash machines (ATMs) to withdraw euros for most purchases, and the credit card to pay for larger items. Some travelers carry a third card as a backup, in case one gets demagnetized or eaten by a temperamental machine.

For an emergency stash, bring several hundred dollars in hard cash in easy-to-exchange $20 bills. Avoid using currency exchange booths (because of their lousy rates and/or outrageous fees).

Cash

Cash is just as desirable in the Low Countries as it is at home. Small businesses (hotels, restaurants, and shops) prefer that you pay your bills with cash. Some vendors will charge you extra for using a credit card, and some won't take American or Canadian credit cards at all. Cash is the best—and sometimes only—way to pay for bus fare, taxis, and local guides.

Throughout Europe, ATMs are the standard for travelers to get cash. Stay away from "independent" ATMs such as Travelex, Euronet, and Forex, which charge huge commissions and have terrible exchange rates.

To withdraw money from an ATM (known as a *geldautomaat* in Dutch and a *distributeur* in French), you'll need a debit card (ideally with a Visa or MasterCard logo for maximum usability),

INTRODUCTION

Exchange Rate

I list prices in euros for the Netherlands and Belgium.

1 euro (€) = about $1.30

To convert prices in euros to dollars, add about 30 percent: €20 = about $26, €50 = about $65. (Check www.oanda.com for the latest exchange rates.) Just like the dollar, one euro (€) is broken down into 100 cents. Coins range from €0.01 to €2, and bills from €5 to €500.

So those €65 wooden clogs are about $85, and the €90 taxi ride through Brussels is...uh-oh.

plus a PIN code. Know your PIN code in numbers; there are only numbers—no letters—on European keypads. Although you can use a credit card for ATM transactions, it's generally more expensive (and only makes sense in an emergency), because it's considered a cash advance rather than a withdrawal. Try to withdraw large sums of money to reduce the number of per-transaction bank fees you'll pay.

Pickpockets target tourists. To safeguard your cash, wear a money belt—a pouch with a strap that you buckle around your waist like a belt and tuck under your clothes. Keep your cash, credit cards, and passport secure in your money belt, and carry only a day's spending money in your front pocket.

Credit and Debit Cards

Credit cards are not as readily accepted in the Netherlands as they are in other European countries: Be prepared to use cash for many transactions. While Dutch hotels, souvenir shops, and most restaurants will take US and Canadian credit cards, some stores only accept Dutch credit cards. Dutch train stations will not accept foreign credit cards at all—not even in a live transaction with a clerk—except at Schiphol Airport and Amsterdam's Central Station. The main Dutch grocery chain—Albert Heijn—only takes Dutch cards. In Belgium, train station ticket machines only take Belgian credit cards, but clerks will accept US and Canadian cards at the ticket windows. Most automated machines in both countries will only take a chip-and-PIN card (described later) or cash. In general, Visa and MasterCard are more commonly accepted than American Express.

When I do use my credit card here, it's only in a few specific situations: to book hotel reservations by phone, to cover major purchases (such as car rentals, plane tickets, and long hotel stays), and to pay for expensive things near the end of my trip (to avoid another visit to the ATM). While you could use a debit card to make most large purchases, using a credit card offers a greater degree of fraud protection (because debit cards draw funds directly from your account).

Ask Your Credit- or Debit-Card Company: Before your trip, contact the company that issued your debit or credit cards.

• Confirm that your **card will work overseas,** and alert them that you'll be using it in Europe; otherwise, they may deny transactions if they perceive unusual spending patterns.

• Ask for the specifics on transaction **fees.** When you use your credit or debit card—either for purchases or ATM withdrawals—you'll often be charged additional "international transaction" fees of up to 3 percent (1 percent is normal) plus $5 per transaction. If your card's fees seem high, consider getting a different card just for your trip: Capital One (www.capitalone.com) and most credit unions have low-to-no international fees.

• If you plan to withdraw cash from ATMs, confirm your **daily withdrawal limit** (€300 is usually about the maximum), and if necessary, ask your bank to adjust it. Some travelers prefer a high limit that allows them to take out more cash at each ATM stop (saving on bank fees), while others prefer to set a lower limit in case their card is stolen. Note that foreign banks also set maximum withdrawal amounts for their ATMs.

• Get your bank's emergency **phone number** in the US (but not its 800 number, which isn't accessible from overseas) to call collect if you have a problem.

• Ask for your credit card's **PIN** in case you need to make an emergency cash withdrawal or encounter Europe's chip-and-PIN system; the bank won't tell you your PIN over the phone, so allow time for it to be mailed to you.

Chip and PIN: If your card is declined for a purchase in Europe, it may be because Europeans are increasingly using chip-and-PIN cards, which are embedded with an electronic chip (in addition to the magnetic stripe used on our American-style cards). Much of Europe is adopting this system, and many Dutch and Belgian merchants rely on it exclusively. You're most likely to encounter chip-and-PIN problems at automated payment machines, such as those at train and subway stations, toll roads, parking garages, luggage lockers, and self-serve gas pumps. If a machine won't take your card, find a cashier who can make your card work (they can print a receipt for you to

sign), or find a machine that takes cash.

But don't panic: Cash still works. It pays to carry plenty of euros (you can always use an ATM with your magnetic-stripe debit card). Memorizing the PIN lets you use it at some chip-and-PIN machines—just enter your PIN when prompted.

If you're still concerned, you can apply for a chip card in the US (though I think it's overkill). While big US banks offer these cards with high annual fees, a better option is the no-annual-fee GlobeTrek Visa, offered by Andrews Federal Credit Union in Maryland (open to all US residents; see www.andrewsfcu.org).

Dynamic Currency Conversion: If merchants offer to convert your purchase price into dollars (called dynamic currency conversion), refuse this "service." You'll pay even more in fees for the expensive convenience of seeing your charge in dollars.

Damage Control for Lost Cards

If you lose your credit or debit card, you can stop people from using it by reporting the loss immediately to the respective global customer-assistance centers. Call these 24-hour US numbers collect: Visa (tel. 303/967-1096), MasterCard (tel. 636/722-7111), and American Express (tel. 336/393-1111). To make a collect call to the US from the Netherlands, dial 0800-022-9111; from Belgium, dial 0800-10010. Press zero or stay on the line for an English-speaking operator. European toll-free numbers (listed by country) can be found at the websites for Visa and MasterCard.

At a minimum, you'll need to know the name of the financial institution that issued you the card, along with the type of card (classic, platinum, or whatever). Providing the following information will allow for a quicker cancellation of your missing card: full card number, whether you are the primary or secondary cardholder, the cardholder's name exactly as printed on the card, billing address, home phone number, circumstances of the loss or theft, and identification verification (your birth date, your mother's maiden name, or your Social Security number—memorize this, don't carry a copy). If you are the secondary cardholder, you'll also need to provide the primary cardholder's identification-verification details. You can generally receive a temporary card within two or three business days in Europe (see www.ricksteves.com/help for more).

If you promptly report your loss within two days, you typically won't be responsible for any unauthorized transactions on your account, although many banks charge a liability fee of $50.

Tipping

Tipping in the Low Countries isn't as automatic and generous as it is in the US, but for special service, tips are appreciated, if not expected. As in the US, the proper amount depends on your resources, tipping philosophy, and the circumstances, but some general guidelines apply.

Restaurants: Tipping is an issue only at restaurants that have table service. If you order your food at a counter, don't tip.

At Dutch and Belgian restaurants that have waitstaff, service is included, although it's common to round up the bill after a good meal (usually 5-10 percent; so, for an €18.50 meal, pay €20).

Taxis: To tip the cabbie, round up. For a typical ride, round up about 5-10 percent (to pay a €4.50 fare, give €5; or for a €28 fare, give €30). If the cabbie hauls your bags and zips you to the airport to help you catch your flight, you might want to toss in a little more. But if you feel like you're being driven in circles or otherwise ripped off, skip the tip.

Services: In general, if someone in the service industry does a super job for you, a small tip of a euro or two is appropriate...but not required. If you're not sure whether (or how much) to tip for a service, ask your hotelier or the TI.

Getting a VAT Refund

Wrapped into the purchase price of your souvenirs is a Value-Added Tax (VAT) of about 21 percent in both the Netherlands and Belgium. You're entitled to get most of that tax back if you purchase more than €50 (about $65) in the Netherlands or €125.01 (about $165) in Belgium worth of goods at a store that participates in the VAT-refund scheme. Typically, you must ring up the minimum at a single retailer—you can't add up your purchases from various shops to reach the required amount.

Getting your refund is usually straightforward and, if you buy a substantial amount of souvenirs, well worth the hassle. If you're lucky, the merchant will subtract the tax when you make your purchase. (This is more likely to occur if the store ships the goods to your home.) Otherwise, you'll need to:

Get the paperwork. Have the merchant completely fill out the necessary refund document, called a "Tax-Free Shopping Cheque." You'll have to present your passport. Get the paperwork done before you leave the store to ensure you'll have everything you need (including your original sales receipt).

Get your stamp at the border or airport. Process your cheque(s) at your last stop in the European Union (such as at the airport) with the customs agent who deals with VAT refunds. Before checking in for your flight, find the local customs office, and be prepared to stand in line. Keep your purchases readily available for viewing by the customs agent (ideally in your carry-on bag—don't make the mistake of checking the bag with your purchases before you've seen the agent). You're not supposed to use your purchased goods before you leave. If you show up at customs wearing Dutch wooden clogs and a Belgian lace wedding veil, officials might look the other way—or deny you a refund.

Collect your refund. You'll need to return your stamped document to the retailer or its representative. Many merchants work with services, such as Global Blue or Premier Tax Free, that have offices at major airports, ports, and border crossings (either before or after security, probably strategically located near a duty-free shop). These services, which extract a 4 percent fee, can refund your money immediately in your currency of choice or credit your card (within two billing cycles). If the retailer handles VAT refunds directly, it's up to you to contact the merchant for your refund. You can also mail the documents from home, or more quickly, from your point of departure (using an envelope you've prepared in advance or one that's been provided by the merchant). Then you'll have to wait—it can take months.

Customs for American Shoppers

You are allowed to take home $800 worth of items per person duty-free, once every 30 days. You can also bring in duty-free a liter of alcohol. As for food, you can take home many processed and packaged foods: vacuum-packed cheeses, dried herbs, jams, baked goods, candy, chocolate, oil, vinegar, mustard, and honey. Fresh fruits and vegetables and most meats are not allowed. Any liquid-containing foods must be packed in checked luggage, a potential recipe for disaster. To check customs rules and duty rates before you go, visit www.cbp.gov, and click on "Travel," then "Know Before You Go."

Sightseeing

Sightseeing can be hard work. Use these tips to make your visits to the Low Countries' finest sights meaningful, fun, efficient, and painless.

Plan Ahead

Set up an itinerary that allows you to fit in all your must-see sights. For a one-stop look at opening hours in Amsterdam, Bruges, and Brussels, see the "At a Glance" sidebars for these destinations. Most sights keep stable hours, but you can easily confirm the latest by checking with the TI or visiting museum websites.

Don't put off visiting a must-see sight—you never know when a place will close unexpectedly for a holiday, strike, or restoration. On holidays (see page 626), expect reduced hours or closures. In summer, some sights may stay open late. Off-season, many museums have shorter hours.

Going at the right time helps avoid crowds. This book offers tips on the best times to see specific sights. Try visiting very early, at lunch, or very late. Evening visits (when possible) are usually peaceful, with fewer crowds.

Study up. To get the most out of the self-guided tours and sight descriptions in this book, reread them the night before your visit. The Rijksmuseum is much more entertaining if you've boned up on ruffs and Dutch Masters the night before.

At Sights

Here's what you can typically expect:

Some important sights require you to check daypacks and coats. To avoid checking a small backpack, carry it under your arm like a purse as you enter. From a guard's point of view, a backpack is generally a problem, while a purse is not.

Flash photography is often banned, but taking photos without a flash is usually allowed. Flashes damage oil paintings and distract others in the room. Even without a flash, a handheld camera will take a decent picture (or buy postcards or posters at the museum bookstore).

Museums may have special exhibits in addition to their permanent collection. Some exhibits are included in the entry price, while others come at an extra cost (which you may have to pay even if you don't want to see the exhibit).

Expect changes—artwork can be on tour, on loan, out sick, or shifted at the whim of the curator. To adapt, pick up any available free floor plans as you enter, and ask museum staff if you can't find a particular item.

Many sights rent audioguides, which generally offer excellent recorded descriptions of the art in English. If you bring your own earbuds, you can enjoy better sound and avoid holding the device to your ear. To save money, bring a Y-jack and share one audioguide with your travel partner. Guided tours in English (widely ranging in quality) are most likely to occur during peak season.

Important sights may have an on-site café or cafeteria (usually a handy place to rejuvenate during a long visit). The WCs at sights are free and generally clean.

Many places sell postcards that highlight their attractions. Before you leave a sight, scan the postcards and thumb through the biggest guidebook (or skim its index) to be sure you haven't overlooked something that you'd like to see.

Most sights stop admitting people 30-60 minutes before closing time, and some rooms may close early (often 45 minutes before the actual closing time). Guards usher people out, so don't save the best for last.

Every sight or museum offers more than what is covered in

this book. Use the information in this book as an introduction—not the final word.

Sleeping

I favor hotels and restaurants handy to your sightseeing activities. Rather than list hotels scattered throughout a city, I choose two or three favorite neighborhoods and recommend the best accommodations values in each, from dorm beds to fancy doubles with all of the comforts.

A major feature of this book is its extensive listing of good-value rooms. I like places that are clean, central, relatively quiet at night, reasonably priced, friendly, small enough to have a hands-on owner and stable staff, run with a respect for Dutch or Belgian traditions, and not listed in other guidebooks. (In the Low Countries, for me, six out of these eight criteria means it's a keeper.) I'm more impressed by a convenient location and a fun-loving philosophy than flat-screen TVs and shoeshine machines.

Book your accommodations well in advance if you'll be traveling during busy times. See page 626 for a list of major holidays and festivals in the Low Countries; for tips on making reservations, see page 18.

Rates and Deals

I've described my recommended accommodations using a Sleep Code (see sidebar). Prices listed are for one-night stays in peak season, generally include breakfast, and assume you're booking directly (not through a TI or online hotel-booking engine).

These days, many hotels change prices from day to day according to demand. Given the economic downturn, hoteliers are often willing to make a deal. I'd suggest emailing several hotels to ask for their best price. Comparison-shop and make your choice.

As you look over the listings, you'll notice that some accommodations promise special prices to my readers who book direct (without using a room-finding service or hotel-booking website, which take a commission). To get these rates, you must mention this book when you reserve, and then show the book upon arrival. Rick Steves discounts apply to readers with ebooks as well as printed books. Discounts may not apply to promotional rates.

In general, prices can soften up if you do any of the following: offer to pay cash, stay at least three nights, or mention this book.

Sleep Code

(€1 = about $1.30)

Price Rankings

To help you easily sort through my listings, I've divided the accommodations into three categories based on the price for a double room with bath during high season:

$$$	**Higher Priced**
$$	**Moderately Priced**
$	**Lower Priced**

I always rate hostels as $, whether or not they have double rooms, because they have the cheapest beds in town.

Prices can change without notice; verify the hotel's current rates online or by email.

Abbreviations

To pack maximum information in a minimum of space, I use the following code to describe accommodations in this book. Prices listed are per room, not per person. When a price range is given for a type of room (such as double rooms listing for "Db-€80-120"), it means the price fluctuates with the season, size of room, or length of stay; expect to pay the upper end for peak-season stays.

S = Single room (or price for one person in a double).

D = Double or twin. "Double beds" can be two twins sheeted together and are usually big enough for nonromantic couples.

T = Triple (generally a double bed with a single).

Q = Quad (usually two double beds; adding an extra child's bed to a T is usually cheaper).

b = Private bathroom with toilet and shower or tub.

s = Private shower or tub only (the toilet is down the hall).

According to this code, a couple staying at a "Db-€85" hotel would pay a total of €85 (about $110) for a double room with a private bathroom. Unless otherwise noted, breakfast is included, hotel staff speak basic English, and credit cards are accepted.

There's almost always Wi-Fi and/or Internet access available, either free or for a fee.

Making Hotel Reservations

Given the good value of the accommodations I've found for this book, reserve your rooms several weeks in advance—or as soon as you've pinned down your travel dates—particularly if you'll be traveling during peak times. Note that some national holidays jam things up and merit your making reservations far in advance (see "Holidays and Festivals" on page 626).

Requesting a Reservation: It's usually easiest to book your room through the hotel's website; many have a reservation-request form built right in. (For the best rates, be sure to use the hotel's official site and not a booking agency's site.) Just type in your preferred dates and the website will automatically display a list of available rooms and prices. Simpler websites will generate an email to the hotelier with your request. If there's no reservation form, or for complicated requests, send an email from your personal address. Other options include calling (see "Phoning" next page, and be mindful of time zones) or faxing. Most recommended hotels are accustomed to guests who speak only English.

The hotelier wants to know these key pieces of information (also included in the sample request form in the appendix):

- number and type of rooms
- number of nights
- date of arrival
- date of departure
- any special needs (such as bathroom in the room or down the hall, twin beds vs. double bed, air-conditioning, quiet, view, ground floor, etc.)

When you request a room, use the European style for writing dates: day/month/year. For example, for a two-night stay in July of 2014, I would request "1 double room for 2 nights, arrive 16/07/14, depart 18/07/14." Consider carefully how long you'll stay; don't just assume you can tack on extra days once you arrive. Make sure you mention any discounts—for Rick Steves readers or otherwise—when you make the reservation.

If you don't get a response to your email, it usually means the hotel is already fully booked—but try sending the message again or call to follow up.

Confirming a Reservation: Most places will request your credit-card number to hold the room. To confirm a room using a hotel's secure online reservation form, enter your contact information and credit-card number; the hotel will email a confirmation.

If you sent an email to request a reservation, the hotel will reply with its room availability and rates. This is not a confirmation. You must email back to say that you want the room at the given rate. While you can email your credit-card information (I do), it's safer to share that confidential info via phone call, two emails (splitting your number between them), or the hotel's secure online reservation form.

Canceling a Reservation: If you must cancel your reservation, it's courteous to do so with as much notice as possible. Simply make a quick phone call or send an email. Family-run places lose money if they turn away customers while holding a room for someone who doesn't show up. Understandably, many hoteliers bill no-shows for one night.

Cancellation policies can be strict: For example, you might lose a deposit if you cancel within two weeks of your reserved stay, or you might be billed for the entire visit if you leave early. Internet deals may require prepayment, with no refunds for cancellations. Ask about cancellation policies before you book.

If canceling via email, request confirmation that your cancellation was received to avoid being accidentally billed.

Reconfirming a Reservation: Always call to reconfirm your room reservation a few days in advance. Smaller hotels and B&Bs appreciate knowing your estimated time of arrival. If you'll be arriving late (after 17:00), let them know. On the small chance that a hotel loses track of your reservation, bring along a hard copy of their confirmation.

Reserving Rooms as You Travel: You can make reservations as you travel, calling hotels and B&Bs a few days to a week before your arrival. If everything's full, don't despair. Call a day or two in advance and fill in a cancellation. If you'd rather travel without any reservations at all, you'll have greater success snaring rooms if you arrive at your destination early in the day. When you anticipate crowds (weekends are worst), call hotels at about 9:00 or 10:00 on the day you plan to arrive, when the receptionist knows who'll be checking out and which rooms will be available. If you encounter a language barrier, ask the fluent receptionist at your current hotel to call for you.

Phoning: To call the Netherlands or Belgium, you'll need to know the country code: 31 for the Netherlands, and 32 for Belgium. To call the Netherlands from the US or Canada, dial 011-31-number in this book (drop the initial 0 from the hotel's number). If calling the Netherlands from another European country, dial 00-31-number in this book (without its initial 0). For Belgium, use "32" instead of "31." For more tips on calling, see page 604.

You can also try asking for a cheaper room or a discount, or offer to skip breakfast.

Before accepting a room, confirm your understanding of the complete price. The only tip my recommended hotels would like is a friendly, easygoing guest.

Types of Accommodations

Hotels

In this book, the price for a double room ranges from $70 (very simple, toilet and shower down the hall) to $300 (maximum plumbing and more), with most clustering at about $140. You'll pay more at Amsterdam hotels, less at Brussels hotels and Bruges B&Bs. There is often a city room tax, which is not included in the prices I list.

Most hotels have lots of doubles and a few singles, triples, and quads. And though groups sleep cheap, traveling alone can be expensive. Singles (except for the rare closet-type rooms that fit only a twin bed) are simply doubles used by one person, so they often cost nearly the same as a double.

A hearty breakfast with cereal, meats, local cheeses, fresh bread, yogurt, juice, and coffee or tea is standard in hotels.

For environmental reasons, towels are often replaced in hotels only when you leave them on the floor. (In cheaper places, they aren't replaced at all, so hang them up to dry and reuse.) Hotel elevators, while becoming more common, are often very small, forcing you to send your bags up separately—pack light.

If you're arriving early in the morning, your room probably won't be ready. You can drop your bag safely at the hotel and dive right into sightseeing.

Hoteliers can be a great help and source of advice. Most know their city well, and can assist you with everything from public transit and airport connections to finding a good restaurant, the nearest launderette, or an Internet café.

Even at the best hotels, mechanical breakdowns occur: air-conditioning malfunctions, sinks leak, hot water turns cold, and toilets gurgle and smell. Report your concerns clearly and calmly at the front desk. For more complicated problems, don't expect instant results.

If you suspect night noise will be a problem (if, for instance, your room is over a pub), ask for a quiet room in the back or on an upper floor. To guard against theft in your room, keep valuables out of sight. Some rooms come with a safe, and other hotels have safes at the front desk. I've never bothered using one.

Checkout can pose problems if surprise charges pop up on your bill. If you settle up your bill the afternoon before you leave, you'll have time to discuss and address any points of contention (before 19:00, when the night shift usually arrives).

Above all, keep a positive attitude. After all, you're on vacation. If your hotel is a disappointment, spend more time out enjoying the city you came to see.

Bed-and-Breakfasts

B&Bs offer double the cultural intimacy and—often—nicer rooms for a good deal less than most hotel rooms. Hosts usually speak English and are interesting conversationalists.

In the Low Countries, B&Bs are common in well-touristed areas outside the big cities. There are plenty to choose from in Haarlem, Antwerp, Ghent, and especially Bruges. Amsterdam also has B&Bs, though they tend to be more expensive and not as good a value as those in small towns (I've listed the better-value B&Bs in Amsterdam). Urban Brussels has only one recommended B&B. Local TIs have lists of B&Bs and can book a room for you, but you'll save money by booking direct with the B&Bs listed in this book.

Hostels

For about $30 a night, you can stay at a youth hostel. Travelers of any age are welcome, if they don't mind dorm-style accommodations or meeting other travelers. Most hostels offer kitchen facilities, Internet access, Wi-Fi, and a self-service laundry. Nowadays, concerned about bedbugs, hostels are likely to provide all bedding, including sheets. Family and private rooms may be available on request.

Independent hostels tend to be easygoing, colorful, and informal (no membership required); see www.hostelz.com, www.hostelseurope.com, www.hostels.com, and www.hostelbookers.com. **Official hostels** are part of Hostelling International (HI) and share an online booking site (www.hihostels.com). HI hostels typically require that you either have a membership card or pay extra per night.

Traveling as a Temporary Local

We travel all the way to the Netherlands and Belgium to enjoy differences—to become temporary locals. You'll experience frustrations. Certain truths that we find "God-given" or "self-evident," such as cold beer, ice in drinks, bottomless cups of coffee, hot showers, and bigger being better, are suddenly not so true. One of the benefits of travel is the eye-opening realization that there are logical, civil, and even better alternatives. A willingness to go local ensures that you'll enjoy a full dose of Dutch and Belgian hospitality.

How Was Your Trip?

Were your travels fun, smooth, and meaningful? If you'd like to share your tips, concerns, and discoveries, please fill out the survey at www.ricksteves.com/feedback. I value your feedback. Thanks in advance—it helps a lot.

Europeans generally like Americans. But if there is a negative aspect to the image Europeans have of Americans, it's that we are loud, wasteful, ethnocentric, too informal (which can seem disrespectful), and a bit naive.

My Dutch and Belgian friends place a high value on speaking quietly in restaurants and on trains. Listen while on the bus or in a restaurant—the place can be packed, but the decibel level is low. Try to adjust your volume accordingly to show respect for their culture.

While the Dutch and Belgians look bemusedly at some of our Yankee excesses—and worriedly at others—they nearly always afford individual travelers all the warmth we deserve.

Judging from all the happy feedback I receive from travelers who have used this book, it's safe to assume you'll enjoy a great, affordable vacation—with the finesse of an independent, experienced traveler.

Thanks, and have a *goede vakantie!*

Back Door Travel Philosophy
From *Rick Steves' Europe Through the Back Door*

Travel is intensified living—maximum thrills per minute and one of the last great sources of legal adventure. Travel is freedom. It's recess, and we need it.

Experiencing the real Europe requires catching it by surprise, going casual..."through the Back Door."

Affording travel is a matter of priorities. (Make do with the old car.) You can eat and sleep—simply, safely, and enjoyably—anywhere in Europe for $120 a day plus transportation costs. In many ways, spending more money only builds a thicker wall between you and what you traveled so far to see. Europe is a cultural carnival, and time after time, you'll find that its best acts are free and the best seats are the cheap ones.

A tight budget forces you to travel close to the ground, meeting and communicating with the people. Never sacrifice sleep, nutrition, safety, or cleanliness to save money. Simply enjoy the local-style alternatives to expensive hotels and restaurants.

Connecting with people carbonates your experience. Extroverts have more fun. If your trip is low on magic moments, kick yourself and make things happen. If you don't enjoy a place, maybe you don't know enough about it. Seek the truth. Recognize tourist traps. Give a culture the benefit of your open mind. See things as different, but not better or worse. Any culture has plenty to share.

Of course, travel, like the world, is a series of hills and valleys. Be fanatically positive and militantly optimistic. If something's not to your liking, change your liking.

Travel can make you a happier American, as well as a citizen of the world. Our Earth is home to seven billion equally precious people. It's humbling to travel and find that other people don't have the "American Dream"—they have their own dreams. Europeans like us, but with all due respect, they wouldn't trade passports.

Thoughtful travel engages us with the world. In tough economic times, it reminds us what is truly important. By broadening perspectives, travel teaches new ways to measure quality of life.

Globetrotting destroys ethnocentricity, helping us understand and appreciate other cultures. Rather than fear the diversity on this planet, celebrate it. Among your most prized souvenirs will be the strands of different cultures you choose to knit into your own character. The world is a cultural yarn shop, and Back Door travelers are weaving the ultimate tapestry. Join in!

THE
NETHERLANDS

THE NETHERLANDS

Holland: windmills, wooden shoes, cheese, tulips, and tranquility. In Holland's 17th-century Golden Age, Dutch traders sailed the seas to find exotic goods, creating a global economy. Tiny Holland was a world power—politically, economically, and culturally— with more great artists per square mile than any other country.

"Holland" is just a nickname for the Netherlands. North Holland and South Holland are the largest of the 12 provinces that make up the Netherlands. Today, the country is Europe's most densely populated and also one of its wealthiest and best organized. In 1944, the neighboring countries of Belgium, the Netherlands, and Luxembourg became the nucleus of a united Europe when they joined economically to form BeNeLux.

The average income in the Netherlands is higher than in the United States. Though only 8 percent of the labor force is made up of farmers, 70 percent of the land is cultivated—if you venture outside of Amsterdam, you'll travel through vast fields of barley, wheat, sugar beets, potatoes, and flowers.

The word *Netherlands* means "lowlands." The country occupies the low-lying delta near the mouth of three of Europe's large rivers, including the Rhine. In medieval times, inhabitants built a system of earthen dikes to protect their land from flooding caused by tides and storm surges. The fictional story of the little Dutch boy who saves the country—by sticking his finger in a leaking dike—summed up the country's precarious situation. (Many Americans know this story from a popular 19th-century novel, but few Dutch people have ever heard of it.) In 1953, severe floods breached the old dikes, killing 1,800 and requiring a major overhaul of the system. Today's 350 miles of dikes and levees are high-tech, with electronic systems to monitor water levels. Dutch experts traveled to Louisiana after Hurricane Katrina to share

The Netherlands

their expertise with US officials after levee failure caused massive flooding. And after Hurricane Sandy, American hydrology experts began looking to the Netherlands for models of how to protect vast areas from flooding.

Much of the Dutch landscape is reclaimed from the sea, rivers, and lakes. That's where Holland's famous windmills came in. After diking off large tracts of land below sea level, the Dutch used windmills to harness wind energy to lift the water up out of the enclosed area, divert it into canals, and drain the land. They cultivated hardy plants that removed salt from the soil, slowly turning marshy estuaries into fertile farmland. The windmills later served a second purpose for farmers by turning stone wheels to grind their grain.

Dutch reclamation projects are essentially finished (though a new province—Flevoland, near Amsterdam—has been drained, dried, and populated in the last 100 years—see the Schokland Museum chapter). But in this era of global warming and rising sea levels, the Dutch are developing plans to upgrade their dikes and bulk up their beaches to hold back the sea. They also continue to innovate, building floatable homes and greenhouses (which rise

NETHERLANDS

Netherlands Almanac

Official Name: Koninkrijk der Nederlanden (Kingdom of the Netherlands), or simply Nederland.

Population: 16.7 million people (1,200 people per square mile; 15 times the population density of the US). About 80 percent are Dutch; 5 percent hail from other EU countries; and the rest are mostly Indonesian, Turkish, Surinamese, or Moroccan. Less than a third are Catholic, 20 percent are Protestant, 6 percent are Muslim, and more than 40 percent have no religious affiliation.

Latitude and Longitude: 52 °N and 5 °E. The latitude is similar to Alberta, Canada.

Area: 16,000 square miles—about twice the size of New Jersey.

Geography: The Netherlands is located at the mouths of three major European rivers: the Rhine, the Waal, and the Meuse. It shares borders with Belgium, Germany, and the North Sea. The Dutch have been beating back the sea for centuries, forming *polders*—flat, low-lying reclaimed lands. The Netherlands has a mild marine climate.

Biggest Cities: Amsterdam is the largest city, with 820,000 people, followed by Rotterdam (617,000) and The Hague (500,000).

Economy: The Netherlands is prosperous, with the planet's 23rd-largest economy ($713 billion), a per-capita GDP in the world's top 20 ($42,700), and one of Europe's lowest unemployment rates. Its port at Rotterdam is Europe's largest, and the country

---

with the tides) and relocating dikes farther back from the rivers (to create wider floodplains). All this technological tinkering with nature prompted a popular local saying: "God made the Earth, but the Dutch made Holland."

Several Dutch icons came directly from the country's flat, reclaimed landscape: As mentioned, windmills and canals drained the land. Wooden shoes *(klompen)* allowed farmers to walk across soggy fields. (They're also easy to find should they come off in high water because they float.) Tulips and other flowers grew well in the sandy soil near dunes.

In the 1630s, Holland was gripped with "tulip mania" (see sidebar on page 30). Financial speculators invested wildly in exotic varieties, causing prices to skyrocket. You could buy a house with just three tulip bulbs. In February of 1637, the bubble burst, investors were ruined, and the economic fallout helped contribute to the decline of the Dutch Golden Age.

The Netherlands' flat land makes it a biker's dream. The Dutch, who average four bikes per family, have put small bike roads (with their own traffic lights) beside nearly every major highway. You can rent bikes at most train stations and drop them off

relies heavily on foreign trade. The nation's highly mechanized farms produce huge quantities of flowers, bulbs, and produce for export. The economy has also benefited from its many natural gas fields—including the huge Groningen field, one of the world's biggest. However, even this notably stable nation has suffered from the worldwide recession.

Government: The Netherlands is a parliamentary democracy, with its seat of government at The Hague, although the country's official capital is Amsterdam. The ceremonial head of state is King Willem-Alexander, whose ascension to the throne on April 30, 2013 is celebrated each spring on King's Day. He is the first Dutch king in 123 years. The Dutch parliament consists of two houses: the 150-member, directly elected Second Chamber (or Lower House); and the 75-member First Chamber (or Upper House), elected by provincial assemblies. The government is led by a prime minister.

Flag: The Netherlands' flag is composed of three horizontal bands of red (top), white, and blue.

The Dutch: They're among the world's tallest people—the average height for a man is 6'1" and for a woman, 5'6". The average age for both men and women is around 41 years old, and they'll live to be 81. They ride their bikes about 1.5 miles a day and smoke half as much marijuana as their American friends.

at most others. And you can take bikes on trains (outside of rush hour) for €6 per day. Dutch pedestrians know to look carefully for bikes before crossing the street—and so should you.

The Dutch can generally speak English, pride themselves on their frankness, and like to split the bill. Thriftiness, efficiency, and a dislike of wastefulness are longstanding Dutch traits. Traditionally, Dutch cities have been open-minded, loose, and liberal (to attract sailors in the days of Henry Hudson). And today, Amsterdam is a capital of alternative lifestyles—a city where nothing's illegal as long as nobody gets hurt. Coffee shops serve cannabis as well as cappuccinos, and prostitutes pose in government-licensed windows. The city is surprisingly diverse, housing many recent immigrants— a trend that, unfortunately, has resulted in tension in recent years. The Netherlands in general and Amsterdam in particular are gay-friendly. Some of the biggest festivals and parades on the social calendar bring out the LGBT crowd.

While freewheeling Amsterdam does have a quiet side (particularly in West Amsterdam, which contains the pleasant Jordaan neighborhood), travelers who prefer more small-town Dutch evenings can sleep in a small town nearby, such as Haarlem, and

NETHERLANDS

Tulip Mania

When we think of the Netherlands, a few images spring to mind: windmills, wooden shoes, and, perhaps most vividly, tulips. A Dutch icon since the 17th century, the colorful flowers are actually native to central Asia ("tulip" comes from a Turkish word for "turban"). When the Holy Roman Emperor's ambassador to Constantinople first sent some bulbs westward in the mid-1500s, a few wound up in the hands of a Dutch botanist—and thus began one of the oddest chapters in the Netherlands' history.

The region's harsh conditions turned out to be ideal for the hardy bulbs, which also benefited from good timing: They arrived in the Netherlands in the middle of the Dutch Golden Age, delighting a relatively affluent populace who were fond of beauty and able to pay for it. Within a generation the popularity of these then-exotic flowers—and for a few rare species in particular—grew from a trendy fad into an all-out frenzy. Prices shot skyward: Forty bulbs could fetch up to 100,000 florins (about $1.7 million in today's dollars); in the context of the times, an average laborer made around 150 florins a year. The most treasured variety was the Semper Augustus, with its distinctive red-and-white petals—just one bulb sold for 12 acres of land.

"Tulip mania" reached a fever pitch in late 1636, and for the next few months, frantic trading consumed the Dutch. Production of other goods declined as people dropped everything to get rich on the tulip exchange. Soon, instead of buying and selling actual bulbs, people began trading promissory vouchers—by that time, it wasn't really the flowers everyone was after, but the opportunity to resell them at a higher price. The number of potential buyers seemed endless...until it wasn't. In February of 1637, one of history's most famous speculative bubbles burst, leaving many tulip investors with empty contracts or bulbs worth only a tiny fraction of what they'd cost. But the demand for tulips never died out—a love of the flowers had  been firmly planted in the Dutch psyche, and they continue to be an integral part of the culture as well as a major export.

side-trip into the big city.

To get a complete taste of the Netherlands, venture beyond Amsterdam and Haarlem. The efficient train system turns much of the country into a feasible day trip (or two). The charming town of Delft (Vermeer's hometown, laced with canals) and its neighbor city, The Hague, make a rewarding day or two of sightseeing. Arnhem has the Arnhem Open-Air Folk Museum and the Kröller-Müller Museum of modern art nearby (in Hogue Veluwe National Park). The Historic Triangle offers a nostalgic loop trip on a steam train and boat. Keukenhof's flower garden is one of the world's best (open in spring only). Explore farther: There's Edam (an adorable village), Alkmaar (best on Friday for its cheese market), Aalsmeer (a bustling modern flower auction), Schokland (for a chance to walk on what was the bottom of the sea at this village/museum), open-air folk museums at Enkhuizen and Zaanse Schans, and more. Your top options are outlined in the Dutch Day Trips chapter.

Wherever you roam, you'll find the Netherlands to be something of an eye-opener. Behind its placid exterior, it's a complex mix of modern technology, honored traditions, quaint countryside, outrageous architecture, and no-nonsense, globally minded people.

Dutch Cuisine

Traditional Dutch food is basic and hearty, with lots of bread, soup, and fish. Dutch treats include cheese, pancakes *(pannenkoeken)*, and "syrup waffles" *(stroopwafels)*. Popular drinks are light, pilsner-type beer and gin *(jenever)*.

Treat your tongue to some new experiences in Holland: Try a pickled herring at an outdoor herring stand, linger over coffee in a "brown café," sip an old *jenever* with a new friend, and consume an Indonesian feast—a *rijsttafel*.

Lunch and dinner are served at typical American times (roughly 12:00-14:00 and 18:00-21:00). At restaurants, tipping is not necessary (15 percent service is usually included in the menu price), but a tip of about 5-10 percent is a nice reward for good service. In bars, rounding up to the next euro ("keep the change") is appropriate if you get table service, rather than ordering at the bar.

When ordering drinks in a café or bar, you can just pay as you go (especially if the bar is crowded), or wait until the end to settle up, as many locals do. If you get table service, take the cue from your waiter.

Cafés with outdoor tables generally do not charge more if you sit outside (unlike in France or Italy).

Waiters constantly say, *"Alstublieft"* (AHL-stoo-bleeft). It's a useful, catchall polite word meaning, "please," "here's your order," "enjoy," and "you're welcome." You can respond with a thank you by saying, *"Dank u wel"* (dahnk yoo vehl).

Dutch Specialties

Cheeses: Edam (covered with red wax) or Gouda (HHHOW-dah). Gouda can be young or old—*jong* is mellow; *oude* is salty, crumbly, and strong, sometimes seasoned with cumin or cloves.

French Fries: Commonly served with mayonnaise (ketchup and curry sauce are often available) on a paper tray or in a newspaper cone. Flemish *(Vlaamse) friets* are made from whole potatoes, not pulp.

Haring **(herring):** Pickled herring, often served with onions or pickles, sometimes with sour cream, on a thick, soft, white bun.

Hutspot: Hearty meat stew with mashed potatoes, onions, and carrots, especially popular on winter days.

Kroketten **(croquettes):** Log-shaped rolls of meats and vegetables (kind of like corn dogs) breaded and deep-fried, such as *bitterballen* (meatballs), *frikandellen* (sausages), or *vlammetjes* (spring rolls).

Pannenkoeken: Either sweet dessert pancakes or crêpe-like, savory dinner pancakes.

Typical Meals

Breakfast: Breakfasts are big by continental standards—bread, meat, cheese, and maybe an egg or omelet. Hotels generally put out a buffet spread, including juice and cereal.

Lunch: Simple sandwiches are called *broodjes* (most commonly made with cheese and/or ham). An open-face sandwich of ham and cheese topped with two fried eggs is an *uitsmijter* (OUTS-mi-ter). Soup is popular for lunch, including *erwtensoep*, a thick, hearty pea soup.

Snacks and Take-Out Food: Small stands sell french fries *(friets)* with mayonnaise, pickled herring, falafels (fried chickpea balls in pita bread), *shoarmas* (lamb tucked in pita bread), and *döner kebabs* (Turkish version of a *shoarma*). Delis have deep-fried croquettes *(kroketten)*.

Dinner: It's the biggest meal of the day, consisting of meat or seafood with boiled potatoes, cooked vegetables, and a salad. Hearty stews are served in winter. These days, many people eat more vegetarian fare.

Sweets: Try *poffertjes* (small, sugared puffy pancakes), *pannen-koeken* (pancakes with fruit and cream), *stroopwafels* (syrup waffles), and *appelgebak* or *appeltaart* (apple pie).

Ethnic Foods

If you're not in the mood for meat and potatoes, sample some of Amsterdam's abundant ethnic offerings.

Indonesian *(Indisch):* The tastiest "Dutch" food is Indonesian, from the former colony. Find any Indisch restaurant and experience a *rijsttafel* (literally, "rice table"). With as many as 30 spicy dishes (ranging from small sides to entrée-sized plates) and a big bowl of rice (or noodles), a *rijsttafel* can be split and still fill two hungry tourists. Vegetarian versions are yours for the asking.

Nasi rames is a cheaper, smaller version of a *rijsttafel*. Another popular dish is *bami goreng*—stir-fried noodles served with meat, vegetables, and *rijsttafel* items. *Nasi goreng* is like *bami*, but comes with fried rice. *Saté* is skewered meat, and *gado-gado* consists of steamed vegetables and hard-boiled eggs with peanut sauce. Among the most common sauces are peanut, red chili *(sambal)*, and dark soy.

Middle Eastern: Try a *shoarma* (roasted lamb with garlic in pita bread, served with bowls of different sauces), falafel, gyros, or a *döner kebab*.

Surinamese *(Surinaamse):* Surinamese cuisine is a mix of Caribbean and Indonesian influences, featuring *roti* (spiced chicken wrapped in a tortilla) and rice (white or fried) served with meats in sauces (curry and spices). Why Surinamese food in Amsterdam? In 1667, Holland traded New York City ("New Amsterdam") to Britain in exchange for the small country of Suriname (which borders Guyana on the northeast coast of South America). For the next three centuries, Suriname (renamed Dutch Guyana) was a Dutch colony, which is why it has indigenous Indians, Creoles, and Indonesian immigrants who all speak Dutch. When Suriname gained independence in 1975, 100,000 Surinamese immigrated to Amsterdam, sparking a rash of Surinamese fast-food outlets.

Types of Eateries

Any place labeled "restaurant" will serve full sit-down meals for lunch or dinner. But there are other places to fill the tank.

An *eetcafé* is a simple restaurant serving basic soups, salads, sandwiches, as well as traditional meat-and-potatoes meals in a generally comfortable but no-nonsense setting.

A *salon de thé* serves tea and coffee, but also croissants, pastries, and sandwiches for a light brunch, a lunch, or an afternoon snack.

Cafés are all-purpose establishments, serving light meals at mealtimes and coffee, drinks, and snacks the rest of the day and night. *Bruin* cafés ("brown cafés") are named for their nicotine-stained walls—until smoking was banned indoors in 2008, they were filled with tobacco smoke. These places are usually a little more bar-like, with dimmer lighting and wood paneling.

A *proeflokaal* is a bar (with snacks) offering wine, spirits, or beer. A "coffeeshop" is the code word for an establishment where marijuana is sold and consumed, though most offer drinks and munchies, too (for details, see the Smoking chapter).

There's no shortage of stand-up, take-out places serving fast food, sandwiches, and all kinds of quick ethnic fare.

No matter what type of establishment you choose, expect it to be *gezellig*—a much-prized Dutch virtue, meaning an atmosphere of relaxed coziness.

Dutch Drinks

Beer: Order "a beer," and you'll get a *pils,* a light lager/pilsner-type beer in a 10-ounce glass with a thick head leveled off with a stick. (Typical brands are Heineken, Grolsch, Oranjeboom, and Amstel.) A common tap beer is Palm Speciale, an amber ale served in a stemmed, wide-mouth glass. Belgian beers are popular, always available in bottles and sometimes on tap (for more information, see page 357). *Witte* (white) beer is light-colored and summery, sometimes served with a lemon slice (it's like Hefeweizen, but yeastier).

Jenever: Try this Dutch gin made from juniper berries. *Jong* (young) is sharper; *oude* (old) is mellow. Served chilled, *jenever* (yah-NAY-ver) is meant to be chugged with a *pils* chaser (this combination is called a *kopstoot*—head-butt). While cheese gets harder and sharper with age, *jenever* grows smooth and soft, so old *jenever* is best.

Liqueur: You'll find a variety of local fruit brandies and cognacs.

Wine: Dutch people drink a lot of fine wine, but it's almost all imported.

Coffee: The Dutch love their coffee, enjoying many of the same drinks (espresso, cappuccino) served in American or Italian coffee shops. Coffee usually comes with a small spice cookie. A *koffie verkeerd* (fer-KEERT, "coffee wrong") is an espresso with a lot of steamed milk.

Soft Drinks: You'll find the full array.

Orange Juice: Many cafés/bars have a juicer for making fresh-squeezed orange juice.

Water: The Dutch drink tap water with meals, but many prefer mineral water, still or sparkling (Spa brand is popular). At restaurants, you can get tap water free for the asking.

AMSTERDAM

ORIENTATION TO AMSTERDAM

Amsterdam still looks much like it did in the 1600s—the Dutch Golden Age—when it was the world's richest city, an international sea-trading port, and the cradle of capitalism. Wealthy, democratic burghers built a city upon millions of pilings, creating a wonderland of canals lined with trees and townhouses topped with fancy gables. Immigrants, Jews, outcasts, and political rebels were drawn here by its tolerant atmosphere, while painters such as young Rembrandt captured that atmosphere on canvas.

Today's Amsterdam is a progressive place of 820,000 people and almost as many bikes. It's a city of good living, cozy cafés, great art, street-corner jazz, stately history, and a spirit of live and let live. In 2013, Amsterdam celebrates the 400th birthday of its canal system with a series of art festivals, concerts, and special exhibits.

Amsterdam also offers the Netherlands' best people-watching. The Dutch are unique, and observing them is a sightseeing experience all in itself. They're a handsome and healthy people, and among the world's tallest. They're also open and honest—I think of them as refreshingly blunt—and they like to laugh. As connoisseurs of world culture, they appreciate Rembrandt paintings, Indonesian food, and the latest French film—but with an unsnooty, blue-jeans attitude.

Be warned: Amsterdam, a bold experiment in freedom, may box your Puritan ears. For centuries, the city has taken a tolerant approach to things other places try to forbid. Traditionally, the city attracted sailors and businessmen away from home, so it was profitable to allow them to have a little fun. In the 1960s, Amsterdam became a magnet for Europe's hippies. Since then, it's become a world capital of alternative lifestyles. Stroll through any neighborhood and see things that are commonplace here but rarely found elsewhere. Prostitution is allowed in the Red Light District, while "smartshops" sell psychedelic drugs and marijuana is openly sold and smoked. (The Dutch aren't necessarily more tolerant or decadent than the rest of us—just pragmatic and looking for smart solutions.)

Approach Amsterdam as an ethnologist observing a strange culture. It's a place where carillons chime quaintly from spires towering above coffeeshops where yuppies go to smoke pot. Take it all in, then pause to watch the clouds blow past stately old gables—and see the Golden Age reflected in a quiet canal.

Amsterdam: A Verbal Map

Amsterdam's Central Station (Amsterdam Centraal), on the north edge of the city, is your starting point, with the TI, bike rental, and trams branching out to all points. Damrak is the main north-south axis, connecting Central Station with Dam Square (people-watching and hangout center) and its Royal Palace. From this main street, the city spreads out like a fan, with 90 islands, hundreds of bridges, and a series of concentric canals—named Herengracht (Gentleman's Canal), Keizersgracht (Emperor's Canal), and Prinsengracht (Prince's Canal)—that were laid out in the 17th century, Holland's Golden Age. Amsterdam's major sights are all within walking distance of Dam Square.

To the east of Damrak is the oldest part of the city (today's Red Light District), and to the west is the newer part, where you'll find the Anne Frank House and the peaceful Jordaan neighborhood. Museums and Leidseplein nightlife cluster at the southern edge of the city center.

Amsterdam by Neighborhood

Amsterdam can feel like a big, sprawling city, but its major sights cluster in convenient zones. Grouping your sightseeing, walks, dining, and shopping thoughtfully can save you time.

Central Amsterdam—the historic core—runs north-south from Central Station along Damrak, passing through two major city squares (Dam and Spui) and ending at the Mint Tower. The central spine of streets (Damrak, Kalverstraat, Rokin) has some of the city's main department, chain, and tourist stores. Flanking Damrak on the east is the city's oldest area (today's Red Light District) and the revitalized waterfront around the train station.

West Amsterdam lies west of Damrak—from Dam Square to the Anne Frank House. This pleasant area is famous for its four grand canals (Singel, Herengracht, Keizersgracht, and Prinsengracht) that circle the historic core. West Amsterdam has tree-lined canals fronted by old, gabled mansions, as well as many of my recommended accommodations and restaurants. Within West

AMSTERDAM ORIENTATION

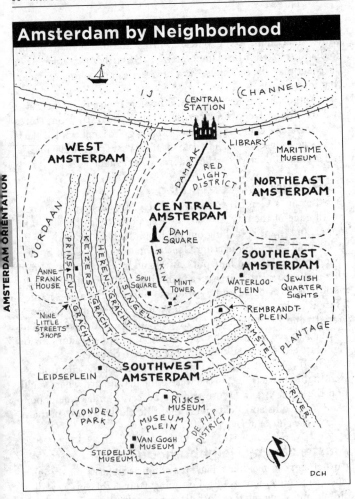

Amsterdam by Neighborhood

Amsterdam is the boutique shopping district known as the Nine Little Streets. Farther west is the quieter, cozier Jordaan neighborhood, which is good for a stroll, though it's mostly residential.

Southwest Amsterdam is defined by two main features: museums and a city park. The city's major art museums (Rijksmuseum, Van Gogh) and other sights cluster together on an expansive square, Museumplein. The museums are just a short walk from Vondelpark, Amsterdam's version of a central park. The lively Leidseplein (a small square that's home to nightlife and restaurants) and the Spiegelkwartier (classy antiques-shopping district) are nearby. While it's less central to stay in Southwest Amsterdam, I've recommended accommodations that are a quick, convenient walk to the area's tram lines.

Amsterdam Landmarks

Dam (pronounced dahm)	Amsterdam's main square
Damrak (DAHM-rock)	main street between Central Station and Dam Square
Spui (spow, rhymes with cow)	both a street and square
Rokin (roh-KEEN)	street connecting Dam Square and Spui
Kalverstraat (KAL-ver-straht)	pedestrian street
Leidseplein (LIDE-zuh-pline)	lively square
Jordaan (yor-DAHN)	neighborhood in west Amsterdam
Museumplein (myoo-ZAY-um-pline)	square with Rijks and Van Gogh museums
gracht (khrockt, pronounced gutturally)	canal
straat (straht)	street
plein (pline)	public square
huis (house)	house
kerk (kerk)	church

Northeast Amsterdam has the Netherlands Maritime Museum and a children's science museum (NEMO).

Southeast Amsterdam contains the former Jewish Quarter and the Jewish Historical Museum. Several sights can be found around the square known as Waterlooplein (Rembrandt's House and a flea market). Additional sights are gathered in a park-dotted area called the Plantage (Dutch Resistance Museum, a theater-turned-Holocaust-memorial, a zoo, and a botanical garden). Rembrandtplein, another nightlife center, is a five-minute walk away.

Planning Your Time

Amsterdam is worth a full day of sightseeing on even the busiest itinerary. And though the city has a couple of must-see museums, its best attraction is its own carefree ambience. The city's a joy on foot—and a breezier and faster delight by bike.

Amsterdam in One Day

9:00   Follow my self-guided Amsterdam City Walk, which takes you from the train station to the Rijksmuseum, with stops at the peaceful Begijnhof, the Amsterdam Museum, and the flower market. Break up the walk with a relaxing hour-long canal cruise (departs from Spui dock or from near Leidseplein).

14:00   Visit Amsterdam's two great art museums, located side by side: the Van Gogh Museum and the Rijksmuseum.

18:30   Tour the Anne Frank House. (Consider reserving online to skip long lines.) Arrive earlier off-season, when it closes at 19:00.

19:30   Wander the Jordaan neighborhood, enjoying dinner by a canal or on a cobbled, quiet street.

21:30   Stroll the Red Light District for some of Europe's most fascinating window-shopping.

Amsterdam in Two or More Days
Day 1

9:00   Follow my self-guided Amsterdam City Walk, leading from the train station to the Rijksmuseum, via the quiet Begijnhof, the Amsterdam Museum (make time to tour this), and the flower market.

12:00   Stop for lunch in the Spui neighborhood before completing the walk.

14:00   Visit Amsterdam's two outstanding art museums, located next to each other: the Van Gogh Museum and the Rijksmuseum.

18:00   Dinner.

20:00   Stroll the Red Light District for some memorable window-shopping.

Day 2

10:00   Start your day with a one-hour canal boat tour (boats leave across from train station).

11:00   Visit the sights of your choice around Rembrandtplein (Rembrandt's House, Waterlooplein flea market— closed Sun), Gassan Diamonds polishing demo, Dutch Resistance Museum).

13:30   Free time for lunch and to shop and explore.

17:00   Tour the Anne Frank House. (Consider reserving online to avoid long lines.)

18:30   Take my self-guided Jordaan Walk.

20:00   Dinner in the Jordaan neighborhood.

Day 3
Visit the nearby town of Haarlem (see Haarlem chapters) or Delft (see the Delft and The Hague chapter).

Day 4
Side-trip by train to an open-air folk museum; choose among Arnhem's, Enkhuizen's, or Zaandijk's (Zaanse Schans Museum).

Daily Reminder

The biggest Amsterdam sights—the Rijksmuseum, the Van Gogh Museum, and the Anne Frank House—are open daily year-round (the Anne Frank House until 22:00 July-Aug). The Westerkerk stays open late in summer (Mon-Sat until 20:00 July-Aug).

The city's naughty sights, as you might expect, stay open late every day (the Hash, Marijuana, and Hemp Museum until 23:00, the Damrak Sex Museum until 23:00, and the Erotic Museum until 1:00 in the morning).

Sunday: These sights have limited, afternoon-only hours today—the Amstelkring Museum (13:00-17:00) and Old Church (13:00-17:00). The Canal House, Westerkerk church and tower, and the Old Church tower are closed altogether, as is the Waterlooplein flea market.

Monday: The Stedelijk Museum, Houseboat Museum, Canal House, the Old Church tower, and Tropical Museum are closed today. From September through May, NEMO is closed today (but open in peak season). Many businesses are closed Monday morning.

Tuesday: All recommended sights are open, except the Old Church tower.

Wednesday: All recommended sights are open, except the Old Church tower.

Thursday: All recommended sights are open. The Stedelijk Museum is open until 22:00.

Friday: The Van Gogh Museum is open until 22:00, and the House of Bols is open until 21:00.

Saturday: The Anne Frank House is open until 22:00 mid-March-mid-Sept, and until 21:00 in the off-season.

Unless you're visiting far-flung Arnhem, you could also easily fit in a short visit to nearby Edam.

Overview

Tourist Information

"VVV" (pronounced "fay fay fay") is Dutch for "TI," a tourist information office. Amsterdam's tourist offices are crowded and inefficient—avoid them if you can. You can save yourself a trip by calling the TI at 020/201-8800 (Mon-Fri 8:00-18:00) or trying 0900-400-4040 (Mon-Fri 9:00-17:00). From the US dial 011-31-20-551-2525.

The main TI at Central Station is busy, but is convenient for anyone arriving by train (July-Aug Mon-Sat 9:00-19:00, Sun 10:00-17:00; Sept-June Mon-Sat 9:00-18:00, Sun 10:00-17:00). An affiliated office is in the AUB/Last Minute Ticket Shop on

Leidseplein, tucked into the side of the giant Stadsschouwburg Theater (Mon-Fri 10:00-19:00, Sat 10:00-18:00, Sun 12:00-18:00; doesn't book hotel rooms). These TIs outside of Amsterdam are helpful and less crowded: at Schiphol Airport (daily 7:00-22:00) and in the town of Haarlem (see pages 227 and 232).

Tickets: Although Amsterdam's main TI sells tickets to the Anne Frank House (€1 extra per ticket, same-day tickets available) and the Van Gogh and Stedelijk museums (no fee), it's quicker to get tickets in advance online (see below).

Maps and Brochures: Given the city's maze of streets and canals, I'd definitely get a good city map (€2.50 at Central Station TI, same map given away free at the TI in the AUB/Last Minute Ticket Shop—go figure). Also consider picking up any of the walking-tour brochures (€3 each, including tours covering city center, former Jewish Quarter, Jordaan, and funky De Pijp neighborhood). For entertainment, get a copy of *Time Out Amsterdam* (€3, €1.50 if bought with city map); for additional entertainment ideas, see the Entertainment in Amsterdam chapter.

Currency Exchange: At Central Station, **GWK Currency Exchange** offices have hotel reservation windows where clerks sell international phone cards and mobile-phone SIM cards, and answer basic tourist questions, with shorter lines than the TI (Mon-Sat 8:00-22:00, Sun 9:00-22:00, near front of station in both the east and west corridors, tel. 020/627-2731).

Resources for Gay Travelers: A short walk from Central Station down Damrak is **GAYtic,** a TI specifically oriented to the needs of gay travelers. The office stocks maps, magazines, and brochures, and dispenses advice on nightlife and general sightseeing (daily 11:00-20:00, Spuistraat 44, tel. 020/330-1461, www.gaytic.nl). **Pink Point,** in a kiosk outside Westerkerk, next to the Homomonument, is less of a resource, but has advice about nightlife (usually daily 10:00-18:00).

Advance Tickets and Sightseeing Cards

During high season (late March-Oct), you can avoid long ticket lines at the **Rijksmuseum, Van Gogh Museum,** and **Stedelijk** modern-art museum either by booking tickets online, or by getting a Museumkaart sightseeing pass (described later) or by buying tickets in advance. At the **Anne Frank House,** the only line-skipping option is booking tickets ahead (or, if you'll be buying a Museumkaart, reserving an entry time). The I amsterdam Card, also described later, only lets you skip the line at the Van Gogh Museum.

Advance Tickets for Major Sights: It's easy to buy tickets online through each museum's website: www.annefrank.org (€0.50 surcharge per ticket, but worth it), www.rijksmuseum.nl, www

.vangoghmuseum.com, and www.stedelijk.nl (no extra fee for Rijks, Van Gogh, or Stedelijk). Print out your ticket and bring it to the ticket-holder's line for a quick entry. Before you get your tickets online, however, consider whether you'll save money by buying a sightseeing card.

You can also buy tickets for these sights in advance at the TIs (main TI only for Anne Frank House), but TI lines seem almost as long as the ones you're trying to avoid at the sights.

If You Don't Have Advance Tickets: If you end up visiting the Anne Frank House without a reservation, trim your wait in line by showing up the minute it opens, or late in the day; this works better in early spring and fall than in summer, when even after-dinner lines can be long. Visit the Van Gogh Museum on a Friday evening, when it's open until 22:00, with no lines and few crowds, even in peak season.

Sightseeing Cards: Two cards merit consideration for heavy-duty sightseers: The Museumkaart and the I amsterdam Card. If your trip includes any other Dutch city, you'll save more money by purchasing the Museumkaart, which covers many sights throughout the Netherlands, than the overpriced I amsterdam Card, which is valid only in Amsterdam. (There's no reason to buy both.) However, if Amsterdam's your only stop in the Netherlands, and if you plan to get around on transit (rather than by bike), the I amsterdam Card makes sense, as it includes a transit pass. Both cards allow you free entry to most sights in Amsterdam (including the Van Gogh Museum), but neither card covers the Heineken Brewery, Westerkerk tower, or any sights dealing with sex or marijuana. The Anne Frank House and Rijksmuseum are covered by the Museumkaart but not by the I amsterdam Card. The Museumkaart is a better option for avoiding crowds (it lets you skip ticket-buying lines everywhere except the Anne Frank House; the I amsterdam Card only lets you skip at the Van Gogh). Note: Even those who skip the ticket line still have to go through security. You'll also see ads for the Holland Pass, but it's not worth it.

The **Museumkaart** costs €50 and is valid for a year throughout the Netherlands, is a no-brainer for anyone visiting at least six museums (for example, an itinerary that includes these museums, for a total of €65: Rijksmuseum-€15, Van Gogh Museum-€15, Anne Frank House-€9, Amsterdam Museum-€10, Amstelkring Museum-€8, and the Dutch Resistance Museum-€8). The Museumkaart is sold at all participating museums (buy it at a less-crowded one to avoid lines).

The **I amsterdam Card,** which focuses on Amsterdam and includes most transportation, is not worth the cost unless you're planning on a day or two of nonstop sightseeing, and connecting it all by public transit (it doesn't cover bike rental). This pass doesn't cover the Rijksmuseum or the Anne Frank House. It does, however, include most other Amsterdam sights (including the Van Gogh Museum), one free canal boat tour (otherwise about €13), and unlimited use of trams, buses, and metro (except for the canal tour, all of these public-transit options are also covered by a normal transit pass—see "Getting Around Amsterdam," later). Remember, this card's line-skipping perks are limited to the Van Gogh Museum. You have a set number of consecutive hours to use it (for example: Visit your first museum at 14:00 Monday with a 24-hour pass, and it's good until 13:59 on Tuesday). It's sold at major museums, TIs, and with shorter lines at the GVB public-transit office across from Central Station, next to the TI (€40/24 hours, €50/48 hours, or €60/72 hours; www.iamsterdamcard.com).

Arrival in Amsterdam

By Train

The portal connecting Amsterdam to the world is its aptly named Central Station (Amsterdam Centraal). Through at least 2014, expect the station and the plaza in front of it to be a construction zone and therefore in a state of some flux.

Trains arrive on a level above the station. Go down the stairs or the escalator (at the "A" end of the platform). As you descend from the platforms, you'll find yourself in one of the corridors leading to the street exit for the city center *(Centrum)*. Those wanting buses and river ferries should head in the opposite direction—to the north *(Noord)* exit.

The station is fully equipped for the traveler. You'll find GWK Travelex counters in both the east and west corridors, and international train-ticket offices near the exit of both corridors. Luggage lockers are in the east corridor, under the "B" end of the platforms (€5-7/24 hours, depending on size of bag, always open, can fill up on busy summer weekends). The station has plenty of shops and places to grab a bite to eat. On the train level, platform 2 is lined with eateries, including the tall, venerable, 1920s-style **First Class Grand Café.** Handy **Albert Heijn** "to go" supermarkets are easy to find at the end of the east corridor and in the main north-south underground passage.

Exiting the station, you're in the heart of the city. Straight ahead, just past the canal, is Damrak street, leading to Dam Square. To your left are the TI and GVB public-transit office. Farther to your left is a fascinating exhibit about the big construction project going on all around you (specifically, the digging of a new subway line). Past the exhibit are two bike rental places: **MacBike** (in the station building), and **Star Bikes** (a five-minute walk past the station), both listed on page 49. To the right of the station are the postcard-perfect neighborhoods of West Amsterdam; some of my recommended hotels are within walking distance.

Just beyond the taxis are the platforms for the city's blue trams, which come along frequently, ready to take you anywhere your feet won't (buy ticket or pass from conductor). Trams #1, #2, and #5 (which run to nearly all my recommended hotels) leave from in front of the station's west (main) entrance. All trams leaving Central Station stop at Dam Square along their route. For more on the transit system, see page 47.

By Plane
For details on getting from Schiphol Airport into downtown Amsterdam, see page 228.

Helpful Hints
Theft Alert: Tourists are considered green and rich, and the city has more than its share of hungry thieves—especially in the train station, on trams, in and near crowded museums, at places of drunkenness, and at the many hostels. Wear your money belt.

Emergency Telephone Number: Throughout the Netherlands, dial 112.

Street Smarts: Beware of silent transportation—trams, electric mopeds, and bicycles—when walking around town. Don't walk on tram tracks or pink/maroon bicycle paths. Before you step off any sidewalk, do a double- or triple-check in both directions to make sure all's clear.

Sightseeing Strategies: To beat the lines at Amsterdam's most popular sights, plan ahead—either buy a sightseeing pass or advance online tickets (see details on page 42). Friday night is a great time to visit the Van Gogh Museum, when it's open until 22:00 (with far smaller crowds). On Saturday nights in summer, the Anne Frank House stays open until 22:00.

Shop Hours: Most shops are open Tuesday through Saturday 10:00-18:00, and Sunday and Monday 12:00-18:00. Some shops stay open later (21:00) on Thursdays. Supermarkets are generally open Monday through Saturday 8:00-20:00 and have shorter hours or are closed on Sundays.

Busy Weekends: Every year, **King's Day** (Koningsdag, April 27 most years, but April 26 in 2014) and **Gay Pride** (Aug 2-4 in 2013, Aug 1-3 in 2014) bring big crowds, fuller hotels, and inflated room prices.

Cash Only: Thrifty Dutch merchants, who hate paying the unusually high fees charged by credit-card companies here, rarely take US credit cards; expect to pay cash in unexpected places, including grocery stores, cafés, budget hotels, train-station machines and windows, and at some museums.

Internet Access: It's easy at cafés all over town, but the best place for serious surfing and email is the towering **Central Library,** which has hundreds of fast terminals and Wi-Fi (€1/30 minutes, Openbare Bibliotheek Amsterdam, daily 10:00-22:00, a 10-minute walk from train station, described on page 70). The café across the street from Central Station (next to the TI) also has pay Internet access and Wi-Fi. "Coffeeshops," which sell marijuana, usually also offer Internet access—letting you surf with a special bravado.

English Bookstores: For fiction and guidebooks, try the **American Book Center** at Spui 12, right on the square (generally daily 10:00-20:00, tel. 020/535-2575). The huge and helpful **Selexyz Scheltema** is at Koningsplein 20 near the Leidsestraat (included in my Amsterdam City Walk; generally daily 9:30-18:00; lots of English novels, guidebooks, and maps; tel. 020/523-1411). **Waterstone's Booksellers,** a UK chain, also sells British newspapers (near Spui at 152 Kalverstraat, generally daily 10:00-18:30, tel. 020/638-3821). Expect shorter hours on Monday and Sunday.

Language Barrier: This is one of the easiest places in the non-English-speaking world for an English speaker. Nearly all signs and services are offered in two languages: Dutch and "non-Dutch" (i.e., English).

Maps: The free tourist maps can be confusing, except for *Amsterdam Museums: Guide to 37 Museums* (includes tram info and stops, ask for it at the big museums, such as the Van Gogh). If you want a top-notch map, buy one (about €2.50). I like the *Carto Studio Centrumkaart Amsterdam.* Amsterdam Anything's virtual "Go Where the Locals Go" city map is worth checking out, especially if you have mobile Internet access (www.amsterdamanything.nl).

Pharmacy: The shop named **DA** (Dienstdoende Apotheek) has all the basics—shampoo and toothpaste—as well as a pharmacy counter hidden in the back (Mon-Sat 9:00-22:00, Sun 11:00-22:00, Leidsestraat 74-76 near where it meets Keizersgracht, tel. 020/627-5351). Near Dam Square, there's **BENU Apotheek** (Mon-Fri 8:30-17:30, Sat 10:00-17:00, Sun 12:00-17:00, Damstraat 2, tel. 020/624-4331).

Laundry: Try **Clean Brothers Wasserij** in the Jordaan (daily 8:00-20:00 for €7 self-service, €9 drop-off—ready in an hour—Mon-Fri 9:00-17:00, Sat 9:00-18:00, no drop-off Sun, Westerstraat 26, one block from Prinsengracht, tel. 020/627-9888) or **Powders,** near Leidseplein (daily 8:00-22:00, €6.50 self-service, €12 drop-off available Mon-Wed and Fri 8:00-17:00, Sat-Sun 9:00-15:00, no drop-off Thu, Kerkstraat 56, one block south of Leidsestraat, mobile 06-2630-6057).

Best Views: Although sea-level Amsterdam is notoriously horizontal, there are a few high points where you can get the big picture. The best city views are from the **Central Library** (Openbare Bibliotheek Amsterdam; see page 70). The **Westerkerk**—a stop on my Jordaan Walk and convenient for anyone visiting the Anne Frank House—has a climbable tower with fine views. The tower of the **Old Church** (Oude Kerk), the top floor of the **Kalvertoren** shopping complex (mentioned in my Amsterdam City Walk), and the rooftop terrace at the **NEMO science museum** also provide good views.

Updates to This Book: Check www.ricksteves.com/update for any significant changes that have occurred since this book was printed.

Getting Around Amsterdam

Amsterdam is big, and you'll find the trams handy. The longest walk a tourist would make is an hour from Central Station to the Rijksmuseum. When you're on foot, be extremely vigilant for silent but potentially painful bikes, trams, and crotch-high bollards.

By Tram, Bus, and Metro

Amsterdam's public transit system includes trams, buses, and an underground metro; of these, trams are most useful for most tourists.

The helpful **GVB public-transit information office** in front of Central Station can answer questions (next to TI, Mon-Fri 7:00-21:00, Sat-Sun 10:00-18:00). Its free, multilingual *Public Transport Amsterdam Tourist Guide* includes a transit map and explains ticket options and tram connections to all the sights. For more public transit information, visit www.gvb.nl.

Tickets: The entire country's public transit network operates on a single ticket system called the OV-Chipkaart (for "Openbaar Vervoer"—public transit). For locals, it couldn't be easier. With a single pre-paid card, they can hop on any form of public transit in the country, scan their card, and the (discounted) fare is immediately deducted. Cards can be reloaded automatically, straight from residents' bank accounts. While it's possible for tourists to purchase an OV-Chipkaart, they cost a non-refundable €7.50 and can only be reloaded at train stations—unless you're staying in the Netherlands for more than a week, don't bother (for more information, see page 617).

Most travelers instead rely on either single tickets or multiday passes. (While officially classified as "OV-Chipkaarten," these tickets and passes with electronic chips are nothing like the reloadable, valid-nationwide, plastic cards locals use.)

Within Amsterdam, a single transit ticket costs €2.80 and is good for one hour on the tram, bus, and metro, including transfers. Passes good for unlimited transportation are available for 24 hours (€7.50), 48 hours (€12), 72 hours (€16.50), and 96 hours (€21). (The I amsterdam sightseeing card, described on page 43, includes a transit pass.) Given how expensive single tickets are, consider buying a pass before you buy that first ticket. (A rental bike—described later—costs about the same as a transit pass...but is way more fun.)

The easiest way to buy a ticket or transit pass is to simply board a tram or bus and pay the conductor (no extra fee). Tickets and passes are also available at metro-station vending machines (which take cash but not US credit cards), at GVB public-transit offices, and at TIs.

Trams: Board the tram at any entrance not marked with a red/white "do not enter" sticker. If you need a ticket or pass, pay the conductor (in a booth at the back); if there's no conductor, pay the driver in front. You must always "check in" as you board by scanning your ticket or pass at the pink-and-gray scanner, and "check out" by scanning it again when you get off. The scanner will beep and flash a green light after a successful scan. Be careful not to accidentally scan your ticket or pass twice while boarding, or it becomes

invalid. Checking in and out is very important, as controllers do pass through and fine violators. To open the door when you reach your stop, press a green button on one of the poles near an exit.

Trams #2 *(Nieuw Sloten)* and #5 *(A'veen Binnenhof)* travel the north-south axis, from Central Station to Dam Square to Leidseplein to Museumplein (Van Gogh and Rijks museums). Tram #1 (marked *Osdorp*) also runs to Leidseplein. At Central Station, these three trams depart from the west side of Stationsplein (with the station behind you, they're to your right).

Tram #14, which doesn't connect to Central Station, goes east-west (Westerkerk-Dam Square-Muntplein-Waterlooplein-Plantage). If you get lost in Amsterdam, don't sweat it—10 of the city's 17 trams take you back to Central Station.

Buses and Metro: Tickets and passes work on buses and the metro just as they do on the trams—scan your ticket or pass to "check in" as you enter and again to "check out" when you leave. The metro system is scant—used mostly for commuting to the suburbs—but it does connect Central Station with some sights east of Damrak (Nieuwmarkt-Waterlooplein-Weesperplein). The glacial speed of the metro-expansion project is a running joke among cynical Amsterdammers.

Bike Theft

Bike thieves are bold and brazen in Amsterdam. Bikes come with two locks and stern instructions to use both. The wimpy

ones go through the spokes, whereas the industrial-strength chains are meant to be wrapped around the actual body of the bike and through the front wheel, and connected to something stronger than any human. (Note the steel bike-hitching racks sticking up all around town, called "staples.") Follow your rental agency's locking directions diligently. Once, I used both locks, but my chain wasn't around the main bar of my bike's body. In the morning, I found only my front tire (still safely chained to the metal fence). If you're sloppy, it's an expensive mistake and one that any "included" theft insurance won't cover.

By Bike

Everyone—bank managers, students, pizza delivery boys, and police—uses this mode of transport. It's by far the smartest way to travel in a city where 40 percent of all traffic rolls on two wheels. You'll get around town by bike faster than you can by taxi. On my last visit, I rented a bike for five days, chained it to the rack outside my hotel at night, and enjoyed wonderful mobility. I highly encourage this for anyone who wants to get maximum fun per hour in Amsterdam. One-speed bikes, with *"brrringing"* bells, rent for about €10 per day (cheaper for longer periods) at any number of places—hotels can send you to the nearest spot.

Rental Shops: Star Bikes Rental has cheap rates, long hours, and inconspicuous black bikes. They're happy to arrange an after-hours drop-off if you give them your credit-card number and pre-pay (€5/3 hours, €7/day, €9/24 hours, €12/2 days, €17/3 days, daily 9:00-19:00, requires ID but no monetary deposit, 5-minute walk from east end of Central Station—walk underneath tracks near Doubletree Hotel and then turn right, De Ruyterkade 127, tel. 020/620-3215, www.starbikesrental.com).

MacBike, with thousands of bikes, is the city's bike-rental powerhouse—you'll see their bright-red bikes all over town (they do stick out a bit). It has a huge and efficient outlet at Central Station (€7/3 hours, €9.50/24 hours, €14/48 hours, €19/72 hours, more for 3 gears, 25 percent discount with I amsterdam Card; either leave €50 deposit plus a copy of your passport, or leave a credit-card imprint; free helmets, daily 9:00-17:45; at east end of station—on the left as you're leaving; tel. 020/620-0985, www.macbike.nl). They have two smaller satellite stations at Leidseplein (Weteringschans 2) and Waterlooplein (Nieuwe Uilenburgerstraat 116). Return your bike to the station where you rented it. MacBike sells several pamphlets outlining bike tours with a variety of themes in and around Amsterdam for €1-2.

Frederic Rent-a-Bike, a 10-minute walk from Central Station, has quality bikes and a helpful staff (€8/3 hours, €15/24 hours—€10 if returned by 17:30, €25/48 hours, €50/week, 10 percent discount with this book, daily 9:00-17:30, no after-hours drop-off, Brouwersgracht 78, tel. 020/624-5509, www.frederic.nl, Frederic and son Marne).

Tips: As the Dutch believe in fashion over safety, no one here wears a helmet. They do, however, ride cautiously, and so should you: Use arm signals, follow the bike-only traffic signals, stay in the obvious and omnipresent bike lanes, and yield to traffic on the right. Fear oncoming trams and tram tracks. Carefully cross tram tracks at a perpendicular angle to avoid catching your tire in the rut. Warning: Police ticket cyclists just as they do drivers. Obey all traffic signals, and walk your bike through pedestrian zones. Fines for biking through pedestrian zones are reportedly €30-50. A handy bicycle route-planner can be found at www.routecraft.com (select "bikeplanner," then click British flag for English). For a "Do-It-Yourself Bike Tour of Amsterdam" and for bike tours, see "By Bike," later in this chapter.

By Boat

While the city is great on foot, bike, or tram, you can also get around Amsterdam by boat. **Rederij Lovers** boats shuttle tourists on a variety of routes covering different combinations of the city's top sights. Their Museum Line, for example, costs €16 and stops near the Hermitage, Rijksmuseum/Van Gogh Museum, and Central Station (at least every 45 minutes, 4 stops, 1.5 hours). Sales booths in front of Central Station (and the boats) offer free brochures listing museum hours and admission prices. Most routes come with recorded narration and run daily 10:00-17:30 (tel. 020/530-1090, www.lovers.nl).

The similar **Canal Bus** is actually a boat, offering 17 stops on three different boat routes (€24/24-hour pass, departures daily 9:30-18:30, until 19:00 April-Oct, leaves near Central Station and Rederij Lovers dock, tel. 020/623-9886, www.canal.nl).

If you're simply looking for a floating, nonstop tour, the regular canal tour boats (without the stops) give more information, cover more ground, and cost less (see "Tours in Amsterdam," below).

For do-it-yourself canal tours and lots of exercise, Canal Bus also rents "canal bikes" (a.k.a. paddleboats) at several locations: near the Anne Frank House, near the Rijksmuseum, near Leidseplein, and where Leidsestraat meets Keizersgracht (€8/hour per person, daily July-Aug 10:00-22:00, Sept-June 10:00-18:00).

By Taxi

For short rides, Amsterdam is a bad town for taxis. Given the good tram system and ease of biking, I use taxis less in Amsterdam than in just about any other city in Europe. The city's taxis have a high drop charge (€7.50) for the first two kilometers (e.g., from Central Station to the Mint Tower), after which it's €2.30 per kilometer (no extra fee for luggage; it's worth trying to bargain a lower rate, as competition among cabbies is fierce). You can wave them down, find a rare taxi stand, or call one (tel. 020/677-7777). You'll also see **bike taxis**, particularly near Dam Square and Leidseplein. Negotiate a rate for the trip before you board (no meter), and they'll wheel you wherever you want to go (€1/3 minutes, no surcharge for baggage or extra weight, sample fare from Leidseplein to Anne Frank House: about €6).

By Car

If you've got a car, park it—all you'll find are frustrating one-way streets, terrible parking, and meter maids with a passion for booting cars parked incorrectly. You'll pay €60 a day to park safely in a central garage. If you must bring a car to Amsterdam, it's best to leave it at one of the city's supervised park-and-ride lots (follow *P&R* signs from freeway, €8/24 hours, includes round-trip transit into city center for up to five people, 4-day maximum).

Tours in Amsterdam

By Boat

▲▲**Canal Boat Tours**—These long, low, tourist-laden boats leave continually from several docks around town for a relaxing, if uninspiring, one-hour introduction to the city (with recorded headphone commentary). Select a boat tour based on convenience of its starting point, or whether it's

included with your I amsterdam Card (which covers Blue Boat Company and Holland International boats). Tip: Boats leave only when full, so jump on a full boat to avoid waiting at the dock. Choose from one of these three companies:

Rederij P. Kooij is cheapest (€9, 3/hour in summer 10:00-22:00, 2/hour in winter 10:00-17:00, at corner of Spui and Rokin streets, about 10 minutes from Dam Square, tel. 020/623-3810, www.rederijkooij.nl).

Blue Boat Company's boats depart from near Leidseplein (€14; every half-hour April-Sept 10:00-18:00, also at 19:00; hourly Oct-March 10:00-17:00; 1.25 hours, Stadhouderskade 30, tel. 020/679-1370, www.blueboat.nl). Their 1.5-hour evening cruise has a live English-speaking guide (€17.50, nightly at 20:00, April-Sept also at 21:00 and 22:00, reservations required).

Holland International offers a standard one-hour trip and a variety of longer tours from the docks opposite Central Station (€14, 1-hour "100 Highlights" tour with recorded commentary, daily 4/hour 9:00-18:00, 2/hour 18:00-22:00; Prins Hendrikkade 33a, tel. 020/625-3035, www.hir.nl).

No fishing allowed—but bring your camera. Some prefer to cruise at night, when the bridges are illuminated.

Hop-On, Hop-Off Canal Boats—Small, 12-person electric Canal Hopper boats leave every 20-30 minutes with live commentary on two different hop-on, hop-off routes (€24 day pass, €17 round-trip ticket, July-Aug daily 10:00-17:00, Sept-June Fri-Sun only, "yellow" west route runs 2/hour and stops near Anne Frank House and Rijksmuseum, "orange" east route runs 3/hour and stops near Red Light District and Damrak, tel. 020/626-5574, www.canal.nl).

Wetlands Safari, Nature Canoe Tours near Amsterdam—If you want some exercise and a dose of the *polder* country and village life, consider this five-hour tour. Majel Tromp, a friendly villager who speaks great English, takes groups limited to 15 people. The program: Meet at the bus stops behind Central Station (leave the station from the west corridor and take the escalator up to the buses) at 9:30, catch a public bus, stop for coffee, take a 3.5-hour canoe trip (2-3 people per canoe) with several stops, tour a village by canoe, munch a rural canalside picnic lunch (included), then canoe and bus back into Amsterdam by 15:00 (€43, €27 for kids ages 7-16, €3 discount with this book, May-mid-Sept Sun-Fri, reservations required, tel. 020/686-3445, mobile 06-5355-2669, www.wetlandssafari.nl, info@wetlandssafari.nl).

On Foot

Red Light District Tours—For a stroll through Amsterdam's most infamous neighborhood, consider my self-guided Red Light

> # Rick Steves Audio Europe
>
> If you're bringing a mobile device, be sure to check out **Rick Steves Audio Europe,** where you can download free audio tours and hours of travel interviews (via the Rick Steves Audio Europe smartphone app, www.ricksteves.com/audioeurope, iTunes, or Google Play).
>
> My self-guided **audio tours** are user-friendly, easy to follow, fun, and informative, covering my Amsterdam City Walk, Red Light District Walk, and Jordaan Walk. Compared to live tours, my audio tours are hard to beat: Nobody will stand you up, the quality is reliable, you can take the tour exactly when you like, and they're free.
>
> Rick Steves Audio Europe also offers a far-reaching library of intriguing **travel interviews** with experts from around the globe.

District Walk on page 69. But if you'd be more comfortable exploring with a group, a guided tour is a good way to go. **Randy Roy's Red Light Tours** consists of one expat American woman, Kimberley. She lived in the Red Light District for years and gives fun, casual, yet informative 1.5-hour walks through this fascinating and eye-popping neighborhood. Though the actual information is light, you'll walk through various porn and drug shops and have an expert to answer your questions. Call or email to reserve (€15 includes a drink in a colorful bar at the end, nightly at 20:00, Fri and Sat also at 22:00, no tours Dec-Feb, tours meet in front of Victoria Hotel—in front of Central Station, mobile 06-4185-3288, www.randyroysredlighttours.com, kimberley@randyroysredlight tours.com).

Free City Walk—New Europe Tours "employs" native, English-speaking students to give irreverent and entertaining three-hour walks (using the same "free tour, ask for tips, sell their other tours" formula popular in so many great European cities). While most guides lack a local's deep understanding of Dutch culture, not to mention professional training, they're certainly high-energy. This long walk covers a lot of the city with an enthusiasm for the contemporary pot-and-prostitution scene (free but tips expected, daily at 11:15 and 13:15, www.neweuropetours.eu). They also offer paid tours (Red Light District—€12, daily at 19:00; coffeeshop scene—€12, daily at 16:00; city by bike—€19, includes bike, daily at 14:00). Their walking tours leave from the National Monument on Dam Square; the bike tour leaves from Central Station.

Adam's Apple Tours—Frank Sanders' walking tour offers a two-hour, English-only look at the historic roots and development of Amsterdam. You'll have a small group of generally 5-6 people and a caring guide, starting off at Central Station and ending up at Dam Square (€25; May-Sept daily at 10:00, 12:30, and 15:00 based on demand; call 020/616-7867 to confirm times and book).

Private Guide—**Albert Walet** is a likeable, hardworking, and knowledgeable local guide who enjoys personalizing tours for Americans interested in knowing his city. Al specializes in history, architecture, and water management, and exudes a passion for Amsterdam (€70/2 hours, €120/4 hours, up to 4 people, on foot or by bike, mobile 06-2069-7882, abwalet@yahoo.com). Al also takes travelers to nearby towns, including Haarlem, Leiden, and Delft.

By Bike

Guided Bike Tours—**Yellow Bike Guided Tours** offers city bike tours of either two hours (€19.50, daily at 10:30) or three hours (€23.50, daily at 13:30), which both include a 20-minute break. They also offer a four-hour, 15-mile tour of the dikes and green pastures of the countryside (€29.50, lunch extra, includes 45-minute break, April-Oct daily at 10:30). All tours leave from Nieuwezijds Kolk 29, three blocks from Central Station (reservations smart, tel. 020/620-6940, www.yellowbike.nl). If you'd prefer a private guide, see Albert Walet, above.

Joy Ride Bike Tours is a creative little company run by English-speaking Sean and Allison Cody. Their most popular tours start just behind the Rijksmuseum (city by bike—€26, 2.5-3 hours, May-Sept departs Fri-Mon at 16:00, none Tue-Thu, no kids under 13; countryside by bike—€30, 4-4.5 hours, May-Sept departs Thu-Mon at 10:30, none Tue-Wed, no kids under 10; no tours off-season). Both tours are limited to 10-15 people, so it's smart to book ahead (save €3 by booking online, €7 cheaper with your own bike—must email or call ahead, tours meet 15 minutes before departure time, helmets and rain gear available, mobile 06-4361-1798, www.joyridetours.nl). Their four-hour "bespoke" tours, offered year-round, are tailored to match your interests (Jewish history, Amsterdam for kids, WWII history, or cannabis; €125/3 people).

Do-It-Yourself Bike Tour of Amsterdam—A day enjoying the bridges, bike lanes, and sleepy, off-the-beaten-path canals on your own one-speed is an essential Amsterdam experience. The real joys of Europe's best-preserved 17th-century city are the countless intimate glimpses it offers: the laid-back locals sunning on their porches under elegant gables, rusted bikes that look as if they've been lashed to the same lamppost since the 1960s, wasted hedonists planted on canalside benches, and happy sailors permanently moored, but still manning the deck.

For a good day trip, rent a bike at or near Central Station (see "By Bike" on page 49). Head west down Haarlemmerstraat,

working your wide-eyed way down Prinsengracht (drop into Café 't Papeneiland at Prinsengracht 2) and detouring through the small, gentrified streets of the Jordaan neighborhood before popping out at the Westerkerk under the tallest spire in the city.

Pedal south to the lush and peaceful Vondelpark, then cut back through the center of town (Leidseplein to the Mint Tower, along Rokin street to Dam Square). From there, cruise the Red Light District, following Oudezijds Voorburgwal past the Old Church (Oude Kerk) to Zeedijk street, and return to the train station.

Then, you can escape into the countryside by hopping on the free ferry behind Central Station (see below). In five minutes, Amsterdam is gone, and you're rolling through your very own Dutch painting.

Taking Bikes Across the Harbor on a Free Ferry—Behind Central Station is a little commuter port where four ferries come and go constantly (free, bikes welcome, signs count down minutes until next departure), offering two quick little excursions. The middle two ferries run immediately across the harbor (3-minute ride). Bring your bike and ride two kilometers (1.25 miles) along the canal, through suburbs, and then into the *polderland* and villages. For a quick visit to the striking new EYE Film Institute Netherlands complex, catch the boat labeled *Buiksloterweg*.

Ferries leaving from the far-left "NDSM" wharf cruise 10 minutes across the North Sea Canal (2/hour, generally departing at :15 and :45). This gives a fun peek at the fifth-biggest harbor in Europe (Rotterdam is number one); old wheat silos now renovated into upscale condos; and the shoreline of north Amsterdam, where the planned metro connection to the center is bringing growth, with lots of new apartments under construction. The ferry deposits you in an industrial wasteland (a vacant old warehouse just past the modern MTV headquarters building is filled with artist studios, wacky ventures, and a noisy skateboard hall). **IJ-Kantine** is a fine modern restaurant/café 30 yards from the ferry landing (daily from 9:00, tel. 020/633-7162).

SIGHTS IN AMSTERDAM

One of Amsterdam's delights is that it has perhaps more small specialty museums than any other city its size. From houseboats to sex, from marijuana to Old Masters, you can find a museum to suit your interests.

For tips on how to save time otherwise spent in the long ticket-buying lines of the big three museums—the Anne Frank House, Van Gogh Museum, and Rijksmuseum—see "Advance Tickets and Sightseeing Cards" on page 42. Admission prices are high: A sightseeing card such as the Museumkaart (or I amsterdam Card) can pay for itself quickly. Entry to most sights is free with a card (I've noted those that aren't covered).

Most museums require baggage check (usually free, often in coin-op lockers where you get your coin back).

The following sights are arranged by neighborhood for handy sightseeing. When you see a ✪ in a listing, it means the sight is covered in much more depth in one of my walks or self-guided tours. This is why Amsterdam's most important attractions get the least coverage in this chapter—we'll explore them later in the book.

Southwest Amsterdam

▲▲▲**Rijksmuseum**—Built to house the nation's great art, the Rijksmuseum (RIKES-moo-zay-oom) owns several thousand paintings, including an incomparable collection of 17th-century Dutch Masters: Rembrandt, Vermeer, Hals, and Steen. The museum recently underwent an extensive renovation that restored this great building to its original 1885 glory—a great event in the world of art.

Cost and Hours: €15, not covered by I amsterdam Card, audioguide-€5, daily 9:00-17:00, last entry 30 minutes before

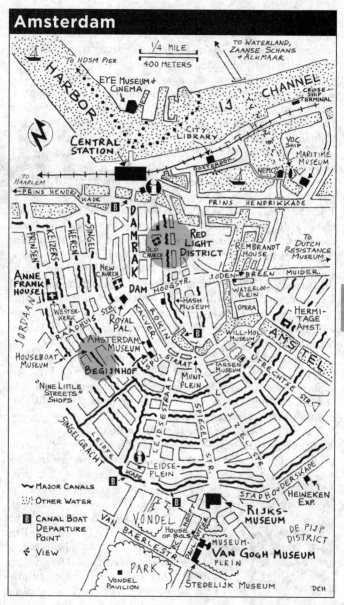

AMSTERDAM SIGHTS

closing, tram #2 or #5 from Central Station to Hobbemastraat. Info tel. 020/674-7047 or switchboard tel. 020/674-7000, www.rijks museum.nl. The entrance is off the passageway that tunnels right through the center of the building.

○ See the Rijksmuseum Tour chapter.

▲▲▲Van Gogh Museum—Near the Rijksmuseum, this remarkable museum features works by the troubled Dutch artist whose

art seemed to mirror his life. Vincent, who killed himself in 1890 at age 37, is best known for sunny, Impressionist canvases that vibrate and pulse with vitality. The museum's 200 paintings—which offer a virtual stroll through the artist's work and life—were owned by Theo, Vincent's younger, art-dealer brother. Highlights include *Sunflowers, The Bedroom, The Potato Eaters*, and many brooding self-portraits. The third floor shows works that influenced Vincent, from Monet and Pissarro to Gauguin, Cézanne, and Toulouse-Lautrec. The worthwhile audioguide includes insightful commentaries and quotes from Vincent himself. Temporary exhibits fill the new wing, down the escalator from the ground-floor lobby.

Cost and Hours: €15, more for special exhibits, audioguide–€5, kids' audioguide–€2.50, daily 9:00-17:00, Fri until 22:00—with no crowds in evening, Paulus Potterstraat 7, tram #2 or #5 from Central Station to Van Baerlestraat stop, tel. 020/570-5200, www.vangoghmuseum.com.

○ See the Van Gogh Museum Tour chapter.

▲▲Stedelijk Museum—The Netherlands' top modern-art museum is filled with a fun, far-out, and refreshing collection that includes

post-1945 experimental and conceptual art as well as works by Picasso, Chagall, Cézanne, Kandinsky, and Mondrian. The Stedelijk (STAYD-eh-lik), like the Rijksmuseum, also boasts a newly spiffed-up building, which now flaunts an architecturally daring entry facing Museumplein (near the Van Gogh Museum).

Cost and Hours: €15, Tue-Wed 11:00-17:00, Thu 11:00-22:00, Fri-Sun 10:00-18:00, closed Mon, café with outdoor seating, top-notch shop, Paulus Potterstraat 13/Museumplein 10, tel. 020/573-2911, www.stede lijk.nl.

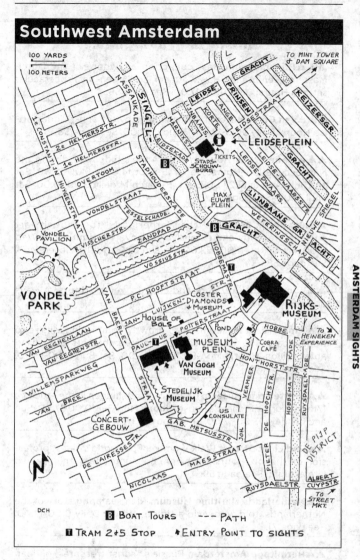

Southwest Amsterdam

100 YARDS
100 METERS

TO MINT TOWER & DAM SQUARE

LEIDSEPLEIN

STADS-SCHOUWBURG

TICKETS

MAX EUWE-PLEIN

VONDEL PAVILION

VONDEL-PARK

COSTER DIAMONDS + MUSEUM

House of BOLS

RIJKS-MUSEUM

To HEINEKEN Experience

MUSEUM-PLEIN

COBRA CAFÉ

Van Gogh Museum

STEDELIJK Museum

US CONSULATE

CONCERT-GEBOUW

DE PIJP DISTRICT

ALBERT CUYPSTR

TO STREET MKT.

DCH

B BOAT TOURS
T TRAM 2 & 5 STOP
- - - PATH
⚑ ENTRY POINT TO SIGHTS

AMSTERDAM SIGHTS

▲**Museumplein**—Bordered by the Rijks, Van Gogh, and Stedelijk museums, and the Concertgebouw (classical music hall), this park-like square is interesting even to art haters. Amsterdam's best acoustics are found underneath the Rijksmuseum, where street musicians perform everything from chamber music to Mongolian throat singing. Mimes, human statues, and crafts booths dot the square. Skateboarders careen across a concrete tube, while locals enjoy a park bench or a coffee at the Cobra Café.

Amsterdam at a Glance

▲▲▲**Rijksmuseum** Best collection anywhere of the Dutch Masters—Rembrandt, Hals, Vermeer, and Steen—in a spectacular setting. **Hours:** Daily 9:00-17:00. See page 56.

▲▲▲**Van Gogh Museum** 200 paintings by the angst-ridden artist. **Hours:** Daily 9:00-17:00, Fri until 22:00. See page 58.

▲▲▲**Anne Frank House** Young Anne's hideaway during the Nazi occupation. **Hours:** March 15-Sept 14 daily 9:00-21:00, Sat and July-Aug until 22:00; Sept 15-March 14 daily 9:00-19:00, Sat until 21:00. See page 64.

▲▲**Stedelijk Museum** The Netherlands' top modern-art museum, recently and extensively renovated. **Hours:** Tue-Wed 11:00-17:00, Thu 11:00- 22:00, Fri-Sun 10:00-18:00, closed Mon. See page 58.

▲▲**Vondelpark** City park and concert venue. **Hours:** Always open. See page 63.

▲▲**Amsterdam Museum** City's growth from fishing village to trading capital to today, including some Rembrandts and a playable carillon. **Hours:** Mon-Fri 10:00-17:00, Sat-Sun 11:00-17:00. See page 68.

▲▲**Amstelkring Museum** Catholic church hidden in the attic of a 17th-century merchant's house. **Hours:** Mon-Sat 10:00-17:00, Sun and holidays 13:00-17:00. See page 69.

▲▲**Red Light District Walk** Women of the world's oldest profession on the job. **Hours:** Best from noon into the evening; avoid late at night. See page 69.

▲▲**Netherlands Maritime Museum** Rich seafaring story of the Netherlands, told with vivid artifacts. **Hours:** Daily 9:00-17:00. See page 71.

▲▲**Hermitage Amsterdam** Russia's Tsarist treasures, on loan from St. Petersburg. **Hours:** Daily 10:00-17:00, Wed until 20:00. See page 76.

▲▲**Dutch Resistance Museum** History of the Dutch struggle against the Nazis. **Hours:** Tue-Fri 10:00-17:00, Sat-Mon 11:00-17:00. See page 80.

▲**Museumplein** Square with art museums, street musicians, crafts, and nearby diamond demos. **Hours:** Always open. See page 59.

▲**Leidseplein** Lively square with cafés and street musicians. **Hours:** Always open, best on sunny afternoons. See page 63.

▲**Royal Palace** Lavish City Hall that takes you back to the Golden Age of the 17th century. **Hours:** Daily 11:00-17:00 when not closed for official ceremonies. See page 66.

▲**Begijnhof** Quiet courtyard lined with picturesque houses. **Hours:** Always open. See page 68.

▲**Hash, Marijuana, and Hemp Museum** All the dope, from history and science to memorabilia. **Hours:** Daily 10:00-23:00. See page 70.

▲**EYE Film Institute Netherlands** Film museum and cinema complex housed in a futuristic new building. **Hours:** Exhibits open daily 11:00-18:00, cinemas open roughly 10:00-24:00. See page 72.

▲**Rembrandt's House** The master's reconstructed house, displaying his etchings. **Hours:** Daily 10:00-17:00. See page 73.

▲**Diamond Tours** Offered at shops throughout the city. **Hours:** Generally daily 9:00-17:00. See page 75.

▲**Willet-Holthuysen Museum** Elegant 17th-century house. **Hours:** Mon-Fri 10:00-17:00, Sat-Sun 11:00-17:00. See page 75.

▲**Jewish Historical Museum** The Great Synagogue and exhibits on Judaism and culture, with Portuguese Synagogue across the street. **Hours:** Daily 11:00-17:00. See page 77.

▲**Dutch Theater** Moving memorial in former Jewish detention center. **Hours:** Daily 11:00-16:00. See page 79.

▲**Tropical Museum** Re-creations of tropical-life scenes. **Hours:** Tue-Sun 10:00-17:00, closed Mon. See page 81.

Houseboat Museum Your chance to see one of these floating homes from the inside. **Hours:** March-Oct Tue-Sun 11:00-17:00, closed Mon; Nov-Dec and Feb Fri-Sun 11:00-17:00, closed Mon-Thu; closed most of Jan. See page 64.

Central Library Architecturally fun spot—with great view terrace—to take a breather among Amsterdam's bookworms. **Hours:** Daily 10:00-22:00. See page 70.

Nearby is **Coster Diamonds,** a handy place to see a diamond-cutting and polishing demo (free, frequent, and interesting 30-minute tours followed  by sales pitch, popular for decades with tour groups, prices marked up to include tour guide kickbacks, daily 9:00-17:00, Paulus Potterstraat 2, tel. 020/305-5555, www.coster diamonds.com). The end of the tour leads you straight into their Diamond Museum, which is worthwhile only for those who have a Museumkaart (which covers entry) or feel the need to see even more diamonds (€7.50, daily 9:00-17:00, tel. 020/305-5300, www.diamantmuseum amsterdam.nl). The tour at **Gassan Diamonds** is free and better (see page 75), but Coster is convenient to the Museumplein scene.

House of Bols: Cocktail & Genever Experience—This leading Dutch distillery runs a pricey and polished little museum/marketing opportunity across the street from the Van Gogh Museum. The "experience" is a self-guided walk through what is essentially an ad for Bols—"four hundred years of working on the art of mixing and blending...a celebration of gin"—with some fun sniffing opportunities and a drink at a modern, mirrored-out cocktail bar for a finale. (It's essentially the gin-flavored version of the Heineken Experience, listed next.) The highlight is a chance to taste up to five different local gins with a talkative expert guiding you. Then have your barista mix up the cocktail of your dreams—based on what you learned during your sniffing.

Cost and Hours: €12.50, not covered by Museumkaart, daily 12:00-17:30, Fri until 21:00, Sat until 19:00, last entry 45 minutes before closing, must be 18, Paulus Potterstraat 14, tel. 020/570-8575, www.houseofbols.com. If you like the booze and hang out and talk, this can be a good deal (but do it after the Van Gogh Museum).

Heineken Experience—This famous brewery, having moved its operations to the suburbs, has converted its original headquarters into a slick, Disneyesque beerfest—complete with a beer-making simulation ride. The "experience" also includes do-it-yourself music videos, photo ops that put you inside Heineken logos and labels, and no small amount of hype about the Heineken family and the quality of their beer. It's a fun trip, if you can ignore the fact that you're essentially paying for an hour of advertising (overpriced at €17, includes two drinks, daily 11:00-19:00, last entry at 17:30; tram #16, #24, or #25 to Heinekenplein; an easy walk from Rijksmuseum, tel. 020/523-9222, www.heinekenexperience.com).

De Pijp District—This former working-class industrial and residential zone (behind the Heineken Experience, near the

Rijksmuseum) is emerging as a colorful, vibrant district. Its spine is Albert Cuypstraat, a street taken over by a long, sprawling produce market packed with interesting people. The centerpiece is **Restaurant Bazar** (marked by a roof-capping golden angel), a church turned into a Middle Eastern food circus (see listing on page 209).

▲**Leidseplein**—Brimming with cafés, this people-watching mecca is an impromptu stage for street artists, accordionists, jugglers, and unicyclists. It's particularly bustling on sunny afternoons. The Boom Chicago theater fronts this square (see the Entertainment in Amsterdam chapter). Stroll nearby Lange Leidsedwarsstraat (one block north) for a taste-bud tour of ethnic eateries, from Greek to Indonesian.

▲▲**Vondelpark**—This huge, lively city park is popular with the Dutch—families with little kids, romantic couples, strolling seniors, and hippies sharing blankets and beers. It's a favored venue for free summer concerts. On a sunny afternoon, it's a hedonistic scene that seems to say, "Parents...relax."

Rembrandtplein and Tuschinski Theater—One of the city's premier nightlife spots is the leafy Rembrandtplein (the artist's statue stands here, along with a jaunty group of statues giving us *The Night Watch* in 3-D) and the adjoining Thorbeckeplein. Several late-night dance clubs keep the area lively into the wee hours. Utrechtsestraat is lined with upscale shops and restaurants. Nearby Reguliersdwarsstraat (a street one block south of Rembrandtplein) is a center for gay and lesbian nightclubs.

The **Tuschinski Theater,** a movie palace from the 1920s (a half-block from Rembrandtplein down Reguliersbreestraat), glitters inside and out. Still a working theater, it's a delightful old place to see first-run movies (always in their original language—usually English—with Dutch subtitles). The exterior is an interesting hybrid of styles, forcing the round peg of Art Nouveau into the square hole of Art Deco. The stone-and-tile facade features stripped-down, functional Art Deco squares and rectangles, but is ornamented with Art Nouveau elements—Tiffany-style windows, garlands,

AMSTERDAM SIGHTS

curvy iron lamps, Egyptian pharaohs, and exotic gold lettering over the door. Inside (lobby is free), the sumptuous decor features fancy carpets, slinky fixtures, and semi-abstract designs. Grab a seat in the lobby and watch the ceiling morph (Reguliersbreestraat 26-28).

Pipe Museum (Pijpenkabinet)—This small and quirky-yet-classy museum holds 300 years of pipes in a 17th-century canal house. (It's almost worth the admission price just to see the inside of one of these elegant homes.) You enter through the street-level shop, Smokiana, which is almost interesting enough to be a museum itself. It sells new and antique pipes, various smoking curiosities, and scholarly books written by the shop's owner. If you want more, pay to enter the museum, and a volunteer docent will accompany you upstairs through a tour of smoking history. You begin with some pre-Columbian terra-cotta pipes (from the discoverers of tobacco, dating from around 500 B.C.), followed by plenty of intricate, finely decorated Baroque and Victorian smoking paraphernalia. Ask questions—your guide is happy to explain why the opium pipes have their bowls in the center of the stem, or why some white clay pipes are a foot long.

Cost and Hours: €8, Wed-Sat 12:00-18:00, usually closed Sun-Tue, tel. 020/421-1779, just off Leidsestraat at Prinsengracht 488, www.pijpenkabinet.nl.

Houseboat Museum (Woonbootmuseum)—In the 1930s, modern cargo ships came into widespread use—making small, sail-powered cargo boats obsolete. In danger of extinction, these little vessels found new life as houseboats lining the canals of Amsterdam. Today, 2,500 such boats—their cargo holds turned into classy, comfortable living rooms—are called home. For a peek into this *gezellig* (cozy) world, visit this tiny museum. Captain Vincent enjoys showing visitors around the houseboat, which feels lived-in because, until 1997, it was.

Cost and Hours: €3.75, not covered by Museumkaart; March-Oct Tue-Sun 11:00-17:00, closed Mon; Nov-Dec and Feb Fri-Sun 11:00-17:00, closed Mon-Thu; closed most of Jan; on Prinsengracht, opposite #296 facing Elandsgracht, tel. 020/427-0750, www.houseboatmuseum.nl.

West Amsterdam

▲▲▲**Anne Frank House**—A pilgrimage for many, this house offers a fascinating look at the hideaway of young Anne during the Nazi occupation of the Netherlands. Anne, her parents, an older sister, and four others spent a little more than two years in a "Secret Annex" behind her father's business. While in hiding, 13-year-old Anne kept a diary chronicling her extraordinary experience. Acting on a tip, the Nazis arrested the group in August of 1944 and sent them to concentration camps in Poland and

Germany. Anne and her sister died of typhus in March of 1945, only weeks before their camp was liberated. Of the eight inhabitants of the Secret Annex, only Anne's father, Otto Frank, survived. He returned to Amsterdam and arranged for his daughter's diary to be published in 1947. It was followed by many translations, a play, and a movie.

The thoughtfully designed exhibit offers thorough coverage of the Frank family, the diary, the stories of others who hid, and the Holocaust.

Cost and Hours: €9, not covered by I amsterdam Card; March 15-Sept 14 daily 9:00-21:00, Sat and July-Aug until 22:00; Sept 15-March 14 daily 9:00-19:00, Sat until 21:00; last entry 30 minutes before closing, often less crowded right when it opens or after 18:00, no baggage check, no large bags allowed inside, Prinsengracht 267, near Westerkerk, tel. 020/556-7100, www .annefrank.org.

○ See the Anne Frank House Tour chapter.

Westerkerk—Located near the Anne Frank House, this landmark church has a barren interior, Rembrandt's body buried somewhere under the pews, and Amsterdam's tallest steeple.

The tower is open only for tours and offers a grand city view. The tour guide, who speaks English and Dutch, tells of the church and its carillon. Only six people are allowed at a time (it's first-come, first-served), so lines can be long.

Cost and Hours: Church—free, generally April-Sept Mon-Sat 11:00-15:00, closed Sun and Oct-March. Tower—€7 for 30-minute tour—departures on the half hour April-Sept Mon-Sat 10:00-18:00, July-Aug until 20:00; Oct Mon-Sat 11:00-16:00; closed Sun year-round, last tour departs 30 minutes before closing, Nov-March tourable only by appointment—call 020/689-2565 or email anna@westertorenamsterdam.nl.

Reypenaer Tasting Rooms—While essentially just a fancy cheese emporium, this place does a great job of showcasing Dutch cheese. You can pop into the delightful shop any time for a few samples, or experience an hour-long cheese tasting in the basement (which has just 20 seats—it's smart to reserve ahead). The tasting session starts with a video that's somewhere between an ad for cheese and dairy soft porn. Then, with an English-speaking guide, you guillotine six different cheeses and taste them with a nice wine accompaniment.

Cost and Hours: €15 for tasting; Mon-Tue at 13:00 and 15:00, Wed-Sun at 12:00, 13:30, 15:00, and 16:30; book by phone or online, Singel 182, tel. 020/320-6333, www.wijngaardkaas.nl/en /proeflokaal.

The Canal House (Het Grachtenhuis)—This recently opened and aggressively promoted museum sounds exciting and tells an

AMSTERDAM SIGHTS

interesting story—but, for most visitors, it's not worth the time or money. There aren't any artifacts on display, and as you shuffle through a series of rooms showing video presentations, you get no sense of the great canalside mansion you came to experience.

Cost and Hours: €12, Tue-Sun 10:00-18:00, closed Mon, Herrengracht 386, www.hetgrachtenhuis.nl.

Nearby: Next door is the **Biblical Museum,** which, like its neighbor, has the potential to be fascinating. Instead, it's an old-school jumble of all things Biblical, with temporary exhibits that'll disappoint most visitors (€8, Mon-Sat 10:00-17:00, Sun 11:00-17:00, Herrengracht 366-368, tel. 020/624-2436, www.bijbels museum.nl).

Central Amsterdam, near Dam Square

▲Royal Palace (Koninklijk Huis)—This palace was built as a lavish City Hall (1648-1655), when Holland was a proud new republic and Amsterdam was the richest city on the planet—awash in profit from trade. The building became a "Royal Palace" when Napoleon installed his brother Louis as king (1806). After Napoleon's fall, it continued as a royal residence for the Dutch royal family, the House of Orange. Today, it's one of King Willem-Alexander's official residences, with a single impressive floor open to the public. Visitors can gawk at a grand hall and stroll about 20 rooms branching off from it, all of them lavishly decorated with chandeliers, paintings, statues, and furniture that reflect Amsterdam's former status as the center of global trade.

Cost and Hours: €7.50, includes audioguide, daily 11:00-17:00 but often closed for official business, tel. 020/620-4060, www.paleisamsterdam.nl.

Visiting the Palace: The huge, white central hall (Gallery or Citizens' Hall) is the palace's highlight—120 feet by 60 feet by 90 feet—and lit by eight big chandeliers. At the far end, a statue of Atlas holds the globe of the world, and the ceiling painting shows Amsterdam triumphant amid the clouds of heaven. On the floor, inlaid maps show the known world circa 1750 (back when the West Coast of the US was still being explored). The hall is used today for hosting foreign dignitaries and for royal family wedding receptions.

The central hall leads directly to a room where Louis Bonaparte's throne once sat in front of the fireplace. The next room has his era's Empire Style furniture (high-polished wood with Neoclassical motifs). After that you'll see then-Princess Beatrix's bedroom (1939-80).

One room, which overlooks Dam Square, is where the council of ex-mayors would meet every year to elect the four new burgomasters, who governed the city. The paintings over the fireplace,

Central Amsterdam

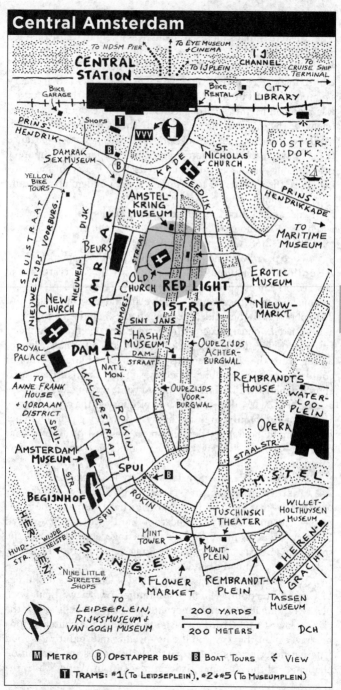

To NDSM Pier · To Eye Museum & Cinema · IJ Channel · To Cruise Ship Terminal

CENTRAL STATION

To IJplein

Bike Garage · Bike Rental · City Library

Prins-Hendrik- · Shops · T · VVV · i

B · B · Damrak Sex Museum

Yellow Bike Tours

St. Nicholas Church · Ooster-Dok

Kade · Zeedijk · Prins-Hendrikkade

Amstel-Kring Museum · To Maritime Museum

Beurs · Straat

Old Church · RED LIGHT DISTRICT · Erotic Museum

New Church · Damrak · Nieuwen- · Nieuwe Zijds Voorburg. · Spuistraat · Dijk · Warmoes- · Sint Jans · Nieuw-Markt

Royal Palace · DAM · Hash Museum · Dam-straat · OudeZijds Achter-Burgwal

To Anne Frank House & Jordaan District · Nat'l. Mon. · Kalverstraat · Rokin · OudeZijds Voor-Burgwal · Rembrandt's House · Water-Loo-Plein

Amsterdam Museum · Spui-Str. · Opera · Staalstr.

Begijnhof · SPUI · B · Rokin · Amstel

Spui · Tuschinski Theater · Willet-Holthuysen Museum

Huid.-Str. · Wijde Heiste · SINGEL · Mint Tower · Munt-Plein · Heren-Gracht

"Nine Little Streets" Shops · Flower Market · Rembrandt-Plein · Tassen Museum

To Leidseplein, Rijksmuseum & Van Gogh Museum

200 YARDS
200 METERS

DCH

Ⓜ METRO   Ⓑ OPSTAPPER BUS   🄱 BOAT TOURS   ⋖ VIEW

🅃 TRAMS: #1 (To Leidseplein), #2 & #5 (To Museumplein)

by Rembrandt's pupils, show righteous Romans whom Golden Age Amsterdammers modeled themselves after (all well-explained by the audioguide).

New Church (Nieuwe Kerk)—Barely newer than the "Old" Church (located in the Red Light District), this 15th-century sanctuary has an intentionally dull interior, after the decoration was removed by 16th-century iconoclastic Protestants seeking to unclutter their communion with God. This is where many Dutch royal weddings and all coronations take place. A steep entrance fee is charged for admission to the church's popular temporary exhibits, but you can view the church itself for free from the landing above the shop (enter to left of main door and go up the stairs in the gift shop).

Cost and Hours: Free to view from gift-shop balcony, special exhibits-€8-15, audioguide-€3, daily 10:00-17:00, on Dam Square, tel. 020/353-8168, www.nieuwekerk.nl.

❂ See page 92 of the Amsterdam City Walk chapter.

▲**Begijnhof**—Stepping into this tiny, idyllic courtyard in the city center, you escape into the charm of old Amsterdam. (Please be considerate of the people who live around the courtyard, and don't photograph the residents or their homes.) Notice house #34, a 500-year-old wooden structure (rare, since repeated fires taught city fathers a trick called brick). Peek into the hidden Catholic church, dating from the time when post-Reformation Dutch Catholics couldn't worship in public. It's opposite the English Reformed church, where the Pilgrims worshipped while waiting for their voyage to the New World—marked by a plaque near the door.

Cost and Hours: Free and always open (though the churches have sporadic hours), on Begijnensteeg lane, just off Kalverstraat between #130 and #132, pick up flier at office near entrance, www.ercadam.nl.

❂ See page 97 of the Amsterdam City Walk chapter.

▲▲**Amsterdam Museum**—Housed in a 500-year-old former orphanage, this creative museum tries hard to make the city's history engaging and fun (almost too hard—it recently dropped "history" from its name for fear of putting people off). But the story of Amsterdam is indeed engaging and fun, and this is the only museum in town designed to tell it.

Your visit starts with a section called "DNA—City on Pilings to City of Freedom," which gives a quick overview. Then, with plenty of interactivity and fancy museum tricks, you'll follow the city's growth from fishing village to world trade center to hippie haven. On the way you'll enjoy Rembrandt paintings, good English descriptions, and a particularly interesting section on challenges of the 20th and 21st centuries (life in World War I, the gay scene in the 1920s, squatter riots, drug policy, immigration issues, prostitution, and so on). The museum's free pedestrian corridor—lined with old-time group portraits—is a powerful teaser.

Cost and Hours: €10, good audioguide-€4.50, Mon-Fri 10:00-17:00, Sat-Sun 11:00-17:00, pleasant restaurant, next to Begijnhof at Kalverstraat 92, tel. 020/523-1822, www.ahm.nl. This museum is a fine place to buy the Museumkaart, which you can then use to skip long lines at various museums (for details, see page 43).

Red Light District

▲▲**Amstelkring Museum (Our Lord in the Attic/Museum Ons' Lieve Heer op Solder)**—Although Amsterdam has long been known for its tolerant attitudes, 16th-century politics forced Dutch Catholics to worship discreetly. At this museum near Central Station, you'll find a fascinating, hidden Catholic church filling the attic of three 17th-century merchants' houses. Don't miss the silver collection and other exhibits of daily life from 300 years ago.

Cost and Hours: €8, includes audioguide, Mon-Sat 10:00-17:00, Sun and holidays 13:00-17:00, no photos, Oudezijds Voorburgwal 40, tel. 020/624-6604, www.opsolder.nl.

✪ See the Amstelkring Museum Tour chapter.

▲▲**Red Light District Walk**—Europe's most popular ladies of the night tease and tempt here, as they have for centuries, in several hundred display-case windows around Oudezijds Achterburgwal and Oudezijds Voorburgwal, surrounding the Old Church (Oude Kerk, described later). Drunks and druggies make the streets uncomfortable late at night after the gawking tour groups leave (about 22:30), but it's a fascinating walk earlier in the evening.

The neighborhood, one of Amsterdam's oldest, has hosted prostitutes since 1200. Prostitution is entirely legal here, and the prostitutes are generally entrepreneurs, renting space and running their own businesses, as well as filling out tax returns and even paying union dues. Popular prostitutes net about €500 a day (for what's called "S&F" in its abbreviated, printable form, charging €30-50 per customer).

✪ See the Red Light District Walk chapter.

Sex Museums—Amsterdam has two sex museums: one in the Red Light District and another one a block in front of Central Station on Damrak street. While visiting one can be called sightseeing, visiting both is harder to explain. The one on Damrak is cheaper and more interesting. Here's a comparison:

The **Erotic Museum** in the Red Light District is five floors of uninspired paintings, videos, old photos, and sculpture (€7, not covered by Museumkaart, daily 11:00-1:00 in the morning, along the canal at Oudezijds Achterburgwal 54, tel. 020/624-7303; see page 123).

The **Damrak Sex Museum** tells the story of pornography from Roman times through 1960. Every sexual deviation is revealed in various displays. The museum includes early French pornographic photos; memorabilia from Europe, India, and Asia; a Marilyn Monroe tribute; and some S&M displays (€4, not covered by Museumkaart, daily 9:30-23:00, Damrak 18, a block in front of Central Station, tel. 020/622-8376).

Old Church (Oude Kerk)—This 14th-century landmark—the needle around which the Red Light District spins—has served as a reassuring welcome-home symbol to sailors, a refuge to the downtrodden, an ideological battlefield of the Counter-Reformation, and, today, a tourist sight with a dull interior.

Cost and Hours: €5, more for temporary exhibits, Mon-Sat 11:00-17:00, Sun 13:00-17:00, tel. 020/625-8284, www.oudekerk.nl. It's 167 steps to the top of the church tower (€7, April-Sept Thu-Sat 13:00-17:00, closed Sun-Wed and Oct-March).

○ See page 114 of the Red Light District Walk chapter.

Marijuana Sights in the Red Light District—Three related establishments cluster together along a canal in the Red Light District. The **Hash, Marijuana, and Hemp Museum,** worth ▲, is the most worthwhile of the three; it shares a ticket with the less substantial **Hemp Gallery.** Right nearby is **Cannabis College,** a free nonprofit center that's "dedicated to ending the global war against the cannabis plant through public education."

Cost and Hours: Museum and gallery—€9, daily 10:00-23:00, Oudezijds Achterburgwal 148, tel. 020/624-8926, www.hashmuseum.com. College—free, daily 11:00-19:00, Oudezijds Achterburgwal 124, tel. 020/423-4420, www.cannabiscollege.com.

○ For more on these sights, see pages 124-125 of the Red Light District Walk chapter. For all the dope on Dutch dope, see the Smoking chapter.

Northeast Amsterdam

Central Library (Openbare Bibliotheek Amsterdam)—This huge, striking, multistory building holds almost 1,400 seats—many with wraparound views of the city—and lots of Internet terminals, not to mention Wi-Fi (€1/30 minutes, sign up at the desk). It's a classy place to check email. The library, which opened in 2007, demonstrates the Dutch people's dedication to a freely educated populace (the right to information, they point out, is enshrined in the UN's Universal Declaration of Human Rights). Everything's relaxed and inviting, from the fun kids' zone and international magazine and newspaper section on the ground floor to the cafeteria, with its dramatic view-terrace dining on the top (La Place, €10 meals, salad bar, daily 10:00-21:00). The library is a 10-minute walk from the east end of Central Station.

Cost and Hours: Free, daily 10:00-22:00, tel. 020/523-0900, www.oba.nl.

NEMO (National Center for Science and Technology)—This kid-friendly science museum is a city landmark. Its distinctive copper-green building, jut-ting up from the water like a sinking ship, has prompted critics to nickname it the *Titanic*. Designed by Italian architect Renzo Piano (known for Paris' Pompidou Center and Berlin's Sony Center complex on Pots-damer Platz), the building's shape reflects its nautical surroundings as well as the curve of the underwater tunnel it straddles.

Several floors feature permanent and rotating exhibits that allow kids (and adults) to explore topics such as light, sound, and gravity, and play with bubbles, topple giant dominoes, and draw with lasers. The museum's motto: "It's forbidden NOT to touch!" Whirring, room-size pinball machines reputedly teach kids about physics. English explanations are available.

Up top is a restaurant with a great city view, as well as a slop-ing terrace that becomes a popular "beach" in summer, complete with lounge chairs, a sandbox, and a lively bar. On the bottom floor is a cafeteria offering €5 sandwiches.

Cost and Hours: €13.50, June-Aug daily 10:00-17:00, Sept-May generally closed Mon, tel. 020/531-3233, www.e-nemo.nl. The roof terrace—open until 19:00 in the summer—is generally free.

Getting There: It's above the entrance to the IJ tunnel at Oosterdok 2. From Central Station, you can walk there in 15 min-utes, or take bus #22, #42, or #43 to the Kadijksplein stop.

▲▲Netherlands Maritime Museum (Nederlands Scheep-vaartmuseum)—This huge, kid-friendly collection of model ships, maps, and sea-battle paintings fills the 300-year-old Dutch Navy Arsenal (cleverly located a little ways from the city cen-ter, as this was where they stored the gunpowder). Just outside the museum is a replica of the *Amsterdam*, an 18th-century cargo ship. Given the Dutch seafaring heritage, this is an appropriately important and impressive place.

AMSTERDAM SIGHTS

Cost and Hours: €15 covers both museum and ship, both open daily 9:00-17:00, bus #22 or #48 from Central Station to Kattenburgerplein 1, tel. 020/523-2222, www.scheepvaart museum.nl.

Visiting the Museum: On the **east side** of the courtyard (to the right as you enter), you'll find the museum's core collection: globes, an exhibit on the city's busy shipping port, original navigational tools, displays of ship ornamentation, and a beautifully lit gallery of maritime paintings, depicting dramatic 17th-century naval battles against the British and Romantic seascapes from the 19th century. Most everything here is described in English. On the **west side** of the courtyard are exhibits on whaling, and seafaring in the Dutch Golden Age.

Moored at the jetty behind the museum is the VOC ship *Amsterdam*. While just a replica, it lets you crawl through a type of ship called an East Indiaman, which had its heyday during the 17th and 18th centuries, sailing for the Dutch East India Company (abbreviated VOC, for Vereenigde Oost-Indische Compagnie—you'll see it on insignias throughout the boat).

Wander the decks, then duck your head and check out the captain and surgeon's quarters, packed with items they would have used. Don't forget to climb down into the hold. The ship is a little light on good historical information, but it's still a shipshape sight that entertains naval history buffs as well as *Pirates of the Caribbean* fans.

▲**EYE Film Institute Netherlands**—The newest and most striking feature of the Amsterdam skyline is EYE, a film museum and cinema housed in an übersleek modern building immediately across the water from Central Station. Heralding the coming gentrification of the north side of the IJ, EYE (a play on "IJ") is a complex of museum spaces and four theaters playing mostly art films (shown in their original language, with selections organized around various themes). Its many other offerings include a monthly program of silent films with live musical accompaniment, special exhibits on film-related themes, a free permanent exhibit in the basement, a shop, and a trendy terrace café with great waterside seating. Helpful attendants at the reception desk can get you oriented.

Cost and Hours: General entry is free, films cost €10, and exhibits cost around €10 (no cash accepted, but standard US credit cards OK), exhibits open 11:00-18:00, cinemas open daily at 10:00 until last screening (ticket office usually closes at 22:00 or 23:00), tel. 020/589-1400, eyefilm.nl.

Getting There: From the docks behind Central Station, catch the free ferry (labeled *Buiksloterweg*) across the river and walk left to IJpromenade 1.

Southeast Amsterdam

To reach the following sights from the train station, take tram #9 or #14. All of these sights (except the Tropical Museum) are close to one another and can easily be connected into an interesting walk—or, better yet, a bike ride. Several of the sights in southeast Amsterdam cluster near the large square, Waterlooplein, dominated by the modern opera house.

For an orientation, survey the neighborhood from the lamp-lined Blauwbrug ("Blue Bridge")—a modest, modern version of Paris' Pont Alexandre III. The bridge crosses the Amstel River. From this point, the river is channeled to form the city's canals.

Scan clockwise. The big, curved, modern facade belongs to the opera house, commonly called the "Stopera," as it's the combo City Hall *(stadhuis)* and opera. Behind the Stopera are these sights (not visible from here, but described next): the Waterlooplein flea market, Rembrandt's House, and Gassan Diamonds. To the right of the Stopera are the twin gray steeples of the Moses and Aaron Church, which sits roughly in the center of the former Jewish Quarter.

Several Jewish sights cluster to the right of the Moses and Aaron Church: the Jewish Historical Museum, the Portuguese Synagogue, and the dockworker statue (a Holocaust memorial). Just east of those is the De Hortus Botanical Garden.

The cute little drawbridge, while not famous, is certainly photogenic. (Its traditional counterbalance design is so effective that even a child can lift the bridge.) Beyond that is the Hermitage Amsterdam (it takes up an entire city block). Crossing the Amstel upstream is one of the city's romantic spots, the Magere Brug ("Skinny Bridge"). A block away is the city's best look at a Dutch Golden Age mansion, the Willet-Holthuysen Museum (a.k.a. Herengracht Canal Mansion).

Waterlooplein Flea Market—For more than a hundred years, the Jewish Quarter flea market has raged daily except Sunday (at the Waterlooplein metro station, behind Rembrandt's House). The long, narrow park is filled with stalls selling cheap clothes, hippie stuff, old records, tourist knickknacks, and garage-sale junk.

▲Rembrandt's House (Museum Het Rembrandthuis)—A middle-aged Rembrandt lived here from 1639 to 1658 after his wife's death, as his popularity and wealth dwindled down to obscurity and bankruptcy. As you enter, ask when the next etching demonstration is scheduled and pick up the excellent audioguide.

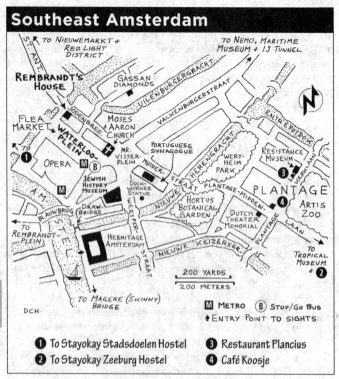

Southeast Amsterdam

TO NIEUWEMARKT &
RED LIGHT
DISTRICT

TO NEMO, MARITIME
MUSEUM & IJ TUNNEL

REMBRANDT'S
HOUSE

GASSAN
DIAMONDS

UILENBURGERGRACHT

ENTREPOTDOK

FLEA
MARKET

JODENBREE

MOSES
& AARON
CHURCH

VALKENBURGERSTRAAT

N

WATERLOO
PLEIN

MR.
VISSER-
PLEIN

PORTUGUESE
SYNAGOGUE

HERENGRACHT

WERT-
HEIM
PARK

RESISTANCE
MUSEUM

3

KERKLAAN

OPERA

M

M

JEWISH
HISTORY
MUSEUM

MUIDER-

STRAAT

NIEUWE

PLANTAGE-
MIDDEN-

PLANTAGE

AM

DRAW-
BRIDGE

DOCK-
WORKER
STATUE

WEESPER

HORTUS
BOTANICAL
GARDEN

4

LAAN

ARTIS
ZOO

BLAUWBRUG

TO
REMBRANDT-
PLEIN

HERMITAGE
AMSTERDAM

STRAAT

DUTCH
THEATER
MEMORIAL

PLANTAGE

NIEUWE KEIZERSGR.

TO
TROPICAL
MUSEUM
& 2

200 YARDS

200 METERS

TO MAGERE (SKINNY)
BRIDGE

DCH

M METRO   B STOP/GO BUS
↟ ENTRY POINT TO SIGHTS

❶ To Stayokay Stadsdoelen Hostel   ❸ Restaurant Plancius
❷ To Stayokay Zeeburg Hostel   ❹ Café Koosje

Tour the place this way: Explore Rembrandt's reconstructed house (filled with exactly what his bankruptcy inventory of 1656

said he owned); imagine him at work in his reconstructed studio; marvel at his personal collection of exotic objects, many of which he included in paintings; attend the etching demonstration and ask the printer to explain the etching process (drawing in soft wax on a metal plate that's then dipped in acid, inked up, and printed); and then, for the finale, enjoy several rooms of original Rembrandt etchings. You're not likely to see a single painting, but the master's etchings are marvelous and well-described. I came away wanting to know more about the man and his art.

Cost and Hours: €10, includes audioguide, daily 10:00–17:00, etching demonstrations almost hourly, Jodenbreestraat 4, tel. 020/520-0400, www.rembrandthuis.nl.

▲**Diamonds**—Many shops in this "city of diamonds" offer tours. These tours come with two parts: a chance to see experts behind magnifying glasses polishing the facets of precious diamonds, followed by a visit to an intimate sales room to see (and perhaps buy) a mighty shiny yet very tiny souvenir.

The handy and professional **Gassan Diamonds** facility fills a huge warehouse one block from Rembrandt's House. A visit

here plops you in the big-tour-group fray (notice how each tour group has a color-coded sticker so they know which guide gets the commission on what they buy). You'll get a sticker, join a free 15-minute tour to see a polisher at work, and hear a general explanation of the process. Then you'll have an opportunity to sit down and have color and clarity described and illustrated with diamonds ranging in value from $100 to $30,000. Before or after, you can have a free cup of coffee in the waiting room across the parking lot (daily 9:00-17:00, Nieuwe Uilenburgerstraat 173, tel. 020/622-5333, www.gassan.com, handy WC). Another company, **Coster,** also offers diamond demos. They're not as good as Gassan's, but convenient if you're near the Rijksmuseum (see page 62).

▲**Willet-Holthuysen Museum (a.k.a. Herengracht Canal Mansion)**—This 1687 townhouse is a must for devotees of Hummel-topped sugar bowls and Louis XVI-style wainscoting.

For others, it's a pleasant look inside a typical (rich) home with much of the original furniture and decor. Forget the history and just browse through a dozen rooms of beautiful saccharine objects from the 19th century.

Cost and Hours: €8, audioguide-€3, Mon-Fri 10:00-17:00, Sat-Sun 11:00-17:00; take tram #4, #9, or #14 to Rembrandtplein—it's a 2-minute walk southeast to Herengracht 605, tel. 020/523-1822, www.willetholthuysen.nl. The museum also hands out a free brochure that covers the house's history.

Visiting the Museum: Upon entering (through the servants' door under the grand entry), see photos of the owners during the house's heyday in the 1860s. The 15-minute video explains how the wealthy heiress Louise Holthuysen and the art-collecting bon vivant Abraham Willet got married and became joined at the hyphen, then set out to make their home the social hub of Amsterdam.

Picture the couple's servants in the kitchen—before electricity and running water—turning meat on the spit at the fireplace or filtering rainwater. Upstairs, where the Willet-Holthuysens entertained, wall paintings introduce you to Abraham's artistic tastes, showing scenes of happy French peasants and nobles frolicking in the countryside. Several rooms are decorated in the Louis XVI style, featuring chairs with straight, tapering legs (not the heavy, curving, animal-claw feet of earlier styles); blue, yellow, and purple-themed rooms; wainscoting ("wallpaper" covering only the lower part of walls); and mythological paintings on the ceiling.

The impressive gilded ballroom contains a painting showing the room in its prime—and how little it's changed. Imagine Abraham, Louise, and 22 guests retiring to the Dining Room, dining off the 275-piece Meissen porcelain set; chatting with friends in the Blue Room by the canal; or sipping tea in the Garden Room, gazing out at symmetrically curved hedges and classical statues. Up another flight is the bedroom, with a canopy bed and matching oak washstand and makeup table (and a chamber pot tucked under the bed). You can even browse the collection virtually using a computer terminal.

When the widow Louise died in 1895, she bequeathed the house to the city, along with its candelabras, snuff boxes, and puppy paintings.

Tassen Museum (Hendrikje Museum of Bags and Purses)—This hardworking little museum fills an elegant 1664 canal house with 500 years of bag and purse history—from before the invention of pockets through the 20th century. The collection, with lots of artifacts, is well-described in English and gives a fascinating insight into fashion through the ages that fans of handbags will love, and their partners might even enjoy. The creative and surreal bag styles of the 1920s and 1930s are particularly interesting.

Cost and Hours: €8.50, daily 10:00-17:00, three floors—one houses temporary exhibits and two hold the permanent collection, start on top floor, behind Rembrandtplein at Herengracht 573, tel. 020/524-6452, www.tassenmuseum.nl.

▲▲**Hermitage Amsterdam**—The famous Hermitage Museum in St. Petersburg, Russia, loans art to Amsterdam for a series of rotating, and often exquisitely beautiful, special exhibits in the Amstelhof, a 17th-century former nursing home that takes up a whole city block along the Amstel River.

Why is there Russian-owned art in Amsterdam? The Hermitage collection in St. Petersburg is so vast that they can only show about 5 percent of it at any one time. Therefore, the Hermitage is establishing satellite collections around the world. The one here in Amsterdam is the biggest, filling the large Amstelhof. By law, the great Russian collection can only be out of the country for six months at a time, so the collection is always changing (check the museum's website to see what's on during your visit). Curators in Amsterdam make a point to display art that complements—rather than just repeats—what the city's other museums show so well. The one small permanent "History Hermitage" exhibit explains the historic connection between the Dutch (Orange) and Russian (Romanov) royal families.

Cost and Hours: Generally €15, but price varies with rotating exhibits; audioguide-€4, daily 10:00-17:00; come later in the day to avoid crowds, mandatory free bag check, café, Nieuwe Herengracht 14, tram #9 from the train station or #14 from Dam Square to Waterlooplein, recorded info tel. 020/530-7488, www .hermitage.nl.

De Hortus Botanical Garden—This is a unique oasis of tranquility within the city (no mobile phones are allowed, because "our collection of plants is a precious community—treat it with respect"). One of the oldest botanical gardens in the world, it dates from 1638, when medicinal herbs were grown here. Today, among its 6,000 different kinds of plants—most of which were collected by the Dutch East India Company in the 17th and 18th centuries—you'll find medicinal herbs, cacti, several greenhouses (one with a fluttery butterfly house—a hit with kids), and a tropical palm house. Much of it is described in English: "A Dutch merchant snuck a coffee plant out of Ethiopia, which ended up in this garden in 1706. This first coffee plant in Europe was the literal granddaddy of the coffee cultures of Brazil—long the world's biggest coffee producer."

Cost and Hours: €7.50, not covered by Museumkaart, daily 10:00-17:00, Plantage Middenlaan 2A, tel. 020/625-9021, www .dehortus.nl. The inviting Orangery Café serves tapas.

▲Jewish Historical Museum (Joods Historisch Museum)— This interesting museum tells the story of the Netherlands' Jews through three centuries, serving as a good introduction to Judaism

and Jewish customs and religious traditions.

Originally opened in 1932, the museum was forced to close during the Nazi years. Recent renovations have brought it into the 21st century. Its current location comprises four historic former synagogues that have been

Jews in Amsterdam

In 1940, one in ten Amsterdammers was Jewish, and most lived in the neighborhood behind Waterlooplein. Jewish traders had long been welcome in a city that cared more about business than religion. In the late 1500s, many Sephardic Jews from Spain and Portugal immigrated, fleeing persecution. (The philosopher Baruch Spinoza's ancestors were among them.) In the 1630s, Yiddish-speaking Eastern European Jews (Ashkenazi) poured in. By 1700, the Jewish Quarter was a bustling, exotic, multicultural world, with more people speaking Portuguese, German, and Yiddish than Dutch.

Despite their large numbers, for several centuries Jews were not first-class citizens. They needed the city's permission to settle here, and they couldn't hold public office (but then, neither could Catholics under Calvinist rule). Still, the Jewish Quarter was not a ghetto per se, as the segregation wasn't forced, and Jews faced no special taxes. Cosmopolitan Amsterdam was well-acquainted with all types of beliefs and customs.

In 1796, Jews were given full citizenship. In exchange, they were required to learn the Dutch language and submit to the city's legal system. Over the next century or so, the Jewish culture began assimilating into the Dutch.

In 1940, Nazi Germany occupied the Netherlands. On February 22, 1941, the Nazis began rounding up Jews and shipping them to extermination camps in Eastern Europe. By war's end, more than 100,000 of the country's 135,000 Jews had died.

Today, about 25,000 Jews live in Amsterdam, and the Jewish Quarter has blended with the modern city. For more information on Amsterdam's many Jewish sights, see www.jhm.nl.

joined by steel and glass to make one modern complex.

Cost and Hours: €12, includes Portuguese Synagogue, more for special exhibits, ticket also covers Dutch Theater—see next listing; museum daily 11:00-17:00, Portuguese Synagogue daily 10:00-16:00, last entry 30 minutes before closing; free audio-guide, displays all have English explanations, children's museum, Jonas Daniel Meijerplein 2, tel. 020/531-0310, www.jhm.nl. The museum has a modern, minimalist, kosher café.

Visiting the Museum: First see the ground floor of the Great Synagogue (for an overview of Jewish culture), then go upstairs to the women's gallery (for history from 1600 to 1900). From there, follow the sky bridge to the New Synagogue (for the 20th century story), and poke into the Aanbouw Annex (contemporary exhibits). Then, with the same ticket, finish your visit by crossing the street to the Portuguese Synagogue, with its treasury.

The centerpiece of the museum is the **Great Synagogue.** Have a seat in the high-ceilinged synagogue, surrounded by religious objects, and picture it during its prime (1671-1943). The hall would be full for a service—men downstairs, women above in the gallery. On the east wall (the symbolic direction of Jerusalem) is the Ark, where they keep the scrolls of the Torah (the Jewish scriptures, comprising the first five books of Old Testament of the Bible). The rabbi and other men, wearing thigh-length prayer shawls, would approach the Ark and carry the Torah to the raised platform in the center of the room. After unwrapping it from its drapery and silver cap, a man would use a *yad* (ceremonial pointer) to follow along while singing the text aloud.

Video displays around the room explain Jewish customs, from birth (circumcision) to puberty (the bar/bat mitzvah, celebrating the entry into adulthood) to Passover celebrations to marriage—culminating in the groom stomping on a glass while everyone shouts "Mazel tov!"

Next, head upstairs to the **women's gallery,** which traces the history of Amsterdam's Jews from 1600 to 1900. From here, a sky bridge leads to the **New Synagogue** and the 20th century. A worthwhile exhibit on the "Jews of the Netherlands" uses personal artifacts and touch-screen computers to tell the devastating history of the Nazi occupation. By purposefully showing everyday objects such as chairs and clothes, the museum helps make an inconceivable period of time meaningful and real. Temporary exhibition space in the **Aanbouw Annex** generally shows the work of Jewish artists from around the world.

Finish your visit by crossing the street to the **Portuguese Synagogue,** which stands about 100 yards from the rest of the museum complex. It's a bold structure, built in the 1670s, when Catholics were worshipping underground. It survived World War II, and stands today as a big, open, and simple place of worship ringed by four Ionic columns. In the courtyard you will find a more intimate winter synagogue and stairs leading down into a treasury with precious ceremonial objects, textiles, and rare books.

▲**Dutch Theater (Hollandsche Schouwburg)**—Once a lively theater in the Jewish neighborhood, and today a moving memorial, this building was used as an assembly hall for local Jews destined for Nazi concentration camps. On the wall, 6,700 family names pay tribute to the 104,000 Jews deported and killed by the Nazis. Some 70,000 victims spent time here, awaiting transfer to

concentration camps. Upstairs is a small history exhibit with a model of the ghetto, plus photos and memorabilia (such as shoes and letters) of some victims, putting a human face on the staggering numbers. Television monitors show actual footage of the Nazis rounding up Amsterdam's Jews. You can also see a few costumes from the days when the building was a theater. While the exhibit is small, it offers plenty to think about. Back in the ground-floor courtyard, notice the hopeful messages that visiting school groups attach to the wooden tulips.

Cost and Hours: Covered by €12 Jewish Historical Museum ticket, daily 11:00-16:00, Plantage Middenlaan 24, tel. 020/531-0340, www.hollandscheschouwburg.nl.

▲▲**Dutch Resistance Museum (Verzetsmuseum)**—This is an impressive look at how the Dutch resisted (or collaborated with) their Nazi occupiers from 1940 to 1945. You'll see propaganda movie clips, study forged ID cards under a magnifying glass, and read about ingenious and courageous efforts—big and small—to hide local Jews from the Germans and undermine the Nazi regime.

Cost and Hours: €8 includes audioguide; Tue-Fri 10:00-17:00, Sat-Mon 11:00-17:00, English descriptions, no flash photos, mandatory and free bag check, tram #9 from station or #14 from Dam Square, Plantage Kerklaan 61. Tel. 020/620-2535, www.verzetsmuseum.org.

Visiting the Museum: The museum does a good job of presenting the Dutch people's struggle with a timeless moral dilemma:

Is it better to collaborate with a wicked system to effect small-scale change—or to resist outright, even if your efforts are doomed to fail? You'll learn why some parts of Dutch society opted for the former, and others for the latter. While proudly describing acts of extraordinary courage, it doesn't shy away from the less heroic side of the story (for example, the fact that most of the population, though troubled by the persecution of their Jewish countrymen, only became actively anti-Nazi after gentile Dutch men were deported to forced-labor camps). The exhibit is interspersed with riveting first-person accounts of what it was like to go underground, strike, starve, or return from the camps—with every tragic detail translated into English.

The first dozen displays set the stage, showing peaceful, upright Dutch people of the 1930s living oblivious to the rise of fascism. Then—bam—it's May of 1940 and the Germans invade the Netherlands, pummel Rotterdam, drive Queen Wilhelmina into exile, and—in four short days of fighting—hammer home the message that resistance is futile. The Germans install local Dutch Nazis in power (the "NSB"), led by Anton Mussert.

Next, in the corner of the exhibition area, push a button to see photos of the event that first mobilized organized resistance. In February of 1941, Nazis start rounding up Jews from the neighborhood, killing nine protesters. Amsterdammers respond by shutting down the trams, schools, and businesses in a massive two-day strike. (This heroic gesture is honored today with a statue of a striking dockworker on the square called Jonas Daniel Meyerplein, where Jews were rounded up.) The next display makes it clear that this brave strike did little to save 100,000 Jews from extermination.

Turning the corner into the main room, you'll see numerous exhibits on Nazi rule (on topics including ID cards, propaganda, and the segregation of Jews) and the many forms of Dutch resistance: vandals turning Nazi V-for-Victory posters into W-for-Wilhelmina, preachers giving pointed sermons, schoolkids telling "Kraut" jokes, printers distributing underground newspapers (such as *Het Parool,* which became a major daily paper), counterfeiters forging documents, and ordinary people hiding radios under floorboards and Jews inside closets. As the war progresses, the armed Dutch Resistance becomes bolder and more violent, killing German occupiers and Dutch collaborators. In September of 1944, the Allies liberate Antwerp, and the Netherlands starts celebrating...too soon. The Nazis dig in and punish the country by cutting off rations, plunging West Holland into the "Hunger Winter" of 1944 to 1945, during which 20,000 die. Finally, it's springtime. The Allies liberate the country, and at war's end, Nazi helmets are turned into Dutch bedpans.

Nearby: Two recommended eateries—Restaurant Plancius and Café Koosje—are on the same block as the museum (see listings on page 210), and Amsterdam's famous zoo is just across the street.

▲**Tropical Museum (Tropenmuseum)**—As close to the Third World as you'll get without lots of vaccinations, this imaginative museum offers wonderful re-creations of tropical life and explanations of Third World problems (largely created by Dutch colonialism and the slave trade). Ride the elevator to the top floor, and circle your way down through this immense collection, opened in 1926 to give the Dutch people a peek at their vast colonial holdings. Don't miss the display case where you can see and hear the world's most exotic musical instruments. The Ekeko cafeteria serves tropical food.

Cost and Hours: €10, Tue-Sun 10:00-17:00, closed Mon, tram #9 to Linnaeusstraat 2, tel. 020/568-8200, www.tropen museum.nl.

AMSTERDAM CITY WALK

*From Central Station to
the Rijksmuseum*

Amsterdam today looks much as it did in its Golden Age, the 1600s. It's a retired sea captain of a city, still in love with life, with a broad outlook and a salty story to tell.

Take a Dutch sampler walk from one end of the old center to the other, tasting all that Amsterdam has to offer along the way. It's your best single stroll through quintessentially Dutch scenes, hidden churches, surprising shops, thriving happy-hour hangouts, and eight centuries of history.

Orientation

Length of This Walk: Allow three hours.

When to Go: The walk is best during the day, when churches and sights are open.

Bike Rental: If you'd like to make this "walk" a much faster "roll," there's a handy bike-rental place in Central Station (MacBike, listed on page 49).

Alert: Beware of silent transport—trams and bikes. Walkers should stay off the tram tracks and bike paths, and yield to bell-ringing bikers.

WCs: You can find public toilets at fast-food places (generally €0.30) and near the entrance to the Amsterdam Museum.

Royal Palace: €7.50, includes audioguide, daily 11:00-17:00 but often closed for official business.

New Church: Free to view from gift-shop balcony, special exhibits-€8-15, audioguide-€3, daily 10:00-17:00.

De Papegaai Hidden Church: Free, daily 10:00-16:00.

Civic Guards Gallery: Free, daily 10:00-17:00.

Accommodating the Amsterdam of the Future

For years now, anyone arriving to this grand city by train has been met by a cacophony of construction chaos, as the city works to extend its metro system. It's proven to be a huge challenge: Workers must tunnel under ancient buildings—which stand on pilings driven centuries ago into the mud below the city—without unsettling everything. While the project is now scheduled to wrap up in 2017, Amsterdammers are skeptical. The whole thing got underway in the "Golden '90s," when the economic climate was much sunnier than now. Since then the project has been riddled with delays, and many think it is bleeding the city economically. But most realize that the city's infrastructure needs to accommodate the tens of thousands of people living in North Amsterdam, the fast-growing suburb beyond the IJ. (The city's also planning a new bus hub across the IJ that'll serve destinations in the northern Netherlands, hopefully moving congestion away from the Central Station area.)

If you're into engineering and/or urban design, pop into the **North-South Line Information Center,** where you'll learn about the 85-yard-long "mole" that's chewing a 23-foot-wide tunnel, and the futuristic vision for the station district (free, Tue-Fri 10:00-17:00, Sun 11:00-16:00, closed Mon and Sat, on the left as you leave the station, look for the blue-and-red sign next to MacBike).

Amsterdam Museum: €10, good audioguide-€4.50, Mon-Fri 10:00-17:00, Sat-Sun 11:00-17:00.

Begijnhof: Free and always open (though churches have sporadic hours).

Rijksmuseum: €15, audioguide-€5, daily 9:00-17:00, last entry 30 minutes before closing.

Van Gogh Museum: €15, more for special exhibits, audioguide-€5, kids' audioguide-€2.50, daily 9:00-17:00, Fri until 22:00.

Audio Tour: You can download this chapter as a free Rick Steves audio tour (see page 53).

Overview

This walk starts at the central-as-can-be Central Station, and ends at the Rijksmuseum. The train station and art museum—designed by the same architect—stand like bookends holding the old town together. You'll walk about three miles, heading down Damrak to Dam Square, continuing south down Kalverstraat to the Mint Tower (Munttoren), then wafting through the flower market (Bloemenmarkt), before continuing south to Leidseplein and jogging left to the Rijksmuseum. To return to Central Station, catch tram #2 or #5 from the southwest corner of the Rijksmuseum.

The Walk Begins

❶ Central Station

Here, where today's train travelers enter the city, sailors of yore disembarked from seagoing ships. They were met by street musicians, pickpockets, hotel-runners, and ladies carrying red lanterns. Central Station, built in the late 1800s, sits on reclaimed land at what was once the harbor mouth. The station, with warm red brick and prickly spires, is the first of several Neo-Gothic buildings we'll see from the late 1800s, built dur-

ing Amsterdam's economic revival. One of the towers has a clock dial; the other tower's dial is a weathervane. Watch the hand twitch as the wind gusts in every direction—N, Z, O, and W.

Let's get oriented: *nord, zuid, ost,* and *vest.* Facing the station, you're facing north. Farther north, on the other side of the station, is the IJ (pronounced "eye"), the body of water that gives Amsterdam access to the open sea.

Now turn around 180 degrees and, with your back to the station, face the city, looking south. The city spreads out before you like a fan, in a series of concentric canals. Ahead of you stretches the street called Damrak, which leads to Dam Square a half-mile away. That's where we'll be heading. To the left of Damrak is the city's old *(oude)* town. More recently, that historic neighborhood has become the Red Light District (for a tour of that neighborhood, ❷ see the Red Light District Walk chapter). The big church towering above the old part of town is St. Nicholas Church. It was built in the 1880s, when

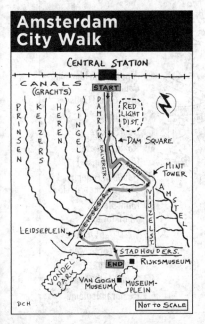

Amsterdam City Walk—First Half

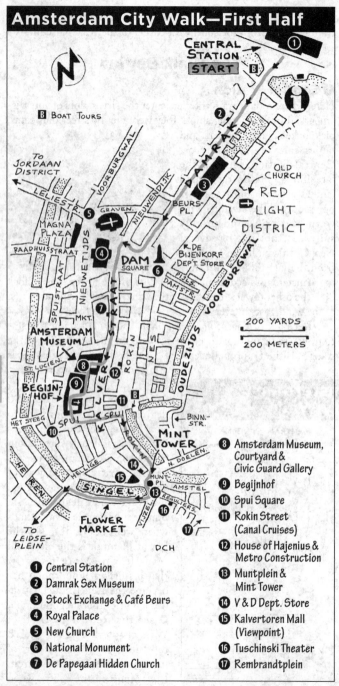

AMSTERDAM CITY WALK

B Boat Tours

① Central Station
② Damrak Sex Museum
③ Stock Exchange & Café Beurs
④ Royal Palace
⑤ New Church
⑥ National Monument
⑦ De Papegaai Hidden Church

⑧ Amsterdam Museum, Courtyard & Civic Guard Gallery
⑨ Begijnhof
⑩ Spui Square
⑪ Rokin Street (Canal Cruises)
⑫ House of Hajenius & Metro Construction
⑬ Muntplein & Mint Tower
⑭ V & D Dept. Store
⑮ Kalvertoren Mall (Viewpoint)
⑯ Tuschinski Theater
⑰ Rembrandtplein

Catholics—after about three centuries of oppression—were finally free to worship in public. To the right of Damrak is the new *(nieuwe)* part of town, where you'll find the Anne Frank House and the peaceful Jordaan neighborhood.

The train station is the city's transportation hub. Many trams and taxis leave from out front. Beneath your feet are the beginnings of a new arm of the city's metro; as you can see, the mess from the construction has spilled above ground (see sidebar). Across the street from the station is the city's main TI, marked by *VVV* sign.

On your far right, in front of the Ibis Hotel, is a huge, multistory **parking garage.** This is for bikes only. Biking in Holland is the way to go—the land is flat, distances are short, and there are designated bike paths everywhere. This bike parking garage is completely free, courtesy of the government, and intended to encourage this green and ultra-efficient mode of transportation.

• *Let's head out. With your back to Central Station, start walking south from the station into the city, to the head of Damrak.*

Again, be careful crossing the street. Be aware of trams, bikes, and cars. When you reach the head of Damrak, keep going straight, following the crowds south on Damrak, walking along the right side of the street.

Damrak

This street was once a riverbed. It's where the Amstel River flowed north into the IJ, which led to a vast inlet of the North Sea called

the Zuiderzee. It's this unique geography that turned Amsterdam into a center of trade. Boats could sail up the Amstel into the interior of Europe, or out to the North Sea, to reach the rest of the world.

As you stroll along Damrak, look left. There's a marina, lined with old brick buildings. Though these aren't terribly historic buildings, the scene still captures a bit of Golden Age Amsterdam. Think of it: Back in the 1600s, this area was the harbor, and those buildings warehoused exotic goods from all over the world.

All along Damrak, you'll pass a veritable gauntlet of touristy shops. These seem to cover every Dutch cliché. You'll see wooden shoes, which the Dutch used to wear to get around easily in the marshy soil, and all manner of tulips; the real ones come from Holland's famed fresh-flower industry. Heineken fridge magnets advertise one of the world's most popular pilsner beers. You'll likely hear a hand-cranked barrel organ and see windmill-shaped salt shakers. And everything seems to be available in bright

Amsterdam's Story

Visualize the physical layout of this man-made city: built on trees, protected by dikes, and laced with canals in the marshy delta at the mouth of the Amstel River. Location, location, location. Boats could arrive here from Germany by riverboat down the Rhine, from England across the Channel and down the IJ, and from Denmark by entering the Zuiderzee inlet of the North Sea. No wonder that St. Nicholas, protector of water travelers, was the city's patron saint.

As early as 1300, Amsterdam was already an international trade center of German beer, locally caught herring, cloth, bacon, salt, and wine. Having dammed and canalized the Amstel and diked out the sea tides, the Dutch drained land, sunk pilings, and built a city from scratch. When the region's leading bishop granted the town a charter (1300), Amsterdammers could then set up law courts, judge their own matters, and be essentially autonomous. The town thrived.

By 1500, Amsterdam was a walled city of 12,000, with the Singel canal serving as the moat. The city had a midcentury growth spurt when its trading rival Antwerp fell to Spanish troops, and a flood of fellow Flemish headed north, fleeing chaos and religious persecution.

In 1602, hardy Dutch sailors (and Englishman Henry Hudson) tried their hand at trade with the Far East. When they returned, they brought with them valuable spices, jewels, luxury goods... and the Golden Age.

The Dutch East India Company (abbreviated as "VOC" in Dutch), a state-subsidized import/export business, combined nautical skills with capitalist investing. With 500 or so 150-foot ships cruising in and out of Amsterdam's harbor, it was the first great multinational corporation. Amsterdam's Golden Age (c. 1600-1650) rode the wave of hard work and good fortune. Over the next two centuries, the VOC would send a half-million Dutch people on business trips to Asia, broadening their horizons.

This city of the Golden Age was perhaps the wealthiest on earth, thriving as the "warehouse of the world." Goods came from

orange—because that's the official color of the Dutch royal family.

At Damrak 18, you'll find the city's most notorious commodity on display. It's the ❷ **Damrak Sex Museum** (described on page 70). As a port town catering to sailors and businessmen away from home, Amsterdam has always accommodated the sex trade.

Continue up Damrak (noting the **canal boats** on your right—see page 52) for more touristy delectables. Teasers (at #36) is the local Hooters. You'll also pass places selling the popular local fast food: French fries. Here they're called *Vlaamse friets* (Flemish fries), since they were invented in the Low Countries. The stand at

everywhere. The VOC's specialties were spices (pepper and cinnamon), coffee and tea, Chinese porcelain (Delftware's Eastern inspiration), and silk. Meanwhile, the competing Dutch West India Company concentrated on the New World, trading African slaves for South American sugar. With its wealth, Amsterdam built in grand style, erecting the gabled townhouses we see today. The city expanded west and south, adding new neighborhoods.

But by 1650, Amsterdam's overseas trade was being eclipsed by new superpowers—England and France. Inconclusive wars with Louis XIV and England drained the economy, destroyed the trading fleet, and demoralized the people. Throughout the 1700s, Amsterdam was a city of backwater bankers rather than international traders, although it remained the cultural center of Holland. In early 1795, Napoleon's French troops occupied the country, and the economy was dismal.

A revival in the 1800s was spurred by technological achievements. The Dutch built a canal reconnecting Amsterdam directly with the North Sea (1824-1876), railroads laced the small country, and the city expanded southward by draining new land. The Rijksmuseum, Central Station, and Magna Plaza were built as proud monuments to the economic upswing.

The 1930s Depression hit hard, followed by five years of occupation under the Nazis, aided by pro-Nazi Dutch. The city's large Jewish population was decimated by Nazi deportations and extermination (falling from about 80,000 Jews in 1940 to just 16,000 in 1945).

With postwar prosperity, 1960s Amsterdam again became a world cultural capital as the center for Europe's hippies, who came here to smoke marijuana. Grassroots campaigns by young, artistic, politically active people promoted free sex and free bikes.

Today, Amsterdam is a city of 820,000 people jammed into small apartments (often with the same floor plan as their neighbors'). Since the 1970s, many immigrants have become locals. One in 10 Amsterdammers is Surinamese, and one in 10 prays toward Mecca.

Damrak 41 is a favorite. Locals dip their fries in mayonnaise, not ketchup.

All along Damrak, you'll pass many restaurants. It quickly becomes obvious that, here in cosmopolitan Amsterdam, international cuisine is almost like going local. Indonesian restaurants are especially popular, since that was a former Dutch colony. Here you can order *rijsttafel*, a sampler assortment of Indonesian dishes that's big enough for two. Also popular in Amsterdam are Argentinian steak houses. Amsterdammers on the go usually just grab a simple sandwich, called a *broodje* (BRODE-juh), or a pita-bread wrap, such as a *shoarma,* from a Middle Eastern take-out joint.

We're walking along what was once the Amstel River. Today, the Amstel is channeled into canals and its former mouth is covered by the Central Station. But Amsterdam still remains a major seaport. That's because, in the 19th century, the Dutch dug the North Sea Canal. These days, more than 100,000 ships a year dock on the outskirts of Amsterdam, making it Europe's fourth-busiest seaport (and those giant cruise ships have begun stopping here as well). For all of Amsterdam's existence, it's been a trading center.

• *The long brick building with the square clock tower, along the left side of Damrak, is the...*

❸Stock Exchange (Beurs van Berlage)

This impressive structure, a symbol of the city's long tradition as a trading town, was built with nine million bricks. Like so many

buildings in this once-marshy city, it was constructed on a foundation of pilings—some 5,000 tree trunks hammered vertically into the soil. When the Beurs opened in 1903, it was one of the world's first modernist buildings, with a geometric, minimal, no-frills style. Emphasizing function over looks, it helped set the architectural tone for many 20th-century buildings.

Continuing along Damrak, make your way to the end of the long building. Though it's only a century old, Amsterdammers have gathered in this neighborhood to trade since medieval times. Back then, "trading stock" meant buying and selling any kind of goods that could be loaded and unloaded onto a boat—goats, chickens, or kegs of beer. Over time, they began exchanging slips of paper, or "futures," rather than actual goods. Traders needed moneychangers, who needed bankers, who made money by lending money. By the 1600s, Amsterdam had become one of the world's first great capitalist cities, loaning money to free-spending kings, dukes, and bishops.

When you reach the end of the building, detour left into the square called **Beursplein.** In 1984, the Beurs building was turned into a cultural center, and the stock exchange moved next door, to the Euronext complex—a joint attempt by France, Belgium, and the Netherlands to compete with the power of Britain's stock exchange. See the stock price readout board. How's your Heineken stock doing? Green means it's going up, and red means it's losing value. Amsterdam still thrives as the center of Dutch business and is home to Heineken, Shell Oil, Philips Electronics, and Unilever.

Before leaving Beursplein, drop into **Café Beurs** and take in its minimalist 1930s interior. The optimistic art heralds a new age of worker-empowering technology, social democracy, and a hope for peace. It's also a nice place for a break.

• *Return to Damrak, and continue south along the busy boulevard until it opens into Dam Square. Make your way—carefully—across the street to the cobblestone pavement. Now, stand in the middle of the square and take it all in.*

Dam Square

This is the historic heart of the city. The city got its start right here in about the year 1250, when fishermen in this marshy delta settled along the built-up banks of the Amstel River. They built a *damme*, blocking the Amstel River, and creating a small village called "Amstel-damme." To the north was the *damrak* (meaning "outer harbor"), a waterway that eventually led to the sea. That's the street we just walked. To the south was the *rokin* (roh-KEEN, "inner harbor"), for river traffic. Nowadays, the Rokin is also a main street. With access to the sea, the fishermen were soon trading with German riverboats traveling downstream and with sea-faring boats from Stockholm, Hamburg, and London. Land trade

routes converged here as well, and a customs house stood in this spot. Dam Square was the center of it all.

Today, Dam Square is still the center of Dutch life, at least symbolically. The Royal Palace and major department stores face the square. Mimes, jugglers, and human statues mingle with locals and tourists. As Holland's most recognizable place, Dam Square is where political demonstrations begin and end.

Circling the Square

Pan the square clockwise, and take in the sights, starting with the Royal Palace—the large domed building on the west side. To its right stands the New Church (Nieuwe Kerk); it's located on the pedestrian-only shopping street called Nieuwendijk, which runs parallel to Damrak and stretches all the way to Central Station. Panning past Damrak, see the proud old De Bijenkorf ("The Beehive") department store. The store's café on the first floor is a great place to rise above it all for a light meal and pleasant views (see page 206).

Farther right, the Grand Hotel Krasnapolsky has a lovely

circa-1900 Winter Garden. The white obelisk is the National
Monument. A few blocks behind the hotel is the edge of the Red
Light District. To the right of the hotel stretches the street called
the Nes, lined with some of Amsterdam's edgy live-theater venues. Panning farther right, find Rokin street—Damrak's southern
counterpart, continuing past the square. Next, just to the right of
the touristy Madame Tussauds, is Kalverstraat, a busy pedestrian-
only shoppers mall (look for *Rabobank* sign).

❹Royal Palace

Despite the name, this is really the former City Hall—and
Amsterdam is one of the cradles of modern democracy. In medieval times, this was where the city
council and mayor met. Amsterdam was a self-governing community that prided itself on its
independence and thumbed its
nose at royalty. In about 1650,
the old medieval town hall was
replaced with this one. Its style is
appropriately Classical, recalling

the democratic Greeks. The triangular pediment features denizens
of the sea cavorting with Neptune and his gilded copper trident—
all appropriate imagery for sea-trading Amsterdam.

The building became known as the "Royal Palace" in 1806,
when Napoleon invaded and installed his brother Louis as king.
Even after Napoleon was defeated, the victorious powers dictated
that the Netherlands remain a monarchy, under a noble Dutch
family called the House of Orange. Today, the palace remains one
of the four official residences of King Willem-Alexander. (Though
Amsterdam is the nominal capital of the Netherlands, all governing activity—and the King's actual permanent home—are in The
Hague, 30 miles away.) Amsterdam's Royal Palace is usually open
to visitors. Inside, you can see a grand hall and about 20 lavishly
decorated rooms (see page 66).

• *A few paces away, to the right as you're facing the Royal Palace, is
the...*

❺New Church (Nieuwe Kerk)

Though called the "New" Church, this building is actually 600
years old—a mere 100 years newer than the "Old" Church in the
Red Light District. The sundial above the entrance once served as
the city's official timepiece.

While it's pricey to enter the church, cheapskates can get a
glimpse for free. Enter through the gift shop (just to the left of the

main church entrance), and climb the stairs to a balcony with a small free museum and great views of the nave.

The church's bare, spacious, well-lit interior (occupied by a new art exhibit every three months) looks quite different from the Baroque-encrusted churches found in the rest of Europe. In 1566, clear-eyed Protestant extremists throughout Holland marched into Catholic churches (including this one), lopped off the heads of holy statues, stripped gold-leaf angels from the walls, urinated on Virgin Marys, and shattered stained-glass windows in a wave of anti-Catholic vandalism.

This iconoclasm (icon-breaking) of 1566 started an 80-year war against Spain and the Habsburgs, leading finally to Dutch independence in 1648. Catholic churches like this one were converted to the new dominant religion, Calvinist Protestantism (today's Dutch Reformed Church). From then on, Dutch churches downplayed the "graven images" and "idols" of ornate religious art.

Take in the church's main highlights. At the far left end is an organ from 1655, still played for midday concerts. Opposite the entrance, a stained-glass window shows Count William IV giving the city its "XXX" coat of arms. And the window over the entrance portrays the inauguration of Queen Wilhelmina, who became the steadfast center of the Dutch Resistance during World War II. The choir, once used by the monks, was, after the Reformation, turned into a mausoleum for a great Dutch admiral.

This church is where many of the Netherlands' monarchs are married, and all are "inaugurated." (Dutch royals never actually wear the official crown.) In April 2013, Willem-Alexander—Wilhelmina's great-grandson—paraded through this church to the golden choir screen, where he was presented with the royal crown, scepter, orb, sword—and a copy of the Dutch constitution—and, with TV lights glaring and cameras flashing, sworn in as the new sovereign.

While on the viewing balcony, see the short video about the most recent royal wedding—it offers a nice chance to see the church in action. Leave the shop via the main church entrance. On your way out, look up to see stained glass windows showing Dutch royals from 1579 to 1898.

• *Back outside, look at the monument standing tall in the middle of Dam square.*

City on a Sandbar

Amsterdam sits in the marshy delta at the mouth of the Amstel River—a completely man-made city, built on millions of wooden pilings. The city was founded on unstable mud, which sits on stable sand. In the Middle Ages, buildings were made of wood, which rests lightly and easily on mud. But devastating fires repeatedly wiped out entire neighborhoods, so stone became the building material of choice. Brick is fire resistant, but was too heavy for a mud foundation, so for more support, pilings were driven 30 feet through the soggy soil and into the sand. The Royal Palace sits upon 13,000 such pilings—still solid after 350 years. (The wood survives if kept wet and out of the air.)

Since World War II, concrete, rather than wood, has been used for the pilings, with foundations driven 60 feet deep through the first layer of sand, through more mud, and into a second layer of sand. Today's biggest buildings have foundations that go down as much as 120 feet deep.

Many of the city's buildings, however, tend to lean this way and that as their pilings settle—and local landowners are concerned that the tunneling for the new metro line will cause their buildings to tilt even further. The snoopy-looking white cameras mounted on various building corners (such as on the Beurs) are monitoring buildings to check for settling.

❻National Monument

This white obelisk was built in 1956 as a WWII memorial. The Nazis occupied Holland from 1940 to 1945; in those years they deported 100,000 Jewish Amsterdammers, driving many—including young Anne Frank and her family—into hiding. Near the end of the war, the "Hunger Winter" of 1944-1945 killed thousands of Dutch and forced many to survive on little more than tulip bulbs. The monument—with its carvings of the crucified Christ, men in chains, and howling dogs—remembers the suffering of that grim time. Now the structure is also considered a monument for peace.

• From Dam Square, *head south (at the* Rabobank *sign) on...*

Kalverstraat

This shopping street (strictly pedestrian-only—even bikers need to dismount and walk) has been a traditional shopping street for centuries. But today it's notorious among locals as a noisy ghetto with chain stores and no soul. For smaller and more elegant stores, try the adjacent district called De Negen Straatjes ("The Nine Little Streets"). Only about four blocks west of Kalverstraat, it's where 200 or so shops and cafés mingle along pleasant canals.

• *About 100 yards along, keep a sharp eye out for the next sight (it's fairly easy to miss): On the right, just before and across from the McDonald's, at #58. Now pop into...*

❼De Papegaai Hidden Church (Petrus en Paulus Kerk)

This Catholic church is an oasis of peace amid crass 21st-century commercialism. It's not exactly a hidden church (after all, you've

found it), but it still keeps a low profile. That's because it dates from an era when Catholics in Amsterdam were forced to worship in secret.

In the 1500s, Protestants were fighting Catholics all over Europe. As a center for trade, Amsterdam has long made an effort to put business above ideological differences, doing business with all parties. But by 1578 the division had become too wide to straddle, and Protestant extremists took political control of the city. They expelled Catholic leaders and bishops and outlawed the religion. Catholic churches were stripped of their lavish decoration and converted into Dutch Reformed churches. Simultaneously, the Dutch were rising up politically against their (Catholic) Spanish overlords, and eventually threw them out.

For the next two centuries, Amsterdam's Catholics were driven underground. While technically illegal here, Catholicism was tolerated (kind of like marijuana is, these days). Catholics could worship so long as they practiced in humble, unadvertised places, like this church. The church gets its nickname from a parrot *(papegaai)* carved over the entrance of the house that formerly stood on this site. Now, a stuffed parrot hangs in the nave to remember that original *papegaai*.

Today, the church asks visitors for a mere "15 minutes for God" (so says the sign: *een kwartier voor God*)—an indication of how religion has long been a marginal part of highly commercial and secular Amsterdam.

• *Return to Kalverstraat and continue south for about 100 yards. At #92, where Kalverstraat crosses Wijde Kapel Steeg, look to the right at an archway that leads to the...*

❽Entrance and Courtyard of the Amsterdam Museum

Pause at the entrance to the museum complex to view the archway. On the slumping arch is Amsterdam's coat of arms—a red

shield with three Xs and a crown. The X-shaped crosses represent the crucifixion of St. Andrew, the patron saint of fishermen. (And here you thought the three Xs referred to the city's sex trade.) They also represent the three virtues of heroism, determination, and mercy—symbolism that was declared by the queen after the Dutch experience in World War II. (Before that, they likely symbolized the three great medieval threats: fire, flood, and plague.) The crown dates from 1489, when Maximilian I—a Habsburg emperor—also ruled the Low Countries. He paid off a big loan with help from Amsterdam's city bankers and, as thanks for the cash, gave the city permission to use his prestigious trademark, the Habsburg crown, atop its shield.

Now check out the relief above the door, dated 1581. It shows boys around a dove, asking for charity, reminding all who pass that this building was once an orphanage. People would donate by putting a coin in the slot of a donation box (find the bronze, nipple-crowned box on the sidewalk).

Go inside. The pleasant café has a shaded courtyard with a pay toilet, and old lockers for the orphans' uniforms. The exhibit here helps you imagine life in the orphanage through the centuries.

• *The courtyard leads to another courtyard with the best city history museum in town, the Amsterdam Museum (described on page 68).*

Between the two courtyards (on the left) is a free, glassed-in passageway lined with paintings. If it's closed, you'll need to backtrack to Kalverstraat to continue our walk (continue south, then turn right on Begijnensteeg, then look for the gate leading to the Begijnhof). Otherwise, step into the...

Civic Guard Gallery (Schuttersgalerij)

This hall features group portraits from Amsterdam's Golden Age, the early 1600s. Giant statues of Goliath and a knee-high David

(from 1650) watch over the whole thing.

Stroll around and gaze into the eyes of the hardworking men and women who made tiny Holland so prosperous and powerful. These are ordinary middle-class people, merchants, and traders, dressed in their Sunday best. They come across as good people—honest, businesslike, and friendly.

The Dutch got rich the old-fashioned way—they earned it. Dutch fishermen sold their surplus catch in distant areas of Europe, importing goods from these far lands. In time, fishermen became traders, and by 1600, Holland's merchant fleets ruled the waves. They had colonies as far away as India, Indonesia, and America (remember—New York was originally "Nieuw Amsterdam"). Back home, these traders were financed by shrewd Amsterdam businessmen on the new frontiers of capitalism. These people are clearly proud of their accomplishments.

The portraits show the men gathered with their Civic Guard militia units. These men defended Holland, but the Civic Guards were also fraternal organizations of business bigwigs—the Rotary Clubs of the 17th century. The weapons they carry—pikes and muskets—are mostly symbolic.

Many paintings look the same in this highly stylized genre. The men usually sit arranged in two rows. Someone holds the militia's flag. Later group portraits showed "captains" of industry going about their work, dressed in suits, along with the tools of their trade—ledger books, quill pens, and money.

Everyone looks straight out, and every face is lit perfectly. Each paid for his own portrait and wanted it right. It took masters like Rembrandt and Frans Hals to take the starch out of the collars and compose more natural scenes.

Find Ervin Olaf's "Dutch School" painting. It's a fun look at the city's cultural leaders in 2006, posing as Golden Age bigwigs.

• *The gallery offers a shortcut to our next stop, a hidden and peaceful little courtyard. To get there, exit out the far end of the Civic Guards Gallery. Once in the light of day, continue ahead one block farther south and find the humble gate on the right, which leads to the...*

❾ Begijnhof

As you enter, keep in mind that this spot isn't just a tourist attraction; it's also a place where people live. Be considerate: Don't photograph the residents or their homes, and if you're here in the evening, be quiet and stick to the area near the churches.

This quiet courtyard, lined with houses around a church, has sheltered women since 1346 (and is quite a contrast with the noisy Kalverstraat just steps away). This was for centuries the home of a community of Beguines—pious and simple women who removed themselves from the world at large to dedicate their lives to God. When it was first established, it literally was a "woman's island"—a circle of houses facing a peaceful courtyard, surrounded by water.

Begin your visit at the **statue** of one of these charitable sisters. You'll find it just beyond the church. The Beguines' ranks swelled during the Crusades, when so many men took off, never to return, leaving society with an abundance of single women. Later, women widowed by the hazards of overseas trade lived out their days as Beguines. Poor and rich women alike turned their backs on materialism and marriage to live here in Christian poverty. And though obedient to a mother superior, the members of the lay order of Beguines were not nuns. The Beguines were very popular in their communities for the lives they led—unpretentious, simple, with a Christ-like dedication to serving others. They spent their days deep in prayer and busy with daily tasks—spinning wool, making lace, teaching, and caring for the sick. In quiet seclusion, they provided a striking contrast to the more decadent and corrupt Roman Church, inspiring one another as well as their neighbors.

Now turn your attention to the brick-faced **English Reformed church** (Engelse Kerk). The church was built in 1420 to serve the Beguine community. But then, in 1578, Catholicism was outlawed, and the Dutch Reformed Church took over many Catholic monasteries. Still, the Begijnhof survived; in 1607, this church became Anglican. The church served as a refuge for English traders and religious refugees fleeing persecution in England. Strict Protestants such as the famous Pilgrims stopped here in tolerant Amsterdam, praying in this church before sailing to religious freedom in America. If the church is open, step inside, and head to the far end, toward the stained-glass window. It shows the Pilgrims praying before boarding the Mayflower. Along the right-hand wall is an old pew they may have sat on, and on the altar is a Bible from 1763, with lotſof old-ſtyle ſ's.

AMSTERDAM CITY WALK

Back outside, find the **Catholic church,** which faces the English Reformed Church. Because Catholics were being persecuted when it was built, this had to be a low-profile, "hidden" church—notice the painted-out windows on the second and third floors. Step inside, through the low-profile doorway; you can pick up an English brochure near the entry. This church served Amsterdam's oppressed 17th-century Catholics, who refused to worship as Protestants. It's decorated lovingly, if on the cheap (try tapping softly on a "marble" column). Amsterdam's Catholics must have eagerly awaited the day when they were legally allowed to say Mass (that day finally came in the 19th century).

Today, Holland still has something of a religious divide, but not a bitter one. Amsterdam itself is, like many big cities in the West, pretty un-churched. But the Dutch countryside is much more religious, including a "Bible Belt" region where 98 percent of the population is Protestant. Overall, in the Netherlands, the country is divided fairly evenly between Catholics, Protestants, and those who see Sunday as a day to sleep in and enjoy a lazy brunch.

Step back outside. The last Beguine died in 1971, but this Begijnhof still thrives, providing subsidized housing to about 100 single women (mostly Catholic seniors). The Begijnhof is just one of a few dozen *hofjes* (little housing projects surrounding courtyards) that dot Amsterdam.

The statue of the Beguine faces a black **wooden house,** at #34. This structure dates from 1477, and is the city's oldest. Originally, the whole city consisted of wooden houses like this one. They were eventually replaced with brick houses, to minimize the fire danger of having so many homes packed together.

Stroll a few steps to the left of the house to find a display of colorfully painted carved gable stones. These once adorned housefronts and served as street numbers.

• *Near the wooden house and gables, find a little corridor leading you back into the modern world. Head up a few steps to emerge into a lively square called Spui.*

⑩Spui and ⑪Rokin

Spui (spow, rhymes with cow), lined with cafés and bars, is one of the city's more popular spots for nightlife and sunny afternoon people-watching.

Head two blocks to the left, crossing busy Kalverstraat,

to the busy street called **Rokin.** A small black statue of Queen Wilhelmina (1880-1962) on the Rokin shows her riding daintily sidesaddle. Remember that in real life, she was the iron-willed inspiration for the Dutch Resistance against the Nazis.

Canal cruises depart from the Rondvaart Kooij dock across the water, in the yellow canal house (see "Canal Boat Tours" on page 51).

Turn left on the Rokin and walk up 50 yards to the ❷ **House of Hajenius** (at Rokin 92). This temple of cigars is a "paradise for the connoisseur" showing "175 years of tradition and good taste." To enter this sumptuous Art Deco building with painted leather ceilings is to step back into 1910. Don't be shy—the place is as much a free museum for visitors as it is a store for paying customers. The brown-capped canisters (under the wall of pipes, to the right) are for smelling fine pipe tobacco. Take a whiff. Sample three, and appreciate the differences between them. The personal humidifiers (read the explanation) allow locals (famous local names are on the cupboard doors) to call in an order and have their cigars waiting for them at just the right humidity. Above the street entry, check out the humidifier pipes pumping moisture into the room. Upstairs in back is a small, free museum. As you leave, read the legal notice on the door—establishing a strict age limit and limits on promotion—no discounts and no freebies. (If you ask me, this is a good, pragmatic "legalize, tax, and regulate" approach to the sale of a soft drug.)

In front of the cigar house is a red cage offering taxpayers (and tourists) an encouraging peek at the massive north-south metro line project. Descend 80 feet into a vast cave—a future metro stop—and get a sense of the work involved as they tunnel and build deep under the city.

• *From here, turn right and backtrack down the Rokin, past the statue of the queen. Stay on the right side of the street until you hit...*

❸Muntplein

On your right, where Kalverstraat hits the square, are two department stores. ❹ **Vroom & Dreesman** is where locals go for basic supplies (nothing fancy). It has a handy place where shoppers and hungry tourists can grab an easy lunch—the cheap and cheery La Place cafeteria. The ❺ **Kalvertoren** complex, across Kalverstraat from V&D, is a modern mall with a slanting glass elevator inside. You can ride this to the top floor, to enjoy something that's rare in altitude-challenged Amsterdam—a nice view.

At the center of the square stands the **Mint Tower** (Munt-toren), which marked the limit of the medieval walled city, and served as one of its original gates. In the Middle Ages, the city walls were girdled by a moat—the Singel canal. Until about 1500, the area beyond here was nothing but marshy fields and a few farms on reclaimed land. The Mint Tower's steeple was added later—in the year 1620, as you can see written below the clock face.

Today, the tower is a favorite within Amsterdam's marijuana culture. Stoners love to take a photo of the clock and its 1620 sign at exactly 4:20 p.m. (On the 24-hour clock, 4:20 p.m. is 16:20...Du-u-u-ude!)

Before moving on, look left (at about 10 o'clock) down Reguliersbreestraat. Midway down the block, the twin green domes mark the exotic ⓰ **Tuschinski Theater.** Here you can see current movies (subtitled in Dutch) in a sumptuous Art Deco setting. If you like, take a quick detour to check out its lobby, and imagine this place in the Roaring '20s (see page 63). Wa-a-ay at the end of the long block (where you see trees) is ⓱ **Rembrandtplein,** another major center for nightlife.

• Continue past the Mint Tower, first walking a few yards south along busy Vijzelstraat (keep an eye out for trams). Then turn right and walk west along the south bank of the Singel canal. The canal is lined with the greenhouse shops of the...

⓲ Flower Market (Bloemenmarkt)

The stands along this busy block sell cut flowers, plants, bulbs, seeds, and garden supplies. Browse your way along while heading for the end of the block.

The Bloemenmarkt is a testament to Holland's long-time love affair with flowers. The Netherlands is by far the largest flower exporter in Europe, and a major force worldwide. If you're looking for a souvenir, note that certain seeds are marked as OK to bring back through customs into the US (the marijuana starter-kit-in-a-can is probably...not).

For more on the history of tulips in Holland, see page 30.

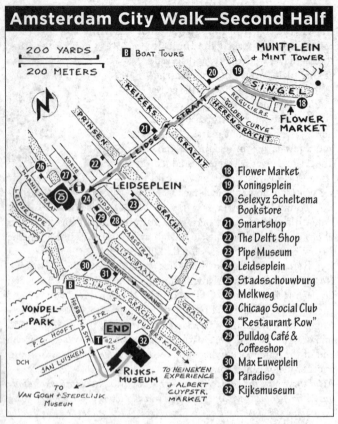

Amsterdam City Walk—Second Half

200 YARDS
200 METERS

B BOAT TOURS

MUNTPLEIN
+ MINT TOWER

SINGEL

KEIZERS GRACHT

PRINSEN

REGULIERS

GOLDEN CURVE

HERENGRACHT

LEIDSE STRAAT

FLOWER MARKET

KONI

LEIDSEPLEIN

LEIDSE KADE

HAARLEM STRAAT

LEIDSE GRACHT

DWARSSTRAAT

LIJNBAANS

WETERING

SINGEL-GRACHT SCHANS

VONDEL-PARK

HOBBEMASTR.

STAD HOUDERSKADE

P.C. HOOFT STR.

DCH

JAN LUIJKEN

END

RIJKS-MUSEUM

TO VAN GOGH + STEDELIJK MUSEUM

TO HEINEKEN EXPERIENCE + ALBERT CUYPSTR. MARKET

⑱ Flower Market
⑲ Koningsplein
⑳ Selexyz Scheltema Bookstore
㉑ Smartshop
㉒ The Delft Shop
㉓ Pipe Museum
㉔ Leidseplein
㉕ Stadsschouwburg
㉖ Melkweg
㉗ Chicago Social Club
㉘ "Restaurant Row"
㉙ Bulldog Café & Coffeeshop
㉚ Max Euweplein
㉛ Paradiso
㉜ Rijksmuseum

AMSTERDAM CITY WALK

• *The long Flower Market ends at the next bridge, where you'll see a square named...*

⑲Koningsplein

This pleasant square, with a popular outdoor food stand, is a great place to choke down a raw herring—a fish that has a special place in every Dutch heart. After all, herring was the commodity that first put Amsterdam on the trading map. It's also what Dutch sailors ate for protein on those long cross-global voyages. Even today, it's a specialty, and locals flock to this popular place. In season you'll see the sign: *Hollandse nieuwe*, alerting locals that the herring are "new" (fresh), caught during the May-June season. They eat it with

onions and pickles—your utensil is your Dutch-flag toothpick. Amsterdammers like to eat the fish whole—you grab it by the tail, tip your head back, and down she goes.

• *From Koningsplein, turn left, heading straight south to Leidseplein along...*

Leidsestraat

At first, the street is just labeled *Koningsplein*. You'll pass by Amsterdam's leading bookstore, ❷⓿ **Selexyz Scheltema,** just before

reaching the first of several grand canals, Herengracht.

Looking left down Herengracht, you'll see the so-called **"Golden Curve"** of the canal. It's lined with townhouses sporting especially nice gables. Amsterdam has many different types of gables—bell-shaped, step-shaped, and so on. This stretch is best known for its "cornice" gables (straight across); these topped the Classical-looking facades of rich merchants—the *heren*. (For more on gables, see the sidebar on page 133.)

After the bridge, Koningsplein becomes Leidsestraat. It's a busy street, crowded with shoppers, tourists, bicycles, and trams (keep your wits about you along here, and don't walk on the tram tracks). Notice that, as the street narrows, trams must wait their turn to share a single track.

• *Cross over the next canal (Keizersgracht), then find the little shop on the right at Kaisersgracht 508.*

❷⓵When Nature Calls Smartshop

While "smartshops" like this one are all just as above-board as any other in the city, they sell drugs— some of them quite strong, most of them illegal back home, and not all of them harmless. But since all these products are found in nature, the Dutch government considers them legal (for more on smartshops, see page 113). You can check out the window displays, or go on in and browse.

• *Where Leidsestraat crosses Prinsengracht, just over the bridge on the right (at Prinsengracht 440), you'll find...*

㉒The Delft Shop

This place sells good examples of the glazed ceramics known as Delftware, famous for its distinctive blue-and-white design (see the sidebar on page 289). It's traditionally made in Delft, a quaint town about 30 miles southwest of here (and described later in this book). Dutch traders learned the technique from the Chinese of the Ming dynasty, and many pieces have an Oriental look. The doodads with arms branching off a trunk are popular "flower pagodas," vases for displaying tulips.

• *Looking left, half a block down Prinsengracht, you can see the home of the* ㉓ *Pipe Museum (at #488; see listing on page 64). Unless you're detouring to visit the museum, turn right on Leidsestraat and follow it to the big, busy square, called...*

㉔Leidseplein

This is Amsterdam's liveliest square: filled with outdoor tables under trees; ringed with cafés, theaters, and nightclubs; bustling

with tourists, diners, trams, mimes, and fire-eaters. No wonder locals and tourists alike come here day and night, to sit under the trees, sip a coffee or beer, in the warmth of the sun or the glow of lantern light.

Do a 360-degree spin: Leidseplein's south side is bordered by the huge Apple Store—

sitting on what may be the city's most expensive piece of real estate. Nearby is the city's main serious theater, the ㉕ **Stadsschouwburg**. The theater company dates back to the 17th-century Golden Age, and the present building is from 1890. Does the building look familiar, with its red brick and fanciful turrets? That's because this building, along with Central Station and the Rijksmuseum, were built by the same architect, Pierre Cuypers. Tucked inside the theater is the **AUB/Last Minute Ticket Shop.** This handy box office sells tickets to all kinds of shows and concerts around town, including half-price, same-day tickets to select shows (after 12:00 Fri-Sat only).

Now look to the right of the Stadsschouwburg, down a lane behind the big theater. There you'd find the ㉖ **Melkweg** ("Milky Way") nightclub. Back in the 1970s, this place was almost mythical—an entertainment complex entirely devoted to the young generation and their desires. Even today it offers an edgy array of new acts—step into the lobby or check out posters nearby to see what's on.

Continue panning to the right. On Leidseplein's west side,

Amsterdam's Canals

Why are there so many canals *(grachten)* in Amsterdam? The city was founded in a marshy river delta, so its citizens needed  to keep the water at bay. They built a dike, near where Central Station stands today, to keep out the sea-tide surge. Then they dammed the Amstel River. The excess water was channeled safely away into canals, creating pockets of dry land to build on. They used windmills to harness wind power to pump the excess water into the canals.

Today, the city has about 100 canals, most of which are about 10 feet deep. They're crossed by some 1,200 bridges, fringed with 100,000 Dutch elm and lime trees, and bedecked with 2,500 houseboats. A system of locks (back near the Central Station) controls the flow. The locks are opened periodically to flush out the system.

The word *gracht* (pronounced, roughly, "khrockt," but with guttural flair) can refer to a canal itself, or to the ensemble of a canal and the lanes that border it on each side. A *straat* is a street without a canal, though a few paved-over canals, such as Elandsgracht, have kept their old name.

Some of the boats in the canals look pretty funky by day, but Amsterdam is an unpretentious, anti-status city. When the sun goes down and the lights come on, people cruise the sparkling canals with an on-board hibachi and a bottle of wine, and even scows can become chick-magnets.

AMSTERDAM CITY WALK

on the far-right corner, is ❷⓿ **Chicago Social Club.** This late-night bar has DJs and killer cocktails. It is affiliated with Boom Chicago, a comedy theater in the Jordaan district that presents English-language spoofs of politics, Amsterdam, and tourists (see the Entertainment in Amsterdam chapter). Pick up theater info here.

Continue panning. The neighborhood beyond Burger King is Amsterdam's ❷❽ **"Restaurant Row,"** featuring countless Thai, Brazilian, Indian, Italian, Indonesian—and even a few Dutch—eateries. Next, on the east end of Leidseplein, is the ❷❾ **Bulldog Café and Coffeeshop,** the flagship of several coffeeshops in town with the Bulldog name.

(Notice the sign above the door: It once housed the police bureau.) A small green-and-white decal on the window indicates that it's a city-licensed "coffeeshop," where marijuana is sold and smoked legally. Incredible as that may seem to visitors from the States, it's been going on here in Amsterdam for over 30 years—another Dutch cliché alongside windmill peppermills and wooden shoes. (For more, see the Smoking chapter.)

• *From Leidseplein, turn left and head along the taxi stand down the broad, busy, tram-filled boulevard called Kleine-Gartman Plantsoen, which becomes Weteringschans. At the triangular garden, cross the street and pass under a row of tall, gray, Greek-style columns, entering...*

③⓪Max Euweplein

The Latin inscription above the colonnade—*Homo Sapiens non urinat in ventum*—means "People, don't pee into the wind." Passing

between the columns, you soon reach a pleasant interior courtyard with cafés and a large chessboard with knee-high kings. (Max Euwe was a Dutch world chess champion; in 1957, he beat 14-year-old Bobby Fischer in 20 moves.) The square gives you access to the Casino, and just over the small bridge is the entrance to **Vondelpark.** Nearby are the Blue Boat Company's **canal boats,** offering one-hour tours (see "Canal Boat Tours" on page 51).

• *Return to Weteringschans street. Turn right and continue 75 yards east to a squat, red-brick building called...*

③①Paradiso

Back when rock-and-roll was a religion, this former church staged intimate concerts by big-name acts such as the Rolling Stones. In the late 1960s, when city fathers were trying hard to tolerate hordes of young pot smokers, this building was redecorated with psychedelic colors and opened up as the first place where marijuana could be smoked—not legally yet, but it was tolerated. Today, the club hosts live bands and DJs, and sells pot—legally.

• *Continue down Weteringschans to the first bridge, where you'll see the Rijksmuseum across the canal.*

③②The Rijksmuseum and Beyond

The best visual chronicle of the Dutch Golden Age is found in the Rijksmuseum's portraits and slice-of-life scenes.

For a tour of the Rembrandts, Vermeers, and others, ✪ see the Rijksmuseum Tour chapter.

On this walk, we've seen landmarks built during the city's late 19th-century revival: Central Station, the Stadsschouwburg, and now the Rijksmuseum. They're all similar, with red-brick and Gothic-style motifs (clock towers, steeples, prickly spires, and stained glass). Pierre Cuypers (1827-1921), who designed the train station and the Rijksmuseum, was extremely influential. Mainly a builder of Catholic churches, he made the Rijksmuseum, with its stained-glass windows, a temple to art.

Behind the Rijksmuseum are the Museumplein (always entertaining) and the Van Gogh Museum (✪ see the tour chapter). The Heineken Experience (beer tour) is a half-mile east of the Rijksmuseum on Heinekenplein (see page 62), and the Albert Cuypstraat street market is a block south of the Heineken Experience.

To return to Central Station (or to nearly anyplace along this walk), catch tram #2 or #5 from the southwest corner of the Rijksmuseum. Or walk north on Nieuwe Spiegelstraat, which leads you (with a little detour) back to the Mint Tower.

RED LIGHT DISTRICT WALK

Amsterdam's oldest neighborhood has hosted the world's oldest profession since the Middle Ages. Today, prostitution and public marijuana use still thrive here, creating a spectacle that's unique in all of Europe.

The Red Light District lies between Damrak and Nieuw-markt. On our walk, we'll see history, sleaze, and cheese: transvestites in windows, drunks in doorways, cruising packs of foreign twentysomethings, cannabis being enjoyed, and sex for sale.

The sex trade runs the gamut from sex shops selling porn and accessories to blue video arcades, from glitzy nightclub sex shows featuring strippers and sex acts to the real deal—prostitutes in bras, thongs, and high heels, standing in window displays, offering their bodies. Amsterdam keeps several thousand prostitutes employed—and it's all legal.

Not for Everyone: The Red Light District seems to have something to offend everyone. Whether it's in-your-face images of graphic sex, exploited immigrant women, whips and chains, passed-out drug addicts, the pungent smells of pot smoke and urine, or just the shameless commercialism of it all, it's not everyone's cup of tea. And though I encourage people to expand their horizons—that's a great thing about travel—it's perfectly OK to say, "No, thank you."

Orientation

Length of This Walk: Allow two hours.
Photography: Consider leaving your camera in your bag. Absolutely avoid taking photos of ladies in windows—even with an inconspicuous camera phone—or a snarly bouncer

may appear from out of nowhere
to forcibly rip it from your hands.
In this district, taking even seemingly harmless pictures of ordinary
people is frowned upon by privacy-
loving locals. Photos of landmarks
like the Old Church and wide
shots of distant red lights from
the bridges are certainly OK, but
remember that a camera is a prime
target in this high-theft area.

When to Go: The best times to visit
are afternoons and early evenings.
Mornings are dead, but are also
when you see more passed-out-drunk-in-a-doorway scenes.
Avoid late nights (after about 22:30), when the tourists disappear and the area gets creepy. Earlier in the evening, the
streets start filling with tourists, and the atmosphere feels
safe, even festive.

Safety: Coming here is asking for trouble, but if you're on the
ball and smart, you'll find that it's quite safe. While there are
plenty of police on horseback keeping things orderly, there
are also plenty of rowdy drunks, drug-pushing lowlifes, con
artists, and pickpockets (not to mention extremely persuasive
women in windows). Assume any fight or commotion in the
streets is a ploy to distract innocent victims who are about to
lose their wallets. As always, wear your money belt and keep
a low profile.

Tours: This walk is enough for most visitors, but if you want a
more in-depth visit with a guide and a group, consider
Randy Roy's Red Light Tours (described on page 53). The
Prostitution Information Center also offers tours (see below).

Old Church (Oude Kerk): €5, more for temporary exhibits, Mon-
Sat 11:00-17:00, Sun 13:00-17:00. You can climb the 167 steps
to the top of the church tower (€7, April-Sept Thu-Sat 13:00-
17:00, closed Sun-Wed and Oct-March).

Prostitution Information Center: €1, Sat 13:30-20:00 only, €15
walking tours offered Sat at 17:00 and Wed at 18:30, tel.
020/420-7328, www.pic-amsterdam.com.

Amstelkring Museum (Our Lord in the Attic): €8, Mon-Sat
10:00-17:00, Sun and holidays 13:00-17:00, no photos.

Cannabis College: Free, daily 11:00-19:00.

Hash, Marijuana, and Hemp Museum: €9, daily 10:00-23:00.

Audio Tour: You can download this chapter as a free Rick Steves
audio tour (see page 53).

Red Light District Walk

1. Warmoesstraat
2. Golden Fleece Condomerie
3. Entering De Wallen
4. Smartshop
5. Sex Shops & Mr. B's
6. Old Church
7. Bulldog Café Coffeeshop
8. Dollebegijnensteeg
9. Prostitution Info Center & Room-Rental Office
10. Princess Juliana Daycare
11. Oudezijds Voorburgwal & Pill Bridge
12. Amstelkring Museum
13. Historical Building (1580)
14. Old Harbor View & Old Wooden House
15. The Zeedijk
16. Café 't Mandje
17. Oudezijds Achterburgwal
18. Banana Bar
19. Erotic Museum
20. Absolute Danny Shop
21. Theatre Casa Rosso
22. Cannabis College
23. Hemp Gallery
24. Hash, Marijuana & Hemp Museum

RED LIGHT WALK

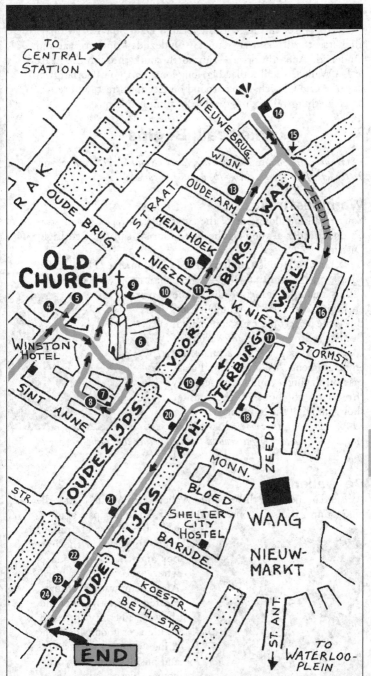

Overview

The walk starts on the centrally located Dam Square. Two parallel streets with similar names—Oudezijds Voorburgwal and Oudezijds Achterburgwal—run north-south through the heart of De Wallen. You'll walk a big, long loop: north on Voorburgwal past the Old Church, hook around on Zeedijk street, and return on Achterburgwal, ending two blocks from Dam Square.

The Walk Begins

• *Start on Dam Square. Face the big, fancy Grand Hotel Krasnapolsky. To the left of the hotel stretches the long street called...*

Warmoesstraat

You're walking along one of the city's oldest streets. It's the traditional border of the neighborhood tourists call the Red Light District.

Our first stop is **Golden Fleece Condomerie** (Het Gulden Vlies), on the right at #141. It's the small shop with the large, yellow triangle sign. Located at the entrance to the Red Light District, this is the perfect place to get prepared. Besides selling an amazing variety of condoms, this place has a knack for entertainment. Inside is a small glass case displaying a condom museum. A three-ring notebook on the counter shows off all of the inventory.

• *From here, pass the two little street barricades with cute red lights around them and enter the traffic-free world of...*

De Wallen

Amsterdammers call this area De Wallen ("The Walls"), after the old retaining walls that once stood here. It's the oldest part of town, with the oldest church. It grew up between the harbor and the Dam Square, where the city was born. Amsterdam was a port town, located where the river met the sea. The city traded in all kinds of goods, including things popular with sailors and businessmen away from home—like sex and drugs.

According to legend, Quentin Tarantino holed up at the Winston Hotel for three months in 1993 to write *Pulp Fiction* (you'll pass the hotel on your right, at #129). It's clear that the area attracts many out-of-towners, especially Brits. Notice all the Irish pubs, advertisements for football (soccer) games, and British, Scottish, and Irish flags. From the British Isles, the Red Light District is just a cheap flight away. Brits come here in droves for "stag" (bachelor) parties or just a wild weekend—and the money-savvy Dutch know their best customers.

Farther down, also on the right, you'll come to an intersection with a small street called Wijde Kerksteeg, which leads to the Old Church (we'll go to the church in a moment). Standing here, note the gay rainbow flags and the S&M flags (black and blue with a heart). Also notice the security cameras and modern lighting. Freedom reigns in this quarter—under the watchful eye of the two neighborhood police departments.

• *Continue down Warmoesstraat a few more steps. At #97 is the...*

Elements of Nature Smartshop

This "smartshop" is a little grocery store of mind-bending natural ingredients. This shop, like the city's other smartshops, is a clean, well-lit, fully professional retail outlet that sells powerful drugs, many of which are illegal in America. Prices are clearly marked, with brief descriptions of the drugs, their ingredients, and effects. The knowledgeable salespeople can give you more information on their "100 percent natural products that play with the human senses."

Their "natural" drugs include harmless nutrition boosters (such as royal jelly), harmful but familiar tobacco, and herbal versions of popular dance-club drugs (such as herbal Ecstasy). Marijuana seeds, however, are the big sellers. You'll also see mind-bending truffles, a recent trend that caught on after the EU forbade the retailing of hallucinogenic mushrooms. (Truffles grow underground—so they're technically not mushrooms.)

Still, my fellow travelers, *caveat emptor!* We've grown used to thinking, "If it's legal, it must be safe. If it's not, I'll sue." Though perfectly legal and aboveboard in the Netherlands, some of these substances can cause powerful, often unpleasant reactions.

• *Continue a bit farther down Warmoesstraat, to an area filled with so-called...*

Sex Shops

These places deal in erotic paraphernalia (dildos, S&M starter kits, and kinky magazines). Browsers are welcome. Some shops have video booths playing porn films, charging by the minute. (Haven't these guys heard of the Internet?) While Amsterdam is notorious for its Red Light District, even small Dutch towns often have a sex shop and a brothel to satisfy their citizens' needs.

Farther down Warmoesstraat, at #93 and #96, you'll see several men-only leather bars, distinguished by their black doors and windows. These places come with a bar, a dance floor, and a dark back room.

A few steps along, at #89, is **Mr. B's Leather and Rubber Land,** proudly flying an S&M flag. This place takes macho to painful—and what seems like anatomically impossible—extremes. (Ouch.) Downstairs, you'll find some irresistible deals on whips and masks.

• *Let's go see the Old Church. Backtrack a few steps to the intersection, and head down Wijde Kerksteeg to the...*

Old Church (Oude Kerk)

As the name implies, this was the medieval city's original church. Returning from a long sea voyage, sailors of yore would spy the

steeple of the Old Church on the horizon and know they were home. Having returned safely, they'd come here to give thanks to St. Nicholas— the patron saint of this church, of seafarers, of Christmas, and of the city of Amsterdam.

The church was begun about 1300. Construction continued in fits and starts for the next 300 years—as is apparent in the building's many gangly parts. Then, in the 15th century, Amsterdam built the New Church

(Nieuwe Kerk) on Dam Square. But the Old Church still had the tallest spire, the biggest organ, and the most side-altars, and remained the city's center of activity, bustling inside and out with merchants and street markets.

The **tower** is 290 feet high, with an octagonal steeple atop a bell tower (you can pay to climb to the top). This tower served as the model for many other Dutch steeples. The carillon has 47 bells, which can chime mechanically or be played by one of Amsterdam's three official carillonneurs. (For more on carillons, see page 136.)

While the church is historic, there's not much to see inside. If you pay to enter, you'll see a big empty church with 2,500 gravestones in the floor. The most famous grave is Rembrandt's wife, Saskia. The church is so bare because it was vandalized during the religious wars of the 16th century. Protestants gutted this Catholic church, smashing windows and removing politically incorrect statues they considered "graven images." One renowned girl threw her shoe at the Virgin statue. (Strict Calvinists at one point even removed the organ as a senseless luxury, until they found they couldn't stay on key singing hymns without it.) Atop the brass choir screen, an inscription *('t misbruyk in Godes...)* commemorates the iconoclasm: "The false practices introduced into God's church were undone here in 1578."

The church, permanently stripped of "pope-ish" decoration, was transformed from Catholic to Dutch Reformed, the name St. Nicholas' Church was dropped, and it became known by the nickname everyone called it anyway—the Old Church.

Nowadays, the church is the holy needle around which the unholy Red Light District spins. This marks the neighborhood's most dense concentration of prostitution.

Back outside, explore around the right side of the church. You'll see a **statue,** dedicated to the Unknown Prostitute. She's nicknamed Belle, and the statue honors "sexworkers around the world." Also nearby you might trip over a bronze breast sculpted into the pavement, being groped by bronze hands.

Attached to the church like barnacles are **small buildings.** These were originally used as homes for priests, church offices, or rental units. The house to the right of the entrance (at #25) is very tiny—32 feet by 8 feet. (An elderly lady lives here, so be discreet.)

Now check out the green metal **urinal** over by the canal. This one gets a lot of use. Consider that, on average, about 12 people drown in Amsterdam every year. When found, most of them turn out to be men with their zippers down. It's not hard to imagine the scene: Some guy is drunk as a skunk at 3 a.m., goes to the edge of the canal to take a pee...and falls in.

• *From the urinal, go half a block south along the canal toward the...*

RED LIGHT WALK

Bulldog Café Coffeeshop

The Bulldog claims to be Amsterdam's very first marijuana coffeeshop, established here in 1975. Now there's a chain of Bulldogs around the city. At "coffeeshops" like this one, customers start the transaction by asking the bartender, "Can I see the cannabis menu?" (As it's illegal to advertise marijuana, buyers must

ask to see a list of what's for sale.) Then the bartender pulls out a display case with different varieties of weed, sold in baggies or pre-rolled joints. It's all clearly priced, and available either to-go or to smoke on the premises. You'll see people at the Bulldog enjoying a joint while they sip a beer or a Coke.

As coffeeshops go, the Bulldog is considered pretty touristy. The staff is unintimidating, though, and timid first-timers are guided through the process. Connoisseurs, however, seek out smaller places with better-quality pot. While the Bulldog caters to a young crowd, other coffeeshops play Donovan and target an older, mellower clientele.

In recent years, various Dutch politicians have proposed new laws that would forbid sales of marijuana to nonresidents. Their big worry is European drug dealers who drive over the Dutch border, buy up large quantities of pot, and return home to sell it illegally. This law would be devastating for these Dutch businesses, who depend on out-of-towners to stay in business. The current mayor of Amsterdam is adamant that the city's coffeeshops will remain open—for the sake of the businesses, and because the city believes that the law would just drive business back into a black market, and cause an increase in street crime.

For more on the Dutch approach to pot, and how coffeeshops work, see the Smoking chapter.

• *Time to dive into the heart of the Red Light District—we're right around the corner from one of the neighborhood's main streets for legal prostitution. Immediately adjacent to the coffeeshop is a three-foot-wide entrance to a narrow alleyway, called...*

Dollebegijnensteeg

You're right in the thick of high-density prostitution. Remember: Don't take any pictures, and watch for pickpockets if crowds jostle together. If you do both these things, you'll be fine.

As you pass window after window of women in panties and bras, notice how they wink at the horny men, rap on the window to attract attention, or look disdainfully at sightseers. You can take your time here and then explore deeper (or you can hurry to the end of the block and turn right to return to the Old Church).

This alleyway is just one of several in this area. You may notice that different zones feature prostitutes from different lands—Asia, Africa, Eastern Europe. This is to cater to customer tastes, as regulars know what they want.

• *Return to the Old Church and start to circle the church clockwise. Around the back (on Oudekerksplein), you'll see older, plumper (and cheaper) prostitutes. In the same area, at Enge Kerksteeg 3, is the...*

Prostitution Information Center (PIC)

This center exists solely to demystify prostitution, giving visitors

matter-of-fact information on how the trade works and what it's like to be a sex worker. It's only open on Saturday evenings, when it doles out pamphlets, books, condoms, T-shirts, and other offbeat souvenirs. They also offer a twice-weekly walking tour (PIC entry-€1; see beginning of chapter for tour details). They have a map showing exactly where prostitution is legal, and sell a small, frank booklet (€1.50) answering the most common questions tourists have about Amsterdam's Red Light District. The center also offers a one-to-one

workshop, for women only, on what it's like to be a sex worker in Amsterdam (must be booked in advance).

Next door is a **room-rental office** (labeled *Kamerverhuurbedrijf*). Prostitutes come here to rent window space and bedrooms to use for their work. Several of the available rooms for rent are just next door. The office also sells supplies—condoms by the case, lubricants, and soft drinks. The man at the desk does not arrange sex. The women who rent space from this business are self-employed, and negotiate directly with their customers.

In return for their rental fees, prostitutes get security. The man in the office keeps an eye on them by video surveillance—you can see the monitors inside. Looking down the street, you can see small cameras and orange alarm lights above the doors. If prostitutes have any trouble, they press a buzzer that swiftly unleashes not a pimp, but a burly bouncer or the police. The area sure looks rough, but, aside from tricky pickpockets, these streets are actually pretty safe.

• *Continue circling clockwise around the church. Amid prostitutes in windows, find the orange brick building on the left at Oudekerksplein 8. (Since it's low-profile and sealed up tight, it might be hard to find— look for the black-and-white photo of the princess near a gunmetal-gray door.) This is the...*

Princess Juliana Daycare

De Wallen is also a residential neighborhood, where ordinary citizens go about their daily lives. Of course, locals need someplace to

Prostitution in Amsterdam

The sex trade has been plied in Amsterdam since the 1200s. For centuries, it existed alongside everyday life. But it's only been legal since the 1980s, when the city designated De Wallen as the neighborhood where prostitution would be allowed and regulated.

The system is simple. A customer browses around. A prostitute catches his eye. If the prostitute is interested in his business (prostitutes are selective for their own safety), she winks him over. They talk at the door as she explains her price and what she has to offer. Many are very aggressive at getting the man inside, where the temptation game revs up. A price is agreed on and paid in advance. A typical visit can cost €30-50 for 20 minutes or so. The man goes in. The woman draws the curtain. Where do they actually do it? The rooms look tiny from the street, but these are just display windows. There's a bigger room behind or upstairs that comes with a bed, a sink, and not much else (or so I've heard).

Are there male prostitutes? Certainly—anything you might want is available somewhere in the Red Light District. But an experiment in the 1990s to put male prostitutes in windows didn't stand up. The district does, however, have plenty of "reconstructed women"—i.e., transvestites, many of them so gorgeous they need to (but don't necessarily) warn customers before they get a rude surprise. Blue lights (rather than red) mark where transvestites do business.

The prostitutes here are self-employed—entrepreneurs,

RED LIGHT WALK

send their kids. The Princess Juliana Daycare is for newborns to four-year-olds. It was built in the 1970s, when the idea was to mix all dimensions of society together, absorbing the seedy into the decent. I don't know about you, but this location would be a tough sell where I come from.

· *Turn left at the canal and continue north along...*

Oudezijds Voorburgwal

Pause at the bridge and enjoy the canal and all the old buildings with their charming gables. Back in the 1970s, this bridge was nicknamed **"Pill Bridge"** for the retail items sold by the seedy guys who used to hang out here. Now it's a pleasant place for a photo-op.

Just past the bridge, at Oudezijds Voorburgwal 40, is one of

renting space and running their own business. They usually work a four- to eight-hour shift. A good spot costs about €100 for a day shift, and €150 for an evening. Prostitutes are required to keep their premises hygienic, make sure their clients use condoms, and avoid minors.

Popular prostitutes can make about €500 a day. They fill out tax returns, and many belong to a loose union called the Red Thread. The law, not pimps, protects prostitutes. If a prostitute is diagnosed with HIV or AIDS, she loses her license. As shocking as legalized prostitution may seem to some, it's a good example of a pragmatic Dutch solution to a persistent problem.

Although some women choose prostitution as a lucrative career, others (likely most) are forced into it by circumstance—poverty, drug addiction, abusive men, and immigration scams. Since the fall of the Iron Curtain, many Eastern Europeans have flocked here, and Russian and East European crime syndicates have muscled in. While the hope here in the Netherlands is that sex workers are smartly regulated small-business-people, in reality the line between victim and entrepreneur is not always so clear.

Amsterdam's current city government is trying to rein in the sex trade by limiting it to De Wallen. It's also hoping to splice other commerce into a district that for centuries has had variations on basically only one product. As many as half of the sex businesses here may close over the next few years—not because of prudishness, but to limit the encroachment of organized crime. A major Red Light District landlord was essentially given the option either to lease many of his booths to the city or be zoned out of business. The city picked up the leases, and windows that once showcased "girls for rent" now showcase mannequins wearing the latest fashions—lit by lights that aren't red.

RED LIGHT WALK

the city's most worthwhile museums: the **Amstelkring Museum,** in Our Lord in the Attic Church. With its triangular gable, this building looks like just another townhouse. But inside, it holds a secret—a small, lavishly decorated place of worship hidden in the attic. Although Amsterdam has long been known for its tolerance, back in the 16th century there was one group they kept in the closet—Catholics. (For more, ✪ see the Amstelkring Museum Tour chapter.)

As we stroll up the canal, remember that this neighborhood is Amsterdam's oldest. It sits on formerly marshy land that was reclaimed by diking off the sea's tidal surge. That location gave Amsterdam's merchants easy access to both river trade and the North Sea. By the 1500s, Amsterdam was booming.

Near the next bridge, at #14, is a **historical building** from that very era—around 1580. At the time of its construction, Amsterdam's citizens were rising up in revolt to throw out their Spanish rulers. Now free to govern themselves, a group of energetic businessmen turned the city into a sea-trading hub. By 1600, brave Dutch sailors were traveling as far as Africa, America and Asia. They returned with shiploads of exotic goods to sell to the rest of Europe.

The 1600s were Amsterdam's heyday. With its canals and fine townhouses, it became known as the "Venice of the North." The part of the canal we're walking along now is known as **"Little Venice"** (a term used Europe-wide for any charming neighborhood with canalside houses). Houses rise directly from the water here, with no quays or streets. Like Venice, the city was built in a marshy delta area, on millions of pilings. And, like Venice, it grew rich on sea trade.

You'll soon reach the end of the canal. Before you go on, notice the collection of fine gable stones embedded in the wall on the right.

• *Continue straight up a small inclined lane called Sint Olofssteeg. At the top, turn left onto a street called the Zeedijk. Walk along the Zeedijk about 100 yards to the end of the block, where it opens up to a...*

View of the Old Harbor

As you survey the marina, Damrak, and Central Station, imagine the scene in the 1600s. The **old wooden house**—now a café—was once a tavern, sitting right at what was then the water's edge (today's marina was the city's harbor). Boats sailed in and out of the harbor through an opening located where Central Station sits today. (The station was built on reclaimed land.) From there, they could sail along the IJ River out to the North Sea.

Amsterdam became home to the Dutch East India Company, the world's first multinational corporation. Goods from all over the world flowed into this harbor, and cargo could be transferred from there to smaller river-trade boats that sailed up the Amstel to Europe's interior. The city grew wealthier and larger, expanding beyond De Wallen to new neighborhoods to the west and south. In its Golden Age, Amsterdam was perhaps the wealthiest city on earth, known as the "warehouse of the world."

Picture a ship tying up in the harbor. The crew has just returned home from a two-year voyage to Bali. They're bringing home fabulous wealth—crates and crates of spices, coffee, and silk. Sailors are celebrating their homecoming, spilling onto the Zeedijk. Here they'll be greeted by swinging ladies swinging red lanterns. Their first stop might be St. Olaf's chapel to say a prayer of thanks—or perhaps they'll head straight to this tavern at Zeedijk 1 and drop anchor for a good Dutch beer. Ahh-hh!

• *But our journey continues on. Backtrack along the same street, to the crest of a bridge, to take in the...*

Zeedijk

See that green box by the railing? It's part of the city's system of **locks:** Once a day a worker opens up this box and presses a button. The locks open, and the tides flush out the city's canals. Look

down—if the gate is open, you might see water flowing in or out.

The Zeedijk runs along the top of the "sea dike" that historically protected sea-level Amsterdam from the North Sea tides. It also connected the harbor, bustling with ocean-going ships, with De Wallen.

In the early 1600s, Zeedijk street was thriving with overseas trade. But Amsterdam would soon lose its maritime supremacy to England and France, and by midcentury, its trading ships and economy had been destroyed by wars with these rivals. The city remained culturally vibrant, and banking flourished—but without all the ships, De Wallen never really recovered. For centuries, the area languished as Amsterdam's grimy old sailors' quarter. It wasn't until the 1960s that this neighborhood began the transformation to the place we see today.

As you continue down the Zeedijk and around the bend, you can see that the area has become fairly gentrified. Residents enjoy a mix of ethnic restaurants—Thai and Portuguese, for example—and bars like the Queen's Head (at #20, on the left) that draw a gay clientele. The apartment building at #30 (on the right) is new, built in "MIIM" (1998).

Back in the 1960s, it was a whole different story. Amsterdam was the world capital of experimental lifestyles, a wide-open city of sex and drugs. By the 1970s, the Zeedijk had become unbelievably sleazy. That's where I come into the story. When I made my first trip here, this street was nicknamed "Heroin Alley." Thousands of hard-drug addicts wandered the neighborhood and squatted in old buildings. "Pill Bridge" (which we passed earlier) became "Needle Bridge." It was a scene with little else besides sex, hard drugs, and wandering lonely souls. The area was a no-man's-land of junkies fighting among themselves, and the police just kept their distance.

Social Control

De Wallen has pioneered the Dutch concept of "social control." In Holland, neighborhood security doesn't come from just the police, but from neighbors looking out for each another. If Geert doesn't buy bread for two days, the baker asks around if anyone's seen him. An elderly man feels safe in his home, knowing he's being watched over by the prostitutes next door. Unlike many big cities, there's no chance that anyone here could die or be in trouble and go unnoticed. Video-surveillance cameras keep an eye on the streets. So do prostitutes, who buzz for help if they spot trouble. As you stroll, watch the men who watch the women who watch out for their neighbors—"social control."

But locals longed to take back this potentially wonderful corner of their city, and the Dutch eventually decided to do something about the problem. The first step was legalizing marijuana and allowing "coffeeshops" to sell small quantities of pot. Then they cracked down on hard drugs—heroin, cocaine, and pills. Almost overnight, the illicit drug trade dropped dramatically. Dealers got stiff sentences. Addicts got treatment. Four decades later, the policy seems to have worked. Pot-smoking has not gone up, hard drug use is down, and the Zeedijk belongs to the people of Amsterdam once again.

Pause at #63, on the left. The **Café 't Mandje** was perhaps Europe's first gay bar. It opened in 1927, closed in 1985, and is now

a working bar once again. It stands as a memorial to the woman who ran it during its heyday in the 1950s and '60s: Bet van Beeren, "Queen of the Zeedijk." Bet was a lesbian, and her bar became a hangout for gay people. It still is, though all are welcome. If you go inside for a drink, you'll enjoy a tiny interior crammed with photos and memorabilia. Bet was the original Zeedyke—you might see a picture of Bet cruising the streets on her motorcycle, decked out in leather. Neckties hang from the ceiling, a reminder of Bet's tradition of scissoring off customers' ties.

• *This tour veers right at the next intersection, back into the heart of the Red Light District. For a quick detour, however, you could continue straight ahead for a peek into the local Chinatown. Otherwise, make the*

RED LIGHT WALK

next right and head a few steps down narrow Korte Stormsteeg street, back to the canalside red lights. Then go left, before the bridge, along the left side of the canal.

Oudezijds Achterburgwal

We're back in the glitzy Red Light District. This beautiful, tree-lined canal is the heart of this neighborhood's nightlife, playing host to most of the main nightclubs.

· *Keep walking along the left side of the canal, making your way to the first bridge. Up ahead, at #37, is the...*

Banana Bar (Bananenbar)

This popular nightclub has an erotic Art Nouveau facade that's far classier than what's offered inside. Basically, this place is a strip club with a-peel: For €50 you get admission for an hour, drinks included. Undressed ladies serve the drinks, perched on the bar. Touching is not allowed, but you can order a banana, and the lady will serve it to you, any way you like. For a full description, step into the lobby.

· *At Molensteeg, cross the bridge to head to the right side of Oudezijds Achterburgwal. Once across the bridge, we'll be turning left. But first, pause and look to the right. At #54 is the...*

Erotic Museum

"Wot a rip-off!" said a drunk British lout to his mates as he emerged from the Erotic Museum. If it's graphic sex you seek, this is not the place. To put it bluntly, this museum is not very good (the Damrak Sex Museum is better; see page 70).

This museum, however, does offer a peek at some of the sex services found in the Red Light District. Besides the self-pleasuring bicycle girl in the lobby, displays include reconstructions of a prostitute's chambers, sex-shop windows, and videos of nightclub sex shows (on the third floor). There's also the S&M room, where S-mannequins torment M-mannequins for their mutual pleasure (€7, daily 11:00-1:00 in the morning).

· *From the bridge, turn left, and walk south along Oudezijds Achterburgwal. On the way, you'll pass by a shop, at #76, called...*

Absolute Danny

This shop bills itself as the place for "all your sensual clothing." It sells leather and rubber outfits with dog collars suggesting

bondage scenarios, in a full array of colors from red to black to... well, that's about it.
• *Continuing south, on the right (lined by pink elephants) you'll find the...*

Theatre Casa Rosso

This is the Red Light District's best-known nightclub for live sex shows. Unlike some strip clubs that draw you in to rip you off with hidden charges, the Casa Rosso is a legitimate operation. Audience members pay a single price that includes drinks and a show. Evening performances feature strippers, but the main event is naked people on stage engaging in sex acts—some simulated, some completely real (€30, €45 includes drinks, nightly until 2:00 in the morning).

As you continue south along the canal, you gotta wonder, Why does Amsterdam embrace prostitution and drugs? It's not that the Dutch are any more liberal in their attitudes—they aren't. They're simply more pragmatic. They've found that when the sex trade goes underground, you get pimps, mobsters, and the spread of STDs. When marijuana is illegal, you get drug dealers, gangs, and violent turf wars. Their solution is to keeping these markets legal, and minimize problems through strict regulation.
• *Had it with the sleaze? We're almost done. But first...more drugs. Along the right side of the next block, you'll find four cannabis-related establishments, starting with the Cannabis College, at #124.*

Cannabis College

This free, non-profit public study center aims to explain the pros and cons (but mostly pros) of the industrial, medicinal, and recreational uses of the green stuff. You can read about practical hemp products, the medical uses of marijuana, and police prosecution/persecution of cannabis users. The pride and joy of the college is downstairs. For a €3 donation, you can visit the organic flowering cannabis garden, where, as the sign reads, "you can admire the plant in all her beauty." The garden is small—it fits the Dutch legal limit of three plants per person or five per household. And if you've brought your own pot, they'll let you try out their vaporizer, a device that lets you inhale without actually smoking, making it less damaging to your lungs.
• *Continue up the street to the next two sights, the...*

RED LIGHT WALK

Hemp Gallery and the Hash, Marijuana, and Hemp Museum

One ticket admits you to both places. The gallery (at #130) focuses mainly on extolling the wonders of industrial hemp, and isn't as meaty as the small, earnestly educational museum (at #148). If you have the patience to read its thorough displays, you'll learn plenty about how valuable the cannabis plant was to Holland during the Golden Age. The leafy, green cannabis plant was grown on large plantations. The fibrous stalks (hemp) were made into rope and canvas for ships, and even used to make clothing and lace.

Certain strains of the cannabis plant—particularly mature females of the species *sativa* and *indica*—contain the psychoactive alkaloid tetrahydrocannabinol (THC) that makes you high. The buds, flowers, and leaves (marijuana) can be dried and smoked. The brown sap/resin/pitch that oozes out of the leaves (hashish, a.k.a. hash) can also be dried and smoked. Both produce effects ranging from euphoria to paranoia to the munchies.

Throughout history, various peoples have used cannabis as a sacred ritual drug—from ancient Scythians and Hindus to modern Nepalis and Afghanis. Modern Rastafarians, following a

Bible-based religion centered in Jamaica, smoke cannabis. To worship, they get high, bob to reggae music, and praise God. They love the Bible verse (Genesis 1:11-12) that says God created "every herb" and called them all "good." All over Amsterdam, you'll see the Rastafarian colors: green, gold, and red, mon.

The museum's highlight is the grow room, where you look through windows at live cannabis plants in various stages of growth, some as tall as me. These plants are grown hydroponically (in water, no soil) under grow lights. At a certain stage they're "sexed" to weed out the boring males and "selected" to produce the most powerful strains. Your ticket includes a souvenir guidebook about the exhibit and a fun photo op.

At the museum's exit you'll pass through the **Sensi Seed Bank Store**, which sells weed seeds, how-to books, and knickknacks geared to growers.

• *We've reached the end of our tour. Dam Square is just two blocks away. Continue a few steps farther up the canal to the big and busy*

Oude Doelen street. Look right, and you'll see the Royal Palace on Dam Square, two blocks away.

Congratulations

We've seen a lot. We've peeked at locals—from prostitutes to drug pushers to the ghosts of pioneer lesbians to politically active heads with green thumbs. We've talked a bit of history, a little politics, and a lot of sleaze. Congratulations. You've survived. Now, go back to your hotel and take a shower.

JORDAAN WALK

This walk takes you from Dam Square—the Times Square of Amsterdam—to the Anne Frank House, and then deep into the characteristic Jordaan neighborhood. Cafés, boutiques, bookstores, and art galleries have gentrified the area. The walk is a cultural scavenger hunt, offering you a chance to experience the laid-back Dutch lifestyle and catch a few intimate details most busy tourists never appreciate. In the Jordaan (yor-DAHN) you'll see things that are commonplace in Amsterdam, but that you won't find in any other city in the world.

This is a short and easygoing walk—nice in the sleepy morning or en route to a Jordaan dinner in the evening. Bring your camera, as you'll enjoy some of Amsterdam's most charming canal scenes.

Orientation

Length of This Walk: Allow 90 minutes.

When to Go: For the best views, and to hit a few minor sights while they're open, do this walk in daylight (and before 18:00, when some of the minor sights along the way close). Sundays aren't ideal, as many shops (and St. Andrew's Courtyard, our last stop) are closed.

Westerkerk: Church—free, generally open April-Sept Mon-Sat 11:00-15:00, closed Sun and Oct-March. Tower—€7 for 30-minute tour—departures on the half hour April-Sept Mon-Sat 10:00-18:00, July-Aug until 20:00, Oct Mon-Sat 11:00-16:00, last tour leaves at 30 minutes before closing, closed Sun; Nov-March tourable only by appointment.

Audio Tour: You can download this chapter as a free Rick Steves audio tour (see page 53).

Overview

The walk begins at Dam Square and ends at the center of the Jordaan, along the Egelantiersgracht canal. From there it's just a short, scenic walk back to your starting point.

The Walk Begins

Start in **Dam Square,** where the city was born. The original residents settled east of here, in the neighborhood now known as the Red Light District. But as Amsterdam grew—from a river-trading village to a worldwide sea-trading empire—the population needed new places to live. Citizens started reclaiming land to the west of Dam Square, and built a "new church" (Nieuwe Kerk) to serve these new neighborhoods. Canal by canal, they created new neighborhoods of waterways lined with merchants' townhouses. This is the area we'll be walking through in the first half of our tour. By the 1600s—Amsterdam's Golden Age—they needed still more land. They opened up a new development farther west, the Jordaan. It was served by a new church to the west—the Westerkerk, which we'll pass on this walk. It was also in the 1600s that the Royal Palace was built here on Dam Square. It didn't house royalty, as the name suggests, but was home to the city council. They passed zoning laws and oversaw the rapid expansion of this growing metropolis. Let's go see it.

• *From Dam Square, leave the fast-food chains, mimes, and tourists behind, and head to the place where real Amsterdammers live. Facing the Royal Palace, slip (to the right) between the palace and the New Church (Nieuwe Kerk), then cross the street called Nieuwezijds Voorburgwal. If it seems like this wide, busy street doesn't really fit the city, that's because it's new—built over what had been a canal up until the 1880s. You'll soon see the facade of the red-brick...*

Magna Plaza Shopping Center

Built in 1899, the Magna Plaza was, like so many buildings in this soggy city, constructed atop a foundation of pilings—some 4,500 of them, in this case. In its day, it was ultra-modern, symbolizing the city's economic revival after two centuries of decline. The North Sea Canal had just opened, industrialization was on the rise, and it was all capped by a World's Fair in 1883.

Until the 1980s, the Magna Plaza was Amsterdam's main post office. Now, however, it's a mall, housing 40 stores.

Jordaan Walk

1. Dam Square
2. Magna Plaza Shopping Center
3. Molsteeg
4. Torensluis Bridge
5. Oude Leliestraat
6. Herengracht
7. Leliegracht
8. Keizersgracht
9. Homomonument
10. Westerkerk
11. Prinsengracht
12. Nieuwe Leliestraat
13. Eerste Leliedwarsstraat
14. Heart of the Jordaan
15. Tweede Egelantiers Dwarsstraat (Main Shopping Street)
16. Electric Ladyland
17. Paradox Coffeeshop
18. St. Andrew's Courtyard

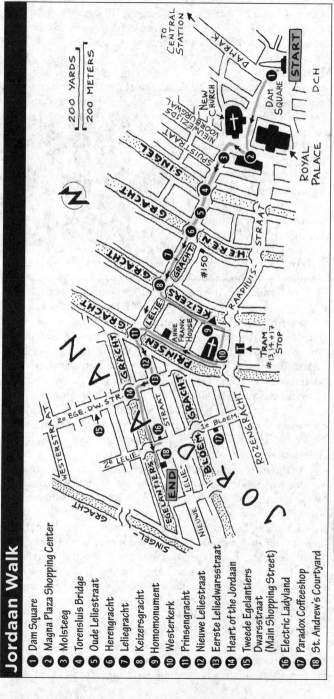

• *Facing Magna Plaza, head right, walking 50 yards down the busy street to the corner of a tiny street called Molsteeg. Before turning left down Molsteeg, stand and survey this slice of Amsterdam.*

Molsteeg

Scan the higgledy-piggledy facades across the busy street. Are you drunk, high...or just in Amsterdam, where the houses were built on mud? Check out the nice line of gables in this row of houses. We'll see more like this on our walk.

Before moving on, notice the T-shirt gallery on the corner. Decades ago, I bought a Mark Raven T-shirt from a street vendor. Now this Amsterdam original has his own upscale shop, selling T-shirts and paintings featuring spindly lined, semi-abstract cityscapes. Raven works primarily with small etchings—as Rembrandt often did.

Now head down tiny Molsteeg street—but don't walk on the reddish pavement in the middle; that's for bikes. Keep to the side. A few steps along, on the left, find house #5: Just one window wide, it's typical of the city's narrow old merchants' houses, with a shop on the ground floor, living space in the middle, and storage in the attic. Look up to see the hooks above warehouse doors. Houses like this lean out toward the street on purpose: Attach a pulley to the hook, and you can hoist cargo without banging it against the house (or, these days, lift up a sofa and send it through a big upper-story window without lugging it up a steep, narrow staircase).

From here this tour's essentially a straight shot west, though the street changes names along the way.

At the intersection with Spuistraat, you'll likely see rows of **bicycles** parked along the street. Amsterdam's 820,000 residents own nearly that many bikes. The Netherlands' 17 million people own 17 million bikes, with many people owning two—a long-distance racing bike and a junky in-city bike, often deliberately kept in poor maintenance, so it's less enticing to the many bike thieves in town. Locals are diligent about locking their bikes twice: They lock the spokes with the first lock, and then they use a heavy chain to attach the bike to something immovable, such as one of the city's U-shaped "staple" hitching racks.

Amsterdam is a great bike town—and indeed, bikes outnumber cars. Notice how 100 bikes might be parked along the road, yet they blend right in. Then imagine if each bike were a car. The efficient Dutch appreciate a self-propelled machine that travels five times faster than a person on foot, while creating zero pollution, noise, parking problems, or high fuel costs. On a *fiets* (bike), a speedy local can traverse the historic center in about 10 minutes. Biking seems to keep the populace fit and good-looking—people here say that Amsterdam's health clubs are more for networking than for working out.

• *The street opens onto a small space (understandably nicknamed "Big Head Square") that's actually a bridge, straddling the Singel canal. It's called...*

Torensluis Bridge

We haven't quite reached the Jordaan yet, but the atmosphere already seems miles away from busy Dam Square. With cafés, art

galleries, and fine benches for picnics, this is a great place to relax and take in a Golden Age atmosphere.

Find a place to enjoy the scene. Belly up to the railing, take a seat on a bench, or even pause the tour for a drink at one of the **characteristic bars** that spill out onto the bridge. Van Zuylen is famous for its variety of beers, and Villa Zeezicht is popular for its sandwiches and apple pie. Take in your surroundings.

The Singel canal was the original moat running around the old walled city. This bridge is so wide because it was the road that led to one of the original city gates. The area still looks much as it might have during the Dutch Golden Age of the 1600s. This was when Amsterdam's sea-going merchants ruled the waves, establishing trading colonies as far away as modern Indonesia. Fueled with this wealth, the city quickly became a major urban center, lined with impressive homes. Each proud merchant tried to outdo his neighbor. Pan 360 degrees and take in the variety of buildings.

The houses crowd together, shoulder-to-shoulder. They're built on top of thousands of logs hammered vertically into the marshy soil to provide a foundation. Over the years, they've shifted with the tides, leaving some leaning this way and that. Notice that some of the brick houses have iron rods strapped onto the sides. These act like braces, binding the bricks to an inner skeleton of wood. Almost all Amsterdam houses have big, tall windows to let in as

JORDAAN WALK

much light as possible.

Although some houses look quite narrow, most of them extend far back. The rear of the building—called the *achterhuis*—is often much more spacious than you might expect, judging from the facade. Real estate has always been expensive on this canal, and owners were taxed by the amount of street frontage. It was especially expensive for homes with a wide facade and minimum usable space in back. A local saying back then was, "Only the wealthy can live on the inside of a canal's curve."

Mingled among the old houses are a few modern buildings. These sleek, gray-metal ones are part of the university. Built in the less affluent 1970s, architecture like this wouldn't be allowed today. Though these buildings try to match the humble, functional spirit of the older ones, they're still pretty ugly. But the students they house inject life into the neighborhood.

The "big head" statue honors a writer known by his pen name: **Multatuli.** Born in Amsterdam in 1820, Multatuli (a.k.a.  Eduard Douwes Dekker) did what many young Dutchmen did back then: He sought his fortune in Indonesia, then a colony of the Netherlands. While working as a bureaucrat in the colonial system, he witnessed first-hand the hard life of Javanese natives slaving away on Dutch-owned planta- tions. His semi-autobiographical novel, *Max Havelaar* (1860), follows a progressive civil servant fighting to reform colonial abuses. He was the first author to crit- icize Dutch colonial practices—a very bold position back then. For his talent and subject matter, Multatuli has been dubbed "the Dutch Rudyard Kipling."

The Singel canal is just one of Amsterdam's many canals—all told, there are roughly 50 miles of them (see sidebar on page 105). In the distance, way down at the north end of Singel, beyond the dome, you can get a glimpse of one of this canal's **locks.** Those white-flagpole thingies, sprouting at 45-degree angles, are part of the apparatus that opens and shuts the gates. While the canals originated as a way to drain diked-off marshland, they eventually became part of the city's sewer system. They were flushed daily: Just open the locks, and let the North Sea tides come in and out.

The Dutch are credited with inventing locks in the 1300s. (Let's not ask the Chinese.) Locks are the single greatest innova- tion in canal-building. Besides controlling water flow in the city, they allow ships to pass from higher to lower water levels, and vice versa. It's because of locks that you can ship something by boat

Gables

Along the rooftops, Amsterdam's famous gables are false fronts to enhance roofs that are, generally, sharply pitched. Gables come in all shapes and sizes. They might be ornamented with animal and human heads, garlands, urns, scrolls, and curlicues. Despite their infinite variety, most belong to a few distinct types. See how many of these you can spot.

A simple "point" gable just follows the triangular shape of a normal pitched roof. A "bell" gable is shaped like...well, guess. "Step" gables are triangular in shape and lined with steps; these are especially popular in Belgium. The one with a rectangular protrusion at the peak is called a "spout" gable. "Neck" gables rise up vertically from a pair of sloping "shoulders." "Cornice" gables make pointed roofs look classically horizontal. (There's probably even a "clark" gable, but frankly, I don't give a damn.)

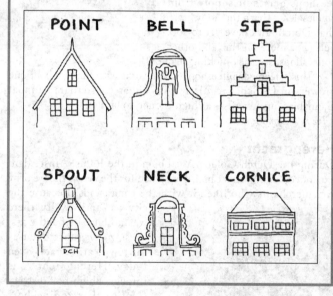

from here inland. Thanks to an extensive system of locks, from this very spot, you could hop a boat and go upriver, connect to the Rhine, and eventually—over the continental divide in Germany—connect to the Danube and then sail downstream, eventually reaching Romania and the Black Sea.

The green copper dome in the distance marks the Lutheran church. To the left of the church is the new city—reclaimed in the 1600s and destined to be the high-rent district. To the right is the old town.

• *Continue west on...*

Oude Leliestraat

On "Old Lily Street," consumers will find plenty of Amsterdam edibles—Reypenaer's cheeses, Puccini's bonbons, Sukabumi's *rijsttafel*, Grey Area's marijuana, Thirsty Dogg's traditional café fare, and *shoarmas*—everything but lilies. (The Reypenaer cheese shop is especially worthwhile, as it offers tasty samples, and has a classroom in the basement for tasting sessions; see page 65.)

The Grey Area is a thriving coffeeshop; like Holland's other "coffeeshops," it sells marijuana. The green-and-white decal in the

window identifies it as #092 in the city's licensing program. While smoking marijuana is essentially legal here, the café's name refers to the murky back-side of the marijuana business—how coffeeshops get their supply from wholesalers. That's the "gray area" that Dutch laws have yet to sort out. (For more on this and other coffeeshops, see the Smoking chapter.)

This esteemed coffeeshop, which works with the best boutique growers in Holland, regularly wins big at Amsterdam's annual Cannabis Cup Awards—a "high" honor, to be sure.

• *The next canal is the...*

Herengracht

During the Dutch Golden Age boom in the 1600s, Amsterdam expanded, adding this canal. It's named for the *heren*, the wealthy city merchants who lined it with their mansions. Because the

city was anti-royalty, there was no blue-blooded class; these *heren* functioned as the town's aristocracy. Even today, Herengracht runs through a high-rent district. (Notice that zoning here forbids houseboats.)

Check out the house that's kitty-corner across the bridge, at Herengracht 150. It has features you'll find on many old Amsterdam buildings. On the roof, rods support the false-front gable (which originally supported only a rich merchant's ego). Also, notice that, because this particular building is at the end of the block, you get a cutaway look of its entire depth—the long side of the building. Most Amsterdam buildings, like this one, are much bigger than they appear from the front.

Before moving on, notice the parking sign along Herengracht, on the left. The sign instructs motorists to put money in the meter at the end of the block. Parking is a major problem in a city like this, designed for boats, not cars.

• *Continue west, walking along…*

Leliegracht

This is one of the city's prettiest small canals, lined with trees and crossed by a series of arched bridges. There are some 400 such

bridges in Amsterdam. It's a pleasant street of trendy furniture shops and bookstores. Notice that some buildings have staircases leading down below the street level to residences. Looking up, you'll see the characteristic beams jutting out from the top with a cargo-hoisting hook on the end.

• *Continue on to the next canal, and pause on the bridge to take in another fine row of gables. After the bridge, we'll take a detour off our westward route, and veer left along…*

Keizersgracht

Walk south about 100 yards along the canal with an eye toward the church tower, rising above the rooftops and capped with a colorful crown. You'll reach a set of steps leading down to the water, where a triangular pink stone juts into the canal. This is part of the so-called **Homomonument**—Amsterdam's AIDS memorial. If you survey the square, you'll see that the pink triangle is just one of three triangles between here and the church. These are contained in a single large triangle that comprises the Homomonument. The pink-triangle design reclaims the symbol that the Nazis used in concentration camps to label homosexual men. It's also a reminder of the persecution gay people still experience today. You may see flowers or cards left here by friends and loved ones.

Near the monument, on Westermarkt square, is a souvenir kiosk called Pink Point. Here the volunteer staff gives out information on gay and lesbian Amsterdam, especially nightlife.

The green metal structure near the Homomonument is a public urinal. It offers just enough privacy. City trucks circulate around town on a regular basis, suds-ing them down.

From here, walk through the square called Westermarkt, between the church and busy Raadhuisstraat. You'll find two very Dutch kiosks. One sells french fries; when it's closed, the shutters feature funny paintings putting *friet*s into great masterpieces of Western art. The other sells fresh herring. If you've yet to try a delicious Dutch herring, this is the perfect opportunity. For €2.75 you get a fresh herring with pickles and onion on a paper plate and instructions from the friendly merchant on how to eat it.

• *Keep walking toward the entrance to...*

Westerkerk

Near the western end of the church, look for a cute little statue. It's of Anne Frank, who holed up with her family in a house just down the block from here (we'll pass it in a minute).

For now, look up at the towering spire of the impressive Westerkerk. The crown shape was a gift of the Habsburg emperor, Maximilian I. As a thanks for a big loan, the city got permission to use the Habsburg royal symbol. The tower also displays the sym-

bol of Amsterdam, with its three Xs. The Westerkerk (Western Church) was built in 1631, as the city was expanding out from Dam Square. Rembrandt's buried inside...but no one knows where. You can pop into the church for free, or pay to climb to the tower balcony (just below the *XXX*) for a grand view (see page 65).

The church tower has a carillon that chimes every 15 minutes. At other times, it plays full songs. Invented by Dutch bellmakers in the 1400s, a carillon is a set of bells of different sizes and pitches. There's a live musician inside the tower who plays a keyboard to make the music. Mozart, Vivaldi, and Bach—all of whom lived during the heyday of the carillon—wrote music that sounds great on this unique instrument. During World War II, the Westerkerk's carillon played every day. This hopeful sound reminded Anne Frank that there was, indeed, an outside world.

• *Continue around the church, and walk north along the canal, past the long line of tourists marking the entrance to the ever-popular* **Anne Frank House** *(⊙ see the Anne Frank House Tour chapter). At the next bridge turn left. Stop at its summit, mid-canal, for a view of...*

Prinsengracht

The "Princes' Canal" runs through what's considered one of the most livable areas in town. It's lined with houseboats, some of the city's estimated 2,500. These small vessels were once cargo ships—but by the 1930s, they had become obsolete, replaced by more modern craft. They found a new use, as houseboats lining the canals of Amsterdam, where dry land was so limited and pricey.

Today, their former cargo holds are fashioned into elegant, cozy living rooms. The once-powerful engines have generally been removed to make room for more living space. Moorage spots are prized and grandfathered in, making some of the junky old boats worth more than you'd think. Houseboaters can plug hoses and cables into outlets along the canals to get water and electricity. (To learn more about houseboats, visit the charming Houseboat Museum, described on page 64.)

Notice the canal traffic. The official speed limit on canals is about four miles per hour. At night, boats must have running

lights on the top, the side, and the stern. Most boats are small and low, designed to glide under the city's bridges. The Prinsengracht bridge is average height, with less than seven feet of headroom (it varies with the water level); some bridges have less than six feet. Boaters need good maps to tell them the height, which is crucial for navigating. Police boats roam on the lookout for anyone CUI (cruising under the influence).

Just across the bridge are several typical Jordaan cafés. The relaxed **Café de Prins** serves food and drink both day and night. The old-timey **De Twee Zwaantjes** (a few doors to the right) occasionally features the mournful songs of a late local legend, balladeer Johnny Jordaan. Finally, there's the **Café 't Smalle**—it's not visible from here, but it's a half-block to the right. It has a deck where you can drink outside along a quiet canal (for details, see listings in the Eating in Amsterdam chapter).

• *Once you cross Prinsengracht, you enter what's officially considered the Jordaan neighborhood. Facing west (toward Café de Prins), cross the bridge and veer left down...*

Nieuwe Leliestraat

Welcome to the quiet Jordaan. Built in the 1600s as a working-class housing area, it's now home to artists and yuppies. The name Jordaan probably was not derived from the French *jardin*—but given the neighborhood's garden-like ambience, it seems like it should have been.

Have your ultra-sharp "traveler's eyes" trained on all the tiny details of Amsterdam life. Notice house #2. While parking is generally not allowed in this area, this prime space—complete with a plug-in—reserves a spot for those investing in an electric car. Signs warn speeding drivers of the speed bumps: *Let op!* and watch out for *drempels*. Notice how the pragmatic Dutch deal with junk mail. On the doors, stickers next to mail slots say *Nee* or *Ja* (no or yes), telling the postman if they'll accept or refuse junk mail. Residents are allowed a "front-yard garden" as long as it's no more than one sidewalk tile wide. The red metal bollards known

as *Amsterdammertjes* ("little Amsterdammers") have been bashing balls since the 1970s, when they were put in to stop people from parking on the sidewalks. Though many apartments have windows right on the street, the neighbors don't stare and the residents don't care.

• *At the first intersection, turn right onto...*

Eerste Leliedwarsstraat

Pause and linger awhile on this tiny lane. Imagine the frustrations of home ownership here. The ugly modern buildings you see date from the 1960s and '70s. This was before the gentrification of the 1980s, when the city started writing more restrictive building codes. Check out house #9. Here, a run-down historic home was torn down, replaced by a cheap and functional building with modern heating and plumbing. Now move ahead to #5. Its owners were probably stuck with rent control, so they didn't invest in the place. They missed the window of time when a cheap and functional rebuild was allowed, and now they can't get permission to renovate this home without making it prohibitively expensive. Across the street, #2A obviously had the cash to do a first-class sprucing up. Even newly renovated homes must preserve their funky leaning angles and original wooden beams. They're certainly nice to look at, but absolutely maddening if you own a building and aren't rich.

• *Just ahead, walk out to the middle of the bridge over the next canal (Egelantiersgracht). This is what I think of as...*

The Heart of the Jordaan

For me, this bridge and its surroundings capture the essence of the Jordaan. Take it all in: the bookstores, art galleries, working artists' studios, and small cafés full of rickety tables. Look down the quiet canal. It's lined with trees and old, narrow buildings with gables—classic Amsterdam.

Look north, farther down the street beyond the bridge. This lane, called Tweede Egelantiers Dwarsstraat, is the laid-back Jordaan neighborhood's main shopping-and-people street. If you venture down there, you'll find boutiques, galleries, antique stores,

JORDAAN WALK

hair salons, restaurants, and cafés.

Now turn around and look south at the Westerkerk, and you'll see a completely different view of the church from the one that the tourists in line at the Anne Frank House get. Framed by narrow streets, crossed with streetlamp wires, and looming over shoppers on bicycles—to me, this is the church in its best light.

Backtrack to the base of the bridge, then turn right. As you walk west along Egelantiersgract, check out the boats. Junky old boats litter the canal. Some aren't worth maintaining and are left abandoned. As these dinghies fill with rainwater and start to rot, the city confiscates them and stores them in a big lot. Unclaimed boats are auctioned off three times a year. But most boats are well used, and even the funkiest scows can become cruising Love Boats when the sun goes down.

At the first intersection, turn left onto Tweede Leliedwarsstraat, and walk a few steps to #5. This small shop, with a flowery window display, is **Electric Ladyland,** which calls itself "The First

Museum of Fluorescent Art." Its funky facade hides an illuminated wonderland within, with a tiny exhibit of black-light art (under the shop, down a very steep set of stairs). It's the creation of Nick Padalino—one cool cat who really found his niche in life. He enjoys personally demonstrating the fluorescence found in unexpected places—everything from minerals to stamps to candy to the tattoo on his arm. Nick seems to get an even bigger kick out of it than his customers. You can see the historic first fluorescent crayon from San Francisco in the 1950s. Wow. Its label says, "Use with black light for church groups." Wow (€5, Tue-Sat 13:00-18:00, closed Sun-Mon).

About 100 yards farther down the street, old hippies might want to visit the **Paradox Coffeeshop.** It's the perfect coffeeshop for the nervous American who wants a friendly, mellow place to go local (see listing in the Smoking chapter).

• *To reach our last stop, backtrack to the canal and turn left, then walk a few dozen yards to Egelantiersgract #107, the entrance to...*

St. Andrew's Courtyard (Sint-Andrieshof)

The black door is marked *Sint-Andrieshof 107 t/m 145*. The doorway looks private, but it's the public entrance to a set of residences. It's

generally open during daytime hours, except on Sundays. Enter quietly; you may have to push hard on the door. Go inside and continue on into a tiny garden courtyard surrounded by a dozen or so residences. Take a seat on a bench. This is one of the city's scores of similar courtyards, called *hofjes*—subsidized residences built around a courtyard, and funded by churches, charities, and the city for low-income widows and pensioners.

And this is where our tour ends—in a tranquil world that seems right out of a painting by Vermeer. You're just blocks from the bustle of Amsterdam, but it feels like another world. You're immersed in the Jordaan, where everything's in its place, and life seems very good.

RIJKSMUSEUM TOUR

At Amsterdam's Rijksmuseum ("Rijks" rhymes with "bikes"), Holland's Golden Age shines with the best collection anywhere of the Dutch Masters—from Vermeer's quiet domestic scenes, to Steen's raucous family meals, to Hals' snapshot portraits, to Rembrandt's moody brilliance.

The 17th century saw the Netherlands at the pinnacle of its power. The Dutch had won their independence from Spain, trade and shipping boomed, wealth poured  in, the people were understandably proud, and the arts flourished. This era was later dubbed the Dutch Golden Age. With no church bigwigs or royalty around to commission big canvases in the Protestant Dutch republic, artists had to find different patrons—and they discovered the upper-middle-class businessmen who fueled Holland's capitalist economy. Artists painted their portraits and decorated their homes with pretty still lifes and nonpreachy, slice-of-life art.

This delightful museum—recently much improved after a long renovation—offers one of the most exciting and enjoyable art experiences in Europe.

Orientation

Cost: €15, not covered by I amsterdam Card.
Hours: Daily 9:00-17:00, last entry 30 minutes before closing, café and gift shop open until 18:00.

Avoiding Crowds: The museum is most crowded from April to September (especially April to June), on weekends, and during morning hours. You can avoid crowds by coming later in the day (it's least crowded after 16:00—but most visitors will want more than an hour here). Avoid waits in the ticket-buying line by buying your ticket or pass in advance. No one can completely avoid the security line.

You can buy and print your ticket in advance online at www.rijksmuseum.nl. The ticket is good any time (no entry time specified). Buying online has the added advantage of letting you enter through the "direct entry" doorway, scooting you to the front of the security line. You can also buy tickets at many hotels.

Getting There: From Central Station, catch tram #2 or #5 (get out at Hobbemastraat). The museum entrance is just off the arched passage that cuts under the building at its center (watch out for bikes).

Information: The helpful information desk in the Atrium has free maps. Info tel. 020/674-7047, www.rijksmuseum.nl.

Videoguide: A multimedia videoguide offers a highlights tour of the collection.

Length of This Tour: Allow 1.5 hours.

Baggage Check: Leave your bag at the free checkroom in the Atrium.

Cuisine Art: The Rijksmuseum Grand Café is in the Atrium above the gift shop. It's outside the ticketed entry, so you don't need a museum ticket to eat here. Beyond the museum complex, you'll find the Cobra Café on Museumplein (daily 10:00-18:00, toward the Van Gogh Museum, tel. 020/470-0111). Vondelpark has the delightful Café Vert-

igo (see page 210) and many picnic spots. Museumplein is perfect for a picnic.

Photography: Permitted but no flash.

Starring: Rembrandt van Rijn, Frans Hals, Johannes Vermeer, Jan Steen.

Overview

Dutch art is meant to be enjoyed, not studied. It's straightforward, meat-and-potatoes art for the common man. The Dutch love the beauty of everyday things painted realistically and with exquisite

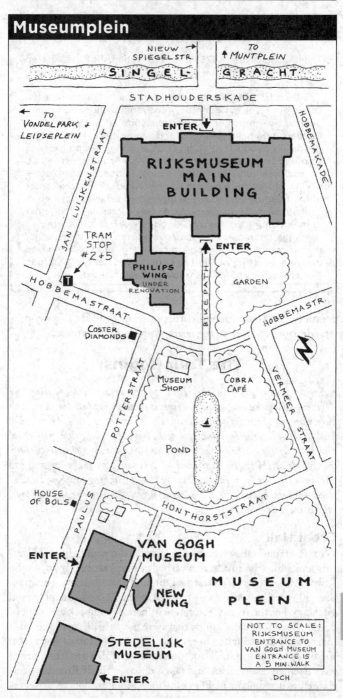

Museumplein

NIEUW SPIEGELSTR →

TO ↑ MUNTPLEIN

SINGEL

GRACHT

STADHOUDERSKADE

← TO VONDELPARK & LEIDSEPLEIN

HOBBEMAKADE

ENTER ↓

RIJKSMUSEUM MAIN BUILDING

JAN LUIJKENSTRAAT

TRAM STOP #2+5 ↓

🅣

HOBBEMASTRAAT

PHILIPS WING UNDER RENOVATION

ENTER ↑

BIKE PATH

GARDEN

HOBBEMASTR.

COSTER DIAMONDS ■

POTTERSTRAAT

MUSEUM SHOP

COBRA CAFÉ

VERMEERSTRAAT

⚡

POND ⛵

HOUSE OF BOLS

PAULUS

HONTHORSTSTRAAT

ENTER →

VAN GOGH MUSEUM

NEW WING

MUSEUM PLEIN

STEDELIJK MUSEUM

← ENTER

NOT TO SCALE: RIJKSMUSEUM ENTRANCE TO VAN GOGH MUSEUM ENTRANCE IS A 5 MIN. WALK

DCH

RIJKSMUSEUM

Renovating the Rijks

Thanks to a 10-year, €375 million renovation, the Rijksmuseum once again matches the vision of its 19th-century architect, Pierre Cuypers.

Built in 1885 to house the Netherlands' greatest art, a series of brutal 20th-century renovations chopped up and painted over much of the Rijksmuseum. But today much of Cuypers' original Gothic-revival design is back: Natural light floods large rooms with high ceilings. Long viewing galleries surround two massive courtyards, which had been walled up for half a century. Rembrandt's most famous masterpiece—*The Night Watch*—is back in its original position at the center of the building, just where Cuypers had originally placed it. Around the museum, many pieces are now displayed together in their cultural context, making the exhibits a lively mix of paintings, photographs, decorative objects, and so on. Rather than encountering painting after painting...after painting, you may see a setting of Delftware displayed next to a Golden Age still life—cultural anthropology meets fine art.

detail. So set your cerebral cortex on "low" and let this art pass straight from the eyes to the heart, with minimal detours.

The Tour Begins

• *As you enter, descend the stairs to the lower level, called the Atrium—a space thoughtfully designed to accommodate the museum's huge number of visitors (more than a million every year). Here you'll find ticket sales, the information desk, baggage check, café, gift shop, and WCs. After getting your ticket and going through security, follow the crowds up the stairway on your left. As you leave the courtyard, you pass into Cuypers' original entryway. Keep climbing on these durable steps—which haven't been replaced since 1885—to the second floor, where you'll find the...*

Great Hall

With its stained-glass windows, vaulted ceiling, and gilt moldings, this looks like the inside of a cathedral—appropriately so, as the Rijksmuseum is a cathedral to Dutch art and history. For more than 50 years, this space was painted over and used as a lobby and gift shop. For the recent restoration, officials went back to Cuypers' design, but chose paint colors that were not as brilliant as the originals—as if they'd faded over time. The late-Victorian murals on the walls are original, restored after a long absence (the murals were deemed chauvinistic and taken down in the 1920s). They celebrate great moments in Dutch history—look for lots of explorers

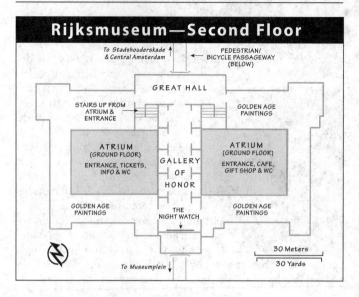

Rijksmuseum—Second Floor

To Stadshouderskade
& Central Amsterdam

PEDESTRIAN/
BICYCLE PASSAGEWAY
(BELOW)

GREAT HALL

STAIRS UP FROM
ATRIUM &
ENTRANCE

GOLDEN AGE
PAINTINGS

ATRIUM
(GROUND FLOOR)
ENTRANCE, TICKETS,
INFO & WC

GALLERY
OF
HONOR

ATRIUM
(GROUND FLOOR)
ENTRANCE, CAFE,
GIFT SHOP & WC

GOLDEN AGE
PAINTINGS

THE
NIGHT WATCH

GOLDEN AGE
PAINTINGS

30 Meters

30 Yards

To Museumplein

and warrior kings. Soak up the ambience. Cuypers wanted to wow you before you'd even entered the Golden Age.

• *Follow the flow into the...*

Gallery of Honor

This grand space was purpose-built to hold the Greatest Hits of the Golden Age, by the era's biggest rock stars: Frans Hals, Vermeer, Jan Steen, and Rembrandt. The best of the era's portraits, still lifes, landscapes, and slice-of-life "genre scenes" give us a close-up look at everyday life in this happy, affluent era.

Frans Hals (c. 1581-1666)

Frans Hals was the premier Golden Age portrait painter. Merchants hired him the way we'd hire a wedding photographer. With a few quick strokes, Hals captured not only the features, but also the personality.

The Merry Drinker (1627)

You're greeted by a jovial man in a black hat, capturing the earthy, exuberant spirit of the Dutch Golden Age. Notice the details—the happy red face of the man offering us a glass of wine, the sparkle in his eyes, the lacy collar, the decorative belt buckle, and so on.

Now move in closer. All these meticulous details are accomplished with a few thick, messy brushstrokes. The beard is a tangle of brown worms, the belt buckle a yellow blur. His hand is a study in smudges. Even the expressive face is created with a few well-chosen patches of color. Unlike the still-life scenes, this canvas is

RIJKSMUSEUM

meant to be viewed from a distance, where the colors and brush-strokes blend together.

Rather than posing his subject, making him stand for hours saying "cheese," Hals tried to catch him at a candid moment. He often painted common people, fishermen, and barflies, such as this one. He had to work quickly to capture the serendipity of the moment. Hals used a stop-action technique, freezing the man in mid-gesture, where the rough brushwork creates a blur that suggests the man is still moving.

Two centuries later, the Impressionists learned from Hals' messy brushwork. In the Van Gogh Museum, you'll see how Van Gogh painted, say, a brown beard by using thick dabs of green, yellow, and red that blend at a distance to make brown.

Wedding Portrait of Isaac Abrahamsz Massa and Beatrix van der Laen (1622)

This wedding portrait of a chubby, pleasant merchant and his bride sums up the story of the Dutch Golden Age. Because this overseas trader was away from home for years at a time on business, Hals

makes a special effort to point out his patron's commitment to marriage. Isaac pledges allegiance to his wife, putting his hand on his heart. Beatrix's wedding ring is prominently displayed dead center between them (on her right-hand forefinger, Protestant-style). The vine clinging to a tree is a symbol of man's support and woman's dependence. And in the distance at right, in the classical love garden, are other happy couples strolling arm-in-arm amid peacocks, a symbol of fertility.

In earlier times, marriage portraits put the man and wife in separate canvases, staring out grimly. Hals' jolly side-by-side couple reflects a societal shift from marriage as business partnership to an arrangement that's more friendly and intimate.

Hals didn't need symbolism to tell us that these two are prepared for their long-distance relationship—they seem relaxed together, but each looks at us directly, with a strong, individual identity. Good as gold, these are the type of people who propelled this soggy little country into its glorious Golden Age.

The Dutch Golden Age (1600s)

Who bought this art? Look around at the Rijksmuseum's many portraits, and you'll see ordinary middle-class people, merchants, and traders. Even in their Sunday best, you can tell that these are hardworking, businesslike, friendly, simple people (with a penchant for ruffled lace collars).

Dutch fishermen sold their surplus catch in distant areas of Europe, importing goods from these far lands. In time, fishermen became traders, and by 1600, Holland's merchant fleets ruled the waves with colonies as far away as India, Indonesia, and America (remember—New York was originally "Nieuw Amsterdam"). The Dutch slave trade—selling Africans to Americans—generated a lot of profit for luxuries such as the art you're viewing. Back home, these traders were financed by shrewd Amsterdam businessmen on the new frontiers of capitalism.

Look around again. Is there even one crucifixion? One saint? One Madonna? This art is made for the people, not for the church. In most countries, Catholic bishops and rich kings supported the arts. But the Republic of the Netherlands, recently free of Spanish rule and Vatican domination, was independent, democratic, and largely Protestant, with no taste for saints and Madonnas.

Instead, Dutch burghers bought portraits of themselves and pretty, unpreachy, unpretentious works for their homes. Even poor people bought art—usually on smaller canvases, painted by "no-name" artists, and designed to fit their budgets and lifestyles. We'll see examples of their four favorite subjects—still lifes (of food and mundane objects), landscapes, portraits (often of groups), and scenes from everyday life.

Johannes Vermeer (1632-1675)

Vermeer is the master of tranquility and stillness. He creates a clear and silent pool that is a world in itself. Most of his canvases show interiors of Dutch homes, where Dutch women engage in everyday activities, lit by a side window.

Vermeer's father, an art dealer, gave Johannes a passion for painting. Late in the artist's career, with Holland fighting draining wars against England, the demand for art and luxuries went sour in the Netherlands, forcing Vermeer to downsize—he sold his big home, packed up his wife and 14 children, and moved in with his mother-in-law. He died two years later, and his works fell into centuries of obscurity.

The Rijksmuseum has the best collection of Vermeers in the world—four of them. (There are only some 34 in captivity.) But each is a small jewel worth lingering over.

RIJKSMUSEUM

Shhh...Dutch Art

You're sitting at home late one night, and it's perfectly calm. Not a sound, very peaceful. And then...the refrigerator motor turns off, and it's *really* quiet.

Dutch art is really quiet art. It silences our busy world, so that every sound, every motion is noticeable. You can hear cows tearing off grass 50 yards away. Dutch art is still. It slows our fast-lane world, so we notice the motion of birds. We notice how the cold night air makes the stars sharp. We notice that the undersides of leaves and cats are always a lighter shade than the tops. Dutch art stills the world so we can hear our own heartbeat and reflect upon that most noble muscle that, without thinking, gives us life.

To see how subtle Dutch art is, realize that one of the museum's most exciting, dramatic, emotional, and extravagant Dutch paintings is probably *The Threatened Swan* (in the Gallery of Honor). It's quite a contrast to the rape scenes and visions of heaven of Italian Baroque paintings from the same time period.

The Milkmaid (c. 1658)

It's so quiet you can practically hear the milk pouring into the bowl.

Vermeer brings out the beauty in everyday things. The subject is ordinary—a kitchen maid—but you could look for hours at the tiny details and rich color tones. These are everyday objects, but they glow in a diffused light: the crunchy crust, the hanging basket, even the rusty nail in the wall with its tiny shadow. Vermeer

had a unique ability with surface texture, to show how things feel when you touch them.

The maid is alive with Vermeer's distinctive yellow and blue—the colors of many traditional Dutch homes—against a white backdrop. She is content, solid, and sturdy, performing this simple task as if it's the most important thing in the world. Her full arms are built with patches of reflected light. Vermeer squares off a little world in itself (framed by the table in the foreground, the wall in back, the window to the left, and the footstool at right), then fills this space with objects for our perusal.

Woman Reading a Letter (c. 1662-1663)

This painting likely will be away for renovation during your visit. If you do get to see it on display, notice how Vermeer's placid

scenes often have an air of mystery. The woman is reading a letter. From whom? A lover? A father on a two-year business trip to Indonesia? Not even taking time to sit down, she reads it intently, with parted lips and a bowed head. It must be important. (She looks pregnant, adding to the mystery, but that may just be the cut of her clothes.)

Again, Vermeer has framed a moment of everyday life. But within this small world are hints of a wider, wilder world—the light coming from the left is obviously from a large window, giving us a whiff of the life going on outside. The map hangs prominently, reminding us of travel, and perhaps of where the letter is from.

The Love Letter (c. 1669-1670)

There's a similar theme here. The curtain parts, and we see through the doorway into a dollhouse world, then through the seascape on the back wall to the wide ocean. A woman is playing a lute when she's interrupted by a servant bringing a letter. The mysterious letter stops the music, intruding like a pebble dropped into the pool of Vermeer's quiet world. The floor tiles create a strong 3-D perspective that sucks

us straight into the center of the painting—the woman's heart.

View of Houses in Delft (a.k.a. The Little Street, c. 1658)

Vermeer was born in the picturesque town of Delft, grew up near its Market Square, and set a number of his paintings there. This may be the view from his front door.

In *The Little Street*, the details actually aren't very detailed—

the cobblestone street doesn't have a single individual stone in it. But Vermeer shows us the beautiful interplay of colored rectangles on the buildings. Our eye moves back and forth from shutter to gable to window...and then from front to back, as we notice the woman deep in the alleyway.

Jan Steen (1626-1679)

Not everyone could afford a masterpiece, but even poorer people wanted works of art for their own homes (like a landscape from Sears for over the sofa). Jan Steen (pronounced "yahn stain"), the Norman Rockwell of his day, painted humorous scenes from the lives of the lower classes. As a tavern owner, he observed society firsthand.

The Burgher of Delft and His Daughter (1655)

This painting is the latest major acquisition of the Rijksmuseum and another star in its lineup. In August of 2004, the museum paid

$15 million for it...and figured they got a great deal. While the rest of the Steen collection is in the next room, the curators often display this one with Vermeer's works because it's pristine and peaceful—more like an exquisite Vermeer than a raucous Steen.

Steen's well-dressed burgher sits on his front porch, when a poor woman and child approach to beg, putting him squarely between the horns of a moral dilemma. On the one hand, we see his rich home, well-dressed daughter, and a vase of flowers—a symbol that his money came from morally suspect capitalism (the kind that produced the folly of 1637's "tulip mania," described on page 30). On the other hand, there are his poor fellow citizens and the church steeple, reminding him of his Christian duty. The man's daughter avoids the confrontation. Will the burgher set the right Christian example? This moral dilemma perplexed many nouveau-riche Dutch Calvinists of Steen's day.

This early painting by Steen demonstrates his mastery of several popular genres: portrait, still life (the flowers and fabrics), cityscape, and moral instruction.

RIJKSMUSEUM

Ruffs

I cannot tell you why men and women of the Dutch Golden Age found these fanlike collars attractive, but they certainly

were all the rage here and elsewhere in Europe. It started in Spain in the 1540s, but the style really took off with a marvelous discovery in 1565: starch. Within decades, Europe's wealthy merchant class was wearing nine-inch collars made from 18 yards of material.

The ruffs were detachable and made from a long, pleated strip of linen set into a neck (or wrist) band. You tied it in front with strings. Big ones required that you wear a wire frame underneath for support. There were various types—the "cartwheel" was the biggest, a "double ruff" had two layers of pleats, and a "cabbage" was somewhat asymmetrical.

Ruffs required elaborate maintenance. First, you washed and starched the linen. While the cloth was still wet, hot metal pokers were painstakingly inserted into the folds to form the characteristic figure-eight pattern. The ruffs were stored in special round boxes to hold their shape.

For about a century, Europeans loved the ruff, but by 1630, Holland had come to its senses, and the fad faded.

The Feast of St. Nicholas

It's Christmas time, and the kids have been given their gifts, including a little girl who got a doll. The mother says, "Let me

see it," but the girl turns away playfully. Everyone is happy except the boy, who's crying. His Christmas present is only a branch in his shoe—like coal in your stocking, the gift for bad boys. His sister gloats and passes it around. The kids laugh at him. But wait—it turns out the family is just playing a trick. In the background, the grandmother beckons to him, saying, "Look, I have your real present in here." Out of the limelight, but smack in the middle, sits the father providing ballast to this family scene and clearly enjoying his children's pleasure.

Steen has frozen the moment, sliced off a piece, and laid it on a canvas. He's told a story with a past, a present, and a future. These are real people in a real scene.

Steen's fun art reminds us that museums aren't mausoleums.

The Merry Family (1668)

This family—three generations living happily under one roof—is eating, drinking, and singing like there's no tomorrow. The broken eggshells and scattered cookware symbolize waste and extravagance. The neglected proverb tacked to the fireplace reminds us that children will follow in the footsteps of their parents. The father in this jolly scene is very drunk—ready to topple over—while in the foreground his mischievous daughter is feeding her brother wine straight from the

flask. Mom and Grandma join the artist himself (playing the bagpipes) in a lively sing-along, but the child learning to smoke would rather follow Dad's lead.

Dutch Golden Age families were notoriously lenient with their kids. Even today, the Dutch describe a rowdy family as a "Jan Steen household."

Rembrandt van Rijn (1606-1669)

Rembrandt van Rijn is the greatest of all Dutch painters. Whereas most painters specialized in one field—portraits, landscapes, still lifes—Rembrandt excelled in them all.

RIJKSMUSEUM

The son of a Leiden miller who owned a waterwheel on the Rhine ("van Rijn"), Rembrandt took Amsterdam by storm with his famous painting of *The Anatomy Lesson* (1632, currently in the The Hague). The commissions poured in for official portraits, and he was soon wealthy and married (1634) to Saskia van Uylenburgh. They moved to an expensive home in the Jewish Quarter (today's Rembrandt's House museum), and decorated it with their collection of art and exotic furniture. His portraits were dutifully detailed, but other paintings explored strong contrasts of light and dark, with dramatic composition.

In 1642, Saskia died, and Rembrandt's fortunes changed, as

the public's taste shifted and commissions dried up. In 1649, he hired an 18-year-old model named Hendrickje Stoffels, and she soon moved in with him and gave birth to their daughter.

Holland's war with England (1652-1654) devastated the art market, and Rembrandt's free-spending ways forced him to declare bankruptcy (1656)—the ultimate humiliation in success-oriented Amsterdam. The commissions came more slowly. The money ran out. His mother died. He had to auction off his paintings and furniture to pay debts. He moved out of his fine house to a cheaper place on Rozengracht. His bitter losses added a new wisdom to his work.

In his last years, his greatest works were his self-portraits, showing a tired, wrinkled man stoically enduring life's misfortunes. Rembrandt piled on layers of paint and glaze to capture increasingly subtle effects. In 1668, his lone surviving son, Titus, died, and Rembrandt passed away the next year. His death effectively marked the end of the Dutch Golden Age.

Isaac and Rebecca (a.k.a. *The Jewish Bride*, 1667)

The man gently draws the woman toward him. She's comfortable enough with him to sink into thought, and she reaches up unconsciously to return the gentle touch. They're young but wizened. This uncommissioned portrait (its subjects remain unknown) is a truly human look at the relationship between two people in love. They form a protective pyramid of love amid a gloomy background. The touching hands form the center of this  somewhat sad but peaceful work. Van Gogh said that "Rembrandt alone has that tenderness—the heartbroken tenderness."

Rembrandt was a master of oil painting. In his later years, he rendered details with a messier, more Impressionistic style. The red-brown-gold of the couple's clothes is a patchwork of oil laid on thick with a palette knife.

The Syndics of the Amsterdam Drapers' Guild (De Staalmeesters, 1662)

Although commissions dwindled, Rembrandt could still paint an official group portrait better than anyone. In the painting made famous by Dutch Masters cigars, he catches the Drapers Guild in a natural but dignified pose (dignified, at least, until the guy on the left sits on his friend's lap).

It's a business meeting, and they're all dressed in black with black hats—the standard power suit of the Dutch Golden Age.

They gather around a table examining the company's books. Suddenly, someone (us) walks in, and they look up. It's as natural as a snapshot, though X-rays show Rembrandt made many changes in posing them perfectly.

The figures are "framed" by the table beneath them and the top of the wood paneling above their heads, making a three-part composition that brings this band of colleagues together. Even in this simple portrait, we feel we can read the guild members' personalities in their faces. (If the table in the painting looks like it's sloping a bit unnaturally, lie on the floor to view it at Rembrandt's intended angle.)

• *Leave the Gallery of Honor, and approach the museum's star masterpiece. The best viewing spot is to the right of center—the angle Rembrandt had in mind when he designed it for its original location.*

The Night Watch (a.k.a. *The Company of Frans Banning Cocq*, 1642)

This is Rembrandt's most famous—though not necessarily greatest—painting. Created in 1642, when he was 36, it was one of his most important commissions: a group portrait of a company of Amsterdam's Civic Guards to hang in their meeting hall.

It's an action shot. With flags waving and drums beating, the guardsmen (who, by the 1640s, were really only an honorary

militia of rich bigwigs) spill onto the street from under an arch in the back. It's "all for one and one for all" as they rush to Amsterdam's rescue. The soldiers grab lances and load their muskets. In the center, the commander (in black, with a red sash) strides forward energetically with a hand gesture that seems to say, "What are we waiting for? Let's move out!" His lieutenant focuses on his every order.

Rembrandt caught the optimistic spirit of Holland in the 1600s. Its war of independence from Spain was heading to victory and the economy was booming. These guardsmen on the move epitomize the proud, independent, upwardly mobile Dutch.

Why is *The Night Watch* so famous? Compare it with other,

less famous group portraits, where every face is visible and everyone is well-lit, flat, and flashbulb-perfect. These people paid good money to have their mugs preserved for posterity, and they wanted it right up front. Other group portraits may be colorful, dignified works by a master...but not quite masterpieces.

By contrast, Rembrandt rousted the Civic Guards off their fat duffs. By adding movement and depth to an otherwise static scene, he took posers and turned them into warriors. He turned a simple portrait into great art.

OK, some *Night Watch* scuttlebutt: First off, "*Night Watch*" is a misnomer. It's a daytime scene, but over the years, as the preserving varnish darkened and layers of dirt built up, the sun set on this painting, and it got its popular title. When the painting was moved to a smaller room, the sides were lopped off (and the pieces lost), putting the two main characters in the center and causing the work to become more static than intended. During World War II, the painting was rolled up and hidden for five years. In 1975, a madman attacked the painting, slicing the captain's legs, and in 1990, it was sprayed with acid (it was skillfully restored after both incidents).

The Night Watch, contrary to popular myth, was a smashing success in its day. However, there are elements in it that show why Rembrandt soon fell out of favor as a portrait painter. He seemed to spend as much time painting the dwarf and the mysterious glowing girl with a chicken (the very appropriate mascot of this "militia" of shopkeepers) as he did the faces of his employers.

Rembrandt's life darkened long before his *Night Watch* did. This work marks the peak of Rembrandt's popularity...and the beginning of his fall from grace. He continued to paint masterpieces. Free from the dictates of employers whose taste was in their mouths, he painted what he wanted, how he wanted it. Rembrandt goes beyond mere craftsmanship to probe into, and draw life from, the deepest wells of the human soul.

• *Near* The Night Watch *are several other Rembrandt masterpieces.*

Self-Portrait at an Early Age

Here we see the young small-town boy about to launch himself into whatever life has to offer. Rembrandt was a precocious kid. His father, a miller, insisted that he become a lawyer. His mother hoped he'd be a preacher (look for a portrait of her reading the Bible). Rembrandt combined the secular and religious worlds by becoming an artist, someone who

Other "Rembrandts"

The Rijksmuseum displays real Rembrandts, paintings by others that look like his, portraits of Rembrandt by his students, and one or two "Rembrandts" that may not be his. A century ago, there were 1,000 so-called Rembrandt paintings in existence. Since then, a panel of five art scholars has declared most of those to be by someone else, winnowing the number of authentic Rembrandts to 300, with some 50 more that may one day be "audited" by the Internal Rembrandt Service. Most of the fakes are not out-and-out forgeries, but works by admirers of his distinctive style. The lesson? Be careful the next time you plunk down $15 million for a "Rembrandt."

can hint at the spiritual by showing us the beauty of the created world.

He moved to Amsterdam and entered the highly competitive art world. Amsterdam was a booming town and, like today, a hip and cosmopolitan city. Rembrandt portrays himself at age 22 as being divided—half in light, half hidden by hair and shadows—open-eyed, but wary of an uncertain future. As we'll see, Rembrandt's paintings are often light and dark, both in color and in subject, exploring the "darker" side of human experience.

Jeremiah Lamenting the Destruction of Jerusalem (1630)

The Babylonians have sacked and burned Jerusalem, but Rembrandt leaves the pyrotechnics (in the murky background at left) to Spielberg and the big screen. Instead, he tells the story of Israel's destruction in the face of the prophet who predicted the disaster. Jeremiah slumps in defeat, deep in thought, confused and despondent, trying to understand why this evil had to happen. Rembrandt turns his floodlight of truth on the prophet's deeply lined forehead.

Rembrandt wasn't satisfied to crank out portraits of fat merchants in frilly bibs, no matter what they paid him. He wanted to experiment, trying new techniques and more probing subjects. Many of his paintings weren't commissioned and were never even intended for sale. His subjects could be brooding and melancholy, a bit dark for the public's taste. His technique set him apart—you can recognize a Rembrandt canvas by his play of light and dark. Most of his paintings are a deep brown tone, with only a few

bright spots glowing from the darkness. This allows Rembrandt to highlight the details he thinks are most important and to express moody emotions.

Light has a primal appeal to humans. (Dig deep into your DNA and remember the time when fire was not tamed. Light! In the middle of the night! This miracle separated us from our fellow animals.) Rembrandt strikes at that instinctive level.

Maria Trip (1639)

This debutante daughter of a wealthy citizen is shy and reserved—maybe a bit awkward in her new dress and adult role, but still self-

assured. When he chose to, Rembrandt could dash off a commissioned portrait like nobody's business. The details are immaculate—the lace and shiny satin, the pearls behind the veil, the subtle face and hands. Rembrandt gives us not just a person, but a personality.

Look at the red rings around her eyes, a detail a lesser painter would have airbrushed out. Rembrandt takes this feature, unique to her, and uses it as a setting for her luminous, jewel-like eyes.

Without being prettified, she's beautiful.

A Young Woman (a.k.a. The Portrait of Saskia, 1633)

It didn't take long for Amsterdam to recognize Rembrandt's great talent. Everyone wanted a portrait done by the young master, and

he became wealthy and famous. He fell in love with and married the rich, beautiful, and cultured Saskia. By all accounts, the two were enormously happy, entertaining friends, decorating their house with fine furniture, raising a family, and living the high life. In this wedding portrait, thought to be of Saskia, the bride's face literally glows. A dash of white paint puts a sparkle in her eye. Barely 30 years old, Rembrandt was the most successful painter in Holland. He had it all.

Self-Portrait as the Apostle Paul (1661)

Rembrandt's many self-portraits show us the evolution of a great painter's style, as well as the progress of a genius's life. For Rembrandt, the two were intertwined.

Compare this later self-portrait (he's 55 but looks 70) with the youthful, curious Rembrandt of age 22 we saw earlier. With

a lined forehead, a bulbous nose, and messy hair, he peers out from under several coats of glazing, holding old, wrinkled pages. His look is...skeptical? Weary? Resigned to life's misfortunes? Or amused? (He's looking at us, but not *just* at us—remember that a self-portrait is done staring into a mirror.)

This man has seen it all—success, love, money, fatherhood, loss, poverty, death. He took these experiences and wove them into his art. Rembrandt died poor and misunderstood, but he remained very much his own man to the end.

• *Wander through both sides of the second-floor galleries to see other 17th-century masterpieces.*

More Golden Age Treasures

Welcome to the Dutch Golden Age. As you view the group portraits, you're gazing into the eyes of the men who made Amsterdam the richest city on earth in the 1600s. Though shown in their military uniforms, these men were really captains of industry—shipbuilders, seamen, salesmen, spice-tasters, bankers, and venture capitalists—all part of the complex economic web that planned and financed overseas trade. These galleries also hold interesting artifacts of the era, including a ship's cannon and a big wooden model of a 74-gun Dutch man-of-war that had escorted convoys of merchant ships loaded with wealth.

Various Still Lifes (c. 1630)

Savor the fruits of Holland's rich overseas trade—lemons from the south, pitchers from Germany, and spices from Asia, including those most exotic of spices...salt and pepper. These carefully composed, photo-realistic still lifes reflect the same sense of pride the Dutch have for their homes, cultivating them like gardens until they're immaculate, decorative, and in perfect order.

Pick one, such as *Still Life with Gilt Goblet* (by Willem Claesz Heda, 1635). Get so close that the guard joins you. Linger over the little things: the pewter-ware, the seafood, the lemon peels, the rolls, and the glowing goblets that cast a warm reflection on the tablecloth. You'd swear you could see yourself reflected in the pewter vessels. At the very least, you can see the faint reflections of the food and even of

surrounding windows. The closer you get, the better it looks.

Hendrick Avercamp (1585-1634)— *Winter Landscape with Ice Skaters*

The village stream has frozen over, and the people all come out to play. (Even today, tiny Holland's speed-skating teams routinely

beat those from much larger nations.) In the center, a guy falls flat on his face. A couple makes out in the hay-tower silo. There's a "bad moon on the rise" in the broken-down outhouse at left and another nearby. We see the scene from above (the horizon line is high), making it seem as if the fun goes on forever.

A song or a play is revealed to the audience at the writer's pace. But in a painting, we set the tempo, choosing where to look and how long to linger. Exercise your right to loiter. Avercamp, who was deaf and mute, presents a visual symphony of small scenes. Just skate among these Dutch people—rich, poor, lovers hand-in-hand, kids, and moms—and appreciate the silent beauty of this intimate look at old Holland.

The Rest of the Rijks

Most visitors are here to see the Golden Age art, but the museum has much, much more, with upward of 8,000 works on display—including a Van Gogh self-portrait, and an airplane (in the 20th-century exhibit). The Special Collections wing on level 0 has elaborately decorated weapons, dolls' houses *(poppenhuizen)*, magic lantern shows, armor, women's fashion, and precious objects of silver, jewelry, glass, and ceramics. Highlights include Delftware inspired by Chinese porcelain and a huge collection of model ships.

The Asian Art Pavilion, a completely new exhibit space, shows off 365 objects from Indonesia—a former Dutch colony—as well as from India, Japan, Korea, and China. The Philips Wing is closed for a makeover (when it's ready in 2015, it'll host temporary exhibits). Outside, the relaxing Rijksmuseum garden, also restored with an eye to Cuypers' original vision, features statues, fountains, ponds, and five centuries of Dutch architectural artifacts.

VAN GOGH MUSEUM TOUR

The Van Gogh Museum (we say "van GO," the Dutch say "van HHHOCK") is a cultural high even for those not into art. Located near the Rijksmuseum, the museum houses the 200 paintings owned by Vincent's younger brother, Theo. It's a user-friendly stroll through the work and life of one enigmatic man. If you like brightly colored landscapes in the Impressionist style, you'll like this museum. If you enjoy finding deeper meaning in works of art, you'll really love it. The mix of Van Gogh's creative genius, his tumultuous life, and the traveler's determination to connect to it makes this museum as much a walk with Vincent as with his art.

Orientation

Cost: €15, more for special exhibits, free for those under 18 and for those with one ear. Credit cards accepted if buying two or more tickets (€25 minimum).

Hours: Daily 9:00-17:00, Fri until 22:00, closed only on Jan 1.

When to Go: Consider visiting on a Friday evening, when crowds are sparse and the atmosphere is cool, with musicians or a DJ and a wine bar in the lobby.

Avoiding Lines: Skip the 15-30-minute wait in the ticket-buying line by getting your ticket in advance (online at www.vangogh museum.com or at the TI), or by getting a Museumkaart or I amsterdam Card at a less-popular sight.

Getting There: It's the big, modern, gray-and-beige place a few blocks behind the Rijksmuseum at Paulus Potterstraat 7 (the entrance may change with renovation). From Central Station, catch tram #2 or #5 to Hobbemastraat.

Information: At the information desk, pick up a free floor plan (containing a brief history of the artist's brief life). The bookstore is understandably popular, with several good, basic "Vincent" guidebooks and lots of posters (with mailing tubes). A watchable 15-minute video with a basic introduction to Van Gogh plays continuously in the downstairs auditorium. Tel. 020/570-5200, www.vangoghmuseum.nl.

Audioguides: The €5 audioguide includes 90 creatively produced minutes of insightful commentaries about Van Gogh's paintings, along with related quotations from Vincent himself. The museum also rents a €2.50 audioguide geared toward kids.

Length of This Tour: Allow one hour.

Baggage Check: Free and mandatory.

Cuisine Art: The museum café (€10 plates, €6 salads, €4 sandwiches) is OK. The recommended Café Vertigo is nearby, in Vondelpark (see page 210).

Photography: No photos allowed.

Overview

The core of the museum and this entire tour is on the first floor, one flight up from the ground floor.

On the ground floor, you'll find the bookstore and café, along with paintings by artists who preceded and influenced Van

Gogh's generation. The second floor has a study area and more paintings (including Van Gogh's smaller-scale works). The third floor shows works by his friends and colleagues, from smooth-surfaced Academy art, to Impressionists Claude Monet and Camille Pissarro, to fellow post-Impressionists Paul Gauguin, Paul Cézanne, and Henri de Toulouse-Lautrec. These painters who influenced and were influenced by Van Gogh. The exhibition wing in the basement showcases temporary exhibitions.

The main collection of Van Gogh paintings on the first floor is arranged chronologically, taking you through the changes in Vincent van Gogh's life and styles. The paintings are divided into five periods of Vincent's life—the Netherlands, Paris, Arles, St. Rémy, and Auvers-sur-Oise—proceeding clockwise around the floor. (Although the busy curators frequently move the paintings around, they *usually* keep them within the same room, so look around; some may be upstairs.) Some background on Vincent's star-crossed life makes the museum even better, so I've included doses of biographical material for each painting.

The Tour Begins

• *Climb the stairs to the first floor. The first room—often displaying self-portraits—introduces you to the artist.*

Vincent van Gogh (1853-1890)

> *I am a man of passions...*
>
> —Vincent van Gogh

You could see Vincent van Gogh's canvases as a series of suicide notes—or as the record of a life full of beauty...perhaps too full of beauty. He attacked life with a passion, experiencing highs and lows more intensely than the average person. The beauty of the world overwhelmed him; its ugliness struck him as only another dimension of beauty. He tried to absorb the full spectrum of experience, good and bad, and channel it onto a canvas. The frustration of this overwhelming task drove him to madness. If all this is a bit overstated—and I guess it is—it's an attempt to show the emotional impact that Van Gogh's works have had on many people, me included.

Vincent, a pastor's son from a small Dutch town, started working at age 16 as a clerk for an art dealership. But his two interests, art and religion, distracted him from his dreary work, and after several years, he was fired.

The next 10 years were a collage of dead ends as he traveled northern Europe pursuing one path after another. He launched into each project with incredible energy, then became disillusioned and moved on to something else: teacher at a boarding school, assistant preacher, bookstore apprentice, preacher again, theology student, English student, literature student, art student. He bounced around England, France, Belgium, and the Netherlands. He fell in love, but was rejected for someone more respectable. He quarreled with his family and was estranged. He lived with a prostitute and her daughter, offending the few friends he had. Finally, in his late 20s, worn out, flat broke, and in poor health, he returned to his family in Nuenen and made peace. He then started to paint.

• *For his stark early work, enter the next room.*

The Netherlands (1880-1885): Poverty and Religion

These dark, gray canvases show us the hard, plain existence of the people and town of Nuenen, in the rural southern Netherlands. We see simple buildings, bare or autumnal trees, and overcast skies—a world where it seems spring will never arrive. What warmth there is comes from the sturdy, gentle people themselves.

The style is crude—Van Gogh couldn't draw very well and would never become a great technician. The paint is laid on thick, as though painted with Nuenen mud. The main subject is almost always dead center, with little or no background, so there's a claustrophobic feeling. We are unable to see anything but the immediate surroundings.

The Potato Eaters (1885)

Those that prefer to see the peasants in their Sunday-best may do as they like. I person-ally am convinced I get better results by painting them in their roughness.... If a peasant picture smells of bacon, smoke, potato steam—all right, that's healthy.

—Vincent van Gogh

In a dark, cramped room lit only by a dim lamp, poor workers help themselves to a steaming plate of potatoes. They've earned

it. Vincent deliberately wanted the canvas to be potato-colored.

Vincent had dabbled as an artist during his wandering years, sketch-ing things around him and taking a few art classes, but it wasn't until age 29 that he painted his first oil canvas. He soon threw himself into it with abandon.

He painted the poor working peasants. He worked as a lay minister among the poorest of the poor, peasants and miners. He joined them at work in the mines, taught their children, and even gave away his own few possessions to help them. The church authorities finally dismissed him for "excessive zeal," but he came away understanding the poor's harsh existence and the dignity with which they bore it.

Still Life with Bible (1885)

I have a terrible need of—shall I say the word?—religion. Then I go out and paint the stars.

—Vincent van Gogh

The Bible and Emile Zola's *La Joie de Vivre*—these two books dominated Van Gogh's life. In his art he tried to fuse his religious upbringing with his

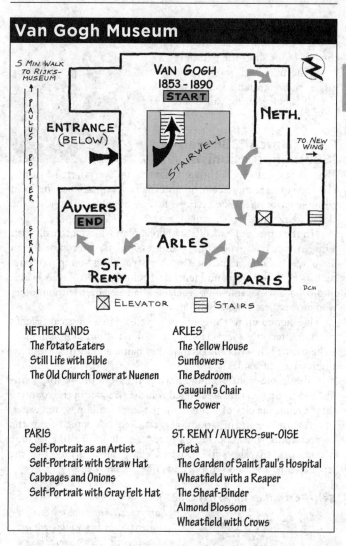

Van Gogh Museum

5 MIN. WALK TO RIJKS-MUSEUM

PAULUS POTTER STRAAT

ENTRANCE (BELOW)

VAN GOGH 1853 - 1890 START

NETH.

TO NEW WING

STAIRWELL

AUVERS END

ARLES

ST. REMY

PARIS

DCH

☒ ELEVATOR   ☰ STAIRS

NETHERLANDS	ARLES
The Potato Eaters	The Yellow House
Still Life with Bible	Sunflowers
The Old Church Tower at Nuenen	The Bedroom
	Gauguin's Chair
	The Sower

PARIS	ST. REMY / AUVERS-sur-OISE
Self-Portrait as an Artist	Pietà
Self-Portrait with Straw Hat	The Garden of Saint Paul's Hospital
Cabbages and Onions	Wheatfield with a Reaper
Self-Portrait with Gray Felt Hat	The Sheaf-Binder
	Almond Blossom
	Wheatfield with Crows

love of the world's beauty. He lusted after life with a religious fervor. The burned-out candle tells us of the recent death of his father. The Bible is open to Isaiah 53: "He was despised and rejected of men, a man of sorrows..."

The Old Church Tower at Nuenen (1885)

The crows circle above the local cemetery of Nuenen. Soon after his father's death, Vincent—in poor health and depressed—moved briefly to Antwerp. He then decided to visit his brother Theo, an art dealer living in Paris, the art capital of the world.

Theo's support—financial and emotional—allowed Vincent to spend the rest of his short life painting.

Vincent moved from rural, religious, poor Holland to Paris, the City of Light. Vincent van Gone.

• Continue to...

Paris (March 1886-Feb 1888): Impressionism

The sun begins to break through, lighting up everything he paints. His canvases are more colorful and the landscapes more spacious, with plenty of open sky, giving a feeling of exhilaration after the closed, dark world of Nuenen.

In the cafés and bars of Paris' bohemian Montmartre district, Vincent met the revolutionary Impressionists. He roomed with Theo and became friends with other struggling young painters, such as Paul Gauguin and Henri de Toulouse-Lautrec. His health improved. He became more sociable, had an affair with an older woman, and was generally happy.

He signed up to study under a well-known classical teacher but quit after only a few classes. He couldn't afford to hire models, so he roamed the streets, sketch pad in hand, and learned from his Impressionist friends.

The Impressionists emphasized getting out of the stuffy studio and setting up canvases outside on the street or in the countryside to paint the play of sunlight off the trees, buildings, and water.

As you see in this room, at first, Vincent copied from the Impressionist masters. He painted garden scenes like Claude Monet, café snapshots like Edgar Degas, "block prints" like the Japanese masters, and self-portraits like...nobody else.

Self-Portrait as an Artist (1888)

I am now living with my brother Vincent, who is studying the art of painting with indefatigable zeal.

—Theo van Gogh to a friend

Here, the budding young artist proudly displays his new palette full of bright new colors, trying his hand at the Impressionist technique of building a scene using dabs of different-colored paint. A whole new world of art—and life—opened up to him in Paris.

Self-Portrait with Straw Hat (1887)

> *You wouldn't recognize Vincent, he has changed so much.... The doctor says that he is now perfectly fit again. He is making tremendous strides with his work.... He is also far livelier than he used to be and is popular with people.*
>
> —Theo van Gogh to their mother

In Paris, Vincent learned the Impressionist painting technique. The shimmering effect comes from placing dabs of different colors side by side on the canvas. At a distance, the two colors blend in the eye of the viewer to become a third color. Here, Vincent uses separate strokes of blue, yellow, green, and red to create a brown beard—but a brown that throbs with excitement.

Still Lifes, such as Cabbages and Onions (1887)

Vincent quickly developed his own style: thicker paint; broad, swirling brushstrokes; and brighter, clashing colors that make even inanimate objects seem to pulsate with life. The many different colors are supposed to blend together, but you'd have to back up to Belgium to make these colors resolve into focus.

Self-Portrait with Gray Felt Hat (1887-1888)

> *He has painted one or two portraits which have turned out well, but he insists on working for nothing. It is a pity that he shows no desire to earn some money because he could easily do so here. But you can't change people.*
>
> —Theo van Gogh to their mother

Despite his new sociability, Vincent never quite fit in with his Impressionist friends. As he developed into a good painter, he became anxious to strike out on his own. Also, he thought the social life of the big city was distracting him from serious work. In this painting, his face screams out from a swirling background of molecular activity. He wanted peace and quiet, a place where he could throw himself into

his work completely. He headed for the sunny south of France.
• *Travel to the next room to reach...*

Arles (Feb 1888–May 1889): Sunlight, Beauty, and Madness

Winter was just turning to spring when Vincent arrived in Arles, near the French Riviera. After the dreary Paris winter, the colors of springtime overwhelmed him. The blossoming trees inspired him to paint canvas after canvas, drenched in sunlight.

The Yellow House (a.k.a. The Street, 1888)

> *It is my intention...to go temporarily to the South, where there is even more color, even more sun.*
>
> —Vincent van Gogh

Vincent rented this house with the green shutters. (He ate at the pink café next door.) Look at that blue sky! He painted in a frenzy,

working feverishly to try and take it all in. For the next nine months, he produced an explosion of canvases, working very quickly when the mood possessed him. His unique style evolved beyond the Impressionists'—thicker paint, stronger outlines, brighter colors (often applied right from the paint tube), and swirling brushwork that makes inanimate objects pulse and vibrate with life.

Sunflowers (1889)

> *The worse I get along with people, the more I learn to have faith in Nature and concentrate on her.*
>
> —Vincent van Gogh

Vincent saw sunflowers as his signature subject, and he painted a half-dozen versions of them, each a study in intense yellow. If he signed the work (look on the vase), it means he was proud of it.

Even a simple work like these sunflowers bursts with life. Different people see different things in *Sunflowers*. Is it a happy painting, or is it a melancholy one? Take your own emotional temperature and see.

The Bedroom (1888)

> *I am a man of passions, capable of and subject to doing more or less foolish things—which I happen to regret, more or less, afterwards.*

—Vincent van Gogh

Vincent was alone, a Dutchman in Provence. And that had its downside. Vincent swung from flurries of ecstatic activity to bouts

of great loneliness. Like anyone traveling alone, he experienced those high highs and low lows. This narrow, trapezoid-shaped, single-room apartment (less than 200 square feet) must have seemed like a prison cell at times. (Psychologists have pointed out that most everything in this painting comes in pairs—two chairs, two paintings, a double bed squeezed down to a single—indicating his desire for a mate. Hmm.)

He invited his friend Paul Gauguin to join him, envisioning a sort of artists' colony in Arles. He spent months preparing a room upstairs for Gauguin's arrival.

Gauguin's Chair (1888)

> *Empty chairs—there are many of them, there will be even more, and sooner or later, there will be nothing but empty chairs.*

—Vincent van Gogh

Gauguin arrived. At first, they got along great, painting and carousing. But then things went sour. They clashed over art, life, and personalities. On Christmas Eve 1888, Vincent went ballistic. Enraged during an alcohol-fueled argument, he pulled out a knife and waved it in Gauguin's face. Gauguin took the hint and quickly left town. Vincent was horrified at himself. In a fit of remorse and madness, he mutilated his own ear and presented it to a prostitute.

The Sower (1888)

A dark, silhouetted figure sows seeds in the burning sun. It's late in the day. The heat from the sun, the source of all life, radiates out

in thick swirls of paint. The sower must be a hopeful man, because the field looks slanted and barren. Someday, he thinks, the seeds he's planting will grow into something great, like the tree that slashes diagonally across the scene—tough and craggy, but with small, optimistic blossoms.

In his younger years, Vincent had worked in Belgium sowing the Christian gospel in a harsh environment (see Mark 4:1-9). Now in Arles, ignited by the sun, he cast his artistic seeds to the wind, hoping.

• *Continue into the next room. Paintings featured in the rest of this tour are shifted around a lot, so they'll likely be in a different order than listed here.*

St. Rémy (May 1889-1890): The Mental Hospital

The people of Arles realized they had a madman on their hands. A doctor diagnosed "acute mania with hallucinations," and the local vicar talked Vincent into admitting himself to a mental hospital. Vincent wrote to Theo: "Temporarily I wish to remain shut up, as much for my own peace of mind as for other people's."

In the mental hospital, Vincent continued to paint whenever he was well enough. He often couldn't go out, so he copied from books, making his own distinctive versions of works by Rembrandt, Delacroix, Millet, and others.

We see a change from bright, happy landscapes to more introspective subjects. The colors are less bright and more surreal, the brushwork even more furious. The strong outlines of figures are twisted and tortured.

Pietà, after Delacroix (1889)

It's evening after a thunderstorm. Jesus has been crucified, and the corpse lies at the mouth of a tomb. Mary, whipped by the cold wind, holds her empty arms out in despair and confusion. She is the tender mother who receives us all in death, as though saying, "My child, you've been away so long—rest in my arms." Christ has a Vincent-esque red beard.

At first, the peace and quiet of

the asylum did Vincent good, and his health improved. Occasionally, he was allowed outside to paint the gardens and landscapes. Meanwhile, the paintings he had sent to Theo began to attract attention in Paris for the first time. A woman in Brussels bought one of his canvases—the only painting he ever sold during his lifetime. In 1987, one of his *Sunflowers* sold for $40 million. Three years later a portrait of Vincent's doctor went for more than $80 million.

The Garden of Saint Paul's Hospital (a.k.a. *The Fall of the Leaves*, 1889)

...a traveler going to a destination that does not exist...

—Vincent van Gogh

The stark brown trees are blown by the wind. A solitary figure (Vincent?) winds along a narrow, snaky path as the wind blows leaves on him. The colors are surreal—blue, green, and red tree trunks with heavy black outlines. A road runs away from us, heading nowhere.

Wheatfield with a Reaper (1889)

I have been working hard and fast in the last few days. This is how I try to express how desperately fast things pass in modern life.

—Vincent van Gogh

The harvest is here. The time is short. There's much work to be done. A lone reaper works uphill, scything through a swirling wheat field, cutting slender paths of calm.

The Sheaf-Binder, after Millet (1889)

I want to paint men and women with that something of the eternal which the halo used to symbolize...

—Vincent van Gogh

Vincent's compassion for honest laborers remained constant following his work with Belgian miners. These sturdy folk, with their curving bodies, wrestle as one with their curving wheat. The world Vincent sees is charged from within by spiritual fires, twisting and turning matter into energy, and vice versa.

The fits of madness returned. During these spells, he lost all sense of his own actions. He couldn't paint, the one thing he felt driven to do. He wrote to Theo, "My surroundings here begin to weigh on me more than I can say—I need air. I feel overwhelmed by boredom and grief."

Auvers-sur-Oise (May-July 1890): Flying Away

> *The bird looks through the bars at the overcast sky where a thunderstorm is gathering, and inwardly he rebels against his fate. 'I am caged, I am caged, and you tell me I have everything I need! Oh! I beg you, give me liberty, that I may be a bird like other birds.' A certain idle man resembles this idle bird...*
>
> —Vincent van Gogh

Almond Blossom (1890)

Vincent moved north to Auvers, a small town near Paris where he could stay at a hotel under a doctor friend's supervision. On the way there, he visited Theo. Theo's wife had just had a baby, whom they named Vincent. Brother Vincent showed up with this painting under his arm as a birthday gift. Theo's wife later recalled, "I had expected a sick man, but here was a sturdy, broad-shouldered man with a healthy color, a smile on his face, and a very resolute appearance."

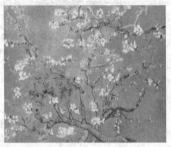

In his new surroundings, he continued painting, averaging a canvas a day, but was interrupted by spells that swung from boredom to madness. His letters to Theo were generally optimistic, but he worried that he'd soon succumb completely to insanity and never paint again. The final landscapes are walls of bright, thick paint.

Wheatfield with Crows (1890)

> *This new attack...came on me in the fields, on a windy day, when I was busy painting.*
>
> —Vincent van Gogh

On July 27, 1890, Vincent left his hotel, walked out to a nearby field, and put a bullet through his chest.

This is the last painting Vincent finished. We can try to search the wreckage of his life for the black box explaining what happened, but there's not much there. His life was sad and tragic, but

the record he left is one not of sadness, but of beauty—intense beauty.

The windblown wheat field is a nest of restless energy. Scenes like this must have overwhelmed Vincent with their incredible beauty—too much, too fast, with no release. The sky is stormy and dark blue, almost nighttime, barely lit by two suns boiling through the deep ocean of blue. The road starts nowhere, leads nowhere, disappearing into the burning wheat field. Above all of this swirling beauty fly the crows, the dark ghosts that had hovered over his life since the cemetery in Nuenen.

ANNE FRANK HOUSE TOUR

On May 10, 1940, Germany's Luftwaffe began bombing Schiphol Airport, preparing to invade the Netherlands. The Dutch army fought back, and the Nazis responded by leveling Rotterdam. Within a week, the Netherlands surrendered, Queen Wilhelmina fled to Britain, and Nazi soldiers goose-stepped past the Westerkerk and into Dam Square, where they draped huge swastikas on the Royal Palace. A five-year occupation began. The Netherlands had been neutral in World War I, and Amsterdam—progressive and modern, but a bit naive—was in for a rude awakening.

The Anne Frank House immerses you, in a very immediate way, in the struggles and pains of the war years. Walk through rooms where, for two years, eight Amsterdam Jews hid from Nazi persecution. Though they were eventually discovered, and seven of the eight died in concentration camps, their story has an uplifting twist—the diary of Anne Frank, which bolsters the human spirit, affirming that it cannot be crushed.

Orientation

Cost: €9, covered by Museumkaart but not I amsterdam Card.
Hours: March 15-Sept 14 daily 9:00-21:00, Sat and July-Aug until 22:00; Sept 15-March 14 daily 9:00-19:00, Sat until 21:00; last entry 30 minutes before closing. Unlike many of Amsterdam's museums, the Anne Frank House is open on most holidays, although it does close for Yom Kippur (Sept

14 in 2013, Oct 4 in 2014).

Avoiding Lines: Skip the long ticket-buying line (which is especially bad in the daytime during summer) by purchasing your

ticket and reserving an
entry time online at www
.annefrank.org (€0.50/
person fee). Museumkaart
holders can purchase an
online reservation without
buying a separate Anne
Frank House ticket. Book
as soon as you're sure of
your itinerary.

You must present a print-out of your ticket and/or reservation; if you don't have access to a printer, try emailing your confirmation to your hotel and asking them to print it—or bring your confirmation number to the museum and explain the situation. With your ticket (or Museumkaart plus reservation) in hand, you can skip the line and ring the buzzer at the low-profile door marked *Entrance: Reservations Only*. Without a reservation, try arriving when the museum opens (at 9:00) or after 18:00.

Getting There: It's at Prinsengracht 267, near Westerkerk and about a 20-minute walk from Central Station. You can also take tram #13, #14, or #17—or bus #170 or #172—to the Westermarkt stop, about a block south of the museum's entrance.

Information: The museum has excellent information in English, including a pamphlet at the door and good descriptions with excerpts from the diary throughout. Use this chapter as background, and then let the displays and videos tell you more. Tel. 020/556-7100, www.annefrank.org. Note that the house has many steep, narrow stairways.

Length of This Tour: Allow one hour.

Baggage Check: The museum has a strict no-big-bags policy—but doesn't offer you a place to check them.

Eating: The museum café serves simple fare and has good views (daily 9:30-18:00).

The Tour Begins

We'll walk through the rooms where Anne Frank's family and four other Jews hid for 25 months. The front half of the building, facing the canal, remained the offices and warehouses of an operating business. The back half, where the Franks and others lived, was the Secret Annex, its entrance concealed by a bookcase.

• *After the ticket desk, enter the ground-floor exhibit. After viewing the important five-minute video, go upstairs to the offices/warehouses of the front half of the building.*

First Floor: Offices

From these offices, Otto Frank ran a successful business called Opekta, selling spices and pectin for making jelly. When the Nazis gained power in Germany in 1933, Otto moved his family from Frankfurt to tolerant Amsterdam, hoping for a better life.

Photos and displays show Otto with some of his colleagues. During the Nazi occupation, while the Frank family hid in the back of the building, these brave people kept Otto's business running, secretly bringing supplies to the Franks. Miep Gies, Otto's secretary (see her in the video), brought food every few days, while bookkeeper Victor Kugler cheered up Anne with the latest movie magazines.

• *Go upstairs to the...*

Second Floor: Warehouse

Two models show the two floors where Anne, her family, and four others lived. Dollhouse furniture helps you envision life in the now-bare living quarters. In the first model, find the swinging bookcase that hid the secret entrance leading to Anne's parents' room (with wood stove). Anne's room is next to it, with a blue bed, a brown sofa, a table/chair/bookcase ensemble, and photos on the wall. On the upper floor (the next model) was the living area and the rooms where another family—the Van Pels—stayed. All told, eight people lived in a tiny apartment smaller than 1,000 square feet.

At first the Nazi overlords were lenient toward, even friendly with, the vanquished Dutch. But soon they began imposing restrictions that affected one in ten Amsterdammers—that is, Jews. Jews had to wear yellow-star patches and register with the police. They were banned from movie theaters and trams, and even forbidden to ride bikes.

In February of 1941, the Nazis started rounding up Amsterdam's Jews, shipping them by train to "work camps," which, in reality, were transit stations on the way to death camps in the east. Outraged, the people of Amsterdam called a general strike that shut down the city for two days...but the Nazis responded with even harsher laws.

In July of 1942, Anne's sister Margot got her **call-up notice** for a "work-force project." Otto handed over the keys to the business to his "Aryan" colleagues, sent a final postcard to relatives, gave the family cat to a neighbor, spread rumors that they were fleeing to Switzerland, and prepared his family to "dive under" *(onderduik,* as it was called) into hiding.

Photos of *The People in Hiding* put faces on the eight people—all Jewish—who eventually inhabited the Secret Annex. First was the Frank family—Otto and Edith and their daughters, 13-year-old Anne and 16-year-old Margot. A week later, they were joined by the Van Pels (called the "Van Daans" in her diary), with their teenage son, Peter. A few months later, Fritz Pfeffer (called "Mr. Dussel" in the diary) was invited in.

• *It's now time to enter the hiding place. At the back of the second floor warehouse is the clever hidden passageway into the Secret Annex.*

Secret Annex

The Bookcase Entrance

On a rainy Monday morning, July 6, 1942, the Frank family—wearing extra clothes to avoid carrying suspicious suitcases—breathed their last fresh air, took a long look at the Prinsengracht canal, and disappeared into the back part of the building, where they spent the next two years. Victor Kugler concealed the entrance to the annex with this swinging bookcase, stacked with business files.

Though not exactly a secret (since it's hard to hide an entire building), the annex was a typical back-house *(achterhuis),* a common feature in Amsterdam buildings, and the Nazis had no reason to suspect anything on the premises of the legitimate Opekta business.

• *Pass through the bookcase entrance into...*

Otto, Edith, and Margot's Room

The family carried on life as usual. Otto read Dickens' *Sketches by Boz,* Edith read from a **prayer book** in their native German, and the children continued their studies, with Margot taking **Latin lessons** by correspondence course. They avidly followed the course of the war by radio broadcasts and news from their helpers. As the tides of war slowly turned and it appeared they might one day be saved from the Nazis, Otto tracked the Allied advance on a **map** of Normandy.

The room is very small, even without the furniture. Imagine yourself and two fellow tourists confined here for two years...

Pencil lines on the wall track Margot's and Anne's heights, marking the point at which these growing lives were cut short.

Anne Frank's Room

Pan the room clockwise to see some of the young girl's idols in photos and clippings she pasted there herself: American actor Robert Stack, the future Queen Elizabeth II as a child, matinee

Life in the Annex

By day, it's enforced silence, so no one can hear them in the offices. They whisper, tiptoe, and step around squeaky places in the floor. The windows are blacked out, so they can't even look outside. They read or study, and Anne writes in her diary.

At night and on weekends, when the offices close, one or two might sneak downstairs to listen to Winston Churchill's BBC broadcasts on the office radio. Everyone's spirits rise and sink with news of Allied victories and setbacks.

Anne's diaries make clear the tensions, petty quarrels, and domestic politics of eight people living under intense pressure. Mr. Van Pels annoys Anne, but he gets along well with Margot. Anne never gets used to Mr. Pfeffer, who is literally invading her space. Most troublesome of all, pubescent Anne often strikes sparks with her mom. (Anne's angriest comments about her mother were deleted from early editions of the published diary.)

Despite their hardships, the group feels guilty: They have shelter, while so many other Jews are being rounded up and sent off.

As the war progresses, they endure long nights when the house shakes from Allied air raids, and Anne cuddles up in her dad's bed.

Boredom tinged with fear—this existentialist hell is captured so well in Anne's journal.

idol Rudy Vallee, figure-skating actress Sonja Henie, and, on the other wall, actress Greta Garbo, actor Ray Milland, Renaissance man Leonardo da Vinci, and actress Ginger Rogers.

Out the window (which had to be blacked out) is the back courtyard, which had a chestnut tree and a few buildings. (In 2010, the tree, which Anne had greatly enjoyed, toppled in a storm.) These things, along with the Westerkerk bell chiming every 15 minutes, represented the borders of Anne's "outside world."

Imagine Anne sitting here at a small desk, writing in her diary.

In November of 1942, the Franks invited a Jewish neighbor to join them, and Anne was forced to share the tiny room. Fritz Pfeffer (known in the diary as "Mr. Dussel") was a middle-aged dentist with whom Anne didn't get along. Pfeffer wrote a farewell letter to his non-Jewish fiancée, who continued to live nearby and receive news of him from Miep Gies without knowing his whereabouts.

The Bathroom

The eight inhabitants shared this bathroom. During the day, they didn't dare flush the toilet.

• *Ascend the steep staircase—silently—to the...*

Common Living Room

This was also the kitchen and dining room. Otto Frank was well off, and early on, the annex was well-stocked with food. Miep Gies would dutifully take their shopping list, buy food for her "family" of eight, and secretly lug it up to them. Buying such large quantities in a coupon-rationed economy was highly suspect, but she knew a sympathetic grocer (a block away on Leliegracht) who was part of a ring of Amsterdammers risking their lives to help the Jews.

The **menu** for a special dinner lists soup, roast beef, salad, potatoes, rice, dessert, and coffee. Later, as war and German restrictions plunged Holland into poverty and famine, they survived on canned foods and dried kidney beans.

At night, the living room became sleeping quarters for Hermann and Auguste van Pels.

Peter van Pels' Room

On Peter's 16th birthday, he got a Monopoly-like board game called "The Broker" as a present.

Initially, Anne was cool toward Peter, but after two years together, a courtship developed, and their flirtation culminated in a kiss.

The staircase (no visitor access) leads up to where they stored their food. Anne loved to steal away here for a bit of privacy. At night they'd open a hatch to let in fresh air.

One hot August day, Otto was in this room helping Peter learn English, when they looked up to see a man with a gun. The hiding was over.

• *From here we leave the Secret Annex, returning to the Opekta storeroom and offices in the front house. As you work your way downstairs, you'll see a number of exhibits on the aftermath of this story.*

The Aftermath

Front House: The Arrest, Deportation, and Auschwitz Exhibits

They went quietly. On August 4, 1944, a German policeman accompanied by three Dutch Nazis pulled up in a car, politely entered the Opekta office, and went straight to the bookcase entrance. No one knows who tipped them off. The police gave the surprised hiders time to pack. They demanded their valuables and stuffed them into Anne's briefcase...after dumping her diaries onto the floor.

Taken in a van to Gestapo headquarters, the eight were processed in an efficient, bureaucratic manner, then placed on a train to Westerbork, a concentration camp northeast of the city (see their 3-inch-by-5-inch **registration cards**).

From there they were locked in a car on a normal passenger train and sent to Auschwitz, a Nazi extermination camp in Poland (see the **transport list,** which includes "Anneliese Frank"). On the platform at Auschwitz, they were "forcibly separated from each other" (as Otto later reported) and sent to different camps. Anne and Margot were sent to Bergen-Belsen.

Don't miss the **video** of one of Anne's former neighbors who, by chance, ended up at Bergen-Belsen with Anne. In English she describes their reunion as they talked through a barbed-wire fence shortly before Anne died. She says of Anne, "She didn't have any more tears."

Anne and Margot both died of typhus in March of 1945, only weeks before the camp was liberated. Five of the other original eight were either gassed or died of disease. Only Otto survived.

The Franks' story was that of Holland's Jews. The seven who died were among the more than 100,000 Dutch Jews killed during the war years. (Before the war, 135,000 Jews lived in the Netherlands.) Of Anne's school class of 87 Jews, only 20 survived.

• *The next room is devoted to Anne's father.*

The Otto Frank Room

Listen to a 1967 video of Anne's father talking about how the diaries were discovered in the annex. The case holds a rotating display: You may find notebooks that Otto kept during the hiding period, or letters he wrote after the war as he tried to get Anne's diaries published.

• *Downstairs you come to...*

The Diaries

See Anne's three diaries, which were published after the war. Anne received the first diary (with a red-plaid binding) as a birthday present when she turned 13, shortly before the family went into hiding. She wrote her diary in the form of a letter to an imaginary friend named Kitty. The other two diaries were written in school-exercise books. Also on display are a book of Anne's short stories, a note-

Photography: No photos allowed.
Length of This Tour: Allow one hour.

The Tour Begins

Exterior

Behind the attic windows of this narrow townhouse sits a 150-seat, three-
story church the size of a four-lane
bowling alley. Beneath it is the home of
the wealthy businessman who built the
church. This 17th-century townhouse,
like many in the city, also has a back
house *(achterhuis)* that was rented out to
another family. On this tour we'll visit
the front house, then the church, then
the back house. Before entering, notice
the emergency-exit door in the alley.
This was once the hidden church's
main entrance.

• *Step inside. Buy your ticket and climb the stairs to the first floor, where
we begin touring the front house. The first stop is a room with a big
fireplace, the...*

Parlor

By humble Dutch standards, this is an enormous, highly ornate
room. Here, in the largest room of the house, the family received
guests and hosted parties. The decor is the Dutch version of classical, where everything comes in symmetrical pairs—corkscrew
columns flank the fireplace, the coffered ceiling mirrors the patterned black-and-white marble floor, and a fake exit door balances
the real entrance door.

Over the fireplace is the coat of arms of Jan Hartman (1619-
1668), a rich Catholic businessman who built this house for his
family and the church for his fellow Catholics in the neighborhood. The family symbol, the crouching hart (deer), became the
nickname of the church—*Het Hert.*

The painting over the fireplace *(The Presentation in the Temple)*
has hung here since Hartman's time and shows his taste for Italian,
Catholic, Baroque-style beauty. On the wall opposite the windows, the family portrait is right out of the Dutch Golden Age,
showing a rich Catholic businessman and his family of four...but
it's not Hartman.

• *Now ascend the small spiral staircase that leads to a room facing the
canal, called the...*

Canal Room

Unlike the rather formal parlor, this was where the family hung out, staring out the windows or warming themselves at the stove. The furnishings are typical of a wealthy merchant's home at the time. The wood stove and the textiles on the walls are re-creations but look like the original s. In the Dutch custom (still occasionally seen today), the family covered tables with exotic Turkish rugs imported by traders of the Dutch East India Company. The Delftware vase would have been filled with tulips, back then still an exotic and expensive transplant from the East. The tall ceramic doodad is a multi-armed tulip vase. Its pagoda shape reminds us that Delftware's designs and techniques originated in China.

Despite the family's wealth, space was tight. In the 1600s, entire families would often sleep together in small bed cabinets. They sat up to sleep, because they believed that if they lay down, the blood would pool in their heads and kill them.

The black ebony knickknack cabinet is painted with a scene right out of the 1600s Red Light District. On the right door, the Prodigal Son spends his inheritance, making merry with barebreasted, scarlet-clothed courtesans—high-rent prostitutes who could also entertain educated, cello-loving clients. On the left door, the Prodigal Son has spent it all. He can't pay his bill, and is kicked out of a cheap tavern—still half-dressed—by a pair of short-changed prostitutes.

• As you climb the staircase up to the church, you can look through a window into the small Chaplain's Room, which shows how humbly the church chaplain lived in the 1800s. Then continue up into the actual hidden church.

Our Lord in the Attic Church—Nave and Altar

The church is long and narrow, with an altar at one end, an organ at the other, and two balconies overhead to maximize the seat-
ing in this relatively small space. Compared with Amsterdam's whitewashed Protestant churches, this Catholic church has touches of elaborate Baroque decor, with statues of saints, garlands, and baby angels. The balconies are suspended from the ceiling and held in place by metal rods.

This attic church certainly is hidden, but everyone knew it was here. In tolerant (and largely Catholic) Amsterdam, it was rare for Catholics to actually be arrested or punished (after the Protestants' initial anger of 1578), but they were socially unacceptable. Hartman was a respected

Anti-Catholic = Anti-Spanish

The anti-Catholic laws were imposed by Protestants, partly as retribution for the Catholics' own oppressive rule, partly from a desire to reform what was seen as a corrupted religion...but mostly for political reasons.

By a quirk of royal marriage, Holland was ruled from afar by Spain, Europe's most militantly Catholic country, home of the Inquisition, the Jesuits, and the pope's own Counter-Reformation army. In 1578, Amsterdam's hard-line Protestants staged the "Alteration"—a coup kicking out their Spanish oppressors and allying the city with the Prince of Orange's rebels.

Catholics in the city—probably a majority of the population—were considered guilty by association. They were potential enemies, suspected as puppets of the pope, spies for Spanish kings, or subverters of the social order. In addition, Catholics were considered immoral worshippers of false idols, bowing down to graven images of saints and the Virgin Mary.

Catholic churches were seized and looted, and prominent Catholics were dragged to Dam Square by a lynch mob, before being freed, unharmed, outside the city gates. Laws were passed prohibiting open Catholic worship. For two centuries, Protestant extremists gave Catholics a taste of their own repressive medicine. However, Amsterdam's long tradition of tolerance meant that Catholics were not actually arrested or prosecuted under these laws. Still, many families over many generations were torn apart by the religious and political strife of the Reformation.

businessman who used his wealth and influence to convince the city fathers to look the other way as the church was built. Imagine the jubilation when the church opened its doors in 1663, and Catholics could finally gather together and worship in this fine space without feeling like two-bit criminals.

The **altar** is flanked by classical columns and topped with an arch featuring a stucco God the Father, a dove of the Holy Spirit, and trumpeting angels.

The **base of the left column**—made of wood painted to look like marble—is hollow. Inside is a foldout wooden pulpit that could be pulled out for the priest to preach from—as shown in photos on the wall opposite.

The **altarpiece painting** (Jacob de Wit's *Baptism of Jesus*) is one of four (three survive) that could be rotated with the feast days. Step into the room behind the altar to see the two spares.

• *Behind the altar is a room called the...*

Calvinism

Holland's Protestant movement followed the stern French (then Swiss) reformer John Calvin more than the beer-drinking German Martin Luther. Calvin's French followers, called Huguenots, fled religious persecution in the 1500s, finding refuge in tolerant Amsterdam. When Catholic Spain began persecuting them in Holland, they entered politics and fought back.

Calvin wanted to reform the Catholic faith by condemning corruption, simplifying rituals, and returning the faith to its biblical roots. Like other Protestants, Calvinists emphasized that only God's grace—and not our good works—can get us to heaven.

He went so far as to say that God predestined some for heaven, some for hell. Later, some overly pious Calvinists even claimed to be able to pick out the lucky winners from the unlucky, sinful losers. Today, the Dutch Reformed Church, as well as some other Reformed and Presbyterian churches, carry on Calvin's brand of Christianity.

Lady Chapel

A 400-year-old altar dedicated to Our Lady—the Virgin Mary, the mother of Christ—contains more of the images that so offended and outraged hard-line Protestants. See her statue with baby Jesus and find her symbols, the rose and crown, in the blue damask altar cloth.

Catholics have traditionally honored Mary, addressing prayers to her or to other saints, asking them to intercede with God on

their behalf. To Calvinist extremists, this was like bowing down to a false goddess. They considered statues of the Virgin to be among the "graven images" forbidden by the Ten Commandments (Exodus 20:4).

The **collection box** (*voor St. Pieter*, on the wall by the staircase down) was for donations sent to fund that most Catholic of monuments, the pope's own church, the Basilica of St. Peter in Rome—to Calvinists, the center of corruption, the "whore of Babylon."

• *Later, we'll head down the stairs here, but first climb the stairs to the first balcony above the church.*

Lower Balcony

The window to the left of the altar (as you face it) looks south across ramshackle rooftops (note the complex townhouse-with-back-house design of so many Amsterdam buildings) to the steeple of the Old Church (Oude Kerk). The Old Church was the main Catholic church until 1578, when it was rededicated as Dutch Reformed (Protestant), the new official religion of the Netherlands. For the next hundred years, Catholics had no large venue to gather in until Our Lord in the Attic opened in 1663.

The 1749 **organ** is small, but more than adequate. These days, music lovers flock here on special evenings for a *Vondelkonzert* (wandering concert). They listen to a few tunes here, have a drink,

then move on to hear more music at, say, the Old Church or the Royal Palace.

Next to the organ, the **painting** *Evangelist Matthew with an Angel* (*De Evangelist Mattheus*, c. 1625, by Jan Lievens) features the wrinkled forehead and high-contrast shadings used by Lievens' more famous colleague, Rembrandt.

• *Stairs next to the organ lead you to the...*

Upper Balcony

Looking down from this angle, the small church really looks small. It can accommodate 150 seated worshippers. From here the tapering roofline creates the "attic" feel that gives the church its nickname.

• *At the back of the upper balcony is the...*

Canalside Room—Religious Art

This kind of religious hardware is standard in Catholic church services—elaborate silver-and-gold monstrances (ornamental holders in which the Communion wafer is displayed), chalices (for the Communion wine), ciboria (chalices with lids for holding consecrated wafers), pyxes (for storing unconsecrated wafers), candlesticks, and incense burners. "Holy earth boxes" were used for Catholics denied burial in consecrated ground. Instead, they put a little consecrated dirt in the box and placed it in the coffin.

While you admire these beautiful pieces, remember that it was this kind of luxury, ostentation, and Catholic mumbo-jumbo that drove thrifty Calvinists nuts.

Looking out the window, you can see that you're literally in

the attic. Straight across the canal is a house with an ornate gable featuring dolphins. This street was once the city's best address.
• *Back down on the lower balcony, circle around to the window just to the right of the altar for a...*

Northern View

Look north across modern junk on rooftops to the impressive dome and twin steeples of St. Nicholas Church, near Central Station. This is the third Amsterdam church to be dedicated to the patron saint of seafarers and of the city. The first was the Old Church (until 1578), then Our Lord in the Attic (1663). Finally, after the last anti-Catholic laws were repealed (1821), St. Nicholas was built as a symbol of the faith's revival.

When St. Nicholas Church was dedicated in 1887, Our Lord in the Attic closed up shop. The next year, wealthy Catholics saved it from the wrecking ball, turning it into one of Amsterdam's first museums.
• *Head back downstairs, passing through the room behind the altar with the Lady Chapel, and taking the stairs (past the offering box) down to the...*

Confessional

The confessional dates from 1740. The priest sat in the left half, while parishioners knelt in the right to confess their sins through a grilled window. Catholic priests have church authority to forgive sins, whereas Protestants take their troubles directly to God.

The sociologist Max Weber theorized that frequently forgiven Catholics more easily accept the status quo, whereas guilt-ridden Protestants are driven to prove their worth by making money. Hence, northern Protestant countries—like the Netherlands— became capitalist powerhouses, while southern Catholic countries remained feudal and backward. Hmm.
• *Go down another flight and turn right, into the...*

Jaap Leeuwenberg Room (Room 10)

We've now left the church premises and moved to the back-house rooms that were rented out to other families. This room's colors are seen in countless old homes—white walls, ochre-yellow beamed ceiling, oxblood-red landing, and black floor tiles. The simple colors, lit here by a light shaft, make small rooms seem bright and spacious.
• *Some very steep stairs lead down to the...*

17th-Century Kitchen

This reconstructed room was inhabited as-is until 1952. Blue-tiled walls show playful scenes of kids and animals. Step into the small pantry, then open a door to see the toilet.

• *Climb the rope back up the stairs and turn left to find exhibits on Amsterdam's other Catholic churches (known to Protestants as "Papist meeting places"). Then descend a different set of stairs just one floor (not all the way down to the basement) into the...*

19th-Century Kitchen

This just looks so Dutch, with blue tiles, yellow walls, and Vermeer-esque lighting from a skylight. The portrait opposite the fireplace depicts the last resident of this house on her First Communion day. When she died, in 1953, her house became part of this museum.

Think of how her age overlaps our age...of all the change since she was born. Consider the contrast of this serene space with the wild world that awaits just outside the door of this hidden church. And plunge back into today's Amsterdam.

SLEEPING IN AMSTERDAM

Greeting a new day by descending steep stairs and stepping into a leafy canalside scene—graceful bridges, historic gables, and bikes clattering on cobbles—is a fun part of experiencing Amsterdam. But Amsterdam is a tough city for budget accommodations, and any hotel room under €140 (or B&B room under €100) will have rough edges. Still, you can sleep well and safely in a great location for €100 per double.

I've grouped my hotel listings into three neighborhoods, each of which has its own character.

West Amsterdam (which includes the Jordaan) has Old World ambience, with quiet canals, old gabled buildings, and candle-lit restaurants. It's also just minutes on foot to Dam Square. Many of my hotels are charming, friendly gabled mansions. The downside here is that you'll pay more and likely have lots of stairs to climb.

Southwest Amsterdam has two main areas for accommodations: near Leidseplein (more central) and near Vondelpark (farther away). The streets near the bustling Leidseplein have restaurants, tourist buzz, nightlife, canalside charm, B&B coziness, and walkable (or easy tram) access to the center of town. Farther afield is the quieter semi-suburban neighborhood around Vondelpark and Museumplein, close to the Rijks and Van Gogh museums. You'll find good hotel values and ready access to Vondelpark and the art museums, but it's a half-hour walk (or 10-minute tram ride) to Dam Square.

Staying in **Central Amsterdam** is ideal for people who like shopping, tourist sights, and easy access to public transportation (including Central Station). On the downside, the area has traffic noise, concrete, and urban grittiness, and the hotels can lack character.

Sleep Code

(€1 = about $1.30, country code: 31, area code: 020)
S = Single, **D** = Double/Twin, **T** = Triple, **Q** = Quad, **b** = bathroom,
s = shower only. Nearly everyone speaks English. Credit cards
are accepted, and prices include breakfast and tax unless
otherwise noted.

To help you easily sort through these listings, I've divided
the accommodations into three categories, based on the
price for a standard double room with bath:

$$$ Higher Priced—Most rooms €140 or more.
$$ Moderately Priced—Most rooms between €80-140.
$ Lower Priced—Most rooms €80 or less.

Prices can change without notice and most do not
include the city's 6 percent room tax; verify the hotel's current
rates online or by email.

Some national holidays merit your making reservations far in advance (see "Holidays and Festivals" on page 626). Amsterdam is jammed during tulip season (late March-mid-May), conventions, festivals, and on summer weekends. During peak season, some hoteliers won't take weekend bookings for those staying fewer than two or three nights.

Around just about every corner in downtown Amsterdam, you'll see construction: cranes for big transportation projects and small crews of bricklayers repairing the wobbly, cobbled streets that line the canals. Canalside rooms can come with great views— and early-morning construction-crew noise. If you're a light sleeper, ask the hotelier for a quiet room in the back. Smoking is illegal in hotel rooms throughout the Netherlands. Parking in Amsterdam is even worse than driving—if you must park a car, ask your hotelier for advice.

Canal houses were built tight. They have steep stairs with narrow treads; almost none have elevators. If steep stairs are potentially problematic, book a hotel with an elevator.

If you'd rather trade big-city action for small-town coziness, consider sleeping in Haarlem, 20 minutes away by train (see Haarlem chapters).

West Amsterdam

Stately Canalside Hotels

These hotels, a half-mile apart, both face historic canals. They come with lovely lobbies (some more ornate than others) and

Hotels & Restaurants in West Amsterdam

T TRAM #13, 14 & 17 STOP

DCH

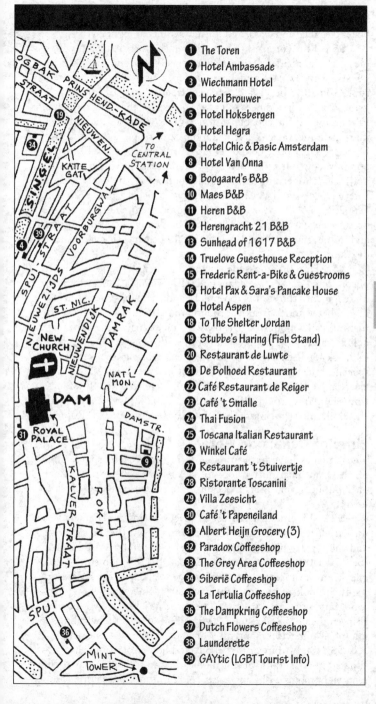

1 The Toren
2 Hotel Ambassade
3 Wiechmann Hotel
4 Hotel Brouwer
5 Hotel Hoksbergen
6 Hotel Hegra
7 Hotel Chic & Basic Amsterdam
8 Hotel Van Onna
9 Boogaard's B&B
10 Maes B&B
11 Heren B&B
12 Herengracht 21 B&B
13 Sunhead of 1617 B&B
14 Truelove Guesthouse Reception
15 Frederic Rent-a-Bike & Guestrooms
16 Hotel Pax & Sara's Pancake House
17 Hotel Aspen
18 To The Shelter Jordan
19 Stubbe's Haring (Fish Stand)
20 Restaurant de Luwte
21 De Bolhoed Restaurant
22 Café Restaurant de Reiger
23 Café 't Smalle
24 Thai Fusion
25 Toscana Italian Restaurant
26 Winkel Café
27 Restaurant 't Stuivertje
28 Ristorante Toscanini
29 Villa Zeesicht
30 Café 't Papeneiland
31 Albert Heijn Grocery (3)
32 Paradox Coffeeshop
33 The Grey Area Coffeeshop
34 Siberië Coffeeshop
35 La Tertulia Coffeeshop
36 The Dampkring Coffeeshop
37 Dutch Flowers Coffeeshop
38 Launderette
39 GAYtic (LGBT Tourist Info)

AMSTERDAM SLEEPING

rooms that can feel like they're from another century. This area oozes elegance and class, and it is fairly quiet at night.

$$$ The Toren is a chandeliered, historic mansion with a pleasant, canalside setting and a peaceful garden out back for guests. Run by Eric and Petra Toren, this smartly renovated, super-romantic hotel is classy yet friendly, with 38 rooms in a great location on a quiet street two blocks northeast of the Anne Frank House. The capable staff is a great source of local advice. The gilt-frame, velvet-curtained rooms are an opulent splurge (tiny Sb-€115, Db-€200, deluxe Db-€250, third person-€40, prices bump way up during conferences and decrease in winter, rates do not include 6 percent tax, breakfast buffet-€14, air-con, elevator, Internet access and Wi-Fi, Keizersgracht 164, tel. 020/622-6033, fax 020/626-9705, www.thetoren.nl, info@thetoren.nl). To get the best prices, check their website for their "daily rate," book direct, and in the "remarks" field, ask for the 10 percent Rick Steves cash discount.

$$$ Hotel Ambassade, lacing together 59 rooms in a maze of connected houses, is elegant and fresh, sitting aristocratically on Herengracht. The staff is top-notch, and the public areas (including a library and a breakfast room) are palatial, with antique furnishings and modern art (Sb-€210, Db-€265, more expensive deluxe canal-view doubles and suites, Tb-€245-295, extra bed-€40, ask for Rick Steves discount when booking, see website for specials, rates do not include 6 percent tax, breakfast-€18, air-con, elevator, free Internet access and Wi-Fi, Herengracht 341, for location see map on page 192, tel. 020/555-0222, www.ambassade -hotel.nl, info@ambassade-hotel.nl, Roos—pronounced "Rose").

Simpler Canalside Hotels

These places have basic rooms—some downright spare, none plush—and most do without an elevator or other extras. Each of them, however, offers a decent night's sleep in a lovely area of town.

$$$ Wiechmann Hotel's 37 pricey rooms are sparsely furnished with just the dark-wood essentials, but they're spacious, and the *gezellig* public areas are chock-full of Old World charm (Sb-€70-110, Db-€150-170, Tb-€210, Qb-€225, Db suite-€265, check online for best price, 15 percent cheaper for 3 or more nights if booking through their website, some canal views, back rooms are quiet, free Internet access and Wi-Fi, nicely located at Prinsengracht 328-332, tel. 020/626-3321, www.hotelwiechmann .nl, info@hotelwiechmann.nl, John and Taz the welcome dog).

$$ Hotel Brouwer is a woody and homey old-time place. It's situated in a tranquil yet central location on the Singel canal and rents eight rooms with canal views, old furniture, and soulful throw rugs. It's so popular that it's often booked four or five months in advance—reserve as soon as possible (Sb-€60, Db-€95, Tb-€120, rates don't include 6 percent tax, cash only, breakfast-€7, small elevator, free Internet access and Wi-Fi, located between Central Station and Dam Square, near Lijnbaanssteeg at Singel 83, tel. 020/624-6358, www.hotelbrouwer.nl, akita@hotelbrouwer.nl).

$$ Hotel Hoksbergen is a welcoming, well-run canalside place in a peaceful location where helpful, hands-on owners Tony and Bert rent 14 rooms with newly remodeled bathrooms (Db-€98, Tb-€143, five Qb apartments-€165-198, fans, free Wi-Fi, Singel 301, tel. 020/626-6043, www.hotelhoksbergen.com, info @hotelhoksbergen.nl).

$$ Hotel Hegra is cozy, with nine rooms filling a 17th-century merchant's house overlooking the canal (Db-€80-€160, Tb-€119-149, breakfast-€6.50, some rooms with canal view, pay Internet access, free Wi-Fi, bike and boat rentals, just north of Wolvenstraat at Herengracht 269, tel. 020/623-7877, www.hotel hegra.nl, info@hotelhegra.nl, Robert).

$$ Hotel Chic & Basic Amsterdam has a boutique-hotel feel, even though it's part of a Spanish chain. With its mod utilitarian design and younger clientele, it provides a break from all the lace curtains. Located in a quiet neighborhood near Central Station, it offers 25 minimalist rooms and public areas that are bathed in space-age white. Rooms with canal views are pricier and breezier (Sb-€95-130, Db-€120-155, €20 more on holiday weekends, less in winter, cheaper prices are for less sleek "vintage" rooms without canal views, free coffee, continental breakfast, fans on request, tangled floor plan connecting three canalside buildings, free Internet access and Wi-Fi, Herengracht 13, tel. 020/522-2345, www.chicandbasic.com, amsterdam@chicandbasic.com, manager Bernardo Campo).

$$ Hotel Van Onna has 41 simple, industrial-strength rooms, some with canal views. The price is right, and the leafy location makes you want to crack out your easel. The popular top-floor attic rooms are cozy hideaways (Sb-€45-65, Db-€80-110, Tb-€125-145, Qb-€170-200, price depends on season, 5 percent more with credit card, cot-like beds are sufficient, no phones or TVs, free Internet access and Wi-Fi, in the Jordaan at Bloemgracht 104, tel. 020/626-5801, www.hotelvanonna.nl, info@hotelvanonna.nl, Leon and Tsibo).

B&Bs and Private-Room Rentals

B&Bs offer a chance to feel like a local during your visit. The first and third listings here are in a peaceful residential neighborhood that's a short walk from Central Station; the second and fourth are in slightly busier areas. The last two listings are services that manage and rent many apartments and rooms in West Amsterdam.

$$ Boogaard's B&B moved to a new location in 2014, just a few blocks from Dam Square and short walk from the Jordaan. The B&B, which has three comfortable rooms and inviting public spaces, is run by Peter, an American expat opera singer, with help from his Jack Russell terriers, Pepe and Curly. Peter, who clearly enjoys hosting Americans in his home, serves his fresh-baked goodies at breakfast and treats you royally. As his place is popular with my readers, it's smart to book as soon as possible—even as much as six months in advance (Db-€130, 2- to 3-night minimum; prices don't include tax, air-con, DVD library, free laundry, laptops in rooms and free Wi-Fi, loaner cell phones, Pieter Jacobszstraat 21, mobile 634-991-941, www.boogaardsbnb.com, info@boogaardsbnb.com).

$$ Maes B&B (pronounced "mahss") is a dynamite value, renting tastefully cozy rooms for much less than you'd pay at a hotel. Instead of a reception desk, you get antique-filled rooms, the use of a full kitchen, and a warm welcome from Ken and Vlad. They also run **Heren B&B,** a crisply modern space around the corner from Maes, with large rooms—one with a canal view (both locations: Sb-€105, Db-€125, extra bed-€30, suites and full apartments also available, free Internet access and Wi-Fi, if street noise bothers you ask for room in back, Herenstraat 26, tel. 020/427-5165, www.bedandbreakfastamsterdam.com, maesinfo@xs4all.nl).

$$ Herengracht 21 B&B has two stylish, intimate rooms in a canal house filled with art and run by lovely Loes Olden (2-floor Db-€125, canal-view Db-€135, air-con, free Wi-Fi, Herengracht 21, tel. 020/625-6305, mobile 06-2812-0962, www.herengracht21.nl, loes@herengracht21.nl).

$$ Sunhead of 1617 B&B justifiably calls itself a "bed and delicious breakfast," but you're just as likely to remember the thoughtfully decorated, flower-filled rooms and the personality of owner Carlos (Db-€90-150, Db apartment-€130-150, more on holidays, free Wi-Fi, mobile 06-2865-3572, Herengracht 152, www.sunhead.com, carlos@sunhead.com).

$$ With **Truelove Guesthouse,** a room-rental service, you'll feel like you're staying at your Dutch friends' house while they're out of town. Sean and Paul—whose tiny antique store on Prinsenstraat doubles as the reception desk for their rental service—have 15 rooms and apartments in houses sprinkled throughout the northern end of the Jordaan neighborhood. The apartments are stylish and come with kitchens and pull-out beds (Db-€90-140, Db apartment-€130-150, prices soft in off-season and midweek, 10 percent more with credit card, 2-night minimum on weekends, no breakfast, pick up keys in store at Prinsenstraat 4, store tel. 020/320-2500, mobile 06-2480-5672, fax 084-711-4950,

AMSTERDAM SLEEPING

www.cosyandwarm-amsterdam.com, trueloveantiek@zonnet.nl).

$ Frederic Rent-a-Bike & Guestrooms, with a bike-rental shop as the reception, is a collection of private rooms on a gorgeous canal just outside the Jordaan, a five-minute walk from Central Station. Frederic has amassed about 100 beds, ranging from dumpy €75 doubles behind the bike-rental shop, to spacious and elegant apartments (from €46/person; these places require a 2-night minimum, occasionally more). Some places are ideal for families and groups of up to eight. He also rents houseboat apartments. All are displayed on his website (phone bookings preferred, book with credit card but pay with cash, no breakfast, Brouwersgracht 78, tel. 020/624-5509, www.frederic.nl, info@frederic.nl, Frederic and Marjolijn). His excellent bike shop, which serves as the reception, is open daily 9:00-17:30 (€15/24 hours). My readers who rent a houseboat or apartment get a 50 percent discount on Frederic's bikes.

Southwest Amsterdam

Charming B&Bs near Leidseplein

The area around Amsterdam's rip-roaring nightlife center (Leidseplein) is colorful, comfortable, and convenient. These canalside mom-and-pop places are within a five-minute walk of rowdy Leidseplein, but generally are in quiet and typically Dutch settings. Within walking distance of the major museums, and steps off the tram line, this neighborhood offers a perfect mix of charm and location.

$$ Hotel de Leydsche Hof, a hidden gem located on a canal, doesn't charge extra for its views. Its four large rooms are a symphony in white, some overlooking a tree-filled backyard, others a canal. Frits and Loes give their big, elegant, old building a stylish air, but be prepared for lots of stairs. Breakfast is served in the grand canal-front room (Db-€120, cash only, 2-night minimum, free Internet access and Wi-Fi, Leidsegracht 14, tel. 020/638-2327, mobile 06-5125-8588, www.freewebs.com/leydschehof, loespiller @planet.nl).

$$ Wildervanck B&B, run by Helene and Sjoerd Wildervanck with the help of their three girls, offers two tasteful rooms in an elegant 17th-century canal house (big Db on first floor-€135, Db with twin beds on ground floor-€130, extra bed-€35, 2-night minimum, breakfast in their pleasant dining room, free Wi-Fi, just west of Leidsestraat at Keizersgracht 498, tel. 020/623-3846, www.wildervanck.com, info@wildervanck.com).

$$ Hotel Keizershof is wonderfully Dutch, with six bright, airy rooms—some with canal views—in a 17th-century canal house with a lush garden and a fine living room. A very steep

Hotels & Restaurants in Southwest Amsterdam

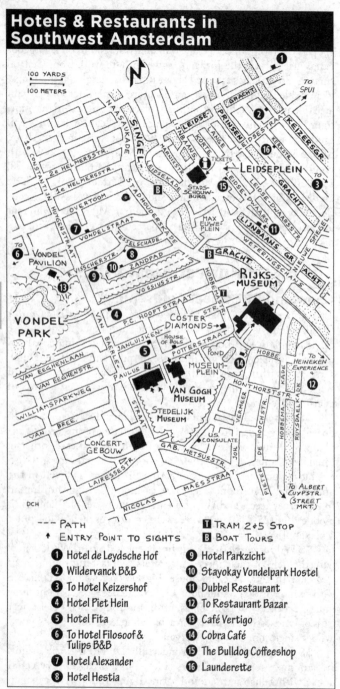

AMSTERDAM SLEEPING

--- Path
↑ Entry Point to Sights

🇹 Tram 2 & 5 Stop
🅱 Boat Tours

① Hotel de Leydsche Hof
② Wildervanck B&B
③ To Hotel Keizershof
④ Hotel Piet Hein
⑤ Hotel Fita
⑥ To Hotel Filosoof & Tulips B&B
⑦ Hotel Alexander
⑧ Hotel Hestia

⑨ Hotel Parkzicht
⑩ Stayokay Vondelpark Hostel
⑪ Dubbel Restaurant
⑫ To Restaurant Bazar
⑬ Café Vertigo
⑭ Cobra Café
⑮ The Bulldog Coffeeshop
⑯ Launderette

spiral staircase leads to rooms named after old-time Hollywood stars. The enthusiastic hospitality of Mrs. de Vries and her daughter, Hanneke, give this place a friendly, almost small-town charm (S-€70, D-€95, Ds-€110, Db-€115, 2-night minimum, reserve with credit card but pay with cash, free Internet access and Wi-Fi; tram #16, #24, or #25 from Central Station; Keizersgracht 618, where Keizersgracht crosses Nieuwe Spiegelstraat; tel. 020/622-2855, www.hotelkeizershof.nl, info@hotelkeizershof.nl).

Near Vondelpark and Museumplein

These options cluster around Vondelpark in a safe neighborhood. Though they don't have a hint of Old Dutch or romantic canalside flavor, they're reasonable values and only a short walk from the action. Unless noted, the places below have elevators. Many are in a pleasant nook between rollicking Leidseplein and the park, and most are a 5- to 15-minute walk to the Rijks and Van Gogh museums. They are easily connected with Central Station by trams #1, #2, and/or #5.

$$$ Hotel Piet Hein offers 81 stylishly sleek yet comfortable rooms as well as a swanky lounge, good breakfast, and a pleasant garden, all on a quiet street (Sb-€100, Db-€165, extra-posh Db-€200-250, Tb-€205, extra bed-€30, specials on website, breakfast-€15, air-con in some rooms, free Internet access and Wi-Fi, Vossiusstraat 51-53, tel. 020/662-7205, www.hotelpiethein .nl, info@hotelpiethein.nl).

$$$ Hotel Fita has 15 bright rooms in a great location—100 yards from the Van Gogh Museum, an even shorter hop from the tram stop, and on a corner with no car traffic. The decor may not be the latest, but all the amenities are there—including espresso machines in every room—and the welcome is very warm (Sb-€109, two small ground-floor Db-€139, Db-€139-169 depending on size, Tb-€205, free laundry service, free Internet access and Wi-Fi in lobby, Jan Luijkenstraat 37, tel. 020/679-0976, fax 020/664-3969, www.fita.nl, info@fita.nl, owner Roel de Haas).

$$ Hotel Filosoof greets you with Aristotle and Plato in the foyer and classical music in its generous lobby. Its 38 rooms, some across the street from reception, are decorated with themes; the Egyptian room has a frieze of hieroglyphics. Philosophers' sayings hang on the walls, and thoughtful travelers wander down the halls or sit in the garden, rooted in deep discussion. The rooms are small, but the hotel is endearing (Db-€110-130 weeknights, €130-150 Fri-Sat, bigger "deluxe" rooms-€20 extra, suites-€60 extra, prices depend on season and don't include 6 percent tax; breakfast-€15, free Internet access and Wi-Fi, 3-minute walk from tram line #1, get off at Jan Pieter Heijestraat, Anna van

Den Vondelstraat 6, tel. 020/683-3013, fax 020/685-3750, www .hotelfilosoof.nl, reservations@hotelfilosoof.nl).

$$ Hotel Alexander is a modern, newly renovated 32-room hotel on a quiet street. Some of the rooms overlook the garden patio out back (Db-€135, prices soft in winter—call or check their website for best deal, breakfast-€10, free Internet access and Wi-Fi, tel. 020/589-4020, fax 020/589-4025, Vondelstraat 44-46, www.hotelalexander.nl, info@hotelalexander.nl).

$$ Tulips B&B, with a bunch of cozy rooms—some on a canal—is run by a friendly Englishwoman, Karen, and her Dutch husband, Paul. Rooms are clean, white, and bright, with red carpeting, plants, and flowers (D-€85, Db-€120, suite-€150, extra bed-€30, discounts for longer stays, cash only, prefer 3-night stays on weekends, includes milk-and-cereal breakfast, no shoes, no elevator but not a lot of stairs, free Wi-Fi, south end of Vondelpark at Sloterkade 65, 7-minute walk from trams #1 and #2, directions sent when you book, tel. 020/679-2753, rooms@bedandbreakfast amsterdam.net, www.bedandbreakfastamsterdam.net).

$$ Hotel Hestia, on a safe street, is efficient and family-run, with 18 clean, airy, and generally spacious rooms (Sb-€83-93, very small Db-€101-107, standard Db-€128-148, Tb-€158-176, Qb-€188-206, Quint/b-€218-236, can be less in winter—check website for best price, Roemer Visscherstraat 7, tel. 020/618-0801, fax 020/685-1382, www.hotel-hestia.nl, info@hotel-hestia.nl, Arnaud).

$$ Hotel Parkzicht, an old-fashioned, no-frills, dark-wood place with extremely steep stairs, rents 13 big, plain, and somewhat frayed rooms on a street bordering Vondelpark (S-€49, Sb-€59, Db-€79-92, Tb-€120-140, closed Nov-March, no elevator, free Wi-Fi, some noise from neighboring youth hostel, Roemer Visscherstraat 33, tel. 020/618-1954, fax 020/618-0897, www.park zicht.nl, hotel@parkzicht.nl).

Central Amsterdam

Basic Hotels in the City Center

You won't get a warm welcome at either of the two following hotels. But if you're looking for a no-nonsense room that's convenient to plenty of tram lines, these hotels fit the bill.

$$$ Hotel Résidence Le Coin offers 42 larger-than-average rooms complete with small kitchenettes. Located near the Mint Tower, this hotel is a two-minute walk to the Flower Market and a five-minute walk to Rembrandtplein (Sb-€125, small Db-€145, bigger Db-€160, Qb-€240, extra bed-€37, breakfast-€12, pay Wi-Fi, by the University at Nieuwe Doelenstraat 5, tel. 020/524-6800, fax 020/524-6801, www.lecoin.nl, hotel@lecoin.nl).

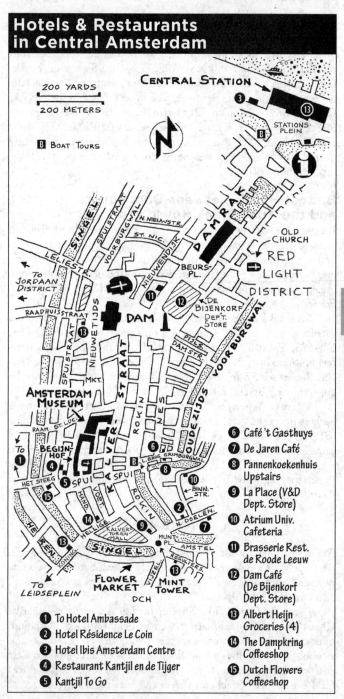

Hotels & Restaurants in Central Amsterdam

200 YARDS

200 METERS

B BOAT TOURS

CENTRAL STATION

STATIONS-PLEIN

OLD CHURCH

RED LIGHT DISTRICT

TO JORDAAN DISTRICT

LELIESTR.

RAADHUISSTRAAT

SINGEL

SPUISTRAAT

VOORBURGWAL

N. NIEUWSTR.

ST. NIC.

NIEUWENDIJK

BEURS-PL.

DAMRAK

DE BIJENKORF DEPT. STORE

DAM

NIEUWEZIJDS

VER. STRAAT

MKT.

AMSTERDAM MUSEUM

RAAM. ST. LUC.

BEGIJN-HOF

HET STEEG

SPUISTRAAT

ROKIN

DAM STR.

PIJLS.

VOORBURGWAL

OUDEZIJDS

L. BRUG GRIMBURGWAL

SPUI

BINN.-STR.

ROKIN

N. DOELEN

MUNT PL.

AMSTEL

HANDB.

COET.

HEILIGE

KALVER-TOREN MALL

SINGEL

REGULIERS.

IJZEL.

TO LEIDSEPLEIN

KONING

HEL REN

FLOWER MARKET

DCH

MINT TOWER

To Hotel Ambassade

AMSTERDAM SLEEPING

6 Café 't Gasthuys

7 De Jaren Café

8 Pannenkoekenhuis Upstairs

9 La Place (V&D Dept. Store)

10 Atrium Univ. Cafeteria

11 Brasserie Rest. de Roode Leeuw

12 Dam Café (De Bijenkorf Dept. Store)

13 Albert Heijn Groceries (4)

14 The Dampkring Coffeeshop

15 Dutch Flowers Coffeeshop

1 To Hotel Ambassade

2 Hotel Résidence Le Coin

3 Hotel Ibis Amsterdam Centre

4 Restaurant Kantjil en de Tijger

5 Kantjil To Go

$$$ Hotel Ibis Amsterdam Centre, located next door to the Central Station, is a modern, efficient, 363-room place. It offers a central location, comfort, and good value, without a hint of charm (Db-€140-160 Nov-Aug, Db-€200 Sept-Oct, breakfast-€16, check website for deals, book long in advance—especially for Sept-Oct, air-con, elevators, free Wi-Fi, pay Internet access; facing Central Station, go left toward the multistory bicycle garage to Stationsplein 49; tel. 020/522-2899, fax 020/522-2889, www.ibishotel.com, h1556@accor.com). When business is slow, usually in mid-summer, they occasionally rent rooms to same-day drop-ins for around €110.

Budget Hotels Between Dam Square and the Anne Frank House

Inexpensive, well-worn hotels line the convenient but noisy and unromantic main drag, Raadhuisstraat. Expect a long, steep, and depressing stairway, with noisy rooms in the front and quieter rooms in the back. Though neither of the places below serves breakfast, they're both steps from a recommended pancake house. For locations, see the map on page 192.

$ Hotel Pax has 11 large, plain, but airy rooms with Ikea furniture—a lot like a European dorm room (S-€35-45, D-€65, Db-€85, T-€100, Tb-€120, prices drop dramatically in winter, no breakfast, five rooms share two showers and two toilets, Raadhuisstraat 37, tel. 020/624-9735, hotelpax@tiscali.nl, run by go-getters Philip and Pieter).

$ Hotel Aspen, a few doors away and a great value for a budget hotel, has eight tidy, stark, and well-maintained rooms (S-€40, tiny D-€55-65, Db-€75-80, Tb-€95, Qb-€110, prices same 365 days a year, no breakfast, free Internet access and Wi-Fi, Raadhuisstraat 31, tel. 020/626-6714, fax 020/620-0866, www.hotelaspen.nl, info@hotelaspen.nl, run by kindhearted Rudy and Esam).

Hostels

Amsterdam has a world of good, cheap hostels located throughout the city. Most are designed for the party crowd, but here are a few quieter options. They all offer dorm beds; Stayokay Vondelpark also has some basic doubles.

In the Jordaan: **$ The Shelter Jordan** is a scruffy, friendly, Christian-run, 90-bed place in a great neighborhood. Although most of Amsterdam's hostels are pretty wild, this place is drug- and alcohol-free, with boys on one floor and girls on another. These are Amsterdam's best budget beds (bunks dorms-€26-31; higher prices for 4-5-bed rooms; includes sheets and breakfast, Internet access in lobby, free Wi-Fi, near Anne Frank House at Bloemstraat 179, tel. 020/624-4717, www.shelter.nl, jordan@shelter.nl). The Shelter serves hot meals; runs a snack bar in its big, relaxing lounge; offers lockers; and leads nightly Bible studies.

In the Red Light District: **$ The Shelter City** is Shelter Jordan's sister—similar, but definitely not preaching to the local choir. And though its 180 beds are buried in the heart of the red lights, it feels very well-run and perfectly safe (same prices as Shelter Jordan, bunks in Qb-€6 extra, D-€49 for spouses or single-sex; same amenities, rules, and Bible study; Barndesteeg 21, see map on page 110, tel. 020/625-3230, fax 020/623-2282, www .shelter.nl, city@shelter.nl).

In Vondelpark: **$ Stayokay Vondelpark (IYHF),** with 536 beds in 130 rooms, is one of Amsterdam's top hostels for the under-25 set—but over-25s will feel comfortable here too (€21-42/bed in 4- to 20-bed dorms, D-€60-105—most with bunk beds, higher prices are for March-Oct, members save €2.50, price depends on demand—cheapest when booked in advance, family rooms, lots of school groups, lockers, laundry, pay Internet access, free Wi-Fi, bike rental, right on Vondelpark at Zandpad 5, tel. 020/589-8996, fax 020/589-8955, www.stayokay.com, vondelpark@stayokay.com). Though Stayokay Vondelpark and Stayokay Stadsdoelen (listed next) are generally booked long in advance, occasionally a few beds open up each day at 11:00.

Near Waterlooplein: **$ Stayokay Stadsdoelen (IYHF),** smaller and simpler than its Vondelpark sister (listed above), has only large dorms and no private bathrooms, but is free of large school groups. Because of the lower prices, this one caters mostly to twentysomethings (€18-35/bed with sheets and breakfast in 10-bed dorms, members save €2.50, price depends on demand— cheapest when booked in advance, lockers, pay Internet access, free Wi-Fi, bike rental, Kloveniersburgwal 97, see map on page 74, tel. 020/624-6832, fax 020/639-1035, www.stayokay.com, stadsdoelen @stayokay.com).

Farthest East: **$ Stayokay Zeeburg (IYHF)** is a 500-bed hostel with all the modern services. While it's pretty far from the center, by tram or bike you're just 15 minutes from Damrak street. Oldsters fit in here with the youngsters (€24-42/bed in 4- to 9-bed dorms, price depends on demand—cheapest when booked in advance, pay Internet access, free Wi-Fi, lockers, games, restau-rant, bike rental, tram #14 to Timorplein 21, tel. 020/551-3190, fax 020/623-4986, www.stayokay.com, zeeburg@stayokay.com).

EATING IN AMSTERDAM

Of Amsterdam's thousand-plus restaurants, no one knows which are best. I'd pick an area and wander. The rowdy food ghetto thrives around Leidseplein; if you don't mind eating in a touristy area, wander along "Restaurant Row" (on Leidsedwarsstraat). The area around Spui Square and that end of Spuistraat is also trendy, and not as noisy. For fewer crowds and more charm, find something in the Jordaan district. Most hoteliers keep a reliable eating list for their neighborhood and know which places keep their travelers happy. I've listed some handy places to consider.

To dine cheaply yet memorably alongside the big spenders, grab a meal to go, then find a bench on a lively neighborhood square or along a canal. Sandwiches *(broodjes)* of delicious cheese on fresh bread are cheap at snack bars, delis, and *broodjes* restaurants. Ethnic restaurants serve cheap, splittable carryout meals. Ethnic fast-food stands abound, offering a variety of meats wrapped in pita bread. Easy to buy at grocery stores, yogurt in the Netherlands (and throughout northern Europe) is delicious and often drinkable right out of its plastic container.

Central Amsterdam

For the locations of these eateries, see the "Hotels and Restaurants in Central Amsterdam" map on page 201.

On and near Spui

Restaurant Kantjil en de Tijger is a thriving place with a plain and noisy ambience, full of happy eaters who know a good value. The food is purely Indonesian; the waiters are happy to explain your many enticing options. Their three *rijsttafels* (traditional "rice tables" with about a dozen small courses) range from €24 to €30 per person. Though they are designed for two people, three people can make a meal by getting a *rijsttafel* for two plus a soup or light dish (daily 12:00-23:00, reservations smart, mostly indoor with a little outdoor seating, Spuistraat 291, tel. 020/620-0994).

Kantjil to Go, run by Restaurant Kantjil, is a tiny take-out bar serving up inexpensive but delicious Indonesian fare. Their printed menu explains the mix-and-match plan (€5 for 300 grams, €6.50 for 600 grams, vegetarian specials, daily 12:00-21:00, store-front at Nieuwezijds Voorburgwal 342, around the back of the sit-down restaurant listed earlier, tel. 020/620-3074). Split a large box, grab a bench on the charming Spui Square around the corner, and you've got perhaps the best cheap, hot meal in town.

Near the Mint Tower

Café 't Gasthuys, one of Amsterdam's many brown cafés (so called for their smoke-stained walls), has a busy dumbwaiter cranking out light lunches, sandwiches, and reasonably priced, if uncreative, dinners. It offers a long bar, a lovely secluded back room, peaceful canalside seating, and sometimes slow service (€6-10 lunch plates, €10 three-course dinner, €11-15 main courses, daily 11:00-16:30 & 17:30-22:00, Grimburgwal 7—from the Rondvaart Kooij boat dock, head down Langebrugsteeg, and it's one block down on the left; tel. 020/624-8230).

De Jaren Café ("The Years") is a chic yet inviting place—clearly a favorite with locals. Upstairs is a minimalist restaurant with a top-notch salad bar and canal-view deck (serving €16-20 dinners after 17:30, prices include salad bar plus fish, meat, and veggie dishes; €14 for salad bar only). Downstairs is a modern café, great for light lunches (soups, salads, and sandwiches served all day and evening) or just coffee over a newspaper. On a sunny day, the café's canalside patio is a fine spot to nurse a drink; this is also a nice place to go just for a drink in the evening and to enjoy the spacious Art Deco setting (daily 9:30-23:00, a long block up from Muntplein at Nieuwe Doelenstraat 20-22, tel. 020/625-5771).

Pannenkoekenhuis Upstairs is a tiny, characteristic perch up some extremely steep stairs, where Arno and Ali cook and serve delicious €6-12 pancakes to four tables throughout the afternoon. They'll tell you that I discovered this place long before Anthony Bourdain did (Mon-Fri 12:00-19:00, Sat 12:00-18:00, Sun 12:00-17:00, Grimburgwal 2, tel. 020/626-5603).

La Place, on the ground floor of the V&D department store, has an abundant, colorful array of fresh, appealing food served cafeteria-style. A multistory eatery that seats 300, it has a small outdoor terrace upstairs. Explore before you make your choice. This bustling spot has a lively market feel, with everything from made-on-the-spot beef stir-fry, to fresh juice, to veggie soups

(€4 pizza and €5 sandwiches, Sun-Mon 11:00-19:00, Tue-Wed 10:00-19:30, Thu-Sat 10:00-21:00, at the end of Kalverstraat near Mint Tower, tel. 020/622-0171). For fast and healthy take-out food (sandwiches, yogurt, fruit cups, and more), try the bakery on the department store's ground floor. (They run another branch, which has the city's ultimate view terrace, on the top floor of the **Central Library**—Openbare Bibliotheek Amsterdam—near Central Station.)

Atrium University Cafeteria, a three-minute walk from Mint Tower, feeds travelers and students from Amsterdam University for great prices, but only on weekdays (€7 meals, Mon-Fri 11:00-15:00 & 17:00-19:30; from Spui, walk west down Landebrug Steeg past canalside Café 't Gasthuys three blocks to Oudezijds Achterburgwal 237, then go through arched doorway on the right; tel. 020/525-3999).

Between Central Station and Dam Square

Brasserie Restaurant de Roode Leeuw ("Red Lion") offers a peaceful respite from the crush of Damrak. While this old standby is somewhat overpriced these days, you can still get a menu filled with traditional Dutch food, good service, and the company of plenty of tourists. The *stamppot* (pickled pork loin with bacon and mashed potatoes) is an adventure in Dutch comfort food. Call ahead to reserve a window seat (€17-25 entrées, €33 three-course fixed-price meal with traditional Dutch choices; daily 12:00-22:00, Damrak 93-94, tel. 020/555-0666).

Dam Café, on the first floor of the De Bijenkorf department store on Dam Square, has a small lineup of tasty salads, sandwiches, and desserts. Enjoying views of busy Damrak, comfortable (but limited) seating, and an upscale café vibe, you'll feel miles above the chaotic streets below (€8-11 salads; Sun-Mon 11:00-20:00; Tue-Sat 10:00-20:00, Thu-Fri until 21:00; Dam 1, tel. 088-245-9080). For a much wider range of dishes and lots of seating—but no Dam views—head up to **Kitchen,** the store's swanky fifth-floor self-service restaurant (similar prices and hours to café).

Munching Cheap

Traditional fish stands sell €4 herring sandwiches and other salty treats, usually from easy photo menus. **Stubbe's Haring,** where the Stubbe family has been selling herring for 100 years, is handy and well-established, a few blocks from Central Station (Tue-Fri 10:00-18:00, Sat 10:00-17:00, closed Sun-Mon, at the locks on Singel canal, near the train station, see map on page 192). Grab a sandwich and have a canalside picnic.

Supermarkets: You'll see **Albert Heijn** grocery stores (daily 8:00-22:00) all over town. They have great deli sections with picnic-perfect take-away salads and sandwiches. Helpful, central locations include behind the Royal Palace on Dam Square (Nieuwezijds Voorburgwal 226), near the Mint Tower (Koningsplein 4), on Leidsestraat (at Konigsplein, on the corner of Leidsestraat and Singel), and inside Central Station (far end of passage under the tracks). Be aware that none of their stores accept US credit cards: Bring cash, and don't get in the checkout lines marked *PIN alleen*.

West Amsterdam

Near the Anne Frank House and in the Jordaan District

Nearly all of these places are within a few scenic blocks of the Anne Frank House, providing handy lunches and atmospheric dinners in Amsterdam's most charming neighborhood. For locations, see the map on page 192.

Restaurant de Luwte is romantic, located on a picturesque street overlooking a canal. It has lots of candles, a muted but fresh modern interior, spacious seating, a few cool outdoor canalside tables, and French Mediterranean cuisine (€20 main dishes, €30 three-course fixed-price dinners, big salads for €18, daily 18:00-22:00, Leliegracht 26-28, tel. 020/625-8548, manager Maarten).

De Bolhoed has serious vegetarian and vegan food in a colorful setting that Buddha would dig, with a clientele that appears to dig Buddha (big splittable portions, €15 dinners, light lunches, daily 12:00-22:00, dinner starts at 17:00, Prinsengracht 60, tel. 020/626-1803).

Café Restaurant de Reiger must offer the best cooking of any *eetcafé* in the Jordaan. Famous for its fresh ingredients and delightful bistro ambience, it's part of the classic Jordaan scene. In addition to an English menu, ask for a translation of the daily specials (€18-20) on the chalkboard. They're proud of their fresh fish and French-Dutch cuisine. The café, which is crowded late and on weekends, takes no reservations, but you're welcome to have a drink (€3 house wine and fun little bar munchies menu) at the bar while you wait (Tue-Sun 17:00-24:00, closed Mon, veggie options, Nieuwe Leliestraat 34, tel. 020/624-7426).

Café 't Smalle is extremely charming, with three zones where you can enjoy a light lunch or a drink: canalside, inside around the bar, and up some steep stairs in a quaint little back room. The café is open late, and simple meals (salads, soup, and fresh sandwiches) are served 11:00-17:30 (plenty of fine €3-4 Belgian beers on tap, interesting wines by the glass, at Egelantiersgracht 12—where it hits Prinsengracht, tel. 020/623-9617).

Thai Fusion, despite the name, serves straight-up top-quality Thai food in a sleekly modern, black-and-white room wedged neatly in the middle of the Nine Little Streets action (€15-20 main courses, €25-30 two-course meals, daily 16:30-22:30, good veggie options, Berenstraat 8, tel. 020/320-8332).

Toscana Italian Restaurant is the Jordaan's favorite place for good, inexpensive Italian cuisine, served in a woody, Dutch-beer-hall setting (€6-9 pizza and pastas, €16 main courses, Sun-Wed 16:00-23:30, Thu-Sat 12:00-23:30, fast service, Haarlemmerstraat 130, tel. 020/622-0353).

Winkel, the North Jordaan's cornerside hangout, serves appetizing Euro-Dutch meals at its plentiful outside tables and easygoing interior. It really gets hopping on Monday mornings, when the Noordermarkt flea market is underway, but Amsterdammers come from across town all week for the *appeltaart* (€11-14 dinner plates, €5 snacks served after 16:00, daily 8:00-late, Noordermarkt 43, tel. 020/623-0223).

Sara's Pancake House is a basic pancake diner where extremely hardworking Sara cranks out sweet and savory €8-12 flapjacks made from fresh, organic ingredients (daily until 22:30, later on weekends, breakfast served until noon, Raadhuisstraat 45, tel. 020/320-0662).

Restaurant 't Stuivertje is a small, family-run neighborhood eatery tucked away in the Jordaan, serving French-inspired Dutch cuisine in an elegantly cozy but unpretentious atmosphere (€15-25 main courses, dinner salads, Wed-Sun 17:30-22:00, closed Mon-Tue, near Elandsgracht at Hazenstraat 58, tel. 020/623-1349).

Ristorante Toscanini is an up-market Italian place that's always packed. It's so popular that the staff can be a bit arrogant, but the lively, spacious ambience and great Italian cuisine more than make up for that—if you can get a seat. Reservations are essentially required (the staff recommends two weeks' notice for Fri and Sat). Otherwise your best bet is to arrive when they open at 18:00 (€10-14 first courses, €16-25 main courses, Mon-Sat 18:00-22:30, closed Sun, deep in the Jordaan at Lindengracht 75, tel. 020/623-2813).

Villa Zeesicht has all the romantic feel of a classic European café. The cozy interior is crammed with tiny tables topped by tall candlesticks, and wicker chairs outside gather under a wisteria-covered awning. The menu is uninventive—come here instead for the famous *appeltaart* and for the great people-watching on Torensluis bridge (€11-16 plates, daily 9:00-21:30, Torensteeg 7, tel. 020/626-7433).

Drinks Only: **Café 't Papeneiland** is a classic brown café with Delft tiles, an evocative old stove, and a stay-awhile perch overlooking a canal with welcoming benches. It's been the neighborhood hangout since the 17th century (drinks but no food, overlooking northwest end of Prinsengracht at #2, tel. 020/624-1989). It feels a little exclusive; patrons who come here to drink and chat aren't eager to see it overrun by tourists. The café's name means "Papists' Island," since this was once a refuge for Catholics; there used to be an escape tunnel here for priests on the run.

Southwest Amsterdam

Near Leidseplein

Stroll through the colorful cancan of eateries on Lange Leidse-dwarsstraat, the "Restaurant Row" just off Leidseplein, and choose your favorite (but don't expect intimacy or good value). Nearby, busy Leidsestraat offers plenty of starving-student options (between Prinsengracht and Herengracht) offering fast and fun food for around €5 a meal.

To escape the crowds without too long a walk from Leidse-plein, wander a few blocks away from the hubbub to Lijnbaans-gracht (via Kleine Gartmanplantsoen, the street to the right of The Bulldog Café). At **Restaurant Dubbel,** for example, the steak, fish, and veggie dishes are reasonably priced (€12-15), the bartenders are extra friendly, and you'll actually hear customers speaking Dutch (daily 17:00-24:00, Lijnbaansgracht 256, tel. 020/620-0909).

Beyond the Rijksmuseum

Restaurant Bazar offers one of the most memorable and fun budget eating experiences in town. Converted from a church, it has spacious seating and mod belly-dance music, and is filled with young locals enjoying good, cheap Middle Eastern and North African cuisine. Reservations are a good idea if you plan to eat after 20:00 (fill up with the €8.50 daily plate, delicious €13 couscous, or €16 main dishes; Mon-Fri 11:00-late, Sat-Sun 9:00-late, Albert Cuypstraat 182, tel. 020/675-0544). Restaurant Bazar marks the center of the thriving Albert Cuyp market, which is wrapped up by about 17:00, though the restaurant stays busy late into the evening.

In Vondelpark

Café Vertigo offers a fun selection of excellent soups, salads, and sandwiches, plus main courses such as steak, fish, and satays. However, due to a change in ownership, it may be closed or have a new name when you visit (daily 10:00-24:00 except opens at 11:00 on off-season weekdays, Vondelpark 3, tel. 020/612-3021).

Southeast Amsterdam

The following eateries are near the Dutch Resistance Museum. For locations, see the map on page 74.

Restaurant Plancius, adjacent to the Dutch Resistance Museum, is a handy, modern spot for lunch. Its good indoor and outdoor seating make it popular with the museum staff and broadcasters from the nearby local TV studios (creative breakfasts, hearty fresh sandwiches, light €6-9 lunches and €16-19 dinners, daily 10:00-22:00, Plantage Kerklaan 61a, tel. 020/330-9469).

Café Koosje, located halfway between the Dutch Resistance Museum and the Dutch Theater, is a corner lunchtime pub/bar ringed with outdoor seating. Inside, casual wooden tables and benches huddle under chandeliers, and the hip, young waitstaff serve beer and salads big enough for two (€5 sandwiches, €11 salads, €14-17 dinners, food served daily 9:00-22:00, on the corner of Plantage Kerklaan at Plantage Middenlaan 37, tel. 020/320-0817).

SMOKING

The Dutch have a long (and complicated) relationship with smoking, whether marijuana or tobacco. This chapter considers Dutch tobacco habits, explains the current (and frequently changing) Dutch laws regarding marijuana, and offers advice both on how marijuana-selling "coffeeshops" work, and which ones in Amsterdam may be worth a visit.

Tobacco

A quarter of Dutch people smoke tobacco. Holland has a long tradition as a smoking culture, being among the first to import the tobacco plant from the New World. (For a history of smoking, visit the fascinating Pipe Museum, described on page 64.)

Tobacco shops, such as the House of Hajenius (described on page 100), glorify the habit, yet the Dutch people are among the healthiest in the world. Tanned, trim, firm, sixtysomething Dutch people sip their beer, take a drag, and ask me why Americans murder themselves with Big Macs.

Still, the Dutch version of the Surgeon General is speaking out loud and clear about the health risks of smoking. Warning stickers bigger than America's are required on cigarette packs, and some of them are almost comically blunt—for example, "Smoking will make you impotent...and then you die."

Since 2008, a Dutch law has outlawed smoking tobacco almost everywhere indoors: trains, hotel rooms, restaurants, bars... and even marijuana-dealing coffeeshops.

Marijuana (a.k.a. Cannabis)

For tourists from lands where you can do hard time for lighting up, the open use of marijuana here can feel either somewhat disturbing, or exhilaratingly liberating...or maybe just refreshingly sane. Several decades after being legalized in the Netherlands, marijuana causes about as much excitement here as a bottle of beer. When tourists call an ambulance after smoking too much pot, medics just say, "Drink something sweet and walk it off."

Marijuana Laws and "Coffeeshops"

Throughout the Netherlands, you'll see "coffeeshops"—cafés selling marijuana, with display cases showing various joints or baggies for sale.

Rules and Regulations: The retail sale of marijuana is strictly regulated, and proceeds are taxed. The minimum age for purchase is 18, and coffeeshops can sell up to five grams of marijuana per person per day. It's also illegal for these shops (or anyone) to advertise marijuana. In fact, in many places, the prospective customer has to take the initiative, and ask to see the menu. In some coffeeshops, you actually have to push and hold down a button to see an illuminated menu—the contents of which look like the inventory of a drug bust.

Shops sell marijuana and hashish both in pre-rolled joints and in little baggies. Joints are generally sold individually (€3-5, depending on the strain you choose), though some places sell only small packs of three or four joints. Baggies usually cost €10-15. Some shops charge per gram. The better pot, though costlier, is actually a better value, as it takes less to get high—and it's a better high.

Each coffeeshop is allowed to keep an inventory of about a pound of pot in stock: The tax authorities don't want to see more than this on the books at the end of each accounting cycle, and a shop can lose its license if it exceeds this amount. A popular shop—whose supply must be replenished five or six times a day—simply has to put up with the hassle of constantly taking small deliveries. A shop can sell a ton of pot with no legal problems, as long as it maintains that tiny stock and just refills it as needed. The reason? Authorities want shops to stay small and not become export bases.

Smoking Tips: Shops have loaner bongs and inhalers, and dispense rolling papers like toothpicks. As long as you're a paying customer (e.g., you buy a cup of coffee), you can pop into any coffeeshop and light up, even if you didn't buy your pot there.

Tourists who haven't smoked pot since their college days are famous for overindulging in Amsterdam. Coffeeshop baristas nickname tourists about to pass out "Whitey"—the color their faces turn just before they hit the floor. They warn Americans (who aren't used to the strength of the local stuff) to try a lighter leaf. If you do overdo it, the key is to eat or drink something sweet to avoid getting sick. Cola is a good fast fix, and coffeeshops keep sugar tablets handy.

Don't ever buy pot on the street in Amsterdam. Well-established coffeeshops are considered much safer, and coffeeshop owners have an interest in keeping their trade safe and healthy. They're also generally very patient in explaining the varieties available.

Types of Cannabis: The Dutch sell several forms of the cannabis plant: They smoke both hashish (the sap of the cannabis plant) and the leaf of the plant (which they call "marihuana" or "grass"). While each shop has different brands, it's all derived from two types of marijuana plant: *Cannabis indica* and *Cannabis sativa*. *Indica* gets you a stoned, heavy, mellow, "couch-weed" high. *Sativa* is light, fun, uplifting, and more psychedelic. *Sativa* makes you giggle.

Most of the pot sold in Dutch coffeeshops is grown locally, as coffeeshops know it's much safer to deal with Dutch-grown plants than to import marijuana (the EU, as you might imagine, prohibits any international drug trade). Technological advances have made it easier to cultivate exotic strains. You may see joints described as if they'd come from overseas, e.g. "Thai"—and indeed the strain in that joint may have originated elsewhere—but it's still Dutch-grown. "Netherlands weed" is now refined, like wine. Most shops get their inventory from the pot equivalent of local home- or micro-brewers. Shops with better "boutique suppliers" develop a reputation for having better-quality weed. (These are the places that proudly display a decal announcing them as winners at Amsterdam's annual Cannabis Cup Awards.)

Tobacco and Marijuana: While most American pot-smokers like their joints made purely of marijuana, the Dutch (like most Europeans) are accustomed to mixing tobacco with marijuana. Back in the 1970s, most "pot smokers" here smoked hash, which needs to be mixed with something else (like tobacco) to light up. Today, more Dutch prefer "herbal cannabis"—the marijuana bud common in the US—but they still keep the familiar tobacco in their joints. Tobacco-mixed joints also go back to hippie days, when pot was expensive and it was simply wasteful to pass around a pure marijuana joint. Mixing in tobacco allowed poor hippies to be generous without going broke. And since the Dutch don't dry and cure their marijuana, it's simply hard to smoke without tobacco.

The Netherlands' indoor-smoking ban pertains to tobacco

smoke, not pot smoke. It might seem strange to an American, but these days, if a coffeeshop is busted, it's for tobacco. Coffeeshops with a few outdoor seats have a huge advantage, as their customers can light up outside. Shops without the outdoor option are in for an extra challenge, as many local smokers would rather get their weed to go than smoke it without tobacco at their neighborhood coffeeshop. Prerolled joints are now sold three ways: pure, with the nontobacco "hamburger helper" herb mix, or with tobacco. Any place that caters to Americans will have joints without tobacco, but you have to ask specifically for a "pure" joint.

The Dutch Approach to Marijuana

To foreign visitors, the Netherlands can seem frighteningly comfortable with—even nonchalant about—drug use. But the Dutch are well aware of the problems associated with drugs, especially addictive ones. (The Dutch word for addiction is "enslavement.") Most also believe that the concept of a "victimless crime" is a contradiction in terms: Any drug-related behavior that affects others is taken seriously. Drive under the influence of anything and you're toast. Because of their wide-reaching social costs, heroin and cocaine are strictly illegal in the Netherlands, and the police stringently enforce laws prohibiting their sale and use.

The Dutch are not even necessarily pro-marijuana; most people here simply believe that outlawing marijuana creates more problems than it solves—and statistics indicate they may be right. No one here would say that smoking pot was healthy. It's a drug. It's dangerous, and it can be abused. But the Dutch have chosen to allow marijuana's responsible adult use as a civil liberty, and treat its abuse as a health-care and education challenge rather than a crime.

Many Dutch believe that America's drug policy is based on fear, misinformation, and electoral politics. After several decades of not arresting pot smokers, the Dutch can point to studies showing that they smoke less than the European average—and fewer than half as many Dutch smoke pot, per capita, as Americans do. (My Dutch friends also enjoy pointing out that, while the three most recent US presidents admitted or implied that they had smoked marijuana, no Dutch prime minister ever has.) The Dutch have found that strict regulation of the soft-drug trade has helped minimize many of the problems associated with it, such as street crime, gang warfare, and hard-drug use.

So what am I? Pro-marijuana? Let's put it this way: I agree with the Dutch people, who remind me that a society either has to allow some room for drug use on the less-harmful end of the spectrum...or build more prisons. About 800,000 Americans are arrested every year for simple possession of marijuana. While a

New Pressure to Re-Criminalize Marijuana

Dutch pot-smokers complain that the generation that ran naked on acid around Amsterdam's Vondelpark during the '60s is now threatening the Netherlands' well-established, regulated marijuana trade.

Responding to international pressure and conservatives in rural and small-town Holland, the federal government is cracking down on coffeeshops. While they're still allowed to sell marijuana, many aspects of these businesses' operations exist in a legal limbo, with certain restrictions usually going unenforced—until now.

Neighboring countries (France and Germany) have complained that it's too easy for citizens to make drug runs across the border, returning home with lots of pot. In response, some Dutch border towns implemented a "weed pass" system, allowing pot sales only to registered Dutch citizens. But the independent-minded Dutch (especially young people) don't want to be registered as pot users, so they're buying it on the street—rekindling the black market, and, many fear, the crime and social problems associated with it.

In 2012, marijuana tourists—and the businesses that rely on them—panicked when it was announced that a similar "weed pass" would go into effect nationwide. But a newly elected national government withdrew the plan, leaving the weed-pass decision up to each individual city. Amsterdam's coffeeshops remain open to the general public.

In general, Amsterdam city leaders recognize that legalized marijuana and the Red Light District's prostitution are part of the city's edgy charm; the mayor wants to keep both, but get rid of the accompanying sleaze. Amsterdam recognizes the pragmatic wisdom of its progressive policies and is bucking the federal shift to the right. Locals don't want shady people pushing drugs in dark alleys; they'd rather see marijuana sold in regulated shops.

A 2011 law sought to close coffeeshops near schools, including the landmark Bulldog Café on Leidseplein (it's still open). And coffeeshop-licenses are not being renewed in some neighborhoods—the number of coffeeshops in Amsterdam has fallen from a peak of more than 700 (in the mid-1990s) to about 200 today. But Amsterdam's mayor has vowed to keep its central coffeeshops open...and with all the talk of new restrictions, coffeeshops are on their best behavior (and are being very careful to nurture good relations with their neighbors).

A 2013 law allows individual coffeeshops to ban foreigners, if they choose (a shop-by-shop variation on the "weed pass"). By the time you visit, new developments will surely have taken place—stay tuned.

wide variety of Americans smoke pot, the people prosecuted for possessing it are disproportionately poor and/or black or Latino.

If you'd like to learn more about marijuana (and don't feel like Googling "Rick Steves marijuana"), drop by Amsterdam's Cannabis College or the Hash, Marijuana, and Hemp Museum (both located on Oudezijds Achterburgwal street—see pages 123-126). Back home, if you'd like to support an outfit dedicated to taking the crime out of pot, read up on the National Organization for the Reform of Marijuana Laws (www.norml.org).

Coffeeshops in Amsterdam

Most of downtown Amsterdam's coffeeshops feel grungy and

foreboding to American travelers who aren't part of the youth-hostel crowd. The neighborhood places (and those in small towns around the countryside) are much more inviting to people without piercings, tattoos, and favorite techno artists. I've listed a few places with a more pub-like ambience for Americans wanting to go local, but within reason. For locations, see the maps in the Sleeping in Amsterdam chapter.

Paradox is the most *gezellig* (cozy) coffeeshop I found—a mellow, graceful place. The managers, Ludo and Wiljan, and their staff are patient with descriptions and happy to walk you through all your options. This is a

rare coffeeshop that serves light meals. The juice is fresh, the music is easy, and the neighborhood is charming (single tobacco-free joints-€3, loaner bongs, games, free Wi-Fi, daily 10:00-20:00, two blocks from Anne Frank House at Eerste Bloemdwarsstraat 2, tel. 020/623-5639, www.paradoxcoffee shop.com).

The Grey Area—a hole-in-the-wall spot with three tiny tables—is a cool, welcoming, and smoky place appreciated among local aficionados as a perennial winner of Amsterdam's Cannabis Cup awards. Judging by the autographed photos on the wall, many famous Americans have dropped in (say hi to Willie Nelson). You're welcome to just nurse a bottomless cup of coffee. It's run by friendly American Jon, with helpful Adam and Stevan. They even have a vaporizer if you want to try "smoking" without smoking (daily 12:00-20:00, they close relatively early out of consideration for their neighbors, between Dam Square and Anne Frank House at Oude Leliestraat 2, tel. 020/420-4301, www.greyarea.nl).

Siberië Coffeeshop is a short walk from Central Station, but feels cozy, with a friendly canalside ambience. Clean, big, and bright, this place has the vibe of a mellow Starbucks (daily 11:00-23:00, Fri-Sat until 24:00, free Wi-Fi for customers, helpful staff, English menu, Brouwersgracht 11, tel. 020/623-5909, www.coffee shopsiberie.nl).

La Tertulia is a sweet little mother-and-daughter-run place with pastel decor and a cheery terrarium atmosphere (Tue-Sat 11:00-19:00, closed Sun-Mon, sandwiches, brownies, games, Prinsengracht 312).

The Bulldog Café is the high-profile, leading touristy chain of coffeeshops. These establishments are young but welcoming,

with reliable selections. They're pretty comfortable for green tourists wanting to just hang out for a while. The flagship branch, in a former police station right on Leidseplein, is very handy, offering alcohol upstairs, pot downstairs, and fun outdoor seating. It's the rare place where you can have a beer while you smoke and watch the world skateboard by (daily 10:00-1:00 in the morning, Fri-Sat until 3:00, Leidseplein 17, tel. 020/625-6278, www.thebull dog.com). Their original café still sits on the canal near the Old Church in the Red Light District (see page 114).

The Dampkring is a rough-and-ready constant party. It's a high-profile, busy place, filled with a young clientele and loud music, but the owners still take the time to explain what they offer. Scenes from the movie *Ocean's Twelve* were filmed here (daily 10:00-1:00 in the morning, close to Spui at Handboogstraat 29, tel. 020/638-0705, www.dampkring.nl).

Dutch Flowers, conveniently located near Spui square on Singel canal, has a very casual "brown café" ambience, with a mature set of regulars. A couple of tables overlooking the canal are perfect for enjoying the late-afternoon sunshine (daily 10:00-23:00, until later Fri-Sat, on the corner of Heisteeg and Singel at Singel 387, tel. 020/624-7624).

SHOPPING IN AMSTERDAM

Amsterdam brings out the browser even in those who were not born to shop. Ten general markets, open six days a week (generally 9:30-17:00, closed Sun), keep folks who brake for garage sales pulling U-turns. Markets include Waterlooplein (the flea market), the huge Albert Cuyp street market, and various flower markets (such as the Singel canal Flower Market near the Mint Tower).

For information on shopping, pick up the TI's *Shopping in Amsterdam* brochure. To find out how to get a VAT (Value-Added Tax) refund on your purchases, see page 13. While the Netherlands has closed most of its post offices, you can still mail your purchases home (ask your hotelier for the nearest ersatz post office, or use Service Point, a shipping service at Schiphol Airport—see page 227).

Most shops in the center are open 10:00-18:00 (Thu until 21:00); the businesslike Dutch know no siesta, but many shopkeepers take Sunday and Monday mornings off. Supermarkets are generally open Monday-Saturday 8:00-20:00, with shorter hours on Sunday; most Albert Heijn grocery stores, however, are open until 22:00 every day.

Department Stores

When you need to buy something but don't know where to go, two chain stores—Hema and Vroom & Dreesmann (V&D)—are handy for everything from inexpensive clothes and notebooks to food and cosmetics. **Hema** is at Kalverstraat 212, in the Kalvertoren mall (Mon 11:00-18:30, Tue-Sat 9:30-18:30 except Thu until 21:00, Sun 12:00-18:30) and at Central Station (similar hours). **Vroom & Dreesmann,** with its great La Place cafeteria, is at Kalverstraat 203 (Sun-Mon 12:00-19:00, Tue-Wed 10:00-19:30, Thu-Sat 10:00-20:00, cafeteria on ground floor has longer hours—

see page 205).

The **De Bijenkorf** department store is old-time fancy and central on Dam Square; its little café on the first floor up is perfect for people-watching out over the square (see page 206).

Amsterdam's Top Shopping Zones

Jordaan—The Jordaan, with its main drag Westerstraat, is a veritable wonderland of funky, artsy shops. Once a working-class district, this colorful, old neighborhood is now upscale. On Mondays you'll find the busy Noordermarkt market at the end of Westerstraat and spilling onto the neighboring street, Lindengracht.

Leidsestraat—This bustling shopping street has trendy, elegant shops.

The Nine Little Streets—De Negen Straatjes is home to 190 diverse shops mixing festive, creative, nostalgic, practical, and artistic items. Trendy cafés dot the area. The cross streets make a tic-tac-toe with a couple of canals and bicycle-friendly canalside streets just west of Kalverstraat. Look for the zone where Harten-straat, Wolvenstraat, and Huidenstraat cross the Keizersgracht and Herengracht canals (see the color map at the beginning of this book). Walking west from the Amsterdam Museum puts you right in the thick of things.

Kalverstraat-Heiligeweg-Spui—This is the busiest shopping corridor in town. Kalverstraat, a pedestrian street, is a human traf-fic jam of low-end shoppers. It feels soulless, but if you explore the fringes, there are some interesting places.

Spiegelkwartier—Located between the Rijksmuseum and the city center, this is *the* place for art and antiques. You'll find 70 dealers offering 17th-century furniture, old Delftware, Oriental art, clocks, jewelry, and Art Nouveau doodads. Wander down Spiegelgracht and Nieuwe Spiegelstraat.

Prinsheerlijk—Along Herenstraat and Prinsenstraat, you'll find high-end fashion, interior design, and gift shops. If you're looking for jewelry, accessories, trendy clothing, and fancy delicatessens, this may be an expensive but rewarding stroll.

Magna Plaza Shopping Center—Formerly the main post office, this grand 19th-century building has been transformed into a stylish mall with 40 boutiques. You'll find fashion, luxury goods, and gift shops galore. It's just behind the Royal Palace a block off Dam Square (see page 128).

P. C. Hooftstraat—The city's most expensive shopping street, with a storefront for nearly every top-name designer, is between Museumplein and Vondelpark.

Albert Cuyp Market—Amsterdam's biggest open-air market, stretching for several blocks along Albert Cuypstraat, bustles daily (roughly 9:00-17:00) except Sunday. You'll find fish, exotic vegetables, bolts of fabric, pantyhose, bargain clothes, native Dutch and ethnic food stands (especially *stroopwafels* and Surinamese *rotis*), and great people-watching. It's located a 10-minute walk east of Museumplein and a block south of the Heineken Experience (tram #16 or #24).

Popular Souvenirs

Amsterdam has lots of one-of-a-kind specialty stores. Poke around and see what you can find. If you want to bring home edibles and drinkables, see page 14 for restrictions.

Wooden Shoes—Once crucial for navigating soggy Amsterdam, these are now simply something fun to clomp around in.

Delftware—Ceramic plates, vases, and tiles decorated with a fake Chinese blue-and-white design popularized in the 1600s. Only a few licensed places sell the real stuff (expensive) and antiques (very expensive). You can find fireplace tiles (cheap) at most gift shops.

Diamonds—Diamonds have been a big Dutch commodity ever since Golden Age traders first exploited the mines of Africa. In Amsterdam, you can get them cut or uncut, expensive or really expensive. Diamond dealers offer free cutting and polishing demos at their shops. Gassan Diamonds, near Rembrandt's House, is best (page 75); Coster is on Potterstraat, behind the Rijksmuseum (page 56).

Jenever—Dutch gin (made from juniper berries) is sold in traditional stone bottles.

Marijuana Pipes—These need to be clean and unused, because even a little residue can get you busted at US Customs (yes, even in Colorado and Washington). Note that, these days, American laws are written in a way that—technically—even importing an unused pipe could get you arrested.

Chocolate—Belgian or Dutch Verkade or Droste cocoa are sold in tins.

Flower Seeds and Bulbs—Look for ones that are packed with a seal that promises they are US Customs-friendly.

Posters and Art Postcards—There's a good selection at the Van Gogh Museum bookshop (also sells protective mailing tubes).

Old Maps—They capture the Dutch Golden Age.

Old Books—You can find treasures in musty bookstores.

ENTERTAINMENT IN AMSTERDAM

Many Amsterdam hotels serve breakfast until 11:00 because so many people—visitors and locals—live for nighttime in this city.

On summer evenings, people flock to the main squares for drinks at outdoor tables. Leidseplein is the liveliest square, surrounded by theaters, restaurants, and nightclubs. The slightly quieter Rembrandtplein (with adjoining Thorbeckeplein and nearby Reguliersdwarsstraat) is the center of gay clubs and nightlife. Spui features a full city block of bars. And Nieuwmarkt, on the east edge of the Red Light District, is a bit rough, but is probably the least touristy.

The Red Light District (particularly Oudezijds Achterburgwal) is less sleazy in the early evening, and almost carnival-like as the neon lights come on and the streets fill with tour groups. But it starts to feel scuzzy after about 22:30 (❂ see the Red Light District Walk chapter).

Information

Newsstands sell *Time Out Amsterdam* and Dutch newspapers (Thu editions generally list events). The free, irreverent *Boom!* has the basics on the youth and nightlife scene, and is packed with practical tips and countercultural insights (includes €5 discount on Boom Chicago comedy theater act described on next page; available at TIs and many bars). *Uitkrant* is in Dutch, but it's just a calendar of events, and anyone can figure out the name of the event and its date, time, and location (available at TIs, bars, and bookstores).

Box Office: The **AUB/Last Minute Ticket Shop** at Stadsschouwburg Theater is the best one-stop-shopping box office for theater, classical music, and major rock shows. The Last Minute window sells half-price, same-day tickets to certain shows;

half-price sales start at noon (Mon-Fri 10:00-19:00, Sat 10:00-18:00, Sun 12:00-18:00, Leidseplein 26, tel. 0900-0191—€0.40/minute, www.lastminuteticketshop.nl).

Music

You'll find classical music at the **Concertgebouw** (free 12:30 lunch concerts on Wed; arrive at 12:00 for best first-come, first-serve seating; at far south end of Museumplein, tel. 0900-671-8345, www.concertgebouw.nl). For chamber music and contemporary works, visit the **Muziekgebouw aan 't IJ,** a mod concert hall on the waterfront, near the train station (Piet Heinkade 1, tel. 020/788-2000, www.muziekgebouw.nl). For opera and dance, try the **opera house** in the Stopera building (Waterlooplein 22, tel. 020/625-5455). In the summer, Vondelpark hosts open-air concerts.

Three of Amsterdam's historic churches have extensive music programs. In summer, the **Westerkerk** has free lunchtime concerts on Fridays at 13:00 (April-Oct) plus an annual Bach organ concert cycle in August (Prinsengracht 281, tel. 020/624-7766, www.westerkerk.nl). The **New Church** offers periodic organ concerts and a religious music festival in June (included in €8 church entry, covered by Museumkaart, Dam Square, tel. 020/638-6909, www.nieuwekerk.nl). The Red Light District's **Old Church** (Oude Kerk) has carillon concerts Tuesday at 14:00 and Saturday at 16:00, and holds an organ music competition in early September (Oudekerksplein, tel. 020/625-8284, www.oudekerk.nl).

Two rock music (and hip-hop) clubs near Leidseplein are **Melkweg** (Lijnbaansgracht 234a, tel. 020/531-8181, www.melkweg.nl) and **Paradiso** (Weteringschans 6, tel. 020/626-4521, www.paradiso.nl; see page 106). They present big-name acts that you might recognize...if you're younger than I am.

Jazz has a long tradition at the **Bimhuis** nightclub, now housed in a black box jutting out from the Muziekgebouw performance hall, right on the waterfront. Its great bar has citywide views, and is open to the public after concerts (Piet Heinkade 3, tel. 020/788-2188, www.bimhuis.nl).

The nearby town of Haarlem offers free pipe-organ concerts on Tuesday evenings in summer at its 15th-century church, the **Grote Kerk** (at 20:15 mid-May-mid-Oct, additional concerts Thu at 16:00 July-Aug, see page 237).

Comedy

Boom Chicago, an R-rated comedy improv act, was started 15 years ago by a group of Americans on a graduation tour. They have been entertaining tourists and locals ever since. The two-hour English-only show is a series of rude, clever, and high-energy improvisational skits offering a raucous look at Dutch culture and local tourism (€22 weekdays, generally €26 Fri-Sat; Sun-Fri shows at 20:15, Sat at 22:00; confirm times when you buy your ticket, ticket office open Wed-Sat from 16:00 until 15 minutes after curtain time, no Tue shows Jan-March, tel. 0900-266-6244, www.boomchicago.nl). It all happens at the Rozentheater, Rozengracht 117, in the Jordaan district (bar service available).

They do *Can't Dutch This* (a collection of their greatest hits over the years) as well as new shows for locals and return customers. They also host stand-up comics on their European tours. When sales are slow, ticket-sellers on the street out front may offer steeply discounted tickets. Drop by that afternoon and see what's up.

Theater

Amsterdam is one of the world centers for experimental live theater (much of it in English). Many theaters cluster around the street called the Nes, which stretches south from Dam Square.

Movies

In the Netherlands, most movies are subtitled, rather than dubbed, so English-only speakers have plenty of cinematic options. It's not unusual for movies at many cinemas to be sold out—consider buying tickets during the day. Catch modern movies in the 1920s setting of the classic **Tuschinski Theater** (between Muntplein and Rembrandtplein, described on page 63).

The new and splashy **EYE Film Institute Netherlands,** across the water from Central Station, is a very memorable place to see a movie (described on page 72).

Museums

Several museums stay open late.

The **Anne Frank House** always stays open until at least 19:00 year-round; it's open daily until 22:00 in July and August and closes late on Saturday year-round (22:00 peak-season, 21:00 off-season). The **Stedelijk Museum's** collection of modern art is on view until 22:00 on Thursday. The **Van Gogh Museum** is open on Friday until 22:00 and sometimes has music and a wine bar in the lobby.

The **Hash, Marijuana, and Hemp Museum** is open daily until 23:00. And the **sex museums** always stay open late (Damrak Sex Museum until 23:00, Erotic Museum until 1:00 in the morning).

Skating After Dark

Amsterdammers get their skating fix every Friday night in summer and early fall in Vondelpark. Huge groups don inline skates and meet at the round bench near the Vondel Pavilion (around 20:15, www.fridaynightskate.com). Anyone can join in. You can rent skates at the shop at the far end of the park (Vondeltuin Rental, daily 11:00-20:00 in good weather; first hour-€5, then €2.50/hour, €20 deposit and ID required; price includes helmet, wrist guards, and knee guards; at southeastern edge of park, mobile 0627-565-576, www.vondeltuin.nl).

AMSTERDAM CONNECTIONS

The Netherlands is so small, level, and well-covered by trains and buses that transportation is a snap. Buses take you where trains don't go, and bicycles take you where buses don't go. Bus stations and bike-rental shops cluster around train stations. The easy-to-navigate airport is well-connected to Amsterdam and other destinations by bus and train. Use the comprehensive transit website www.9292.nl to plan connections inside the Netherlands by train, bus, or both.

By Train

Amsterdam is the country's hub, but all major cities are linked by speedy trains that come and go every 15 minutes or so. For information on tickets, deals, and railpasses, see page 614. Dutch rail schedules are online at www.ns.nl (domestic) and www.nshispeed .nl (international).

Amsterdam Central Station

Amsterdam's Central Station is being renovated—a messy construction project that's expected to last through 2014 (see "Arrival in Amsterdam" on page 44 for more details on the station). The station's train-information center can require a long wait. Save lots of time by getting train tickets and information at a small-town station (such as Haarlem), the airport upon arrival (wonderful service), or a travel agency. You can buy tickets ahead of time for travel the next day.

If you have a railpass, it's quicker to validate it when you arrive at Schiphol Airport than in Amsterdam's Central Station, where ticket-counter lines are long; you can stretch your railpass by buying an inexpensive ticket from the airport into Amsterdam and using your first "flexi" day for a longer trip.

From Amsterdam Central Station by Train to Domestic Destinations: Schiphol Airport (4-6/hour, 15 minutes, €4.30, have coins handy to buy from a machine to avoid lines), **Haarlem** (6/hour, 20 minutes, €3.80 one-way, €7.60 same-day round-trip; see page 240 for a train-window tour of the countryside), **Keukenhof** (catch train to Leiden—4/hour, 35 minutes; then bus #854, called Keukenhof Express, to garden—4/hour, 30 minutes), **Aalsmeer** (take bus instead; see next page), **Zandvoort** (2/hour, 30 minutes), **Delft** (3/hour direct, 1 hour, more with transfer in Leiden or The Hague), **The Hague/Den Haag** (2/hour, 50 minutes, more with change in Leiden), **Rotterdam** (3/hour, 40 minutes), **Arnhem** (4/hour, 1 hour, half with transfer in Utrecht), **Kröller-Müller Museum/Hoge Veluwe National Park** (get off at Ede-Wageningen—4/hour, 1 hour, half with transfer in Utrecht; from Ede-Wageningen, take bus to Otterlo near park entrance—1-2/hour, 15 minutes), **Utrecht** (4/hour, 30 minutes), **Edam/Volendam/Marken** (take bus; see next page), **Hoorn** (start of Historic Triangle; 2/hour, 35 minutes; more with change in Zaandam, 45 minutes), **Enkhuizen/Zuiderzee Museum** (2/hour, 1 hour), **Alkmaar** (4/hour, 40 minutes), **Zaanse Schans Open-Air Museum** (get off at Koog-Zaandijk; train direction: Uitgeest; 4/hour, 15 minutes).

By Train to International Destinations: Bruges (hourly, 3 hours, transfer at Antwerp Central or Brussels Midi; transfer can be tight—be alert and check with conductor), **Brussels** (hourly, 2 hours), **Ostend** (for ferries to UK; hourly, 4 hours, 3 changes), **London** (6/day, 4.75-5.5 hours, with transfer to Eurostar Chunnel train in Brussels; Eurostar discounted with railpass, www.eurostar.com), **Copenhagen** (3/day, 11.25 hours, multiple transfers; one direct night train), **Bacharach/St. Goar** (roughly every 2 hours, 4.5-6 hours), **Frankfurt** (every 2 hours, 4 hours direct), **Berlin** (5/day, 6.5 hours; 1 direct night train, 9.5 hours), **Munich** (roughly hourly, 7.5-8.75 hours, 1-2 transfers; one direct night train, 10.5 hours), **Bern** (5/day, 8-9 hours, fastest trains change once in Frankfurt), **Paris** (nearly hourly, 3.25 hours direct on fast Thalys train or 4 hours with change to Thalys train in Brussels, www.thalys.com). When booking Thalys trains, even railpass-holders need to buy a seat reservation (generally €26-33 in second class or €41-54 in first class—the first-class reservation generally gets you a meal). If your railpass covers France but not BeNeLux, the reservation will cost more. (Railpasses that don't include France are not accepted on Thalys trains.) Save money by taking a bus to Paris—described on the next page.

By Bus

The biggest companies serving towns near Amsterdam include Arriva (www.arriva.nl) and Connexxion (www.connexxion.nl).

From Amsterdam by Bus to: Edam/Volendam (EBS bus #314 or #317; 2/hour, 30 minutes), **Marken** (bus #311, 2/hour, 40 minutes), **Aalsmeer Flower Auction** (Connexxion bus #172, 4/hour, 1 hour). Buses depart from just north of Amsterdam's Central Station (exit station through the back of the west passageway, and head up the escalator).

To Paris by Bus: If you don't have a railpass, the cheapest way to get to Paris is by Eurolines bus (about 6/day, 8 hours, €46 one-way, €70-86 round-trip; price depends on demand—nonrefundable, advance-purchase one-way tickets as cheap as €17 and round-trip as cheap as €28, check online for deals, Julianaplein 5, Amstel Station, five stops by metro from Central Station, tel. 020/560-8788, www.eurolines.com).

By Plane

Amsterdam's Schiphol Airport

Schiphol (SKIP-pol) Airport is located about 10 miles southwest of Amsterdam's city center. Like most of Holland, it is user-friendly and below sea level. With an appealing array of shops, eateries, and other time-killing opportunities, Schiphol is a fine place to arrive, depart, or change planes. A truly international airport, Schiphol has done away with Dutch—signs are in English only.

Information: Schiphol flight information can give you flight times and your airline's contact info (airport code: AMS, toll tel. 0900-0141, from other countries dial +31-20-794-0800, www.schiphol.nl).

Orientation: Schiphol has four terminals. Terminal 1 is for flights to the Schengen European countries (not including the UK); Terminals 2 and 3 are for flights to the UK, US, and other non-European countries; and the new, smaller Terminal 4 (attached to Terminal 3) is for low-cost carriers. Inside the airport, the terminal waiting areas are called lounges; an inviting shopping and eating zone called Holland Boulevard runs between Lounges 2 and 3.

Arrival at Schiphol: Baggage-claim areas for all terminals empty into the same arrival zone, called Schiphol Plaza—with ATMs, shops, eateries, a busy **TI** (near Terminal 2, daily 7:00-22:00), a train station, and bus stops for getting into the city. You can validate your railpass and hit the rails immediately, or, to stretch your railpass, buy an inexpensive ticket into Amsterdam today and start the pass later.

Airport Services: The ABN/AMRO **banks** offer fair exchange rates (in both arrivals and lounge areas). **Service Point,** in Schiphol Plaza at the end of the shopping mall near Terminal 4, is a useful all-purpose service counter that sells SIM cards, has an ATM, and ships packages. The **GWK Travelex** currency-exchange office is located in Arrivals 3 and sells SIM cards for mobile phones. Avoid the Orbitel mobile shop just outside Terminal 2; it sells only one brand of SIM cards, and for an exorbitant rate.

You can surf the **Internet** (for a price) and make phone calls at the Communication Centres (one on the top level of Lounge 2, another on the ground floor of Lounge 1; both are behind customs and not available once you've left the security checkpoint). Convenient luggage **lockers** are at various points around the airport—allowing you to leave your bag here on a lengthy layover (both short- and long-term lockers, credit card only; biggest bank of lockers near the train station at Schiphol Plaza).

Airport Train Ticket Counter: To get train information, buy a ticket, or validate your railpass, take advantage of the fantastic "Train Tickets and Services" counter (Schiphol Plaza ground level, just past Burger King). They have an easy info desk and almost no lines (much quicker than the ticket desk at Amsterdam's Central Station—but they only accept US credit cards with a smart chip) and issue tickets for a fee (€0.50 for domestic tickets, €3.50 for tickets to Belgium, Luxembourg, and nearby German cities; up to €10 for other international tickets).

Time-Killing Tips: If you have extra time at Schiphol, check out the Rijksmuseum Amsterdam Schiphol, a little art gallery and museum store on Holland Boulevard, the lively shopping/eating zone between Lounges 2 and 3. The Rijksmuseum loans a dozen or so of its minor masterpieces from the Dutch Golden Age to this unique airport museum, including actual Dutch Masters by Rembrandt, Vermeer, and others (free, daily 6:00-20:00).

To escape the airport crowds, follow signs for the Panorama Terrace to the third floor of Terminal 2, where you'll find a quieter, full-of-locals cafeteria, a kids' play area, and a view terrace where you can watch planes come and go while you nurse a coffee. If you plan to visit the terrace on arrival, stop there before you pass through customs.

From Schiphol Airport to Amsterdam: Direct **trains** to Amsterdam's Central Station run frequently (4-6/hour, 15 minutes, €4.30). The Connexxion **shuttle bus** takes you to your hotel neighborhood; there are three different routes, so ask the attendant which one works best for your hotel (2/hour, 20 minutes, €16 one-way, €26 round-trip, one route stops at Westerkerk near Anne Frank House and many recommended hotels, other routes may cost a couple euros more, departs from lane A7 in front of airport, reserve at least 2 hours ahead for shuttles to airport, tel. 088-339-4741, www.airporthotelshuttle.nl). Allow about €60-70 for a **taxi** to downtown Amsterdam. **Bus #197** is handiest for those staying in the Leidseplein district (€4, buy ticket from driver, departs from lane B9 in front of airport).

From Schiphol Airport to Haarlem: The big red #300 **bus** is direct, stopping at Haarlem's train station and near the Grote Markt/Market Square (4-10/hour, 40 minutes, €4—buy ticket from driver, departs from lane B6 in front of airport). The **train** is just as quick, but you'll have to transfer at the Amsterdam-Sloterdijk station (6/hour, 30-40 minutes, €5.40). Figure about €30-40 to Haarlem by **taxi.**

From Schiphol Airport by Train to: Delft (6/hour, 45 minutes, transfer in The Hague, Rotterdam, or Leiden; less frequent direct trains take 20 minutes longer), **The Hague/Den Haag** (2/hour, 35 minutes, more with change in Leiden), **Rotterdam** (3/hour, 30 minutes), **Bruges** (10/day, 2.75 hours, change in Antwerp), **Brussels** (hourly, 1.75 hours).

From Schiphol Airport by Bus to: Keukenhof (bus #858, 8/hour, 40 minutes), **Aalsmeer** (Connexxion bus #198, 4/hour, 18 minutes).

By Cruise Ship

Things here are simple for cruisers: The Passenger Terminal Amsterdam (PTA) is just a 15-minute walk or three-minute tram ride along the water east of Central Station. There's an ATM (with poor rates) inside the terminal, and many better ones at the station.

To ride the **tram,** simply exit the cruise terminal, follow the *Town Center* sign, cross the busy portside street, and look for the stop for tram #26. Buy a ticket from the driver (either a single ticket or a day pass, pay cash) and ride it one stop to Central Station. To **walk,** head out the same door, turn right, and stroll with the water on your right for about 15 minutes toward the station's glass-and-steel arch. You'll pass between the station and the river, then turn left at the major crosswalk to enter the lower level of Central Station. Once you've reached Central Station—by tram or by foot—turn to the arrival instructions on page 44.

From the cruise terminal, a **taxi** to the Rijksmuseum or Van Gogh Museum should cost about €16. The **Canal Bus** blue line stops at the Passenger Terminal (for details, see page 50). The nearest **bike rental** is AmsterBike, in the parking garage under the Mövenpick Hotel next door (daily 9:00-18:00 except closed Wed in winter, tel. 020/419-9063, www.amsterbike.eu); more bike rental options are near Central Station.

HAARLEM

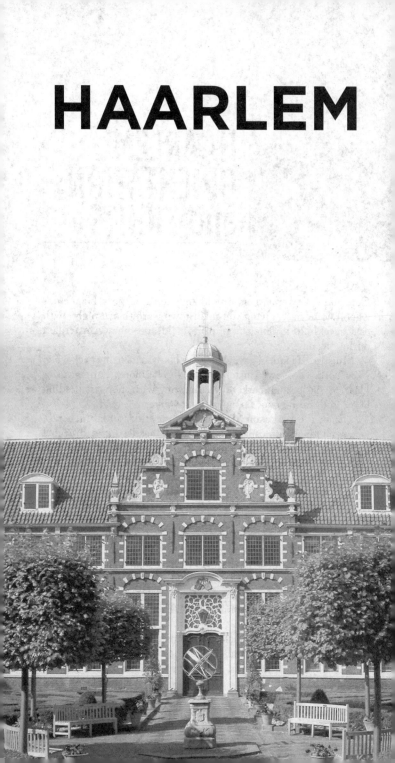

HAARLEM ORIENTATION and SIGHTS

Cute and cozy, yet authentic and handy to the airport, Haarlem is a good home base, giving you small-town warmth overnight, with easy access (20 minutes by train) to wild-and-crazy Amsterdam during the day.

Bustling Haarlem gave America's Harlem its name back when New York was New Amsterdam, a Dutch colony. For centuries Haarlem has been a market town, buzzing with shoppers heading home with fresh bouquets, nowadays by bike.

Enjoy the market on Monday (clothing) or Saturday (general), when the town's atmospheric main square bustles like a Brueghel painting, with cheese, fish, flowers, and families. Make yourself at home; buy some flowers to brighten your hotel room.

Overview

Tourist Information

Haarlem's TI (VVV), in the town center, is friendlier, more helpful, and less crowded than Amsterdam's, so ask your Amsterdam questions here (April-Sept Mon-Fri 9:30-18:00, Sat 9:30-17:00, Sun 12:00-16:00; Oct-March Mon 13:00-17:30, Tue-Fri 9:30-17:30, Sat 10:00-17:00, closed Sun; across from V&D department store at Verwulft 11, toll tel. 0900-616-1600—€0.50/minute, www.haarlem.nl, info@vvvhaarlem.nl).

The TI offers a good selection of maps and sightseeing- and walking-tour brochures, and sells discounted tickets (€1-2 off) for the Frans Hals Museum and the Teylers Museum.

Arrival in Haarlem

By Train: Lockers are available at the station at the very end of platform 3A (€3.70/day, no coins—use a credit card or buy a

"Chipknip" prepaid debit card at a ticket window). Two parallel streets flank the train station (Kruisweg and Jansweg). Head up either street, and you'll reach the town square and church within 10 minutes. If you need help, ask a local person to point you toward Grote Markt (Market Square). If you're arriving by train from Amsterdam, see the end of this chapter for a description of sights you'll see out the train window along the way.

By Bus: Buses from Schiphol Airport stop both in the center (Centrum/Verwulft stop, a short walk from Grote Markt) and at the train station.

By Car: Parking is expensive on the streets (€2.70/hour). It's cheaper (€1/30 minutes; €2.50 overnight—19:00-8:00) in these central garages: at the train station, at the southern end of Gedempte Oude Gracht (the main thoroughfare), near the recommended Die Raeckse Hotel, and near the Frans Hals Museum. The most central garage, near the Teylers Museum, is pricier (€1.50 every 40 minutes—essentially, €2.75/hour).

By Plane: For details on getting from Schiphol Airport to Haarlem, see page 229.

Helpful Hints

Blue Monday and Early Closures: Most sights are closed on Monday, except the church, De Adriaan Windmill (closed Tue), and History Museum Haarlem. The **Corrie ten Boom House** is closed Sunday-Monday, and closes early the rest of the week (15:00).

Internet Access: Try **Suny Teletechniques** (€2/hour, daily 10:00-24:00, near train station at Lange Herenstraat 4, tel. 023/551-0037) or **High Times Coffeeshop** (free if you buy some pot, Lange Veerstraat 47—see sidebar on page 268).

Post Office: There isn't one. To buy stamps, head to a newsstand with the orange *TNT* logo; if you need to send a package, ask your hotelier for help.

Laundry: My Beautiful Launderette is handy and fairly central (€6 self-service wash and dry, daily 8:30-20:30, €9 full service available Mon-Fri 9:00-17:00, near V&D department store at Boter Markt 20).

Bike Rental: You can rent bikes from **Pieters Fietsverhuur** inside the train station (fixed-gear bike only—€6.50/day, €50 deposit and passport number required, Mon-Sat 6:00-24:00, Sun 7:30-24:00, Stationsplein 7, tel. 023/531-7066). They have only 50 bikes to rent and often run out by midmorning—especially when the weather's good. **Rent a Bike Haarlem** charges more, but is friendly and efficient, and carries plenty of new, good-quality bikes. If you're renting for less than a full day, negotiate a cheaper price (fixed-gear bike—€10/day,

3-speed bike—€13.50/day, mountain bikes available, after-hours drop-off possible, ID required for deposit—if you don't want to leave ID, there's a €150 cash deposit; April-Sept daily 9:00-18:00; Oct-March Tue-Fri 10:00-17:30, Thu until 18:00, Sat 10:00-17:00, closed Sun-Mon; near station at Lange Herenstraat 36, tel. 023/542-1195, www.rentabikehaarlem.nl).

Taxi: The drop charge of €7.50 gets you a little over a mile.

Local Guide: Consider hiring **Walter Schelfhout,** a bearded repository of Haarlem's historical fun facts. If you're into beer lore, Walter's your guy (€85/2 hours, also leads a beer walk sponsored by the Jopenkerk brewpub, tel. 023/535-5715, mobile 06-1258-9299, schelfhout@dutch.nl).

Best View: At **La Place** (top-floor cafeteria of the V&D departmentment store—see page 267), you get wraparound views of the city as you sip your €2 self-serve tea.

Best Ice Cream: Gelateria Bartoli (on the south side of the Grote Kerk) is the local favorite (daily April-Sept 10:00-22:00, March and Oct-Dec 12:00-17:30 in good weather, closed Jan-Feb).

Sights in Haarlem

▲▲Grote Markt (Market Square)

Haarlem's Grote Markt, where 10 streets converge, is the town's delightful centerpiece...as it has been for 700 years. To enjoy a coffee or beer here, simmering in Dutch good living, is a quintessential European experience. Observe. Sit and gaze at the church, appreciating essentially the same scene that Dutch artists captured centuries ago in oil paintings that now hang in museums.

Just a few years ago, trolleys ran through the square, and cars were parked everywhere. But today it's a pedestrian zone, with market stalls filling the square on Mondays and Saturdays, and café tables dominating on other days.

This is a fun place to build a picnic with Haarlem finger foods and enjoy great seating on the square. Look for pickled herring

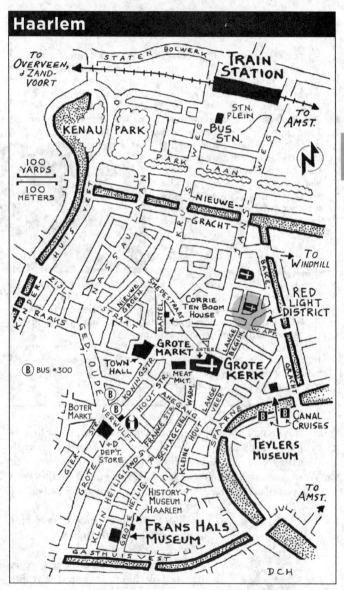

Haarlem

TO Overveen, & ZANDVOORT

STATEN BOLWERK

TRAIN STATION

TO AMST.

STN. PLEIN

BUS STN.

KENAU PARK

PARK LAAN

NIEUWE-

GRACHT

100 YARDS

100 METERS

HUIS VEST

KINDERZIJL

RAAKS

GEDEMPTE OUDE GRACHT

NIEUWE GRACHT

NIEUWE GROEN MARKT

SMEDESTRAAT

BARTEL

BAKENESSERGRACHT

W. APP.

TO WINDMILL

RED LIGHT DISTRICT

Corrie Ten Boom House

GROTE MARKT

ENTER

LANGE BEGIN.

GROTE KERK

Ⓑ BUS #300

TOWN HALL

KONINGSTR.

MEAT MKT.

BOTER MARKT

VERWULFT

HOUT STR.

ANEGANG

FRANKESTRAAT

LANGE VEER

SPAARNE

Ⓑ

Ⓑ CANAL CRUISES

TEYLERS MUSEUM

GIERSTR.

V & D DEP'T. STORE

SCHAGCHELSTRAAT

KLEINE HOUT

HISTORY MUSEUM HAARLEM

GROTE HEILIG.

KLEIN HEILIGLAND

FRANS HALS MUSEUM

GASTHUISVEST

TO AMST.

DCH

Haarlem of the Golden Age

Parts of Haarlem still look like they did four centuries ago, when the city was a bustling commercial center rivaling Amsterdam. It's easy to imagine local merchants and their wives dressed in black with ruff collars, promenading on Grote Markt.

Back then, the town was a port on the large Haarlemmer Lake, with the North Sea only about five miles away. As well as being the tulip capital of the country, Haarlem was a manufacturing center, producing wool, silk, lace, damask cloth, furniture, smoking pipes (along with cheap, locally grown tobacco), and mass quantities of beer. Haarlemmers were notorious consumers of beer—it was a popular breakfast drink, and the average person drank six pints a day.

In 1585, the city got an influx of wealthy merchants when Spanish troops invaded the culturally rich city of Antwerp, driving Protestants and Jews north. Even when hard-line, moralistic Calvinists dominated Haarlem's politics, the city remained culturally and religiously diverse.

In the 1700s, Haarlem's economy declined, along with that of the rest of the Netherlands. In the succeeding centuries, industry—printing, textiles, ship building—once again made the city an economic force.

(take-away stand on the square), local cheese (Gouda and Edam—tasty shop a block away on Barteljorisstraat), french fries with mayonnaise (recommended old-time fries place behind the church on Warmoesstraat), and, in the summer, *stroopwafels* (waffles with built-in syrup) and *poffertjes* (little sugar doughnuts, cooked on the spot).

As you enjoy a snack, take this simple spin tour of the square.

• *Overseeing the square is the...*

L. J. Coster Statue: Forty years before Gutenberg invented movable type, this man carved the letter *A* out of wood, dropped it into some wet sand, and saw the imprint it left. He got the idea of making movable type out of wood (and later, he may have tried using lead). For Haarlemmers, that was good enough, and they credit their man, Coster, with inventing modern printing. In the statue, Coster (c. 1370-1440) holds up a block of movable type and points to himself, saying, "I made this." How much Coster did is uncertain, but Gutenberg trumped him by building a printing press, casting type in metal, and pounding out the Bible.

• *Coster is facing the...*

Town Hall: Whereas most of medieval Europe was ruled by kings, dukes, and barons, Haarlem has been largely self-governing since 1425. This building—built from a royal hunting lodge in the mid-1200s, then rebuilt after a 1351 fire—has served as Haarlem's Town Hall since about 1400. The facade dates from 1630.

The town drunk used to hang out on the bench in front of the Town Hall, where he'd expose himself to newlyweds coming down the stairs. Rather than arresting the man, the townspeople simply moved the bench (a typical Dutch solution to the problem).

• *Next to the church is the...*

Meat Market (Vleeshal), 1603: The fine Flemish Renaissance building nearest the cathedral is the old meat hall, built by the rich butchers' and leatherworkers' guilds. The meat market was on the ground floor, the leather was upstairs, and the cellar was filled with ice to preserve the meat. It's decorated with carved bits of early advertising—sheep and cows for sale. Today, rather than meat, the hall shows off temporary art exhibits in the Museum De Hallen (€6, Tue-Sat 11:00-17:00, Sun 12:00-17:00, closed Mon, Grote Markt 16, tel. 023/511-5775, www.dehallen.nl) and bits of the town's past in the Archaeology Museum (free, Wed-Sun 13:00-17:00, closed Mon-Tue, in the cellar of the Museum De Hallen, tel. 023/542-0888).

More Sights in Haarlem

▲**Church (Grote Kerk)**—This 15th-century Gothic church (now Protestant) is worth a look, if only to see Holland's greatest pipe organ (from 1738, 100 feet high). Its more than 5,000 pipes impressed both Handel and Mozart. Note how the organ, which fills the west end, seems to steal the show from the altar. Quirky highlights of the church include a replica of Foucault's pendulum, the "Dog-Whipper's Chapel," and a 400-year-old cannonball.

To enter, find the small *Entrée* sign behind the Coster statue on Grote Markt.

Cost and Hours: €2.50, not covered by Museumkaart, Mon-Sat

10:00-17:00, closed Sun to tourists, tel. 023/553-2040, www.bavo.nl.

Concerts: Consider attending (even part of) a **concert** to hear the Oz-like pipe organ (regular free concerts Tue at 20:15 mid-May-mid-Oct, additional concerts Thu at 16:00 July-Aug; bring a sweater—the church isn't heated).

For a self-guided tour, see the ✪ Grote Kerk Tour chapter.

▲▲Frans Hals Museum—Haarlem is the hometown of Frans Hals, the foremost Dutch portrait painter of the 17th-century Golden Age. This refreshing museum, once an almshouse for old men back in 1610, displays many of Hals' greatest paintings, crafted in his nearly Impressionistic style. You'll see group portraits and paintings of old-time Haarlem.

Cost and Hours: €10, often €13 with special exhibits, Tue-Sat 11:00-17:00, Sun 12:00-17:00, closed Mon, Groot Heiligland 62, tel. 023/511-5775, www.franshalsmuseum.nl.

For a self-guided tour, see the ✪ Frans Hals Museum Tour chapter.

History Museum Haarlem—This small museum, across the street from the Frans Hals Museum, offers a glimpse of old Haarlem. Request the English version of the 10-minute video, low-key Haarlem's version of a sound-and-light show. Study the large-scale model of Haarlem in 1822 (when its fortifications were still intact), and wander the three rooms without English descriptions.

Cost and Hours: Overpriced at €5, Mon-Sat 12:00-17:00, Sun 13:00-17:00, Groot Heiligland 47, tel. 023/542-2427, www.historischmuseumhaarlem.nl. The adjacent architecture center (free) may be of interest to architects.

▲Corrie ten Boom House—Haarlem was home to Corrie ten Boom, popularized by her inspirational 1971 book (and the 1975 movie that followed), *The Hiding Place*. Both tell about the Ten Boom family's experience protecting Jews from the Nazis. Corrie ten Boom gives the other half of the Anne Frank story—the point of view of those who risked their lives to hide Dutch Jews during the Nazi occupation (1940-1945).

The Ten Boom House is open only for English tours—check the sign on the door for the next start time. The gentle and loving one-hour tours come with a little evangelizing that some may find objectionable.

Cost and Hours: Free, but donations accepted; April-Oct Tue-Sat first tour at 10:00, last tour at 15:30; Nov-March Tue-Sat first tour at 11:00, last tour around 15:00; closed Sun-Mon year-round; 50 yards north of Grote Markt at Barteljorisstraat 19; the clock-shop people get all wound up if you go inside—wait in the little side street at the door, where tour times are posted; tel. 023/531-0823, www.corrietenboom.com.

Background: The clock shop was the Ten Boom family business. The elderly father and his two daughters—Corrie and Betsy, both in their 50s—lived above the store and in the brick building attached in back (along Schoutensteeg alley). Corrie's bedroom was on the top floor at the back. This room was tiny to start with, but then the family built a second, secret room (less than a yard deep) at the very back—"the hiding place," where they could hide six Jews at a time. Devoutly religious, the family had a long tradition of tolerance, having hosted prayer meetings here in their home for both Jews and Christians for generations.

The Gestapo, tipped off that the family was harboring Jews, burst into the Ten Boom house. Finding a suspicious number of ration coupons, the Nazis arrested the family, but failed to find the six Jews (who later escaped) in the hiding place. Corrie's father and sister died while in prison, but Corrie survived the Ravensbrück concentration camp to tell her story in her memoir.

▲**Teylers Museum**—Famous as the oldest museum in Holland, Teylers is a time-warp experience, filled with all sorts of fun curios for science buffs: fossils, minerals, primitive electronic gadgetry, and examples of 18th- and 19th-century technology (it also has two lovely painting galleries and hosts good temporary exhibits).

The science-oriented sections of this place feel like a museum of a museum. They're serious about authenticity here: The presentation is perfectly preserved, right down to the original labels. Since there was no electricity in the olden days, you'll find little electric lighting...if it's dark outside, it's dark inside. The museum's benefactor, Pieter Teyler van der Hulst, was a very wealthy merchant who willed his estate, worth the equivalent of €80 million today, to a foundation whose mission was to "create and maintain a museum to stimulate art and science." The museum opened in 1784, six years after Teyler's death (his last euro was spent in 1983—now it's a national museum). Add your name to the guest book, which goes back to before Napoleon's visit here. The freshly renovated oval room—a temple of science and learning—is the core of the museum; in the art salons paintings are hung in the old style.

Cost and Hours: Overpriced at €10, includes excellent (and I'd say, essential) audioguide, Tue-Sat 10:00-17:00, Sun 12:00-17:00, closed Mon, Spaarne 16, tel. 023/516-0960, www.teylers museum.nl. The museum's modern café has good prices and faces a delightful garden.

▲**De Adriaan Windmill**—Haarlem's old-time windmill, located just a 10-minute walk from the station and Teylers Museum, welcomes visitors with a short video, a little museum, and fine town views.

Cost and Hours: €3, not covered by Museumkaart; April-Oct Mon and Wed-Fri 13:00-17:00, Sat-Sun 10:30-17:00, closed Tue;

same hours in winter except only open Fri-Sun, Papentorenvest 1, tel. 023/545-0259, www.molenadriaan.nl.

Canal Cruise—Making a scenic 50-minute loop through and around Haarlem with a live guide who speaks Dutch and sometimes English, **Post Verkade Cruise**'s little trips are more relaxing than informative (€11; April-Oct daily departures at the top of the hour 12:00-16:00; Nov-March same hours Wed-Sun, reservations required; also evening cruises, across canal from Teylers Museum at Spaarne 11a, tel. 023/535-7723, www.postverkadecruises.nl). For a similar experience in an open boat, find **Haarlem Canal Tours,** farther down Spaarne, across from #17 (€13.50, reservations smart, 70-75 minutes, leaves every 1.5 hours daily 10:00-19:00, may not run in bad weather and off-season, www.haarlemcanaltours.com).

▲**Red Light District**—Wander through a little Red Light District that's as precious as a Barbie doll—and legal since the 1980s (2 blocks northeast of Grote Markt, off Lange Begijnestraat, no senior or student discounts). Don't miss the mall on Begijnesteeg marked by the red neon sign reading *'t Steegje* ("free"). Just beyond that, the nearby 't Poortje ("office park") costs €6 to enter. Jog to the right to pop into the much more inviting "Red Lantern" (window-shopping welcome, at Korte Begijnestraat 27). As you wander through this area, remember that the people here don't condone prostitution any more than your own community back home probably does; they just find it practical not to criminalize it and drive it underground, but instead to regulate it and keep the practice as safe as possible.

Amsterdam to Haarlem Train Tour

Since you'll probably take the train from Amsterdam to Haarlem, here's an out-the-window tour to keep you entertained while you travel. Departing from Amsterdam, grab a seat on the right (with your back to Amsterdam, top deck if possible). Everything is on the right unless I say it's on the left.

You're riding the oldest train line in Holland. Leaving Amsterdam, you'll see the cranes and ships of its harbor—sizable, but nothing like Europe's biggest in nearby Rotterdam.

On your left, a few minutes out of Amsterdam, you should be able to see an old **windmill** (you can visit a similar one in Haarlem). In front of it, the little garden plots and cottages are escapes for big-city people who probably don't even have a balcony.

Coming into the **Sloterdijk Station** (where trains connect for Amsterdam's Schiphol Airport), you'll see huge office buildings, such as Dutch telecom giant KPN. These sprouted after the station made commuting easy. On the horizon, sleek and modern windmills whirl.

Passing through a forest and by some houseboats, you enter a

The Haarlemmermeer

The land between Haarlem and Amsterdam—where trains speed through, cattle graze, and 747s touch down—was once a lake the size of Washington, DC, called the Haarlemmermeer.

In the 1500s, a series of high tides and storms caused the IJ River to breach its banks, flooding this sub-sea-level area and turning a bunch of shallow lakes into a single one nearly 15 feet deep, covering 70 square miles. By the 1800s, floods were licking at the borders of Haarlem and Amsterdam, and the residents needed to act. First, they dug a ring canal to channel away water (and preserve the lake's shipping business). Then, using steam engines, they pumped the lake dry, turning marshy soil into fertile ground. The Amsterdam-Haarlem train line that soon crossed the former lakebed was the country's first.

polder—an area of reclaimed land. This is part of an ecologically sound farm zone, run without chemicals. Cows, pigs, and chickens run free—they're not raised in cages. The train tracks are on a dike, which provides a raised foundation less susceptible to flooding, so the transportation system generally keeps running, even in bad weather. Looking out at another dike in the distance (visible on clear days), consider that you're actually in the most densely populated country in Europe.

On the right, just after the Ikea building, find a big beige-and-white building. This is the **mint,** where currency is printed (top security, no advertising). This has long been a family business—see the name: Joh. Enschedé.

As the train slows down, you're passing through the Netherlands' biggest train-car-maintenance facility, and entering Haarlem. Look left. The domed building is a **prison,** built in 1901 and still in use. The **De Adriaan windmill** that you see was rebuilt in 2002, after the original burnt down in 1932 (the windmill is open for afternoon visits—see page 239).

When you cross the Spaarne River, you'll see the great **church spire** of the Grote Kerk towering over Haarlem, as it has since medieval times, back when a fortified wall circled the town. Notice the white version of the same spire capping the smaller church (between the prison and the big church): This was the original sandstone steeple that stood atop the big church. However, structural problems forced its move to another church, and a new spire was built for the big church.

Exit the train into one of Holland's oldest stations, adorned with Art Nouveau decor from 1908. Welcome to Haarlem.

GROTE KERK TOUR

Haarlem's impressive Grote Kerk (Great Church), one of the best-known landmarks in the Netherlands, is visible from miles around, rising above the flat plain that surrounds it. From the Grote Markt (Market Square), you see the church at a three-quarters angle, emphasizing both its length (240 feet) and its height (260 feet).

Orientation

Cost: €2.50, not covered by Museumkaart.

Hours: Mon-Sat 10:00-17:00, closed Sun to tourists, Sun service at 10:00 (May-Oct). The church also holds a daily 15-minute prayer service at 12:45 (May-Oct). Occasionally, the church is closed for a wedding or a funeral; if you see a closed sign when it's supposed to be open, return in a couple of hours.

Getting There: The church is on the main square, a 10-minute walk south of the train station.

Information: The leaflet at the ticket desk offers basic information in English. Tours are offered on Saturdays, by request (€4). Tel. 023/553-2040, www.bavo.nl.

WC: Nice WCs are inside, just after the ticket desk.

Music: Consider attending even just part of a concert to hear Holland's greatest pipe organ. Free concerts generally are offered throughout the summer (Tue at 20:15 mid-May-mid-Oct, additional concerts Thu at 16:00 July-Aug; concerts last about one hour). In even years, an organ competition is held here in July, bringing nearly nightly performances at 20:15. If you're coming for a concert, bring a sweater—the thick stone walls keep the church cool, even during summer. Entrance to the evening concerts is through the south transept, around the back of the church.

Length of This Tour: Allow one hour.

Overview

After a fire destroyed the old church (1328), the Grote Kerk was built over a 150-year period (c. 1390-1540) in the late Gothic style of red-and-gray brick, topped with a slate-covered wood roof and a stacked tower bearing a golden crown and a rooster weathervane.

Originally Catholic, the church was named after St. Bavo, a local noble who frequented seventh-century Red Light Districts during his youth. After his conversion, he moved out of his castle and into a hollow tree, where he spent his days fasting and praying. In the late 1500s, the St. Bavo Church became Protestant (Dutch Reformed) along with much of the country. From then on, the anti-saint Protestants simply called it the Great Church.

The Tour Begins

• *Before entering, take a few minutes to walk around this incredible building.*

Exterior

Notice the rough buttress anchors, which were never needed. Money ran out, and the planned stone ceiling (which would have

required these buttresses) was replaced by a lighter wooden one. Some windows are bricked up because the organ fills the wall.

The original stone tower crowned the church from 1522 until 1530, when the church began sinking under its weight. The tower was removed and replaced by the lighter, lead-covered-wood version you see today. (The frugal Dutch recycled the old tower, using it to cap the Bakenesser church, a short walk away.)

Because the tower was used as a lookout by Napoleon, it was classified as part of the town's defense. As a result, the tower (but not the rest of the church) became city property, and, since Haarlem's citizens own it, they must help pay to maintain it.

The base of the church is encrusted, barnacle-like, with shops—selling jewelry, souvenirs, haircuts, and artwork in the colonnaded former fish market—harkening back to medieval times,

Grote Kerk

ENTER (TICKETS, SHOP & WC INSIDE)

GROTE MARKT

ORGAN

NAVE

PULPIT

CHOIR   ALTAR

30 YARDS

30 METERS

DCH

❶ Center of Church Viewpoint
❷ Poor Peasant Bending
❸ Grave of Frans Hals
❹ "Pillar Biter"
❺ Three Little Ships
❻ Memorial to Hydraulic Engineers
❼ Brewers' Chapel & Café
❽ Giant & Dwarf Marks
❾ Old Map of "Harlemum"
❿ Church Rosters
⓫ Pelican Lectern
⓬ Mary's Chapel
⓭ Foucault's Pendulum
⓮ Dog-Whipper's Chapel
⓯ Model of the Church
⓰ Cannonball
⓱ Evening Concert Entrance

GROTE KERK

when religion and commerce were more intertwined. The little shops around the cathedral have long been church-owned, rented out to bring in a little cash.

During the day, a machine plays music on the bells of the Grote Kerk's carillon (live carillonneurs play occasionally). If you're in Haarlem at night, you'll hear the carillon chiming a simple "de dong dong, de dong dong" ("Don't worry, be hap-py") at 21:00. In days gone by, this used to warn citizens that the city gates would soon close for the night.

• *Enter the church on the Grote Markt side, near the north transept (look for the small* Entrée *sign). Walk to the **center of the church** and take it all in.*

Interior

Simple white walls, a black floor, a brown ceiling, and a mahogany-colored organ make this spacious church feel vast, light, and airy. Considering it was built over a span of 150 years, its architecture is surprisingly homogenous. Originally, much of the interior was painted in bright patterns, similar to the carpet-like frescoes on some columns near the center of the church. But in 1566, Protestant extremists stripped the church of its graven images and ornate Catholic trappings, leaving it relatively stark, with minimal decoration. They whitewashed everything. The frescoes

you see today were restored when the whitewash was removed in the 1980s.

Look up to see the fan-vaulted cedar ceiling from 1530. Look

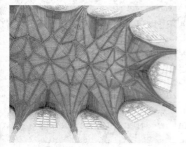

down to see tombstones paving the floor. And look midway up the walls to catch squatting characters supporting the pilasters. The three-story organ fills the west wall.

• *We'll circle the church, but first stand at the candle-lined, fence-like brass barrier and look into an enclosed area of wooden benches ("stalls") and the altar, known as the...*

Choir

After the church's foundation was laid, the choir was built first and used for worship for more than a century while the rest of the building was completed.

Today, the brass-and-wood barrier keeps tourists from entering the most sacred area, just as peasants were

kept out in medieval times. While the commoners had to stand during services, local big shots got to perch their heinies on the little ledges (called misericords, carved in 1512) of the **wooden stalls** that line the choir; the eighth stall along the left-hand side shows a poor peasant bending over to bear a rich guy's bum on his back. The stalls are also decorated with the coats of arms of noble families, whose second sons traditionally became priests.

The choir's floor holds a simple slab marked with a lantern—the **grave of Frans Hals** *(graf van Frans Hals)*, Haarlem's own master artist of the Golden Age. When he was a child, Hals' family moved to Haarlem, and he lived and worked here all his life, worshipping in the Grote Kerk. A friend of mayors and preachers, he chronicled middle-class citizens and tavern life, producing hundreds of masterpieces...and 10 kids.

At both ends of the brass barrier, look for the endearing knee-level carvings of the **"pillar biter."** The message of these carvings,

aimed at those who were "more Catholic than even the pope," was this: Don't go overboard on devotion.

More than a thousand wealthy people are buried under the church's pavement stones. Only those with piles of money to give to the church could be buried in a way that gave them an advantage in the salvation derby. But even though the dead bodies were embalmed, they stunk. Imagine being a peasant sitting here, trying to think about God...and thinking only of the stench of well-fed bodies rotting below. Here is where the phrase "stinking rich" was born.

• *To your right (as you face the choir), suspended between columns, are...*

Three Little Ships

Sailing under the red-white-and-blue Dutch flag and the flag of a rearing lion, ships like these helped make Holland the world's number-one sea-trading nation in the 1600s.

The biggest model ship of the three is a frigate. These fast, heavily armed, three-masted, fully rigged ships rode shotgun for merchant vessels, protecting them from pirates in their two-year journey to the Far East and back. This one has a flat-bottomed hull, which was necessary to ply Amsterdam's shallow harbor. It could fire a 21-gun salute from each side, and extra cannons on the poop deck and forecastle made it more powerful than the average frigate. The keel has an iron saw, a Dutch military specialty for slicing through the chains that commonly blocked harbors (see

the chain between two towers near the bow).

• *At the next column down, just to the right, is the...*

Memorial to Hydraulic Engineers

The marble relief shows Neptune in his water chariot. In low-lying Holland of the 1800s, when flooding could mean life or death, hydraulic engineers were heroes, specifically the two commemorated here.

• *Behind the columns, set into the wall of the church, is the...*

Brewers' Chapel (Brouwerskapel)

This chapel, with its humble café, marks the long and short of the city's 750-year history—literally. On the chapel's central pillar, black lines on the column show the height of Haarlem's shortest citizen, thigh-high (33 inches) Simon Paap, who supposedly died in a dwarf-tossing incident, and—wow!—8-foot-8-inch-tall Daniel Cajanus.

• *On the wall to the left of the café hangs an...*

Old Map of "Harlemum"

The map shows the walled city in 1688, with ramparts and a moat. Surrounding panels showcase Haarlem's 750-year history. The

lower-left panel shows the 1572-1573 Siege of Haarlem, as brave Haarlem women join their menfolk in battle—bombs exploding around them—to fight off invading Spanish troops.

The lower-right panel shows knights kneeling before a king in the 12th century, while in the distance, ships sail right along the city walls. Up until the 1840s, when it was drained and reclaimed, there was a large lake (the Haarlemmermeer) standing between Haarlem and Amsterdam. The Grote Kerk, when viewed by distant travelers, seemed to float like a stately ship on the lake, as seen in the landscape along the bottom of the map.

• *From here, circle the church counterclockwise, heading around the altar. Just after rounding the bend, on the wall, you'll see the first of the church's many lists of prominent church members, dating back to 1577, when the church became Protestant. The first roster, from 1770, has mesmerizingly ornate calligraphy. Opposite this list, inside the choir, is the...*

Pelican Lectern

According to medieval lore, pelicans are so attentive to their chicks that mothers, when necessary, feed their young with their own blood. Because of this myth, the pelican became a symbol of Christ's self-sacrifice. This lectern from 1499 has a brass bird that looks just like other symbolic pelicans—shown stabbing itself with its own beak—except for one important difference: It looks like an eagle. Apparently, its creator had never come across an actual pelican.

• *Just past the end of the choir is...*

Mary's Chapel (Maria Kapel)

Inside the iron cage on the chapel's back wall is an old wood-and-iron chest that served as a safe for the church's cash and precious documents—such as those papers granting the power to sell forgiveness. See the board of keys for the many doors in this huge complex. Notice also the sarcophagi. Once filled with the "stinking rich," boxes like this were buried five deep below the church floor. Such high-density burying maximized the revenue generated by selling burial spots.

Foucault's Pendulum

In the north transept, a ball on a wire hangs from the ceiling (see the brass sphere in the far-right corner). When set in motion (by a church tour guide, mostly on Saturdays), it swings across a dial on the floor, re-creating physicist Léon Foucault's pendulum experiment in Paris in 1851. If it's swinging, stand here patiently and watch the earth rotate on its axis.

As the pendulum swings steadily back and forth, the earth rotates counterclockwise underneath it, making the pendulum appear to rotate clockwise around the dial. The earth rotates once every 24 hours, of course, but at Haarlem's latitude of 52 degrees, it makes the pendulum (appear to) sweep 360 degrees every 30 hours, 27 minutes (to knock over the bowling pin). Stand here for five minutes, and you'll see the earth move one degree.

As the world turns, find several small relief statues (in a niche on the right-hand wall) with beheaded bodies and defaced faces—victims of the 1566 Iconoclastic Fury, when angry Protestant extremists vandalized Dutch Catholic churches (as this once was).

• *Ten yards farther on, the shallow niche is the...*

Dog-Whipper's Chapel

In a sculpted relief (top of column at left end of chapel, above eye level), an angry man whips an angry dog while striding over another angry dog's head. Back when churches served as rainy-day marketplaces, this man's responsibility was to keep Haarlem's dogs out of the church.

The Organ

Even when silent, this organ impresses. Finished in 1738 by Amsterdam's Christian Muller, it features a mahogany-colored casing with tin pipes and gold trim, studded with statues of musicians and an eight-piece combo of angels. Lions on the top hold Haarlem's coat of arms—a sword, surrounded by stars, over a banner reading *Vicit Vim Virtus* ("Virtue Conquers Violence"). There are larger pipe organs in the world, but this is one of the best.

With three keyboards, a forest of pedals, and 65 stops (the knobs on either side of the keyboards), this magnificent organ produces an awesome majesty of sound. Picture 10-year-old Mozart at the controls of this 5,000-pipe sound machine. In 1766, he played Haarlem at the tail end of his triumphant, three-year whirlwind tour of Europe. He'd just returned from London, where he met J. C. Bach, the youngest son of Johann Sebastian Bach (1685-1750), the grandfather of organ music. Mozart had recently written several pieces inspired by Bach, and he may have tried them out here.

"Hal-le-lu-jah!" That famous four-note riff may have echoed around the church when Handel played here in 1740, the year before his famous oratorio, *Messiah*, debuted. The 20th-century organist/humanitarian Albert Schweitzer also performed here.

The organist sits unseen amid the pipes, behind the section that juts out at the bottom. While the bellows generate pressurized air, the organist presses a key, which opens a valve, admitting forced air through a pipe and out its narrow opening, producing a tone. An eight-foot-long pipe plays middle C. A four-foot-long pipe plays C exactly one octave up. A 20-foot pipe rumbles the rafters. With 5,068 pipes ranging from more than 20 feet tall to just a few inches, this organ can cover eight octaves (a piano plays seven), and each key can play a variety of sounds. By pulling one of the stops (such as "flute" or "trumpet"), the organist can channel the air into certain sets of pipes tuned to play together to mimic other instruments. For maximum power, you "pull out all the stops."

• *Cross in front of the organ to find the glass box holding a...*

Model of the Church

A hundred times smaller than the church itself, this model still took a thousand work-hours to build. See if you can spot the matchsticks, washers, screens, glue, wire, and paper clips used to make it.

• *Just beyond the model, to the left of the chapel with the green metal gate and above eye level, is...*

A Cannonball in the Wall

Duck! Placed here in 1573, this cannonball commemorates the city's finest hour: the Siege of Haarlem.

In the winter of 1572-1573, Holland rebelled against its Spanish oppressors. Haarlem proclaimed its alliance with William of Orange (and thus, independence from Spain). In response, the angry Spanish governor—camped in Amsterdam—laid siege to Haarlem. The winter was cold, food ran low, and the city was bombarded by Spanish cannons. Inside huddled 4,000 cold, hungry Calvinists. At one point, the city's women even joined the men on the barricades, brandishing kitchen knives.

But Spain had blockaded the Haarlem Lake (the Haarlemmermeer), and by June 12, 1573, Haarlem had to surrender. The Spanish rounded up 1,500 men (three-quarters of Haarlem's able-bodied male population) and executed them to send a message to the rest of the country. Still, Haarlem's brave seven-month stand against overwhelming odds became a kind of Dutch Alamo, inspiring their countrymen to fight on.

Following Haarlem's brave lead, other Dutch towns rebelled, including Amsterdam (see page 592). Though Holland and Spain would skirmish for another five decades, the battles soon moved southward, and Spanish troops would never again seriously penetrate the country's borders.

• *Back in the middle of the nave, returning to where you began, you'll pass the impressive wooden...*

Pulpit

Elaborately carved from oak in 1679, the pulpit is topped with a tower-shaped roof. Brass handrails snake down the staircase— serpents fleeing the word of God. In this simply decorated Protestant church, the pulpit is perhaps the most ornate element, directing worshippers' eyes to the speaker. During the Reformation, Protestants changed the worship service. As teaching became more important than ritual, the pulpit was given a higher profile.

• *This ends our tour—complete with pillar biters, dwarves and giants, a towering wall of organ pipes, and hanging ships. Who said, "When you've seen one Gothic church, you've seen them all"?*

FRANS HALS MUSEUM TOUR

Frans Hals (c. 1582-1666) is Haarlem's most famous son. He was a bold humanist who painted everyday people in their warts-and-all glory, a forerunner of Impressionist brushwork, a master of composition, and an articulate visual spokesman for his generation—the generation of Holland's Golden Age.

Stand eye-to-eye with life-size, lifelike portraits of Haarlem's citizens—brewers, preachers, workers, bureaucrats, and housewives. Take a close look at the people who built the Dutch Golden Age, and then watched it start to fade.

Orientation

Cost: €10 (often €13 when entry includes a special exhibit), audioguide-€2.

If you'll be visiting six or more museums in the Netherlands, consider buying the €50 Museumkaart pass here. It covers your entry to both the Frans Hals and Teylers museums in Haarlem, and lets you skip the ticket-buying line at some bigger sights, such as the Van Gogh Museum in Amsterdam (for more on sightseeing passes, including the Museumkaart, see page 43).

Hours: Tue-Sat 11:00-17:00, Sun 12:00-17:00, closed Mon.

Getting There: The museum is at Groot Heiligland 62, a delightful five-minute stroll from the main square.

Information: Frans Hals' masterpieces never leave room 14 (and nearby rooms), but the other paintings can rotate—ask a guard if you can't locate them easily. The entire museum has been thoroughly renovated and is thoughtfully described in English. Tel. 023/511-5775, www.franshalsmuseum.nl.

Length of This Tour: Allow one hour.

Cuisine Art: The Frans Hals Lunchcafé serves sandwiches and other simple food (daily 12:00-16:30, only drinks and dessert served after 15:30).

Overview

Frans Hals' paintings are just one part of the collection. The museum fancies itself as *the* museum of the Dutch Golden Age, offering you the rare opportunity of enjoying 17th-century art in a 17th-century building. Well-described exhibits unfold as the rectangular museum wraps around a peaceful central courtyard. The building's layout makes sense when you realize it was built as subsidized housing for poor old men (in 1610).

The Tour Begins

Your visit starts with an exhibit called "Haarlem in the 17th Century," showing Dutch slice-of-life paintings alongside short background stories on the issues and items that concerned every-day Dutch Golden Agers: tulips, trading, linen-weaving, militias, "women power," and beer. For those of us who weren't Dutch tradesmen in the 1600s, this well-done exhibit puts the rest of the museum's artwork in an interesting context.

• *From this room, find your way to room 14. Circle the museum counterclockwise, through the art of Hals' predecessors and colleagues, to the back of the complex. Don't be shy about opening a door to the next wing; because of a new climate-control system, there are lots of closed doors here. You'll know you've arrived in the right place when you find yourself well-guarded by canvases full of companies of uniformed men. We'll start with the men in the bright red sashes.*

Banquet of the Officers of the
St. George Civic Guard (1616)

In 1616, tiny Holland was the richest country on earth, and these Haarlem men are enjoying the fruits of their labor. The bright red sashes, the jaunty poses, the smiles, the rich food, the sweeping tilt of the flags...the exuberant spirit of the Dutch Golden Age. These weekend warriors have finished their ceremonial parade through town and hung their weapons on the wall, and now they sit down for a relaxed, post-show party.

The man in the middle (next to the flag-bearer, facing us) is about to carve the chicken, when the meal is interrupted. It's us,

Frans Hals Museum—Room 14

③ **①** **②**

⑤

④

ROOM 14

⑥ **⑧** FORMER

STAIRS → |||| CHAPEL **⑦**

⑨

① Banquet of the Officers of the St. George Civic Guard (1616)
② Banquet of the Officers of the St. George Civic Guard (1627)
③ Banquet of the Officers of the Civic Guard of St. Adrian (1627)
④ Meeting of the Officers and Subalterns of the Civic Guard
    of St. Adrian (1633)
⑤ Officers and Subalterns of the St. George Civic Guard (1639)
⑥ Still Lifes
⑦ Dollhouse
⑧ Bed Curtain
⑨ Flemish Proverbs

arriving late through the back door, and heads turn to greet us. Rosy-cheeked Nicolaes Woutersz van der Meer (see his portrait on page 258), hand on hip, turns around with a friendly look, while the man to the right, the colonel in charge, waves us in. Frans Hals knew these men well as friends and colleagues, since he himself was a lifelong member of this Civic Guard company.

Frans Hals
(c. 1582-1666)

At age 10, Frans Hals, the son of a weaver, moved with his family to Haarlem. He would spend the rest of his life there, rarely traveling even to nearby Amsterdam.

His early years are known to us only through his paintings of taverns and drunks, musicians and actors, crafted in a free and colorful style (like the Rijksmuseum's *The Merry Drinker* on page 145). In 1610, he married and joined Haarlem's St. Luke's Guild of painters. In 1612, he was admitted to the prestigious St. George Civic Guard. In 1617, widowed Hals married again, producing (altogether) ten children, five of whom took up painting.

Hals' group portrait of the St. George Civic Guard (1616) put him on the map as Haarlem's premier portrait painter. For the next five decades, he abandoned the lighthearted slice-of-life scenes of his youth and dedicated himself to chronicling Haarlem's prosperous, middle-class world of businessmen and professionals—people he knew personally, as well as professionally.

Despite his success, Hals had trouble with money. In 1654, he had to sell his belongings to pay debts, and he fought poverty for the rest of his life. Commissions became scarce, as the public now preferred more elegant, flattering portraits. His final works (1650-1666) are dark and somber, with increasingly rough and simple brushwork.

In 1664, the city granted him a pension for his years of service. When he died two years later, his work quickly passed out of fashion, dismissed as mere portraiture. In the 1800s, the Impressionists rediscovered him, and today he's recognized for his innovations, craftsmanship, and unique style.

This band of brothers is united by common gestures—two men have hands on hips, three turn their palms up, two plant their hands downward, three clutch wine glasses. But mostly, they're joined by the uniform sashes. The red sashes slant both left and right, perfectly forming opposing diagonals.

With this painting, Frans Hals broke the mold of stuffy group portraits. He relegates the traditional symbolic weapons to the shelf (upper right) and breaks up the traditional chorus line of soldiers by placing the men naturally around a table. Van der Meer sticks his elbow in our faces (another Hals trademark) to define a distinct foreground, while the flag-bearer stakes out the middle ground, and a window at the back opens up to a distant, airy background.

Then Hals sets the scene in motion. A guy on the left leans over to tell a joke to his friend. The dashing young flag-bearer in the middle turns back to listen to the bald-headed man. An ensign (standing, right side) enters and doffs his cap to Captain Van der Meer. And then we barge in, interrupting the banquet, but welcomed as one of the boys.

Banquet of the Officers of the St. George Civic Guard (1627)

A decade later, Hals painted the same militia again. Familiar faces appear (Captain Van der Meer is in the upper left), but most of the old men have been replaced by a crop of younger, battle-tested officers. These men had recently seen action in the Battle of Breda (1625), fighting for Dutch independence from Spain. The man in the center—facing us and turning his empty glass down to show he needs a refill—was a well-known Haarlem pub owner. (Find him again, in the same tan coat with blue sash, in the 1639 painting described later.)

The banquet looks spontaneous, but the men's poses were carefully planned. Hals painted the bodies first, then brought in the men one by one for their portraits. As colorful as these Civic Guard paintings appear, much of the canvas is black, white, or gray. Van Gogh marveled at Hals' ability to capture "27 shades of black."

Banquet of the Officers of the Civic Guard of St. Adrian (1627)

The men are bunched into two symmetrical groups, left and right, with a window in the back. The figures form a Y, with a tilted flag marking the right diagonal (echoed by several tilted ruffs), and a slanting row of heads forming the left diagonal (echoed by several slanting sashes). The diagonals meet at the back of the table, marking the center of the composition, where the two groups of men exchange food, drink, and meaningful eye contact.

Meeting of the Officers and Subalterns of the Civic Guard of St. Adrian (1633)

Six years later, Hals painted many of these same men gathered around an outdoor table. The horizontal row of faces is

> # Civic Guard Portraits
>
> The fathers of the men pictured in this room fought, suffered imprisonment, and died in the great Siege of Haarlem (1572-1573), which helped turn the tide against Spanish oppression. But their sons were bankers, merchants, traders, and sailors, boldly conquering Europe on the new frontier of capitalism. The Civic Guards became less of a militia, and more a social club for upwardly mobile men. Their feasts—huge eating and drinking binges, punctuated by endless toasts, poems, skits, readings, dirty limericks, and ceremonial courses—could last for days on end.
>
> Standard Civic Guard portraits (like many of those in the Rijksmuseum in Amsterdam) always showed the soldiers in the same way—two neat rows of men, with everyone looking straight out, holding medieval weapons that tell us their ranks. It took master artists like Hals and Rembrandt to turn these boring visual documents into art.

punctuated by three men standing sideways, elbows out. Again, the men are united by sashes that slant in (generally) the same direction and by repeated gestures—hands on hips, hands on hearts, and so on.

Officers and Subalterns of the St. George Civic Guard (1639)

When 57-year-old Frans Hals painted this, his last Civic Guard portrait, he included himself among his St. George buddies. (Find Frans in the upper left, second from left, under the faint gray—number 19.)

As he got older, Hals refined and simplified his group-portrait style, using quieter colors, the classic two horizontal rows of soldiers, and the traditional symbolic weapons.

A decade after this was painted, Holland officially ended its war with Spain (Treaty of Munster, 1648), the Civic Guards lost their military purpose, businessmen preferred portraits showing themselves as elegant gentlemen rather than crusty soldiers, and the tradition of Civic Guard group portraits quickly died.

• *Backtrack and pause to enjoy the exquisite* **still lifes** *in room 13. These lush paintings give us a sense of how good life is, and how important it is to embrace it before it all rots and falls away. Just after this room, look on your left for the five steps leading up to the...*

Frans Hals' Style

- Hals' forte is portraits. Of his 240 paintings, 195 are individual or group portraits, mostly of Haarlem's citizens.
- His paintings are life-size and realistic, capturing everyday people—even downright ugly people—without airbrushing out their blemishes or character flaws.
- Hals uses rough, Impressionistic brushwork, where a few thick, simple strokes blend at a distance to create details. He works quickly, often making the rough sketch the final, oil version.
- His stop-action technique captures the sitter in mid-motion. Aided by his rough brushwork, this creates a blur that suggests the person is still moving.
- Hals adds 3-D depth to otherwise horizontal, widescreen canvases. (Men with their elbows sticking out sometimes serve to define the foreground.)
- His canvases are unified by people wearing matching colors, using similar poses and gestures, and gathered in symmetrical groups.
- His paintings have a relaxed, light-hearted, even comical atmosphere. In group portraits, the subjects interact with one another. Individual portraits meet your eyes as if meeting an old friend.
- His works show nothing religious—no Madonnas, Crucifixions, angels, or Bible scenes. If anything, he imbues everyday objects with heavenly beauty and grants ordinary people the status of saints.

Former Chapel

Take a look inside. You'll find a **fancy dollhouse** *(poppenhuis)*, the hobby of the lady of the house (her portrait is on the left). Handmade by the finest local craftsmen, this delicately crafted dollhouse offers a glimpse of wealthy 18th-century living.

The exquisite **bed curtain,** brought back from New England, decorated the bed of a wealthy Dutch family who lived in colonial America. It's embroidered with bulb flowers known during the 17th century—and well-described in English.

On the wall is *Flemish Proverbs (Vlaamse Spreekwoorden),*

a fun painting that shows 72 charming Flemish scenes representing different folk sayings. (It's a copy of a 17th-century work by Pieter Brueghel the Younger.) Pick up the chart to identify these clever bits of everyday wisdom. True to form, this piece of Flemish art isn't preachy religious art or political propaganda; rather, it shares the simple, decent morals of these hardworking people.

• *Continue counterclockwise around the museum. When you reach the hallway that is room 17, look for the...*

Portrait of Jacobus Zaffius (1611)

Arr-r-r-r-rh! This fierce, intense, rough-hewn man is not a pirate, but a priest, the rogue leader of an outlawed religion in Haarlem—Catholicism. In the 1600s, Haarlem was a Protestant town in the midst of a war against Catholic Spain, and local Catholics were guilty by association. But Zaffius refused to be silenced. He turns to glare and snarl at the Protestant town fathers. He was so personally imposing that the city tolerated his outspokenness.

The face jumps out from a background of neutral gray-brown-black. His features are alive—head turning, mouth twisting, face wrinkling up, beard bristling. Hals captures him in action, using a slow shutter speed. The rough brushstrokes of the fur coat and beard suggest the blur of motion of this agitated individual. This is Frans Hals' first known portrait, painted when he—a late starter in the art world—was nearly 30.

• *Make a left into room 18 to see the...*

Portraits of Nicolaes Woutersz van der Meer and his wife, Cornelia Claesdr Vooght (1631)

Hals knew Nicolaes van der Meer, a fellow Civic Guard lodge member, personally. Van der Meer was a brewer, an important

post in a city where average beer consumption was six pints a day per person (man, woman, and child). He was also the mayor, so his pose is official and dignified, larger than life-size. But the face is pure Dutch Golden Age—red-cheeked and healthy, confident and intelligent, his even gaze tinged with wisdom. This mayor kept a steady hand on the tiller of Haarlem's ship of state.

The face is the focus of this otherwise messy painting. The ruffled collar is a tangle of simple, figure-eight swirls of white paint; the brocaded coat is a patchwork of white lines; and the lace cuffs are a few broad outlines. But out of the rough brushwork and somber background, Van der Meer's crystal-clear eyes meet ours. The finely etched crow's-feet around his eyes suggest that Hals had seen this imposing man break into a warm smile. Hey, I'd vote for him as my mayor.

The companion painting shows Van der Meer's companion, his wife, **Cornelia.** Husband-and-wife portraits were hung together—notice that they share the same background, and the two figures turn in toward each other. Still, both people are looking out at us, not clinging to each other, suggesting mature partners more than lovey-dovey newlyweds. Married couples in Golden Age Holland divvied up the work—men ran the business, women ran the home—and prided themselves on their

mutual independence. (Even today, in progressive Holland, fewer women join the workforce than in many other industrial nations.) Cornelia's body is as imposing as her husband's, with big, manly hands and a practical, slightly suspicious look. The intricate work in her ruff collar tells us that Hals certainly could sweat the details when it suited his purpose.

Regents of the St. Elisabeth Hospital of Haarlem (1641)

These aren't the Dutch Masters cigar boys, though it looks like Rembrandt's famous (and later) *De Staalmeesters* (described in the Amsterdam Rijksmuseum Tour chapter). It's a board meeting, where five men in black hats and black suits with lace collars and cuffs—the Dutch Golden Age power suit—sit around a table in a brown room.

Pretty boring stuff, but Hals was hired to paint their portraits, and he does his best. Behind the suits, he captures five distinct men (this photo shows three of them). The man on the far left is pondering the universe or raising a belch. The man on the right (facing us) looks like the classic

Dutch Golden Age poster boy, with moustache, goatee, ruddy cheeks, and long hair. The middle guy is nearly clean-shaven. Hals links these unique faces with one of his trademark techniques—similar poses and gestures. The burping man and the goateed man are a mirror image of the same pose—leaning on the table, hand on chest. Several have cupped hands; several have hands laid flat, or on their chests, or on the table. And the one guy keeps working on that burp.

• *Continue to room 19. On the wall straight ahead are the...*

Regents of the Old Men's Almshouse (1664)

These men look tired. So was Holland. So was Hals. At 82, Hals, despite years of success, was poor and dependent on the charity

of the city, which granted him a small pension.

He was hired to paint the board of directors of the Old Men's Almshouse, located here in the building that now houses the Frans Hals Museum. Though Hals himself never lived in the almshouse, he fully understood what it was to be penniless and have to rely on

money doled out by men like these.

The portrait is unflattering, drained of color. Somber men dressed in black peer out of a shadowy room. These men were trying to administer a dwindling budget to house and feed an aging population. Holland's Golden Age was losing its luster.

The style is nearly Impressionistic—collars, cuffs, and gloves rendered with a few messy brushstrokes of paint. Hands and faces are a patchwork of light and dark splotches. Despite the sketchiness, each face captures the man's essence.

Historians speculate that this unflattering portrait was Hals' revenge on tightwad benefactors, but the fact is that the regents were satisfied with their portrait. By the way, the man just to the right of center isn't drunk, but suffering from facial paralysis. To the end, Hals respected unvarnished reality.

• *Directly behind you, find the...*

Regentesses of the Old Men's Almshouse (1664)

These women ran the women's wing of the almshouse, located across the street. Except for a little rouge on the women's pale faces, this canvas is almost a study in gray and black, as Hals pared his palette down to the bare essentials. The faces are subtle variations on old age. Only the woman on the right resolutely returns our gaze.

The man who painted this was old, poor, out of fashion, in failing health, perhaps bitter, and dying. In contrast with the lively group scenes of Hals' youth, these individuals stand forever isolated. They don't look at one another, each lost in her own thoughts, perhaps contemplating mortality (or stifling belches). Their only link to one another is the tenuous, slanting line formed by their hands, leading to the servant who enters the room with a mysterious message.

Could that message be...death? Or just that this tour is over?

HAARLEM SLEEPING, EATING, NIGHTLIFE & CONNECTIONS

Jet-lagged travelers arriving in the Netherlands should consider Haarlem a convenient home base: There's fast-and-easy access to Amsterdam or Schiphol Airport, and other side-trips are a quick train trip away. This chapter describes Haarlem's best places to sleep, eat, and relax at night, along with transportation connections.

Sleeping in Haarlem

The helpful Haarlem TI can nearly always find you a €29 bed in a private home (€5.50/person fee, plus a cut of your host's money; two-night minimum). Avoid this if you can; it's cheaper to reserve by calling direct. Nearly every Dutch person you'll encounter speaks English.

Haarlem is most crowded in April, particularly on Easter weekend (April 18-21 in 2014, April 3-6 in 2015), during the flower parade (April 26 in 2014), on King's Day (also on April 26 in 2014, but usually on April 27), and in May, July, and August (especially during Haarlem's jazz festival on the third weekend of August). Also see the list of holidays in the appendix.

The prices listed here include breakfast (unless otherwise noted) but don't include the €2.20-per-person-per-day tourist tax. To avoid excessive street noises, forgo views for a room in the back. Hotels and the TI have a useful parking brochure.

In the Center
Hotels and B&Bs
$$$ **Hotel Lion D'Or** is a classy 34-room business hotel with all the professional comforts, pleasingly posh decor, and a handy but less-than-quaint location (Db-€150, Fri-Sat Db-€125, extra bed-€15, check website for special deals, 8 percent Rick Steves discount

Sleep Code

(€1 = about $1.30, country code: 31, area code: 023)
S = Single, **D** = Double/Twin, **T** = Triple, **Q** = Quad, **b** = bathroom,
s = shower only. Nearly everyone speaks English. Credit cards
are accepted and breakfast is included unless otherwise
noted.

To help you easily sort through these listings, I've divided
the accommodations into three categories, based on the
price for a standard double room with bath:

$$$ Higher Priced—Most rooms €85 or more.
$$ Moderately Priced—Most rooms between €60-85.
$ Lower Priced—Most rooms €60 or less.

Prices can change without notice; verify the hotel's
current rates online or by email.

with 2-night stay if you book direct, air-con, elevator, free Internet
access and Wi-Fi, across the street from train station at Kruisweg 34, tel. 023/532-1750, fax 023/532-9543, www.hotelliondor.nl,
reservations@hotelliondor.nl, friendly Dirk Pauw).

$$$ Stempels Hotel, modern yet elegant, is located in a
renovated 300-year-old building. With bare floors, comfy high-
quality beds, and minimalist touches in its 17 rooms, what it lacks
in warmth it makes up for in style and value. Double-paned win-
dows help keep down the noise—it's just a block east of Grote
Markt, with a bustling brasserie and bar downstairs (standard
Sb-€95, standard Db-€112-150, pricier rooms and suites available,
breakfast-€12.50, in-room computers with free Internet access and
Wi-Fi, elevator, Klokhuisplein 9, tel. 023/512-3910, www.stempels
inhaarlem.nl, info@stempelsinhaarlem.nl).

$$$ Hotel Amadeus, on Grote Markt, has 15 small, bright,
and basic rooms, some with views of the square. This charming
hotel, ideally located above an early 20th-century dinner café,
is relatively quiet, especially if you take a room in the back. Its
lush old lounge/breakfast room on the second floor overlooks the
square, and Mike and Inez take good care of their guests (Sb-€60,
Db-€85, check website for special deals, 5 percent Rick Steves discount off full price with 2-night stay and cash, free Wi-Fi, Grote
Markt 10—from square it's a steep climb to lounge, elevator inside
ground-floor café if you need it, tel. 023/532-4530, fax 023/532-
2328, www.amadeus-hotel.com, info@amadeus-hotel.com). Hotel
Amadeus' breakfast room overlooking the main square is a great
place to watch the town greet a new day—and one of my favorite
Haarlem moments.

Haarlem Hotels & Restaurants

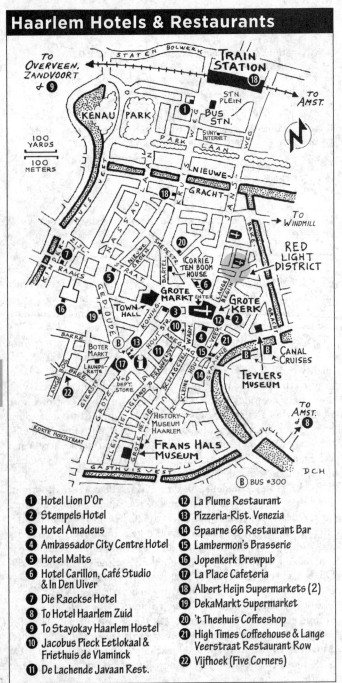

1. Hotel Lion D'Or
2. Stempels Hotel
3. Hotel Amadeus
4. Ambassador City Centre Hotel
5. Hotel Malts
6. Hotel Carillon, Café Studio & In Den Uiver
7. Die Raeckse Hotel
8. To Hotel Haarlem Zuid
9. To Stayokay Haarlem Hostel
10. Jacobus Pieck Eetlokaal & Friethuis de Vlaminck
11. De Lachende Javaan Rest.
12. La Plume Restaurant
13. Pizzeria-Rist. Venezia
14. Spaarne 66 Restaurant Bar
15. Lambermon's Brasserie
16. Jopenkerk Brewpub
17. La Place Cafeteria
18. Albert Heijn Supermarkets (2)
19. DekaMarkt Supermarket
20. 't Theehuis Coffeeshop
21. High Times Coffeehouse & Lange Veerstraat Restaurant Row
22. Vijfhoek (Five Corners)

$$$ Ambassador City Centre Hotel, with 46 comfortable rooms in a big, plain hotel, is located just behind the Grote Kerk. If you're willing to trade some street noise for amazing church views, ask for a room in the front (Db-€100, often less off-season, breakfast buffet-€13.50, free Internet access and Wi-Fi, Oude Groenmarkt 20, tel. 023/512-5300, www.acc-hotel.nl, info@acc -hotel.nl). They also run **Hotel Joops,** with 32 rooms, a block away (rooms are €10 cheaper; studios and apartments with kitchenettes for 2-4 people-€110-140 depending on season and number of people).

$$ Central Hotel Malts rents 12 bright, simple, and fresh rooms for a good price. The rooms in front are big, but not recommended for light sleepers (small D-€75, small Db-€79, standard Db-€89, big Db-€95, check website for best prices, no elevator, free Wi-Fi, Zijlstraat 56, tel. 023/551-2385, www.maltshotel.nl, info@maltshotel.nl, Marco and Andrea). They also offer €65 studio apartments with kitchenettes near the Red Light District.

Rooms in Restaurants

These places are all run as sidelines by restaurants, and you'll know it by the style of service and rooms. Lobbies are in the restaurant, and there are no public spaces. Still, they are handy and—for Haarlem—inexpensive.

$$ Hotel Carillon overlooks the town square and comes with bell-tower chimes and a little traffic. With run-down public spaces and st-e-e-e-p stairs, it's an old-school, over-the-restaurant place. The rooms themselves, however, are freshly updated and pleasant. The front rooms come with more street noise and great townsquare views (tiny loft S-€45, Db-€80-90, Tb-€110, Qb-€150, 5 percent Rick Steves discount if you ask when you reserve and show book on arrival, no elevator, free Wi-Fi, Grote Markt 27, tel. 023/531-0591, fax 023/531-4909, www.hotelcarillon.com, info @hotelcarillon.com, owners Kelly Kuo, Andres Haas, and June).

$$ Die Raeckse Hotel, family-run and friendly, is not as central as the others and has less character and more traffic noise—but its 21 rooms are decent and comfortable. Quiet rooms in back cost more than the noisy rooms on the street—but they're worth it (Sb-€55, smaller Db-€80-85, big Db-€85-90, Tb-€120, Qb-€130-145, €5/night discount for 2-night stay, ask for Rick Steves discount if you book direct and show this book on arrival—good only Nov-March, free but time-limited Internet access, free Wi-Fi, Raaks Straat 1, tel. 023/532-6629, fax 023/531-7937, www.die-raeckse.nl, dieraeckse@zonnet.nl).

Near Haarlem

$$$ Hotel Haarlem Zuid, with 300 modern rooms, is sterile but a good value for drivers. It sits in an industrial zone a 20-minute walk from the center, on the road to the airport. They are renovating about two-thirds of the rooms; rates may rise as a result (Db-€89-140, breakfast-€13, elevator, free Wi-Fi, free parking, laundry service, free fitness center, reasonable hotel restaurant, Toekanweg 2, tel. 023/536-7500, fax 023/536-7980, www.hotelhaarlemzuid .nl, haarlemzuid@valk.com). Bus #300 conveniently connects the hotel with the train station, Grote Markt, and the airport (every 10 minutes, stop: Europaweg).

$ Stayokay Haarlem Hostel, completely renovated and with all the youth-hostel comforts, charges €25-30 for beds in four- and six-bed dorms. They also rent simple €60-80 doubles (€2.50 less for members, includes sheets and breakfast, save by booking on their website, pay Internet access, free Wi-Fi, laundry service, reception open 8:00-23:00, Jan Gijzenpad 3, two miles from Haarlem station—take bus #2 from station, or a 10-minute walk from Santpoort Zuid train station, tel. 023/537-3793, www.stay okay.com/haarlem, haarlem@stayokay.com).

Eating in Haarlem

Restaurants

Jacobus Pieck Eetlokaal is popular with locals for its fine-value "global cuisine," good salads, and unpretentious flair. Sit in the peaceful garden courtyard, at a sidewalk table, or in the romantically cozy interior. The Oriental Peak Salad is a perennial favorite, and the dish of the day (*dagschotel*, €12.50) always sells out (great €7 sandwiches at lunch, Tue-Sat 11:00-16:00 & 17:30-22:00, closed Sun-Mon, cash only, Warmoesstraat 18, behind church, tel. 023/532-6144).

De Lachende Javaan ("The Laughing Javanese") is a long-established Indonesian place serving a memorable *rijsttafel* (€20-24, Tue-Sun 17:00-22:00, closed Mon, Frankestraat 27, tel. 023/532-8792).

La Plume Restaurant steakhouse is noisy, with a happy, local, and carnivorous crowd enjoying the candlelit scene (€20-25 meals, Mon-Fri 17:30-23:00, Sat-Sun 17:00-23:00, *satay* and ribs are favorites, Lange Veerstraat 1, tel. 023/531-3202). The relaxing outdoor seating faces the church and a lively pedestrian street.

Pizzeria-Ristorante Venezia, run for 25 years by the same Italian family from Bari, is *the* place to go for pizza or pasta (€8-10 choices, daily 13:00-23:00, facing V&D department store at Verwulft 7, tel. 023/531-7753). You'll feel like you're in Rome at a good indoor table, or sit outdoors for good people-watching.

Lange Veerstraat Restaurant Row: If you don't know what you want to eat, stroll the delightful Lange Veerstraat behind the church and survey a fun range of restaurants (from cheap falafels to Cuban, and much more).

On the Spaarne River Canal: Haarlem seems to turn its back on its river with most of the eating energy a couple of blocks away. To enjoy a meal with a nice canal view, consider the **Spaarne 66 Restaurant Bar.** The Lemmers girls (a mom and her daughters) run this cozy eatery, with a woody, old-time interior and fine outdoor canalside seating (light €7 lunches, €20 Mediterranean/Dutch dinner plates, €31.50 three-course fixed-price meal, daily in summer 10:00-24:00, closed Mon-Tue in winter, Spaarne 66, tel. 023/551-3800).

Dressy Splurge: At **Lambermon's,** expert chef Michèl Lambermon serves chichi pan-European cuisine in a suave, modern, corner restaurant. The Michelin-rated brasserie offers €29 two-course fixed-price lunches and €45 three-course dinners (€29-32 main courses, daily 12:00-15:00 & 18:00-22:00; Korte Veerstraat 1, tel. 023/542-7804).

Trendy Brewpub: While beer-drinking is a religion in Belgium, it's also getting that way in Haarlem, where the Jopen brewery has converted a church into a flashy gastropub called **Jopenkerk.** With 18 brews on tap, including a *Hoppenbier* from a 1501 recipe, this is a beer lover's mecca. Budget pub grub is served on the ground floor, or try the upstairs restaurant for more elegant fare (€8-10 burgers, salads, and quiche in the pub, €15-23 main dishes in the restaurant, daily 10:00-1:00 in the morning, Gedempte Voldersgracht 2, tel. 023/533-4114).

Budget Options

La Place is a snazzy chain cafeteria that dishes up fresh, healthy budget food. Sit on the top floor or the roof garden of the V&D department store with Haarlem's best view. If you're too hungry to ride six floors of escalators, they offer the same food on the ground floor (Mon 11:00-18:00, Tue-Sat 9:30-18:00, Thu until 21:00, Sun 12:00-17:00, Grote Houtstraat 70, on corner of Gedempte Oude Gracht, tel. 023/515-8700).

Friethuis de Vlaminck is your best bet for a cone of old-fashioned, fresh Flemish-style fries (€2, Tue-Sun 12:00-17:00, closed Mon, Warmoesstraat 3, behind church, tel. 023/532-1084). Ali offers a dazzling array of sauces. With his help, you can be adventurous.

Supermarkets: **Albert Heijn** has two convenient locations. One is in the train station (Mon-Fri 6:30-21:00, Sat 10:00-21:00, Sun 9:00-21:00, cash only); the other is at Kruisstraat 10 (Mon-Sat 8:00-22:00, closed Sun, cash only). The **DekaMarkt** is a few

HAARLEM EATING

Marijuana in Haarlem

Haarlem is a laid-back place for observing the Dutch approach to recreational marijuana. The town is dotted with about a dozen coffeeshops, where pot is sold and smoked by relaxed, noncriminal types. These easygoing coffeeshops are more welcoming than they may feel—bartenders understand that Yankee travelers might feel a bit out of their element and are happy to answer questions.

If you don't like the smell of pot, avoid places sporting wildly painted walls; plants in the windows; or Rastafarian yellow, red, and green colors. The following two shops are inviting and particularly friendly to American visitors:

The tiny **'t Theehuis,** which feels like a hippie teahouse, was Haarlem's first coffeeshop (c. 1984). Along with a global selection of pot, it has 50 varieties of tea on the menu and a friendly staff. The staff is happy to roll you a €2.50-3.50 joint of your choice (daily 11:00-20:00, Fri-Sat until 1:00 in the morning, a block off Grote Markt at Smedestraat 25).

High Times, with a living-room ambience and loaner bongs, offers smokers 12 varieties of joints in racks behind the bar (neatly pre-packed in trademarked "Joint Packs," €3-4.50, Mon-Fri 8:00-23:00, Sat from 9:00, Sun from 11:00, free Internet access for customers, Lange Veerstraat 47). Across the street, at Crackers Pub, you can see what too much alcohol does to people.

blocks west of Grote Markt (Mon-Sat 8:00-20:00, Thu-Fri until 21:00, Sun 16:00-21:00, Gedempte Oude Gracht 54, near the V&D department store).

Nightlife in Haarlem

Haarlem's evening scene is great. Consider four basic zones: Grote Markt in the shadow of the Grote Kerk; Lange Veerstraat; Boter Grote Markt; and Vijfhoek (Five Corners).

Grote Markt is lined with trendy bars that seem made for nursing a drink—**Café Studio** is generally the hot spot for a drink here (at Grote Markt 25); I'd also duck into the dark interior of **In Den Uiver** (near the Grote Kerk entry at Riviervischmarkt 13, live jazz Thu and Sun). Lange Veerstraat (behind the Grote Kerk) is colorful and bordered with lively spots. Boter Grote Markt is more convivial and local, as it's less central and away from the tourists—try the nearby **Jopenkerk** brewpub (described earlier). Vijfhoek, named for the five lanes that converge here, is incredibly charming, although it has only one pub (with plenty of drinks, bar snacks, a relaxed crowd, and good indoor or outdoor seating). Also worth exploring is the area from this cutest corner in town to the New Church (Nieuwe Kerk), a couple blocks away. If you want a more high-powered scene, Amsterdam is just 20 minutes away by train.

Haarlem Connections

For general tips about public transportation in the Netherlands—including types of trains, reading timetables, and how and where to buy tickets—see the appendix. If you take the train from Amsterdam to Haarlem, see page 240 for a train-window tour of the countryside.

From Haarlem by Train to: Zandvoort (2/hour, 11 minutes), **Amsterdam** (6/hour, 20 minutes, €3.70 one-way, €7.10 same-day round-trip), **The Hague/Den Haag** (6/hour, 40 minutes, some transfer in Leiden), **Delft** (2/hour, 40 minutes), **Rotterdam** (4/hour, 55 minutes, half require change in Leiden), **Hoorn** (2/hour, 1 hour, more with change in Amsterdam Sloterdijk), **Alkmaar** (2/hour, 35 minutes), **Brussels** (hourly, 2.75 hours, transfer in Rotterdam), **Bruges/Brugge** (hourly, 3.5 hours, 2-3 changes—avoid Thalys connections if traveling with a railpass).

From Haarlem by Bus to Aalsmeer: Connexxion bus #140 connects Haarlem to bus #172, which goes to the flower auction in Aalsmeer (4/hour, 1 hour, see "Getting There" on page 276).

To Schiphol Airport: Your best option is the **bus** (4-10/hour, 40 minutes, €4—buy ticket from driver, bus #300). For most of the trip, this bus travels on its own limited-access roadway—what transit wonks call a "busway." To catch the bus from the middle of Haarlem, head to the Centrum/Verwulft stop, near the V&D department store. To catch it from the train station, look for the "A" bus stop marked *R Net*. You can also get there by **train** (6/hour, 30-40 minutes, transfer at Amsterdam-Sloterdijk station, €5.40 one-way) or **taxi** (about €30-40).

DUTCH
DAY TRIPS

Any Dutch native will tell you: To really experience everyday life in the Netherlands, get out of Amsterdam. In a country as tiny as Holland, day-tripping is easy to do. Within a half-hour of leaving Central Station, you can be deep in the Dutch country-side—lush, green, and filled with tulips, red-brick houses, quaint canals, and black-and-white cows. It's a refreshing break from urban Amsterdam. Match your interest with the village's spe-cialty: flower auctions, open-air folk museums, fresh cheese, Delft Blue porcelain, or modern art. Take some time to learn a few basic Dutch phrases for the sake of politeness (see the appendix), but don't obsess—even outside of Amsterdam, just about everyone speaks English.

If you're based in Amsterdam, note that Haarlem (covered in the preceding chapters) makes a great day trip in itself. This chap-ter introduces many other easy day trips from Amsterdam (or from Haarlem).

For those interested in Dutch culture, I describe three open-air museums: Arnhem, Zuiderzee in Enkhuizen, and Zaanse Schans. Doing more than one is overkill for most visitors—read my descriptions and choose one. Arnhem's is the best, but the far-thest from Amsterdam. Enkhuizen's Zuiderzee is also good and can be conveniently combined with the Historic Triangle route. Zaanse Schans is the least appealing and most entrepreneurial, but the closest to Amsterdam.

Planning Your Time

If you only have a day or two to venture outside of Amsterdam or Haarlem, use this list to help you decide where to go. I've listed the destinations in the chapter order they appear in this book.

Dutch Day Trips

Keukenhof, Aalsmeer, and Zandvoort

Any of these is an easy half-day side-trip from Haarlem or Amsterdam, but note that Keukenhof's gardens are open only in spring (see dates below), Aalsmeer's auction operates only on weekday mornings (closed Sat-Sun), and Zandvoort's beach is best in summer.

▲▲▲Keukenhof This can't-miss garden show, in the town of Lisse, is open for only two months every spring (mid-March through mid-May).

▲▲FloraHolland Aalsmeer Flower Auction Close to the airport, this vast auction warehouse shows you the business side of the Netherlands' beautiful flower scene (open weekday mornings year-round).

Zandvoort This lively beach resort town, practically a suburb of Haarlem, is handy for a quick getaway.

Delft and The Hague

Allow a full day to visit the adjacent towns of Delft and The Hague—though either destination makes a fun day trip on its own. Delft is also a fine place to spend the night. (Delft's morning markets are on Thu and Sat; The Hague's Peace Palace is closed Sat-Sun, and its minor museums are closed Mon.)

▲▲**Delft** This lovely hometown of the painter Vermeer and the Delftware factory is a delightful place to relax by a canal. For more activity, zip into The Hague, just next door.

▲▲**The Hague** This big-city seat of Dutch government offers good museums, including the excellent Mauritshuis art gallery, housed until mid-2014 at the Gemeentemuseum.

Museums near Arnhem

Allow an extremely long day to visit the open-air and modern-art museums (but not on Mon, when art museum is closed); you'll need to leave Amsterdam by 8:00. If you stay overnight near the art museum (in Otterlo), you'll have more time to fit in the train museum on your return to Amsterdam.

▲▲**Arnhem Open-Air Folk Museum** Holland's original, biggest, and best open-air folk museum, Arnhem sprinkles traditional buildings from around Holland across a delightful park, and populates them with chatty docents to give you a flavor of old-time lifestyles.

▲▲**Kröller-Müller Museum** This excellent modern-art museum has dozens of Van Goghs and a sculpture garden. It's located on the outskirts of the city of Arnhem, within the vast Hoge Veluwe National Park, which has free loaner bikes you can ride to the museum.

▲**Spoorwegmuseum** Holland's biggest and best train museum is located in the crossroads town of Utrecht.

Schokland Museum

Easiest by car, it takes about a half-day to visit this far-flung sight.

▲**Schokland** A former island left high and dry when the surrounding sea was drained, this village is now a museum in the middle of reclaimed farmland.

Edam, Volendam, and Marken

Figure on a day (leaving Amsterdam by 10:00) to visit these picturesque villages, in the region aptly called Waterland. If you have only a half-day, choose Edam. (Edam's museum is closed Mon and its market is held Wed morning.)

▲▲**Edam** In this quiet town, you can mellow out like a hunk of aging cheese. There are no real sights, but its tiny main square and peaceful canals may win you over.

Volendam A transit hub for the Waterland region, this workaday town has an extremely touristy seafront promenade and a boat across to Marken.

Marken Once an island, and now connected by a causeway to the mainland, this time-warp fishing village preserves traditional buildings and lifestyles.

The Historic Triangle

Allow a full day for this excursion. Leave Amsterdam for Hoorn by 9:38 (confirm time at station) if you want to have enough time to visit the Zuiderzee Museum before it closes. The Triangle trip is usually offered daily in peak season (not always on Mondays) and less frequently off-season; ✪ see the Historic Triangle chapter for details.

▲▲**The Historic Triangle** Take this enjoyable trip by catching a steam train in the town of Hoorn to the town of Medemblik, and then sailing on a 1920s-era boat to Enkhuizen to visit the Zuiderzee open-air folk museum.

▲**Enkhuizen Zuiderzee Museum** With an emphasis on seaside lifestyles, this well-presented open-air folk museum is the grand finale of a Historic Triangle day, or can be visited directly from Amsterdam.

Alkmaar and Zaanse Schans

Allow a half-day for Alkmaar—ideally Friday morning for the town's cheese market, held in spring and summer. Allow a full day to add the open-air museum. Both are described in the Alkmaar and Zaanse Schans chapter.

▲**Alkmaar** This likeable town is especially fun to visit, and easily worth ▲▲ during its Friday-morning cheese market (early April-early Sept only, 10:00-12:30).

Zaanse Schans Open-Air Museum Packed with windmills (and greedy shops), this sight is just a quick 15-minute train ride (plus a 15-minute walk) from central Amsterdam.

Transportation Tips

Train: If you're day-tripping, ask about "day return" tickets (same-day round-trip), which are cheaper than two one-way tickets. Before you board at Amsterdam's Central Station, check the yellow train-schedule boards or ask at the information counter to confirm the details of your trip (such as times, necessary transfers, delays, and the name of the station you'll be using—for example, to get to Zaanse Schans, you'll get off at the Koog-Zaandijk station). When riding a train to any big town, note that "CS" always stands for "Central Station"—usually the one you want (unless I note otherwise). You'll find train information online at www.ns.nl or for all public transit, including trains, use www.9292.nl.

Driving: Although the roads are excellent, densely populated Holland can be a time-consuming place for drivers. Traffic congestion is notoriously bad, especially around rush hour near Amsterdam, Rotterdam, The Hague, Utrecht, and other big cities. Everything in this book is covered by the excellent, detailed ANWB Wegenkaart *Nederland midden* map (1:200,000, sold at bookstores).

Of all the Amsterdam day trips, these three side-trips near Haarlem require the least brainpower: two flower experiences (a garden show and a flower auction) and a beach retreat.

▲▲▲Keukenhof

This is the greatest bulb-flower garden on earth, open for only two months in spring. Each spring, seven million flowers, enjoying the sandy soil of the Dutch dunes and *polderland,* conspire to thrill even the most horticulturally challenged. This 80-acre park is packed with tour groups daily; for the least crowds and the best light, go late in the day. Keukenhof is located at the northern tip of the town of Lisse, at the center of the "Dune and Bulb Region."

Cost and Hours: €15, not covered by Museumkaart, open mid-March through mid-May, daily 8:00-19:30, last entry at 18:00, tel. 0252/465-564, www.keukenhof.nl.

Combo-Ticket: €22.50 combo-ticket covers park entry and round-trip bus transport from Leiden, Schiphol Airport, or Haarlem; €27.50 from Amsterdam (available on Keukenhof website).

Getting There: From Amsterdam's Leidseplein, take bus #197 to Schiphol and change to bus #858 (2/hour, 1.25 hours). From Haarlem, take bus #50 to Lisse (4/hour, 1 hour). From Schiphol Airport, catch bus #858 (8/hour, 40 minutes). From Amsterdam or Haarlem you can also take a train to Leiden, then bus #854 (Keukenhof Express). Drivers will find Lisse well-marked from the A-6 expressway south of Amsterdam.

▲▲FloraHolland Aalsmeer Flower Auction (Bloemenveiling)

Get a bird's-eye view of the huge Dutch flower industry in this cavernous building where the world's flower prices are set. You'll wander on elevated walkways (through what's claimed to be the biggest commercial building on earth) over literally trainloads of freshly cut flowers. About half of all the flowers exported from Holland are auctioned off here, in four huge auditoriums. The flowers are shipped here overnight (for maximum freshness), auctioned at

the crack of dawn, and distributed as quickly as possible.

Cost and Hours: €5, Mon-Wed and Fri 7:00-11:00, Thu 7:00-9:00, closed Sat-Sun, gift shop, cafeteria, tel. 0297/393-939, www.floraholland.com.

Getting There: By bus, you can reach the flower auction from Amsterdam (Connexxion bus #172 from Central Station, 4/hour, 1 hour, get off at "BVFH Hoofdingang" stop) or from Haarlem (take bus #140 to the town of Aalsmeer, transfer to bus #172, 4/hour, 1 hour). Aalsmeer, which is close to the airport, makes a handy last fling for drivers before dropping off your car at the airport and catching a late-morning weekday flight out (bus #198 also runs between the auction and the airport; 4/hour, 20 minutes). From the A-6 expressway south of Amsterdam, drivers take the Aalsmeer exit (#3) and follow signs for *Aalsmeer*, then *Bloemenveiling*. Once you reach the complex, carefully follow the *P Tourist* signs to park on top of the garage, then take the elevator downstairs and follow *Tourist* signs to the visitors center.

Visiting the Flower Auction: For the best floral variety and auction action, the earlier, the better (best before 9:30, and the auction closes down by 11:00).

Standing above all those blooms, take a deep, fragrant breath and hold it in. As you wander, keep an eye out for tulip-shaped "listening posts," and press the English button for on-the-spot information. Peering into the auction halls, you'll see that clocks are projected on two big screens. This is a "Dutch auction," meaning that the price starts high and then ticks down, until buyers push the button at the price they're willing to pay. Think about the high stakes and the need for decisiveness...there's no time to think things over as the auctioneer calls, "Going once, going twice..."

Most of the flowers are purchased by wholesalers and exporters. You'll see the busy beehive of the distribution process as workers scurry to load carts of flowers onto little tractors to zip to awaiting buyers. Up along the ceiling, look for the suspended orange trams. This "Aalsmeer Shuttle" zips loads of flowers over the workers' heads to the distribution center across the street, far more quickly and efficiently than trucks.

You'll wind up at the even more elaborate Rose Market, where 450 buyers keep their eyes peeled on three different auction clocks as they jostle to buy the auction's most popular item. As you circle back to the entrance, you'll see the company's testing lab, where they actually create and test new varieties of flowers.

Zandvoort

For a quick and easy look at the windy coastline in a shell-lover's Shangri-la, visit the beach burg of Zandvoort. This pretty, mani-

cured resort has plenty of cafés, ice-cream parlors, *Vlaamse friet* stands, restaurants, and bou-tiques. Just beyond the town is the vast and sandy beach, lined with cafés and rentable chairs. Above it all is a pedestrian promenade and a line of high-rise hotels. South of the main beach, sunbathers work on all-over tans. Come to Zandvoort if the weather's hot and you want a taste of the sea and sun, if you want to see how Dutch and German holiday-makers have fun, or if you just want an excuse for a long bike ride from Haarlem.

Tourist Information: The helpful TI is on Bakkerstraat (Mon-Fri 9:00-17:00, Sat 10:00-17:00, Sun 11:00-16:00, tel. 023/571-7947, www.vvvzandvoort.nl).

Getting There: It's easy to reach by train (2/hour, 30 min-utes from Amsterdam, 11 minutes from Haarlem). For a breezy 45-minute bike ride west of Haarlem, follow road signs for *Bloem-endaal*, then *Zandvoort*.

DELFT and THE HAGUE

These adjoining cities, both conveniently situated just an hour southwest of Amsterdam, are as different as night and day. Sleepy Delft is the charming cultural capital, with soothing canals, an inviting square, royal tombs squirreled away under an exclamation-point church tower, and ties to Vermeer. The citified Eurocrat center of The Hague offers sightseers a few busy but rewarding hours of urban museum-hopping, including the chance to meet a famous girl with a pearl earring.

The two cities are linked by a simple tram or train ride. Together, they form a handy yin and yang of enjoyable experiences.

Planning Your Time

It's easy to day-trip to Delft and The Hague from Amsterdam or Haarlem—but if you spend the night anywhere in the Netherlands outside the capital, make it Delft.

Whether side-tripping or home-basing, for a busy day of contrasts, visit both Delft and The Hague. In the morning, take in The Hague's sights (the Mauritshuis collection—temporarily housed at the Gemeen-

temuseum—is tops). Then continue to Delft to visit its churches, Vermeer Center, and Royal Dutch Delftware Manufactory (closes at 17:00)...or to simply mellow out by a canal.

Delft

Peaceful as a Vermeer painting and as lovely as its porcelain, Delft has a special soul. Enjoy this typically Dutch, "I could live here"

 town best by simply wandering around, watching people, munching local syrup waffles, or daydreaming on the canal bridges. If you're eager for some sightseeing, visit a pair of churches, learn more about favorite son Vermeer, or tour the famous porcelain factory.

Think of Delft as an alternative to Haarlem: a low-key, mid-sized city with fast and easy connections to a big metropolis (The Hague). And, laced with tranquil and picturesque canals, Delft would easily win the cuteness contest. If you love Vermeer's quiet, exquisite paintings, you understand why it's said that the painter's muse was his hometown of Delft.

Orientation to Delft

Delft feels much smaller than its population of 95,000. (Because they're squeezed between the two giant cities of Rotterdam and The Hague, locals describe Delft as a "small town.") Almost everything of interest (except the porcelain factory) clusters within the former walls of the canal-lined Old Town, across the street from the train station. The vast Markt (Market Square), with the tall and skinny spire of the New Church, marks the center of the Old Town. A couple of blocks to the southeast is the lively, restaurant-lined Beestenmarkt. You could walk from one end of the Old Town to the other in about 15 minutes.

Tourist Information

This TI is a tourist's dream. Pick up the good free brochure, which includes a map, or just get the map separately (April-Sept Sun-Mon 10:00-16:00, Tue-Fri 9:00-18:00, Sat 10:00-17:00; Oct-March Mon 11:00-16:00, Tue-Sat 10:00-16:00, Sun 11:00-15:00; free Internet access, free baggage storage for day-trippers, near the New Church and the Markt at Kerkstraat 3, tel. 015/215-4051, www.delft.nl). If you want to visit the Royal Dutch Delftware Manufactory, pick up a discount coupon here (may also be available at your hotel).

Walking Tours: The TI sells a brochure describing a pleasant self-guided walking tour (€3.50); it also has a €2 "Vermeer Trail"

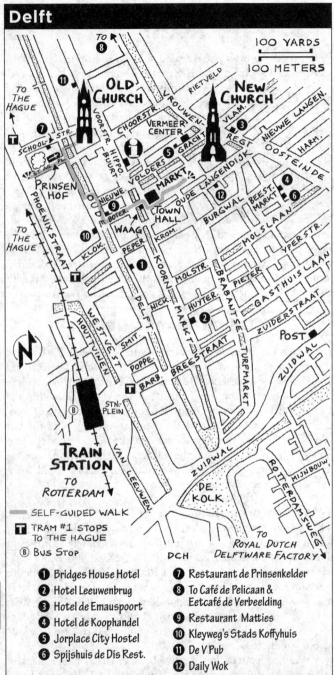

Delft

100 YARDS
100 METERS

TO
THE
HAGUE

OLD CHURCH

NEW CHURCH

VROUWEN-GRACHT · RIETVELD

VLAM.

NIEUWE LANGEN.

OOSTEINDE

HARM.

CHOORSTR.

VOORSTR. · HIPPO. BUURT.

VERMEER CENTER

SCHOOL-STR.

ST. AG. PL.

PRINSEN HOF

VOLDERS

MARKT

REGT

NIEUWE · M. BOTER.

OUDE LANGENDIJK

BURGWAL

BEEST. MARKT

MOLSLAAN

YPER STR.

GASTHUISLAAN

ZUIDERSTRAAT

TOWN HALL

WAAG

KLOK.

PEPER

KROM.

DELFT · NICK.

KOORN. MARKT

MOLSTR.

HUYTER.

SMIT.

POPPE.

BARB.

BREESTRAAT

PIETER

BRABANTSE TURFMARKT

POST

ZUIDWAL

PHOENIX STRAAT

TO THE HAGUE

WESTVEST

HOUTTUINEN

STN-PLEIN

VAN LEEUWEN.

ZUIDWAL

DE KOLK

ROTTERDAMSEWEG

MIJNBOUW.

TRAIN STATION

TO ROTTERDAM

TO ROYAL DUTCH DELFTWARE FACTORY

DCH

SELF-GUIDED WALK

TRAM #1 STOPS TO THE HAGUE

BUS STOP

① Bridges House Hotel
② Hotel Leeuwenbrug
③ Hotel de Emauspoort
④ Hotel de Koophandel
⑤ Jorplace City Hostel
⑥ Spijshuis de Dis Rest.
⑦ Restaurant de Prinsenkelder
⑧ To Café de Pelicaan & Eetcafé de Verbeelding
⑨ Restaurant Matties
⑩ Kleyweg's Stads Koffyhuis
⑪ De V Pub
⑫ Daily Wok

DELFT

pamphlet. In the summer (Easter-Sept), the TI offers a €10 two-hour walking tour of town that includes a canal-boat trip (Sun-Fri at 11:30, Sat at 12:30, also in Oct on weekends only).

Arrival in Delft

By Train: Delft's train station likely will be a mess during your visit, as the station and trains are being moved underground. If lockers are unavailable because of the construction, you can leave bags for free at the TI.

From the train station, it's about a 10-minute walk to the Markt at the center of the Old Town: Exit through the construction mess, walk across the canal, then continue into town, following yellow signs for *Centrum*.

To head straight to the porcelain factory, find the bus stop on the other (west) side of the tracks, away from the construction. For now, the taxi stand is also located on the west side of the station.

By Car: Drivers take the Delft exit #9 off the A-13 expressway. Parking garages are scattered around the city (€14/24 hours, higher per-hour rates for shorter time periods, Marktgarage at Willem Naghelstraat 1 is best for the town center, tel. 015/214-6250, www.parkingdelft.nl/en).

Tours in Delft

Local Guides—Private tours led by licensed guides can be booked through the local guide bureau (€120/2 hours, tel. 062/242-9010, www.delftguidedtours.com, bureau@delft-guide.nl). I enjoyed a walk led by Sybrand de Jong.

Canal Boat Tour—Rondvaart Delft offers a 45-minute boat tour of the Old Town (€7, April-Oct daily 11:00-17:00, boats depart hourly from along Koornmarkt canal, tel. 015/212-6385, www.rondvaartdelft.nl). They also rent paddleboats (€12.50/hour).

Bike/Rickshaw Tour—Bryan, a hard-working young man with a funky bicycle-rickshaw, pedals visitors around town while delivering commentary. He's no historian, but he offers a quirky glimpse at the city—and a special price with this book. It's a fun before-dinner activity: He'll meet you at your hotel and drop you at the restaurant of your choice at the end of the tour (1-2 people: €10/half-hour, €20/hour, tel. 061/886-1552, info@fietsdienstdelft.com). He also provides bike taxi service.

Self-Guided Walk

Welcome to Delft

• *Stand in the center of Delft's market square—the Markt—and face the towering New Church.*

The Markt

This is clearly a city with a rich history and a wealthy past. Its look today was defined in 1536, when lightning struck the spire of the **New Church** (Nieuwe Kerk; interior described later under "Sights in Delft"), starting a fire that destroyed two-thirds of the town. While all the buildings that ring the square have cellars dating from before the fire, what you see above ground made of brick was built after 1536.

Delft recovered well from the fire. In the 17th century, its Golden Age, this was a thriving market town, with an economy stoked by textiles and breweries. (With 200 breweries, the city exported 80 percent of its beer.) Then, in the 18th century, the economy collapsed. Without the infrastructure of a trading city—there's no river, local harbor, or major roads—Delft was left behind. It became a sleeping-beauty town, cocooned in an intact medieval structure, awaiting awakening.

Building of the New Church, with its Late Gothic lines, began in 1393 and took 100 years to complete. The stone tower you see today houses a carillon, proudly considered the Stradivarius of carillons by locals. Its chimes, played on request by the town bell ringer, are a favorite of brides being married at the Town Hall.

The **square** has never really been renovated, perhaps because it must always be ready, on a day's notice, to host a royal funeral. In 1584, William I of Orange (b. 1533), leader of the Dutch revolt against Spain, was assassinated in Delft. Under normal circumstances, he would have been buried in his family's hometown of Breda, but the Spanish had occupied the city. So William was laid to rest in Delft, and to this day, the house of Orange—the Dutch royal family—buries its nobility in the New Church.

The statue dominating the square honors **Hugo Grotius.** Born in Delft in 1583, Grotius was the first to establish international rules of the sea, putting forth the idea that all the oceans were free-trade territory, open to every nation. That didn't go over so well with the rival English, who claimed dominion over all the sea around Britain. The controversy went on for nearly a century, during which the two nations fought a two-year war over it. (The eventual agreement—the sea within the range of a cannonball fired from your shore is yours; any waters beyond that are open to all nations—forms the basis for today's maritime laws.)

Part of Delft's economic heritage is in printing. At #57 (above the Subway sandwich place) a Bible on the building's corner recalls the first printed Dutch Bible, produced here in 1477.

Opposite the New Church stands the **Town Hall,** rebuilt in 1620 in the Renaissance style after a fire. It's a law court, with Lady Justice and her scales prominently positioned on the facade. Of the 17 states in the Spanish Netherlands, seven seceded and created the Dutch Republic—the United Provinces of the Netherlands. Holland was one of these; look for the coat of arms with the red lion. The independent Netherlands were dominated by Holland (which contained Amsterdam and drove 85 percent of the country's economy). The lower banner (above the door) is Delft's—it features a canal, which is what "Delft" means.

• *Step behind the Town Hall, where you'll find the Waag.*

The Waag

The city's medieval trading center, the Waag, was the weighing or **customs house,** with workspaces for goldsmiths and silversmiths upstairs. To the left is the Stadsboterhuis, where butter was traded in barrels. At the far right, the Vleeshal, or meat market, is decorated with cow heads above its doors. Fish was traded in the Visbanken (left of the meat market).

The old sturdy tower around which the Town Hall is built was originally a **prison.** For security, the prison needed to be built of weighty stone—a potential problem in this naturally marshy place. The builders chose this spot, on a clay foundation, as the best place for the structure. It just made sense that the county seat—Delft—would be here, too.

• *With your back to the Town Hall, walk down Waagsteeg lane, a narrow alley to the right of the Waag, to reach Boterbrug.*

Boterbrug to the Oude Delft Canal

At the back side of the Waag, on the right, is the **water gate** where produce was off-loaded from boats to be weighed and taxed. Continue walking straight down Boterbrug (literally, "butter bridge"), a wide street that once was the approach canal to the customs house. Merchants knew the drill for all their goods: Before you traded, you first weighed, then you paid. During Spanish rule, taxation got so out of hand that the Dutch revolted—much as high British taxes angered American colonists during the same period.

Boterbrug leads one block to the 11th-century **Oude Delft canal,** the town's first and major trading canal. Boats passing the town used this waterway. On the black iron fence on the corner is a memorial to Anton van Leeuwenhoek (1632-1723), who invented the microscope and then used it to discover bacteria. He's buried in the Old Church visible in the distance (to the right; look for the tilting spire).

• *Turn right and walk along the Oude Delft canal toward the Old Church.*

Oude Delft Canal

Barges are allowed to line the canal from April through September. Historically barges like these brought in the goods and produce that fueled Delft's economy—today they provide the city's restaurants with sunny outdoor tables.

• *Cross left over the first bridge (Nieuwstraat) and continue on to the ornate facade at #167.*

This building is the headquarters of the **water authority,** responsible for keeping waterways dredged and managing water levels in towns and *polders* (lowlands). The colorful coats of arms of the various 17th-century water authority directors decorate the exterior wall.

Water levels are a big deal here. Turn around and look at the yardstick across the canal; the red *NAP* marking—"normal Amsterdam point"—is the average sea level in Amsterdam. The wide-open Dutch countryside plots reclaimed from the sea, known as *polders*, are generally three yards below this point. According to the NAP, we're above sea level and the canal is below, so we're standing on what was an island.

• *Keep walking along this side of the canal. Across from the Old Church, find the photo cube recalling the painter Vermeer, who's buried in the church. Turn left from the photo cube and church into a tiny lane (you'll have to look for it). A series of courtyards will take you to the...*

Prinsenhof

This is the former convent of St. Agatha. William of Orange took refuge here after the king of Spain put a bounty on his head in 1580 for his role in the revolt of the Netherlands. Figuring the convent was a safe place in a safe city, William hid here until 1584, when an assassin finally killed him (the bullet holes are still visible in a wall inside).

• *Step into the green park, an old herb garden.*

The statue here honors William, considered the founder of the Netherlands. When the provinces broke away from Spain, they also broke from the Roman Catholic Church. The Dutch became "reformed" and dissolved the Catholic convents and monasteries. Although they had declared their freedom in 1579, a treaty ending the war for Dutch independence (which formally established their freedom) didn't come until 1648.

Back outside the little park, in the courtyard, the three blue-and-white lampposts were made in Delft's Chinese sister city and are reminders of the 400-year relationship between porcelain makers in China and Delft. The only color that could survive the extremely hot fire of the Chinese porcelain technique was blue, and that's the color of Delftware.

• *A few steps farther take you to...*

Phoenixstraat

You've arrived at the edge of the old town. Along this street (to

DELFT

the right) you'll see a tower and windmill. Twenty such structures once stood on the 11th-century city wall. The **windmills,** which ground the city's grain, go back to the 13th century. Tram line #1 heads (right) along Phoenixstraat to The Hague.

• *Turn around and finish this walk by retracing your steps, through the Prinsenhof, to the Old Church (with the tilting spire).*

Old Church (Oude Kerk)

The Old Church—while smaller and less impressive (inside and out) than the New Church—feels more lived-in. For 150 years, its spire was the tallest in Delft; it leans because it's built on an unstable foundation, over a filled-in canal. (For cost and hours, see the listing next, under "Sights in Delft.")

The church is Dutch Reformed (English service Sun at 12:00) and has been around for a long time: The names of its ministers, going back to 1592, fill a wall. The pulpit dates from 1548. With a carving showing impressive perspective, it's considered one of the finest in the Netherlands. The church is sober and clean because of iconoclastic riots, in 1566 and 1572, that made a violent point of destroying all hints of Roman Catholicism and its imagery. Within the church are the tombs of two local boys done good: the inventor of the microscope, Anton van Leeuwenhoek, and the painter Johannes Vermeer. Vermeer's actual tombstone is just a simple stone plaque in the floor (across from the pulpit). The grander Vermeer monument, installed in 2007, is a reflection of his greater popularity now than in previous generations.

Sights in Delft

In the Old Town

▲**New Church (Nieuwe Kerk) and Old Church (Oude Kerk)**—Delft has two grand churches that hold tombs of prominent local residents. A single flier explains both churches very well, locating and describing all points of interest.

Cost and Hours: Both churches are covered by the same €3.50 ticket (not covered by Museumkaart) and are open the same hours: April-Oct Mon-Sat 9:00-18:00; Nov-Jan Mon-Fri 11:00-16:00, Sat 10:00-17:00; Feb-March Mon-Sat 10:00-17:00; closed to tourists Sun year-round, tel. 015/212-3025, www.oudeennieuwekerkdelft.nl.

Visiting the New Church: The giant, Gothic New Church boldly presides over the town from its prominent position overlooking the Markt. Inside are buried the beloved Dutch ruler William I of Orange and the Dutch royalty that succeeded him. (Look for a TV monitor running a video showing three royal burials here.)

The church has been through a lot. It was devastated by a fire in 1536 and ransacked by iconoclasts in the 1560s. The first "reformed" service was held here in 1572. After a nearby gun-powder depot exploded and ruined its windows in 1654, the church was rebuilt, giving it the look you see today. Until 1829, city leaders were buried under the floor stones. Because of the "stinking rich" problem, only royals have been buried here since then. The chandeliers, produced in 1981 in traditional 17th-century style, marked the 600th birthday of the church.

William I was the founder of the House of Orange, the dynasty that still (in name) rules the Netherlands. It was William who rallied the Dutch to begin their revolt against the Spanish Habsburg rulers. That's why he's considered the father of the country. William's ornate **tomb**—a canopied monument to his greatness—dominates the choir area. It features two representations of William: one of white marble, reclining peacefully; and a strong, armored king in bronze, sitting royally. The sweet dog at his feet symbolizes loyalty. Above the pooch, the angel of Fame blows a trumpet (notice that this whole bronze statue is supported by just one slim foot). At the corners of his monument are female statues representing Liberty, Justice, Religion, and Fortitude. Unfortunately, all these fine virtues could not save William from being gunned down by an assassin's bullet right here in Delft.

Most of William I's descendants of the House of Orange are also buried in this church. A few paces in front of William (near the transept), a large stone slab marks the entrance to the sprawling underground labyrinth that holds crates of Oranges. (The crypt is strictly off-limits for anyone unrelated.) Besides ruling Holland, the Orange family had owned the independent principality of Orange in the south of France since medieval times. The royal family's official color is—what else?—orange, which is why today's Dutch wear orange to soccer matches and consider it their national color (despite having a flag that's red, white, and blue).

If you want to work off your *pannenkoeken*, you can climb the New Church's **tower** (€3.50, three levels and 376 steps in a very narrow staircase). This is a particularly dizzying tower climb, one of Europe's more dramatic. On a clear day you can see the towers of The Hague and, in the other direction, Rotterdam.

DELFT

Johannes Vermeer
(1632-1675)

The great Dutch Golden Age painter Johannes Vermeer was born in Delft, grew up near the Markt, and set a number of his paintings here. His father, an art dealer, gave Johannes a passion for painting. Late in the artist's career, with Holland fighting draining wars against England, the demand for art and luxuries went sour in the Netherlands, forcing Vermeer to downsize—he sold his big home, packed up his wife and 14 children, and moved in with his mother-in-law. He died two years later.

Vermeer painted some 37 surviving works (though experts debate whether all of them were actually his). Although Vermeer painted landscapes and scenes from mythology and the Bible, he specialized in depicting the everyday actions of regular people. And though his scenes are usually still and peaceful, he artfully conveys deep tension, and suggests a complicated story with subtle body language (the subject glances at something out of view) or the inclusion of a small item (a letter that seems pregnant with significance). Vermeer also was a master of light, capturing it with an artistry that would make the Impressionists jealous two centuries later.

After centuries of relative obscurity—we still know very little about him—Vermeer and his paintings are now appreciated. Delft owns none of his works (you'll have to visit Amsterdam's Rijksmuseum, with four masterpieces, or The Hague's Mauritshuis museum). However, the town's Vermeer Center pays tribute to this great artist and his talent.

Visiting the Old Church: From the New Church, you can walk a few blocks up pretty Hippolytusbuurt street (or follow my self-guided town walk, earlier), to find the smaller Old Church. For more on its interior, see page 285.

▲Vermeer Center (Vermeercentrum)—Although it doesn't have any Vermeer originals, this intelligent exhibit does a good job of tracing the career and unique creative mind of Delft's favorite resident. Everything is well-described in English.

Begin in the basement, where a short movie orients you to Vermeer and his ties to Delft. Then view copies of all 37 known Vermeer paintings, arranged chronologically and accompanied by brief and interesting commentary. The top floor hosts an exhibit explaining the hidden symbols of love found in many of Vermeer's paintings. On the middle floor, a mock-up of Vermeer's studio thoughtfully analyzes and explains some of Vermeer's techniques.

Cost and Hours: €7, essential audioguide-€1, daily 10:00-17:00, a block from the Markt—through the gap where Vermeer's

house used to be—at Voldersgracht 21, tel. 015/213-8588, www
.vermeerdelft.nl.

Markets—Various all-day markets are held on Thursdays (general
market on the Markt, flower market on Hippolytusbuurt Square)
and on Saturdays (general market on Brabantse Turfmarkt and
Burgwal, flea market at Hippolytusbuurt Square in summer, and
sometimes an art market at Heilige Geestkerkhof).

Royal Dutch Delftware Manufactory

The Delft Blue earthenware made at this factory (known as the
Koninklijke Porceleyne Fles in Dutch) is famous worldwide, making this the biggest tourist attraction in town. The Dutch East
India Company, partly headquartered
in Delft, imported many exotic goods
from the Far East, including Chinese
porcelain. The Chinese designs became
trendy and were copied by many local
potters. Three centuries later, their
descendants are still going strong, and
you can see them at work in this factory—the only one left of an original
32. While some may think this is just
an excuse to shop for Delftware, it's a worthwhile stop for those
who enjoy porcelain.

Cost and Hours: €12, 25 percent discount with coupon available at TI and many hotels, not covered by Museumkaart, daily
9:00-17:00 except closed Sun Nov-March, Rotterdamsweg 196,
tel. 015/251-2030, www.royaldelft.com.

Getting There: It's about a 15-minute walk south of the Old
Town, on Rotterdamsweg (just off map on page 280). Because of
the canal crossings and railroad construction, the route can be
confusing. Get detailed directions from the TI or your hotelier.

To get from the train station to the factory, catch bus #40 or
#121 (€2.50, 2/hour, 5 minutes, buy ticket from driver, get off at
the second bus stop: Julianalaan, continue walking in the same
direction as the bus to the next street—Jaffalaan, then turn right
and walk one long block to Rotterdamsweg).

From the town center, you can take a canal boat in the summer (€16 includes factory admission, July-Aug at 13:00 and 14:00,
2.5-hour round-trip, catch along Koornmarkt canal, more expensive "full-service" tour includes lunch, tel. 015/212-6385, www
.rondvaartdelft.nl). Or you can take a bike-taxi (€5/person one-
way, see "Bike/Rickshaw Tour," earlier).

Visiting the Factory: There's an included audioguide, but
it's not essential, as English descriptions are posted throughout.

DELFT

Delft Blue Manufacturing Process

Delft Blue earthenware is made from a soupy mix of clay and water. To make plates, the glop is rotated on a spinning disk

until it looks like a traditional Dutch pancake. This "pancake" is then placed in a plate mold, where a design is pressed into it.

To make vases, pitchers, cups, and figurines, the liquid clay is poured into hollow plaster molds. These porous molds work like a sponge, sucking the water out of the clay to leave a layer of dry clay along the mold walls. Once the interior walls have reached the correct thickness, all excess clay within is poured off and recycled.

After the clay object is removed from the mold, it's fired in the kiln for 24 hours. The pottery removed from the kiln is called "biscuit." Next, painters trace traditional decorations with sable-hair pencils onto the biscuit pottery; these are then painted with a black paint containing cobalt oxide. The biscuit immediately soaks up the paint, making it a very unforgiving medium for mistakes.

The objects are dipped into an opaque white glaze and then fired a second time. A chemical reaction transforms the black paint into the famous Delft Blue, and the white glaze melts into a translucent, glass-like outer layer.

At the beginning you'll watch two short videos—the first on the history of Royal Delft and the second on the production process. Then comes the highlight of the tour: a chance to watch the artists as they paint the designs on the fired pottery "biscuit." After rather kitschy exhibits that reconstruct Vermeer's dining room (with Royal Delft china, of course) and trace the firm's connections with the Dutch royal family, you'll see the company's priceless collection. Along with tableware and vases, there are gorgeous pictures made from tiles (including a giant replica of Rembrandt's *The Night Watch* that took two artists a year to paint) and outdoor architectural elements (such as chimneys). After the museum, you'll walk through part of the factory, past racks upon racks of unfired pieces. Take some time to watch artisans at work—and feel free to stop and chat with them.

The tour ends in the gift shop. For bargain hunters, the factory store offers a bonus—"seconds" with slight blemishes for 20-40 percent off. The clerks can also prepare VAT refund documents for you (see page 13).

Near Delft: Rotterdam

The Hague isn't the only big Dutch city near Delft. About the same distance in the opposite direction is the Netherlands' (and Europe's) largest port, Rotterdam—which bounced back after being bombed flat in World War II. And though it lacks the charm of Delft and the great museums of The Hague, it might be worth a visit if you're curious to round out your Dutch urban experience. See its towering Euromast, take a harbor tour, and stroll its great pedestrian zone (TI tel. 010/790-0140, www.rotterdam.info).

Sleeping in Delft

Delft's accommodations aren't cheap, but the ones listed here are well-run and offer good value for the money. If I don't mention an elevator, expect lots of stairs.

$$$ Bridges House Hotel, with 11 rooms around the corner from the Markt, is wood-beamed elegant and was once the home of painter Jan Steen. Energetic Robbert Willemse works hard to bring class and charm to this lovely canalside splurge (Sb-€99-112, Db-€112-142, higher prices are for very roomy junior suites, prices can be lower in winter, extra bed-€20, free Internet access and Wi-Fi, air-con, Oude Delft 74, tel. 015/212-4036, fax 015/213-3600, www.bridges-house.com, info@bridges-house.com).

$$ Hotel Leeuwenbrug, a former warehouse and now a business-class hotel, has 36 classic Dutch rooms (some with canal views), Old World atmosphere, a generous breakfast buffet, and a helpful staff (very small Sb-€55, standard Sb-€69-78, deluxe Sb-€125, standard Db-€75-88, deluxe Db-€95-125, may be cheaper July-Aug—check their website for best rates, elevator, free Internet access and Wi-Fi, Koornmarkt 16, tel. 015/214-7741, fax 015/215-9759, www.leeuwenbrug.nl, sales@leeuwenbrug.nl, Mr. Wubben).

$$ Hotel de Emauspoort, picture perfect and family-run, is relaxed and friendly. It's ideally located one block from the Markt. The 26 rooms, decorated with pleasantly old-fashioned wooden furniture and named for sea heroes and Delft artists, overlook a canal or peek into the courtyard. Romantics can stay in one of their two "Gypsy caravans"—wooden trailers in the courtyard (Sb-€88, Db-€99, stunning "Vermeer Room" Db-€150, Tb-€138, Qb-€175, caravan-€95—sleeps two, Wi-Fi, behind church/Markt at Vrouwenregt 9-11, tel. 015/219-0219, fax 015/214-8251, www.emauspoort.nl, info@emauspoort.nl, Jeroen and Desiree).

$$ Hotel de Koophandel has 25 painting-over-the-bed rooms right on the charming, lively, tree-and-restaurant-lined Beestenmarkt square (Sb-€94, Db-€114, Tb-€144, extra bed-€30, 3 ground-floor rooms, reception closed 23:00-7:00, free Internet

Sleep Code

(€1 = about $1.30, country code: 31, area code: 015)
S = Single, **D** = Double/Twin, **T** = Triple, **Q** = Quad, **b** = bathroom, **s** = shower only. Unless otherwise noted, credit cards are accepted, breakfast is included, and hoteliers speak English.

To help you easily sort through these listings, I've divided the accommodations into three categories, based on the price for a standard double room with bath:

$$$ **Higher Priced**—Most rooms €120 or more.
$$ **Moderately Priced**—Most rooms between €70-120.
$ **Lower Priced**—Most rooms €70 or less.

Prices can change without notice; verify the hotel's current rates online or by email.

access and Wi-Fi, Beestenmarkt 30, tel. 015/214-2302, fax 015/212-0674, www.hoteldekoophandel.nl, info@hoteldekoophandel.nl).

$ Jorplace City Hostel is modern, well-run, and just off the Markt, renting beds in dorm rooms that sleep 6, 12, or 24 (150 beds, bunk-€20, tel. 015/887-5088, next to the Vermeer Center at Voldersgracht 17, www.jorplace.nl, delft@jorplace.nl).

Eating in Delft

As Delft is a university town, lively, affordable eateries abound. Most places have outdoor seating, sometimes on an inviting square or on a little barge floating in the canal out front.

Spijshuis de Dis is driven by the creative energy of chef Jan Boheemen, who cooks Dutch with attitude. With an open kitchen, inviting menu, friendly service, and a characteristic interior—not to mention great food—the entire eating experience is a delight (€17 vegetarian plates, €20 main courses, kitchen opens at 17:00, closed Sun-Mon, Beestenmarkt 36, tel. 015/213-1782, reservations smart). They serve fine Belgian Westmalle beer.

Restaurant de Prinsenkelder, set in a dressy, candlelit cellar, dishes up French cuisine with formal service. Their outdoor courtyard is equally elegant (€15 starters, €25 entrées, Mon-Sat 17:30-21:30, closed Sun, near the Prinsenhof at Schoolstraat 11, tel. 015/212-1860).

Café de Pelicaan, with candles and well-worn tables, is a favorite of students, who eat well on classic Italian food—no pizza. On balmy evenings, tables move out onto their canal barge (€8 pastas, €16 entrées, Tue-Sun 18:00-22:00, closed Mon, Verwersdijk 47, tel. 015/213-9309).

DELFT

Restaurant Matties is a tight and stylish little place with a few nice canalside tables. They serve dressy modern Dutch dishes (€20 plates, Mon-Tue 17:00-22:00, Wed-Sun 13:30-22:00, Oude Delft 92, tel. 015/215-9837).

Eetcafé de Verbeelding ("The Imagination") serves Dutch pub grub in an intimate, woody, yet high-energy place. Choose their dark and candlelit interior or take a spot outside on their canal barge. Their steak and shrimp are very popular (€13 plates, €25 three-course fixed-price meal, daily 17:00-22:00, Verwersdijk 128, tel. 015/212-1328).

Kleyweg's Stads Koffyhuis is a local institution that's won prizes for its sandwiches (see the trophies above the counter). This is a great spot for an affordable bite, either in the country-cozy interior or out on a canal barge (€6-8 sandwiches and hamburgers, €6-10 savory or sweet pancakes, big €12 salads, Mon-Fri 9:00-20:00, Sat 9:00-18:00, closed Sun, shorter hours off-season, just down the canal from the Old Church at Oude Delft 133, tel. 015/212-4625).

De V is a lively pub with a pleasantly cozy ambience and a local following loyal to its straightforward and well-priced food—from ribs and burgers to Asian. Sit in the crowded area near the bar, elbow your way up top to the glassed-in patio, or enjoy the barge tables on the canal (€8.50 daily specials, €10-15 main dishes, daily 16:00-24:00, food served 18:00-22:00, just past the TI and Old Church along the canal at Voorstraat 9, tel. 015/214-0916).

Around the Markt (Market Square): Delft's giant Markt, under the looming tower of the New Church, is a scenic spot for a meal. Most of the places around here are interchangeable, but tucked behind the Town Hall (across the square from the church) are some good options with outdoor seating.

Asian: For a break from flapjacks, try **Daily Wok,** a mod Thai eatery just a few steps off the Markt. It serves up affordable but good fare—either take-out or fast-food sit-down (€4-7 meals, daily 12:30-21:30, Oude Langendijk 230, tel. 015/213-7222).

Delft Connections

From Delft to The Hague

It's easy and cheap to travel between these neighboring towns by train or tram. For tram and bus information, call toll tel. 0900-486-4636, consult www.htm.net, or use the Netherlands' slick public-transit site, www.9292.nl.

Tram #1 leaves from in front of the Delft train station and clatters through residential neighborhoods to The Hague. This connection is frequent, comes with nice urban scenery, and delivers you right into the center of The Hague's tourist zone (€2.50 to town center, €3.50 to Peace Palace or beach, buy ticket from driver or at TI—where you can also buy a €7.50 day pass; about 6/hour, 4/hour on weekends, direction: Scheveningen Noorderstrand; get off after about 30 minutes at The Hague's Centrum stop for TI, parliament area, and most sights). You can continue on this tram directly to the Peace Palace (Vredespaleis stop, about 5 minutes beyond Centrum stop) or go all the way to the beach at Scheveningen (Kurhaus stop, about 15 minutes beyond Centrum stop).

Regular **trains** depart from Delft's station for The Hague (€3.70 one-way, €7.40 round-trip, 4/hour, 15 minutes). Get off at The Hague's Central Station (CS), not the Hollands Spoor station (HS). The train appears to be faster than the tram, but from The Hague's Central Station it's still a 15-minute walk or a 5-minute tram ride to reach the tourist zone (for details, see "Arrival in The Hague," later).

By Train from Delft
From Delft, trains go to **Amsterdam**'s Central Station (3/hour direct, 1 hour, more with transfer in Leiden or The Hague), **Haarlem** (2/hour direct, 40 minutes), and **Arnhem** (2-4/hour, 1.75 hours, transfer in The Hague or Rotterdam, then Utrecht). To reach **Bruges** (hourly, 3 hours), you'll need to change in Ghent, Antwerp, and Rotterdam.

The Hague (Den Haag)

The Dutch constitution may identify Amsterdam as the official "capital," but The Hague has been the Netherlands' seat of government since 1588. Or, as locals say, the money is made in Rotterdam, divided in The Hague, and spent in Amsterdam.

The Hague is the home of several fine museums—including the excellent Mauritshuis art gallery—and international organizations such as the International Court of Justice (at the tourable Peace Palace, where nations try to settle their disputes without

bloodshed) and the UN International Criminal Tribunal for the Former Yugoslavia (not tourable). Urban but still manageable—if not exactly charming—The Hague is ideal for a few engaging hours of sightseeing.

Orientation to The Hague

Though it has a half-million residents (the Netherlands' third-largest city), The Hague feels manageable for a sightseer. On a quick visit, begin at the Centrum tram stop, between the TI and the parliament complex; most worthwhile museums are near here. I list no hotels for The Hague because Delft—so close it's practically a neighborhood of this city—is a much more appealing place to hang your hat.

Tourist Information

The TI is in City Hall (Stadhuis); it's nearest the Centrum stop on tram #1 (two stops after the Station HS stop). Pick up the free map; the better €2.50 map isn't worth it, but the free information guide—while heavy on glossy promotion—is worth having for a longer visit (Mon 12:00-20:00, Tue-Fri 10:00-20:00, Sat 10:00-17:00, Sun 12:00-17:00, Spui 68, tel. 070/361-8860, www.denhaag .com).

Arrival in The Hague

The major sights in The Hague are well-signed—just look for the black-and-gold directional arrows.

By Tram: If coming on tram #1 from Delft, get off at the Centrum stop.

By Train: The Hague has two train stations: Central Station ("CS," "Den Haag CS," or just "Centraal Station") and Hollands Spoor ("HS" or "Den Haag HS," used by more international trains). Central Station is closer to the tourist area.

To get from Central Station to the TI, follow Rijnstraat (which parallels the tram tracks that pass the station, to your left as you leave the station), walking back under the train tracks to where Rijnstraat ends. Turn right through the imposing glass building, and follow Turfmarkt for five minutes to the City Hall (Stadhuis), near the corner of Turfmarkt and Spui. To get from the station to the main sights, exit toward the sign for *Uitgang Centrum* (to the left with your back to the tracks, near the Burger King). Here you can catch tram #16 (direction: Wateringen) and take it two stops to the Centrum stop. Or, for a 15-minute walk, turn right and walk past the big bike-parking lot, then turn left, cross the tram tracks, and head up Bezuidenhoutseweg. After the road changes names a few times, it leads you to Hofweg; the Binnenhof parliament complex will be on your right.

From the Hollands Spoor station, you can reach the TI by backtracking along the tram tracks on Spui to find Spuiplein, home of the TI and City Hall (Stadhuis). To reach the main

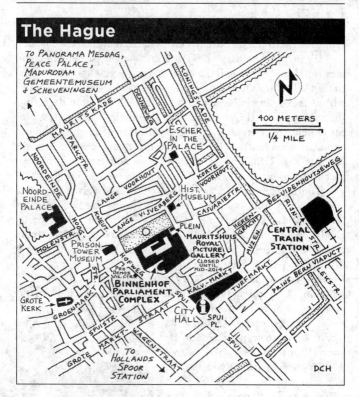

The Hague

TO PANORAMA MESDAG,
PEACE PALACE,
MADURODAM
GEMEENTEMUSEUM
& SCHEVENINGEN

400 METERS
¼ MILE

ESCHER
IN THE
PALACE

NOORD-
EINDE
PALACE

HIST.
MUSEUM

PLEIN

PRISON
TOWER
MUSEUM

PRO'
DEMOS
VIS. CTRS

MAURITSHUIS
ROYAL
PICTURE
GALLERY
CLOSED
UNTIL
MID-2014

CENTRAL
TRAIN
STATION

BINNENHOF
PARLIAMENT
COMPLEX

KALV-MARKT

TURFMARKT

GROTE
KERK

GROENMARKT

CITY
HALL

SPUI
PL.

TO
HOLLANDS
SPOOR
STATION

DCH

sights, walk out in front of the station and take tram #1 (direction: Scheveningen Noorderstrand) to the Centrum stop.

Sights in The Hague

In the City Center
These attractions are all within a 10-minute walk of the TI (most are even closer).

Binnenhof Parliament Complex—The castle-like Binnenhof complex, overlooking a giant pond right in the center of The

Hague, is the seat of Dutch political power. The prime minister's office is here, and it's also the meeting place of the two-house parliament, or Staten-Generaal. The power resides in the directly elected Second Chamber (a.k.a. House of Representatives), whereas the mostly figurehead

First Chamber (a.k.a. Senate, but actually more like the UK's House of Lords) meets once weekly to harrumph their approval.

It's surprisingly easy to dip into the low-key parliament complex (just saunter through the brick gateway across the street from the TI). In the inner courtyard—surrounded by orange-and-white-striped awnings—you'll find a golden fountain depicting the recently retired Queen Beatrix, a reminder that the respectful Dutch parliamentarians govern with the monarch's symbolic approval. Dominating the middle of the complex is the historic Knights' Hall (Ridderzaal), where the two houses meet jointly on special occasions.

Tours: Daily guided tours of the complex are given in Dutch (English handout available) through the ProDemos Visitors Center (tours-€4-6, Mon-Sat 10:00-17:00, Sun 11:00-16:00, English tour runs Sun at 14:00). Tours depart across the street from the Binnenhof next to Café Brasserie Dudok at Hofweg 1 (tel. 070/364-6144, www.prodemos.nl).

Prison Tower Museum (Gevangenpoort)—This torture museum, in a 13th-century gatehouse that once protected a castle on the site of today's parliament,

shows you the medieval mind at its worst. You can wander around by yourself or tour the sight on a free 30-minute tour (usually in Dutch, but you can use a free English guidebook). You'll get the full story on crime and punishment here from 1420 to 1823.

Cost and Hours: €7.50, Tue-Fri 10:00-17:00, Sat-Sun 12:00-17:00, closed Mon, tours depart at :45 after the hour, also at :15 after the hour during busy times, last tour usually leaves at 15:45, across from parliament at Buitenhof 33, tel. 070/346-0861, www.gevangenpoort.nl.

Panorama Mesdag—For a look at the 19th century's attempt at virtual reality, stand in the center of this 360-degree painting of nearby Scheveningen in the 1880s, with a 3-D, sandy-beach foreground. As you experience this nostalgic attraction, ponder that this sort of "art immersion" experience was once mind-blowingly cutting-edge.

Cost and Hours: €7, Mon-Sat 10:00-17:00, Sun 12:00-17:00, a few blocks east of the parliament area at Zeestraat 65, tel. 070/310-6665, www.panorama-mesdag.com.

Escher in the Palace (Escher in Het Paleis)—Compared with The Hague's other museums, this place is just a trifle...but an entertaining one. (Think of it as "art museum lite.") Celebrating Dutch optical illusionist M. C. Escher (1898-1972), the exhibit displays replicas of many of his works and traces his artistic evolution—from the Mediterranean landscapes of his beloved Italy, to shapes that melt into one another, to mind-bending experiments in angles and perspective. Hands-on displays on the top floor let you step right into an Escher engraving. The entry price is worth it, given the museum's extras: fun temporary exhibits, far-out chandeliers by Dutch artist Hans van Bentem, and the chance to stroll the former winter palace of Queen Emma, who lived here for three decades—it remained a royal residence until 1991. I'm guessing the skull-and-crossbones chandelier wasn't around then.

Cost and Hours: €8.50, not covered by Museumkaart, Tue-Sun 11:00-17:00, closed Mon, last entry 30 minutes before closing, mandatory bag check-€1 deposit, Lange Voorhout 74, tel. 070/427-7730, www.escherinhetpaleis.nl.

Historical Museum of The Hague (Haagshistorisch-museum)—This museum's eclectic collection includes landscapes of The Hague in the Golden Age, portraits of its movers and shakers, dollhouses, tile panels, and the well-preserved tongue and finger of a 17th-century murderer.

Cost and Hours: €7.50, Tue-Fri 10:00-17:00, Sat-Sun 12:00-17:00, closed Mon, across the pond from parliament at Korte Vijverberg 7, tel. 070/364-6940, www.haagshistorischmuseum.nl.

▲▲Mauritshuis Royal Picture Gallery

The Hague's top art museum features Dutch Golden Age art, including top-notch pieces by Vermeer (his famous *Girl with a Pearl Earring* lives here), Rembrandt, Rubens, and many others. While calling the Mauritshuis a "mini-Rijksmuseum" might be a stretch, these Golden Age masterpieces are worth a visit.

Temporary Location: The gallery is under renovation until mid-2014, but don't despair—until then much of the collection is on view at the Gemeentemuseum, The Hague's modern art museum. Before you visit, ask at the TI for the latest details or consult the websites listed below.

Cost and Hours: Gemeentemuseum location—€13.50, includes audioguide, Tue-Sun 11:00-17:00, closed Mon; café, free bag check, Stadhouderslaan 41, tel. 070/338-1111, www.gemeentemuseum.nl. For details about the Mauritshuis location or for visits in or after late 2014, see www.mauritshuis.nl.

Getting There: To reach the **Gemeentemuseum** location from the TI, take tram #17 to the Gemeentemuseum stop; from Central Station, take bus #24. The **Mauritshuis** gallery is on the far side of the parliament; cut straight through the Binnenhof courtyard and look left when you pop out on the other side.

Collection Highlights: This list covers the basics; if you have more time, take advantage of the excellent, included audioguide.

Some of the following artworks may be out on tour when you visit.

Vermeer, *Girl with a Pearl Earring* (c. 1665): Sometimes called "the Dutch *Mona Lisa*" for its enigmatic qualities, this canvas became a sensation in recent years as the subject of a popular book and film. This is a "tronie"—a type of picture in which the painter's goal is not to depict an individual person, but to capture mood or character by focusing on the expression of the subject. In fact, we don't even know who this mysterious girl is. Wearing a blue turban and with a gigantic pearl dangling from her earlobe, she glances over her shoulder and catches the viewer's gaze expectantly, maybe even seductively. Vermeer's portrayal subtly implies a much more complicated story than we'll ever know. The artist was a master of color and at suggesting shape with light—look closely and you'll see that the famous pearl is essentially formed by two simple brushstrokes. For more on Vermeer, see page 287.

Vermeer, *View of Delft* (c. 1660-1661): If this were a photograph, it'd be a bad one—you'd want to wait for the clouds to pass to snap another one with the entire scene bathed in light. But Vermeer, an expert at capturing light effects on canvas, uses the cloudy/sunny contrast to his advantage, illuminating the foreground and the distant, inner part of town instead of the more predictable middle ground. This makes your eye probe deep into the canvas, subconsciously immersing you in Vermeer's world.

Rembrandt, *The Anatomy Lesson of Dr. Nicolaes Tulp* (1632): Notice Rembrandt's uniquely engaging version of a (typically dull) group portrait—inquisitive faces lean in, hanging on the doctor's every word. The cadaver resembles a notorious criminal of the day. For more on Rembrandt, see page 152.

Rembrandt, *Portrait of an Elderly Man* (1667): Painted when Rembrandt was 61, this portrait is typical of his style: The clothes are painted lightly, but the face is caked on. Look closely at his ruddy cheeks, built up by layer after layer of paint, carefully slathered on by the master.

Peter Paul Rubens, *Old Woman and a Boy with Candles* (c. 1616-1617): In this touching scene, the elderly woman passes her light to the boy—encouraging him to enjoy life in a way that she perhaps hasn't. Her serene smile suggests her hope that he won't have the same regrets she does.

Frans Hals, *Laughing Boy* (c. 1625): This loveable painting depicts an exuberant scamp grinning widely despite his decaying teeth and rat's-nest hair. Like *Girl with a Pearl Earring,* this is a character study, rather than a portrait of an important person. For more on Hals, see page 254.

Jan Steen, *Girl Eating Oysters* (c. 1658-1660): This seemingly innocent scene—a still life combined with a portrait, on the smallest canvas Steen ever painted—is loaded with 17th-century sexual innuendo. Oysters were considered a powerful aphrodisiac, and behind the subject, peeking through the curtains, we can see a bed. The girl's impish grin suggests that she's got more than shell-fish on her mind.

And Lots More: These paintings are just the beginning. Look around to find works by Jan Brueghel the Elder (a painting of the Garden of Eden, done jointly with Rubens), Hans Holbein, Anthony van Dyck, Hans Memling, and many other famous painters.

Outside the City Center

The following sights lie north of the main tourist zone. Though worthwhile for the thorough sightseer, they're more difficult to reach than the previous sights.

▲**Peace Palace (Vredespaleis)**—The palace houses the International Court of Justice and the Permanent Court of Arbitration. These two Peace

Palace courts attempt to reach amicable settlements for inter-national disagreements, such as border disputes. While the judicial process is interesting, the building itself is the big draw. A gift from American industrialist Andrew Carnegie, it's filled with opulent deco-rations (donated by grateful nations who found diplomatic peace here), from exquisite Japanese tapestries, to a Hungarian tile foun-tain, to French inlay floors.

A free visitors center offers modest multimedia exhibits about the building and international courts. There's also a persuasive video about the history of the Peace Palace and the role of inter-national law. However, if you want to see the inside of the build-ing itself, you must book a weekend tour in advance (see below). You'll see the judicial chambers and the grandly decorated halls, and learn how modern nations attempt to resolve their disputes here instead of on the battlefield. Don't confuse this place with the International Criminal Tribunal for the Former Yugoslavia, which is not open to the public.

Cost and Hours: Visitors center—free, Tue-Sun 10:00-17:00, closes at 16:00 in winter, closed Mon year-round, Carnegieplein 2, tel. 070/302-4242, www.vredespaleis.nl.

Tours: €8.50; Sat-Sun 11:00-16:00 only, 45 minutes; most tours offered in English, you must reserve in advance online and bring your passport (required to enter), due to court schedules you can only book about six weeks in advance, www.vredespaleis.nl. It is possible to attend a hearing (conducted in English or French) of the International Court of Justice; see www.icj-cij.org for details.

Getting There: Take tram #1 directly from Delft, or tram #10 or bus #24 from The Hague's Central Station, and get off at the Vredespaleis stop (right in front of the palace).

Scheveningen—This Dutch Coney Island, with its broad sandy beach, is at its liveliest on sunny summer afternoons (but is dead when the weather cools). Its biggest appeal is watching urbanites from The Hague and Delft enjoy a day at the seashore. Dominating the scene is the long double-decker pleasure pier, with shops down below, a boardwalk up top, and a bungee-jumping pavilion at the far end. A café-lined promenade stretches along the sand.

By the way, if you can't pronounce this tongue-twisting name (roughly SKHHHEH-veh-ning-eh), you're not alone. In World War II, Dutch soldiers would quiz suspicious visitors on how to pronounce this name as a test to determine who was Dutch-born and ferret out potential German spies.

Getting There: Take northbound tram #1 from Delft or from Hofweg/Spui (the street in front of the Binnenhof and The Hague's TI), or take tram #9 from The Hague's Central Station. Get out at Kurhaus (one stop before the end of the line) and follow signs for *Boulevard/Strand* and *Pier*.

Madurodam—This mini-Holland amusement park, with miniature city buildings that make you feel like Godzilla, is fun for kids.

Cost and Hours: Adults-€14.50, kids 3-11-€10.50, not covered by Museumkaart, daily April-June 9:00-20:00, July-Aug 9:00-23:00, Sept-March 9:00-18:00, last entry one hour before closing, George Maduroplein 1, tram #8 and #9 or bus #22 from Central Station, tel. 070/416-2400, www.madurodam.nl.

The Hague Connections

The Hague's Central Station (CS) is handier for sightseers; the Hollands Spoor station (HS) is used mostly by international trains.

From The Hague's Central Station by Train to: Delft (4/hour, 15 minutes), **Amsterdam** (2/hour, 50 minutes, more with change in Leiden), **Haarlem** (6/hour, 40 minutes, some transfer in Leiden), **Arnhem** (4/hour, 1.5 hours, transfer in Utrecht), **Bruges** (hourly, 3 hours, change in Antwerp).

By Tram to Delft: Take tram #1 from any stop (€2.50 from city center, €3.50 from sights outside the city center, about 6/hour, 4/hour on weekends, direction: Delft Tanthof, about 30 minutes). If you're headed to the Markt in Delft, get off at the Prinsenhof stop (a little north of the Markt) or at Binnenwatersloot (the next stop south). The tram also stops at the train station.

MUSEUMS NEAR ARNHEM

Arnhem Open-Air Folk Museum •
Kröller-Müller Museum •
Spoorwegmuseum

While the city of Arnhem itself is nothing special, it's close to a pair of fun and worthwhile side-trips: the Arnhem Open-Air Folk Museum and the exceptional Kröller-Müller Museum. Of all the Netherlands' open-air folk museums, Arnhem's—set just within the city limits—feels the most authentic. Its classically Dutch buildings sprawl across rolling hills, with rich details around every corner. Nearby, the Kröller-Müller Museum, located in the middle of Hoge Veluwe National Park, displays a world-class collection of modern art (including roomfuls of Van Goghs—they own 87 of them). It's also a delight to pedal through the park on free white bikes.

Rail enthusiasts can make a pilgrimage to the Spoorweg-museum in Utrecht, an easy stop (and a common transfer point) on the train route, located roughly midway between Amsterdam and Arnhem.

Planning Your Time

Arnhem, an hour southeast of Amsterdam by train, is doable as a side-trip from Amsterdam. Unfortunately, the two main sights— the folk museum and the art museum—are far from each other and far from Arnhem's Central Station—so you'll need to allow extra time to catch the bus to either one. Both are superb and worth the time and effort, but if you want to see both, you should either spend the night in the town of Otterlo (recommended) or be prepared for a long day of somewhat-rushed sightseeing. Note that the Kröller-Müller Museum is closed on Monday.

By Car: Drivers with short attention spans can visit both the open-air folk museum and Kröller-Müller Museum within a day...and might have time left to park the car and go for a pedal through the national park. Figure just over an hour's drive from

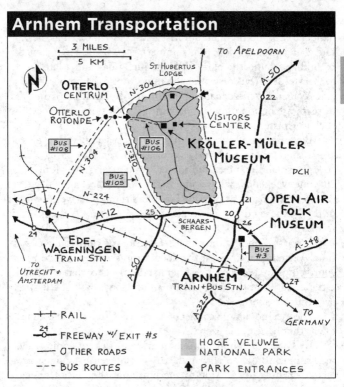

Arnhem Transportation

3 MILES
5 KM

N

TO APELDOORN

ST. HUBERTUS LODGE

A-50

OTTERLO CENTRUM

N-304

22

OTTERLO ROTONDE

VISITORS CENTER

BUS #108

BUS #106

N-304

N-310

KRÖLLER-MÜLLER MUSEUM

DCH

BUS #105

N-224

21

OPEN-AIR FOLK MUSEUM

A-12

25

SCHAARS-BERGEN

20

26

A-50

BUS #3

A-348

24

EDE-WAGENINGEN TRAIN STN.

TO UTRECHT & AMSTERDAM

ARNHEM TRAIN & BUS STN.

A-325

27

TO GERMANY

+++ RAIL

24 FREEWAY W/ EXIT #S

—— OTHER ROADS

--- BUS ROUTES

HOGE VELUWE NATIONAL PARK

⬆ PARK ENTRANCES

Amsterdam to Arnhem, then about a 20-minute ride into the national park, then an hour back to Amsterdam.

By Public Transportation: It's possible to get to both the Arnhem Open-Air Folk Museum and the Kröller-Müller Museum in one very long but fulfilling day of sightseeing—but it's only worthwhile if you get an early start. Because no bus connects the open-air folk museum and the Kröller-Müller Museum, you'll have to return to Arnhem's bus station between sights—limiting the amount of time you'll have at each place.

To do everything in one day, I'd catch an early train (around 8:00) from Amsterdam Central Station to Arnhem (4/hour, 1 hour, half transfer in Utrecht), then walk to the bus station and hop a bus (2/hour, 15 minutes) for the Arnhem Open-Air Folk Museum. Plan to arrive when it opens at 10:00. To make this schedule work, you need to leave the folk museum by 13:00, which gives you enough time to bus back to the Arnhem station and catch another bus to Otterlo (2/hour), near Hoge Veluwe National Park. Once in Otterlo, you can take yet another bus directly to the Kröller-Müller Museum (in the middle of the national park), or walk 15 minutes to the entrance of the park and borrow a bike to ride there (for all the details on Otterlo, see page 314). In the national park, do the museum first (closes at 17:00), then the visitors center (closes at 18:00 in summer), then wind down your day by biking around the park. Plan on a long day and a late return to Amsterdam (bus or walk back into Otterlo, catch bus #108 to Ede-Wageningen—departs from Otterlo Rotonde near the edge of town at the top of each hour until 23:00, then take the train back to Amsterdam).

Bus prices are high—each trip will cost you between €2 and €6. If there are two of you, ask for a "Buzzer" day pass (€13.50, covers two adults, buy from driver, good after 9:00 Mon-Fri or anytime weekends, www.connexxion.nl/buzzer_english/174). If you are traveling alone or using buses and trams for a week or more in the Netherlands, it may make sense to get an OV-Chipkaart; see page 617.

If you're spending the night in Otterlo, you can get a later start from Amsterdam, linger at the open-air folk museum (having left your things in a locker at Arnhem station), relax that evening in Otterlo, and tour the art museum and national park at a leisurely pace the next morning.

For specifics on the connections between these sights, and the towns they're near, see each listing.

By Bike: Pedal enthusiasts may want to rent some wheels in Arnhem to get to the open-air folk museum; it's a strenuous 20-minute uphill ride to the museum, then a breezy, easy 10-minute glide back into town (ask for directions at bike shop, listed under "Arrival in Arnhem," later).

Orientation to Arnhem

Arnhem is a dreary urban city of about 140,000 people. Tourists view Arnhem as a transit hub useful only for reaching the open-air folk museum on its outskirts and the nearby Kröller-Müller Museum and national park. A few hotels line up across from the train station, but I'd rather sleep in charming little Otterlo, near the park entrance (see "Sleeping in Otterlo" on page 315). Arnhem's old town—nowhere near as charming as similar towns in the Netherlands—is just across the busy ring road from the train and bus stations. Restaurants with outdoor seating cluster around the square called Korenmarkt and, a few steps deeper into the old town, around Jaansplaats.

Tourist Information

Arnhem's TI is across the street from the bus station (Mon-Fri 9:30-17:30, Sat 9:30-17:00, closed Sun, Stationsplein 13, tel. 0900-112-2344—€0.45/minute, www.vvvarnhem.nl). The TI provides a free city map and sells a €6.50 tourist map that includes the national park and Kröller-Müller Museum (the national park's visitors center sells a cheaper map).

Arrival in Arnhem

By Train: Arnhem's train station is surrounded by a sea of construction and urban blight, as they're in the midst of a multiyear project to build a super-modern station complex. Expect changes to the following information.

The station has **WCs** (€0.50) and **lockers** (€3.70/24 hours, credit cards only). You'll also find a Rijwiel **bike-rental shop** (€7.50/day for 3-speed bike—you'll need all 3 speeds—plus €50 refundable deposit, open daily very long hours). While the construction continues, the location of the shop changes—look for it near the front of the station.

By Bus: The bus station is to the right as you exit the train station in a large parking garage along the busy street. Check the sign near the entry to the bus area to find the departure bay for your bus. For the Arnhem Open-Air Folk Museum (Openluchtmuseum), take bus #3 (in July-Aug, #13 works as well, but it may stop running in 2013); for Otterlo (near the Kröller-Müller Museum and national park), take bus #105.

Arnhem Open-Air Folk Museum (Openluchtmuseum)

Arnhem has the Netherlands' first, biggest, and best folk museum, rated ▲▲. You'll enjoy a huge park of windmills, old farmhouses and other buildings (relocated from throughout the Netherlands), traditional crafts in action, and a pleasant education-by-immersion in Dutch culture. It's great for families.

Orientation

Cost and Hours: €15, April-Oct daily 10:00-17:00, Dec-mid-Jan daily 11:00-19:00; €4 in Nov and mid-Jan-March, when the buildings are closed but the grounds are open shorter hours.

Getting There: To reach the open-air folk museum from the

Arnhem bus station, take one of two **buses** (check the board for the departure bay): In July and August (and on some holidays), bus #13 zips you directly to the town's zoo, then to the museum entrance—but confirm locally that this bus is still running (3-4/hour, €3). At other times, or if bus #13 is not operating, take bus #3 (make sure it's marked *Alteveer*, as some #3 buses go elsewhere; about 2/hour, 20 minutes, €3). Bus #3 drops you a five-minute walk from the museum entrance: Cross the street, head right, then left down the tree-lined avenue to the roundabout, then turn right (following signs for *Openluchtmuseum*). From the Arnhem train station, you can also **walk** or ride a **bike** (uphill most of the way, figure 30 minutes by foot or 20 minutes by bike). A **taxi** from the station costs about €20.

By **car** from Amsterdam, take A-2 south to Utrecht, then A-12 east to Arnhem. Just before Arnhem, take the Arnhem Nord exit (#26) and follow *Openluchtmuseum* signs to the museum (€5 parking, buy parking ticket when you buy entrance ticket). If driving from Haarlem, skirt Amsterdam to the south on A-9, take A-2 south to Utrecht, and then follow the previous instructions (via A-12).

Information: Tel. 026/357-6111, www.openluchtmuseum.nl.

Getting Around: A free, old-fashioned tram does a lazy counterclockwise circle around the museum grounds, making six stops (well-marked on park maps).

Self-Guided Tour

You could spend the whole day exploring this wonderful open-air museum. But to hit a few highlights, follow this tour. Because the layout of the grounds can be confusing, pick up the good free map at the entry—I've used the numbers on that map to help you navigate this tour. Don't hesitate to dip into any buildings that intrigue you, even if they're not on this tour—most have brief English explanations outside, and some have English-speaking docents inside. (Ask them questions...that's their job.) Especially with kids, it would be a shame to do this place in a rush—there's so much to experience.

• *Start in the...*

Entrance Pavilion: Consider buying the in-depth English guidebook, and ask about special events and activities, especially for kids. Downstairs are exhibits on traditional Dutch costumes and replicas of various storefronts. You'll also find Arnhem's effort to keep up with the Disneys: the high-tech **"HollandRama"** multimedia experience (inside the big copper blob you saw out front; runs about hourly—schedule posted by stairs). You'll sit on a giant platform that rotates inside a spherical theater to gradually reveal various Dutch dioramas: windmills, a snowy countryside, house and store interiors, and so on. Although the narration is in Dutch, the 20-minute presentation is an enjoyable rest.

• *To hit the park, exit straight out of the entrance pavilion and walk up the path. You're likely to see animals in the pasture on your right—if so, take a closer look: They're rare Dutch breeds, not the high-yield animals used in modern farms. No longer cost-effective, these special animals are raised by the museum as part of its mission to preserve a piece of Dutch folk life.*

After a few buildings on the left, step inside the one-story...

"Cheese-Cover" Farmhouse (#4.1, just before the pond): The cows lived on one side of this house from 1745, and the people on the other (notice the claustrophobic cupboard-beds). Along the cow stalls, see the patterns the farmwife would make with fresh sand and seashells each summer to show off family status.

• *Nearby, cross the...*

Yellow Drawbridge (#4.2): Dating from 1358, this takes you to perhaps the most scenic part of the park: a pond surrounded by

windmills and cabins (inspired by the Waterland area around Marken—described in the Edam, Volendam, and Marken chapter). Pause on the bridge to look toward the sawmill. You might see kids playing with a small rope-pulled ferryboat.

Continue across the drawbridge into the little **village.** Along the way are some tempting shops where you can pick up an edible souvenir, including a well-stocked general store, a bakery, and a fragrant candy store.

Village Square (#4.13): You can play here with toys from the 1800s. See if you can make the "flying Dutchman" fly, or try to ride an original "high-wheeled velocipede" without falling off. On the square is a restaurant specializing in *poffertjes* (puffy mini-pancakes dusted with powdered sugar), with indoor and outdoor seating.

• *Behind the* poffertje *shop, cross the little bridge toward the windmills, pass the boat workshop, and enter the...*

Fisherman's Cottage (#4.11): The black-tarred exterior hides a bright and colorful interior. Notice the rope-controlled smoke hatch, rather than a chimney. Wooden cottages like these were nicknamed "smokehouses." In front of the cottage is the boatyard, where vessels could be pulled out of the water to scrape off the barnacles.

• *Backtrack through the village square, then continue on to the...*

Laundry (#5.1, on the right): Inside, an industrial-strength agitator furiously pounds stubborn stains to smithereens. (There was no "delicate cycle" back then.) On nice days, the clean sheets are spread out on the lawn to dry.

• *For an optional detour (best for train buffs), hook around through the little cottages across the street, then turn right to reach the...*

Train Depot (#6.1): Inside, you can actually walk underneath a train to check out its undercarriage. The adjacent **goods shed** (#6.8) holds a virtual-reality postal carriage.

• *Head back past the laundry, then go beyond the cafeteria to reach the small, yellow windmill. Here, turn left and walk up the path, watching for the low-profile brown building through the trees on your right, near the bridge.*

Paper Mill (#5.4): At this building, dating from around 1850, you'll learn that farmers often made paper in their spare time to help make ends meet. Inside, you might see a demonstration of linen rags being turned into pulp, and then into paper. Peek upstairs at the finished paper hanging to dry.

• *Leaving the mill, walk straight ahead on the brick path, passing various buildings on your right-hand side until you reach the...*

Herb Garden (#11.1): This tranquil, hedge-lined garden is worth exploring. The map at the entry explains the various parts of the garden, each growing herbs for different purposes: dyes, food, medicine, and so on. Listen for the squeals of lively children from the playground behind the garden.

• *Continue past the garden and cross the tram tracks to the...*

Freia Steam-Dairy Factory (at #7.1, with the big smoke-stack): Named after Freia, the Norse goddess of agriculture, this was the Netherlands' first privately owned cheese and butter factory. Borrow the English explanations at the entry, sample some free cheese, and try to follow the huge belt of the steam engine as it whirls through the factory.

• *Leaving the factory, loop around to the right—past the little black-and-green windmill—then turn right again, down the path just before the brick-and-thatch forest hut. On the right, look for the...*

Peat Hut (#7.6): Humble little huts like these were used by day laborers and covered with the same turf that those laborers were paid so poorly to gather.

• *Continue to a big, thatched-roof...*

Farmhouse (#8.1): Step into the vast and rough 1700s interior, listen to recorded animal noises, and scope out the layout: grain stored up above, cows along the main room, and at the far end, a (no doubt smelly) residential zone for people.

• *Cross the tram tracks in front of the farmhouse to reach the tiny...*

Schoolhouse (#8.2): Aside from its brick construction (most were made of clay), this is typical of village schoolhouses from around 1730. Only kids from 6 to 12 years old, mostly boys, attended school, with an emphasis on reading and writing, with summers off to help on the farm. Imagine the schoolhouse back then, fragrant with smoke from the peat fire. Notice the slates used to follow along with lessons (stored in the wooden "lockers" on the walls). An underperforming student would have to wear the donkey picture around his neck.

Just beyond the schoolhouse is the **Pancake House** (#9.1; good for a snack or meal—see "Eating at the Arnhem Open-Air Museum," below), with an adjacent playground.

• *Cross the tram tracks to peek into the...*

Church (#10.1): In the typical Dutch style, the church has an austere white interior, a central pulpit, and wooden pews.

• *Then continue along the tracks through the village, past the **Brabant Café** (#12.3), to the modern, working **brewery** (#12.4, on the left), where you can duck inside for a free sample.*

Just beyond, on the left, look for the...

Four Laborers' Houses (#12.5): These houses offer a fascinating glimpse into the lifestyles of four generations of workers: from 1870, 1910, 1954, and 1970. See how home fashion and amenities progressed from the rustic 1870s to the garish 1970s.

• *Continuing through the village, the **hospital** on the left (#12.9), from 1955, really does smell like a hospital. Next, the long **collection center** (#13.8) shows off a mind-numbing array of Dutch bric-a-brac, with futuristic exhibits about recycling and conservation. Just beyond it is a formal hedge garden. Finally, cross the tram tracks and walk to the big, white...*

Platform Windmill (#15.6): Hike up the steep steps of the park's centerpiece for an aerial view over the museums.

• *Our tour is over. Head back to the entrance, or continue exploring to your heart's content.*

Eating at the Arnhem Open-Air Museum

The open-air museum has several good budget restaurants and covered picnic areas. The **café** in the entrance pavilion is inexpensive but has limited choices (€5-6 sandwiches)—it's more enjoyable to eat inside the park. The rustic **Pancake House** (Pannekoeken Huis, a.k.a. "Restaurant de Hanekamp") serves hearty and sweet splittable Dutch flapjacks (€6-9 pancakes, soups, salads, and sandwiches). **Brabant Café,** in the "village" of Budel, resembles an old-fashioned farmhouse café and offers desserts and snacks. The **De Kasteelboerderij Café-Restaurant** at the Oud-Beijerland Manor is a giant place that can feed 300 visitors at once (traditional €8 *dag-menu*—plate of the day; open daily July-Aug, otherwise Sun only).

Arnhem Connections

From Arnhem by Train to: Amsterdam (4/hour, 1 hour, half with transfer in Utrecht), **The Hague** (4/hour, 1.5 hours, transfer in Utrecht; then another 15 minutes to **Delft**).

Kröller-Müller Museum

The Kröller-Müller Museum of top-notch modern art, rated ▲▲, is located within Hoge Veluwe National Park, the Netherlands' largest at 13,000 acres. While the south end of the park is just outside Arnhem, the museum is buried deep in the forest close to the opposite end of the park, near the town of Otterlo. Because the museum is situated within the national park, you must buy a ticket for both the museum and the park.

This memorable museum shows off the collection of Helene Kröller-Müller (1869-1939), who was a wealthy fan of avant-garde art, and includes an outstanding collection of Van Goghs. The modern museum seamlessly blends artistic beauty and its own peaceful park setting. Stroll through the delightfully landscaped sculpture garden, and spend some time with virtually all the top artists of the late 19th and early 20th centuries.

Because it's difficult to get to, the Kröller-Müller Museum doesn't suffer from the hordes who descend on the Van Gogh Museum in Amsterdam. This is your best chance to get up close and personal with Vincent.

Orientation

Cost and Hours: €16.40 combo-ticket includes national park entry, covered by Museumkaart, open Tue-Sun 10:00-17:00, sculpture garden closes at 16:30, closed Mon, Houtkampweg 6, tel. 031/859-1241, www.kmm.nl.

Getting There: Public-transportation connections to the Kröller-Müller Museum and Hoge Veluwe National Park are complicated, potentially involving several changes. (Even the park's employees don't bother trying to commute by bus.) Give yourself plenty of time, and try to confirm bus schedules when planning your day. These instructions get you to the northwest entrance of the park, near Otterlo, just over a mile from the Kröller-Müller Museum.

   From Amsterdam: First, take the train to Ede-Wageningen (4/hour, 1 hour, half with a transfer in Utrecht). Exit the Ede-Wageningen station toward signs marked

Centrum to find the bus stops, where you can catch bus #108 to Otterlo (bus marked *Apeldoorn*, runs hourly about :40 past the hour, or 2/hour on weekday mornings before 11:00, 15 minutes, €6, €13.50 "Buzzer" day pass covers two adults, buy from driver). A handy reader board in the bus displays the next stop. Hop off the bus at Otterlo Rotonde (a roundabout on the edge of town). The #106 bus usually meets the #108 at this stop—making it an easy transition to get to the museum. Jump on board. When you enter the park, the driver will stop at the ticket booth so that you can buy tickets for the park and the museum. Ask the driver to let you off at the Kröller-Müller Museum; turn right at the giant blue trowel and follow the road for a few minutes past the parking lot with all the white bikes; the museum entrance is on the left.

If you miss the #106, walk five minutes into the town center, and then hang a left to the park entrance (about 20 minutes total), where you can buy your combo-ticket at the northwest entrance and hop on a free white bike to ride to the Kröller-Müller Museum or the park's visitors center. If you'd rather take a taxi, it costs about €40 one-way from the Ede-Wageningen station to the museum.

If the schedules don't line up well, you can also get from Amsterdam to the park via Arnhem (see below).

From Arnhem Central Station: Arnhem is a one-hour train ride from Amsterdam. From Arnhem Central Station, the Kröller-Müller Museum is 12 miles away. There's no direct bus to the museum, so you'll go via the town of Otterlo: Go next door to Arnhem's bus station (see "Arrival in Arnhem" on page 305), take bus #105 marked *Barneveld/Syntus*, and get off at Otterlo Centrum (1-2/hour, 20 minutes, €5, €13.50 "Buzzer" day pass covers two adults, buy from driver). Once in Otterlo, you can take bus #106 or walk to the park (both options described under "Arrival in Otterlo" on page 315). You can hire a taxi from Arnhem's station, but it's expensive (about €45).

By Car: From Amsterdam, take A-1 southeast, then exit on N-310 to Otterlo. From Arnhem, take A-12 north, then pick up N-310 to Otterlo. Parking inside the park costs €6, or you can pay €2 to park at the entrance and bike or walk in.

Getting Around Hoge Veluwe National Park: Once at Hoge Veluwe, you have various options for connecting the attractions. My favorite plan: Bus from Otterlo directly to the Kröller-Müller Museum, pick up a free white bike to pedal to the park's visitors center, then bike back to the museum (or, with more time, bike around the park).

By Bike: The park has 1,700 white bikes—an endearing

remnant of Holland's hippie past—that you're free to use to make your explorations more fun. The one-speed bikes, with no hand brakes (just pedal brakes), are good enough to get around on, but not good enough to get stolen. Just pick one up (or drop one off) wherever you see a bike rack, including at park entrances or at any attraction. While riding through the vast green woods, make a point of getting off your bike to climb an inland sand dune.

By Bus: Bus #106 does a convenient circuit around the park, connecting the "Otterlo Rotonde" stop (at the edge of town), the "Otterlo Centrum" stop (in the town center), the Otterlo entrance to the park, a stop 200 yards from the Kröller-Müller Museum, and the park's visitors center. Unfortunately, its frequency isn't ideal (hourly on weekdays, 2/hour on weekends until 18:00; last bus at 20:00 May-Aug, earlier in off-season). But it can be a handy way to connect the dots if you're tired or in a hurry.

Visiting the Museum

A stern-looking statue of Monsieur Jacques (the museum's mascot) greets you on the entry path. Once inside, pick up the informative guidebooklet and drop your bag at the mandatory bag check. Computers near the entry let you tailor a self-guided tour to your interests. Each work is labeled (but not described) in English, and there is no audioguide.

There are two parts to the museum: the outside sculpture garden and the interior art collection.

The **sculpture garden** shows off more than a hundred sculptures, displayed on 60 rolling acres of lawn. You can appreciate works by Auguste Rodin, Barbara Hepworth, Claes Oldenburg, Christo, and others—or just enjoy this excuse for a walk in a pretty park with something fun to look at. Look for Jean Dubuffet's beloved *Garden of Enamel*, a giant, psychedelic, black-and-white roller rink you can climb around on. Since the garden closes at 16:30, head here first if you're arriving later in the day.

Inside, the permanent **art collection** is like a Who's Who

of modern art. The works are displayed chronologically and grouped by movement, in keeping with Helene Kröller-Müller's wishes to foster understanding and appreciation of new art styles. You'll go from the hazy landscapes of the Impressionists (Monet, Manet, Renoir), to the intricate compositions of the Pointillists (Seurat, Pissarro), to the bold innovations of the Post-Impressionists (Gauguin, Van Gogh), to the slinky scenes of Art Nouveau (Toulouse-Lautrec), to the shattered-glass canvases of the Cubists (Picasso, Braque, and Gris), and, finally, to the colorful grids of Dutchman Piet Mondrian.

The museum's highlight is its Vincent van Gogh collection, the second-largest in the world (after Amsterdam's Van Gogh Museum; Kröller-Müller usually displays about 50 of their 87 Vincent canvases). Look for some famous pieces, including various self-portraits; some *Sunflowers*— including one with a blue background; and *Café de Nuit,* the famous scene of an al fresco café on a floodlit Arles square. Notice how thickly the paint is caked on to create the almost-3-D lamp, the work's focal point.

Eating at the Kröller-Müller Museum: Consider the self-service restaurant Monsieur Jacques (€6 soups and sandwiches, €11 salads, Tue-Sun 10:00-16:30, closed Mon).

After visiting the museum, grab a free white bike for the three-quarter-mile pedal to the national park's visitors center, described later.

Sights in Hoge Veluwe National Park

Hoge Veluwe National Park

The Netherlands' biggest national park, rated ▲▲, is a delight to explore. On a quick visit, a short pedal and a visit to the Kröller-Müller Museum are enough; with more time, also swing by the visitors center and bike to your heart's content. The hunting lodge within the park, the former residence of the Kröller-Müller family (described on next page), makes a fun destination. If you head deeper into the park, you'll find a surprising diversity of terrain, from inland sand dunes to lakes to peat bogs to moorland. Get advice, maps, and brochures at the park entrances or at the visitors center.

Cost and Hours: Park entry-€8.20, €16.40 combo-ticket includes the Kröller-Müller Museum, covered by Museumkaart. The park is open daily June-July 8:00-22:00, May and Aug 8:00-21:00, April 8:00-20:00, Sept 9:00-20:00, Oct 9:00-19:00, Nov-March 9:00-18:00, last entry one hour before closing (tel. 055/378-8100, www.hogeveluwe.nl).

Visitors Center (Bezoekerscentrum)—This is a good place to get your bearings in the park, with a helpful information desk, a nature exhibit, WCs, a playground, a restaurant, and a hub for free loaner bikes (daily April-Oct 9:30-18:00, Nov-March 9:30-17:00). Browse the collection of brochures and maps, including the good €2.50 map of the park, and the €1 self-guided bike tour in English, with commentary on the main stops.

The **nature exhibit** features interactive, kid-oriented exhibits, well-explained in English. It's divided into two parts: An above-ground section focuses on the parks' various landscapes and the animals that live above ground; then you'll go through a tunnel to reach the second section, called the "Museonder," which shows life underground (animals, fossils, the water table), with conservation-themed displays. Ask for an English showing of the nature films when you enter (a favorite is the 30-minute movie about park deer).

Eating at the Visitors Center: The good **Restaurant de Koperen Kop** serves up surprisingly tasty self-service cafeteria food, with indoor or outdoor seating (€8-12 plates, daily April-Oct 9:30-18:00, Nov-March 9:30-17:00).

St. Hubertus Lodge—This dramatic hunting lodge, at the north end of the park, is another popular excuse for a bike ride. Once the countryside residence of the modern art-collecting Kröller-Müller family, it's perched on the edge of a lake with a tower looming overhead. Designed to resemble the antlers of a stag, this structure evokes the story of St. Hubert, who supposedly discovered a crucifix miraculously dangling between a deer's antlers (sporadic tours, in Dutch only). The 45-minute walk around the adjacent lake is dotted with sculptures. Combining this lodge, the Kröller-Müller Museum, and the visitors center makes for a fun 6.5-mile biking loop.

Otterlo

The tiny village of Otterlo is located just outside the northwest entrance to the park, which is the closest one to the Kröller-Müller Museum. Though not exciting, it's a good place to spend the night near the park (see "Sleeping in Otterlo," next page). The town has tandem-bike tourists zipping through on their way to the park, cafés, and a meager **TI** (in the middle of the town center, open Mon-Thu 8:00-18:00, Fri 8:00-20:00, Sat 8:00-17:00, closed Sun, Dorpsstraat 9, tel. 0318/614-444).

Arrival in Otterlo: There are two different bus stops in Otterlo. "Otterlo Rotonde" is at a roundabout on the busy road that skirts the edge of town; from here it's about a five-minute walk into the town center. "Otterlo Centrum" is right in the middle of town (described below). Buses #105 (from Arnhem) and #106 (into the park itself) stop at both the Rotonde and Centrum stops; bus #108 (from Ede-Wageningen and trains to Amsterdam) stops only at the Rotonde stop.

From **Otterlo Centrum,** follow the directional signs: The TI is along the main road, and the park is down the major intersecting road. From here it's about a 15-minute walk to the park entrance (or a very fast ride on bus #106).

Sleeping in Otterlo

Consider spending the night in Otterlo if you'd like to have a relaxing time at the museum, the national park, and nearby Arnhem. Both of these accommodations are on the road between Otterlo Centrum and the northwest entrance to the park; Sterrenberg is closer to the park, and Kruller is closer to the town center.

$$ Boutique Hotel Sterrenberg, located about half a mile from the park entrance, is a Dutch designer's take on a traditional hunting lodge. With woodsy touches and modern flair in its 33 rooms, it's a pleasant splurge (Sb-€97, Db-€145-195, price depends on season and room size, pricier "luxury" rooms, great Sunday-night deals include dinner, elevator, free Internet access and Wi-Fi,

---

Sleep Code

(€1 = about $1.30, country code: 31, area code: 0318)
S = Single, **D** = Double/Twin, **T** = Triple, **Q** = Quad, **b** = bathroom, **s** = shower only. Unless otherwise noted, credit cards are accepted, breakfast is included, and hoteliers speak English.

To help you easily sort through these listings, I've divided the accommodations into two categories, based on the price for a standard double room with bath:

$$ Higher Priced—Most rooms €125 or more.
$ Lower Priced—Most rooms less than €125.

Prices can change without notice; verify the hotel's current rates online or by email.

restaurant with terrace, swimming pool, sauna, 6 rentable bikes for guests—€8.50/day—or use free white bikes within nearby park gates, about 1.5 miles to Kröller-Müller Museum, Houtkampweg 1, tel. 0318/591-228, fax 0318/591-693, www.sterrenberg.nl, info @sterrenberg.nl).

$ Hotel Kruller has 17 stylishly simple rooms over a busy restaurant (small Sb-€59, mid-size Sb-€79, small Db-€79, mid-size Db-€99, large Db-€119, cheaper for 2 or more nights, no elevator, free Internet access and Wi-Fi, Dorpsstraat 19, tel. 0318/591-231, fax 0318/592-034, www.kruller.nl, info@kruller.nl).

Utrecht

The bustling student city of Utrecht lies smack-dab between Arnhem to the east, The Hague (and Delft and Rotterdam) to the west, and Amsterdam to the north (4 trains/hour, 30 minutes). You might change trains here; if so, and if you have time to kill, consider poking around the central zone, which is charming compared to Utrecht's grossly commercial train station. Utrecht has plenty to keep you busy for an hour or a day (the station's lockers are near the elevator to track 7, €4/24 hours).

▲Spoorwegmuseum (Railway Museum)—The most interesting sight in town is Holland's biggest and best display of all things locomotive. It's full of vintage engines and cars (including the Dutch royal family's official train), model railways, a ride for kids, and a Disneyesque re-creation of an Industrial Age mining village. Even the most train-blasé will want to spend at least two hours here.

Cost and Hours: Pricey at €14.50, Tue-Sun 10:00-17:00, closed Mon, at east edge of town in old-fashioned Maliebaanstation, tel. 030/230-6206, www.spoorwegmuseum.nl.

Getting There: The easiest way to get to the museum is by a special "Maliebaan" train that leaves hourly from Utrecht's Central Station (departs at about :45 after the hour, last train at 15:45, 15 minutes, €2). It's a pleasant 20-minute walk from the train station to the museum (well-signed all the way). If you'd prefer the bus, hop the GVU bus #3 from Central Station (direction: Fockema Andrealaan, get off at Maliebaan stop).

Museum Speelklok (Musical Clock Museum)—This fun museum is worthwhile only if you take the 50-minute included tour, which shows you musical clocks, calliopes, and street organs in all their clicking, clanking, and tooting glory.

Cost and Hours: €9.50 includes tour, €13.50 combo-ticket includes Domtoren, Tue-Sun 10:00-17:00, closed Mon, tours depart on the hour, last tour at 16:00, well-signed 10-minute walk from station, located on busy shopping street in city center at Steenweg 6, tel. 030/231-2789, www.museumspeelklok.nl.

Domtoren (Cathedral Tower)—Utrecht's exact center is unmistakably marked by this impressive tower. At 368 feet, it's Holland's highest tower—so big that city buses can drive through the arch at its base. It was once the west entrance of the city's cathedral, before most of the High Gothic church was destroyed in a storm in 1674. The tower is even more remarkable considering that it's also the central spire of an even bigger (imaginary) cathedral. To help cement Utrecht's standing as a seat of Church power, four churches were built at the endpoints of an invisible city-sized cross—symbolically making Utrecht one gigantic mega-cathedral. At the tower's base is a lively cluster of cafés.

Cost and Hours: Tower climbable only with €9 guided tour—must reserve in advance by phone, €13.50 combo-ticket includes Museum Speelklok; April-Sept Tue-Sat 11:00-16:00, Sun-Mon 12:00-16:00; Oct-March daily 12:00-16:00; tour leaves from nearby TI at Domplein 9/10, no elevator, tel. 030/236-0010, www.domtoren.nl.

SCHOKLAND MUSEUM

About a fifth of the Netherlands is reclaimed land—much of it a short drive northeast of Amsterdam. To appreciate the Dutch quest to show the sea who's boss (and what the sea did to deserve it), visit the museum at Schokland.

Once a long, skinny island with a few scant villages, Schokland was gradually enveloped by the sea, until the king condemned and evacuated it in 1859. But after the sea around it was tamed and drained, Schokland was turned into a museum of Dutch traditions...and engineering prowess.

Today Schokland is a long way to go for a little museum, and it only makes sense by car, but the area offers a fascinating drive for engineers or anyone else who wants to understand how the Dutch have confidently grabbed the reins from Mother Nature.

Orientation

Cost and Hours: €5; July-Aug daily 10:00-17:00; April-June and Oct Tue-Sun 11:00-17:00, closed Mon; Nov-March Fri-Sun 11:00-17:00, closed Mon-Thu; Middelbuurt 3, tel. 0527/251-396, www.schokland.nl.

Getting There: It's about an hour's **drive** north of Amsterdam (assuming there's no traffic), but the trip offers travelers an insightful glimpse at Dutch land reclamation. From Amsterdam's ring freeway, follow signs for *Almere*—first southeast on A-1, then northeast on A-6. You'll drive the

Taming the Zuiderzee

The Dutch have always had a love/hate relationship with the tempestuous Zuiderzee ("South Sea"). While it provided the Dutch with a convenient source of fish and trade—and an outlet to the Atlantic—the unpredictable bay also made life challenging. Over the centuries, entire towns were gradually eroded off the map.

But in 1918, the Dutch fought back and began to ingeniously tame the sea and "reclaim" their land with the Zuiderzee Works: First they built a sturdy dike (the Afsluitdijk) across the mouth of the sea to turn a dangerous, raging ocean into a mild puddle (the IJsselmeer); then they began to partition pieces of the sea floor, dike them off, and drain the water. The salty new seabed soil was treated organically and eventually became fertile farmland.

The best place to see the result of this process is in Flevoland, the Netherlands' newest state and home to Schokland. Some of the residents are older than the land they live on, which was reclaimed in the 1960s. An area that was once a merciless sea is now dotted with tranquil towns. The roads, commercial centers, and neighborhoods—made affordable to the masses—are all carefully planned and as tidy as can be.

length of the very flat reclaimed island of Flevoland (past the towns of Almere and Lelystad), and pass a striking line of power-generating windmills spinning like gigantic pinwheels as you cross out of Flevoland and into Noordoostpolder—the reclaimed "Northeast Polder" that includes Schokland. Take the Urk exit (#13), turn right, and follow blue signs for *Schokland*.

By **public transportation,** it's possible but not worth the effort (6:00 departure by train from Amsterdam, change at Weesp for Lelystad, then take bus #315 to Nagele, then bus #681 to Schokland; takes 2 hours).

Self-Guided Tour

After buying your ticket, you'll watch a 15-minute **film** (press button to start in English) about the history of the town, its loss to the sea, and its reclamation.

Then tour the exposition called **Schokland: An Island in Time,** which explains how Schokland was reclaimed as part of what would become the Northeast Polder, beginning in 1936. After being enclosed by a sturdy dike, a yearlong project drained this area of water in 1942 (while the Netherlands was occupied by the Nazis). Various Allied bombers were shot down and crashed

into this area (including one whose mangled propeller is displayed just outside the museum), joining the dozens of shipwrecks that already littered the seafloor.

A model shows the full territory of the Northeast Polder, which is carefully planned in concentric circles around the central town of Emmeloord (with Schokland and another former island, Urk, creating a pair of oddball bulges in the otherwise tidy pattern).

The exhibit explains that this isn't the first time this area has been dry land. From prehistoric times through the Middle Ages, much of what is today the Northeast Polder was farmed (many old tools have been discovered). In 1100, medieval engineers even attempted a primitive (and ultimately unsuccessful) effort to reclaim the land. Other remains from former residents include bones from mammoths and other prehistoric mammals, and a primitive 2,450-year-old canoe.

Then you'll head into the **Schokkerhuisje** to learn about the people who lived here (called *Schokkers*) until they were evacuated in 1859. Up to 650 people at a time lived on Schokland, residing in settlements on hills called *terpen* while they farmed the often-flooded land below. Like the rest of the Netherlands, this little island was divided in half by religion: part Catholic, part Protestant. This museum holds artifacts from the former town of Middelbuurt. You'll see traditional *Schokker* costumes (abandoned when they left the island) and a map of the entire island.

Back outside, go into the former **town church,** with a ceiling like the hull of a ship, a pulpit like a crow's nest, and a model ship hanging from the ceiling—appropriate for the seafaring residents of a once nearly submerged island.

Finally, follow the path (below the church) to walk around the base of the former island—now surrounded by **farm fields.** When farmers first tilled their newly reclaimed soil a half-century ago, they uncovered more than just muck and mollusks. You'll see a pair of rusty anchors and a giant buoy that used to bob in the harbor—now lying on its side and still tethered to the ground. Examine the stone dike and black wooden seawall built by residents in a futile attempt to stay above water. The post with the blue strip helped residents keep an eye on the ever-rising water level.

Nearby: If you're intrigued by all of this, you can walk a six-mile path (with posted information) that covers the entire length of the former island (get a map from the museum). Or, for a quick look, drive to the forlorn old **lighthouse,** improbably perched

overlooking a vast field of grazing cows—without a coastline in sight. In fact, the lighthouse marks the far tip of what was Schokland Island—and, because it was situated along a major trade route, this lighthouse was once extremely important. Today, this white elephant is an evocative symbol of Holland's complex relationship with the sea. To get there by car, leave the museum parking lot and turn left onto the main road, then take the first right (marked *Oude Haven Schokland*) and follow the road through the woods for about three minutes. When you reach the next big road, turn right, then look for the lighthouse on the left (with parking nearby).

EDAM, VOLENDAM & MARKEN

The aptly named region of Waterland (VAH-ter-land), just north of Amsterdam on the west shore of the IJsselmeer, is laced with canals and sprinkled with picturesque red-brick villages. Three in particular—the homey cheesemaking village of Edam, the touristy waterfront town of Volendam, and the trapped-in-a-time-warp hamlet of Marken—offer visitors an enticing peek at rural Holland.

If choosing just one Waterland town, make it Edam—and consider spending the night. Because of its charm and its proximity to Amsterdam, this region is popular. But if you'd like to get a taste of traditional Dutch living, it's worth joining the crowds.

Planning Your Time

The most efficient way to see this area is as a one-day loop trip by public transportation from Amsterdam (or Haarlem); to have enough time for the whole loop, get started by 10:00. Begin with a bus from Amsterdam to Edam. Then, after enjoying Edam, continue by bus to Volendam for a stroll and to catch the boat across to Marken. Leave Edam by around 14:00 in order to have sufficient time in Volendam (you'll want at least an hour there), and to be able to reach Marken before its museum and shops close at 17:00. Poke around salty Marken before taking the bus back to Amsterdam.

All of the bus rides in this loop are covered by the €7.50 "Waterland Ticket" from the Arriva bus company (not covered by Amsterdam transit passes). The Volendam-Marken boat costs extra and doesn't take cars. The drive from Volendam to Marken is a delight.

Edam

This adorable cheesemaking village is sweet but not saccharine, and is just 30 minutes by bus from Amsterdam. It's mostly the ter-rain of day-trippers, who can mob the place on summer weekends. For the ultimate in cuteness and peace, make your home in tiny Edam (ay-DAHM) and stay overnight.

Although Edam is known today for cheese, it was once an industrious shipyard and port. But having a canal to the sea caused such severe flooding in town—cracking walls and spill-ing into homes—that one frustrated resident even built a floating cellar (which you can visit in what's now Edam's oldest house). To stop the flooding, the harbor was closed off with locked gates (you'll see the gates at Dam Square next to the TI). Eventually the harbor silted up, forcing the decline of the shipbuilding trade.

Edam's Wednesday market is held year-round, but it's best in July and August, when the focus is on cheese. You, along with piles of other tourists, can meet the cheese traders and local farmers.

Orientation to Edam

Edam is a very small town—you can see it all in a lazy 20-minute stroll. It's so nice, though, that you may be tempted to stay longer. Dam Square, with the City Hall and its TI, is right along the big canal called Spui (rhymes with "cow"); the town's lone museum is just over the big bridge.

Tourist Information

The TI, often staffed by volunteers, is in City Hall on Dam Square. Pick up a free simple map or the €0.50 *Edam Holland* brochure, and consider the €2.50 *A Stroll Through Edam* brochure outlining a self-guided walking tour (mid-March-Oct Mon-Sat 10:00-17:00, closed Sun except July-Aug open Sun 11:00-16:00; Nov-mid-March Mon-Sat 10:00-15:00, closed Sun; WC and ATM just out-side, tel. 0299/315-125, www.vvv-edam.nl).

Arrival in Edam

The bus "station"—really just a parking lot for buses—is a five-minute walk from Dam Square and the TI. At the canal by the bus lot, turn right and walk along the water (on Schepenmakersdijk). Cross the next bridge (Kwakelbrug; a white bridge just wide enough for two people), and head straight up the street toward the gray-and-gold bell tower. Hook right around the church, pass one bridge, and you'll wind up across the canal from Dam Square.

Helpful Hints

Cheese Market: In July and August, farmers bring their cheese by boat and horse to the center of town on Wednesday mornings (10:30-12:30), where it's weighed and traded by Edamers in traditional garb.

Internet Access: You can get online at the library, a 10-minute walk south of Dam Square (daily 9:00-17:00, follow Hoogstraat south as it crosses three bridges and changes names, William Pontstraat 27).

Services: Free WCs are located behind City Hall near the canal.

Bike Rental: Tiny Edam has two bike shops full of friendly folks. **Ronald Schot** is near the cheese market, between Dam Square and the Grote Kerk (€7/half-day, €8.50/day, €14/24 hours; Tue-Fri 8:30-18:00, Sat 8:30-16:00, closed Sun-Mon except by appointment; sells regional maps with bike routes, Grote Kerkstraat 7/9, tel. 0299/372-155, www.ronaldschot.nl). **Ton Tweewielers** is between Dam Square and the bus station (€8/day, tandem-€17.50/day, April-Oct daily 8:00-18:00, closed Nov-March, free maps, Schepenmakersdijk 6, tel. 0299/371-922, www.tontweewielers.nl, Friet).

Sights in Edam

▲Edam's Museum: Edam's Oldest House—The 400-year-old historical home across the bridge from Dam Square provides a fun peek at what all these old canal houses once looked like inside. This house is particularly interesting for its floating cellar, designed to accommodate changes in water level without destabilizing the house. A classic town map shows how Edam would have been a mighty sight in 1698. Exhibits on the town's history and how people lived are invigorated by the included and essential audioguide. The top floor has an exhibit on the locally produced Fris art pottery. An extension of this museum with a few (lackluster) exhibits is across the bridge in City Hall (covered by the same ticket).

Cost and Hours: €4, Easter-Oct Tue-Sat 10:00-16:30, Sun 13:00-16:30, closed Mon and Nov-Easter, Dam Square 8, tel. 0299/372-644, www.edamsmuseum.nl.

▲Take a Stroll—The best thing to do in Edam is to just wander its storybook lanes and canals. Consider taking the short walking tour outlined in the TI's booklet *A Stroll Through Edam*.

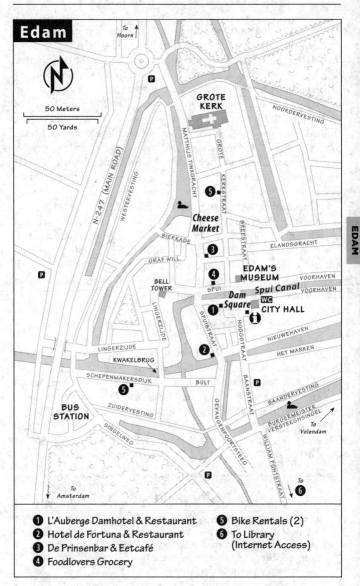

Edam

50 Meters
50 Yards

To Hoorn

GROTE KERK

NOORDERVESTING

N-247 (MAIN ROAD)

WESTERVESTING

MATTHIJS TINGRACHT

GROTE KERKSTRAAT

Cheese Market

BIERKADE

BREESTRAAT

ELANDSGRACHT

GRAF WILL.

❺

❸

EDAM'S MUSEUM

VOORHAVEN

BELL TOWER

❹

SPUI

Spui Canal

VOORHAVEN

LINGERZIJDE

Dam Square

WC

❶

CITY HALL

SPUISTRAAT

HOOGSTRAAT

NIEUWEHAVEN

LINGERZIJDE

❷

HET MARKEN

KWAKELBRUG

SCHEPENMAKERSDIJK

BULT

BAANSTRAAT

BAANDERVESTING

❺

BUS STATION

ZUIDERVESTING

GEVANGENPOORTSTEEG

BURGERMEISTER VERSTEEGHSINGEL

To Volendam

SINGELWEG

WILLIAM PONTSTRAAT

To Amsterdam

To ❻

❶ L'Auberge Damhotel & Restaurant
❷ Hotel de Fortuna & Restaurant
❸ De Prinsenbar & Eetcafé
❹ Foodlovers Grocery
❺ Bike Rentals (2)
❻ To Library (Internet Access)

EDAM

Grote Kerk—Perched on the edge of town, the Grote Kerk (Big Church) feels surprisingly huge for tiny Edam. Like other fine churches in Holland, it was built around 1500, then gutted by iconoclasts during the tumult that came with the Reformation; it's been Dutch Reform since 1566.

The church's vast interior is covered by a ceiling constructed just like a stone vault—but built of wood, because heavier stone would have made the building sink into the wet ground. The wooden catwalks are original. Near the pulpit, find the massive "cabinet organ," dating from 1640, interesting for the big painted side panels that can swing around like shutters to cover it. Many 19th-century Dutch homes had one of these, cleverly disguised to evade a tax on organs. Pick up the church's €2 booklet for more on the church's interior, including some good background on the stained-glass windows. If you haven't landed in Edam on cheese-market day, look for the TV tucked in the side wall on the right, which plays a 12-minute loop video of scenes around town, including the cheese market. The church has a cute café corner and free WCs.

Cost and Hours: Free, daily April-Sept 13:30-17:00.

Getting There: From Dam Square, walk over the bridge, turn left, then head right down Prinsenstraat to Nieuwenhuizenplein, the traditional cheese-market square. Find the "cheese weigh house" on the left—the one with the cheese frieze—and peek inside if it's open (tasty samples). Continue through the square to the canal, which leads to the church.

Sleeping in Edam

These two hotels are both distinctive and classy. For cheaper rooms in private homes, check www.vvv-edam.nl or ask at the TI.

$$ L'Auberge Damhotel, centrally located on a canal across the street from City Hall, has 11 overpriced rooms with over-the-top plush décor that doesn't quite seem to fit (Db-€125-165, Tb-€185, Qb-€195, air-con, free Wi-Fi, Keizersgracht 1, tel. 0299/371-766, fax 0299/374-031, www.damhotel.nl, info@damhotel.nl).

Sleep Code

(€1 = about $1.30, country code: 31, area code: 0299)
S = Single, **D** = Double/Twin, **T** = Triple, **Q** = Quad, **b** = bathroom, **s** = shower only. Unless otherwise noted, credit cards are accepted, breakfast is included, and hoteliers speak English.

To help you easily sort through these listings, I've divided the accommodations into two categories, based on the price for a standard double room with bath:

$$ Higher Priced—Most rooms €125 or more.
$ Lower Priced—Most rooms less than €125.

Prices can change without notice; verify the hotel's current rates online or by email.

$ Hotel de Fortuna is a canalside wonderland with flowers and the sounds of ducks and other birds. It offers steep stairs and

23 low-ceilinged rooms in a cozy collection of five ancient buildings in the old center of Edam. A fine value, it's been run by the Dekker family for more than 30 years (Sb-€85-95, Db-€110-117, luxury Db-€148, free Wi-Fi, Spuistraat 3, tel. 0299/371-671, fax 0299/371-469, www.fortuna -edam.nl, fortuna@fortuna-edam.nl).

Eating in Edam

Considering how close it is to Amsterdam, coming to Edam for a romantic dinner in the countryside and then heading back to your hotel in the big city can be a fine plan. The restaurant at **L'Auberge Damhotel** (listed earlier) dominates the main square with outdoor seating and a dressy interior, and Edam's lanes are lined with tourist-friendly restaurants (within a block or two of Dam Square).

Hotel de Fortuna, listed earlier, has a lovely restaurant, with a romantic dining room and seating in a gorgeous garden alongside a picturesque canal (€20-25 main dishes, three-course "Fortuna *menu*" for €32.50, pricier fixed-price meals also available, daily 12:00-15:00 & 18:00-21:30).

De Prinsenbar and Eetcafé is a good bet for a light lunch or a midday snack. Their €8 *Portie gemengde Hollandse Kaas* is a

sampler of five regional cheeses with bread—a nibbler plate that goes well with a little Belgian *beerje* (€4 soups, €5 salads, €7 pancakes, €6-10 pub grub meals, pub open nightly until 24:00, food served all day June-Aug but only Sat-Sun 12:00-16:00 in off-season, Prinsenstraat 8, tel. 0299/372-

911). The pub offers darts and stay-awhile stools.

Picnickers can stock up on gourmet groceries or pick up a sandwich at **Foodlovers** (daily 8:30-18:00, until 17:00 on weekends, next door to cheese shop overlooking Spui canal across from Dam Square, tel. 0299/373-069). Ask them to heat up a handmade pizza for you.

Edam Connections

EBS runs frequent buses between Edam and **Amsterdam.** From Amsterdam, buses leave from the bus platforms behind Central Station (from the station's west corridor, exit the station and take escalators up to the bus stops). Bus #314 and #317 are the most direct options (2/hour, 30-minute trip, less after 18:30 and on weekends). For bus schedules, see www.9292ov.nl. The €10 all-day transit pass covers everything between Amsterdam and Hoorn.

By Bus to Volendam on the "Waterland Loop": Buses #110 and #118 zip you from Edam to Volendam in about 12 minutes (2/hour daily). Hop off at the Zeestraat stop (other buses also go to Volendam, but not to this handy town-center stop).

Volendam

Less cute and more functional than the other two Waterland towns, Volendam enjoys some workaday charm of its own—including a lively dike-top walkway stretch-ing along a shimmering bay, and a fun town museum.

Tourist Information: Stop by the TI to pick up a free Volendam/Marken map (mid-March–Oct Mon–Sat 10:00–17:00, Sun 11:00–16:00; Nov–mid-March Mon–Sat 10:00–15:00, closed Sun; tel. 0299/363-747, www.vvv-volendam.nl).

Arrival in Volendam: If arriving by bus from Edam, get off at the Zeestraat stop. The museum and TI are within a block, in the modern part of town. To reach the boat to Marken, walk straight from the bus stop toward the water, then turn left and walk along the dike.

Volendams Museum: The town's lone sight is located in the same building as the TI. Its hokey but endearing little collection oozes local pride. You'll wander through displays of traditional costumes, replica house and shop interiors, scenes from village life, and nostalgic old grainy black-and-white movies that are worth watching even if you don't speak Dutch. The corner display show-ing Waterland life during World War II is worth a look, but the museum's highlight is the Cigarband House, where a local artist glued 11 million cigarbands to big boards to create giant images—from Dutch windmills to Venice to a sour-looking Statue of Liberty (€3, borrow English descriptions at entry, mid-March–

Oct daily 10:00-17:00, closed Nov-mid-March, Zeestraat 41, tel. 0299/369-258, www.volendamsmuseum.nl).

To reach the waterfront from the museum, walk two blocks down Zeestraat to Europaplein, head left, cross the dark-green bridge, turn right, then zigzag back across the next bridge and follow the brick steps up to the harbor.

Along the Waterfront: Volendam's extremely touristy **promenade** has a lively boardwalk appeal and is lined with souvenir shops, indoor/outdoor eateries, and Dutch clichés. The walls inside **Hotel Spaander** (eight houses down from the northern end of the harbor, on the right) are decorated with paintings by starving artists who slept or ate there. Don't miss the maze of sleepy residential courtyards below sea level just behind the promenade, with an adorable dollhouse charm and fewer crowds.

"Marken Express": This boat connects Volendam with Marken (€5.50 one-way, €8 round-trip, bike-€1 extra each way, mid-March-Oct daily about 11:00-17:30, departs every 30-45 minutes, in March and Oct sails only if there's enough passengers, by appointment only Nov-mid-March, 30-minute crossing, leaves from northern corner of harbor, no outside food allowed on board, tel. 0299/363-331, www.marken-express.nl).

Marken

Famous as one of the Netherlands' most traditional fishing communities, Marken is a time-passed hamlet in a bottle—once virtually abandoned, now revived but

kept alive solely as a tourist attraction. This island town once had a harbor for whaling and herring fishing, but when the Zuiderzee began to silt up in the late 17th century, it became more and more difficult to eke out a living here, and many people from Marken fled to easier conditions on the mainland. When the Zuiderzee was diked off in 1932 to become a giant freshwater lake (the IJsselmeer), it forced saltwater fishermen to adapt or to find a new calling (which most did). Marken became a virtual ghost town. But in 1957, a long causeway was constructed from the mainland to the island hamlet, which allowed easy access for visitors—who today come in droves to walk its tiny lanes and marvel at its cuteness.

Arrival in Marken: From the boat dock at the little harbor, follow signs to the museum in the town center. Marken has no TI;

the nearest one is in Volendam.

Sights: The village of Marken has two districts connected by counterweight bridges named after Dutch queens. The Havenbuurt district is near the harbor; Kerkbuurt is near the church. Arriving by boat, you'll first wander through the colorful Havenbuurt, then head for the charming Kerkbuurt to get a taste of Marken's old-time charm. As you walk, notice the unique local architecture, adapted to survive the challenging local conditions: Because the tides could be so temperamental, houses here tend to cluster on little hills called *werven,* or are built on pilings to keep them high and dry. Traditional Marken homes, while dull and black-tarred outside, are painted a cheerful yellow and blue inside.

The town's main attraction, in the extremely charming neighborhood of Kerkbuurt, is the modest **Marker Museum,** celebrating the 16th-century costumes (still worn for special events) and traditional lifestyles of the people of Marken. As you enter, ask for an English showing of the good eight-minute movie (€2.50; April-Oct Mon-Sat 10:00-17:00, Sun 12:00-16:00; closed Nov-March; tel. 0299/601-904, www.markermuseum.nl).

For sustenance, enjoy some *kibbeling* (local fish-and-chips) at an idyllic eatery on the harbor.

Just outside town, on the way to the parking lot and the bus stop, you'll pass Marken's raised **cemetery.** Open the black iron gates and step in. Because of the very limited land (so high and dry), plots are shared. That's why the graves are marked with numbers rather than names. With more time, you can walk (about 40 minutes) out to the **lighthouse,** picturesquely situated at the far end of the island, at the tip of a sandy spit.

At the far end of town is a parking lot where you'll find the bus stop, bike rental (from the ice cream wagon), and a wooden shoe factory that is just a touristy shop unless a bus tour stops by (when they demonstrate the traditional way to carve a set of shoes).

Marken Connections: Bus #311 connects Marken with **Amsterdam's** Central Station (2/hour, 40 minutes, leaves at :15 and :45 past the hour until midnight). In Marken, catch the bus along the main road that skirts the town, a little past the south end of the harbor and just past the big parking lot. For info on the boat to Volendam, see "Marken Express," page 329.

Driving to and from Marken, you'll enjoy a scenic road taking you under majestic modern windmills along a four-mile spit. Bikers have their own lane running along the top of the dike. You'll notice lots of cows and sheep but no fences separating the farms. As the animals can't pole-vault, the canals keep them from roaming.

THE HISTORIC TRIANGLE

Hoorn • Medemblik • Enkhuizen
Zuiderzee Museum

The Historic Triangle (De Historische Driehoek) is a manageable and enjoyable one-day journey through the Dutch countryside north of Amsterdam. You'll start in the small town of Hoorn (an easy train trip from Amsterdam or Haarlem), catch a toot-toot steam train to the town of Medemblik, and then sail on a 1920s-era boat to Enkhuizen, home of an excellent open-air folk museum (see page 336). Particularly good for families—and a fantasyland for trainspotters—the Historic Triangle trip is a charming way to pass a day. Dutch grandmothers feed snacks to towheaded toddlers, gusts of steam billow gracefully behind the engine, and cows nod sleepily in the fields. When you reach Enkhuizen, a collection of engaging time-warp villages at the Zuiderzee Museum caps it all off.

Orientation

Cost: Allow about €55 per adult for the entire trip, including the open-air museum in Enkhuizen. If you have a Museumkaart, you're in luck: It covers the museum, the steam train, and the boat trip (but not the Amsterdam-Hoorn and Enkhuizen-Amsterdam sections—about €18, covered by railpass).

Without a Museumkaart, a variety of **combo-tickets** will save you a couple of euros. You can buy these only at the station in Hoorn; buy the regular train tickets at the station in Amsterdam.

If you're not doing the museum in Enkhuizen, get the €21 ticket covering just the steam train and the boat. If you're doing the train, boat ride, and museum, get the €34 combo-ticket (buy your Amsterdam-Hoorn and Enkhuizen-Amsterdam train tickets separately—or use a railpass).

Without any discounts, here's how the price breaks down per leg (2012 prices): Train from Amsterdam to Hoorn-€7.40; steam train to Medemblik-€12.15; boat to Enkhuizen-€9.60; museum entry-€15; train from Enkhuizen back to Amsterdam-€10.10 (Enkhuizen to Hoorn-€3.70). If you're in a hurry and just want to see the museum, skip the steam train and boat, and go directly by train from Amsterdam to Enkhuizen (€10.10 day return ticket, 1 hour).

Schedule: The Historic Triangle trip is offered most of the year, with the frequency determined by the season. Trains leave Hoorn at 11:00 every Sat and Sun from the last weekend of March until mid-November. From April to the end of October, trains also leave Hoorn at 11:00 Tue-Fri. During peak times (first week of May, late July-mid Aug, and third week of Oct), trains leave Hoorn twice daily at 11:00 and 13:45. The trip doesn't run from mid-November to late March. Because holidays or special events can affect the schedule, it's smart to confirm train departure times (tel. 0229/214-862, www.museumstoomtram.nl, info@museumstoomtram.nl). Reservations are not necessary or even possible, except for big groups (if they run out of room, they just add more cars to the train).

Note that on summer days when there are two (or more) departures, you must take the 11:00 steam train from Hoorn if you want to arrive in Enkhuizen in time to see the open-air museum. The museum closes at 17:00, and you can likely get back to Amsterdam at about 18:30.

At peak times, when trains leave twice a day, the extra departures open up more options beyond the basic route I've described here. For example, you could hop off the steam train in Twisk, get on a shuttle bus (included in either combo-ticket) to Medemblik's steam engine museum, then continue on the bus directly to the boat. Or you could just do the boat and steam train both ways (skipping the open-air museum). For more on these options, ask at the station in Hoorn or contact the folks at the Museumstoomtram.

Historic Triangle Tour

Train from Amsterdam to Hoorn

To do the basic trip in time to see the open-air museum in Enkhuizen, catch the 11:00 steam train in Hoorn. To make this connection, leave Amsterdam's Central Station on the 9:38 train to Hoorn (2/hour, 35 minutes). Once in Hoorn, you'll have about 45 minutes to buy your tickets and poke around the interesting old station (opens at 10:00) before boarding the steam train. (Take the

9:08 train from Amsterdam if you want more time to peruse the Hoorn station exhibits; late risers can leave Amsterdam at 10:08, which gives you a tight 18 minutes in Hoorn to make a beeline for the steam train.)

▲Hoorn Station

While pleasant, the town of Hoorn itself has little to offer. The **TI** is a 2-minute walk from the train station—across the park and on the corner (Mon 13:00-18:00, Tue-Fri 9:30-17:30, Thu also 19:00-21:00, until 17:00 Sept-April, Sat 10:00-17:00, closed Sun, Veemarkt 44, tel. 0229/218-343, www.vvvhoorn.nl).

Arriving at Hoorn's modern train station, exit the train and find the modern pedestrian overpass (following *stoomtram* signs) that runs up and over the tracks, leading to the small, old-timey station. (Both old and new trains share the same train tracks, but on opposite sides.) Buy your combo-ticket here for the steam train, boat, and open-air museum. Then poke around to kill time while you wait for the steam train's departure.

The station has a genteel little waiting room where you can buy coffee or snacks (also available on the train). Outside you can climb the stairs to the cute signal house *(seinhuis)*, where the con-

ductor pulls a long line of levers to change tracks (see the complex diagram posted overhead). As he demonstrates pulling the levers, watch the signals flip at the far end of the tracks to notify the trains.

Then head alongside those tracks and into the workshop *(werkplaats)*, where a crew of devoted engineers keeps all those proud, old steam trains in working order. You can actually climb the steep stepladders into some of the gorgeously reconstructed locomotives, and imagine pulling levers, turning valves, and shoveling coal to keep the "iron horse" moving.

Before long...all aboooard!

▲▲"Museum Steam Train" (Museumstoomtram) from Hoorn to Medemblik

From Hoorn it's a relaxing 1.5-hour steam-train ride to Medemblik (1.25 hours in peak season). The trains are the kind that ran through Holland from 1879 through 1966; the train you'll be riding has a chassis from the 1920s, but the cars are furnished circa 1950s. It's a time warp back to when train trips really had style, with wooden-bench seats, leather belts to keep windows secured in place, and nattily uniformed conductors.

After you choose a seat inside the train, you can get up and walk around. The best views (farthest from the soot, noise, and vibrations of the engine) are standing on the train balcony at the very back of the train. You'll feel like a whistle-stop presidential candidate as the train plods through the Dutch countryside.

The train makes three stops: ten minutes in Wognum-Nibbixwoud, and about three minutes each in Twisk and Opperdoes. All three have dollhouse-cute stations,

recently renovated and decorated to evoke times past. Notice the little potbellied stoves between rooms and the old travel posters on the walls. At Wognum, peek into the old-fashioned outhouses. Stops are also a good chance to walk around and peer inside the locomotive, where you can see engineers constantly adjusting valves and levers, and opening the little door to shovel in more coal from the pile at their feet.

The costumed conductor occasionally walks through the cars, giving instructions in Dutch (if you're curious, ask him to repeat what he said in English when he passes). The train periodically stops so a conductor can hop out, scurry out in front of the engine, and flag traffic to a stop the old-fashioned way.

Enjoy the purely Dutch countryside on this serene, old-fashioned joyride. Count sheep. Moo at cows. Watch horses playfully run alongside the train. Look for ducks in the canals and pheasants in the fields. Go ahead, order the *poffertjes* (puffy mini-pancakes, €3.30). If you see Dutch kids waving to the train from their backyards, wave back. The modern white windmills in the distance jolt you back into the 21st century, just in time to arrive at...

Medemblik

You'll have about an hour in this pleasant one-street town before boarding the boat (confirm the boat's exact departure time before leaving the train station). Exit the station and bear left, then right, to walk up the main drag—a pretty market street lined with cafés, bakeries, shops, and postcard stands. Because time is short here, you'll have to pick and choose: If you're hungry, you could grab a quick sandwich or a coffee and a snack at an outdoor café, but you likely won't have time for a full meal. Basic food is available on the upcoming boat ride.

Or, if you feel like sightseeing, head to the first block of the main street (on the right), where you'll find a cute, if overpriced, **bakery museum.** Displayed on two floors of an old bakery, the exhibit shows off baking bric-a-brac and covers everything from Christmas spice cookies and sugar sculptures to chocolate and marzipan. The live demonstrations are the highlight—depending on the day, you might see a baker making cookies, candies, or ice cream in an old-fashioned machine (€6, covered by Museumkaart; Tue-Sun 12:00-17:00, closed Mon; closed Jan-mid-Feb, Nieuwstraat 8, tel. 0227/545-014, www.deoudebakkerij.nl).

Two other Medemblik sights—a steam-engine museum and a castle museum—are too far from the station to visit in the one hour between the steam train and boat. But if you have more time, the **TI**—at the end of the main street on the right—has information on both, as well as a €3 self-guided tour brochure for the town (July-Aug Mon-Sat 10:00-12:30 & 13:00-17:00, May-June and Sept Mon-Sat 11:00-16:00, April and late Oct Mon-Sat 11:00-15:00 except only open 10:00-12:00 in mid-April; closed Sun, in early Oct, and Nov-March; Kaasmarkt 1, tel. 0227/542-852, www.vvvhartvannoordholland.nl).

Shortcut Back to Hoorn: If you want to skip the boat trip and open-air museum at Enkhuizen, and instead return to Hoorn, you can ride back on the steam train, or catch the bus (bus #239, 2/hour in afternoon, otherwise 1/hour, 40 minutes, €3.50, buy ticket from driver; after 18:30 same route called #139). Note that there's usually no direct overland connection from Medemblik to Enkhuizen—if you miss the boat, you'll have to take the bus back to Hoorn, then the train or bus from there to Enkhuizen.

Boat from Medemblik to Enkhuizen

Catch the *MS Friesland* to Enkhuizen just over the dike from the Medemblik station (you'll see the boat moored there as your

train pulls in, tel. 0229/214-862, www.msfriesland.nl). It's a 75-minute putter along the coast to the Zuiderzee Museum in Enkhuizen. You can grab a bite in the boat's surprisingly comfortable dining room (€2-2.50 sandwiches and meatloaf-like "hamburgers," no food served toward end of ride). If you've brought a picnic, grab a wicker chair and enjoy the peaceful, windswept deck. Kids can safely run around on the open spaces of the top deck, or play wooden board games in the lounge. In good weather, you'll pass small pleasure craft—little sailboats and wind-surfers—close enough to shake hands.

▲Enkhuizen Zuiderzee Museum

The boat from Medemblik drops you right at the rear entrance of this wonderful open-air folk museum. The museum's original buildings were collected from around the Zuiderzee (ZOW-der-zay, "South Sea"), which was diked off in 1932 to become a lake called the IJsselmeer. With the ensuing transition from saltwater to fresh-water, and the later reclamation and repurposing of land, the traditional culture on display at this museum became virtually extinct;  this museum was created to preserve that culture. You'll meet people who do a convincing job of role-playing no-nonsense 1905 villagers. You're welcome to take their picture, but they won't smile—no one said "Have a nice day" back then. On weekends, children enjoy trying out old-time games, playing at the dress-up chest, and making sailing ships out of old wooden shoes (small fee for some activities).

Cost and Hours: €15, kids 4-12-€8.70, free for kids under 4, family ticket-€40, April-Oct daily 10:00-17:00; also open Nov-March daily 10:00-17:00, but the buildings are closed, making it a pricey ticket to see just the indoor museum and deserted grounds; tel. 0228/351-111, www.zuiderzeemuseum.nl.

Getting There: If you don't want to do the whole Historic Triangle trip, you can just take the train to the museum from Amsterdam (or Haarlem). Trains make the one-hour trip between Amsterdam and Enkhuizen every half-hour. From the Enkhuizen station, take the shuttle boat or walk 20 minutes to the museum (see "Back to Amsterdam," later). Drivers pay €5 to park here.

❺ Self-Guided Tour: The Zuiderzee Museum is a delight to explore, with something for all the senses—smell the wood fires and tanning vats, savor a bite of aged cheese, watch a windmill turn, hold a lump of coal, and catch the sound of wooden clogs on a brick road. This tour is a start, but don't be afraid to poke into houses (even if they seem to be populated) and backyards.

A museum attendant greets you at the **dock** where the boats arrive. Show your Historic Triangle ticket, or (if you don't have one) buy a museum ticket. From here, head to the left of the museum buildings (a nature preserve lies off to the right). Follow signs for *Informatiecentrum* into the row of brick houses, where you can pick up a map at the information center.

The museum is organized into units. Use the map to visit these in counterclockwise order. Throughout the open-air museum, notice that every building has a little plaque with a brief English description and a map showing the building's original location in the Zuiderzee region. The first section, the **fishing village,** includes many fun-to-explore homes. On some days, dressed-up locals populate the ramshackle village street from Urk—once a remote island across the Zuiderzee, now a strange little lump on a vast, flat *polder.*

Head to the ***polder*** area, near the windmill. Windmills harness the power of the wind to turn Archimedes' screws, which,

by rotating in a tube, pump water up over a dike and into the sea—continuing to drain reclaimed *polder* land. Nearby vats are used to cure fishing nets and a smokehouse where you can buy a tasty snack of smoked herring or eel.

Next, circle around to the **urban canal** zone (near the pavilion), lined with shops—such as a bakery, a gift shop, and a cheese shop where 15,000 clumps of Gouda could be aged (the vacuum-packed samples make another fun snack). Don't miss the pharmacy (marked *Apotheke "De Groote Gaper,"* under the queen with her mouth hanging open). Past the counter where the pharmacist weighs out little bottles of camphor, you'll find a room full of open-mouthed giant heads. Traditionally, Dutch pharmacies were marked by a head with a gaping mouth (opening wide to say "aaaah" for the doctor, or for taking a pill). Many of these original heads are dark-skinned—medicine, like people from the east or south of Europe, was considered mysterious and magical. A nearby theater shows a

dramatic film that includes some grainy black-and-white footage of traditional Zuiderzee life (with English subtitles). As you curl around along the little canal, you'll find other trades represented, such as a barber and a cooper (barrel-maker).

Afterward, head into the **church district,** surrounding a reconstructed church dating from the 15th century. Because local builders were more familiar with boats than buildings, standing inside this church feels like being under an overturned boat (a common feeling in many Dutch village churches). Around the church are more shops, including the blacksmith. Don't miss the schoolhouse, with two period classrooms: one from 1905 and another from 1930. Just across the canal from the church area is a big self-service restaurant, with indoor and outdoor seating (€3 sandwiches, €5-10 meals).

Finally, walk toward the cute, enclosed **harbor**, filled with Zuiderzee watercraft from ages past (just beyond it is a modern harbor, filled with pleasure boats). The little cluster of houses just beyond the harbor (where you may be able to catch a rope-making demonstration) is based on the island village of Marken (for info on visiting the real Marken, see the previous chapter).

As you leave the park through the main entrance, you can visit the **indoor museum** if you have time to spare (same ticket and hours): Exit to the left and walk two blocks, watching for the museum on your right. This space shows off temporary exhibits (only some of which relate to the Zuiderzee), as well as an impressive hall filled with nine old Zuiderzee boats. Notice that many of them have big, flat fins on the sides. Because the Zuiderzee could be very shallow, these boats didn't have a keel; the fins could be extended down into the water to provide more stability.

Back to Amsterdam

From the indoor museum, it's a scenic 15-minute walk, mostly along the water, through the bricks-and-canals town to the Enkhuizen train station: Exit the indoor museum to the right, follow the wall, and cross three bridges (watching for *Station* directional signs). Or go back to the dock at the Zuiderzee Museum and catch a shuttle boat to the station (free with museum ticket, 4/hour, 10 minutes, last boat from museum at 17:30).

ALKMAAR and ZAANSE SCHANS

Two handy day trips line up north of Amsterdam: Alkmaar is a famous cheesemaking town with a charming square and a bustling cheese market; Zaanse Schans, while the least interesting of Holland's open-air museums, is also its most convenient—offering a taste of traditional life a stone's throw from the capital. Consider combining the two destinations for a full day of sightseeing, ideally on a Friday in spring or summer, when Alkmaar's festive cheese market enlivens the town.

Alkmaar

Alkmaar is Holland's cheese capital (and, perhaps, the unofficial capital of high cholesterol). In addition to being an all-around delightful city, Alkmaar has a rich history and a zesty cheese-loving spirit. And though it's enjoyable to visit any time, don't miss this town during its bustling Friday-morning cheese market (early April-early Sept).

Orientation to Alkmaar

Once a stoutly walled city, Alkmaar (pop. 95,000) now has a tidy Old Town laced by canals. The main square, Waagplein, is named for Alkmaar's cheese-weighing. The mighty Weigh House, containing the TI and Cheese Museum, is at one end of the square, and the Beer Museum is at the other. (Think of it as "Holland's Wisconsin.") From this area, the main pedestrian drag, Langestraat, leads visitors to the Grote Kerk and Stedelijk Museum.

Tourist Information

Alkmaar's TI, in the old Weigh House, sells a €2.50 town walking tour brochure (April-Oct Mon-Sat 10:00-17:00, Fri opens at 9:00; Nov-March Mon 13:00-17:00, Tue-Sat 10:00-17:00; closed Sun year-round, Waagplein 2, tel. 072/511-4284, www.vvvalkmaar.nl).

Arrival in Alkmaar

From the train station, it's a 15-minute walk to the town center. The route is well-marked (just follow signs for *Centrum*): Exit the station to the right and veer left with the arterial down Stationsweg, then turn left (onto Scharlo) when the street dead-ends. Soon you'll cross a canal and see the big church (Grote Kerk), with the modern Stedelijk Museum to the left. From the church, walk straight up the main pedestrian street (Langestraat). When you reach the next canal, turn left and walk one more block to the main square and TI.

Sights in Alkmaar

ALKMAAR

▲▲**Cheese Market (Kaasmarkt)**—Tellingly, Alkmaar's biggest building isn't the church or the town hall, but the richly decorated **Weigh House** (Waaggebouw), used since the 16th century for weighing cheese. (It was converted from an old chapel.) The right to weigh, sell, and tax cheese is what put Alkmaar on the map in the Middle Ages, and it's still what the town is celebrated for today.

Think about the udder importance of cheese to this culture—wheying the fact that it has long kept the Dutch economy moo-ving. If you travel through the Dutch countryside, you'll pass endless fields filled with cows, which are more reliable than crops in this marshy landscape. Because cheese offers similar nutritional value to milk, but lasts much longer without refrigeration, it was a staple on long sea voyages—and Holland was the first country to export it. Today the Netherlands remains the world's biggest cheese exporter.

There's no better time to sample a sliver of this proud wedge of Dutch culture than during Alkmaar's **cheese market,** which takes place on Fridays in the spring and summer (early April-early Sept, 10:00-12:30). Early in the morning, cheesemakers line up their giant orange wheels in neat rows on the square. Prospective buyers (mostly wholesalers) examine and sample the cheeses and make their selections. Then the cheese is sold off with much fanfare, as an emcee narrates the action (in Dutch and English). To close the deal, costumed cheese carriers run the giant wheels back and forth to the Weigh House just as they have for centuries: They load a wheel onto a "cheese-barrow"—kind of a wooden stretcher—then

sling each end over their shoulders on ropes and run it to and fro. The cheese carriers' guild has four "fraternities" of seven carriers each: red, yellow, blue, and green (with color-coded hats, cheese-barrows, and scales). Each fraternity is headed by a "cheese father," who enforces the strict rules and levies fines on carriers who show up late or drink beer before carrying cheese (which is strictly forbidden).

On cheese-market days, the town erupts in a carnival atmosphere, becoming one big street fair with festive entertainers and vendors selling souvenirs, snacks...and, of course, cheese. It can get crowded—especially midmorning—but the Cheese Museum (below) is surprisingly empty, and its windows allow great unobstructed views of the action below.

▲**Cheese Museum (Het Hollands Kaas Museum)**—This is probably the Netherlands' best cheese museum...and in this country, that's saying something. With displays on two floors above the TI in the Weigh House, the museum explains both traditional and modern methods of cheesemaking. You'll learn that as the economy evolved, cheesemaking went from being the work of farmers' wives to factory workers. You'll find old equipment (much of it still used for today's cheese market), such as big scales, wagons, cheese-barrows, and (upstairs) old presses for squeezing the last bit of whey out of the cheese molds. Ask for an English showing of the 15-minute movie that traces the history and traditions of Alkmaar cheesemaking. (You'll find out what a "cheesehead" really is, and the technical difference between Gouda and Edam cheeses.) Other, smaller screens around the museum show informative movies—press the flag for English subtitles.

Cost and Hours: €3; April-Oct Mon-Sat 10:00-16:00, Fri from 9:00 during cheese market, closed Sun; closed Nov-March except open Sat 10:00-16:00; enter TI at Waagplein 2 and walk up stairs to museum, tel. 072/515-5516, www.cheesemuseum.com.

Beer Museum (Nationaal Biermuseum De Boom)—This hokey old museum, in a former brewery, shows off an endearing collection about beer production across the centuries—from the days of barrels to the earliest bottling plants. The 1700s-era replica bar has sand on the floor, from a time when men were men and didn't have to aim into a spittoon. While interesting, the museum's explanations are scant (pick up the English descriptions as you enter). If you're not a beer lover or a backyard brewer, I'd skip it.

Cost and Hours: €4, Mon-Sat 13:00-16:00, Fri from 10:00 during cheese market, closed Sun, across Waagplein from Weigh House at Houttil 1, tel. 072/511-3801, www.biermuseum.nl.

Grote Kerk—Alkmaar's "Great Church" is similar to others in Holland (such as Haarlem's and Delft's). Visit if you want to see a typically austere Dutch interior.

Cost and Hours: Free, April-early Sept Tue-Sat 10:00-17:00, Sun 12:00-17:00, closed Mon; off-season open only for concerts and special events. The church hosts frequent concerts (for schedules, call 072/514-0707 or see www.grotekerk-alkmaar.nl).

Stedelijk Museum Alkmaar—The Stedelijk, which has its primary collection in Amsterdam, also runs this worthwhile branch in little Alkmaar (next to Grote Kerk). The museum has two parts: a permanent collection about the history of Alkmaar and a space for temporary exhibits. The 15-minute movie in the town history section is excellent, enlivened by props and sound effects (ask to see it in English). But the rest of the history exhibit—with stiff group portraits, other paintings, and artifacts from the town's illustrious past—is only in Dutch and difficult for nonlocals to appreciate. Visit here only if the temporary exhibit intrigues you.

Cost and Hours: €8.50, Tue-Sun 10:00-17:00, closed Mon, Canadaplein 1, tel. 072/548-9789, www.stedelijkmuseumalkmaar .nl.

Alkmaar Connections

Alkmaar is connected by frequent fast trains to **Amsterdam** (4/hour, 40 minutes). However, these trains do not stop at the Zaanse Schans museum (see next page). To visit the **Zaanse Schans** museum on your way back to Amsterdam, take a train from Alkmaar to Uitgeest (2/hour), where you can transfer to a slower regional train (typically just across the platform) to Koog-Zaandijk (sometimes abbreviated as "Koog Z"; trip takes 40 minutes total). On busy days, the info desk in the tunnel of the Alkmaar train station hands out schedules for this connection.

Zaanse Schans
Open-Air Museum

This re-created 17th-century town puts Dutch culture—from cheesemaking to wooden-shoe carving—on a lazy Susan. Located on the Zaan River in the town of Zaandijk, the museum is devoted to the traditional lifestyles along the Zaan—once lined with hundreds of windmills, used for every imaginable purpose, and today heavily industrialized (including a giant corporate chocolate factory you'll pass on the way). In the 1960s, houses from around the region were transplanted here to preserve traditional culture. Most of the exhibits are run by quirky locals who've found their niche in life, and do it with gusto.

Zaanse Schans (ZAHN-ze skhahns), a hodgepodge of loosely related attractions in a pretty park with old houses, feels less like a museum than Arnhem's or Enkhuizen's open-air museums. And, since each attraction charges a separate entry fee (and those that are free are either selling or promoting something), it also feels more crassly commercial...you'll be nickel-and-dimed for your cultural education. But it's undeniably handy, just 15 minutes by train (plus a 15-minute walk) from downtown Amsterdam. Two of the attractions here—the Dutch Clock Museum and the tourable, working windmills—are unique and genuinely interesting. Because it's the easiest one-stop look at the Netherlands' traditional culture, Zaanse Schans can be flooded at midday by busloads of tour groups. To avoid the hordes, come early or late.

Orientation

Cost: Entry is free, but it costs a euro or two to visit each historical presentation. If you'll be visiting the main Zaans Museum and at least one windmill, you'll save a little money with the €10 **Zaanse Schans Card** (also gives you discounts at some shops and cafés).

Hours: The grounds are open all the time because people actually live here. During the spring and summer (April-Sept), most of the building interiors are open daily 9:00-17:00 (though many are closed Mon, and individual opening and closing times can vary by up to an hour, as noted in each listing). After about 16:30, things get really quiet. In the off-season (Oct-March), only some of the buildings are open (roughly 9:00-17:00 on Sat-Sun, shorter hours or closed entirely Mon-Fri; specific month-to-month hours listed at www.zaanseschans -museum.nl).

Getting There: From Amsterdam, catch a slow **train** going toward Uitgeest (4/hour), ride for about 15 minutes, then hop out at Koog-Zaandijk (or "Koog Z"). Reaching Koog-Zaandijk from Alkmaar requires a change in Uitgeest (see "Alkmaar Connections," earlier).

Once at the Koog-Zaandijk station, it's about a 15-minute walk to the museum (well-marked, just follow the signs... and the other tourists). Go through the underpass and exit straight ahead, watching on your left for a TI machine where you can pull the crank to get a map. Then continue straight until the road forks. (If this area seems surprisingly sweet-smelling for an industrial district, thank the nearby chocolate factory.) From the fork, follow *Zaanse Schans* signs. Turn left, then right across the river, which puts you at the "back entrance" to the park, near the Clock Museum (signs to *Ned. Uurwerkmuseum*).

If **driving** from Amsterdam, take A-8 (direction: Zaanstad/Purmerend), turn off at *Purmerend A-7*, then follow signs to *Zaanse Schans* (parking-€7.50).

Information and Services: The visitors center, located in the Zaans Museum building, has a good, free map of the grounds. Ask if any events are scheduled for that day (daily 9:00-17:00, lockers, free WCs in museum, otherwise €0.50 in park, tel. 075/681-0000, www.zaanseschans-museum.nl).

Sights at Zaanse Schans

I've arranged these sights in order from the train station. Drivers should park at the Zaans Museum and then visit these in reverse order, or walk five minutes to the Dutch Clock Museum and begin there.

▲**Dutch Clock Museum (Museum van het Nederlandse Uurwerk)**—More interesting than it sounds, this collection is brought to life by its curator, clock enthusiast Pier van Leeuwen. If he's not too busy, Pier can show you around and will lovingly describe his favorite pieces. (Or pick up the free brochure and explore seven centuries' worth of timepieces on your own.) Upstairs is a big, bulky, crank-wound turret clock from around 1520. Back then, the length of an "hour" wasn't fixed—there were simply 12 of them between sunrise and sunset, so the clock's weights could be adjusted to modify the length of an hour at different times of year. Also up here are the museum's prized possessions: two of the world's four surviving, original 17th-century pendulum clocks, which allowed for more precision in timekeeping. Downstairs, appreciate the fine craftsmanship of the Zaans clocks (one clock is wound by being pushed up on a rack, rather than pulling a chain) and Amsterdam clocks.

Cost and Hours: €8; April-Oct Tue-Sun 11:00-17:00, closed Mon; Nov-March Sun only 11:00-17:00, closed Mon-Sat; tel. 075/617-9769, www.mnuurwerk.nl.

• *Next door is the...*

Albert Heijn Grocery "Museum" (Museumwinkel)—Little more than a thinly veiled advertisement for the Dutch supermarket chain, this replica grocery store from the 1880s re-creates the first shop run by Albert Heijn. The scant exhibits lead you to a room promoting Heijn coffee.

Cost and Hours: Free, get English description sheet; Easter-Oct Tue-Sun 10:30-13:00 & 13:30-16:00, closed Mon; Nov-Easter Sat-Sun only 12:00-16:00, closed Mon-Fri; tel. 075/616-9619.

• *A few doors up the street is the recommended De Hoop op d'Swarte Walvis restaurant. Just beyond is the dock for the...*

Boat Cruise (Rederij de Schans Rondvaarten)—This 45-minute boat tour floats visitors through the park and adjacent town.

Cost and Hours: €6; departs on the hour; July-Aug daily 11:00-16:00; April-June and Sept Tue-Sun 12:00-15:00, closed Mon; closed Oct-March; tel. 065/329-4467, www.rederijdeschans.nl.

• *From here, enjoy a lovely view of the windmills. But before you go on to visit them, poke into the little village area across from the boat landing. First you'll pass an adorable curiosity shop that's a pack rat's heaven. Then you'll encounter the...*

Bakery Museum (Bakkerijmuseum)—This fragrant and very modest "museum" displays old bakery equipment (including cookie molds) and sells what it bakes. Borrow the English descriptions to navigate the slapdash exhibit.

Cost and Hours: €1 to enter museum, various treats available—most around €2.50, March-Oct Tue-Sun 10:00-17:00; Nov-April Sat-Sun only 11:00-17:00, closed Tue-Fri; closed Mon year-round, tel. 075/617-3522.

• *Now head for the...*

▲Windmills (Molens)—The very industrious Zaan region is typified by these hardworking windmills, which you'll see everywhere. Mills are built with sturdy oak timber frames to withstand the constant tension of movement. To catch the desired amount of wind, millers—like expert sailors—know just how much to unfurl the sails. When the direction of the wind shifts, the miller turns the cap of the building, which weighs several tons, to face the breeze. You can tour several of Zaanse Schans' old-fashioned windmills, each one used for a different purpose.

Cost and Hours: €3 per mill, hours vary, tel. 075/621-5148, www.zaanschemolen.nl).

Visiting the Windmills: **De Gekroonde Poelenburg** is a sawmill, where stout logs are turned into building lumber (open sporadically). **De Kat** ("The Cat") grinds dyes. Watch its gigantic millstones rolling over the colored dust again and again, as wooden chutes keep it on its path. Climb the steep steps (practically a lad-

der) for a closer look at the wooden gears and the fine views out over the museum grounds (July-Aug daily 9:00-17:00; March-June and Sept-Oct Tue-Sun 9:00-17:00, closed Mon; closed Nov-Feb). **De Zoeker** ("The Seeker") crushes oil from seeds and nuts, a drop at a time—up to an incredible 100 quarts per day (March-Oct daily 9:30-16:30, closed Nov-Feb). Other mills may also be open for your visit. If deciding which mill to visit, choose one that's spinning—you'll see more action inside. And though these structures appear graceful, and even whimsical from the out-side, on a windy day you can really experience the awesome power of the mills by getting up close to their grinding gears.

• *After exploring the windmills, cross the little canal to the big...*

De Catharina Hoeve Cheese Farm (Kaasmakerij)—Essentially a giant cheese shop, this is worthwhile only if you catch one of their presentations. A movie shows how cheese is made, and periodically a costumed Dutch maiden explains the process in per-son (about five quarts of milk are used to make about a pound of cheese) and dispenses samples...followed by a confident sales pitch.

Cost and Hours: Free entry, daily 8:00-18:00, tel. 075/621-5820, www.cheesefarms.com.

• *Walk past the mini-windmill to a shopping zone, which includes the...*

Wooden Shoe Workshop (Klompenmakerij)—More engag-ing than the park's other free attractions, this shoe store features a well-presented display of clogs from different regions of the Netherlands. You'll see how clogs were adapted for various pur-poses, including wooden clogs with boot-like leather to the knee, frilly decorative bridal clogs, high-heel clogs, roller-skate clogs, and spiky clogs for ice fishing. Watch the videos, and try to catch the live demonstration that sends wood chips flying as a machine carves a shoe. Your visit ends—where else?—in the vast clog shop.

Cost and Hours: Free entry, daily April-Sept 8:00-18:30, Oct-March 9:00-17:00, tel. 075/617-7121, www.woodenshoework shop.nl.

• *Nearby is the recommended De Kraai restaurant, and just across the big parking lot is the final attraction, the...*

▲**Zaans Museum and Verkade Pavilion**—This museum, with a modern structure that evokes both the hull of a ship and the curved body of a whale, is the focal point of the complex.

In addition to housing the visitors center, the museum has a fresh, modern multimedia presentation that explains Holland's industrial past and present with the help of a good, included audio-guide. The exhibit, with some English descriptions, is thematically divided into four parts: life, work, wind, and water.

The other half of the building is given over to Verkade, a beloved Dutch brand of cookie (translations here use the British "biscuit"). The pavilion is essentially a very slick version of several other "museums" around the park—thinly disguised branding opportunities for major Dutch companies. Nonetheless, this re-created cookie factory is a fun treat, thanks to the free samples, well-written explanations, and clever computer-based games. Don't miss your chance to make like Lucy and Ethel and try to see how many virtual cookies you can pack off a speeding conveyor belt and into a box—my score: 1,253.

Cost and Hours: €9, daily 10:00-17:00, tel. 075/681-0000, www.zaanseschans-museum.nl.

Eating at the Zaanse Schans Open-Air Museum

Pannenkoeken Restaurant de Kraai, located in the open-air museum, is a self-service eatery offering traditional sweet and savory pancakes (€8-10 pancakes; Feb-Oct daily 9:00-18:00; Nov-Dec daily 10:00-17:00; Jan Sat-Sun only 10:00-17:00, closed Mon-Fri; on slow days may close earlier, indoor and outdoor seating).

De Hoop op d'Swarte Walvis ("The Hope of the Black Whale") is the park's splurge, with a white-tablecloth interior, out-door seating, and an ambitiously priced menu (€6-7 sandwiches, €30-35 main dishes at dinner, daily 11:00-22:00 except closed Sun in Feb, dinner served 18:00-21:30, tel. 075/616-5629).

ZAANSE SCHANS

BELGIUM

BELGIUM

Belgium falls through the cracks. It's nestled between Germany, France, and the Netherlands, and it's famous for waffles, sprouts, and a statue of a little boy peeing. No wonder many travelers don't even consider a stop here. But visitors find that Belgium is one of Europe's best-kept secrets. There are tourists—but not as many as the country's charms merit. After all, Belgium produces some of Europe's best beer, creamiest chocolates, most beloved comic strips, and tastiest french fries. From funky urban neighborhoods to tranquil *begijnhof*s, from old-fashioned lace to high-powered European politics, from cows mooing in a pastoral countryside to gentrified Hanseatic cityscapes bristling with spires...Belgium delights.

Ten and a half million Belgians are packed into a country only a little bigger than Maryland. With nearly 900 people per square mile, it's the second most densely populated country in Europe (after the Netherlands). This population concentration, coupled with a well-lit rail and road system, causes Belgium to shine at night when viewed from space—a phenomenon NASA astronauts call the "Belgian Window."

Belgium is divided—linguistically, culturally, and politically—between Wallonia in the south, where they speak French, and Flanders in the north, where they speak Dutch with a Flemish accent—an old sailors' dialect that's even more guttural than textbook Dutch (insert your own "phlegmish" pun here). There's also a small minority of German speakers, in a far-eastern region that once belonged to Germany. Even though about 60 percent of the population speaks Dutch, French speakers have politically dominated the nation for most of its history—a source of much resentment for the Flemish. Talk to locals to learn how deep the cultural rift is (for starters, read the sidebar on page 352).

Belgium

NORTH SEA
ZEEBRUGGE
OSTENDE
DAMME
BRUGES
YPRES SALIENT
YPRES
GHENT ANTWERP
FLANDERS
BRUSSELS
WATER-LOO
HASSELT
BELGIUM
CHAREROI
NAMUR
LIEGE
WALLONIE
BASTOGNE
ARDENNES
NETHER-LANDS
GERMANY
MAAS-TRICHT
AACHEN
VIANDEN
TRIER
ECHTER-NACH
LUX.
LUX.CITY
FRANCE
MEUSE
AIRPORT
50 MILES
50 KM
DCH

Though mostly French-speaking, Belgium's capital, Brussels, is officially bilingual. Because of Brussels' international importance as the capital of the European Union, more than 25 percent of its residents are foreigners.

It's here in Belgium that Europe comes together: where Romance languages meet Germanic languages; Catholics meet Protestants; and the Benelux union was established 40 years ago, planting the seed that today is sprouting into the unification of Europe. Belgium flies the flag of Europe more vigorously than any other place on the Continent.

That could be, in part, because history hasn't been very kind to little Belgium—surrounded, as it is, by much bigger and more powerful nations: France, Germany, the Netherlands, and Britain, each of which has at one time or another found Belgium a barrier on its march to empire. After putting up with tyrants from Charlemagne to the Austrian Habsburgs to Napoleon, Belgium paid the costliest price in both World Wars—most notably at Flanders Fields near Ypres (Ieper) in World War I, and at the Battle of the Bulge near Bastogne in World War II. But its crossroads location has also made Belgium stronger: Belgians are savvy businesspeople, excellent linguists, and talented chefs who've

Belgium Almanac

Official Name: Royaume de Belgique/Koninkrijk België, or simply Belgique in French and België in Dutch.

Population: Of its 10.5 million people, 58 percent are Flemish, 31 percent are Walloon, and 11 percent are "mixed or other." About three-quarters are Catholic, and the rest are Protestant or other.

Latitude and Longitude: 50°N and 4°E. The latitude is similar to Calgary, Canada.

Area: With only 12,000 square miles, it's slightly smaller than the state of Maryland, and one of the smallest countries in Europe.

Geography: Belgium's flat coastal plains in the northwest and central rolling hills make it easy to invade (just ask Napoleon or Hitler). There are some rugged mountains in the southeast Ardennes Forest. The climate is temperate.

Biggest Cities: The capital city of Brussels has about one million people; Antwerp has 490,000.

Economy: With few natural resources, Belgium imports most of its raw materials and exports a large volume of manufactured goods, making its economy unusually dependent on world markets. It can be a sweet business—Belgium is the world's number-one exporter of chocolate. It's prosperous, with a Gross Domestic Product of $383 billion and a GDP per capita of $36,800. As the "crossroads" of Europe, Brussels is the headquarters of NATO and the capital of the European Union.

Government: A parliamentary democracy, Belgium's official head of state is King Albert II. Regional tensions dominate politics: Dutch-speaking, entrepreneurial Flanders wants more autonomy, while the French-speaking "rust belt" of Wallonia is reluctant to give it. The division has made it increasingly difficult for the Belgian Parliament to form a stable coalition government. One prime minister recently said that Belgians are united only by the king, a love of beer, and the national soccer team. Voting is compulsory. More than 90 percent of registered voters participated in the last general election (compared with approximately 62 percent in the US).

Flag: Belgium's flag is composed of three vertical bands of black, yellow, and red.

The Average Belgian: The average Belgian is 42 years old—five years older than the average American—and will live to be 79. He or she is also likely to be divorced—Belgium has the highest divorce rate in Europe, with 60 for every 100 marriages. Beer is the national beverage: On average, Belgians drink 26 gallons a year, just behind the Austrians and just ahead of the Brits.

learned how to blend together delicious culinary influences from various cultures. I recently asked a local, "What is a Belgian?" He said, "We are a melting pot. We're a mix culturally: one-third English for our sense of humor, one-third French for our love of culture and good living, and one-third German for our work ethic."

Belgians have a directness that some find refreshing (and others term brusque), and revel in their sardonic sense of humor. They're not particularly romantic or melodramatic, and—with the wry glimmer in their eye—it can be hard to tell whether they're putting you on. This ties in with their appreciation for a good comic strip. The "ninth art" of comics is deeply respected in Belgium. Some of the world's most beloved comic characters—including the Smurfs and Tintin—were created by Belgians. If you ask a twentysomething Belgian what career they're pursuing, and he or she says "comic books," nobody snickers.

From an accommodations point of view, the Flemish forte is its variety of cozy, funky, affordable B&Bs well-run by gregarious entrepreneurs and typically located up a flight or two of steep, narrow stairs. I've listed my favorite B&Bs in each town (but just one in Brussels, where they're rare).

Bruges and Brussels are the best two first bites of Belgium. Bruges is a wonderfully preserved medieval gem that expertly nurtures its tourist industry, bringing the town a prosperity it hasn't enjoyed for 500 years, when—as one of the largest cities in the world—it helped lead northern Europe out of the Middle Ages.

Brussels is simply one of Europe's great cities. With the finest town square in the country (if not the Continent), a chocolate shop on every corner, a French taste for class and cuisine, and a smattering of intriguing museums, it's equally ideal for a quick stopover as it is for a multiday visit.

With more time, two other Belgian cities are worth visiting. Historic, Old World Ghent—once an important trading and university town—is well-preserved and picturesque, packed with charming little museums. And big, bustling Antwerp—with a port that rivals Rotterdam as Europe's largest—has recently enjoyed a dramatic renaissance. It's gone from being a dirty, dangerous, and depressing city to a trendy, newly spiffed-up mecca with fun boutiques, lively neighborhoods, fine museums, and a youthful vibe. To round out your Belgian experience, spend a few hours in the Flemish countryside around the town of Ypres—both for the pastoral scenery, and to visit World War I's Flanders Fields.

While not "undiscovered" (especially popular Bruges), Belgium is certainly underrated. Those who squeeze in a day or two for Belgium wish they had more time. Like sampling a

The Battle for Belgium: Flanders vs. Wallonia

Although little, peace-loving Belgium—whose capital, Brussels, is also the capital of the European Union—seems like a warm and cozy place, its society is split right down the middle by a surprisingly contentious linguistic divide with roots dating back to the nation's inception: the Dutch-speaking people of Flanders versus the French speakers of Wallonia.

In 1830, Belgium's Francophone (French-speaking) aristocracy led the drive for independence from the Netherlands. They said, "Belgium will be French, or will not be." And so it was: Linguistic and cultural oppression ruled the day, as the Dutch language spoken in Flanders was suppressed as unworthy of higher thinking. Even in Flanders, where Flemish people are the majority, most power has traditionally been in the hands of the Francophone bourgeoisie. Education at prestigious universities, for example, was only in French.

The Flemish often feel they'd have been better off had Belgium remained part of the Netherlands...which would have respected their native tongue in their homeland. That's why most Flemish people are not particularly nationalistic about their language—rather than being blinded by Flemish pride, they readily acknowledge that what they speak is a dialect of Dutch.

Today's Flemish baby boomers remember feeling picked on by their Francophone classmates. To travelers, it almost seems

flavorful praline in a chocolate shop, that first enticing taste just leaves you wanting more. Go ahead, it's OK...buy a whole box of Belgium.

Belgian Cuisine

Belgians brag that they eat as much as the Germans and as well as the French. They are among the world's leading carnivores and beer consumers. Belgium is where France meets northern Europe, and you'll find a good mix of both Germanic and French influences here. The Flemish were ruled by the French and absorbed some of the fancy cuisine and etiquette of their overlords. (The Dutch, on the other hand, were ruled by the Spanish for 80 years and picked up nothing.) And yet, once Belgian, always Belgian: Instead of cooking with wine, Belgians have perfected the art of cooking with their own unique beers, imbuing the cuisine with a hoppy sweetness.

Belgians eat lunch when we do, but they eat dinner later (if you dine earlier than 19:30 at a restaurant, you'll eat alone or with other tourists). Tax and service are always included in your bill

as if Flanders and Wallonia are different countries. For example, each region has its own "national" tourist office, which effectively ignores the other half of the country.

In 1970, Belgium began a gradual process of decentralizing its government (loosely following the Swiss cantonal model), and giving more administrative autonomy to its three regions: Dutch-speaking Flanders, French-speaking Wallonia, and the bilingual city-state of Brussels. Incremental reforms over the last 40 years have separated the Flemish and the Walloons more and more. Each group can now more closely pursue its own agenda, but the flipside is that the country is not as effortlessly bilingual as before. A generation ago, virtually every Belgian spoke both Dutch and French. Today, Flemish students can choose whether to take French or English as a second language...and many choose English. On my last visit to Brussels, I saw a sign in a shop window saying, "Bilingual staff wanted." What used to be commonplace is becoming a rarity.

The longstanding Flemish-Walloon rivalry has flared up again in the last couple of years. Of Belgium's many political parties, the Nieuw-Vlaamse Alliantie (N-VA), which advocates for the secession of Flanders from Belgium altogether, won the highest percentage of the vote in 2010 elections (both in Flanders and in Belgium overall). It's conceivable that a day may come in the not-too-distant future when a unified "Belgium" no longer exists on the map of Europe.

(though a 5-10 percent tip is appreciated). You can't get free tap water; Belgian restaurateurs are emphatic about that. Tap water comes with a smile in the Netherlands, France, and Germany, but that's not the case in Belgium, where you'll either pay for water, enjoy the beer, or go thirsty.

BELGIUM

Belgian Specialties

Although this book's coverage focuses on the Flemish part of the country, people speak French first in Brussels—so both languages are given below (Dutch/French); if I've listed only one word, it's used nationwide. While the French influence is evident everywhere, it's ratcheted up around Brussels.

Traditional Dishes

Stoofvlees/Carbonnade: Rich beef stew flavored with onions, beer, and mustard. It's often quite sweet (sweetened with brown sugar or gingerbread). It's similar to the French beef bourguignon, but made with beer instead of red wine.

(Gentse) Waterzooi: Creamy soup made with chicken, eel, or fish; originated in Ghent.

Konijn met pruimen/lapin à la flamande: Marinated rabbit braised in onions and prunes.

Filet américain: Beware—for some reason, steak tartare (raw) is called "American."

Biersoep/soupe à la bière: Beer soup—though remember that beer can be included in just about any dish.

...à la flamande: Anything cooked in the Flemish style, which generally means with beer.

Seafood

Mosselen/moules: Mussels are served everywhere, either cooked plain *(natuur/nature)*, with white wine *(witte wijn/vin blanc)*, with shallots or onions *(marinière)*, or in a tomato sauce *(provençale)*. You get a big-enough-for-two bucket and a pile of fries. Go local by using one empty shell to tweeze out the rest of the *mosselen*. When the mollusks are in season, from about mid-July through April, you'll get the big Dutch mussels (most are from the coastal area called Zeeland, just north of Belgium). Locals take a break from mussels in May and June, when only the puny Danish kind are available.

Noordzee garnalen/crevettes: Little gray shrimp, generally served in one of two ways: inside a carved-out tomato or in croquettes (minced and stuffed in breaded, deep-fried rolls).

Paling in het groen/anguilles au vert: Eel in green herb sauce. Although a classic dish, this is less common these days, as good-quality eel is in short supply.

Caricoles: Sea snails. Very local, seasonal, and (like eel) hard to find, these are usually sold hot by street vendors.

Vegetables and Side Dishes

Rode kol/chou rouge à la flamande: Red cabbage with onions and prunes.

Asperges: White asparagus, available only for a short time in spring, and usually served in cream sauce.

Witloof/chicoree or *chicon:* Endive, the classic Belgian vegetable, usually served as a side dish. This coarse, bitter green is eaten both raw and cooked.

Spruitjes/choux de Bruxelles: Brussels sprouts (in cream sauce).

Stoemp: Mashed potatoes and vegetables, most common in Brussels.

Snacks

Friets: Belgian-style fries taste so good because they're deep-fried twice—once to cook, and once to brown. The natives eat them with mayonnaise or other flavored sauces, but not ketchup. The Dutch call them *Vlaamse frieten*—"Flemish fries"—but the Flemish just call them *frieten*. Look for a *frituur* (fry shop) or a *frietkot* (fry wagon).

Cheeses: While the French might use wine or alcohol to rub the rind of their cheese to infuse it with flavor, the Belgians use (surprise, surprise) beer. There are 350 types of Belgian cheeses. From Flanders, look for Vieux Brugge ("Old Bruges") and Chimay (named for the beer they use on it); from Wallonia, Remoudou and Djotte de Nivelles are good.

Croque monsieur: Grilled ham-and-cheese sandwich.

Tartine de fromage blanc: Open-face cream-cheese sandwich, often enjoyed with a cherry Kriek beer and found mostly in traditional Brussels bars.

Desserts and Sweets

Chocolates: The two basic types of Belgian chocolates are **pralines** (what we generally think of as "chocolates"—a hard chocolate shell with various fillings) and **truffles** (a softer, crumblier shell, often spherical, and also filled).

Wafels/Gaufres: Belgians recognize two general types of waffles: **Liège-style** (dense, very sweet—with a sugary crust, and heated up) and **Brussels-style** (lighter and fluffier, dusted with powdered sugar and sometimes topped with marmalade). And though Americans think of "Belgian" waffles for breakfast, Belgians generally have them (or pancakes, *pannenkoeken*) as a late-afternoon snack (around 16:00)—though the delicious Liège-style waffles are sold 'round the clock to tourists as an extremely tempting treat. You'll see little windows, shops, and trucks selling these *wafels*, either  plain (for Belgians and purists) or topped with fruit, jam, chocolate sauce, ice cream, or whipped cream (for tourists). You'll find the Brussels-style waffles mostly in teahouses, and only in the afternoon (14:00-18:00).

Speculoos: Spicy gingerbread biscuits served with coffee.

Dame blanche: Chocolate sundae.

Pistolets: Round sandwiches.

Chocolade mousse: Just what it sounds like.

Belgian Beers

Belgium has about 120 different varieties of beer and 580 different brands, more than any other country—the locals take their beers as seriously as the French do their wines. Even small café menus include six to eight varieties. Connoisseurs and novices alike can be confused by the many choices, and casual drinkers probably won't like every kind offered, since some varieties don't even taste like beer. Belgian beer is generally yeastier and higher in alcohol content than beers in other countries.

In Belgium, certain beers are paired with certain dishes. To bring out their flavor, different beers are served cold, cool, or at room temperature, and each has its own distinctive glass. Whether wide-mouthed, tall, or fluted, with or without a stem, the glass is meant to highlight a particular beer's qualities. The choice of glass is so important that if, for some reason, a pub doesn't have the proper glass for a particular beer, they will ask the customer if a different glass will be acceptable—or if they'd like to change their beer order.

To get a draft beer in Bruges, where Dutch is the dominant language, ask for *een pintje* (ayn pinch-ya; a pint); in Brussels, where French prevails, request *une bière* (oon bee-yair). Don't insist on beer from the tap. The only way to offer so many excellent beers fresh is to serve them bottled, and the best varieties generally are available only by the bottle. "Cheers" is *proost* or *gezondheid* in Dutch, and *santé* (sahn-tay) in French. The colorful cardboard coasters make nice, free souvenirs.

Until 2007 there was no age limit for drinking alcohol. Now you must be 16 years old to legally enjoy a good Belgian beer, and 18 to drink wine and harder liquor.

Here's a breakdown of types of beer, with some common brand names you'll find either on tap or in bottles. (Some beers require a second fermentation in the bottle, so they're only available in bottles.) This list is just a start, and you'll find many beers that don't fall into these neat categories.

Ales (Blonde/Red/Amber/Brown): Ales are easily recognized by their color. Try a blonde or golden ale (Leffe Blonde, Duvel), a rare and bitter sour red (Rodenbach), an amber (Palm, De Koninck), or a brown (Leffe Bruin).

Lagers: These are light, sparkling, Budweiser-type beers. Popular brands include Jupiler, Stella Artois, and Maes.

Lambics: Perhaps the most unusual and least beer-like, *lambics*—popular in Brussels—are stored for years in wooden casks, fermenting from wild yeasts that occur naturally in the air. Tasting more like a dry and bitter farmhouse cider, pure *lambic* is often blended with fruits to counter the sour flavor. Some brand names include Cantillon, Lindemans, and Mort-Subite ("Sudden Death").

Fruit *lambics* include those made with cherries *(kriek)*, raspberries *(frambozen)*, peaches *(pêche)*, or blackcurrants *(cassis)*. The result for each is a tart but sweet beer, similar to a dry pink champagne. People who don't usually enjoy beer tend to like these fruit-flavored varieties.

White *(Witte):* Based on wheat instead of hops, these are milky-yellow summertime beers. White beer, similar to a Hefeweizen, is often flavored with spices such as orange peel or coriander.

Trappist Beers: For centuries, between their vespers and matins, Trappist monks have been brewing heavily fermented, malty beers. Three typical Trappist beers (from the Westmalle monastery) are Tripel, with a blonde color, served cold with a frothy head; Dubbel, which is dark, sweet, and served cool; and Single, made especially by the monks for the monks, and considered a fair trade for a life of celibacy. Other Trappist monasteries include Rochefort, Chimay, and Orval. Try the Trappist Blauwe Chimay—extremely smooth, milkshake-like, and complex.

Strong Beers: The potent brands include Duvel (meaning "devil," because of its high octane, camouflaged by a pale color), Verboten Vrucht ("forbidden fruit," with Adam and Eve on the label), and the not-for-the-fainthearted brands of Judas, Satan, and Lucifer. Gouden Carolus is good, and Delerium Tremens speaks for itself.

Mass-Produced Beers: Connoisseurs say you should avoid the mass-produced labels (Leffe, Stella, and Hoegaarden—all owned by InBev, which owns Budweiser in America) when you can enjoy a Belgian microbrew (such as Westmalle or Chimay) instead.

BRUGES
Brugge

ORIENTATION TO BRUGES

With pointy gilded architecture, stay-a-while cafés, vivid time-tunnel art, and dreamy canals dotted with swans, Bruges is a heavyweight sightseeing destination, as well as a joy. Where else can you ride a bike along a canal, munch mussels and wash them down with the world's best beer, savor heavenly chocolate, and see Flemish Primitives and a Michelangelo, all within 300 yards of a bell tower that jingles every 15 minutes? And do it all without worrying about a language barrier?

The town is Brugge (BROO-ghah) in Dutch, and Bruges (broozh) in French and English. Its name comes from the Viking word for wharf. Right from the start, Bruges was a trading center. In the 11th century, the city grew wealthy on the cloth trade.

By the 14th century, Bruges' population was 35,000, as large as London's. As the middleman in the sea trade between northern and southern Europe, it was one of the biggest cities in the world and an economic powerhouse. In addition, Bruges had become the most important cloth market in northern Europe.

In the 15th century, while England and France were slugging it out in the Hundred Years' War, Bruges was the favored residence of the powerful Dukes of Burgundy—and at peace. Commerce and the arts boomed. The artists Jan van Eyck and Hans Memling had studios here.

But by the 16th century, the harbor had silted up and the economy had collapsed. The Burgundian court left, Belgium became a minor Habsburg possession, and Bruges' Golden Age abruptly ended. For generations, Bruges was known as a mysterious and dead city. In the 19th century, a new port, Zeebrugge, brought renewed vitality to the area. And in the 20th century, tourists discovered the town.

Today, Bruges prospers because of tourism: It's a uniquely

well-preserved Gothic city and a handy gateway to Europe. It's no secret, but even with the crowds, it's the kind of place where you don't mind being a tourist.

Bruges' ultimate sight is the town itself, and the best way to enjoy it is to get lost on the back streets, away from the lace shops and ice-cream stands.

Planning Your Time

Bruges needs at least two nights and a full, well-organized day. Even nonshoppers enjoy browsing here, and the Belgian love of life makes a hectic itinerary seem a little senseless. With one day—other than a Monday, when the Groeninge and Memling museums are closed—a speedy visitor could do the Bruges blitz described below (also included in my Bruges City Walk):

9:30	Climb the bell tower on the Markt (Market Square).
10:00	Tour the sights on Burg Square.
11:30	Tour the Groeninge Museum.
13:00	Eat lunch and buy chocolates.
14:00	Take a short canal cruise.
14:30	Visit the Church of Our Lady and see Michelangelo's *Madonna and Child*.
15:00	Tour the Memling Museum.
16:00	Catch the De Halve Maan Brewery tour (note that on winter weekdays, their last tour runs at 15:00).
17:00	Relax in the Begijnhof courtyard.
18:00	Ride a bike around the quiet back streets of town or take a horse-and-buggy tour.
20:00	Enjoy the low light of magic hour on the Markt, then lose the tourists and find dinner elsewhere.

If this schedule seems insane, skip the bell tower and the brewery—or stay another day.

Bruges Overview

The tourist's Bruges—and you'll be sharing it—is less than one square mile, contained within a canal (the former moat). Nearly everything of interest and importance is within a convenient cobbled swath between the train station and the Markt (Market Square; a 20-minute walk). Many of my quiet, charming, recommended accommodations lie just beyond the Markt.

Tourist Information

The main TI, called **In&Uit** ("In and Out"), is in the big, red concert hall on the square called 't Zand (daily 10:00-18:00, take a number from the touch-screen machines and wait, 't Zand 34, tel. 050-444-646, www.brugge.be). They have three terminals with

Bruges

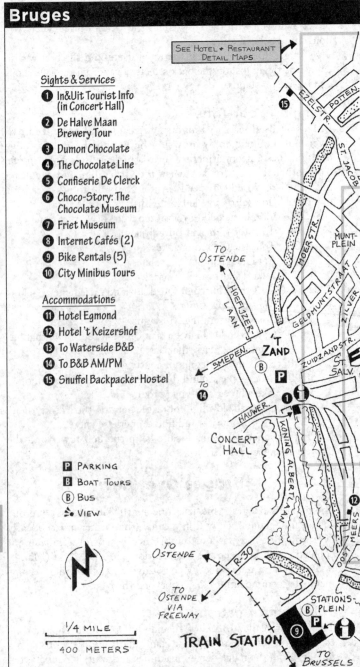

SEE HOTEL & RESTAURANT DETAIL MAPS

Sights & Services

❶ In&Uit Tourist Info (in Concert Hall)

❷ De Halve Maan Brewery Tour

❸ Dumon Chocolate

❹ The Chocolate Line

❺ Confiserie De Clerck

❻ Choco-Story: The Chocolate Museum

❼ Friet Museum

❽ Internet Cafés (2)

❾ Bike Rentals (5)

❿ City Minibus Tours

Accommodations

⓫ Hotel Egmond

⓬ Hotel 't Keizershof

⓭ To Waterside B&B

⓮ To B&B AM/PM

⓯ Snuffel Backpacker Hostel

P PARKING

B BOAT TOURS

Ⓑ BUS

🔭 VIEW

¼ MILE

400 METERS

BRUGES ORIENTATION

TO OSTENDE

HOEFIJZER-LAAN

SMEDEN.

'T ZAND

HAUWER.

CONCERT HALL

KONING ALBERT I-LAAN

MOER STR.

EZEL-STR.

POTTEN.

ST. JACOB

MUNT-PLEIN

GELDMUNTSTRAAT

ZILVER.

ZUIDZANDSTR.

ST. SALV.

OOST MEERS

TO OSTENDE

TO OSTENDE VIA FREEWAY

R-30

STATIONS-PLEIN

TRAIN STATION

TO BRUSSELS

TO ⓮

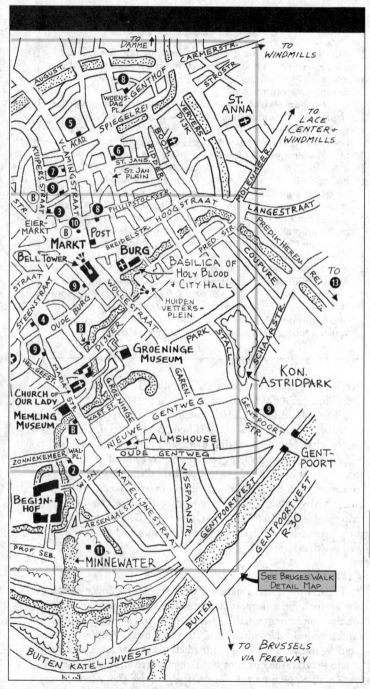

Bruges Museum Tips

Admission prices are steep, but they include great audio-guides—so plan on spending some time and really getting into it. For information on all the museums, call 050-448-711 or visit www.brugge.be.

Museum Passes: The 't Zand TI and city museums sell a "Museumpas" **combo-ticket** (any five museums for €20, valid for 3 days). Because the Groeninge and Memling museums cost €8 each, art lovers will save money with this pass.

The **Brugge City Card** is a more extensive pass covering entry to 26 museums, including all the major sights (€35/48 hours, €40/72 hours, sold at TIs and many hotels). If you'll be doing some serious sightseeing, this card can save you money. Its long list of bonuses and discounts includes a free canal boat ride (March-Nov), a visitors' guide, and discounts on bike rental, parking, and some performances.

Blue Monday: In Bruges, nearly all museums are open Tuesday through Sunday year-round from 9:30 to 17:00 and are closed on Monday. If you're in Bruges on a Monday, the following attractions are open: bell-tower climb on the Markt, Begijnhof, De Halve Maan Brewery Tour, Basilica of the Holy Blood, City Hall's Gothic Room, chocolate shops and museum, and Church of Our Lady. You can also join a boat, bus, or walking tour, or rent a bike and pedal into the countryside.

---

free Internet access and printers. The other TI is at the train station (Mon-Fri 10:00-17:00, Sat-Sun 10:00-14:00).

The TIs sell the €2.50 *Love Bruges Visitors' Guide*, which comes with a map (costs €0.50 if bought separately), a few well-described self-guided walking tours, and listings of all the sights and services (free with Brugge City Card). You can also pick up a free monthly English-language program called *events@brugge*, and information on train schedules and tours (see "Tours in Bruges," later). Many hotels give out free maps with more detail than the map the TIs sell. The TI also has a fine free "Use-It" map available for young-at-heart travelers—filled with tips for backpackers and well worth asking for.

Arrival in Bruges

By Train: Bruges' train station is what all stations under construction aspire to: in a clean, park-like setting, where travelers step out the door and are greeted by a taxi stand and a roundabout with center-bound buses circulating through every couple minutes. Coming in by train, you'll see the bell tower that marks the main square (Markt, the center of town). Upon arrival, stop by the train station TI to pick up the *Love Bruges Visitors' Guide* (with map).

The station has ATMs and lockers (€3-4).

The best way to get to the town center is by **bus.** Buses #1, #3, #4, #6, #11, #13, #14, and #16 go to the Markt (all marked *Centrum*). Simply hop on, pay €2 (€1.20 if you buy in advance at Lijnwinkel shop just outside the train station), and you're there in four minutes (get off at third stop— either Markt or Wollestraat). Buses #4 and #14 continue to the northeast part of town (to the windmills and rec-

ommended accommodations on and near Carmersstraat, stop: Gouden Handstraat). If you arrive after 20:30, when the daytime bus routes end, you can still take the bus, but the "evening line" buses run much less frequently (buses marked *Avondlijn Centrum, Avondlijn Noord*—#91, *Avondlijn Oost*—#92, and *Avondlijn Zuid*—#93 all go to the Markt).

The **taxi** fare from the train station to most hotels is about €8.

It's a 20-minute **walk** from the station to the center—no fun with your luggage. If you want to walk to the Markt, cross the busy street and canal in front of the station, head up Oostmeers, and turn right on Zwidzandstraat. You can rent a **bike** at the station for the duration of your stay, but other bike-rental shops are closer to the center (see "Helpful Hints," below).

By Car: Park in front of the train station in the handy two-story garage for just €3.50 for 24 hours. The parking fee includes a round-trip bus ticket into town and back for everyone in your car. There are pricier underground parking garages at the square called 't Zand and around town (€9/day, all of them well-marked). Paid parking on the street in Bruges is limited to four hours. Driving in town is very complicated because of the one-way system. The best plan for drivers: Park at the train station, visit the TI at the station, and rent a bike or catch a bus into town.

Helpful Hints

Market Days: Bruges hosts markets on Wednesday morning (on the Markt) and Saturday morning ('t Zand). On good-weather Saturdays, Sundays, and public holidays, a flea market hops along Dijver in front of the Groeninge Museum. The Fish Market sells souvenirs daily and seafood Wednesday through Saturday mornings until 13:00.

Shopping: Shops are generally open from 10:00 to 18:00 and closed Sundays. Grocery stores usually are closed on Sunday. The main shopping street, Steenstraat, stretches from the

Markt to 't Zand Square. The **Hema** department store is at Steenstraat 73. **FNAC,** the electronics/department store for all your needs, is on the Markt. There's a fine travel bookstore (which carries my guidebooks) at #12 on the Markt.

Internet Access: There are three free terminals at the **TI** on 't Zand. **Call Shop,** just a block off the Markt, is the most central of the city's many "telephone shops" offering Internet access (€1.50/30 minutes, €2.50/hour, daily 9:00-20:00, Philipstockstraat 4). **Bean Around the World** is a cozy coffeehouse with imported Yankee snacks and free Wi-Fi for customers (€1/15 minutes on their computers, Thu-Mon 10:00-19:00, Wed 11:30-19:00, closed Tue, Genthof 5, tel. 050-703-572, run by American expat Olene).

Post Office: It's on the Markt near the bell tower (Mon-Fri 9:00-18:00, Sat 9:30-15:00, closed Sun, tel. 050-331-411).

Laundry: Bruges has three self-service launderettes, each a five-minute walk from the center; ask your hotelier for the nearest one.

Bike Rental: Bruges Bike Rental is central and cheap, with friendly service and long hours (€3.50/hour, €5/2 hours, €7/4 hours, €10/day, show this book to get student rate—€8/day, no deposit required—just ID, daily 10:00-22:00, free city maps and child seats, behind the far-out iron facade at Niklaas Desparsstraat 17, tel. 050-616-108, Bilal). **Fietsen Popelier Bike Rental** is also good (€4/hour, €8/4 hours, €12/day, 24-hour day is OK if your hotel has a safe place to store bike, no deposit required, daily 10:00-19:00, sometimes open later in summer, free Damme map, Mariastraat 26, tel. 050-343-262). **Koffieboontje Bike Rental** is just under the bell tower on the Markt (€4/hour, €9/day, €20/day for tandem, these prices for Rick Steves readers, daily 9:00-22:00, free city maps and child seats, Hallestraat 4, tel. 050-338-027). **De Ketting** is less central, but cheap (€6/day, Mon-Fri 9:00-12:15 & 13:30-18:30 except Mon opens at 10:00, Sat 9:30-12:15, closed Sun, Gentpoortstraat 23, tel. 050-344-196, www.deketting.be). **Fietspunt Brugge** is a huge outfit at the train station (7-speed bikes, €12/24-hours, €7/4 hours, free maps, Mon-Fri 7:00-19:30, Sat-Sun 9:00-21:30, just outside the station and to the right as you exit, tel. 050-396-826).

Best Town View: The bell tower overlooking the Markt rewards those who climb it with the ultimate town view.

Updates to This Book: Check

BRUGES ORIENTATION

www.ricksteves.com/update for any significant changes that have occurred since this book was printed.

Getting Around Bruges

Most of the city is easily walkable, but you may want to take the bus or taxi between the train station and the city center at the Markt (especially if you have heavy luggage).

By Bus: A bus ticket is good for an hour (€1.20 if you buy in advance at Lijnwinkel shop just outside the train station, or €2 on the bus). And though you can buy various day passes, there's really no need to buy one for your visit. Nearly all city buses go directly from the train station to the Markt and fan out from there; they then return to the Markt and go back to the train station. Note that buses returning to the train station from the Markt also leave from the library bus stop, a block off the square on nearby Kuiperstraat (every 5 minutes). Your key: Use buses that say either *Station* or *Centrum*.

By Taxi: You'll find taxi stands at the station and on the Markt (€8/first 2 km; to get a cab in the center, call 050-334-444 or 050-333-881).

Tours in Bruges

Bruges by Boat—The most relaxing and scenic (though not informative) way to see this city of canals is by boat, with the captain narrating. The city carefully controls this standard tourist activity, so the many companies all offer essentially the same thing: a 30-minute route (roughly 4/hour, daily 10:00-17:00), a price of €7.60 (cash only), and narration in three or four languages. Qualitative differences are because of individual guides, not companies. Always let them know you speak English to ensure you'll understand the spiel. Two companies give the group-rate discount to individuals with this book: Boten Stael (just over the canal from Memling Museum at Katelijnestraat 4, tel. 050-332-771) and Gruuthuse (Nieuwstraat 11, opposite Groeninge Museum, tel. 050-333-393).

Bruges by Bike—**QuasiMundo Bike Tours** leads daily five-mile English-language bike tours around the city (€25, €3 discount with this book, 2.5 hours, departs March-Oct at 10:00, in Nov only with good weather, no tours Dec-Feb). For more details and contact info, see their listing under "Near Bruges," later.

City Minibus Tour—City Tour Bruges gives a rolling overview of the town in an 18-seat, two-skylight minibus with dial-a-language headsets and video support (€16, 50 minutes, pay driver). The tour leaves hourly from the Markt (10:00-19:00, until 18:00 in fall, less in winter, tel. 050-355-024, www.citytour.be). The narration, though clear, is slow-moving and a bit boring. But the tour is a lazy way to cruise past virtually every sight in Bruges.

Walking Tour—Local guides walk small groups through the core of town (€9, 2 hours, daily July-Aug, Sat-Sun only mid-April-June and Sept-Oct, depart from TI on 't Zand Square at 14:30—just drop in a few minutes early and buy tickets at the TI desk). Though earnest, the tours are heavy on history and given in two languages, so they may be less than peppy. Still, to propel you beyond the pretty gables and canal swans of Bruges, they're good medicine. In the off-season, "winter walks" leave from the same TI four evenings a week (€9, Nov-Feb Sat-Mon and Wed at 17:00).

Local Guide—A private two-hour guided tour costs €70 (reserve at least one week in advance through TI, tel. 050-448-686). Or contact Daniëlle Janssens, who gives two-hour walks for €80, three-hour walks for €120, and full-day tours of Bruges, Antwerp, Brussels, Bastogne, and other Belgian destinations for around €210 (mobile 0476-493-203, www.tourmanagementbelgium.be, tmb@skynet.be).

Horse-and-Buggy Tour—The buggies around town can take you on a clip-clop tour (€36, 35 minutes; price is per carriage, not per person; buggies gather in Minnewater, near entrance to Begijnhof, and on the Markt). When divided among four or five people, this can be a good value.

Near Bruges

Popular tour destinations from Bruges are Flanders Fields (famous WWI sites about 40 miles to the southwest; see that chapter for more information) and the picturesque town of Damme (4 easy-to-bike miles to the northeast).

Quasimodo Countryside Tours—This company offers those with extra time two entertaining, all-day, English-only bus tours through the rarely visited Flemish countryside. The "Flanders Fields" tour concentrates on WWI battlefields, trenches, memorials, and poppy-splattered fields (Tue-Sun at 9:15, no tours Mon or in Jan, 8 hours, visit to In Flanders Fields Museum not included). The other tour, "Triple Treat," focuses on Flanders' medieval past and rich culture, with tastes of chocolate, waffles, and beer (departs Mon, Wed, and Fri at 9:15, 8 hours). Be ready for lots of walking.

Tours cost €63, or €53 if you're under 26 (cash preferred, €10 discount on second tour if you've taken the other, includes sandwich lunch, 9- or 30-seat bus depending on demand, non-

smoking, reservations required—call 050-370-470, www.quasimodo
.be). After making a few big-hotel pickups, the buses leave town
from the Park Hotel on 't Zand Square (arrange for pickup when
you reserve).

Bike Tours—**QuasiMundo Bike Tours,** which runs bike tours
around Bruges (listed earlier), also offers a daily "Border by Bike"

tour through the nearby countryside
to Damme (€25, €3 discount with
this book, March-Oct, departs at
13:00, 15 miles, 4 hours, tel. 050-330-
775, www.quasimundo.com). Both
their city and border tours include
bike rental, a light raincoat (if necessary), water, and a drink in a local
café. Meet at the metal "car wash"
fountain on Burg Square 10 minutes
before departure. If you already have a bike, you're welcome to
join either tour for €15. Jos, who leads most departures, is a high-
energy and entertaining guide.

Charming Mieke of **Pink Bear Bike Tours** takes small groups
on an easy and delightful 3.5-hour guided pedal along a canal to

the historic town of Damme
and back, finishing with a
brief tour of Bruges. English
tours go daily through peak
season and nearly daily the
rest of the year (€23, €2 discount with this book, €16 if
you already have a bike, meet
at 10:25 under bell tower on

the Markt, tel. 050-616-686, mobile 0476-744-525, www.pinkbear
.freeservers.com).

For a do-it-yourself bike tour, see page 379. For bike rental
shops in Bruges, see page 368.

SIGHTS IN BRUGES

These sights are listed in walking order, from the Markt (Market Square), to Burg Square, to the cluster of museums around the Church of Our Lady, to the Begijnhof (10-minute walk from beginning to end, without stops). For a self-guided walk and more information on the major sights, see the Bruges City Walk chapter. Be aware that many sights stop admitting visitors 30 minutes before closing.

▲**Markt (Market Square)**—Ringed by a bank, the post office, lots of restaurant terraces, great old gabled buildings, and the iconic bell tower, this square is the modern heart of the city (most city buses run from near here to the train station—use the library bus stop, a block down Kuiperstraat from the Markt). Under the bell tower are two great Belgian-style french-fry stands, a quadrilingual Braille description of the old town, and a metal model of the tower. In Bruges' heyday as a trading center, a canal came right up to this square. Geldmuntstraat, just off the square, is a delightful street with many fun and practical shops and eateries.

▲▲**Bell Tower (Belfort)**—Most of this bell tower has presided over the Markt since 1300, serenading passersby with carillon music. The octagonal lantern was added in 1486, making it 290 feet high—that's 366 steps. The view is worth the climb and probably even the pricey admission.

Cost and Hours: €8, daily 9:30-17:00, 16:15 last-entry time strictly enforced—best to show up before 16:00, €0.30 WC in courtyard.

▲▲**Burg Square**—This opulent square is Bruges' civic center, the historic birthplace of Bruges, and the site of the ninth-century castle of the first count of Flanders. Today, it's an atmospheric place to take in an outdoor concert while surrounded by six centuries of architecture.

▲**Basilica of the Holy Blood**—Originally the Chapel of Saint

Basil, this church is famous for its relic of the blood of Christ, which, according to tradition, was brought to Bruges in 1150 after the Second Crusade. The lower chapel is dark and solid— a fine example of Romanesque style. The upper chapel (separate entrance, climb the stairs) is decorated Gothic. An interesting treasury museum is next to the upper chapel.

Cost and Hours: April-Sept daily 9:30-12:00 & 14:00-18:00; Oct-March daily 10:00-12:00 & 14:00-16:00 except closed Wed afternoon; Burg Square, tel. 050-336-792, www.holyblood.com.

▲**City Hall**—This complex houses several interesting sights. Your €2 ticket includes an audioguide; access to a room full of old town maps and paintings; the grand, beautifully restored **Gothic Room** from 1400, starring a painted and carved wooden ceiling adorned with hanging arches (daily 9:30-17:00, last entry 30 minutes before closing, Burg 12); and the less impressive **Renaissance Hall** (Brugse Vrije), basically just one ornate room with a Renaissance chimney (same hours, separate entrance—in corner of square at Burg 11a).

▲▲**Groeninge Museum**—This museum houses a world-class collection of mostly Flemish art, from Memling to Magritte. While there's plenty of worthwhile modern art, the highlights are the vivid and pristine Flemish Primitives. ("Primitive" here means "before the Renaissance.") Flemish art is shaped by its love of detail, its merchant patrons' egos, and the power of the Church. Lose yourself in the halls of Groeninge: Gaze across 15th-century canals, into the eyes of reassuring Marys, and through town squares littered with leotards, lace, and lopped-off heads.

Cost and Hours: €8, Tue-Sun 9:30-17:00, closed Mon, Dijver 12, tel. 050-448-743, www.brugge.be.

✪ See the Groeninge Museum Tour chapter.

▲▲**Church of Our Lady (Onze-Lieve-Vrouwekerk)**—The church stands as a memorial to the power and wealth of Bruges in its heyday. A delicate *Madonna and Child* by Michelangelo is near the apse (to the right if you're facing the altar). It's said to be the only Michelangelo statue to leave Italy in his lifetime (thanks to the

BRUGES SIGHTS

Bruges at a Glance

▲▲**Groeninge Museum** Top-notch collection of mainly Flemish art. **Hours:** Tue-Sun 9:30-17:00, closed Mon. See page 373.

▲▲**Bell Tower** Overlooking the Markt, with 366 steps to a worthwhile view and a carillon close-up. **Hours:** Daily 9:30-17:00. See page 372.

▲▲**Burg Square** Historic square with sights and impressive architecture. **Hours:** Always open. See page 372.

▲▲**Memling Museum/St. John's Hospital** Art by the greatest of the Flemish Primitives. **Hours:** Tue-Sun 9:30-17:00, closed Mon. See page 374.

▲▲**Church of Our Lady** Tombs and church art, including Michelangelo's *Madonna and Child*. **Hours:** Church open Mon-Sat 9:30-17:00, Sun 13:30-17:00. See page 373.

▲▲**Begijnhof** Benedictine nuns' peaceful courtyard and Beguine's House museum. **Hours:** Courtyard open daily 6:30-18:30; museum open Mon-Sat 10:00-17:00, Sun 14:30-17:00, shorter hours off-season. See page 374.

▲▲**De Halve Maan Brewery Tour** Fun tour that includes beer. **Hours:** April-Oct daily on the hour 11:00-16:00, Sat until 18:00;

wealth generated by Bruges' cloth trade). If you like tombs and church art, pay to wander through the apse.

Cost and Hours: The rear of the church is free to the public. To get into the main section costs €4; church open Mon-Sat 9:30-17:00, Sun 13:30-17:00, Mariastraat, www.brugge.be.

▲▲**Memling Museum/St. John's Hospital (Sint Janshospitaal)**—The former monastery/hospital complex has a fine museum in what was once the monks' church. It contains six much-loved paintings by the greatest of the Flemish Primitives, Hans Memling. His *Mystical Wedding of St. Catherine* triptych is a highlight, as is the miniature, gilded-oak shrine to St. Ursula.

Cost and Hours: €8, includes fine audioguide, Tue-Sun 9:30-17:00, closed Mon, last entry 30 minutes before closing, across the street from the Church of Our Lady, Mariastraat 38, Bruges museums tel. 050-448-713, www.brugge.be.

✪ See the Memling Museum Tour chapter.

▲▲**Begijnhof**—Inhabited by Benedictine nuns, the Begijnhof courtyard (free, daily 6:30-18:30) almost makes you want to don a

Nov-March Mon-Fri at 11:00 and 15:00 only, Sat-Sun on the hour 11:00-17:00. See page 376.

▲▲**Biking** Exploring the countryside and pedaling to nearby Damme. **Hours:** Rental shops generally open daily 10:00-19:00. See page 378.

▲**Markt** Main square that is the modern heart of the city, with carillon bell tower (described on opposite page). **Hours:** Always open. See page 372.

▲**Basilica of the Holy Blood** Romanesque and Gothic church housing a relic of the blood of Christ. **Hours:** April-Sept daily 9:30-12:00 & 14:00-18:00; Oct-March daily 10:00-12:00 & 14:00-16:00 except closed Wed afternoon. See page 373.

▲**City Hall** Beautifully restored Gothic Room from 1400, plus the Renaissance Hall. **Hours:** Daily 9:30-17:00. See page 373.

▲**Chocolate Shops** Bruges' specialty, sold at Dumon, The Chocolate Line, Confiserie De Clerck, and on and on. **Hours:** Shops generally open 10:00-18:00. See page 376.

▲**Choco-Story: The Chocolate Museum** The whole delicious story of Belgium's favorite treat. **Hours:** Daily 10:00-17:00. See page 377.

habit and fold your hands as you walk under its wispy trees and whisper past its frugal little homes. For a good slice of Begijnhof life, walk through the simple Beguine's House museum.

Cost and Hours: €2, Mon-Sat 10:00-17:00, Sun 14:30-17:00, shorter hours off-season, English explanations, museum is left of entry gate.

Minnewater—Just south of the Begijnhof is Minnewater, an idyllic world of flower boxes, canals, and swans.

Almshouses—As you walk from the Begijnhof back to the town center, you might detour along Nieuwe Gentweg to visit one of about 20 almshouses in the city. At #8, go through the door marked *Godshuis de Meulenaere 1613* into the peaceful courtyard (free). This was a medieval form of housing for the poor. The rich would pay for someone's tiny room here in return for lots of prayers.

Bruges Experiences: Beer, Chocolate, Windmills, and Biking

▲▲**De Halve Maan Brewery Tour**—Belgians are Europe's beer connoisseurs, and this handy tour is a great way to pay your respects. The brewery makes the only beers brewed in Bruges: Brugse Zot ("Fool from Bruges") and Straffe Hendrik ("Strong Henry"). The happy gang at this working-family brewery gives entertaining and informative 45-minute tours in two languages. Avoid crowds by visiting at 11:00.

During your tour, you'll learn that "the components of the beer are vitally necessary and contribute to a well-balanced life pattern. Nerves, muscles, visual sentience, and healthy skin are stimulated by these in a positive manner. For longevity and lifelong equilibrium, drink Brugse Zot in moderation!"

Their bistro, where you'll drink your included beer, serves quick, hearty lunch plates. You can eat indoors with the smell of hops, or outdoors with the smell of hops. This is a good place to wait for your tour or to linger afterward. For more on Belgian beer, see page 357.

Cost and Hours: €6.50 includes a beer, lots of very steep steps, great rooftop panorama; tours run April-Oct daily on the hour 11:00-16:00, Sat until 18:00; Nov-March Mon-Fri 11:00 and 15:00 only, Sat-Sun on the hour 11:00-17:00; Walplein 26, tel. 050-444-223, www.halvemaan.be.

▲**Chocolate Shops**—Bruggians are connoisseurs of fine chocolate. You'll be tempted by chocolate-filled display windows all over town. While Godiva is the best big-factory/high-price/high-quality brand, there are plenty of smaller family-run places in Bruges that offer exquisite handmade chocolates. All three of the following chocolatiers are proud of their creative varieties, generous with their samples, and welcome you to assemble a 100-gram assortment of five or six chocolates.

Dumon: Perhaps Bruges' smoothest, creamiest chocolates are at Dumon, just off the Markt (a selection of 5 or 6 chocolates are a deal at €2.30/100 grams). Natale Dumon runs the store with Madame Dumon still dropping by to help make their top-notch chocolate daily and sell it fresh (Wed-Mon 10:00-18:00, closed

Tue, old chocolate molds on display in basement, Eiermarkt 6, tel. 050-346-282). The Dumons don't provide English labels because they believe it's best to describe their chocolates in person—and they do it with an evangelical fervor. Try a small mix-and-match box to sample a few out-of-this-world flavors, and come back for more of your favorites.

The Chocolate Line: Locals and tourists alike flock to The Chocolate Line (pricey at €5.60/100 grams) to taste the *gastronomique* varieties concocted by Dominique Person—the mad scientist of chocolate. His unique creations mix chocolate with various, mostly savory, flavors. Even those that sound gross can be surprisingly good (be adventurous). Options include Havana cigar (marinated in rum, cognac, and Cuban tobacco leaves—so, therefore, technically illegal in the US), lemongrass, lavender, ginger (shaped like a Buddha), saffron curry, spicy chili, Moroccan mint, Pop Rocks/cola chocolate, wine vinegar, fried onions, bay leaf, sake, lime/vodka/passion fruit, wasabi, and tomatoes/olives/basil. The kitchen—busy whipping up 80 varieties—is on display in the back. Enjoy the window display, refreshed monthly (daily 9:30-18:00 except Sun-Mon opens at 10:30, between Church of Our Lady and the Markt at Simon Stevinplein 19, tel. 050-341-090).

Confiserie De Clerck: Third-generation chocolate maker Jan sells his handmade chocolates for just €1.20/100 grams, making this one of the best deals in town. Some locals claim his chocolate's just as good as at pricier places—taste it and decide for yourself. The time-warp candy shop itself is so delightfully old-school, you'll want to visit no matter what (Mon-Wed and Fri-Sat 10:00-19:00, closed Sun and Thu, Academiestraat 19, tel. 050-345-338).

▲Choco-Story: The Chocolate Museum—The Chocolate Fairy leads you through 2,600 years of chocolate history—explaining why, in the ancient Mexican world of the Mayas and the Aztecs, chocolate was considered the drink of the gods, and cocoa beans were used as a means of payment. With lots of artifacts well-described in English, this kid-friendly museum fills you in on the production of truffles, bonbons, hollow figures, and solid bars of

chocolate. You'll view a delicious little video (8 minutes long, runs continuously, English subtitles). Your finale is in the "demonstration room," where—after a 10-minute cooking demo—you get a taste.

Cost and Hours: €7, €11 combo-ticket includes nearby Friet Museum, daily 10:00-17:00; where Wijnzakstraat meets Sint Jansstraat at Sint Jansplein, 3-minute walk from the Markt; tel. 050-612-237, www.choco-story.be.

Nearby: The Chocolate Museum owner's wife got tired of his ancient lamp collection...so he opened a **Lamp Museum** next door (€11 combo-ticket with Chocolate Museum). While obscure, it's an impressive and well-described collection showing lamps through the ages.

Friet Museum—While this fun-loving and kid-friendly place tries hard to elevate the story of the potato, this is—for most—one museum too many. Still, it's the only place in the world that enthusiastically tells the story of french fries, which, of course, aren't even French—they're Belgian.

Cost and Hours: €6, €11 combo-ticket includes Chocolate Museum, daily 10:00-17:00, Vlamingstraat 33, tel. 050-340-150, www.frietmuseum.be.

Windmills and Lace by the Moat—A 15-minute walk from the center to the northeast end of town (faster by bike) brings you to four windmills strung along a pleasant grassy setting on the "big moat" canal. The St. Janshuys **windmill** is open to visitors (€2; May-Aug Tue-Sun 9:30-12:30 & 13:30-17:00, closed Mon, last entry at 16:30; Sept same hours but open Sat-Sun only; closed Oct-April; go to the end of Carmersstraat and hang a right).

The **Folklore Museum,** in the same neighborhood, is cute but forgettable (€2, Tue-Sun 9:30-17:00, last entry at 16:30, closed Mon, Balstraat 43, tel. 050-448-764). To find it, ask for the Jerusalem Church. On the same street is a lace shop with a good reputation, **'t Apostelientje** (Tue 13:00-17:00, Wed-Sat 9:30-12:15 & 13:15-17:00, Sun 10:00-13:00, closed Mon, Balstraat 11, tel. 050-337-860, mobile 0495-562-420).

▲▲Biking—The Dutch word for bike is *fiets* (pronounced "feets"). And though Bruges' sights are close enough for easy walking, the town is a treat for bikers, and a bike quickly gets you into dreamy back lanes without a hint of tourism. Take a peaceful evening ride through the town's nooks and crannies and around the outer canal. Consider keeping a bike for the duration of your stay—it's the way the locals get around. Along the canal that circles the town is a park with a delightful bike lane. Rental shops have maps and ideas (see "Bike Rental" on page 366 for more info).

⊙ **Self-Guided Bike Ride to Damme:** For the best short bike trip out of Bruges, rent a bike and pedal four miles each way to the nearby town of Damme. You'll enjoy a whiff of the countryside and see a working windmill while riding along a canal to a charming (if well-discovered) small market town. Allow about two hours for the leisurely round-trip bike ride and a brief stop in Damme. The Belgium/Netherlands border is a 40-minute pedal (along the same canal) beyond Damme.

• *Head east from Bruges' Markt through Burg Square and out to the canal. (You could stop to see the Jerusalem Church and a lace shop— described earlier—on the way.) At the canal, circle to the left, riding along the former town wall and passing four windmills (one is open for viewing, described earlier). After the last windmill, named Dampoort, turn right across the second of two bridges (at the locks), then continue straight along the north/left bank of the Damme Canal (via Noorweegse Kaai/Damse Vaart-West).*

The Damme Canal (Damse Vaart): From Dampoort you'll pedal straight and level along the canal directly to Damme. There's

no opportunity to cross the canal until you reach the town. The farmland to your left is a *polder*—a salt marsh that flooded each spring, until it was reclaimed by industrious local farmers. The Damme Canal, also called the Napoleon Canal, was built in 1811 by Napoleon (actually by his Spanish prisoners) in a failed attempt to reinvigorate the city as a port. Today locals fish this canal for eels and wait for the next winter freeze. Old-timers have fond memories of skating to Holland on this canal—but nowadays it's a rare event (ask locals about the winter of 2008-2009).

Schelle Windmill (Schellemolen): Just before arriving in Damme, you'll come upon a working windmill that dates from 1867. More clever than the windmills in Bruges, this one is designed so just the wood cap turns to face the wind—rather than the entire building. If it's open, climb up through the creaking,

spinning, wind-powered gears to the top floor (free, April-Sept Sat-Sun 9:30-12:30 & 13:00-18:00, closed Mon-Fri and Oct-March).

In its day (13th-15th centuries), Bruges was one of the top five European ports...and little Damme was important as well. Today all you see is land—the once-bustling former harbors silted up, causing the sea to retreat. Pause atop the bridge just beyond the windmill, with the windmill on your right and the spire of Bruges' Church of Our Lady poking up in the distance. It's easy to imagine how, at Napoleon's instructions, the canal was designed to mimic a grand Parisian boulevard—leading to the towering church back in Bruges.

• *From here, the canal continues straight to Holland. (If tempted...you're a third of the way to the border.) Instead, cross the bridge and follow Kerkstraat, which cuts through the center of town, to Damme's main square and City Hall.*

Damme: Once a thriving medieval port, and then a moated garrison town, Damme is now a tourist center—a tiny version of Bruges. It has a smaller-but-similar City Hall, a St. John's Hospital, and a big brick Church of Our Lady. You can tell by its 15th-century City Hall that, 500 years ago, Damme was rolling in herring money. Rather than being built with Belgian bricks (like other buildings around here), the City Hall was made of French limestone. Originally the ground floor was a market and fish warehouse, with government offices upstairs.

• *Continue on Kerkstraat as it leads two blocks farther to the Church of Our Lady. Along the way, you could side-trip to the left, down Pottenbakkersstraat, which takes you to a quaint little square called Haringmarkt (named for the Herring Market that made Damme rich in the 15th century). The trees you see from here mark the lines of the town's long-gone 17th-century ramparts.*

Returning to Kerkstraat, continue on to the big church.

The Church of Our Lady: This church, which rose and fell with the fortunes of Damme, dates from the 13th century. Inside are two Virgin Marys: To the right of the altar is a 1630 wooden statue of Mary, and to the left is Our Lady of the Fishermen

(c. 1650, in a glass case). Over the nave stands Belgium's oldest wooden statue, St. Andrew, with his X-shaped cross.

Outside, behind the 13th-century church tower, is a three-faced, modern fiberglass sculpture by the Belgian artist Charles Delporte. Called *View of Light,* it evokes three lights: morning (grace), midday (kindness), and evening (gentleness). If you like his work, there's more at his nearby gallery.

• *To return to Bruges, continue past the church on Kerkstraat. Just before crossing the next bridge, follow a scenic dirt lane to the right that leads you back to the Damme Canal (and Damse Vaart-Zuid). Take this road back to Bruges. If you want a change of pace from the canal, about halfway back turn off to the left (at the white bridge and brick house), then immediately turn right on Polderstraat and follow the smaller canal back to the outskirts of Bruges.*

BRUGES CITY WALK

This walk, which takes you from the Markt (Market Square) to the Burg to the museums around the Church of Our Lady (the Groeninge and Memling), shows you the best of Bruges in a day. Note that many sights stop admitting visitors 30 minutes before closing.

Orientation

Length of This Walk: Allow two hours for the walk, plus time for Bruges' two big museums (Groeninge and Memling—see chapters covering these museums).

Museum Passes: If you're planning to visit all the sights listed on this walk, save money by buying one of the city's sightseeing passes (explained on page 366).

Bell Tower (Belfort): €8, daily 9:30-17:00, 16:15 last entry strictly enforced.

Basilica of the Holy Blood: April-Sept daily 9:30-12:00 & 14:00-18:00; Oct-March daily 10:00-12:00 & 14:00-16:00 except closed Wed afternoon.

City Hall's Gothic Room: €2, includes audioguide and entry to Renaissance Hall, daily 9:30-17:00.

Renaissance Hall (Brugse Vrije): €2, includes audioguide and admission to City Hall's Gothic Room, daily 9:30-17:00.

Groeninge Museum: €8, Tue-Sun 9:30-17:00, closed Mon.

Church of Our Lady: Free peek at church from its west (back) end, €4 to see art-filled apse and choir; church open Mon-Sat 9:30-17:00, Sun 13:30-17:00.

Memling Museum: €8, includes good audioguide, Tue-Sun 9:30-17:00, closed Mon.

De Halve Maan Brewery Tour: €6.50 tour includes a beer; April-Oct daily on the hour 11:00-16:00, Sat until 18:00; 11:00 is least crowded; Nov-March Mon-Fri at 11:00 and 15:00 only, Sat-Sun on the hour 11:00-17:00.

Begijnhof: Courtyard free, open daily 6:30-18:30; Beguine's House museum costs €2, open Mon-Sat 10:00-17:00, Sun 14:30-17:00, shorter hours off-season.

The Walk Begins

Markt (Market Square)

Ringed by the post office, lots of restaurant terraces, great old gabled

buildings, and the bell tower, this is the modern heart of the city. And, in Bruges' heyday as a trading city, this was also the center. The "typical" old buildings here were rebuilt in the 19th century in an exaggerated Neo-Gothic style (Bruges is often called "more Gothic than Gothic"). This pre-Martin

Luther style was a political statement for this Catholic town.

A canal came right up to this square. Imagine boats moored where the post office stands today. In the 1300s, farmers shipped their cotton, wool, flax, and hemp to the port at Bruges. Before loading it onto outgoing boats, the industrious locals would spin, weave, and dye it into a finished product.

By 1400, the economy was shifting away from textiles and toward more refined goods, such as high-fashion items, tapestry, chairs, jewelry, and paper—a new invention (replacing parchment) made in Flanders with cotton that was shredded, soaked, and pressed. One of the Continent's first bookmakers worked here in Bruges.

The square is adorned with **flags,** including the red-white-and-blue lion flag of Bruges, the yellow-with-black-lion flag of Flanders, the black-yellow-and-red flag of Belgium, and the blue-with-circle-of-yellow-stars flag of the European Union.

The **statue** depicts two friends, Jan Breidel and Pieter de Coninc, clutching sword and shield and looking toward France as they lead a popular uprising against the French king in 1302. The rebels identified potential French spies by demanding they repeat two words—*schild en vriend* (shield and friend)—that only Flemish locals (or foreigners with phlegm) could pronounce. They won Flanders its freedom. Cleverly using hooks to pull knights

Bruges City Walk

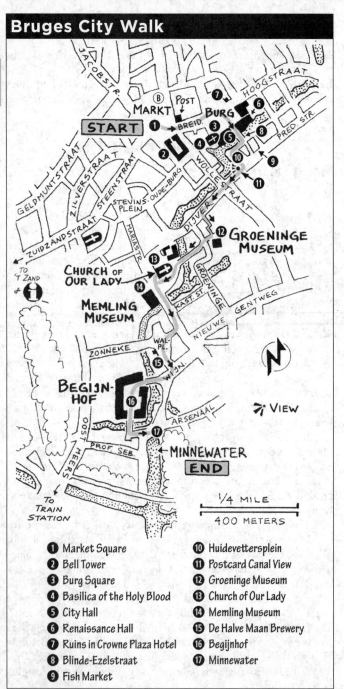

1 Market Square
2 Bell Tower
3 Burg Square
4 Basilica of the Holy Blood
5 City Hall
6 Renaissance Hall
7 Ruins in Crowne Plaza Hotel
8 Blinde-Ezelstraat
9 Fish Market

10 Huidevettersplein
11 Postcard Canal View
12 Groeninge Museum
13 Church of Our Lady
14 Memling Museum
15 De Halve Maan Brewery
16 Begijnhof
17 Minnewater

from their horses, they scored the medieval world's first victory of foot soldiers over cavalry, and of common people over nobility. The French knights, thinking that fighting these Flemish peasants would be a cakewalk, had worn their dress uniforms. The peasants had a field day afterward scavenging all the golden spurs from the fallen soldiers after the Battle of the Golden Spurs (1302).

Geldmuntstraat, a block west of the square, has fun shops and eateries. Steenstraat is the main shopping street and is packed with people. More than ever, in peak season, the crowds here include cruise groups following the numbered ping-pong paddles of their guides. Want a coffee? Stop by the Café-Brasserie Craenenburg on the Markt. Originally the house where Maximilian of Austria was imprisoned in 1488, it's been a café since 1905 (daily 7:30-23:00, Markt 16).

While on the Markt, especially in the early evening, enjoy the peace—the result of closing the square to all traffic except buses and taxis.

Bell Tower (Belfort)

Most of this bell tower has stood over the Markt since 1300. The octagonal lantern was added in 1486, making it 290 feet high. The tower combines medieval crenellations, pointed Gothic arches, round Roman arches, flamboyant spires, and even a few small flying buttresses (two-thirds of the way up).

Try some Belgian-style fries from either stand at the bottom of the tower. While the fries come with an array of exotic sauces, traditionally Belgians dip in mayonnaise—while kids and Americans enjoy ketchup.

Look for the small metal model of the tower and the Braille description of the old town. Enter the courtyard. The public sits on benches here to enjoy free carillon concerts (normally Wed, Sat, and Sun at 11:00, plus mid-June-mid-Sept Mon and Wed at 21:00). A schedule listing visiting musicians who perform free concerts at other times is usually posted. A WC is in the courtyard (€0.30).

Climb the tower (the price is steeper than its 366 steps). Just before you reach the top, peek into the carillon room. The 47 bells can be played mechanically with the giant barrel and movable tabs (as they are on each quarter hour), or with a manual keyboard (as they are during concerts). The carillonneur uses his fists and feet,

rather than fingers. Be there on the quarter hour, when things ring. The bell experience is best at the top of the hour.

Atop the tower, survey Bruges. On the horizon, you can see the towns along the North Sea coast.

• *Leaving the bell tower, turn right (east) onto Breidelstraat, and thread yourself through the lace and waffles to Burg Square.*

Burg Square

This opulent square is Bruges' historical birthplace, political center, and religious heart. Today it's the scene of outdoor concerts and local festivals.

Pan the square to see six centuries of architecture. Starting with the view of the bell tower above the gables, sweep counterclockwise 360 degrees. You'll go from Romanesque (the interior of the fancy, gray-brick **Basilica of the Holy Blood** in the corner), to the pointed Gothic arches and prickly steeples of the white sandstone **City Hall,** to the well-proportioned Renaissance windows of the **Old Recorder's House** (next door, under the gilded statues), to the elaborate 17th-century Baroque of the **Provost's House** (past the park behind you). The park at the back of the square is the site of a cathedral that was demolished during the French Revolutionary period. Today, the foundation is open to the public in the **Crowne Plaza Hotel** basement (we'll visit it in a few minutes).

• *Complete your spin and walk to the small, fancy, gray-and-gold building in the corner of Burg Square.*

Basilica of the Holy Blood

The gleaming gold knights and ladies on the church's gray facade remind us that this double-decker church was built (c. 1150) by a brave Crusader to house the drops of Christ's blood he'd brought back from Jerusalem.

Lower Chapel: Enter the lower chapel through the door labeled *Basiliek.* The stark and dim decor reeks of the medieval piety that drove crusading Christian Europeans to persecute Muslims. With heavy columns and round arches, the style is pure

The Legend of the Holy Blood

Several drops of Christ's blood, washed from his lifeless body by Joseph of Arimathea, were preserved in a rock-crystal vial in Jerusalem. In 1150, the patriarch of Jerusalem gave the blood to a Flemish soldier, Derrick of Alsace, as thanks for rescuing his city from the Muslims during the Second Crusade. Derrick (also called Dedric or Thierry) returned home and donated it to the city. The old, dried blood suddenly turned to liquid, a miracle repeated every Friday for the next two centuries, and verified by thousands of pilgrims from around Europe who flocked here to adore it. The blood dried up for good in 1325.

Every year on Ascension Day (May 29 in 2014, May 14 in 2015), Bruges' bankers, housewives, and waffle vendors put on old-time costumes for the parading of the vial through the city. Crusader knights re-enact the bringing of the relic, Joseph of Arimathea washes Christ's body, and ladies in medieval costume with hair tied up in horn-like hairnets come out to wave flags. Most of the remaining Bruges citizens just take the day off.

Romanesque. The annex along the right aisle displays somber statues of Christ being tortured and entombed, plus a 12th-century relief panel over a doorway showing St. Basil (a fourth-century scholarly monk) being baptized by a double-jointed priest, and a man-size dove of the Holy Spirit.

• *Go back outside and up the staircase to reach the...*

Upper Chapel: After being gutted by Napoleon's secular-humanist crusaders in 1797, the upper chapel's original Romanesque decor was redone by 19th-century Romantics in a Neo-Gothic style. The nave is colorful, with a curved wooden ceiling, painted walls, and stained-glass windows of the dukes who ruled Flanders, along with their duchesses.

The painting at the main altar tells the story of how the Holy Blood got here. Derrick of Alsace, having helped defend Jerusalem *(Hierosolyma)* and Bethlehem *(Bethlema)* from Muslim incursions in the Second

Crusade, kneels (left) before the grateful Christian patriarch of Jerusalem, who rewards him with the relic. Derrick returns home (right) and kneels before Bruges' bishop to give him the vial of blood.

Notice the spherical pulpit carved from a single massive oak. The relic itself—some red stuff preserved inside a clear, six-inch tube of rock crystal—is kept in the adjoining room (through the three arches). It's in the tall, silver tabernacle on the altar. (Each Friday—and most other days as well—the tabernacle's doors will be open, so you can actually see the vial of blood.) On holy days, the relic is shifted across the room and displayed on the throne under the canopy.

Treasury (next to Upper Chapel): For €2, you can see the impressive gold-and-silver, gem-studded, hexagonal reliquary (c.

1600, left wall) that the vial of blood is paraded around in on feast days. The vial is placed in the "casket" at the bottom of the four-foot-tall structure. On the wall, flanking the shrine, are paintings of kneeling residents who, for centuries, have tended the shrine and organized the pageantry as part of the 31-member Brotherhood of the Holy Blood. Elsewhere in the room are the Brothers' ceremonial necklaces, clothes, chalices, and so on.

In the display case by the entrance, find the lead box that protected the vial of blood from Protestant extremists (1578) and French Revolutionaries (1797) bent on destroying what, to them, was a glaring symbol of Catholic mumbo jumbo. The broken rock-crystal tube with gold caps on either end is a replica of the vial, giving you an idea of what the actual relic looks like. Opposite the reliquary are the original cartoons (from 1541) that provided the designs for the basilica's stained glass.

• Go back out into the square.

City Hall (Stadhuis)

Built in about 1400, when Bruges was a thriving bastion of capitalism with a population of 35,000, this building served as a model for town halls elsewhere, including Brussels. The white sandstone facade is studded with statues of knights, nobles, and saints with prickly Gothic steeples over their heads. A colorful double band of cit-

ies' coats of arms includes those of Bruges (Brugghe) and Dunkirk (Dunquerke). Back then, Bruges' jurisdiction included many towns in present-day France. The building is still the City Hall, and, on Fridays and Saturdays, it's not unusual to see couples arriving here to get married.

Entrance Hall: The ground-level lobby leads you to a picture gallery (free, closed Mon) with scenes from Belgium's history, from the Spanish king to the arrival of Napoleon, shown meeting the mayor here at the City Hall in 1803.

• *You can pay to climb the stairs for a look at the...*

Gothic Room: Some of modern democracy's roots lie in this ornate room, where, for centuries, the city council has met to discuss the town's affairs (entry includes audioguide—which explains both the upstairs and the ground floor—and entrance to the adjacent Renaissance Hall). In 1464, one of Europe's first parliaments, the Estates General of the Low Countries, convened here. The fireplace at the far end bears a proclamation from 1305, which says, "All the artisans, laborers...and citizens of Bruges are free—all of them."

The elaborately carved and painted wooden ceiling (a Neo-Gothic reconstruction from the 19th century) features tracery in gold, red, and black. Five dangling arches ("pendentives") hang down the center, now adorned with modern floodlights. Notice the New Testament themes carved into the circular medallions that decorate the points where the arches meet.

The **wall murals** are late 19th-century Romantic paintings depicting episodes in the city's history. Start with the biggest painting along the left wall, and work clockwise, following the numbers found on the walls:

1. Hip, hip, hooray! Everyone cheers, flags wave, trumpets blare, and dogs bark, as Bruges' knights, dressed in gold with black Flemish lions, return triumphant after driving out French oppressors and winning Flanders' independence. The Battle of the Golden Spurs (1302) is remembered every July 11.

2. Bruges' high-water mark came perhaps at this elaborate ceremony, when Philip the Good of Burgundy (seated, in black) assembled his court here in Bruges and solemnly founded the knightly Order of the Golden Fleece (1429).

3. The Crusader knight, Derrick of Alsace, returns from the Holy Land and kneels at the entrance of St. Basil's Chapel to present the relic of Christ's Holy Blood (c. 1150).

4. A nun carries a basket of bread in this scene from St. John's Hospital.

5. A town leader stands at the podium and hands a sealed document to a German businessman, renewing the Hanseatic League's business license. Membership in this club of trading cities was a key to Bruges' prosperity.

6. As peasants cheer, a messenger of the local duke proclaims the town's right to self-government (1190).

7. The mayor visits a Bruges painting studio to shake the hand of Jan van Eyck, the great Flemish Primitive painter (1433). Jan's wife, Margareta, is there, too. In the 1400s, Bruges rivaled Florence and Venice as Europe's cultural capital. See the town in the distance, out Van Eyck's window.

8. Bruges' book printer—the first on the Continent—sells his modern books in 1446.

9. City fathers grab a ceremonial trowel from a pillow to lay the fancy cornerstone of the City Hall (1376). Bruges' familiar towers (before the lantern was added to the bell tower) stand in the background.

10. The city's best-known medieval poet gazes out the window for inspiration.

11. It's a typical market day at the Halls (the courtyard behind the bell tower). Arabs mingle with Germans in fur-lined coats and beards in a market where they sell everything from armor to lemons.

12. A bishop blesses a new canal (1404) as ships sail right by the city. This was Bruges in its heyday, before the silting of the harbor. At the far right, the two bearded men with moustaches are the brothers who painted these murals.

In the adjoining room, old paintings and **maps** show how little the city has changed through the centuries. A **map** (on the left wall) shows in exquisite detail the city as it looked in 1562. Find the bell tower, the Church of Our Lady, and Burg Square, which back then was bounded on the north by a cathedral. Notice the canal (on the west) leading from the North Sea right to the Markt. A moat encircled the city with its gates, unfinished wall, and 28 windmills (four of which survive today). The mills pumped water to the town's fountains, made paper, ground grain, and functioned as the motor of the Middle Ages. Most locals own a copy of this map that shows how their neighborhood looked 400 years ago.

• *Back on the square, leaving the City Hall, turn right and go to the corner.*

Renaissance Hall (Brugse Vrije)

Present your Gothic Room ticket to enter this elaborately decorated room with its grand Renaissance chimney carved from oak

by Bruges' Renaissance man, Lancelot Blondeel, in 1531. If you're into heraldry, the symbolism makes this room worth a five-minute stop. (A free audioguide gives it meaning.) If you're not, you'll wonder where the rest of the museum is.

The centerpiece of the incredible carving is the Holy Roman Emperor Charles V. The hometown duke, on the far left, is related to Charles V. By making the connection to the Holy Roman Emperor clear, this carved family tree of Bruges' nobility helped substantiate their power. Notice the well-guarded family jewels. And check out the expressive little cherubs. Notice the painting that features this same hall in action in 1659, with a repentant man standing before the court to hear his punishment.

• *Leaving the building, walk straight ahead and hook around the cream-colored building to your right.*

Ruins in the Crowne Plaza Hotel

One of the old town's newest buildings (1992) sits atop the ruins of the town's oldest structures. In about A.D. 900, when Viking ships regularly docked here to rape and pillage, Baldwin Iron Arm built a fort *(castrum)* to protect his Flemish people. In 950, the fort was converted into St. Donatian's Church, which became one of the city's largest.

Ask politely at the hotel's reception desk to see the archaeological site—ruins of the fort and the church—in the basement. If there's no conference in progress, they'll let you walk down the stairs and have a peek. (They were only allowed to build here on condition they allow visitors to see the antiquities upon which the building sits.)

In the basement of the modern hotel are conference rooms lined with old stone walls and display cases of objects found in the ruins of earlier structures. On the immediate left hangs a photo of a document announcing the *Vente de Materiaux* (sale of material). When Napoleon destroyed the church in the early 1800s, its bricks were auctioned off. A local builder bought them at auction, and now the pieces of the old cathedral are embedded in other buildings throughout Bruges.

See oak pilings, carved to a point, once driven into this former peat bog to support the fort and shore up its moat. Paintings show the immensity of the church that replaced it. The curved stone walls you walk among are from the foundations of the ambulatory around the church altar.

Excavators found a town water hole—a bonanza for archaeologists—turning up the refuse of a thousand years of habitation: pottery, animal skulls, rosary beads, dice, coins, keys, thimbles, pipes, spoons, and Delftware.

Don't miss the 14th-century painted sarcophagi—painted quickly for burial, with the crucifixion on the west end and the Virgin and Child on the east.

• *Back on Burg Square, walk under the Goldfinger family (through the small archway, just to the left of City Hall) down the alleyway called...*

Blinde-Ezelstraat

Midway down on the left side (knee level, past the doorway), see an original iron hinge from the city's south gate, back when the city was ringed by a moat and closed nightly at 22:00. On the right wall, at eye level, a black patch shows you just how grimy the city had become before a 1960s cleaning. Despite the cleaning and a few fanciful reconstructions, the city today looks much as it did in centuries past.

The name "Blinde-Ezelstraat" means "Blind Donkey Street." Perhaps in medieval times, the donkeys, carrying fish from the North Sea on their backs, were stopped here so that their owners could put blinders on them. Otherwise, the donkeys wouldn't cross the water between the old city and the fish market.

• *Cross the bridge over what was the 13th-century city moat. On your left are the arcades of the...*

Fish Market (Vismarkt)

The North Sea is just 12 miles away, and the fresh catch is sold here (Wed-Sat 6:00-13:00, closed Sun-Tue). Locals love the shrimp—cooked on the boat and sold fresh here. Once a thriving market, today it's mostly souvenirs...and the big catch is the tourists.

• *Take an immediate right (west), entering a courtyard called...*

Huidevettersplein

This tiny, picturesque, restaurant-filled square was originally the headquarters of the town's skinners and tanners. On the facade of the Hotel Duc de Bourgogne, four old relief panels above the windows show scenes from the leather trade—once a leading Bruges industry. First, tan the hide in a bath of acid; then, with tongs, pull it out to dry; then beat it to make it soft; and, finally, scrape and clean it to make it ready for sale.

• *Continue a few steps to Rozenhoedkaai street, where you can look back to your right and get a great...*

Postcard Canal View

The bell tower reflected in a quiet canal lined with old houses—this view is the essence of Bruges. Seeing buildings rising straight from the water makes you understand why this was the Venice of the North. Can you see the bell tower's tilt? It leans about four feet. The tilt has been carefully monitored since 1740, but no change has been detected.

To your left (west) down the Dijver canal (past a flea market on weekends) looms the huge spire of the Church of Our Lady, the tallest brick spire in the Low Countries. Between you and the church are the Europa College (a postgraduate institution for training future "Eurocrats" about the laws, economics, and politics of the European Union) and a fine museum.

• *Continue walking with the canal and the bell tower on your right. About 100 yards ahead, on the left, is the copper-colored sign that points the way to the Groening Museum. This sumptuous collection of paintings takes you from the 15th to the 20th century. The highlights are its Flemish Primitives, with all their glorious detail. If you decide to visit, ✪ see the Groeninge Museum Tour chapter. You could tour it now, or continue this walk and tour it later.*

Facing the Groeninge Museum, go right, into a courtyard. You'll see the prickly church steeple ahead, across a canal. Head up and over the picture-perfect 19th-century pedestrian bridge. From the bridge, look to the right and up at the corner, where there's a teeny-tiny window, a tollkeeper's lookout. The bridge gives you a close-up look at Our Lady's big buttresses and round apse. After pausing to savor the beauty of this spot, cross the bridge, veer left along the hedge-lined path, and find the church entry on the right.

Church of Our Lady

This towering brick church stands as a memorial to the power and wealth of Bruges in its heyday. Step inside. While you can stand in the back and marvel at its interior in general, to get a close-up look at the Michelangelo and historic tombs and art, you'll need to pay for a ticket.

Interior: Stand in the back and admire the Church of Our Lady. Its 14th- and 15th-century stained glass was destroyed by iconoclasts, so the church is lit more brightly today than originally. Like most of Belgium, it is Catholic. The medieval-style screen divided the clergy from the commoners who gathered here in the nave. Worshippers are still attended by 12 Gothic-era statues of apostles, each with his symbol and a grandiose Baroque wooden pulpit, with a roof that seems to float in midair. It was from this fancy perch that the priest would interpret word of God.

Madonna and Child by **Michelangelo:** Pay and pass through the turnstile, entering first a chapel featuring a small marble Michelangelo statue. The delicate statue is somewhat over-whelmed by the ornate Baroque niche it sits in. It's said to be the only Michelangelo statue to leave Italy in his lifetime, bought in

Tuscany by a wealthy Bruges businessman, who's buried in the same chapel (to the right).

As Michelangelo chipped away at the masterpiece of his youth, *David,* he took breaks by carving this one in 1504. Mary, slightly smaller than life-size, sits while young Jesus stands in front of her. Their expressions are mirror images—serene, but a bit melancholy, with downcast eyes, as though pondering the young child's dangerous future. Though they're lost in thought, their hands instinctively link, tenderly. The white Carrara marble is highly polished, something Michelangelo only did when he was certain he'd gotten it right.

Tombs at the High Altar: The reclining statues mark the tombs of the last local rulers of Bruges: Mary of Burgundy, and her father, Charles the Bold. The dog and lion at their feet are symbols of fidelity and courage. Underneath the tombs are the actual excavated gravesites with mirrors to help you enjoy the well-lit centuries-old tomb paintings.

Bruges residents would stand before these tombs and ponder the great decline of their city. In 1482, when 25-year-old Mary of Burgundy tumbled from a horse and died, she left behind a toddler son and a husband who was heir to the Holy Roman Empire. Beside her lies her father, Charles the Bold, who also died prematurely, in war. Their twin deaths meant Bruges belonged to

Austria, and would soon be swallowed up by the empire and ruled from Vienna by Habsburgs—who didn't understand or care about its problems. Trade routes shifted, and goods soon flowed through Antwerp, then Amsterdam, as Bruges' North Sea port silted up. After these developments, Bruges began four centuries of economic decline. The city was eventually mothballed. The sleeping beauty of Flemish towns was later discovered by modern-day tourists to be remarkably well-pickled, which explains its current affluence. The first tourists were Americans and Canadians who came to visit the graves of loved ones in nearby WWI cemeteries after that war.

The Rest of the Church: The wooden balcony to the left of the painted altarpiece is part of the Gruuthuse mansion next door, providing the noble family with prime seats for Mass. Along the outside of the choir, to the left as you face the balcony, notice the row of dramatic wooden statues. (Contrast these with the meek figures in the apse's stained glass.)

In a side chapel in the apse you'll see excavations in 1979 turned up fascinating grave paintings on the tombs below and near the altar. Dating from the 14th and 15th centuries, these show Mary represented as Queen of Heaven (on a throne, carrying a crown and scepter) and Mother of God (with the baby Jesus on her lap). Since Mary is in charge of advocating with Jesus for your salvation, she's a good person to have painted on the wall of your tomb. Tombs also show lots of angels—generally patron saints of the dead person—swinging thuribles (incense burners).

• *Just across Mariastraat from the church entrance and about 20 yards farther south on Mariastraat and to the left is the entrance to perhaps the city's most visit-worthy museum, the...*

Memling Museum

Located in the former wards and church of St. John's Hospital, the Memling Museum offers a glimpse into medieval medicine, displaying surgical instruments, documents, and visual aids as you work your way to the museum's climax: several of Hans Memling's glowing masterpieces.

Hans Memling's art was the culmination of Bruges' Flemish Primitive style. His serene, soft-focus, motionless scenes capture a medieval piety that was quickly fading. The popular style made Memling (c. 1430-1494) one of Bruges' wealthiest citizens, and his work was gobbled up by visiting Italian merchants, who took it home with them, cross-pollinating European art.

✪ See the Memling Museum Tour chapter.

• *Leaving the museum, turn right and go about 20 paces and enjoy a fine canal view. Before you is one of many canal tour boat companies. (As they share city waterways, they all have the same price and standards.) The canal here was part of the city moat. Standing here in the 15th century, you would have just left town through the Maria Gate. Continuing on about 100 yards, turn right and go down a tiny lane, Stoofstraat ("Stove Street"—where the neighborhood's public bathhouse stood). It leads you into the pleasant square called Walplein, where you'll find the...*

De Halve Maan Brewery

If you like beer, take a tour here (Walplein 26). See page 376.

• Leaving the brewery, head right, and make your first right. Just past the horse-head fountain, where the horse-and-buggy horses stop to drink, turn right and pause in the center of a picturesque pedestrian bridge. Before you, above the gate, a sign reads Sauve Garde—*you are entering the protection of the sisters and leaving the jurisdiction of the city. The relief above shows St. Elizabeth taking care of the handicapped. Walk through the gate and, as the lacy charm of Bruges crescendos, enter the...*

Begijnhof

*Begijnhof*s (pronounced gutturally: buh-HHHINE-hof) were built to house women of the lay order, called Beguines, who spent

their lives in piety and service without having to take the same vows a nun would. Primarily because of military fatalities, there were more women than men in the medieval Low Countries. The order of Beguines offered women (often single or widowed) a dignified place to live and work. When the order died out, many *begijnhof*s were taken over by towns for subsidized housing. Today, single religious women live in the small homes. Benedictine nuns live in a building on the far side. You can tour the simple museum to get a sense of Beguine life.

On the far left of the courtyard you'll find a church. Enjoy its peaceful interior. The rope that dangles from the ceiling is yanked by a nun to announce a sung vespers service. The Benedictine nuns gather at 11:55, proceed through the garden, and sing and chant a capella in the choir of the church. The public is welcome for this service.

• Exiting the church, turn left, leave the courtyard, and follow the canal through the gate to the lake.

Minnewater

Just south of the Begijnhof is Minnewater ("Water of Love"), a peaceful, lake-filled park with canals and swans. This was once far from quaint—it was a busy harbor where small boats shuttled cargo from the big, ocean-going ships into town. From this point, the cargo was transferred again to flat-bottomed boats that went through the town's canals to their respective warehouses and to the Markt.

When locals see these swans, they recall the 15th-century mayor—famous for his long neck—who collaborated with the Austrians. The townsfolk beheaded him as a traitor. The Austrians warned them that similarly long-necked swans would inhabit the place to forever remind them of this murder. And they do. With this sweet little murder story, we end our tour of perhaps the cutest town in Europe.

• *You're a five-minute walk from the train station (where you can catch a bus to the Markt) or a 15-minute walk from the Markt—take your pick.*

GROENINGE MUSEUM TOUR

In the 1400s, Bruges was northern Europe's richest, most cosmopolitan, and most cultured city. New ideas, fads, and painting techniques were imported and exported with each shipload. Beautiful paintings were soon an affordable luxury, like fancy clothes or furniture. Internationally known artists set up studios in Bruges, producing portraits and altarpieces for wealthy merchants from all over Europe.

Understandably, the Groeninge Museum has one of the world's best collections of the art produced in the city and surrounding area. This early Flemish art is less appreciated and understood today than the Italian Renaissance art produced a century later. But by selecting 11 masterpieces, you'll get an introduction to this subtle, technically advanced, and beautiful style. Hey, if you can master the museum's name (HHHROON-ih-guh), you can certainly handle the art.

Orientation

Cost and Hours: €8, more for special exhibits, Tue-Sun 9:30-17:00, closed Mon.

Information: Tel. 050-448-743, www.brugge.be.

Getting There: The museum is well-signed on Dijver, near the Church of Our Lady.

Length of This Tour: Allow one hour.

The Tour Begins

The collection fills 10 rooms on one easy floor, arranged chronologically from the 15th to the 20th centuries. As the collection is far bigger than the actual gallery, some of the paintings featured here may be rotated out or moved.

• In room 1, look for...

Gerard David (c. 1455-1523)—
Judgment of Cambyses (1498)

That's gotta hurt.

A man is stretched across a table and skinned alive in a very businesslike manner. The crowd hardly notices, and a dog just

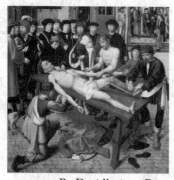

scratches himself. According to legend, the man was a judge arrested for corruption (left panel) and flayed (right panel), then his skin was draped (right panel background) over the new judge's throne.

Gerard David, Memling's successor as the city's leading artist, painted this for the City Hall. City councilors could ponder what might happen to them if they abused their offices.

By David's time, Bruges was in serious decline, with a failing economy and struggles against the powerful Austrian Habsburg family. The Primitive style also was fading. Italian art was popular, so David tried to spice up his retro-Primitive work with pseudo-Renaissance knickknacks—*putti* (baby angels, over the judgment throne), Roman-style medallions, and garlands. But he couldn't quite master the Italian specialty of 3-D perspective. We view the flayed man at an angle from slightly above, but the table he lies on is shown more from the side.

• Head to room 2 for...

Jan van Eyck (c. 1390-1441)—
Virgin and Child with Canon Joris van der Paele (1436)

Jan van Eyck was the world's first and greatest oil painter, and this is his masterpiece—three debatable but defensible assertions.

Mary, in a magnificent red gown, sits playing with her little baby, Jesus. Jesus glances up as St. George, the dragon-slaying knight, enters the room, tips his cap, and says, "I'd like to introduce my namesake, George (Joris)." Mary glances down at the kneeling Joris, a church official dressed in white. Joris takes off his glasses and looks up from his prayer book to see a bishop in

GROENINGE MUSEUM

blue, St. Donatian, patron of the church he hopes to be buried in.

Canon Joris, who hired Van Eyck, is not a pretty sight. He's old and wrinkled, with a double chin, weird earlobes, and blood-shot eyes. But the portrait isn't unflattering; it just shows unvar-nished reality with crystal clarity.

Van Eyck brings Mary and the saints down from heaven and into a typical (rich) Bruges home. He strips off their haloes, banishes all angels, and pulls the plug on heavenly radiance. If this is a religious painting, then where's God?

God's in the details. From the bishop's damask robe and Mary's wispy hair to the folds in Jesus' baby fat and the oriental carpet to "Adonai" (Lord) written on St. George's breastplate, the painting is as complex and beautiful as God's creation. The color scheme—red Mary, white canon, and blue-and-gold saints—are Bruges' city colors, from its coat of arms.

Mary, crowned with a jeweled "halo" and surrounded by beautiful things, makes an appearance in 1400s Bruges, where she can be adored in all her human beauty by Canon Joris...and by us, reflected in the mirror-like shield on St. George's back.

Jan van Eyck—*Portrait of Margareta van Eyck* (1439)

At 35, shortly after moving to Bruges, Jan van Eyck married 20-year-old Margareta. They had two kids, and after Jan died, Margareta took charge of his studio of assistants and kept it run-ning until her death. This portrait (age 33), when paired with a matching self-portrait of Jan, was one of Europe's first husband-and-wife companion sets.

She sits half-turned, looking out of the frame. (Jan might have seen this "where-have-you-been?" expression in the window late one night.) She's dressed in a red, fur-lined coat, and we catch a glimpse of her wedding ring. Her hair is invisible—very fashionable at the time—pulled back tightly, bunched into horn-like hairnets, and draped with a headdress. Stray hairs along the perimeter were plucked to achieve the high forehead look.

This simple portrait is revolution-ary—one of history's first individual por-traits that wasn't of a saint, a king, a duke,

Flemish Primitives

Despite the "Primitive" label, the Low Countries of the 1400s (along with Venice and Florence) produced the most refined art in Europe. Here are some common features of Flemish Primitive art:

- **Primitive 3-D Perspective:** Expect unnaturally cramped-looking rooms; oddly slanted tables; and flat, cardboard-cutout people with stiff posture. Yes, these works are more primitive (hence the label) than those with the later Italian Renaissance perspective.
- **Realism:** Everyday bankers and clothmakers in their Sunday best are painted with clinical, warts-and-all precision. Even saints and heavenly visions are brought down to earth.
- **Details:** Like meticulous Bruges craftsmen, painters used fine-point brushes to capture almost microscopic details—flower petals, wrinkled foreheads, intricately patterned clothes, the sparkle in a ruby. The closer you get to a painting, the better it looks.
- **Oil Painted on Wood:** They were the pioneers of new-fangled oil-based paint (while Italy still used egg-yolk tempera), working on wood, before canvas became popular.
- **Portraits and Altarpieces:** Wealthy merchants and clergymen paid to have themselves painted either alone or mingling with saints.
- **Symbolism:** In earlier times, everyone understood that a dog symbolized fidelity, a lily meant chastity, and a rose was love.
- **Materialism:** Rich Flanders celebrated the beauty of luxury goods—the latest Italian dresses, jewels, carpets, oak tables—and the ordinary beauty that radiates from flesh-and-blood people.

or a pope, and wasn't part of a religious work. It signals the advent of humanism, celebrating the glory of ordinary people. Van Eyck proudly signed the work on the original frame, with his motto saying he painted it *"als ik kan" (ALC IXH KAN)*..."as good as I can."

Rogier van der Weyden (c. 1399-1464)— *St. Luke Drawing the Virgin's Portrait* (c. 1435)

Rogier van der Weyden, the other giant among the Flemish Primitives, adds the human touch to Van Eyck's rather detached precision.

As Mary prepares to nurse, baby Jesus can't contain his glee, wiggling his fingers and toes, anticipating lunch. Mary, dressed in everyday clothes, doesn't try to hide her love as she tilts her

Oil Paint

Take vegetable oil pressed from linseeds (flax), blend in dry powdered pigments, whip to a paste the consistency of room-temperature butter, then brush onto a panel of white-washed oak—you're painting in oils. First popularized in the early 1400s, oil eventually overshadowed egg-yolk-based tempera. Though tempera was great for making fine lines shaded with simple blocks of color, oil could blend colors together seamlessly.

Watch a master create a single dog's hair: He paints a dark stroke of brown, then lets it dry. Then comes a second layer painted over it, of translucent orange. The brown shows through, blending with the orange to match the color of a collie. Finally, he applies a third, transparent layer (a "glaze"), giving the collie her healthy sheen.

Many great artists were not necessarily great painters (e.g., Michelangelo). Van Eyck, Rembrandt, Hals, Velázquez, and Rubens were master painters, meticulously building objects with successive layers of paint...but they're not everyone's favorite artists.

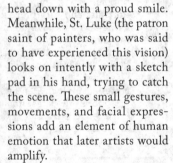

head down with a proud smile. Meanwhile, St. Luke (the patron saint of painters, who was said to have experienced this vision) looks on intently with a sketch pad in his hand, trying to catch the scene. These small gestures, movements, and facial expressions add an element of human emotion that later artists would amplify.

The painting is neatly divided by a spacious view out the window, showing a river stretching off to a spacious horizon. Van der Weyden experimented with 3-D effects like this one (though ultimately it's just window-dressing).

Rogier van der Weyden—
Duke Philip the Good (c. 1450)

Tall, lean, and elegant, this charismatic duke transformed Bruges from a commercial powerhouse to a cultural one. In 1425, Philip moved his court to Bruges, making it the de facto capital of a Burgundian empire stretching from Amsterdam to Switzerland.

Philip wears a big hat to hide his hair, a fashion trend he himself began. He's also wearing the gold-chain necklace of the

Order of the Golden Fleece, a distinguished knightly honor he gave himself. He inaugurated the Golden Fleece in a lavish ceremony at the Bruges City Hall, complete with parades, jousting, and festive pies that contained live people hiding inside to surprise his guests.

As a lover of painting, hunting, fine clothes, and many mistresses, Philip was a role model for Italian princes, such as Lorenzo the Magnificent—the *uomo universale,* the Renaissance Man.

GROENINGE MUSEUM

Hugo van der Goes (c. 1430-c. 1482)— *Death of the Virgin* (c. 1470)

The long deathwatch is over—their beloved Mary has passed on, and the disciples are bleary-eyed and dazed with grief, as though

hit with a spiritual two-by-four. Each etched face is a study in sadness, as they all have their own way of coping—lighting a candle, fidgeting, praying, or just staring off into space. Blues and reds dominate, and there's little eye-catching ornamentation, which lets the lined faces and expressive hand gestures do the talking.

Hugo van der Goes painted this, his last major work, the same year he attempted suicide. Hugo had built a successful career in Ghent, then abruptly dropped out to join a monastery. His paintings became increasingly emotionally charged, his personality more troubled.

Above the bed floats a heavenly vision, as Jesus and the angels prepare to receive Mary's soul. Their smooth skin and serene expressions contrast with the gritty, wrinkled death pallor of those on Earth. Caught up in their own grief, the disciples can't see the silver lining.

• *Head to room 3 for the surreal scene that's...*

Attributed to Hieronymus Bosch (c. 1450-1516)— *Last Judgment* (late 15th century)

It's the end of the world, and Christ descends in a bubble to pass judgment on puny humans. Little naked people dance and cavort in a theme park of medieval symbolism, desperately trying to

squeeze in their last bit of fun. Meanwhile, some wicked souls are being punished, victims either of their own stupidity or of genetically engineered demons. The good are sent to the left panel to frolic in the innocence of paradise, while the rest are damned to hell (right panel) to be tortured under a burning sky. Bosch paints the scenes with a high horizon line, making it seem that the chaos extends forever.

The bizarre work of Bosch (who, by the way, was not from Bruges) is open to many interpretations, but some see it as a warning for the turbulent times. He painted during the dawn of a new age. Secular ideas and materialism were encroaching, and the pious, serene medieval world was shattering into chaos.

• *The following paintings tend to move around. At the entrance to room 4 you'll generally find...*

Jan Provoost (c. 1465-1529)—*Death and the Miser*

A Bruges businessman in his office strikes a deal with Death. The grinning skeleton lays coins on the table and, in return, the man—looking unhealthy and with fear in his eyes—reaches across the divide in the panels to give Death a promissory note, then marks the transaction  in his ledger book. He's trading away a few years of his life for a little more money. The worried man on the right (the artist's self-portrait) says, "Don't do it."

Jan Provoost (also known as Provost) worked for businessmen like this. He knew their offices, full of moneybags, paperwork, and books. Bruges' materialistic capitalism was at odds with Christian poverty, and society was divided over whether to praise or condemn it. Ironically, this painting's flip side is a religious work bought and paid for by...rich merchants.

Petrus Christus (c. 1420-c. 1475)—
Annunciation and Nativity (1452)

Italian art was soon all the rage. Ships from Genoa and Venice

would unload Renaissance paintings, wowing the Northerners with their window-on-the-world, 3-D realism. Petrus Christus, one of Jan van Eyck's students, studied the Italian style and set out to conquer space.

The focus of Christus' *Annunciation* panel is not the winged angel announcing Jesus' coming birth, nor is it the swooning, astonished Mary—it's the empty space between them. Your eye focuses back across the floor tiles and through the

open doorway to gabled houses on a quiet canal in the far distance.

In the *Nativity* panel, the three angels hovering overhead really should be bigger, and the porch over the group looks a little rickety. Compared with the work of Florence's Renaissance painters, this is quite...primitive.

• *Fast-forward a few centuries, past paintings by no-name artists from Bruges' years of decline, to a couple of Belgium's 20th-century masters.*

Paul Delvaux (1897-1994)—
Serenity (1970)

Perhaps there's some vague connection between Van Eyck's medieval symbols and the Surrealist images of Paul Delvaux. Delvaux gained fame for his nudes sleepwalking through moonlit, video-game landscapes.

René Magritte (1898-1967)—*The Assault* (c. 1932)

Magritte had his own private reserve of symbolic images. The cloudy sky, the female torso, windows, and a horsebell (the ball with the slit) appear in other works as well. They're arranged here

side by side as if they should mean something, but they—as well as the title—only serve to short-circuit your thoughts when you try to make sense of them. Magritte paints real objects with photographic clarity, then jumbles them together in new and provocative ways.

Scenes of Bruges

Remember that Jan van Eyck, Petrus Christus, Hans Memling, Gerard David, Jan Provoost, and possibly Rogier van der Weyden (for a few years) all lived and worked in Bruges.

In addition, many other artists included scenes of the picturesque city in their art, proving that it looks today much as it did way back when. Enjoy the many painted scenes of old Bruges as a slice-of-life peek into the city and its people back in its glory days.

GROENINGE MUSEUM

MEMLING MUSEUM TOUR

*Memling in Sint-Jan
Hospitaalmuseum*

Located in the former hospital wards and church of St. John's Hospital, the Memling Museum offers a glimpse into medieval medicine, displaying surgical instruments, documents, and visual aids as you work your way to the museum's climax: several of Hans Memling's glowing masterpieces.

Orientation

Cost: €8, includes good audioguide and free loaner folding chairs (if you'd like to sit and study the paintings).

Hours: Tue-Sun 9:30-17:00, closed Mon, last entry 30 minutes before closing.

Getting There: The museum is at Mariastraat 38, across the street from the Church of Our Lady.

Information: Bruges museums tel. 050-448-713, www.brugge.be.

Length of This Tour: Allow one hour.

Overview

Hans Memling's art was the culmination of Bruges' Flemish Primitive style. His serene, soft-focus, motionless scenes capture a medieval piety that was quickly fading. The popular style made Memling (c. 1430-1494) one of Bruges' wealthiest citizens, and his work was gobbled up by visiting Italian merchants, who took it home with them, cross-pollinating European art.

The displays on medieval medicine are all on one floor of the former sick hall, with the Memlings in a chapel at the far end.

The Tour Begins

The Hospital

Some 500 years ago, Bruges was a major destination for pilgrims. People both healthy and frail trekked here from all over this part of Europe to see the relic of the blood of Christ (at the Church of the Holy Blood). Many were or became ill and had to be cared for. And that's what this building was all about.

The building itself, which has housed a hospital since 1188, is impressive. It grew in importance as the precious relic of the holy blood grew in notoriety. This hall was lined with beds filled with the sick and dying. Nuns served as nurses. At the far end was the high altar, which once displayed Memling's *St. John Altarpiece* (which we'll see). Bedridden patients could gaze on this peaceful, colorful vision and gain a moment's comfort from their agonies.

A painting by Jan Beerblock, *De Oude Ziekenzalen* (1778), gives an intimate peek at "the old sick hall" in action. Study it for a sense of what it was like. The soup's on, dogs are welcome, a nun administers last rites, the sedan chair ambulance taxi awaits a patient (an actual sedan chair ambulance still stands nearby). Snacks and drinks are served in bed. The floor needs mopping. A VIP clergyman drops in to see that all's OK.

As the museum displays make clear, medicine of the day was well-intentioned but very crude. In many ways, this was less a hospital than a hospice, helping the dying make the transition from this world to the next. Religious art (displayed further along in the museum) was therapeutic, addressing the patients' mental and spiritual health. The numerous Crucifixions reminded the

sufferers that Christ could feel their pain, having lived it himself.
• *Continue through the displays of religious art—past paintings that make you thankful for modern medicine. Head through the wooden doorway to the black-and-white tiled room where Memling's paintings are displayed. A large triptych (three-paneled altarpiece) dominates the space.*

St. John Altarpiece
(a.k.a. *The Mystical Marriage of St. Catherine,* 1474)

Sick and dying patients lay in their beds in the hospital and looked at this colorful, three-part work, which sat atop the hospital/church's high altar. The piece was dedicated to the hospital's patron saints, John the Baptist and John the Evangelist

---

Some Memling Trademarks

- Serene symmetry, with little motion or emotion
- Serious faces that are realistic but timeless, with blemishes airbrushed out
- Eye-catching details such as precious carpets, mirrors, and brocaded clothes
- Glowing colors, even lighting, no shadows
- Cityscape backgrounds

(see the inscription along the bottom of the frame), but

Memling broadened the focus to take in a vision of heaven and the end of the world.

Central Panel: Mary, with baby Jesus on her lap, sits in a canopied chair, crowned by hovering blue angels. It's an imaginary gathering of conversing saints *(Sacra Conversazione)*, though nobody in this meditative group is saying a word or even exchanging meaningful eye contact.

Mary is flanked by the two Johns—John the Baptist to the left, and John the Evangelist (in red) to the right. Everyone else

sits symmetrically around Mary. An organist angel to the left is matched by a book-holding acolyte to the right. St. Catherine (left, in white, red, and gold) balances St. Barbara, in green, who's absorbed in her book. Behind them, classical columns are also perfectly balanced left and right.

At the center of it all, baby Jesus tips the balance by leaning over to place a ring on Catherine's finger, sealing the "mystical marriage" between them.

St. Catherine of Alexandria, born rich, smart, and pagan to Roman parents, joined the outlawed Christian faith. She spoke out against pagan Rome, attracting the attention of the emperor, Maxentius, who sent 50 philosophers to talk some sense into her—but she countered every argument, even converting the emperor's own wife. Maxentius killed his wife, then asked Catherine to marry him. She refused, determined to remain true to the man she'd already "married" in a mystical vision—Christ.

Frustrated, Maxentius ordered Catherine to be stretched across a large, spiked wheel (the rather quaint-looking object at her feet), but the wheel flew apart, sparing her and killing many of her torturers. So they just cut her head off, which is why she has a sword, along with her "Catherine Wheel."

Looking through the columns, we see scenes of Bruges. Just to the right of the chair's canopy, the wooden contraption is a crane, used to hoist barrels from barges on Kraanplein.

Left Panel—The Beheading of John the Baptist: Even this gruesome scene, with blood still spurting from John's severed

neck, becomes serene under Memling's gentle brush. Everyone is solemn, graceful, and emotionless—including both parts of the decapitated John. Memling depicts Salomé (in green) receiving the head on her silver platter with a humble servant's downcast eyes, as if accepting her role in God's wonderful, if sometimes painful, plan.

In the background, left, we can look into Herod's palace, where he sits at a banquet table with his wife while Salomé dances modestly in front of him. Herod's lust is only hinted at with the naked statues—a man between two women—that adorn the palace exterior.

Right Panel—John the Evangelist's Vision of the Apocalypse: John sits on a high, rocky bluff on the island of Patmos and sees the end of the world as we know it...and he feels fine.

Overhead, in a rainbow bubble, God appears on his throne, resting his hand on a sealed book. A lamb steps up to open the seals, unleashing the awful events at the end of time. Standing at the bottom of the rainbow, an angel in green gestures to John

and says, "Write this down." John starts to dip his quill into the inkwell (his other hand holds the quill-sharpener), but he pauses, absolutely transfixed, experiencing the Apocalypse now.

He sees wars, fires, and plagues on the horizon, the Virgin in the sky rebuking a red dragon, and many other wonders. Fervent fundamentalists should bring their Bibles along, because there are many specific references brought to life in a literal way.

In the center ride the dreaded Four Horsemen, wreaking havoc on the cosmos (galloping over either islands or clouds). Horseman number four is a skeleton, followed by a human-

eating monster head. Helpless mortals on the right seek shelter in the rocks, but find none.

Memling has been criticized for building a career by copying the formulas of his predecessors, but this panel is a complete original. Its theme had never been so fully expressed, and the bright, contrasting colors and vivid imagery are almost modern. In the *St. John Altarpiece*, Memling shows us the full range of his palette, from medieval grace to Renaissance symmetry, from the real to the surreal.

• *In a glass case, find the...*

St. Ursula Shrine (c. 1489)

On October 21, 1489, the mortal remains of St. Ursula were brought here to the church and placed in this gilded oak shrine,

built specially for the occasion and decorated with paintings by Memling. Ursula, yet another Christian martyred by the ancient Romans, became a sensation in the Middle Ages when builders in Germany's Köln (Cologne) unearthed a huge pile of bones believed to belong to her and her 11,000 slaughtered cohorts.

The shrine, carved of wood and covered with gold, looks like a miniature Gothic church (similar to the hospital church). Memling was asked to fill in the "church's" stained-glass windows with six arch-shaped paintings describing Ursula's well-known legend.

• *Stand with your back to the wall, facing the shrine. "Read" the shrine's story from left to right, circling counterclockwise, but begin with the...*

Left Panel: Ursula—in white and blue—arrives by boat at the city of Köln and enters through the city gate. She's on a pilgrimage to Rome, accompanied by 11,000 (female) virgins. That night (look in the two windows of the house in the background, right), an angel appears and tells her this trip will mean her death, but she is undaunted.

Center Panel: Continuing up the Rhine, they arrive in Basel. (Memling knew the Rhine, having grown up near it.) Memling condenses the 11,000 virgins to a more manageable 11, making each one pure enough for a thousand. From Basel they set out on foot (in the background, right) over the snowy Alps.

Right Panel: They arrive in Rome—formally portrayed by a round Renaissance tower decorated with *putti* (little angels)—where Ursula falls to her knees before the pope at the church steps. Kneeling behind Ursula is her fiancé, Etherus, the pagan prince of England. She has agreed to marry him only if he becomes a Christian and refrains from the marriage bed long enough for her to make this three-year pilgrimage as a virgin (making, I guess, number 11,001). Inside the church, on the right side, he is baptized a Christian.

Opposite Side—Left Panel: They head back home. They're leaving Basel, boarding ships to go north on the Rhine. The pope was so inspired by these virgins that he joined them. These "crowd" scenes are hardly realistic—more like a collage of individual poses and faces. And Memling tells the story with extremely minimal acting. Perhaps his inspiration was the pomp and ceremony of Bruges parades, which were introduced by the Burgundian dukes. He would have seen *tableaux vivants*, where Brugeois would pose in costume like human statues to enact an event from the Bible or from city history. (Today's "living Christmas crèches" carry on this medieval art form.)

Middle Panel: Back in Köln, a surprise awaits them—the city has been taken over by vicious Huns. They grab Etherus and stab him. He dies in Ursula's arms.

Right Panel: The Hun king (in red with turban and beard) woos Ursula, placing his hand over his heart, but she says, "No way." So a Hun soldier draws his arrow and prepares to shoot her dead. Even here, at the climax of the story, there are no histrionics. Even the dog just sits down, crosses his paws, and watches. The whole shrine cycle is as posed, motionless, and colorful as the *tableaux vivants* that may have inaugurated the shrine here in this church in 1489.

In the background, behind Ursula, a Bruges couple looks on sympathetically. This may be Memling himself (in red coat with fur lining) and his wife, Anna, who bore their three children. Behind them, Memling renders an accurate city skyline of Köln, including a side view of the Köln Cathedral (missing its still-unfinished tall spires).

• *In the small adjoining room, find more Memlings.*

Diptych of Martin van Nieuwenhove (1489)

Three-dimensional effects—borrowed from the Italian Renaissance style—enliven this traditional two-panel altarpiece. Both Mary and Child and the 23-year-old Martin, though in different panels, inhabit the same space within the painting.

Stand right in front of Mary, facing her directly. If you line up the paintings' horizons (seen in the distance, out the room's win-

dows), you'll see that both panels depict the same room—with two windows at the back and two along the right wall.

Want proof? In the convex mirror on the back wall (just to the left of Mary), the scene is reflected back at us, showing Mary and Martin from behind, silhouetted in the two "windows" of the picture frames. Apparently, Mary makes house calls, appearing right in the living room of the young donor Martin, the wealthy, unique-looking heir to his father's business.

• *Before leaving this area, find, to your right, a...*

Portrait of a Young Woman (1480)

Memling's bread-and-butter was portraits created for families of wealthy merchants (especially visiting Italians and Portuguese). This portrait takes us right back to that time.

The young woman looks out of the frame as if she were look-ing out a window. Her hands rest on the "sill," with the fingertips sticking over. The frame is original, but the banner and Van Eyck-like lettering are not.

Her clothes look somewhat sim-ple, but they were high-class in their day. A dark damask dress is bright-ened by a red sash and a detachable white collar. She's pulled her hair into a tight bun at the back, pinned there with a fez-like cap and draped with a transparent veil. She's shaved her hairline and plucked her brows to get that clean, high-forehead look. Her ensemble is animated by a well-placed necklace of small stones.

Memling accentuates her fashionably pale complexion and gives her a pensive, sober expression, portraying her like a medi-eval saint. Still, she keeps her personality, with distinct features like her broad nose, neck tendons, and realistic hands. She peers out from her subtly painted veil, which sweeps down over the side of her face. What's she thinking? (My guess: "It's time for a waffle.")

BRUGES SLEEPING, EATING, NIGHTLIFE & CONNECTIONS

Bruges is the most inviting town in Belgium for an overnight. This chapter describes the town's top accommodations, eateries, and nightlife options, as well as train connections to other cities.

Sleeping in Bruges

Bruges is a great place to sleep, with Gothic spires out your window, little traffic noise, and the cheerily out-of-tune carillon heralding each new day at 8:00 sharp. (Thankfully, the bell tower is silent from 22:00 to 8:00.) Most Bruges accommodations are located between the train station and the old center, with the most distant (and best) being a few blocks to the north and east of the Markt (Market Square).

B&Bs offer the best value (listed on page 418), but hoteliers have lobbied City Hall to make it harder to have more than two "official" rooms. Creative B&B owners have found ways to get around the new restrictions. All are on quiet streets and (with a few exceptions) keep the same prices throughout the year.

Bruges is most crowded Friday and Saturday evenings from Easter through October—July and August weekends are the worst. Many hotels charge a bit more on Friday and Saturday, and won't let you stay just one night if it's a Saturday.

Hotels

$$$ Hotel Heritage offers 24 rooms, with chandeliers that seem hung especially for you, in a solid and completely modernized old building with luxurious public spaces. Tastefully decorated and offering all the amenities, it's one of those places that does everything just right yet still feels warm and inviting—if you can afford it (Db-€178, superior Db-€229, deluxe Db-€283, extra bed-€60,

Sleep Code

(€1 = about $1.30, country code: 32)
S = Single, **D** = Double/Twin, **T** = Triple, **Q** = Quad, **b** = bathroom,
s = shower only. Everyone speaks English. Unless otherwise
noted, breakfast is included and credit cards are accepted.

To help you easily sort through these listings, I've divided
the accommodations into three categories, based on the
price for a standard double room with bath:

$$$ Higher Priced—Most rooms €125 or more.
  $$ Moderately Priced—Most rooms between €80-125.
   $ Lower Priced—Most rooms €80 or less.

Prices can change without notice; verify the hotel's
current rates online or by email.

wonderful buffet breakfast-€24, continental breakfast-€12, iPad
in every room, air-con, elevator, free Internet access and Wi-Fi,
sauna, tanning bed, fitness room, bike rental, free 2-hour guided
city tour, parking-€35/day, Niklaas Desparsstraat 11, a block north
of the Markt, tel. 050-444-444, fax 050-444-440, www.hotel
-heritage.com, info@hotel-heritage.com). It's run by cheery and
hardworking Johan and Isabelle Creytens.

$$$ Hotel Adornes is small and classy—a great value situ-
ated in the most charming part of town. This 17th-century canal-
side house has 20 rooms with full modern bathrooms, free parking
(reserve in advance), free loaner bikes, and a cellar lounge with
games and videos (small Db-€125, larger Db-€145-155, Tb-€175,
Qb-€185, elevator, free Wi-Fi in lobby, some street noise, near
Carmersstraat at St. Annarei 26, tel. 050-341-336, fax 050-342-
085, www.adornes.be, info@adornes.be). Nathalie runs the family
business with the help of courteous Rik.

$$ Hotel Patritius, family-run and centrally located, is a
grand, circa-1830 Neoclassical mansion with hardwood oak floors
in its 16 stately, high-ceilinged rooms. It features a plush lounge,
a chandeliered breakfast room, and a courtyard garden. If you
get a room at the lower end of the price range, this can be a great
value (Db-€100-140, Tb-€140-165, Qb-€165-200, cheaper in off-
season, rates depend on room size and demand—check site for
best price, extra bed-€25, air-con, elevator, free Internet access and
Wi-Fi, coin-op laundry, parking-€9/day, garage parking-€15/day,
Riddersstraat 11, tel. 050-338-454, fax 050-339-634, www.hotel
patritius.be, info@hotelpatritius.be, cordial Garrett and Elvi Spaey).

$$ Hotel Egmond is a creaky mansion located in the middle
of the quietly idyllic Minnewater. Its eight 18th-century rooms are

BRUGES SLEEPING

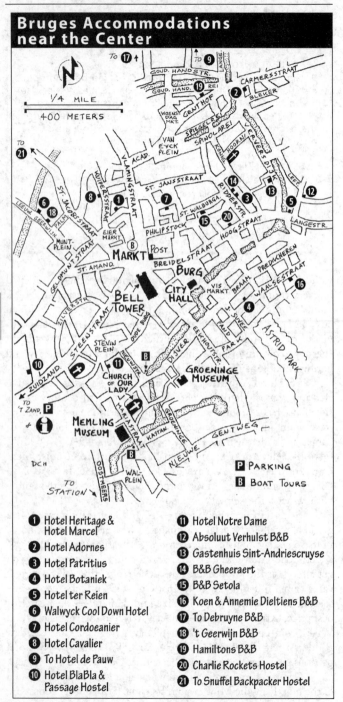

Bruges Accommodations near the Center

1/4 MILE
400 METERS

P PARKING
B BOAT TOURS

1 Hotel Heritage & Hotel Marcel
2 Hotel Adornes
3 Hotel Patritius
4 Hotel Botaniek
5 Hotel ter Reien
6 Walwyck Cool Down Hotel
7 Hotel Cordoeanier
8 Hotel Cavalier
9 To Hotel de Pauw
10 Hotel BlaBla & Passage Hostel

11 Hotel Notre Dame
12 Absoluut Verhulst B&B
13 Gastenhuis Sint-Andriescruyse
14 B&B Gheeraert
15 B&B Setola
16 Koen & Annemie Dieltiens B&B
17 To Debruyne B&B
18 't Geerwijn B&B
19 Hamiltons B&B
20 Charlie Rockets Hostel
21 To Snuffel Backpacker Hostel

plain, with small modern baths shoehorned in, and the guests-only garden is just waiting for a tea party. This hotel is ideal for romantics who want a countryside setting—where you sleep surrounded by a park, not a city (Sb-€95, small twin Db-€105, larger Db-€115, Tb-€150, cheaper in winter, free Wi-Fi, parking-€10/day, Minnewater 15, for location see map on page 364, tel. 050-341-445, fax 050-342-940, www.egmond.be, info@egmond.be, Steven).

$$ Hotel Botaniek, quietly located a block from Astrid Park, is a pint-sized hotel with a comfy lounge, renting nine slightly worn rooms—some of them quite big (Db-€95 weekday special for my readers, €99 Fri-Sat; Qb-€145, €149 Fri-Sat; less for longer and off-season stays, elevator, Waalsestraat 23, tel. 050-341-424, fax 050-345-939, www.botaniek.be, info@botaniek.be, Andy).

$$ Hotel ter Reien is big and basic, with 26 rooms overlooking a canal in the town center (Db-€70-110, Tb-€95-130, Qb-€140-160, rates vary widely with demand—check their website for best prices; cheapest rates for weekdays, stays of at least 3 nights, or rooms without canal views; extra bed-€24-29, pay Internet access and Wi-Fi, Langestraat 1, tel. 050-349-100, fax 050-340-048, www.hotelterreien.be, info@hotelterreien.be, owned by Diederik and Stephanie Pille-Maes).

$$ Walwyck Cool Down Hotel—a bit of modern comfort, chic design, and English verbiage in a medieval shell—is a nicely located hotel with 21 spacious rooms. If you're getting tired of Bruges cute, this is the place (small Db-€100, standard Db-€110, "superior" Db-€120, Tb-€150, family room-€155, "superior" family room-€180, free Wi-Fi, Leeuwstraat 8, tel. 050-616-360, fax 050-616-560, www.walwyck.com, rooms@walwyck.com).

$$ Hotel Cordoeanier, a charming family-run hotel, rents 22 simple, compact, hardwood-floor rooms on a quiet street two blocks off the Markt. It's one of the best deals in town (Sb-€75-105, Db-€80-110, twin Db-€90-120, Tb-€110-150, Qb-€135, cheaper with cash if you show this book, breakfast buffet served in their pleasant Café Rose Red, no elevator, pay Internet access, free Wi-Fi, patio, Cordoeanierstraat 16-18, tel. 050-339-051, fax 050-346-111, www.cordoeanier.be, info@cordoeanier.be, Kris).

$$ Hotel Marcel (formerly the Hotel B underwent a complete makeover in 2012, so expect its 20 big rooms to have all the amenities—and higher prices. The location is ideal—on a quiet street a block off the Markt (Db-€90-130, elevator, Niklaas Desparsstraat 9, tel. 050-335-502, fax 050-343-544, www.hotelmarcel.be, info@hotelmarcel.be, Sophie).

$ Hotel Cavalier, with lots of stairs and lots of character, rents eight rooms decorated with quirky knickknacks; some units have remodeled bathrooms. The staff serves a hearty buffet breakfast in a once-royal setting (Sb-€60, Db-€73, Tb-€95, Qb-€105, 2 lofty en-suite "backpackers' doubles" on fourth floor-€45-50, book direct and mention this book for special Rick Steves price, free Wi-Fi, Kuipersstraat 25, tel. 050-330-207, fax 050-347-199, www.hotelcavalier.be, info@hotelcavalier.be, run by friendly Viviane De Clerck).

$ Hotel de Pauw is tall, skinny, flower-bedecked, and family-run, with eight straightforward rooms on a quiet street next to a church (Sb-€70-75, Db-€85-95, no elevator, free and easy street parking, Sint Gilliskerkhof 8, tel. 050-337-118, fax 050-345-140, www.hoteldepauw.be, info@hoteldepauw.be, Philippe and Hilde).

$ Hotel 't Keizershof is a dollhouse of a hotel that lives by its motto, "Spend a night...not a fortune." (Its other motto: "When you're asleep, we look just like those big fancy hotels.") It's simple and tidy, with seven small, cheery, old-time rooms split between two floors, with a shower and toilet on each (S-€30-45, D-€45, T-€66, Q-€84, cash only, free Wi-Fi, free and easy parking, laundry service-€7.50, Oostmeers 126, a block in front of station, for location see map on page 364, tel. 050-338-728, www.hotel keizershof.be, info@hotelkeizershof.be). The hotel is run by Stefaan and Hilde, with decor by their children, Lorie and Fien; it's situated in a pleasant area near the train station and Minnewater, a 15-minute walk from the Markt.

$ Hotel BlaBla is an newly renovated hotel with seven simple, white rooms. It's well-run and in a charming building on a handy, quiet street (Db-€85-105, no elevator, free Wi-Fi, 2-night minimum on weekends, Dweersstraat 24, tel. 050-339-014, www .hotelblabla.com, info@hotelblabla.com).

$ Hotel Notre Dame has seen better days, but new owner Gauthier is renovating its 12 well-worn rooms. Since this place is in the thick of things, it's worth considering, but stay in the renovated rooms only (Db-€70-75, free Internet access and Wi-Fi, Mariastraat 3, tel. 050-333-193, fax 050-337-608, www.hotelnotre dame.be, info@hotelnotredame.be).

Bed-and-Breakfasts

These B&Bs, run by people who enjoy their work, offer a better value than hotels. Most families rent out their entire top floor—several rooms and a small sitting area. And most are mod and stylish—they're just in medieval shells. Each is central, with lots of stairs and €70 doubles you'd pay €100 for in a hotel. Many places charge €10-15 extra for one-night stays. It's possible to find parking on the street in the evening (pay 9:00-19:00, 2-hour maximum for metered parking during the day, free overnight).

$$ Absoluut Verhulst is a great, modern-feeling B&B with three rooms in a 400-year-old house, run by friendly Frieda and

Benno (Db-€95; huge and lofty suite-€130 for 2, €160 for 3, €180 for 4; €10 more for one-night stays, cash only, free Wi-Fi, 5-minute walk east of the Markt at Verbrand Nieuwland 1, tel. 050-334-515, www.b-bverhulst.com, b-b.verhulst@pandora.be).

$$ Gastenhuis Sint-Andriescruyse offers warmly decorated rooms with high ceilings in a spacious, cheerfully red canalside house a short walk from the Old Town action. Owners Luc and Christiane treat guests like long-lost family, and proudly share their photo albums with pictures of previous guests (S-€75, D/Db-€100, T-€125, Q-€150, family room for up to 5 comes with board games, cash only, free soft drinks, free Internet access, free pick-up at station, Verversdijk 15A, tel. 050-789-168, mobile 0477-973-933, www.gastenhuisst-andriescruyse.be, luc.cloet @telenet.be).

$$ B&B Gheeraert is a Neoclassical mansion where Inne rents three huge, bright, comfy rooms (Sb-€75, Db-€85, Tb-€95, two-night minimum stay required, cash only but credit card required to hold reservation, strictly non-smoking, fridges in rooms, free Internet access and Wi-Fi, Riddersstraat 9, 5-minute walk east of the Markt, tel. 050-335-627, fax 050-345-201, www .bb-bruges.be, bb-bruges@skynet.be).

$ B&B Setola, run by Lut and Bruno Setola, offers three expansive rooms and a spacious breakfast/living room on the top floor of their house. Wooden ceiling beams give the modern rooms a touch of Old World flair, and the family room has a fun loft for the kids (Sb-€65, Db-€75, extra person-€25, add €15 for one-night stays, free Wi-Fi, 5-minute walk from the Markt, Sint Walburgastraat 12, tel. 050-334-977, fax 050-332-551, www.bed andbreakfast-bruges.com, setola@bedandbreakfast-bruges.com).

$ Koen and Annemie Dieltiens are a friendly couple who enjoy getting to know their guests while sharing a wealth of information on Bruges. You'll eat a hearty breakfast around a big table in their comfortable house (Sb-€60, Db-€70, Tb-€90, €10 more for one-night stays, cash only, free Internet access and Wi-Fi, Waalsestraat 40, three blocks southeast of Burg Square, tel. 050-334-294, www.bedandbreakfastbruges.be, dieltiens@bedand breakfastbruges.be).

$ Debruyne B&B, run by Marie-Rose and her architect husband, Ronny, offers three rooms with artsy, modern decor (check out the elephant-size yellow doors—Ronny's design). The glass walls in the breakfast room open to a cloister-like garden. The architecture is cool but the hosts have genuine warmth (Sb-€65, Db-€70, Tb-€90, €10 more for one-night stays, cash only, Internet access, free Wi-Fi, 7-minute walk north of the Markt, 2 blocks from the little church at Lange Raamstraat 18, tel. 050-347-606, www.bedandbreakfastbruges.com, mietjedebruyne@yahoo.co.uk).

$ 't Geerwijn B&B, run by Chris de Loof, offers homey rooms in the old center. Check out the fun, lofty A-frame room upstairs (Ds/Db-€75-80 depending on season, Tb-€85-90, cash only, pleasant breakfast room and royal lounge, free Wi-Fi, Geerwijnstraat 14, tel. 050-340-544, fax 050-343-721, www.geerwijn .be, info@geerwijn.be). Chris also rents an apartment that sleeps five.

$$$ Hamiltons B&B, formerly Royal Stewart B&B, has new owners. It offers two luxury suites in a quiet, convent-style 17th-century house (D/Db-€130, book direct and mention Rick Steves for this price, cash preferred, homemade breakfast in garden room, Genthof 27, 5-minute walk from the Markt, mobile 0479-445-134, www.hamiltons.be, nicola@hamiltons.be, English Nicola and Olivier).

$ Waterside B&B has two fresh, Zen-like rooms, one floor above a peaceful canal south of the town center (D-€80, €5 more on Sat, continental breakfast, free Wi-Fi, 15-minute walk from Burg Square at Kazernevest 88, for location see map on page 364, tel. & fax 050-616-686, mobile 0476-744-525, www.water side.be, waterside@telenet.be, run by Mieke of recommended Pink Bear Bike Tours).

$ B&B AM/PM sports three ultra-modern rooms in a residential neighborhood just west of the old town (Db-€70, Tb-€90, €10 more for one-night stay, cash only, free Internet access—mornings only, free Wi-Fi, 5-minute walk from 't Zand at Singel 10, for location see map on page 364, mobile 0485-071-003, www .bruges-bedandbreakfast.com, info@bruges-bedandbreakfast.com, artsy young couple Tiny and Kevin). From the train station, head left down busy Buiten Begijnevest to the roundabout. Stay to the left, take the pedestrian underpass, then follow the busy road (now on your left). Just before the next bridge, turn right onto the footpath called Buiten Boevrievest, then turn left onto Singel; the B&B is at #10.

Hostels

Bruges has several good hostels offering beds for around €16 in 4- to 12-bed rooms. Breakfast is about €3 extra. The American-style **$ Charlie Rockets** hostel (and bar), a backpacker dive, is the liveliest and most central. The ground floor feels like a 19th-century sports bar, with a foosball-and-movie-posters party ambience. Upstairs is an industrial-strength pile of hostel dorms (90 beds, €18/bed with sheets, €22/bed with sheets and breakfast, 4-6 beds/ room, D-€55 includes breakfast, lockers, free Wi-Fi, Hoogstraat 19, tel. 050-330-660, www.charlierockets.com). Other small and loose places are the minimal, funky, and central **$ Passage** (€16/ bed with sheets, 4-7 beds/room, D-€52, Db-€67, Dweerstraat 26,

tel. 050-340-232, www.passagebruges.com, info@passagebruges
.com) and **$ Snuffel Backpacker Hostel,** which is less central
and pretty grungy, but friendly and laid-back (60 beds, €16-18/
bed includes sheets and breakfast, 4-12 beds/room, Ezelstraat 47,
tel. 050-333-133, www.snuffel.be).

Eating in Bruges

Bruges' specialties include mussels cooked a variety of ways (one
order can feed two), fish dishes, grilled meats, and french fries (for

more on Belgian cuisine, see page 354). The
town's two indigenous beers are the prizewin-
ning Brugse Zot ("Bruges Fool"), a golden ale,
and Straffe Hendrik, a potent, bitter triple ale.

You'll find plenty of affordable, touristy restaurants on floodlit squares and along
dreamy canals. Bruges feeds 3.5 million
tourists a year, and most are seduced by a
high-profile location. These can be great experiences for the magical setting and views, but
the quality of food and service will likely be
mediocre. I wouldn't blame you for eating at
one of these places, but I won't recommend

any. I prefer the candle-cool bistros that flicker on back streets.

Restaurants

Rock Fort is a chic spot with a modern, fresh coziness and a high-
powered respect for good food. Two young chefs, Peter Laloo and
Hermes Vanliefde, give their French cuisine a creative, gourmet
twist. At the bar they serve a separate tapas menu. Reservations
recommended. This place is a winner (€6-12 tapas, great pastas
and salads, €15 lunch special, beautifully presented €19-34 dinner
plates, €40 five-tapas special, fancy €50 fixed-price four-course
meal, open Mon-Fri 12:00-14:30 & 18:30-23:00, closed Sat-Sun,
Langestraat 15, tel. 050-334-113).

Bistro in den Wittenkop, very Flemish, is a stylishly small,
laid-back, old-time place specializing in local favorites, where
Lindsey serves while Patrick cooks. It's a classy spot to enjoy
hand-cut fries, which go particularly well with Straffe Hendrik
beer (€37 three-course meal, €20-25 plates, Tue-Sat 18:00-21:30,
closed Sun-Mon, reserve ahead, terrace in back in summer, Sint
Jakobsstraat 14, tel. 050-332-059).

Bistro den Amand, with a plain interior and a few outdoor
tables, exudes unpretentious quality the moment you step in. In
this mussels-free zone, Chef An is enthusiastic about stir-fry and
vegetables, as her busy wok and fun salads prove. Portions are

Bruges Restaurants

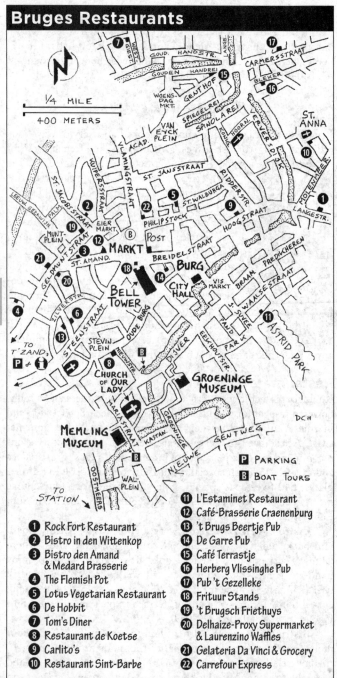

BRUGES EATING

P PARKING
B BOAT TOURS

1 Rock Fort Restaurant
2 Bistro in den Wittenkop
3 Bistro den Amand & Medard Brasserie
4 The Flemish Pot
5 Lotus Vegetarian Restaurant
6 De Hobbit
7 Tom's Diner
8 Restaurant de Koetse
9 Carlito's
10 Restaurant Sint-Barbe
11 L'Estaminet Restaurant
12 Café-Brasserie Craenenburg
13 't Brugs Beertje Pub
14 De Garre Pub
15 Café Terrastje
16 Herberg Vlissinghe Pub
17 Pub 't Gezelleke
18 Frituur Stands
19 't Brugsch Friethuys
20 Delhaize-Proxy Supermarket & Laurenzino Waffles
21 Gelateria Da Vinci & Grocery
22 Carrefour Express

splittable and there are always good vegetarian options. The creative dishes—some with a hint of Asian influence—are a welcome departure from Bruges' mostly predictable traditional restaurants. It's on a bustling pedestrian lane a half-block off the Markt (€35 three-course meal, €20-25 plates; Mon-Tue and Thu-Sat 12:00-14:00 & 18:00-21:00, closed Wed and Sun; Sint-Amandstraat 4, tel. 050-340-122, An Vissers and Arnout Beyaert). Reservations are smart for dinner.

The Flemish Pot is a busy eatery where enthusiastic chefs Mario and Rik cook up a traditional menu of vintage Flemish specialties—from beef and rabbit stew to eel—served in little iron pots and skillets. Seating is tight and cluttered, and service can be spotty. But you'll enjoy huge portions, refills from the hovering "fries angel," and a good selection of local beers (€26-30 three-course meals, €16-24 plates, daily 12:00-22:00, reservations smart, just off Geldmuntstraat at Helmstraat 3, tel. 050-340-086).

Lotus Vegetarian Restaurant serves serious lunch plates (€10 *plat du jour* offered daily), salads, and homemade chocolate cake in a pleasantly small, bustling, and upscale setting. To keep carnivorous companions happy, they also serve several very good, organic meat dishes (Mon-Fri from 11:45, last orders at 14:00, closed Sat-Sun, just north of Burg Square at Wapenmakersstraat 5, tel. 050-331-078).

De Hobbit, featuring an entertaining menu, is always busy with happy eaters. For a swinging deal, try the all-you-can-eat spareribs with bread and salad for €18.50. It's nothing fancy, just good, basic food served in a fun, crowded, traditional grill house (daily 18:00-23:00, family-friendly, Kemelstraat 8-10, reservations smart, tel. 050-335-520).

Tom's Diner is a trendy, cozy little candlelit bistro in a quiet, cobbled residential area a 10-minute walk from the center. Young chef Tom gives traditional dishes a delightful modern twist, such as his signature Flemish meat loaf with rhubarb sauce. If you want to flee the tourists and experience a popular neighborhood joint, this is it—the locals love it (€15-20 plates, Tue-Sat 12:00-14:00 & 18:00-23:00, closed Sun-Mon, north of the Markt near Sint-Gilliskerk at West-Gistelhof 23, tel. 050-333-382).

Restaurant de Koetse is handy for central, good-quality, local-style food. The feeling is traditional, a bit formal (stuffy even), and dressy, yet accessible. The cuisine is Belgian and French, with an emphasis on grilled meat, seafood, and mussels (€30 three-course meals, €20-30 plates include vegetables and a salad, Fri-Wed 12:00-14:30 & 18:00-22:00, closed Thu, non-smoking section, Oude Burg 31, tel. 050-337-680, Piet).

Carlito's is a good choice for basic Italian fare. Their informal space, with whitewashed walls and tea-light candles, is two blocks from Burg Square (€8-13 pizzas and pastas, daily 12:00-14:00 & 18:00-22:30, patio seating in back, Hoogstraat 21, tel. 050-490-075).

Restaurant Sint-Barbe, on the eastern edge of town, is a homey little neighborhood place where Evi serves classy Flemish dishes made from local ingredients in a fresh, modern space on two floors (€12 soup-and-main lunch, €14-25 main courses, Thu-Mon 11:30-14:30 & 18:00-22:00, closed Tue-Wed, food served until 21:00, St. Annaplein 29, tel. 050-330-999).

L'Estaminet is a youthful, jazz-filled eatery, similar to one of Amsterdam's brown cafés. Don't be intimidated by its lack of tourists. Local students flock here for the Tolkien-chic ambience, hearty €9 spaghetti, and big dinner salads. This is Belgium—it serves more beer than wine. For outdoor dining under an all-weather canopy, enjoy the relaxed patio facing peaceful Astrid Park (Fri-Wed 11:30-24:00, Thu 16:00-24:00, Park 5, tel. 050-330-916).

Restaurants on the Markt: Most tourists seem to be eating on the Markt with the bell tower high overhead and horse carriages clip-clopping by. The square is ringed by tourist traps with aggressive waiters expert at getting you to consume more than you intended. Still, if you order smartly, you can have a memorable meal or drink here on one of the finest squares in Europe at a reasonable price. Consider **Café-Brasserie Craenenburg,** with a straightforward menu, where you can get pasta and beer for €15 and spend all the time you want ogling the magic of Bruges (daily 7:30-23:00, Markt 16, tel. 050-333-402). While it's overpriced for dining, it can be a fine place to savor a before- or after-meal drink with the view.

Cheap Eats: **Medard Brasserie,** just a block off the Markt, serves the cheapest hot meal in town—hearty meat spaghetti (big plate-€3, huge plate-€5.50, sit inside or out, Fri-Wed 11:00-20:30, closed Thu, Sint Amandstraat 18, tel. 050-348-684).

Bars Offering Light Meals, Beer, and Ambience

My best budget-eating tip for Bruges: Stop into one of the city's bars for a simple meal and a couple of world-class beers with great Bruges ambience. For information on beer, see page 357. The last three pubs listed are in the wonderfully *gezellig* (cozy) quarter, northeast of the Markt. Just walking out here is a treat as it gets you away from the tourists.

The **'t Brugs Beertje** is young and convivial. Although any pub or restaurant carries the basic beers, you'll find a selection here of more than 300 types, including seasonal brews. They serve light meals, including pâté, spaghetti, toasted sandwiches, and a traditional cheese plate. You're welcome to sit at the bar and talk with the staff (€12 for splittable plate with 5 cheeses, bread, and salad; Thu-Tue 16:00-24:00, closed Wed, Kemelstraat 5, tel. 050-339-616, run by fun-loving manager Daisy). Daisy's on a mission to sell the world on the wonders of beer and cheese rather than wine and cheese.

De Garre (deh-HHHHAHR-rah) is another good place to gain an appreciation of the Belgian beer culture. Rather than a noisy pub scene, it has a dressy, sit-down-and-focus-on-your-friend-and-the-fine-beer vibe. It's mature and cozy with tables, light meals (cold cuts, pâtés, and toasted sandwiches), and a huge selection of beers, with heavy beers being the forte (Tue-Sun 12:00-24:00, closed Mon, additional seating up tiny staircase, off Breidelstraat between Burg and the Markt, on tiny Garre alley, tel. 050-341-029).

Café Terrastje is a cozy pub serving light meals. Enjoy the subdued ambience inside, or relax on the front terrace overlooking the canal and heart of the *gezellig* district (€6-8 sandwiches, €10-18 dishes; food served Fri-Mon 12:00-21:00, open until 23:30; Tue 12:00-18:00; closed Wed-Thu; corner of Genthof and Langerei, tel. 050-330-919, Ian and Patricia).

Herberg Vlissinghe is the oldest pub in town (1515). Bruno keeps things basic and laid-back, serving simple plates (lasagna, grilled cheese sandwiches, and famous €8 angel-hair spaghetti) and great beer in the best old-time tavern atmosphere in town. This must have been the Dutch Masters' rec room. The garden outside comes with a *boules* court—free for guests to watch or play (Wed-Sat 11:00-24:00, Sun 11:00-19:00, closed Mon-Tue, Blekersstraat 2, tel. 050-343-737).

Pub 't Gezelleke lacks the mystique of the Vlissinghe, but it's a true neighborhood pub offering spaghetti and a few basic plates and a good chance to drink with locals (if you sit at the bar). Its name is an appropriate play on the word for "cozy" and the name of a great local poet (daily 11:00-24:00, but closed Sun and Wed, Carmersstraat 15, tel. 050-338-381, Jean de Bruges). Don't come here to eat outdoors.

Fries, Fast Food, and Picnics

Local french fries *(friets)* are a treat. Proud and traditional *frituur*s serve tubs of fries and various local-style shish kebabs. Belgians dip their *friets* in mayonnaise, but ketchup is there for the Yankees (along with spicier sauces). For a quick, cheap, hot, and scenic snack, hit a *frituur* and sit on the steps or benches overlooking the Markt (convenient benches are about 50 yards past the post office).

Markt *Frituur*s: Twin take-away fry carts are on the Markt at the base of the bell tower (daily 10:00-24:00). Skip the ketchup and have a sauce adventure. I find the cart on the left more user-friendly.

't Brugsch Friethuys, a block off the Markt, is handy for fries you can sit down and enjoy. Its forte is greasy, deep-fried Flemish fast food. The €12 "Big Hunger menu" comes with all the traditional gut bombs: shrimp, *frikandel* minced-meat sausage, and "gypsy stick" sausage (daily 11:00-late, at the corner of Geldmuntstraat and Sint Jakobstraat, Luc will explain your options).

Delhaize-Proxy Supermarket is ideal for picnics. Its push-button produce pricer lets you buy as little as one mushroom (Mon-Sat 9:00-19:00, closed Sun, 3 blocks off the Markt on Geldmuntstraat). For midnight snacks, you'll find Indian-run corner grocery stores scattered around town.

Carrefour Express is handy for picnics and stocking your hotel room pantry. It's just off the Markt on Vlamingstraat (daily 8:00-19:00).

Belgian Waffles and Ice Cream

You'll see waffles sold at restaurants and take-away stands. **Laurenzino** is particularly good, and a favorite with Bruges' teens when they get the waffle munchies. Their classic waffle with chocolate costs €3 (daily in summer 10:00-22:00, until 23:00 Fri-Sat; winter 10:00-20:00, until 22:00 Fri-Sat; across from Gelateria Da Vinci at Noordzandstraat 1, tel. 050-333-213).

Gelateria Da Vinci, the local favorite for homemade ice cream, has creative flavors and a lively atmosphere. As you approach, you'll see a line of happy lickers. Before ordering, ask to sample the Ferrero Rocher (chocolate, nuts, and crunchy cookie) and plain yogurt (daily 11:00-23:00, later in summer, Geldmuntstraat 34, run by Sylvia from Austria).

Nightlife in Bruges

Herberg Vlissinghe (page 425) and **De Garre** (page 425) are great places to just nurse a beer and enjoy new friends.

Charlie Rockets is an American-style bar—lively and central—with foosball games, darts, and five pool tables (€9/hour) in the inviting back room. It also runs a youth hostel upstairs and therefore is filled with a young, international crowd who take full advantage of the guest-only happy hour prices (a block off the Markt at Hoogstraat 19). It's open nightly until 4:00 in the morning with nonstop rock 'n' roll.

Nighttime Bike Ride: Great as these pubs are, my favorite way to spend a late-summer evening in Bruges is in the twilight on a rental bike, savoring the cobbled wonders of its back streets, far from the touristic commotion.

Evening Carillon Concerts: The tiny courtyard behind the bell tower has a few benches where people can enjoy the free carillon concerts (generally Mon, Wed, and Sat at 21:00 in the summer; schedule posted on courtyard wall).

Bruges Connections

For information on rail deals in Belgium, see page 614.

From Bruges by Train to: Brussels (2/hour, usually at :31 and :58, 1 hour), **Brussels Airport** (2/hour, 1.5 hours, transfer at Brussels Nord), **Ghent** (4/hour, 30 minutes), **Antwerp** (2/hour, 1.5 hours, half the trains change in Ghent), **Ypres/Ieper** (hourly, 2 hours, change in Kortrijk), **Ostende** (3/hour, 15 minutes), **Delft** (hourly, 3 hours, change in Ghent, Antwerp, and Rotterdam), **The Hague** (hourly, 3 hours, change in Antwerp), **Köln** (8/day, 3.25 hours, change to fast Thalys train at Brussels Midi), **Paris** (roughly hourly via Brussels, 2.5 hours on fast Thalys trains—it's best to book by 20:00 the day before), **Amsterdam** (hourly, 3 hours, transfer at Antwerp Central or Brussels Midi; transfer can be tight—be alert and check with conductor; some trips via Thalys train, which requires supplement), **Amsterdam's Schiphol Airport** (10/day, 2.75 hours, change in Antwerp), **Haarlem** (hourly, 3.5 hours, 2-3 changes—avoid Thalys if traveling with a railpass)

Trains from London: Bruges is an ideal "Welcome to Europe" stop after London. Take the Eurostar train from London to Brussels (10/day, 2.5 hours), then transfer, backtracking to Bruges (2/hour, 1 hour, entire trip just a few dollars more with Eurostar ticket; see Eurostar details on page 527).

FLANDERS FIELDS

These World War I battlefields, about 40 miles southwest of Bruges, remain infamous in military history. In Flanders Fields, the second decade of the 20th century saw the invention of modern warfare: machine guns, trenches, poison gas, and a war of attrition. The most intense fighting occurred in the area called the Ypres Salient, a nondescript but hilly—and therefore terrifically strategic—bulge of land just east of the medieval trading town of Ypres (which the Flemish call "Ieper"). Over a period of three and a half years, it was here that hundreds of thousands of soldiers from fifty nations and five continents drew their last breath. Fields and forests were turned first to trenches and battlefields, and then to desolate wastelands with mud several feet deep, entirely devoid of life.

Poppies are the first flowers to bloom in a desolate battlefield once the dust (and mustard gas) clears. And today, this far-western corner of Belgium is blooming once more, having adopted that flower as its symbol. It represents sacrifice and renewal.

Today visitors can't drive through this part of Flanders without passing countless artillery craters, monuments and memorials, stones marking this advance or that conquest, and war cemeteries standing stoically between the cow-speckled pastures. Local farmers pull live shells and ammunition from the earth when they till their fields each spring and fall. (It's so commonplace, most don't even bother to call the bomb squad... they just throw it on a pile with the rest of the rusty ordnance.) Every local has his own garage collection of rusty "Great War" debris

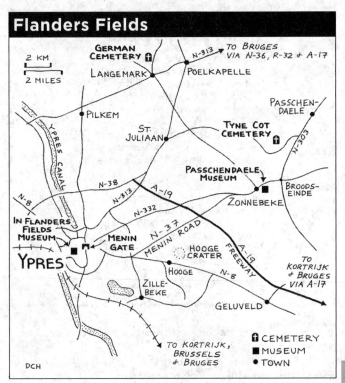

Flanders Fields

2 KM
2 MILES

GERMAN CEMETERY ✝
LANGEMARK
N-313
TO BRUGES VIA N-36, R-32 & A-17
POELKAPELLE

PILKEM

PASSCHEN-DAELE

ST. JULIAAN

TYNE COT CEMETERY ✝

YPRES CANAL

N-303

N-38
N-313
A-19

PASSCHENDAELE MUSEUM

BROODS-EINDE
ZONNEBEKE

N-8
N-332

N-37

A-19 FREEWAY

IN FLANDERS FIELDS MUSEUM

YPRES

MENIN GATE

MENIN ROAD

HOOGE CRATER

TO KORTRIJK & BRUGES VIA A-17

HOOGE
N-8

ZILLE-BEKE

GELUVELD

TO KORTRIJK, BRUSSELS & BRUGES

✝ CEMETERY
■ MUSEUM
● TOWN

DCH

FLANDERS FIELDS

he fished out of a field. Human remains are also regularly disinterred here, with every effort made to identify the fallen soldier and notify any surviving family.

If you're interested in this chapter of history, you can visit several Flanders Fields sites in a one-day side-trip from Bruges (best by car or guided tour). The most important and accessible sites are the pleasant and completely rebuilt market town of Ypres, with its impressive In Flanders Fields Museum; the town of Passchendaele (a.k.a. "Passiondale"), with a nearby, more humble, but still interesting museum; and Tyne Cot Cemetery, where thousands of enlisted men from the British Commonwealth are buried and honored. Because most of the fighting here involved British Commonwealth troops, the vast majority of visitors are Brits, Canadians, Australians, and New Zealanders, for whom the stories of Flanders Fields are etched, like names on gravestones, into their national consciousness. You'll notice on maps that many places have English names—often anglicized approximations of the Flemish names (Passiondale for Passchendaele), or more blunt new names for existing locales (Mount Sorrow, Hellfire Corner).

The years 2014 through 2018 will be a banner time in this

In Flanders Fields

In Flanders fields the poppies blow
Between the crosses, row on row,
That mark our place; and in the sky
The larks, still bravely singing, fly
Scarce heard amid the guns below.

We are the Dead. Short days ago
We lived, felt dawn, saw sunset glow,
Loved and were loved, and now we lie,
In Flanders fields.

Take up our quarrel with the foe:
To you from failing hands we throw
The torch; be yours to hold it high.
If ye break faith with us who die
We shall not sleep, though poppies grow
In Flanders fields.

John McCrae

area, as the centennial of various battles and other events are commemorated.

Between the sites, you'll drive through idyllic Belgian countryside, streaked with cornfields, dotted with pudgy cows, and punctuated by the occasional artillery crater—now overgrown with grass or trees, or serving as a handy little pond. On your Flanders Fields journey, be sure to take time to slow down and smell the cabbage.

Planning Your Time

By Tour: If you really want to delve into Flanders Fields, your best bet is to take a **tour.** These come with a rolling history lecture, and take you to off-the-beaten-path sites you'd likely not find on your own. Several companies based in Ypres run tours of the area (for information, check with the TI listed on page 436); if you're coming from Bruges, it's more convenient to take the Quasimodo big-bus tour (described on page 370).

By Car: Drivers can easily link the three main sites in a day. Be aware that road signs use the Flemish "Ieper," not "Ypres." Shop around locally for a good guidebook to point you to additional options. The local tourist board publishes a free guidebooklet called

The Flanders Fields Country & The Great War, which is a good starting place.

Here's a one-day plan for seeing the sites listed in this chapter. There's much more to see; if you're a WWI battlefield buff, invest in a good local guidebook and map to hunt down the many sites.

From Bruges, head south on the A-17 expressway. If you want to make a beeline to Ypres, take this all the way to A-19, which you'll take east and follow *Ieper Centrum* signs. For a slower, much more scenic route that takes you to more sites, exit the A-17 expressway at R-32 and circle around the northern edge of Roeselare, then head west on N-36, then south on N-313. This takes you to Langemark and the German cemetery there. Then take Zonnebaekestraat southeast to the village of Zonnebaeke and the Passchendaele Museum. From there follow the Menin Road (N-37) right on into Ypres, crossing under the Menin Gate as you enter town. After touring Ypres' excellent In Flanders Fields Museum, you can explore more countryside sites, or head directly back to Bruges (fastest route between Ypres and Bruges: A-19 expressway east to the A-17 interchange near Kortrijk, then zip north on A-17).

By Public Transportation: Non-drivers will find it time-consuming to get from Bruges to Ypres (2 hours one-way with a transfer in Kortrijk; note that Ypres is "Ieper" on timetables). Once at Ypres, it's very difficult to see the scattered sites using public transit. Taking a tour (from Ypres or Bruges) or renting a car is a must.

Background

Flanders Fields and the Ypres Salient

Because American forces played a relatively minor role in the fighting at Flanders Fields, its history is obscure to many visitors from the US. If visiting the sites, it helps to get up to speed by doing a little homework to make it all more meaningful. This section will give you a good start.

From 1830, Belgium was established as an independent and neutral state—an essential buffer zone to protect European peace, surrounded as it was by four big powers: France, Prussia, the Netherlands, and Britain. After defeating France and unifying in 1870, Germany was on the rise—an upstart powerhouse hungry for overseas colonies to fuel its growing economy. Germany amassed an intimidating army, and the rest of Europe worriedly watched flickering newsreel footage of wave after wave of German soldiers, goose-stepping past the camera in perfect sync, followed by gleaming, state-of-the-art cannons. Some of Europe's nations scrambled to ally with their neighbors against potential German encroachment; others allied with Germany. Because many alliances were secret, and often conflicting, no one knew for sure exactly where anyone else stood. As H. G. Wells said, "Every intelligent person in the world knew that disaster was impending and knew no way to avoid it."

On June 28, 1914, while on a visit to Sarajevo, the heir to the Austro-Hungarian throne, Archduke Franz Ferdinand, and his wife were assassinated by a teenage terrorist working for Bosnian Serb separatists. The Austrians held Serbia responsible and declared war. Germany joined Austria, and Russia (allied with France) backed Serbia. Through an intricate web of alliances—which ironically had been created to prevent war—soon all of Europe was drawn in the conflict. On August 4, 1914, Germany sent some 800,000 troops across the border into neutral Belgium en route to France. By August 20, they had already taken Brussels, and four days later they were in western Flanders. The Germans expected to blow through the country quickly. Their ultimate goal: Paris to the south and, to the north, the French ports of Dunkerque and Calais. If they could control those, Germany would command the English Channel.

However, the small but determined Belgian army—less than a quarter the size of the German army—pushed back hard, as they waited for British reinforcements to come from across the Channel. In the **Battle of the IJzer River,** the Belgians opened a sea gate at a pivotal moment to flood a low-lying plain just before a German advance. This diverted the German effort slightly to the south, around the town of Ypres.

Ypres (Ieper in Dutch)—an important market center in the Middle Ages (similar to Bruges)—was just an ordinary town. But its location, surrounding terrain, and modern weaponry turned it into a perpetual battlefield. This conflict saw the advent of the machine gun—a new invention that, before the war, had been called "the peacekeeper," because it was assumed that no sane commander would ever send his boys into its fire. The extremely flat terrain of Flanders Fields, combined with these newly emerging battlefield techniques, made even the slightest gain in elevation strategically important. From any ridge, machine guns and artillery could be used to mow down enemy troops—advancing armies would be sitting ducks. (The names of some of the land features here—such as "Hill 60," as in 60 meters above sea level—indicate how the surrounding flatness emphasized even the most modest gain in elevation.) Consequently, the low-lying ridges just

FLANDERS FIELDS

east of Ypres—which came to be known as the **Ypres Salient** (the French term for "bulge")—saw some of the fiercest, most devastating fighting of World War I.

The **First Battle of Ypres** began on October 20, 1914, when German troops attempted to invade the town. It became a priority of the Allies—Belgians, French, and British Commonwealth troops—to hold the Germans at bay. Both sides sustained huge losses, but the German troops—mostly inexperienced young conscripts who had underestimated the opposition—were devastated; to this day, Germans call the battle *Kindermord*, "Massacre of the Innocents." For a while, at least, the Allies succeeded in preventing Germany from pushing through. It was the last mobile combat of a conflict that would come to be known for its grueling trench warfare.

Both sides regrouped and prepared for a harsh winter. They dug trenches. Nobody planned it—it was simply human nature for soldiers ducking machine-gun bullets to burrow down. Separated by as little as 50 yards, enemy armies were close enough to offer each other a *Gesundheit!* after each sneeze. It was during this time that the famous "Christmas Truce" took place, in which the German soldiers erected little candlelit *Tanenbaum*s beside their trenches and even approached the English trenches with gifts, kind words, and a pick-up soccer game.

In the spring of 1915, the Germans tried again in the **Second Battle of Ypres.** During this battle, the Germans used poison gas for the first time on a large scale, catching the Allies off-guard. Chlorine gas (a.k.a. bertholite) reacts with moisture in the lungs to form hydrochloric acid—choking soldiers from the inside out. It was also one of the first times flamethrowers were used in battle. Despite these gruesome innovations, Germany was still unable to take the town. By May of 1915, the opposing forces were deadlocked near the town of Passchendaele, seven miles east of Ypres; for two years, little progress was made in either direction.

Although the Western Front appeared to be "all quiet," each side fortified its positions. The Germans in particular established an elaborate network of five successive trenches, connected to and supplied by one another with perpendicular "switches." They built stout fortresses with flat tops, designed to protect troops from British artillery while allowing them to quickly emerge to man nearby machine-gun nests. These flat-topped German fortresses—which you'll still see everywhere—were dubbed "pillboxes." The British opted for underground wooden tunnels called "dugouts," and reserved concrete bunkers for more specialized use, as command posts and shelters for the wounded. (Their rounded-top bunkers proved to be a more effective deterrent to artillery blasts than the Germans' flat-top design—leading the Germans to adopt the

Dulce et Decorum Est

Bent double, like old beggars under sacks,
Knock-kneed, coughing like hags, we cursed
   through sludge,
Till on the haunting flares we turned our backs
And towards our distant rest began to trudge.
Men marched asleep. Many had lost their boots
But limped on, blood-shod. All went lame; all
   blind;
Drunk with fatigue; deaf even to the hoots
Of tired, outstripped Five-Nines that dropped
   behind.

Gas! Gas! Quick, boys!—An ecstasy of fumbling,
Fitting the clumsy helmets just in time;
But someone still was yelling out and stumbling,
And flound'ring like a man in fire or lime...
Dim, through the misty panes and thick green
   light,
As under a green sea, I saw him drowning.

In all my dreams, before my helpless sight,
He plunges at me, guttering, choking, drowning.

If in some smothering dreams you too could
   pace
Behind the wagon that we flung him in,
And watch the white eyes writhing in his face,
His hanging face, like a devil's sick of sin;
If you could hear, at every jolt, the blood
Come gargling from the froth-corrupted lungs,
Obscene as cancer, bitter as the cud
Of vile, incurable sores on innocent tongues, —
My friend, you would not tell with such high zest
To children ardent for some desperate glory,
The old Lie: *Dulce et decorum est
Pro patria mori*.

Wilfred Owen

round British style in World War II.)

In the summer of 1917, the Allies attempted their own offensive against the newly strengthened German threat, the **Third Battle of Ypres** (a.k.a. the Battle of Passchendaele). After a sustained two-week artillery bombardment of German positions, some four million projectiles turned the countryside into a desolate wasteland. One solider said that "the earth had been churned and rechurned"; another termed it "as featureless as the Sahara."

Then British infantry took to the battlefield...going "over the top" (giving us that phrase), rather than staying in the trenches. They faced barbed wire, machine-gun fire, dangerously exposed high ground, and liquid mud. The utter devastation of the shelling, combined with historic rainfall (the most in the history of Flanders), turned the Ypres Salient into a sea of mud. The same flatness that made the high ground here so strategic turned the low ground into quicksand in heavy rain. Fields became flooded with stagnant water. Troops' boots and tank treads could barely move, causing the British to gain only two of the four miles they so desperately needed to conquer. This battle was also the first time the Germans used the notorious mustard gas, which causes exposed skin to blister agonizingly on contact.

As the summer of 1917 turned to fall, and the heavy rains continued to deluge the area, British soldiers made more and more inroads, bunker by bunker. Their goal was the destroyed village of **Passchendaele,** perched on a modest ridge with a strategic view over the flat lands below. The village's name literally meant "passing the valley," but the Brits dubbed it "Passiondale"...the valley of suffering. Menin Road, which connected Ypres to Passchendaele (now road N-37), was the focus of much warfare—especially the notorious intersection dubbed "Hellfire Corner."

But British forces never succeeded in taking Passchendaele (Canadian forces finally took it in November of 1917). By this point, it was clear that this was a **war of attrition.** Each side had lost about a quarter of a million men. And, as both sides poured troops and resources into the fighting, neither could actually make a definitive breakthrough—they simply wanted to be the last man standing.

Two pivotal events took place over the winter of 1917-1918: The United States entered the war on the side of the Allies; and Germany agreed to a separate peace with Russia, allowing it to steer more resources to the Ypres Salient. In spring of 1918, the **Fourth Battle of Ypres** (a.k.a. the Battle of the Lys) saw German forces trying to push through to the town of Ypres before US troops could arrive. They were emboldened by the collapse of Russia in the Bolshevik Revolution, which freed up more German troops and resources to direct at this front. Always innovative on the battlefield, the Germans introduced an elite squad of storm troopers (*Stosstruppen,* literally "shock troops")—lightly armed but well-trained and highly mobile special units tasked with breaking through enemy lines.

But by late April, the German advance stalled for lack of supplies; meanwhile, American troops had come to the rescue. By summer it was evident that Germany was losing the war of attrition, and in September and October of 1918, in the **Fifth Battle** of Ypres, Allied forces made huge gains. Less than a month later, Armistice Day (Nov 11, 1918) brought an end to the war to end all wars...until the next war.

World War I claimed the lives of an estimated nine million people; about a million were killed, wounded, or declared missing in action here in the Ypres Salient. By war's end, the British Commonwealth forces had suffered 720,000 casualties, including (officially) 185,000 dead. In the century since, Flanders Fields has recovered, and has become a compelling tourist attraction for the descendants of the victims and survivors of the fighting here. As you tour the place, keep in mind that everything you see—every building, every tree—dates from after 1918.

Sites in Flanders Fields

Ypres (Ieper)

About 40 miles southwest of Bruges is the town most English-speakers call Ypres (EE-preh, though some pronounce it "Wipers"); its official Flemish name is Ieper (YEE-per). By the

end of the war, Ypres was so devastated that Winston Churchill advocated keeping it in ruins as a monument to the travesty of warfare. But locals did rebuild, resurrecting its charming main market square (Grote Markt), watched over by the grand and impressive Cloth Hall (which houses the In Flanders Fields Museum). Today's Ypres is a downright pleasant market town, with a steady stream of mostly British tourists interested in the WWI sites. The **TI,** downstairs in the Cloth Hall, has information on tours (below the museum; April-mid-Nov Mon-Sat 9:00-18:00, Sun 10:00-18:00; mid-Nov-March Mon-Sat 9:00-17:00, Sun 10:00-17:00; tel. 057-239-220, www.toerisme-ieper.be). Saturday morning is **market** day.

Getting There: If you're based in Bruges without a car, take a tour (see recommended tours on page 369). Less than an hour away, Ypres is easy for drivers (see route tips under "Planning Your Time," earlier). There's parking right on the main market square, next to the giant Cloth Hall that houses the museum (€0.50/hour, 3-hour limit).

▲▲**In Flanders Fields Museum**—This excellent museum provides a moving look at the battles fought near Ypres. The focus is not on the strategy and the commanders, but on the ordinary people who fought and died here. The evocative descriptions personalize the miserable day-to-day existence in the trenches, and interactive computer displays trace the wartime lives of individual soldiers and citizens. Actual artifacts, engaging descriptions, and thoughtful presentations all bring the war-torn places to life.

The museum was renovated in 2011, with an expanded focus on the entire Belgian front rather than just the Ypres Salient, a renewed focus on specific locations where wartime events took place (tying the museum's exhibits to the actual sites in the surrounding countryside), and a look at the century of remembrances that have passed since the war's end.

The Cloth Hall's **belfry** (200 steps to the top, likely €2 extra), offers a panoramic view of the surrounding countryside, which was so prized and so costly in human lives a century ago.

Cost and Hours: €8; April-mid-Nov daily 10:00-18:00; mid-Nov-March Tue-Sun 10:00-17:00, closed Mon and for three weeks in Jan; last entry one hour before closing, in Ypres' huge Cloth Hall at Grote Markt 34, tel. 057-239-220, www.inflanders fields.be.

▲**Menin Gate**—This impressive Victorian archway is an easy two-block walk from the museum (past the end of Grote Markt). Built

into the old town wall of Ypres, it's etched with the names of British Commonwealth victims of the fighting here. It marks the Menin Road, where many Brits, Canadians, Aussies, and Kiwis left this town for the grueling battlefields and trenches, never to return. The gate is formally a mausoleum for "the Missing," 54,896 troops who likely perished at Flanders Fields but whose remains were never found. To honor the hundreds of thousands of British subjects who gave their lives, every night under the arch at 20:00, a Belgian bugle corps plays the **"Last Post"** to honor the dead.

Other Sites

Most of the following sites are on or near Menin Road between Ypres and Passchendaele (to the northeast), where the most famous battles took place. The German Cemetery is a bit to the north (but still within a few miles).

▲**Passchendaele Museum**—Although not as extensive or well-presented as the In Flanders Fields Museum, this good exhibit supplements it nicely, with a focus on the strategy and battles of the fighting here. Presented chronologically on the top floor of a chalet-like mansion, it details each advance and retreat from the first German boot on Belgian soil to Armistice Day. You'll see displays of uniforms, medical instruments, and objects illustrating day-to-day life at the front. One exhibit explains—and lets you sniff—the four basic types of poison gas used here. You'll exit through a simulation of the wooden underground "dugout" tunnels used by British forces as their headquarters, after the ground level was so scorched by artillery that nothing was left up above.

Cost and Hours: €5, Feb-Nov daily 9:00-17:00, closed Dec-Jan, Ieperstraat 5, in Zonnebeke about 5 miles east of Ypres and 2 miles west of Passchendaele, tel. 051-770-441, www.passchendaele.be.

▲**Tyne Cot Cemetery**—This evocative site is the largest cemetery honoring soldiers of the British Commonwealth. It's the final

resting place of 11,956 British, Canadian, Australian, New Zealander, South African, and other British Commonwealth soldiers. Named for a blockhouse on this site that was taken by British forces, who nicknamed it "Tyne Cottage" after the river in North England, the cemetery grounds also hold three German pillbox bunkers. Between those are seemingly endless rows of white headstones, marked with the deceased soldier's name and the emblem from his unit (many of these are regional, such as the maple leaf of Canada). Many graves are marked simply "A soldier of the Great War, known to God." In the center of the cemetery, near the tallest cross (marking the location of Tyne Cottage), notice the higgledy-piggledy arrangement of graves. During the war, when this cottage was a makeshift medic station, this area became an impromptu burial ground. (In contrast, any cemetery that's neat and symmetrical—like the surrounding headstones—dates from after the war.) Running along the top of the cemetery is a wall inscribed with the names of 34,857 "officers and men to whom the fortune of war denied the known and honoured burial given to their comrades in death." Inside the visitors center, you'll see a few artifacts and exhibits about the fighting here.

Cost and Hours: Cemetery and visitors center free, visitors center open daily 10:00-18:00, closed Dec-Jan, just northeast of Zonnebeke, off of N37 toward Passchendaele, about 6.5 miles east of Ypres, www.cwgc.org.

Hooge Crater—This giant flooded crater, about three miles east of Ypres, was created when British forces detonated a vast store of artillery that destroyed the château they had been using as a headquarters. This desperate act was only partly successful, as the strategic high ground around the château (now a crater) switched hands repeatedly throughout the war. Today the Hooge Crater area has a large British Commonwealth **cemetery,** the **Hooge Crater Museum** (a touristy exhibit with historic information about the fighting here, €4.50, Tue-Sun 10:00-18:00, closed Mon, www.hoogecrater.com), and—hiding out in the woods just down the road—a hotel/restaurant called **Kasteelhof 't Hooghe,** where you can pay €1 to stroll around the adjacent crater-pond and see some old bunkers and trenches (www.hotelkasteelhofthooghe.be).

German Military Cemetery (Deutscher Soldatenfriedhof) at Langemark—A relatively rare site dedicated to the invaders

of this region, this is the final resting place of 44,324 Central Powers soldiers (along with two Brits who were originally mis-identified). Compared with the gleaming British Commonwealth cemeteries nearby, it's dull and drab. That's because the Treaty of Versailles (which concluded World War I) forbade German WWI cemeteries from using white stones; instead, it uses basalt and even oak. As you wander the cemetery, you'll notice that many of these "German" troops have Slavic names, as they were imported here to fight from the far-eastern corners of the multiethnic Austro-Hungarian Empire. In the center is a mass grave with 25,000 soldiers (free, always open, on the northern outskirts of Langemark, about five miles north/northeast of Ypres).

Other Cemeteries, Memorials, and Craters—The sites listed above are just the beginning. You can't drive a mile or two without passing a monument or a memorial. Tranquil forests suddenly open into clearings with eerily rippled contours—overgrown trenches, pockmarks, and craters. Several nondescript ponds and lakes in the area are actually huge, flooded artillery craters. Joining a tour helps you find some of the more out-of-the-way remnants of the war, but if you're exploring on your own, be sure to get a good guidebook on the region (several are available at local bookstores and tourist offices—find one that suits your needs). If you have a special interest—for example, a nationality or a specific battle an ancestor participated in—just ask around, and you'll find it's easy to seek out related sites.

BRUSSELS
Bruxelles

ORIENTATION TO BRUSSELS

Six hundred years ago, Brussels was just a nice place to stop and buy a waffle on the way to Bruges. With no strategic importance, it was allowed to grow as a free trading town. Today it's a city of one million people, the capital of Belgium, the headquarters of NATO, and the seat of the European Union.

The Bruxelloise are cultured and genteel—even a bit snobby compared to their more earthy Flemish cousins. And yet you may notice an impish sparkle and joie de vivre, as evidenced by their love of comic strips (giant comic-strip panels are painted on buildings all over town) and their civic symbol: a statue of a little boy peeing.

About 500,000 people who call Brussels home, however, aren't Bruxelloise, or even Belgian. As the unofficial capital of Europe, Brussels is multicultural, hosting politicians and businesspeople (not to mention immigrants) from around the globe, and featuring a world of ethnic restaurants. The city hosts 400 embassies (the US has three here, one each to the EU, NATO, and Belgium). Every sizable corporation has a lobbyist in Brussels.

Brussels speaks French. Bone up on *bonjour* and *s'il vous plaît* (see the French survival phrases on page 635). While the city spoke mostly Dutch until 1900 and is entirely contained within the Dutch-speaking region of Flanders, today 65 percent of Bruxelloise speak French as their first language, and only 5 percent speak Dutch. The remaining third are non-natives who speak their own languages, including Brussels' businesspeople, diplomats, and politicians who use English as their default. Many predict that in 20 years, English will be the city's first language. But language aside, the whole feel of the town is urban French, not rural Flemish.

Brussels enjoyed a Golden Age of peace and prosperity

(1400-1550) while England and France were duking it out in the Hundred Years' War. It was then that many of the fine structures that distinguish the city today were built. In the late 1800s, Brussels had another growth spurt, fueled by industrialization, wealth taken from the Belgian Congo, and the exhilaration of the country's recent independence (1830). City expansion peaked at the end of the 19th century, when the "Builder King" Leopold II erected grand monuments and palaces.

Tourists zipping between Amsterdam and Bruges or Paris by train usually miss Brussels, but its rich, chocolaty mix of food and culture pleasantly surprises those who stop.

Planning Your Time

For a city of its size and prominence, Brussels is low on great sights, but high on ambience. On a quick trip, a day and a night are enough for a good first taste (but if you have more time, Brussels has enjoyable ways to fill it). Even better, if you're in a hurry, Brussels can be done as a day trip by train from Bruges, Ghent, or Antwerp (frequent trains, less than an hour from any of these) or a stopover on the Amsterdam-Paris or Amsterdam-Bruges ride (hourly trains). The main reason to visit Brussels—the Grand Place—takes only a few minutes to see. With very limited time, skip the indoor sights and just enjoy a coffee or a beer on the square.

Brussels in Three to Five Hours

Brussels makes a great stopover between trains. First toss your bag in a locker at Central Station and confirm your departure time and station (if you're catching a fast international train, factor in any necessary transit time to the Midi/Zuid/South Station—described on page 447). Then walk about five minutes into town and do this Brussels blitz:

Head directly for the Grand Place and take my Grand Place Walk. To streamline, skip the *Manneken-Pis* until later, and end the walk at the Bourse (stock-exchange building), where you can catch a taxi to Place Royale/Koningsplein. Enjoy the Royal Museums of Fine Arts and the Magritte Museum. If you're rushing to get back to your train, make a beeline to the station; if you have another hour or two to kill, do my Upper Town Walk, which ends back at the *Manneken-Pis* and the Grand Place. Buy a box of chocolates and a bottle of Belgian beer, and pop the top as your train pulls out of the station. You did the Brussels blitz.

Brussels in a Day or More

A full day (with one or two overnights) is about right to get a more complete taste of Brussels. With a second day, you can slow things down and really delve into the city. A side-trip to Bruges, Antwerp, or Ghent (each a short train-ride away) is more satisfying than a third day in Brussels.

Get your bearings in the morning with my Grand Place Walk, then tour the Royal Museums of Fine Arts of Belgium and the Magritte Museum (enjoyable to art-lovers and novices alike), and do the Upper Town Walk. With additional time, choose from a good selection of other sights. Very near the Royal Museums, historians enjoy the excellent story of Belgium at the BELvue Museum, and even the tone-deaf can appreciate the Musical Instruments Museum. In the Lower Town, aficionados of the funny pages head for the Belgian Comic Strip Center (a 15-minute walk from the Grand Place). And political-science majors visit the EU Parliament complex for a lesson in Euro-civics. In the evening, consider exploring the fun and colorful streets around Place St-Géry and Ste. Catherine, where you'll find plenty of good dinner options. With more time or a special interest, head out to the museums at the Park of the Cinquantenaire, visit the kitschy former fairgrounds at the giant Atomium, or venture to the adjacent town of Tervuren to tour the Royal Museum of the Belgian Congo and relax in a big park.

Brussels Overview

Central Brussels is surrounded by a ring of roads (which replaced the old city wall) called the Pentagon. (Romantics think it looks more like a heart.) All hotels and nearly all the sights I mention are within this ring. The epicenter holds the main square (the Grand Place), the TI, and Central Station (all within three blocks of one another).

What isn't so apparent from maps is that Brussels is a city divided by altitude. A ridgeline that runs north-south splits the town into the Upper Town (east half, elevation 200 feet) and Lower Town (west, at sea level), with Central Station in between. The Upper Town, traditionally the home of nobility and the rich, has big marble palaces, broad boulevards, and the major museums.

The Lower Town, with the Grand Place (grahn plahs; in Dutch: Grote Markt, HHHROH-teh markt), narrow streets, old buildings, modern shops, colorful eateries, and the famous *Manneken-Pis* peeing-boy statue, has more character. Running along the western edge of the touristic center is a bustling boulevard (Boulevard Anspach/Anspachlaan) that runs over the city's forgotten river. Just beyond that—past a block or two of high-rise ugliness—is the lively market square called Place St-Géry/Sint-Goriksplein, and a charming village-within-a-city huddled around the old fish market: the Ste. Catherine neighborhood,

Brussels Overview

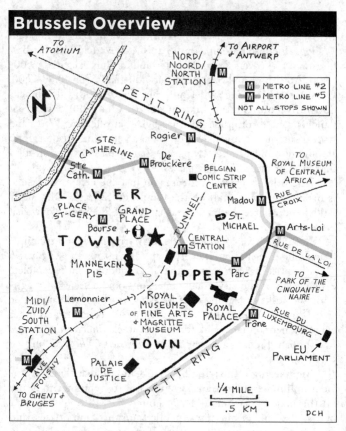

Brussels Overview

TO ATOMIUM

TO AIRPORT & ANTWERP

NORD/ NOORD/ NORTH STATION

Ⓜ METRO LINE #2
ⓂⓂ METRO LINE #5
NOT ALL STOPS SHOWN

PETIT RING

Rogier Ⓜ

STE. CATHERINE

De Brouckère Ⓜ

BELGIAN COMIC STRIP CENTER

Ste. Cath. Ⓜ

L O W E R

PLACE ST-GERY

Bourse Ⓜ

GRAND PLACE

T O W N

Madou Ⓜ

ST. MICHAEL

CENTRAL STATION Ⓜ

Arts-Loi Ⓜ

RUE CROIX

TO ROYAL MUSEUM OF CENTRAL AFRICA

RUE DE LA LOI

TUNNEL

MANNEKEN-PIS

UPPER

Parc Ⓜ

TO PARK OF THE CINQUANTE-NAIRE

MIDI/ ZUID/ SOUTH STATION

Lemonnier Ⓜ

ROYAL MUSEUMS OF FINE ARTS & MAGRITTE MUSEUM

ROYAL PALACE

Trône Ⓜ

RUE DU LUXEMBOURG

EU PARLIAMENT

T O W N

AVE. FONSNY Ⓜ

PALAIS DE JUSTICE

PETIT RING

TO GHENT & BRUGES

¼ MILE

.5 KM

DCH

home to several recommended hotels and restaurants.

Outside the pentagon-shaped center, sprawling suburbs and vast green zones contain more tourist attractions. To the east are the European Parliament and, beyond that, the Park of the Cinquantenaire (Royal Museum of the Army and Military History, Autoworld, and a lesser art museum). And far to the north is the 1958 World's Fair site, with the Atomium and Mini-Europe.

Because the city is officially bilingual, most of Brussels' street signs and maps are in both French and Dutch; I've tried to follow suit in this text, but due to space constraints, on my maps I've generally only given the French name. Because the languages are so different (French is a Romance language, Dutch is Germanic), many places have two names that barely resemble each other (for example, Marché-aux-Herbes/Grasmarkt, or Place Royale/ Koningsplein). This can make navigating the city confusing. Use one of the good local maps (such as the TI's €0.50 map), which list both languages, so you'll know both street names to look for.

Tourist Information

Brussels has two competing TIs (indicative of Belgium's latent Walloon-Flemish tension). The TI at Rue du Marché-aux-Herbes/ Grasmarkt 63 covers **Brussels and Flanders** (July-Aug daily 9:00-18:00; April-June and Sept Mon-Sat 9:00-18:00, Sun 10:00-17:00; Oct-March Mon-Sat 9:00-17:00, Sun 10:00-16:00; three blocks downhill from Central Station, tel. 02-504-0390, www.visit flanders.com, fun Europe store nearby). They offer free Wi-Fi and several Internet terminals where you can get online free for up to 15 minutes (and print a few pages—handy for checking in for a flight and printing boarding passes).

The other TI, which focuses on just the **city of Brussels,** is inside the Town Hall on the Grand Place (April-Nov daily 9:00-18:00, shorter hours off-season; tel. 02-513-8940, www.visit brussels.be).

Both TIs have countless fliers. Day-trippers should pick up a free public transit map. The city map costs €0.50. The €3 *Brussels Guide* booklet is an overview of the city, including a more complete explanation of the city's many museums, and a series of neighborhood walks (including ones focusing on Art Nouveau, comic strips, and shopping). For current listings of concerts and other entertainment options, look for the free weekly magazines *Agenda* (in English, French, and Dutch) and *Brussels Unlimited* (only in English).

Sightseeing Deals: The **Brussels Card,** sold at the TIs, provides unlimited public transportation and free entrance to nearly all the major museums (€24/24 hours, €34/48 hours, €40/72 hours, also sold at museums, public transportation offices, and some hotels, www.brusselscard.be). If you're in town for less than a day, it's unlikely this pass will pay for itself; but with more time here, busy sightseers will get their money's worth. The TIs also offer a deal called **Must of Brussels**—you pay €19 for 10 vouchers that you can mix and match for discounted entries into top sights. Though complicated to figure out, it could save you a few euros (www.mustofbrussels.com).

Alternative Tourist Information: The excellent, welcoming **USE-IT** information office, which is geared toward youthful backpackers, offers free Internet access and Wi-Fi, free coffee and tea, and in-the-know advice about Brussels and other Belgian destinations, including Bruges, Antwerp, and Ghent (Mon-Sat 10:00-13:00 & 14:00-18:00, closed Sun, Quai à la Houille/ Steenkoolkaai 9B, Metro: Ste. Catherine/Sint-Katelijne, www .use-it.be). They also publish free user-friendly maps of Brussels and several other Belgian cities; all of their maps are packed with homegrown insight.

Arrival in Brussels
By Train
Brussels has three stations: Centraal/Central, Nord/Noord/ North, and Midi/Zuid/South. Although none is officially the "main" train station, Central Station (a short walk from the Grand Place) is by far the easiest for arriving sightseers, whereas Midi/ Zuid/South Station is the only one served by high-speed trains (with the fastest connections to Paris, London, Amsterdam, and Germany). If you're arriving on one of these fast trains, you'll enter the city through Midi/Zuid/South Station; all other trains stop at all three stations. No matter how you arrive, your goal is eventually to reach Central Station (pay close attention and ask your conductor for help to ensure you get off at the right stop).

Nord/Noord/North Station
Any train that goes through North Station (surrounded by a seedy red light district, far from any significant sightseeing) will also stop at the other two. Don't bother getting off at North Station— disembark at Central Station instead.

Midi/Zuid/South Station
About a mile and a half southwest of the city center, this station's various names mystify tourists (especially since *midi* is French for "middle," not "south"). But as Brussels' lone station for speedy, long-distance trains, it's considered the city's primary international hub. Fortunately, the station is a lot more user-friendly than its name.

South Station serves the fastest high-speed connections: Eurostar (to/from London); Thalys (to/from Amsterdam, Paris, Köln in Germany, and a few other destinations—such as Marseille, France, in the summer and the French Alps in the winter); TGV (to/from Paris' Charles de Gaulle Airport—but not central Paris, as Thalys has a monopoly there, and then on to destinations in southern France); and ICE (to/from Frankfurt). These special fast trains stop only at South Station, not at the other two Brussels stations. All other trains—including slower trains to many of these same destinations, and trains to anywhere in Belgium—stop at all three stations. Unless your train only stops here, get off at Central Station instead (explained later).

South Station's tracks are connected by a long, gloomy, gray-steel concourse with ample computer screens showing upcoming trains. High-speed trains use tracks 1-6 (1-2 for Eurostar and 3-6 for the others). The station has plenty of luggage lockers (€3-4, between tracks 6 and 7), as well as three separate Travel Centre ticket offices (for domestic, international, and international/immediate departures). The area around South Station is a rough-and-tumble immigrant neighborhood (marked by its towering Ferris wheel).

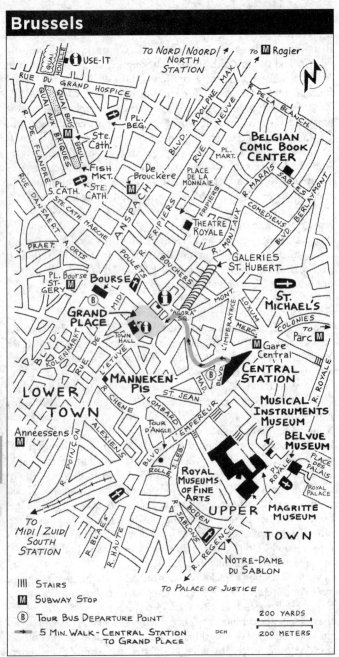

Brussels

BRUSSELS ORIENTATION

USE-IT

TO NORD/NOORD/ NORTH STATION

TO Rogier

RUE DU GRAND HOSPICE

PL. BEG.

Ste. Cath.

Fish Mkt.

Ste. CATH.

PL. S. CATH.

De Brouckère

PLACE DE LA MONNAIE

PL. MART.

BELGIAN COMIC BOOK CENTER

THEATRE ROYALE

GALERIES St. HUBERT

PL. ST-GERY

PL. Bourse

Bourse

GRAND PLACE

"AGORA" SQ.

St. MICHAEL'S

Gare Central

CENTRAL STATION

TO Parc

TOWN HALL

MANNEKEN-PIS

LOWER TOWN

Anneessens

MUSICAL INSTRUMENTS MUSEUM

BELVUE MUSEUM

PLACE DES PALAIS

TOUR D'ANGLE

St. JEAN

Royal MUSEUMS of FINE ARTS

UPPER TOWN

MAGRITTE MUSEUM

ROYAL PALACE

PL. ROYALE

TO MIDI/ZUID/ SOUTH STATION

NOTRE-DAME DU SABLON

TO PALACE OF JUSTICE

IIII STAIRS

M SUBWAY STOP

B TOUR BUS DEPARTURE POINT

→ 5 MIN. WALK - CENTRAL STATION TO GRAND PLACE

DCH

200 YARDS

200 METERS

Getting from Midi/Zuid/South Station to Central Station: If you must disembark at South Station, your first step on arrival will be to make your way to Central Station. It's fast and easy by train, but also possible by taxi.

Trains zip under the city, connecting all three stations every few minutes or so. The €2 fare between the stations is covered by any train ticket into or out of Brussels (or an activated railpass). Scan the computer departure screens for trains leaving in the next few minutes. While these boards usually don't list Central Station as a destination, trains headed for any of the following places will stop there: the airport, Alost/Aalst, Antwerpen, Leuven, Liège, Namur, and many others. If you see a train going to any of these places in the next few minutes, just head to that track. (But note that trains headed in the opposite direction—including those to Ghent and Bruges—do *not* stop at Central Station.)

Alternatively, you can take a **taxi** from South Station into the city center. It should cost you no more than €10; however, cabbies from this station are notorious for taking a roundabout route to overcharge arriving tourists. If you do opt for a taxi, insist on the meter, follow the route on a map, and if the total fare seems too high, enlist the help of your hotel receptionist.

Centraal/Central Station

This station, nearest to the sights and my recommended hotels, has handy services: a small grocery store, fast food, waiting rooms, and luggage lockers (€3-4, between tracks 3 and 4). Walking from Central Station to the Grand Place takes about five minutes: Exit the station from the top floor (to the left of the ticket windows), where you'll see Le Meridien Hôtel across the square. Pass through the arch of Le Meridien Hôtel, turn right, and walk one block downhill on l'Infante Isabelle street to a small square with a fountain (officially "Herb Market"—Rue du Marché-aux-Herbes/Grasmarkt—but nicknamed "Agora"). For the Grand Place, turn left at the far end of the little square. Or, to head directly to one of the TIs, exit the small square at the far end and continue straight for one block, then look left.

Competitive hop-on, hop-off tourist buses depart from Central Station (you may meet ticket hustlers as you leave). You could hop on one of these buses upon arrival to orient yourself from the top deck (see "Tours in Brussels," later).

By Plane

Brussels is served by two airports. Most flights use the primary Brussels Airport, a.k.a. Zaventem; no-frills carriers use the Brussels South Charleroi Airport. For details on both, see "Brussels Connections" on page 525.

Helpful Hints

Theft Alert: Though the tourist zone—the area within the pentagon-shaped ring road—is basically safe at any hour of day or night, muggings do occur in some rough-and-tumble areas farther afield. (Near the Midi/Zuid/South Station is a mostly Muslim immigrant neighborhood; near the North Station is a red-light district. Locals joke that as you walk from one end of town to the other, you go from seeing women entirely covered to women entirely uncovered.)

Sightseeing Schedules: Brussels' most important museums are closed on Monday. Of course, the city's single best sight—the Grand Place—is always open. You can also enjoy a bus tour any day of the week, or visit the more far-flung sights (which *are* open on Monday), such as the Atomium/Mini-Europe and the European Parliament. Most importantly, this is a city to browse and wander.

Internet Access: The **USE-IT** information office (listed earlier) has four free Internet terminals and free Wi-Fi; the **Brussels and Flanders TI** on Rue du Marché-aux-Herbes/ Grasmarkt has one Internet terminal and offers 15 minutes free (plus unlimited free Wi-Fi). There's also an **Internet café** in a dreary urban area between the Grand Place and Ste. Catherine (€1.50/hour, also cheap calls and printing, calling cabins downstairs, computer terminals upstairs, daily 9:30-23:15, 18 Rue Marché aux Poulets/Kiekenmarkt).

Laundry: Coin-op launderettes aren't too hard to find. There's one near the Grand Place at Rue du Midi/Zuidstraat 65 (daily 7:00-21:00, change machine) and another in Ste. Catherine, at Rue Flandres/Vlaamsesteenweg 51 (daily 7:00-22:00, no change machine).

Travel Bookstore: Anticyclone des Açores has a wide selection of maps and travel books, including many in English (Mon-Sat 11:00-18:00, closed Sun, Rue Fossé aux Loups/Wolvengracht 34, tel. 02-217-5246, www.anticyclonedesacores.be).

Updates to This Book: Check www.ricksteves.com/update for any significant changes that have occurred since this book was printed.

Getting Around Brussels

Most of central Brussels' sights can be reached on foot. But public transport is handy for connecting the train stations, climbing to the Upper Town (bus #95 from Rue du Lombard near the Grand Place), or visiting sights outside the central core. To reach these outlying sights, such as the European Parliament, take the Métro or jump on a hop-on, hop-off tour bus from Central Station (described under "Tours in Brussels," next page; check tour bus route map to make sure it covers the sights you want to see).

By Métro, Bus, Tram, and Train: A single €2 ticket is good for one hour on all public transportation—Métro, buses, trams, and even trains shuttling between Brussels' three train stations. Validate your ticket when you enter, feeding it into one of the breadbox-size orange machines. Notice the time when you first stamp it (you have an hour). Transit info: tel. 02-515-2000, www.mivb.be.

A five-ride card costs €7.50, and a 10-ride card is €13. An all-day pass is €6—the same price as three single tickets—and on Sat-Sun and holidays, this pass covers two people. (Skip the prepaid card for public transit that gives a small discount but is practical only for locals.)

Buy individual tickets at newsstands, in Métro stations (vending machines accept credit cards or coins), or (for €0.50 extra) from the bus driver. Get multiride cards and passes from the Brussels and Flanders TI or at Métro stations. The excellent, free *Métro Tram Bus Plan* is available at either TI or any Métro station.

Like the streets, Brussels' transit stops are labeled in both French and Dutch (unless the spelling is the same in both languages); I've followed suit in this book.

Brussels' Métro has four lines: Line 1 runs west-east (from Gare de l'Ouest/Weststation to Stockel/Stokkel); the circular line 2 starts and ends at Simonis; line 5 runs west-east from Erasme/Erasmus to Herrmann-Debroux; and line 6 starts at Roi Baudouin/Koning Boudewijn in the northwest, then ties into the circular line at Simonis. A series of tram lines run north-south through the city center, connecting the Métro lines and the North, Central, and Midi/Zuid/South train stations; two of these are considered part of the Métro (lines 3 and 4). Buses go where the Métro and trams don't (buses marked *Noctis* travel at night, after other transit stops running).

Near the Grand Place are two transportation hubs: Central Station and the Bourse. If you're staying at a hotel northwest of the Grand Place, you've got good access to the Métro system via the Ste. Catherine/Sint-Katelijne and De Brouckère stops.

By Taxi: Cabbies charge a €2.40 drop fee, as well as €1.70 per additional kilometer. After 22:00, they hit you with a €2 surcharge. You'll pay about €10 to ride from the center to the European Parliament. Convenient taxi stands are at the Bourse (near the Grand Place), at the "Agora" square near the Grand Place (Rue du Marché-aux-Herbes/Grasmarkt), and at Place du Grand Sablon (in the Upper Town). To call a cab, try **Taxi Bleu** (tel. 02-268-0000) or **Autolux** (tel. 02-512-3123).

By Bike: The city of Brussels subsidizes a network of cheap bikes designed to be borrowed for short rides within the city. The program, called **Villo**, has rental stations around town. After you register at the automated kiosk with your credit card (€1.60/day, €7.50/week), you can borrow bikes at will for short durations, then drop them off at any other station (free for up to 30 minutes, €0.50/30-60 minutes, €1/1-1.5 hours, €2/1.5-2 hours, www.villo .be). Stations with an automated kiosk also show you which nearby stations have bikes available, and how many. Bike stands at higher altitudes (in the Upper Town) are often empty, whereas they're full—surprise, surprise—at lower altitudes (in the Lower Town).

Tours in Brussels

Hop-On, Hop-Off Bus Tours—Various companies offer nearly identical introductory city tours: **City Tours** (tel. 02-513-7744, www.brussels-city-tours.com), **CitySightseeing/Open Tours** (tel. 02-466-1111, www.citysightseeingbrussel.be), and **Golden Tours** (mobile 0486-053-981, www.goldentours.be). The 1.5-hour loop and recorded narration give you a once-over-lightly of the city from the top deck (open on sunny days) of a double-decker bus. You can hop on and off for 24 hours with one ticket, but schedules are sparse (figure €20-22 for each company, about 2/hour, times listed on each flier; all companies run roughly April-Oct daily 10:00-16:00, Sat until 17:00; Nov-March daily 10:00-15:00, Sat until 16:00). Except for the trip out to the European Parliament and Cinquantenaire Park (which hosts the military and auto museums), I'd just stay on to enjoy the views and the minimal commentary. The fiercely competitive companies often have hustlers at Central Station trying to get you on board (offering "student" discounts to customers of all ages). The handiest starting points are Central Station and the Bourse.

Bus Tours—City Tours also offers a typical three-hour guided (in up to five languages) bus tour, providing you an easy way to get the grand perspective on Brussels. You start with a walk around the Grand Place, then jump on a tour bus (€26, year-round daily at 10:00, they'll pick you up at your hotel or depart from their office a block off Grand Place at Rue du Marché-aux-Herbes/Grasmarkt 82; you can buy tickets there, at TI, or in your hotel; tel. 02-513-7744, www.brussels-city-tours.com). You'll get off the bus at the Atomium for a quick photo stop.

Local Guides—You can hire a private guide through **Visit Brussels** (€117/3 hours, €216/full day, tel. 02-548-0448, guides@visit brussles.be; I enjoyed the guiding of Didier Rochette). **Claude and Dominique Janssens** are a father-and-son team who lead tours both in Brussels and to other Belgian cities, including

Bruges, Ghent, and Antwerp (€120/3 hours, €240/full day plus €25 for lunch, Claude's mobile 0485-025-423, Dominique's mobile 0486-451-155, www.discover-b.be, claude@discover-b .be). **Christian Scharlé** and **Daniëlle Janssens,** who are based in Bruges, offer a three-hour tour of Brussels for €120 (for contact info, see "Local Guide" on page 370).

SIGHTS IN BRUSSELS

The Grand Place may be Brussels' top sight, but the city offers a variety of museums, big and small, to fill your time here. I've divided the sights between the Lower Town, the Upper Town, and the outskirts.

Lower Town

On the Grand Place

Brussels' Grand Place—as well as some of the sights fronting it, including the Town Hall, City Museum, and chocolate shops—are described in more detail in the ☉ Grand Place Walk chapter.

▲▲▲**Grand Place**—Brussels' main square, aptly called the Grand Place (grahn plahs; in Dutch: Grote Markt, HHHROH-teh markt), is the heart of the old town and Brussels' greatest sight. Any time of day, it's worth swinging by to see what's going on. Concerts, flower markets, sound-and-light shows, endless people-watching—it entertains (as do the streets around it). The museums on the square are well-advertised but dull.

Town Hall (Hôtel de Ville)—With the Grand Place's tallest spire, this is the square's centerpiece, but its interior is no big deal. Admission is only possible with a 45-minute English tour, which also covers city history and the building's tapestries and architecture. Only 25 people are allowed per tour; assure a spot by buying tickets from the guide exactly 40 minutes before the tour starts (in the courtyard behind the spire.

Cost and Hours: €3, Tue-Wed at 15:15, Sun at 10:45 and 12:15 except no Sun tours Oct-March.

▲**City Museum (Musée de la Ville de Bruxelles)**—Inside the King's House (Maison du Roi) building, across the Grand Place from the Town Hall, is the one museum on the square that's

Grand Place

actually worth visiting. The museum's top floor has a roomful of goofy costumes the *Manneken* statue has pissed through (and an engrossing video of tourists' reactions to the statue), the middle floor features maps and models of old Brussels, and the bottom floor has some old artwork.

Cost and Hours: €4, borrow English descriptions in each room, Tue-Sun 10:00-17:00, Thu until 20:00, closed Mon, Grand Place, tel. 02-279-4350. For local history, the best choice is not this museum, but the BELvue Museum (see page 465).

▲**Chocolate Shops on the Grand Place**—For many, the best thing about the Grand Place is the chocolate sold at its venerable chocolate shops: Godiva, Neuhaus, Galler, and Leonidas (shops generally open Mon-Sat 9:00-22:00, Sun 10:00-22:00). Each has inviting displays and sells mixes of 100 grams (your choice of 8 pieces) or individual pieces for about €1. It takes a lot of sampling to judge. For more info, see the "choco-crawl" described in the Grand Place Walk chapter.

Brussels at a Glance

▲▲▲**Grand Place** Main square and spirited heart of the Lower Town, surrounded by mediocre museums and delectable chocolate shops. **Hours:** Always open. See page 454.

▲▲▲**Royal Museums of Fine Arts of Belgium** Museums displaying ancient art (14th-18th centuries) and turn-of-the-century art (19th-20th centuries). **Hours:** Tue-Sun 10:00-17:00, closed Mon. See page 463.

▲▲**Manneken-Pis** World-famous statue of a leaky little boy. **Hours:** Always peeing. See page 458.

▲▲**Magritte Museum** Biographical collection of works by the prominent Belgian Surrealist painter René Magritte. **Hours:** Tue-Sun 10:00-17:00, Wed until 20:00, closed Mon. See page 464.

▲▲**BELvue Museum** Interesting Belgian history museum with a focus on the popular royal family. **Hours:** Tue-Fri 10:00-17:00, Sat-Sun 10:00-18:00, closed Mon. See page 465.

▲**City Museum** Costumes worn by the *Manneken-Pis* statue and models of Brussels' history. **Hours:** Tue-Sun 10:00-17:00, Thu until 20:00, closed Mon. See page 454.

▲**Chocolate on Grand Place** Choco-crawl through Godiva, Neuhaus, Galler, and Leonidas. **Hours:** Generally Mon-Sat 9:00-22:00, Sun 10:00-22:00. See page 455.

▲**Costume and Lace Museum** World-famous Brussels lace, as well as outfits, embroidery, and accessories from the 17th-20th centuries. **Hours:** Thu-Tue 10:00-17:00, closed Wed. See page 458.

▲**St. Michael's Cathedral** White-stone Gothic church where Belgian royals are married and buried. **Hours:** Mon-Fri 7:00-18:00, Sat-Sun 8:30-18:00. See page 459.

▲**Belgian Comic Strip Center** Homage to hometown heroes including the Smurfs, Tintin, and Lucky Luke. **Hours:** Tue-Sun 10:00-18:00, closed Mon. See page 460.

▲**Musical Instruments Museum** Exhibits with more than 1,500 instruments, complete with audio. **Hours:** Tue-Fri 9:30-16:45,

Sat-Sun 10:00-16:45, closed Mon. See page 464.

▲**European Parliament** Soaring home of Europe's governing body. **Hours:** Parlamentarium exhibit open Mon 13:00-18:00, Tue-Wed 9:00-20:00, Thu-Fri 9:00-18:00, Sat-Sun 10:00-17:00. See page 467.

▲**Royal Army and Military History Museum** Vast collection of weaponry and uniforms. **Hours:** Tue-Sun 9:00-16:45, closed Mon. See page 471.

▲**Autoworld** Hundreds of historic vehicles, including Mr. Benz's 1886 motorized tricycle. **Hours:** Daily April-Sept 10:00-18:00, Oct-March 10:00-17:00. See page 472.

▲**Royal Museum of Central Africa** Excellent but far-flung exhibit about the former Belgian Congo, featuring ethnology, artifacts, and wildlife. **Hours:** Tue-Fri 10:00-17:00, Sat-Sun 10:00-18:00, closed Mon. See page 474.

Town Hall Focal point of the Grand Place, with arresting spire but boring interior. **Hours:** Tours depart Tue-Wed at 15:15, Sun at 10:45 and 12:15, no Sun tours Oct-March. See page 454.

Ste. Catherine Neighborhood and Place St-Géry Pleasant areas with fun eateries west of the Grand Place. **Hours:** Always buzzing. See pages 458-459.

Royal Belgian Institute of Natural Sciences Europe's largest dinosaur gallery. **Hours:** Tue-Fri 9:30-17:00, Sat-Sun 10:00-18:00, closed Mon. See page 470.

Cinquantenaire Museum Eclectic but unexciting art and archaeology museum. **Hours:** Tue-Fri 9:30-17:00, Sat-Sun 10:00-17:00, closed Mon. See page 472.

Atomium Giant homage to the atomic age with fun exhibit and panorama deck. **Hours:** Exterior always viewable; interior open daily 10:00-18:00, later in summer. See page 473.

Mini-Europe Models of 350 famous European landmarks. **Hours:** Mid-March-Sept daily 9:30-18:00, July-Aug until 20:00; Oct-Dec 10:00-18:00, closed Jan-mid-March. See page 473.

Brewery Museum—This little bar-like place has one room of old brewing paraphernalia and one room of new, plus a beer video in English. It's pretty lame...but a good excuse for a beer.

Cost and Hours: €5 includes an unnamed local beer, daily 10:00-17:00 except Dec-March Sat-Sun opens at 12:00, Grand Place 10, tel. 02-511-4987, www.beerparadise.be.

Museum of Cocoa and Chocolate—This touristy exhibit, just off the Grand Place to the right of Town Hall, is a delightful concept and tries hard, but it's overpriced at €5.50 for three floors of meager displays, a ho-hum video, a look at a "chocolate master" at work (live demos 2/hour), and a choco-sample.

Cost and Hours: Tue-Sun 10:00-16:30, closed Mon, Rue de la Tête d'Or 9, tel. 02-514-2048, www.mucc.be.

Near the Grand Place

▲▲**Manneken-Pis**—Brussels is a great city with a cheesy mascot: a statue of a little boy urinating (apparently symbolizing the city's irreverence and love of the good life). Read up on his story at any postcard stand. He's three short blocks off the Grand Place: For exact directions, take my Grand Place Walk; look for small, white *Manneken-Pis* signs; or just ask a local, *"Où est le Manneken-Pis?"* (oo ay luh man-ay-kehn peese). The little squirt may be wearing some clever outfit, as costumes are sent to Brussels from around the world. Cases full of these are on display in the City Museum (described earlier).

▲**Costume and Lace Museum**—This fine little museum showcases historic costumes and fashion as well as the art of lace. You'll enjoy exquisite costumes, feathery fans, and baby baptismal gowns. As the lace is fragile, much of it is stored in drawers—be sure to pull them out. At the entry, borrow the necessary English booklet that describes each exhibit.

Cost and Hours: €4, Thu-Tue 10:00-17:00, closed Wed, Rue de la Violette 12, a block off the Grand Place, tel. 02-213-4450.

West of the Grand Place

These two fun-to-explore neighborhoods, just across the busy Boulevard Anspach from the Bourse, offer some of Brussels' most appealing restaurants (far less touristy than those near the Grand Place). Ste. Catherine is also a fine place to sleep. If you're looking for a bustling nighttime neighborhood full of inviting eateries and bars, you'll enjoy strolling these two areas and the five-minute walk between them. For details, see page 524.

Ste. Catherine and the Old Fish Market (Vieux Marché aux Poissons/Vismet)—Two blocks northwest of the Bourse is the ragtag Church of Ste. Catherine, which marks an inviting "village in the city" area with great eating options. The church itself is falling apart—during its construction, the architect got the commission for the Place of Justice in the Upper Town, and rushed to complete this church so he could begin the more lucrative new job as quickly as possible. In front of the church stretches the long, skinny former fish market, lined with a range of upscale fish restaurants. Alongside the church is Place Ste. Catherine/Sint-Katelijneplein, with more restaurants, bars, and the city's best cheap-and-fast lunch options (including a charming little cheese shop and a pair of seafood bars).

Place St-Géry/Sint-Goriksplein—This square was actually once an island, and the market hall in the middle of the square evokes a time when goods—which were offloaded a few blocks away, at the old fish market (see above)—were brought here for sale. Today the hall houses a café and special exhibits. On Sunday mornings, the surrounding square is filled with a comics market. Across from the southwest corner of the hall, at #23 (next to the *Au Lion d'Or* information board), duck through the little gateway to find a relaxing courtyard. You might see businesspeople dozing on their lunch break here in this oasis in the heart of the city. At the far end of the courtyard you'll see a small stretch of the river that used to be Brussels' trading lifeline, but was long ago covered over and forgotten.

North of Central Station

For locations, see the map on page 448.

▲**St. Michael's Cathedral**—One of Europe's classic Gothic churches, built between roughly 1200 and 1500, Brussels' cathe-

dral is made from white stone and topped by twin towers. For nearly 1,000 years, it's been the most important church in this largely Catholic country. (Whereas the Netherlands went in a Protestant direction in the 1500s, Belgium remains 80 percent Catholic—although only about 20 percent attend Mass.)

Cost and Hours: Free, but small fees to visit the underwhelming crypt and treasury, Mon-Fri 7:00-18:00, Sat-Sun 8:30-18:00.

Visiting the Cathedral: The white-themed nave is bare but impressive, with a few nice stained-glass windows and a marvelous carved pulpit of Adam and Eve supporting the preacher. On top, St. Michael stabs Satan in serpent form.

This church is where royal weddings and funerals take place. Photographs (to the right of the entrance) show the funeral of the popular King Baudouin, who died in 1993. He was succeeded by his younger brother, Albert II (whose face is on Belgium's euro

Tintin 101

The Belgian comic character Tintin is beloved to several generations of Europeans who have grown up reading of his adventures. Tintin is still relatively unknown in the United States, despite Steven Spielberg's 2011 film *The Adventures of Tintin*, which won the Golden Globe for best animated feature.

In 1929, a French-speaking Brussels comics artist named Georges Rémi (1907-1983) created a dedicated young reporter with a shock of blond hair who's constantly getting into and out of misadventures. The artist reversed his initials to create the pseudonym Hergé (the French pronunciation for "R. G."). A precise artist, Hergé used a simple, uncluttered style called *ligne claire* ("clear line").

Combining fantasy, mystery, and sci-fi, with a dash of humor, the Tintin stories quickly found an appreciative audience. *The Adventures of Tintin* spanned 47 years and 24 books (selling some 200 million copies—and counting—in 50 languages). Tintin's popularity continues even today, as nostalgic parents buy the comics they grew up on for their own kids.

Tintin (pronounced a nasal "tan-tan" in French) is the smart, upbeat, inquisitive, noble, brave-but-not-foolhardy young man whose adventures propel the plot. His newspaper sends him on

coins). Albert will be succeeded by his son, Prince Philippe. Traditionally, the ruler was always a male, but in 1992 the constitution was changed to allow the oldest child of either gender—boy or girl—to take the throne. In 1999, Prince Philippe and his bride, Mathilde—after a civil ceremony at the Town Hall—paraded up here for a two-hour Catholic ceremony with all the trimmings. Their daughter Elisabeth, born in 2001, is in line to become Belgium's queen.

Before leaving, pause on the outer porch to enjoy the great view of the Town Hall spire with its gold statue of St. Michael.

▲**Belgian Comic Strip Center (Centre Belge de la Bande Dessinée)**—Belgians are as proud of their comics as they are of their beer, lace, and chocolates. Something about the comic medium resonates with the wry and artistic-yet-unpretentious Belgian sensibility. Belgium has produced some of the world's most popular comic characters, including the Smurfs, Tintin, and Lucky Luke. You'll find these, and many less famous local comics, at the Comic Strip Center.

assignments all over the world. **Snowy** (Milou in French), Tintin's loyal fox terrier, is his constant canine companion—and often saves the day. The grizzled, grouchy, heavy-drinking **Captain Haddock** is as cynical as Tintin is optimistic, with a penchant for colorful curses ("Blistering barnacles!"). **Professor Calculus** (a.k.a. Professeur Tournesol) is as brilliant as he is absentminded and hard of hearing, and comic relief is provided by the bumbling, nearly identical detectives called **Thomson and Thompson** (Dupont et Dupond).

Throughout his swashbuckling adventures, Tintin travels far and wide to many exotic destinations. Hergé has been acclaimed for his meticulous research—he studied up on the actual places he portrayed, and tried to avoid basing his stories on assumptions or stereotypes (though by today's standards, some of the comics still betray an ugly Eurocentrism—one of the earliest, *Tintin in the Congo*, Hergé himself later acknowledged was regretfully racist).

And though the supporting characters are dynamic and colorful, Tintin himself has a rather bland personality. His expressions are usually indistinct (Hergé wanted the young reader to project his or her own emotions onto Tintin's blank-canvas face). While presumably a teenager, Tintin's age is unclear—at times we imagine him to be a young boy, while others he's seen drinking a beer, piloting a plane, or living in his own apartment (we never meet his family, if he has one). All of this is intentional: Hergé's style subconsciously encourages each reader to put him- or herself in Tintin's everyman shoes.

Even if you don't have time or interest to visit the museum's collection, pop in to the lobby to see the groundbreaking Art Nouveau building (a former department store designed in 1903 by Belgian architect Victor Horta), browse through comics in the bookshop, and snap a photo with a three-foot-tall Smurf. That's enough for many people. Kids might find the museum,

like, totally boring, but those who appreciate art in general will enjoy this sometimes humorous, sometimes probing, often beautiful medium. The displays are mostly in French and Dutch, but there is some English. The free, essential English guidebooklet describes the comics-making process (comparing it to the filmmaking process) and has short bios of famous cartoonists.

462 Rick Steves' Amsterdam, Bruges & Brussels

Shopping in Brussels

The obvious temptations—available absolutely everywhere—are **chocolate** and **lace**. (For tips on specific shops for each one, see the Grand Place Walk chapter.) Other popular Brussels souvenirs include EU gear (flags, T-shirts, etc., with the gold circle of stars on a blue background) and miniature reproductions of the *Manneken-Pis*.

To get beyond the touristy city center, consider browsing along some of the following streets:

Rue Neuve/Nieuwstraat, a few blocks north of the Grand Place, is where you'll find big department stores and other international shops. The giant **City2** complex on this street is the downtown's primary modern shopping mall.

Antoine Dansaert street, directly across the boulevard from the Bourse, is lined with boutiques and galleries.

The somewhat seedy **Marolles neighborhood** is well-known for its secondhand shops. Rue Blaes/Blaesstraat and Rue Haute/Hoogstraat, which run southwest from near the old Tour d'Angle (described in the Upper Town Walk chapter) to the Midi/Zuid/South Train Station, are lined with several characteristic stores. There's a lively flea market each morning (7:00-14:00, best on weekends) on Place du Jeu de Balle/Vossenplein, just off of Rue Blaes/Blaesstraat.

Cost and Hours: €8, Tue-Sun 10:00-18:00, closed Mon, 10-minute walk from the Grand Place to Rue des Sables 20, tel. 02-219-1980, www.comicscenter.net.

Getting There: From Central Station, walk north along the big boulevard, then turn left down the stairs at the giant comic character.

Visiting the Comic Strip Center: The collection changes often, but no matter what's on you'll see how comics are made and watch early animated films. The heart of the collection is the golden age of comics in the 1950s and 1960s. You'll likely see a sprawling exhibit on Tintin, the intrepid young reporter with the button eyes and wavy shock of hair, launched in 1929 by Hergé and much loved by older Europeans (see sidebar). Brussels' own Peyo (a.k.a. Pierre Culliford, 1928-1992) invented the Smurfs—the little blue forest creatures that stand "three apples high." First popular across much Europe, especially in Belgium (where they're known as Les Schtroumpfs), the Smurfs became well-known to a generation of Americans after they starred in Hanna-Barbera's 1980s televised cartoons. The cowboy Lucky Luke (by Morris, a.k.a. Maurice De Bevere, 1923-2001) exemplifies Belgians' fascination for exotic locales, especially America's Wild West.

The top floor's temporary exhibits are often dedicated to

BRUSSELS SIGHTS

"serious" comics, where more adult themes and high-quality drawing aspire to turn kids' stuff into that "Ninth Art." These works can be grimly realistic, openly erotic or graphic, or darker in tone, often featuring flawed antiheroes. The museum's bookstore is nearly as interesting, giving you the chance to page through reproductions of classic comics.

Nearby: The related **Marc Sleen Museum,** across the street, is dedicated to one Belgian cartoonist in particular. Sleen's big-nosed, caricatured drawings are recognizable even to many Americans, and is oh-so-typically Belgian. His *Adventures of Nero and Co.,* which he churned out in two strips a day for a staggering 55 years, holds the record for the longest-running comic by a single artist. Still, the collection is worth a visit only to his fans (€1 extra with Comic Strip Center entry, or €2.50 alone; Tue-Sun 11:00-18:00, closed Mon; tel. 02-219-1980, www.marc-sleen.be).

Upper Town

Brussels' grandiose Upper Town, with its huge palace, is described in the ✪ Upper Town Walk chapter. Along that walk, you'll pass the following sights (for locations, see map on page 448).

▲▲▲**Royal Museums of Fine Arts of Belgium (Musées Royaux des Beaux-Arts de Belgique)**—This sprawling complex is worth visiting for its twin museums that show off the country's best all-around art collection (as well as

the Magritte Museum—described next—which is in the same complex). The **Museum of Ancient Art** and the new **Fin de Siècle Museum** are covered by the same ticket. The Museum of Ancient Art—featuring Flemish and Belgian art of the 14th-18th centuries—is packed with a dazzling collection of masterpieces by Van der Weyden, Bruegel, Bosch, and Rubens. The Fin de Siècle Museum gives visitors a contextual look at art of the late 19th and early 20th centuries, including an extensive Art Nouveau collection.

Cost and Hours: €9 for Ancient Art and Fin de Siècle museums, €13 combo-ticket adds Magritte Museum, free first Wed of month after 13:00; Ancient Art audioguide-€4, Fin de Siècle videoguide-€5, tour booklet-€2.50; open Tue-Sun 10:00-17:00, closed Mon, last entry 30 minutes before closing; pricey cafeteria with salad bar, Rue de la Régence 3, recorded info tel. 02-508-3211, www.fine-arts-museum.be.

✪ See the Royal Museums of Fine Arts and Magritte Museum Tour chapter.

▲▲**Magritte Museum (Musée Magritte)**—This exhibit, examining Surrealist painter René Magritte, is in the same museum complex as the Royal Museums of Fine Arts (earlier), and contains more than 200 works housed on three floors of a Neoclassical building. Although you won't see many of Magritte's most famous pieces, this lovingly presented museum offers an unusually intimate look at the life and work of one of Belgium's top artists.

Cost and Hours: €8, €13 combo-ticket with Royal Museums of Fine Arts, free first Wed of month after 13:00, audioguide-€4; open Tue-Sun 10:00-17:00, Wed until 20:00, closed Mon, last entry 30 minutes before closing; tel. 02-508-3333, www.musee-magritte-museum.be.

✪ See the Royal Museums of Fine Arts and Magritte Museum Tour chapter.

▲**Musical Instruments Museum (Musée des Instruments de Musique)**—One of Europe's best music museums (nicknamed "MIM") is housed in one of Brussels' most impressive Art Nouveau

buildings, the beautifully renovated Old England department store. This museum has more than 1,500 instruments—from Egyptian harps, to medieval lutes, to groundbreaking harpsichords, to the Brussels-built saxophone.

Inside you'll be given an included audioguide and set free to wander several levels: folk instruments from around the world on the ground floor, a history of Western musical instruments on the first, and an entire floor devoted to strings and pianos on the second. As you approach an instrument, you hear it playing on your headphones. It's all color-coordinated so that you can easily access the music. On the upper floor is an exhibit about the history of the building and Brussels Art Nouveau in general. The audioguide covers the territory in English—but the music you'll hear is an international language.

Cost and Hours: €5, Tue-Fri 9:30-16:45, Sat-Sun 10:00-16:45, closed Mon, last entry 45 minutes before closing, mandatory free coat and bag check, Rue Montagne de la Cour 2, just downhill and toward Grand Place from the Magritte wing of the Royal Museums of Fine Arts, tel. 02-545-0130, www.mim.be.

Cuisine Art and City Views: The 10th floor has a restaurant, a terrace, and a great view of Brussels (€10-15 *plats du jour*, same hours as museum, pick up free access pass at museum entrance). The corner alcoves on each level (accessible as you tour the museum) have even better views.

▲▲**BELvue Museum**—This remarkable museum makes Belgian history fascinating. The exhibit—which fills two palatial floors with lots of real historical artifacts—illustrates the short sweep of this nation's story, from its 1830 inception to today. To make the most of your visit, follow along with the wonderful and extensive flier translating all of the descriptions. The €2.50 audioguide simply repeats the information on the flier.

Cost and Hours: €5, €8 combo-ticket includes Coudenberg Palace, Tue-Fri 10:00-17:00, Sat-Sun 10:00-18:00, closed Mon, to the right of the palace at place des Palais 7, tel. 070-220-492, www.belvue.be.

Cuisine Art: Healthy lunches are served in the cool "Green Kitchen" café in the lobby and leafy courtyard of this former princess' palace (€10-15 plates, same hours as museum).

Visiting the Museum: At the top of the stairs, start by enjoying the monitor showing the changing map of Europe from 1000 to 1830. With rooms that proceed in chronological order, the museum explains Belgium's push for independence from the Netherlands, the roots of the ongoing friction between its Francophone-dominated ruling class and its generally Flemish peasant class, and how Belgium cleverly managed to assert itself as a fledgling nation in a changing world.

The exhibit illustrates how, after the political Revolution of 1830, the Industrial Revolution spread from England first to Belgium, and then to other countries on the Continent. A section covers science, industry, and exploration as justification for Belgium's colonization of the Congo.

The WWI section explains how King Albert I refused to give command of Belgian troops to the French or English—so his country lost only 30,000 men. Upstairs, the exhibit continues with a fascinating look at how Albert, who loved mountain climbing, died in a climbing accident.

After outlining the devastation of the World Wars (Belgium surrendered 18 days into World War II), the exhibit examines postwar Belgium's recovery (the optimism of the 1950s, and the World's Fair, which accelerated the rise of modern commercialism), its successful implementation of one of Europe's most socialistic governments, and its gradual emergence as the capital of Europe. A video screen traces the growth of the EU from Benelux in 1948 to today. The conclusion explains how even now, the Flemish-Walloon conflict festers, while reforms implemented since 1970 aspire to prevent Belgium from splitting completely in half.

Outside in the hallway, biographical sketches and intimate family photos provide a chance to get to know the (generally) much-loved royal family. Since these imported German monarchs arrived in 1830, each of the six "Kings of the Belgians" (as they're officially known) has had his own style and claim to fame—or infamy: visionary Leopold I; "Builder King" and Congo exploiter Leopold II; appreciated World War I leader Albert I (who won many fans for the monarchy); controversial World War II-era Leopold III (who abdicated in disgrace); well-respected Baudouin (r. 1950-1993); and his equally popular brother, current King Albert II.

Coudenberg Palace—The BELvue Museum stands atop the barren archaeological remains of a 12th-century Brussels palace. Though well-lit and well-described, these long, vaulted cellars require too much imagination to make them meaningful. A small museum explains artifacts from the palace. The best thing is the free orientation video you see before descending. If you do tour the palace ruins, do so after you're finished at the BELvue Museum, because you'll exit the Coudenberg downhill, near the Musical Instruments Museum.

Cost and Hours: €5, €8 combo-ticket includes BELvue Museum; €2.50 audioguide does not cover BELvue Museum, yet must be (inconveniently) returned to BELvue entrance; same hours as BELvue Museum.

Greater Brussels

East of Downtown

Several interesting sights lie just east of the city center: First, the European Parliament (just beyond the Pentagon ring road); beyond that, the museums at the Park of the Cinquantenaire. Because these are in the same direction and connected by a quick bus ride (explained next), they're easy to visit in one fell swoop.

Connecting the Sights: Handy public-transportation connections make it easy to see both the European Parliament and the Park of the Cinquantenaire. The Métro zips you from the center out to the Park of the Cinquantenaire in minutes (Métro stop: Merode). From the park, catch bus #27 behind the Autoworld building on Avenue des Gaulois (bus stop: Gaulois/Galliërs, direction: Gare du Midi/Zuidstation, 4-5/hour Mon-Fri, 2-3/hour Sat-Sun) to the Luxembourg stop (for the European Parliament) and on to the Royale/Koning stop (for the Royal Palace and great nearby museums). It's cheap and easy, plus you'll feel quite clever doing it.

▲European Parliament

Europe's governing body welcomes visitors with an exhibit about the EU, an entertaining information center, and audioguide tours.

This sprawling complex of glass skyscrapers is a cacophony of black-suited politicians speaking 23 different Euro-languages. It's exciting just to be here—a fly on the wall of a place that aspires to chart the future of Europe "with respect for all political thinking... consolidating democracy in the spirit of peace and solidarity." The 785 parliament members, representing 27 countries and more than 500 million citizens, shape Europe with a €130 billion budget.

Getting There: The European Parliament is next to Place du Luxembourg. From downtown Brussels, take bus #38 or #95; from the museums at the Park of the Cinquantenaire or the Royal Palace, take bus #27. Place du Luxembourg is also a seven-minute walk from the Trône/Troon Métro stop (straight ahead up Luxembourg street—Europe's K Street which teems with lobbyists). To find the Parlamentarium (described next) from Place du Luxembourg, go behind the old train station and beneath the semicircular glass walkway, and turn left. To return to the old center, catch bus #38 or #95 departing from in front of the Gare de Bruxelles-Luxembourg/Station Brussels-Luxemburg just to the right as you leave the EU center.

Parlamentarium: This high-tech fun and informative exhibit is designed to let you meet the EU and understand how it works. Pick up your headset and wander freely through its many exhibits (free, Mon 13:00-18:00, Tue-Wed 9:00-20:00, Thu-Fri 9:00-18:00, Sat-Sun 10:00-17:00, www.europarl.europa.eu).

Visitors Center: The **Info Point** is a welcoming place, with racks of entertaining freebies—including maps outlining the member states, the free *Troubled Waters* comic book that explains how the parliament works, and bins of miniature *My Fundamental Rights in the EU* booklets—everything in 23 different languages, of course (free entry, Mon-Thu 9:00-17:15, Fri 9:00-13:00, closed Sat-Sun).

Visiting the Parliament: The only way to get inside the European Parliament itself is to join a free 45-minute **audio-guide tour.** These leave from the visitors' entrance, down the stairs and across the street from the Info Point (around the left side of the round, glassy building; Mon-Thu at 10:00 and 15:00, additional tours in July-Aug—last one usually departs at 16:00; Fri only at 10:00; busiest on Mon). While you can't make an advance

The European Union

Brussels is the capital of one of the biggest, most powerful, and most idealistic states in the world (and, arguably, in history): The European Union (EU). In just one genera-tion, more than two dozen European countries have gone from being bitter rivals to compatriots. This union of such a diverse collection of separate nations—with different languages, cultures, and soccer teams—is almost unprecedented. And it all started in the rubble of a devastating war.

World War II left 40 million dead and a continent in ruins, and it convinced Europeans that they had to work together to maintain peace. Poised between competing superpowers (the US and the USSR), they also needed to cooperate economically to survive in an increasingly globalized economy. Just after the war ended, visionary "Eurocrats" began the task of convincing reluctant European nations to relinquish elements of their sovereignty and merge into a united body.

The transition happened very gradually, in fits and starts. It began in 1948, when Belgium, the Netherlands, and Luxembourg—jointly called "BeNeLux"—established a free-trade zone. That evolved into an ever-broadening alliance of states (the European Coal and Steel Union, then the European Economic Community, or "Common Market"). In 1992, with the Treaty of Maastricht, the 12 member countries of the Common Market made a leap of faith: They created a "European Union" that would eventually allow for free movement of capital, goods, services, and labor.

In 2002, most EU members adopted a single currency (the euro), and for all practical purposes, economic unity was a reality. Ten additional member states joined in 2004 and two more in 2007, bringing the total to 27—encompassing the British Isles, nearly all of Western Europe, and much of Eastern Europe and Scandinavia. Almost all EU members have joined the open-borders Schengen Agreement, making passport check-

reservation, you can drop by the starting point up to an hour before the tour to pick up your free ticket, then spend your waiting time at the Parlamentarium. There's a slice of the Berlin Wall in the scruffy park a few steps from the tour point.

When you check in, you'll be sent through security and then given an audioguide. Head up the stairs and wait for your tour to begin in the atrium, with exhibits and a gift shop. At the appointed time, your escort leads you to various viewpoints in the

points obsolete. This makes the EU the world's seventh-largest "country" (1.7 million square miles), with the third-largest population (more than 500 million people), and an economy that beats the US's as the world's biggest ($16 trillion GDP).

The EU is governed from Brussels (though some EU institutions meet in Strasbourg, Frankfurt, Luxembourg, and other cities). While it has a parliament, the EU is primarily led by the European Commission (with commissioners appointed by individual member governments and approved by its parliament) and the Council of Ministers. Daily business is conducted by an army of bureaucrats and policy wonks.

Unlike America's federation of 50 states, Europe's member states retain the right to opt out of some EU policies. Britain, for example, belongs to the EU but chose not to adopt the euro as its currency. While the Lisbon Treaty (enacted in 2009) streamlines EU responses to conflicts and issues, there's no unified foreign or economic policy among the member countries. The EU also lacks a powerful chief executive—the president of the European Council, appointed for a two-and-a-half-year term, is much weaker than the US president, as EU laws require consensus on taxes, foreign policy, defense, and social programs.

The EU is currently financing an ambitious 21st-century infrastructure of roads, high-speed trains, high-tech industries, and communication networks. The goal is to create a competitive, sustainable, environmentally friendly economy that improves the quality of life for all Europeans.

Still, many "Euroskeptics" remain unconvinced that the EU is a good thing. Some chafe at the highly regulated business environment and high taxes. They complain about the bureaucracy and worry that their national cultures will be swallowed up and Euro-fied. The wealthier member countries (mostly in the north) are reluctant to bail out their economically unsound compatriots (mostly in the south) in order to prop up the euro, while the troubled countries resent the cuts demanded by the richer ones.

Despite the problems facing them, Europeans don't want to go back to the days of division and strife. Most recognize that a strong, unified Europe is necessary to keep the peace and compete in a global economy.

complex where you'll be instructed to listen to the related audio-guide commentary.

The slow-paced audioguide—with helpful video illustrations—dryly takes you through the history of the EU, as well as its current structure and procedures. You'll learn how early visionary utopians (like Churchill, who in 1946 called for a "United States of Europe" to avoid future wars) led the way as Europe gradually evolved into the European Union (1992).

From the balcony overlooking the building's lobby, you can see the giant *Confluence* sculpture with moving metal-wire pieces—representing people coming together for a common purpose. The audioguide tells you all about the building itself: In line with EU idealism, it's functional, transparent, and very "green."

The grand finale is the vast "hemicycle," where the members of the European Parliament sit. Here you'll listen to a political-science lesson about the all-Europe system of governance. Parliament-arians representing 160 different national political parties, organized into seven different voting blocs based on political ideals (rather than nationality), hash out pan-European issues in this hall. It's the largest multilingual operation on the planet. Yet somehow things get done; recent pieces of legislation include a crackdown on mobile-phone roaming fees within EU member states and a cap on carbon dioxide emissions.

Near the European Parliament
Royal Belgian Institute of Natural Sciences (Institut Royal des Sciences Naturelles de Belgique)—Dinosaur enthusiasts come to this museum, practically next door to the European Parliament, for the world's largest collection of iguanodon skeletons.

Cost and Hours: €7, Tue-Fri 9:30-17:00, Sat-Sun 10:00-18:00, closed Mon, last entry 30 minutes before closing, Rue Vautier 29; bus #95 from Rue du Lombard near Grand Place to Luxembourg, plus a 10-minute walk; or bus #34 from the Porte de Namur/Naamsepoort or Trône/Troon Métro stops to Museum; tel. 02-627-4211, www.naturalsciences.be.

Park of the Cinquantenaire (Parc du Cinquantenaire)
Standing proudly in a big park in eastern Brussels is a trio of sprawling museums housed in cavernous halls: the Royal Army

and Military History Museum, Autoworld, and the Cinquantenaire Museum. These attractions thrill specialists but bore most others. The complex itself is interesting to see and has a grandiose history: The ambitious 19th-century Belgian King

Leopold II wanted Brussels to rival Paris. In 1880 he celebrated the 50th anniversary *(cinquantenaire)* of Belgian independence by building a huge monumental arch flanked by massive exhibition halls, which today house the museums.

Getting There: The Merode Métro stop is 200 yards from the museums (exit the Métro station following signs to *Yser/IJzer,* then cross the street toward the big arch). All of these are also within steps of the Gaulois/Galliërs stop for bus #27 (with handy connections to the European Parliament, then the Royal Palace and Upper Town—see "Connecting the Sights" on page 466).

▲Royal Army and Military History Museum (Musée Royal de l'Armée et d'Histoire Militaire)—Wander through this enormous collection of weaponry, uniforms, tanks, warplanes, and

endless exhibits about military history, focusing on the 19th and 20th centuries. The museum—which is getting a much-needed makeover—is filled with real, tangible history. This impressively complete museum made me want to watch my favorite war movies all over again. It's a nirvana for fans of military history and aviation, but skippable for those who think a "panzer" is a pretty flower. Current renovation work might close some sections—especially parts of the aviation wing—during your visit, and staff cuts may temporarily close some sections midday.

Cost and Hours: Free, Tue-Sun 9:00-16:45, closed Mon, Parc du Cinquantenaire 3, tel. 02-737-7811, www.klm-mra.be. Most of the museum (except for the aviation section) closes from 12:00 to 13:00.

Visiting the Museum: Exploring the whole place is exhausting, so be selective and use the floor plan and directional signs to navigate. Each item is labeled in French and Dutch, but some good English descriptions are available; to get the most out of your visit, pay €3 for the essential audioguide (available 9:00-11:30 & 13:00-16:30).

From the entrance, to the right is a hall with historic exhibits, then a large and very good section on World War I, with the best collection of WWI weaponry anywhere. Don't miss the primitive WWI tanks—able to break through the stalemated "Western Front," but so clumsy that they couldn't do anything in enemy territory. The grand finale of this wing is the vast (and I mean vast) hall filled with warplanes. You'll see WWI and WWII classics, plus a Soviet MiG 23 fighter that crashed in Belgium in 1989 (one of the last airspace violations of the Cold War). Some of these planes are one-of-a-kind relics—including a French Nieuport fighter, a Schreck seaplane, and two German observation planes from World War I. To the left from the entrance are impressively displayed armor and weapons, and a huge hall with information on modern conflict (including World War II) and temporary exhibits.

From atop the grand arch, enjoy free access to "Napoleonic" views over the park complex and the Brussels skyline (some of the best views in the city). It's best to ask directions as you enter— basically you turn left at the gift shop, wander through the armory exhibit following *Panorama* signs, and then take a cramped elevator to the fourth floor (open in summer only).

▲**Autoworld**—Starting with Mr. Benz's motorized tricycle of 1886, stroll through a giant hall filled with 400 historic cars, each one labeled and briefly explained in four languages. Car buffs can ogle circa-1905 models from Peugeot, Renault, Oldsmobile, Cadillac, and Rolls-Royce. It's well-described in English.

Cost and Hours: €9, daily April-Sept 10:00-18:00, Oct-March 10:00-17:00, in Palais Mondial, Parc du Cinquantenaire 11, tel. 02-736-4165, www.auto world.be.

Cinquantenaire Museum—This varied, decent (but not spectacular) collection features both European and non-European items from prehistoric times to the present. As you wander the almost-empty halls, you'll see fine tapestries, exquisite altarpieces, an impressive Islamic collection, gorgeous Art Nouveau and Art Deco, and a "museum of the heart" (featuring various creative depictions of everyone's favorite organ, donated by a local heart doctor). The collection is arranged somewhat haphazardly; pick up the brochure at the entry to figure out which items you'd like to find, then follow the signposts. While it's sometimes called the "Belgian Louvre," that's an overstatement; this place pales in comparison to the excellent Royal Museums of Fine Art in the Upper Town.

Cost and Hours: €5, includes audioguide that covers only some of the museum, limited English information posted, Tue-Fri 9:30-17:00, Sat-Sun 10:00-17:00, closed Mon, hiding behind Autoworld at Jubelpark 10, Parc du Cinquantenaire, tel. 02-741-7211, www.kmkg-mrah.be.

North of Downtown:
The 1958 World's Fair Grounds

These sights are next to each other about four miles north of the Grand Place at Bruparck, a complex of tacky-but-fun attractions at the old 1958 World's Fair grounds.

Getting There: It's easy but fairly time-consuming to reach from the center. Ride the Métro to Heysel/Heizel and walk about five minutes toward the can't-miss-it Atomium. You'll come to a little pavilion with a walkway going over the train tracks; to reach Mini-Europe, take this walkway and enter "The Village," a corny food circus (with a giant cineplex and a water park) done up like a European village. Entering this area, turn left and head down the stairs to reach the Mini-Europe entrance. If you're only going to the Atomium, simply go straight through the pavilion and head for the big silver balls.

Atomium—This giant, silvery iron molecule, with escalators and stairs connecting the various "atoms" and a view from the top sphere, was the über-optimistic symbol of the 1958 World's Fair. It's Brussels' answer to Paris' Eiffel Tower, Seattle's Space Needle, and St. Louis' Gateway Arch. Recently reopened after an extensive renovation, the Atomium celebrates its kitschy past with fun space-age videos and displays.

Your ticket includes an elevator ride to the panorama deck, with views over the fairgrounds and Mini-Europe (which looks *really* mini from up here)—but, disappointingly, you can't actually see the landmarks of downtown Brussels. Then meander on endless escalators and stairs through five of the nine balls on your way back down. The good €2 audioguide explains the building and the 1958 World Expo, including sound clips from people who actually attended the festivities. If you don't like heights or tight spaces, tell your friends you'll wave to them...from the ground.

Cost and Hours: €11, €23 combo-ticket with Mini-Europe, daily 10:00-18:00, later in summer, last entry 30 minutes before closing, overpriced restaurant inside, tel. 02-475-4777, www.atomium.be.

Mini-Europe—This kid-pleasing sight, sharing a park with the Atomium, has 1:25-scale models of 350 famous European landmarks, such as Big Ben, the Eiffel Tower, and Venice's canals. The "Spirit of Europe" section is an interactive educational exhibit about the European Union.

Cost and Hours: €14, €23 combo-ticket with Atomium; mid-March-Sept daily 9:30-18:00, July-Aug until 20:00; Oct-Dec 10:00-18:00, closed Jan-mid-March; last entry one hour before closing, tel. 02-474-1313, www.minieurope.com.

In Tervuren, East of Brussels

▲Royal Museum of Central Africa (Musée Royal de l'Afrique Centrale)—Remember the Belgian Congo? About an hour by public transit from downtown Brussels, this worthwhile museum covers the Congo and much more of Africa, including ethnography, sculpture, jewelry, colonial history, flora, and fauna. It's a great place to learn about both the history of Belgian adventure in the Congo (when it was the king's private plantation) and the region's natural wonders. Unfortunately, there's barely a word of English. The museum, housed in an immense palace, is surrounded by a vast, well-kept park. A trip out here puts you in a lush, wooded oasis a world away from the big, noisy city. The palace was built by the king in 1907 to promote the beauties of living and working in the Congo.

Cost and Hours: €4, more for special exhibits, audioguide-€2, Tue-Fri 10:00-17:00, Sat-Sun 10:00-18:00, closed Mon, Leuvensesteenweg 13 in the town of Tervuren, tel. 02-769-5211, www.africamuseum.be.

Getting There: Take Métro line 1 (direction: Stockel/ Stokkel) to Montgomery, and then catch tram #44 and ride it about 20 minutes to its final stop, Tervuren. From there, walk 300 yards through the park to the palace.

GRAND PLACE WALK

This walk takes in Brussels' delightful old center, starting at its spectacular main square. After exploring the Grand Place, we'll loop a couple blocks north, see the Bourse, and then end south of the Grand Place at the *Manneken-Pis*.

Orientation

Length of This Walk: Allow two hours.

Brewery Museum: €5, daily 10:00-17:00 except Dec-March Sat-Sun opens at 12:00.

City Museum: €4, Tue-Sun 10:00-17:00, Thu until 20:00, closed Mon.

Chocolate Shops: Generally Mon-Sat 9:00-22:00, Sun 10:00-22:00.

The Walk Begins

The Grand Place

This colorful cobblestone square is the heart—historically and geographically—of heart-shaped Brussels. As the town's market square for 1,000 years, this was where farmers and merchants sold their wares in open-air stalls, enticing travelers from the main east-west highway across Belgium, which ran a block north of the square. Today, shops and cafés sell chocolates, *gaufres* (waffles), beer, mussels, fries, *dentelles* (lace), and flowers.

Brussels was born about 1,000 years ago at a strategic spot on the banks of the Senne (not Seine) River, which today is completely bricked over. The river crossed the main road from Köln to Bruges.

Pan the square to get oriented. Face the Town Hall, with

Grand Place Walk

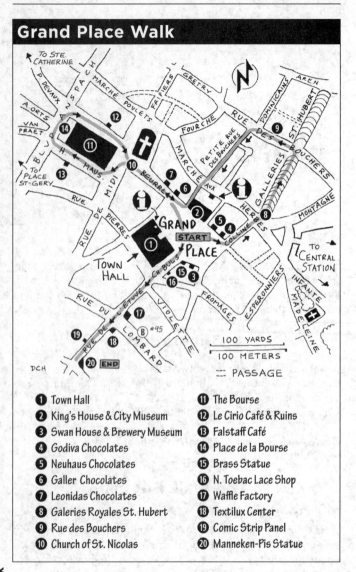

1. Town Hall
2. King's House & City Museum
3. Swan House & Brewery Museum
4. Godiva Chocolates
5. Neuhaus Chocolates
6. Galler Chocolates
7. Leonidas Chocolates
8. Galeries Royales St. Hubert
9. Rue des Bouchers
10. Church of St. Nicolas
11. The Bourse
12. Le Cirio Café & Ruins
13. Falstaff Café
14. Place de la Bourse
15. Brass Statue
16. N. Toebac Lace Shop
17. Waffle Factory
18. Textilux Center
19. Comic Strip Panel
20. Manneken-Pis Statue

your back to the King's House. The TI is one block behind you, and "restaurant row" is another block beyond that. To your right, a block away (downhill), catch a glimpse of the Bourse building. The Upper Town is to your left, rising up the hill beyond the Central Station. Over your left shoulder a few blocks away is St. Michael's Cathedral. And most important? The *Manneken-Pis* is three blocks ahead, down the street that runs along the left side of the Town Hall.

The **Town Hall** (Hôtel de Ville) dominates the square with its 300-foot-tall tower, topped by a golden statue of St. Michael slaying a devil (open only by tour; see page 454 for tour times if you're interested). This was where the city council met to rule this free trading town. Brussels proudly maintained its self-governing independence while dukes, kings, and clergymen ruled much of Europe. These days, the Town Hall hosts weddings— Crown Prince Philippe got married here in 1999. (The Belgian government demands that all marriages first be performed in simple civil ceremonies.)

Opposite the Town Hall is the impressive, gray **King's House** (Maison du Roi), used by the Habsburg kings not as a house, but as an administrative center. Rebuilt in the 1890s, it's a stately and prickly Neo-Gothic building. Inside is the mildly interesting **City Museum** (described later).

The fancy smaller buildings giving the square its uniquely grand medieval character are former **guild halls** (now mostly

shops and restaurants), their impressive gabled roofs topped with statues. Once the home offices for the town's different professions (brewers, bakers, and *Manneken-Pis*-corkscrew-makers), they all date from shortly after 1695—the year French king Louis XIV's troops surrounded the city, sighted their cannons on the Town Hall spire, and managed to level everything around it (4,000

mostly wooden buildings) without ever hitting the spire itself. As a matter of pride, these Brussels businessmen rebuilt their offices better than ever, completing everything within seven years. They're in stone, taller, and with ornamented gables and classical statues. While they were all built at about the same time, the many differences in styles reflect the independent spirit of the people and the many cultural influences that converged in this crossroads trading center.

The **Swan House** (#9, just to the left of the Town Hall—find the plaque) once housed a bar where Karl Marx and Friedrich Engels met in February of 1848 to write their *Communist Manifesto*, and where the first German Workers' Association (the proto-communist party) met. Later that year, when their treatise sparked socialist revolution around Europe, Brussels exiled Marx and Engels. Today, the once-proletarian bar is one of the city's most expensive restaurants. Next door (#10) was and still is the brewers' guild, now housing the **Brewery Museum** (see page 455).

Each rooftop **statue** comes with its own uninteresting legend, but the Bruxelloise have an earthier explanation: "What's that smell?" say the statues on the roof of the Swan House. "Someone farted." "Yeah," says the golden man riding a horse atop the Brewery Museum next door, "it was that guy over there," and he points north across the square to another statue. "It wasn't me," says that statue, "it was him—way over there." Follow his gaze to the middle of the northwest side of the square, where the statue of a saint with a shepherd's staff hangs his head in shame.

Imagine this already glorious square filled with a carpet of flowers. Every other year (next in August of 2014; www.flower carpet.be), florists create a colorful 19,000-square-foot pattern of tightly packed begonias—that's about three-quarters of a million individual flowers. Begun in 1971 by a begonia salesman as a way to promote his wares, this gorgeous display has become a biannual Brussels fixture that makes this grand space even grander.

• *Inside the King's House (Maison du Roi)—across the Grand Place from the Town Hall—is the only museum of any importance on the square, the...*

City Museum

This museum has three stories of exhibits: The top floor displays a chronological history of the city and an enjoyable room full of

costumes dampened by the *Manneken-Pis* statue (see page 487); the middle floor has a 20-minute film on city history and maps and models of 13th- and 17th-century Brussels; and the ground floor features tapestries and paintings. Borrow the English descriptions in each room.

Most visitors aim straight for the *Manneken-Pis* outfits, **upstairs.** It's a longstanding tradition for the statue to be outfitted in clothing—the little guy goes through several costume changes each week. Many of the costumes you'll see here were donated by other countries—you'll see everything from a Civil War Union soldier to an El Salvadorian farmer, from a Polish hussar to a Japanese samurai, from an Indian maharajah to a Spanish bull-fighter, from a Russian cosmonaut to a Fiji islander...and much more. Once up here, sit down and enjoy the video showing visitors' reactions to the ridiculous little statue.

On the **middle floor,** be sure to find the model of the city in the 13th century. (To follow the directions in this description, uphill is east.) The largest structure is St. Michael's Cathedral (northeast). The Upper Town hasn't a hint of its monumental future. The Grand Place's embryonic beginning is roughly in the center of town, amid a cluster of houses.

The city was a port town—see the crane unloading barges—since it was at this point that the shallow Senne became navigable. Grain from the area was processed in the watermills, then shipped downstream to Antwerp and on to the North Sea.

By the 1200s, Brussels—though tiny by today's standards—was an important commercial center, and St. Michael's was the region's religious hub. Still, most of the area inside the 2.5-mile-long city wall was farmland, dotted with a few churches, towers, markets, and convents (such as the Carmelite convent hugging the south wall).

The model in the far end of the room shows the city a couple centuries later—much bigger, but still within the same wall. By this time, the Upper and Lower Towns are clearly defined. In the Upper Town, the huge palace of the dukes of Burgundy marks the site of today's Royal Palace (described on page 491).

On the **ground floor** you'll see the original statues that once adorned the Town Hall. The limestone is no match for the corrosive acidic air, so they were brought inside for protection. Also on this floor are a few old paintings, fine carved altarpieces, tapestries, sculpture, and porcelain.

Tasty Treats on the Grand Place

Cafés: Mussels in Brussels, Belgian-style french fries, yeasty local beers, waffles...if all you do here is plop down at a café on the square, try some of these specialties, and watch the world go by—hey, that's a great afternoon in Brussels.

The outdoor cafés are casual and come with fair prices (a good Belgian beer costs €4.50—with no cover or service charge). Have a seat, and a waiter will serve you. The half-dozen or so cafés on the downhill side of the square are all roughly equal in price and qual-ity for simple drinks and foods—check the posted menus. As they are generally owned by breweries, you won't have a big selection of beers.

A Brief History of Chocolate

In 1519, Montezuma served Cortés a cup of hot cocoa (xocoatl) made from cocoa beans, which were native to the New World.

It ignited a food fad in Europe—by 1700, elegant "chocolate houses" in Europe's capitals served hot chocolate (with milk and sugar added) to wealthy aristocrats. By the 1850s, the process of making chocolate candies for eating was developed, and Brussels, with a long tradition of quality handmade luxuries, was at the forefront.

Cocoa beans are husked, fermented, and roasted, then ground into chocolate paste. (Chocolate straight from the bean is very bitter.) The vegetable fat is pressed out to make cocoa butter. Cocoa butter and chocolate paste are mixed together and sweetened with sugar to make chocolates. In 1876, a Swiss man named Henry Nestlé added concentrated milk, creating milk chocolate—a lighter, sweeter variation, with less pure chocolate.

Choco-Crawl: The best chocolate shops all lie along the north (uphill) side of the square, starting with Godiva at the high end (higher in both altitude and price). The cost goes down slightly as you descend to the other shops. Each shop has a mouth-watering display case of 20 or so chocolates and sells mixes of 100 grams—your choice of 8 pieces—for about €5, or individual pieces for about €1. Americans use the word "chocolates" indiscriminately to describe the different varieties you'd find in a box of chocolates, but the Belgians call them either "truffles" (soft, crumbly chocolate shells filled with buttercream) or "pralines" (made of a hard chocolate shell with a wide range of fillings—uniquely Belgian and totally different from the sugar-and-nuts French praline). Chocolate shops are generally open Monday to Saturday from 9:00 to 22:00 and Sunday from 10:00 to 22:00.

Godiva, with the top reputation internationally, is synonymous with fine Belgian chocolate. Now owned by a Turkish company, Godiva still has its management and the original factory (built in 1926) in Belgium. This store, at Grand Place 22, was Godiva's first (est. 1937). The almond and honey goes way beyond almond roca.

Neuhaus, a few doors down at #27, has been encouraging local chocoholics since 1857. Their main store is in the Galeries St. Hubert (described later). Neuhaus publishes a good little pamphlet explaining its products. The "caprice" (toffee with vanilla crème) tastes like Easter. Neuhaus claims to be the inventor of the praline.

Galler, just off the square at Rue au Beurre 44, is homier and less famous because it doesn't export. Still family-run (and the royal favorite), it proudly serves less sugary chocolate—dark. The new top-end choice, 85 percent pure chocolate, is called simply "Black 85"—and worth a sample if you like chocolate without the sweetness. Galler's products are well-described in English.

Leonidas, four doors down at Rue au Beurre 34, is where cost-conscious Bruxelloise get their fix, sacrificing 10 percent in quality to nearly triple their take (machine-made, only €2.20/100 grams). White chocolate is their specialty.

If all the chocolate has made you thirsty, wash it down with **250 Beers,** next to Leonidas.

• *Exit the Grand Place next to Godiva (from the northeast, or uphill, corner of the square), and go north one block on Rue de la Colline (passing a popular Tintin shop at #9) to Rue du Marché-aux-Herbes/ Grasmarkt, which was once the main east-west highway through Belgium. The little park-like square just to your right—a modest gathering place with market stalls—is nicknamed "Agora" (after the marketplaces of ancient Greece).*

Looking to the right, notice that it's all uphill from here to the Upper Town, another four blocks (and 200-foot elevation gain) beyond. Straight ahead, you enter the arcaded shopping mall called...

Galeries Royales St. Hubert

Built in 1847, Europe's oldest still-operating shopping mall served as the glass-covered model that inspired many other shopping galler-

ies in Paris, London, and beyond. It celebrated the town's new modern attitude (having recently gained its independence from the Netherlands). Built in an age of expansion and industrialization, the mall demonstrated efficient modern living, with elegant apartments upstairs above trendy shops, theaters, and cafés. Originally, you had to pay to get in to see its fancy shops, and that elite sensibility survives today. Even today, people live in the upstairs apartments.

Looking down the arcade, you'll notice that it bends halfway down, designed to lure shoppers farther. Its iron-and-glass look is still popular, but the decorative columns, cameos, and pastel colors evoke a more elegant time. It's Neo-Renaissance, like a pastel Florentine palace.

There's no Gap (yet), no Foot Locker, no Karmelkorn.

Instead, you'll find hat, cane, and, umbrella stores that sell... hats, canes, and umbrellas—that's it, all made on the premises. **Philippe** (halfway down the first section, on the left), carries shoes made especially for the curves of your feet, handcrafted by a family that's been doing it for generations. Since 1857, **Neuhaus** (near the end of the first section, on the right) has sold chocolates from here at its flagship store, where many Brussels natives buy their pralines—invented in this very house in 1912. Across from Neuhaus, the **Taverne du Passage** restaurant serves the same local specialties that singer Jacques Brel used to come here for: *croquettes de crevettes* (shrimp croquettes), *tête de veau* (calf's head), *anguilles au vert* (eels with herb sauce), and *fondue au fromage* (cheese fondue; €15-25 meals, daily 12:00-24:00).

• *Midway down the mall, where the two sections bend, turn left and exit the mall onto...*

Rue des Bouchers

Yikes! During meal times, this street is absolutely crawling with tourists browsing through wall-to-wall, midlevel-quality restau-

rants. Brussels is known worldwide for its food, serving all kinds of cuisine, but specializing in seafood (particularly mussels). You'll have plenty to choose from along this table-clogged "restaurant row." To get an idea of prices, compare their posted *menùs*—the fixed-price, several-course meal offered by most restaurants. But don't count on getting a good value—better restaurants are just a few steps away (for specifics, see page 518).

Many diners here are day-trippers. Colin from London, Marie from Paris, Martje from Holland, and Dietrich from Frankfurt could easily all "do lunch" together in Brussels—just three hours away.

The first intersection, with Petite Rue des Bouchers, is the heart of the restaurant quarter, which sprawls for several blocks around. The street names reveal what sorts of shops used to stand here—butchers *(bouchers)*, herbs, chickens, and cheese.

• *At this intersection, turn left onto Petite Rue des Bouchers and walk straight back to the Grand Place. (You'll see the Town Hall tower ahead.) At the Grand Place, turn right (west) on Rue du Beurre. Comparison-shop a little more at the Galler and Leonidas chocolate stores and pass by the little "Is it raining?" fountain. At the intersection with Rue du Midi is the...*

Church of St. Nicolas

Since the 12th century, there's been a church here. Inside, along the left aisle, see rough stones in some of the arches from the early church. Outside, notice the barnacle-like shops, such as De Witte Jewelers, built right into the church. The church was rebuilt 300 years ago with money provided by the town's jewelers. As thanks, they were given these shops with apartments upstairs. Close to God, this was prime real estate. And jewelers are still here.

• *Just beyond the church, you run into the back entrance of a big Neoclassical building.*

The Bourse (Stock Exchange) and Art Nouveau Cafés

The stock exchange was built in the 1870s in the Historicist style—a mix-and-match, Neo-everything architectural movement. Plans are in the works for the former stock exchange to host a big beer museum. The **ruins** under glass on the right side of the Bourse are from a 13th-century convent; there's a small museum inside.

Several **historic cafés** huddle around the Bourse. To the right (next to the covered ruins) is the woody **Le Cirio,** with its delightful circa-1900 interior. Around the left side of the Bourse is the **Falstaff Café,** which is worth a peek inside. Some Brussels cafés, like the Falstaff, are still decorated in the early 20th-century style called Art Nouveau. Ironwork columns twist and bend like flower stems, and lots of Tiffany-style stained glass and mirrors make them light and spacious. Slender, elegant, willowy Gibson Girls decorate the wallpaper, while waiters in bowties glide by.

• *Circle around to the front of the Bourse, toward the busy Boulevard Anspach.*

Place de la Bourse and Boulevard Anspach

Brussels is the political nerve center of Europe (with as many lobbyists as Washington, DC), and the city sees several hundred

demonstrations a year. When the local team wins a soccer match or some political group wants to make a statement, this is where people flock to wave flags and honk horns.

It's also where the old town meets the new. To the right along Boulevard Anspach are two shopping malls and several first-run movie theaters. Rue Neuve, which parallels Anspach, is a bustling pedestrian-only shopping street.

Boulevard Anspach covers the still-flowing Senne River (which was open until 1870). Remember that Brussels was once a port, with North Sea boats coming as far as this point to unload their goods. But with frequent cholera epidemics killing thousands of its citizens, the city decided to cover up its stinky river.

Beyond Boulevard Anspach—two blocks past the black, blocky skyscraper—is the charming **Ste. Catherine** neighborhood, clustered around the former fish market and the Church of Ste. Catherine. This village-like zone is the easiest escape from the bustle of downtown Brussels, and features two ideal lunch stops: the Mer du Nord/Nordzee fish bar and the delightful Belgian cheese shop Cremerie de Linkebeek (both worth a detour and described on page 522).

• *For efficient sightseeing, consider catching a taxi across the street from the Bourse to the Place Royale, where you can follow my Upper Town Walk (see next chapter), also ending at the* Manneken-Pis. *But if you'd rather stay in the Lower Town, return to the Grand Place.*

From the Grand Place to the *Manneken-Pis*

• *Leave the square kitty-corner, heading south down the street running along the left side of the Town Hall, Rue Charles Buls (which soon changes its name to Stoofstraat). Just five yards off the square, under the arch, are two interesting monuments honoring illustrious Brussels mayors:*

The first monument features a beautiful young man—an Art Nouveau allegory of knowledge and science (which brings illumination, as indicated by the Roman oil lamp)—designed by Victor Horta. It honors **Charles Buls,** mayor from 1888 to 1899. If you enjoyed the Grand Place, thank him for saving it. He stopped King Leopold II from blasting a grand esplanade from Grand Place up the hill to the palace.

A few steps farther you'll see tourists and locals rubbing a brass statue of a reclining man. This was **Mayor Evrard 't Serclaes,** who in 1356 bravely refused to surrender the keys of the city to invaders, and so was tortured and killed. Touch him, and his misfortune becomes your good luck. Judging by the reverence with which locals treat this ritual, I figure there must be something to it.

A half-block farther (on the left), the **N. Toebac Lace Shop** shows off some fine lace. Brussels

Lace

In the 1500s, lace collars, sleeves, headdresses, and veils were fashionable among rich men and women. For the next 200 years, the fashion raged (peaking in about 1700). All this lace had to be made by hand, and many women earned extra income from the demand. But the French Revolution of 1789 suddenly made lace for men undemocratic and unmanly. Then, in about 1800, machines replaced human hands, and except for ornamental pieces, the fashion died out among women, too.

These days, handmade lace is usually also homemade—not produced in factories, but at home by dedicated, sharp-eyed hobbyists who love their work. Unlike knitting, it requires total concentration as the lacemaker follows intricate patterns. Lacemakers create their own patterns or trace tried-and-true designs. A piece of lace takes days, not hours, to make—which is why a handmade tablecloth can easily sell for €250.

There are two basic kinds of lace: bobbin lace (which originated in Bruges) and needle lace. To make bobbin lace, the lacemaker juggles many different strands tied to bobbins, "weaving" a design by overlapping the threads. Because of the difficulties, the resulting pattern is usually rather rough and simple compared with other techniques.

Needle lace is more like sewing—stitching pre-made bits onto a pattern. For example, the "Renaissance" design is made by sewing a pre-made ribbon onto a pattern in a fancy design. This is then attached as a fringe to a piece of linen—to make a fancy tablecloth, for instance.

In the "Princess" design, pre-made pieces are stitched onto a cotton net. This method is often used to make all sorts of pieces, from small doilies to full wedding veils.

"Rose point"—no longer practiced—used authentic bits of handmade antique lace as an ornament in a frame or to fill a pendant. Antique pieces can be very expensive.

is perhaps the best-known city for traditional lacemaking, and this shop still sells handmade pieces in the old style: lace clothing, doilies, tablecloths, and ornamental pieces. The shop gives travelers with this book a 15 percent discount. For more on lace, the Costume and Lace Museum is a block away and just around the corner (closed Wed, see page 458).

A block farther down the street on the left (at the little yellow window before the busy street) is the always-popular **Waffle**

Tapestries

In 1500, tapestry workshops in Brussels were famous, cranking out high-quality tapestries for the walls of Europe's palaces. They were functional (as insulation and propaganda for a church, king, or nobleman) and beautiful—an intricate design formed by colored thread. Even great painters, such as Rubens and Raphael, designed tapestries, which rivaled Renaissance canvases. The best Belgian tapestries are in Madrid, because the Golden Age of Belgian tapestries was under Spanish rule in the 16th and 17th centuries.

To make a tapestry, neutral-colored threads are stretched vertically over a loom. (In Renaissance Belgium, the threads were made from imported English wool.) The design of the tapestry is created with the horizontal weave, from the colored threads that (mostly) overlay the vertical threads. Tapestry-making is much more difficult than basic weaving, as each horizontal thread is only as long as the detail it's meant to create. A single horizontal row can be made up of many individual pieces of thread. Before weaving begins, an artist designs a pattern for the larger picture, called a "cartoon," which weavers follow for guidance as they work.

Flanders and Paris (in the Gobelins workshop) were the two centers of tapestry-making until the art died out, mirroring the decline of Europe's noble class.

Factory, where €2 gets you a freshly made take-away "Belgian" (Liège-style) waffle (up to €7 more if you opt for any of the fun toppings).

Across the busy street, step into the **Textilux Center** (Rue Lombard 41, on the left) for a good look at Belgian tapestries—both traditional wall-hangings and modern goods, such as tapestry purses and luggage in traditional designs.

High on the wall to the right, notice the delightful **comic strip panel** depicting that favorite of Belgian comic heroes, Tintin, climbing a fire escape. (For those unfamiliar with this character—beloved by virtually all Europeans—his dog is named Snowy, Captain Haddock keeps an eye out for him, and the trio are always getting into misadventures. For more details, see the sidebar on page 460.) Dozens of these building-sized comic-strip panels decorate Brussels (marked on the TI's €0.50 map), celebrating the Belgians' favorite medium. Just as Ireland has its writers, Italy its painters, and France its chefs, Belgium has a knack for turning out world-class comic artists.

• *Follow the crowds, noticing the excitement build, because in another block you reach the...*

Manneken-Pis

Even with low expectations, this bronze statue is smaller than you'd think—the little squirt's under two feet tall, practically the size of a newborn. Still, the little peeing boy is an appropriately low-key symbol for the unpretentious Bruxelloise. The statue was made in 1619 to provide drinking water for the neighborhood. Notice that the baby, sculpted in Renaissance style, actually has the musculature of a man instead of the pudgy limbs of a child. The statue was knighted by the occupying King

Louis XV—so French soldiers had to salute the eternally pissing lad when they passed.

As it's tradition for visiting VIPs to bring the statue an outfit, and he also dresses up for special occasions, you can often see the *Manneken* peeing through a colorful costume. A sign on the fence lists the month's festival days and how he'll be dressed. For example, on January 8, Elvis Presley's birthday, he's an Elvis impersonator; on Prostate Awareness Day, his flow is down to a slow drip. He can also be hooked up to a keg to pee wine or beer.

There are several different legends about the story behind *Manneken*—take your pick: He was a naughty boy who peed inside a witch's house, so she froze him. A rich man lost his son and declared, "Find my son, and we'll make a statue of him doing what he did when found." Or—the locals' favorite version—the little tyke loved his beer, which came in handy when a fire threatened the wooden city: He bravely put it out. Want the truth? The city commissioned *the Manneken* to show the freedom and joie de vivre of living in Brussels—where happy people eat, drink...and drink... and then pee.

The gathering crowds make the scene more interesting. Hang out for a while and watch the commotion this little guy makes as tour groups come and go. When I was there, a Russian man marveled at the statue, shook his head, and said, "He never stop!"

UPPER TOWN WALK

The Upper Town has always had a more aristocratic feel than the medieval, commercial streets of the Lower Town. With broad boulevards, big marble buildings, palaces, museums, and so many things called "royal," it also seems much newer and a bit more sterile. But the Upper Town has plenty to offer.

Use this walk to get acquainted with this less-touristed part of town, sample some world-class museums, see the palace, explore art galleries, and get the lay of the land from a panoramic viewpoint. The tour starts a half-block from the one essential art sight in town, the complex that holds the Royal Museums of Fine Arts of Belgium (Ancient Art and Fin de Siècle) and the Magritte Museum. Consider a visit while you're here (see next chapter). The Musical Instruments Museum is also in the neighborhood.

Orientation

Length of This Walk: Allow 1.5 hours.

Getting There: The walk begins at Place Royale/Koningsplein in the Upper Town. You have several ways to get there:

    1. From the Grand Place, walk uphill for 15 minutes (follow your map).

    2. Catch a taxi (figure €6 from the Bourse).

    3. From Rue du Lombard south of the Grand Place, take bus #95, which leaves every few minutes for Place Royale (bus signs call it *Royale/Koning;* buy €2.50 ticket from driver, validate in machine).

    4. Hop off here during a hop-on, hop-off bus tour (see page 452).

Route Overview: From Place Royale, walk south along the ridge. On the way, pop in to a stained-glass-filled Gothic church, then continue on to reach the towering Palace of Justice, which has the best view of the city. Backtrack a bit and descend through the well-worn tapestry of the Sablon Quarter's antiques stores, art galleries, and cafés, ending down to the *Manneken-Pis* at the foot of the hill.

Starring: Brussels' genteel Upper Town, with its best museums, top views, and a bit of personality poking out from behind its stuffy veneer.

The Walk Begins

❶ Place Royale (Koningsplein)

At the crest of the hill sits Place Royale, encircled by cars and trams and enclosed by white Neoclassical buildings forming a mirror image across a cobblestone square. A big, green statue of a horseman stands in the center.

The **statue** depicts the local hero, Godfrey de Bouillon, who led the First Crusade (in 1096). The ultimate Catholic knight, he

rides forward with his flag, gazing down on the Town Hall spire. If Godfrey turned and looked left down Rue de la Régence, he'd see the domed Palace of Justice at the end of the boulevard. Over his right shoulder, just outside the square, is the Royal Palace, the king's residence.

In the 1870s, as Belgium exerted itself to industrialize and modernize, this tight ensemble of planned buildings and squares was rebuilt as a sign that Brussels had arrived as a world capital. Broad vistas down wide boulevards end at gleaming white, Greek-columned monuments—this look was all the rage, seen in Paris, London, Washington, DC...and here.

The cupola of the **Church of St. Jacques sur Coudenberg**—the central portion of the square's ring of buildings—makes the church look more like a bank building. But St. Jacques' church goes back much further than this building (from 1787); the original was built here in the 13th century near a 12th-century castle. Nobles chose to build their mansions in the neighborhood—and, later, so did the king. And when locals stand here, they remember that it was on the porch of this building, on July 21, 1931, that their first king took the oath that established modern Belgium.

The square has several worthwhile museums: the Royal Museums of Fine Arts of Belgium (main entrance a half-block to the right) and the associated Magritte Museum (facing the crusader statue; see tour chapter), and the Musical Instruments

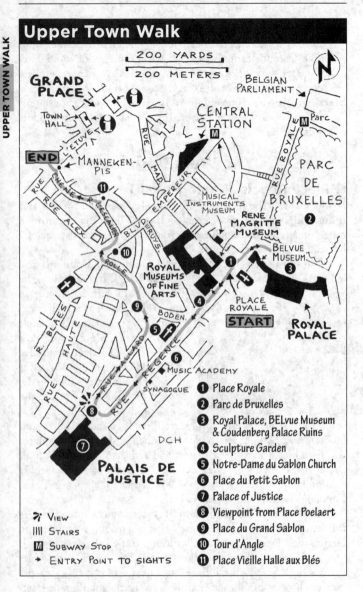

Upper Town Walk

200 YARDS
200 METERS

N

GRAND PLACE

TOWN HALL

BELGIAN PARLIAMENT

CENTRAL STATION M

Parc
M Parc

RUE DE L'ETUVE

MANNEKEN-PIS

END

RUE MAD.

EMPEREUR

RUE CHENE - R. LESCAILLE

RUE ALEX.

BLVD. R. LESCAILLE

BLVD. (RUYS.)

11

10

9

5

8

7

MUSICAL INSTRUMENTS MUSEUM

RENE MAGRITTE MUSEUM

ROYAL MUSEUMS OF FINE ARTS

BODEN.

ROLLE.

RUE BLAES

R. HAUTE

RUE ALLARD

RUE REGENCE

MUSIC ACADEMY

SYNAGOGUE

DCH

PALAIS DE JUSTICE

PARC DE BRUXELLES

2

BELVUE MUSEUM

3

PLACE ROYALE

1

4

START

ROYAL PALACE

6

7i VIEW
|||| STAIRS
M SUBWAY STOP
→ ENTRY POINT TO SIGHTS

1 Place Royale
2 Parc de Bruxelles
3 Royal Palace, BELvue Museum & Coudenberg Palace Ruins
4 Sculpture Garden
5 Notre-Dame du Sablon Church
6 Place du Petit Sablon
7 Palace of Justice
8 Viewpoint from Place Poelaert
9 Place du Grand Sablon
10 Tour d'Angle
11 Place Vieille Halle aux Blés

Museum, straight downhill from the square—if Godfrey spurred his horse straight ahead, he'd pass it on his right. It's housed in an early 20th-century iron-and-glass former department store. Its Art Nouveau facade was a deliberate attempt to get beyond the retro-looking Greek columns and domes of the Place Royale. Even if you don't visit the Musical Instruments Museum, you can ride the elevator up to the museum café for a superb Lower Town view.

• *Before heading south, exit Place Royale on the north side (to the left as you face Godfrey), which opens up to the large, tree-lined...*

❷ Parc de Bruxelles

Copying Versailles, the Habsburg empress Maria Theresa of Austria (Marie-Antoinette's mom) had this symmetrical park laid out in 1776, when she ruled (but never visited) the city. This is just one of many large parks in Brussels, which started with an awareness of the importance of city planning.

At the far (north) end of the park (directly opposite the Royal Palace, no need to actually walk there) is the Parliament building. Which parliament? The city hosts several: the European Parliament, the Belgian Parliament, and several local, city-council-type parliaments. This is the Belgian Parliament, seen on nightly newscasts as a backdrop for talking heads and politicians.

In 1830, Belgian patriots rose up and converged on the park, where they attacked the troops of the Dutch king. This was the first blow in a short, almost bloodless revolution that drove out the foreign-born king and gave the Belgians independence...and a different foreign-born king.

• *The long building facing the park is the...*

❸ Royal Palace (Palais Royale)

Belgium struck out twice trying to convince someone to be its new king. Finally, Leopold I (r. 1831-1865), a nobleman from

Germany, agreed to become "King of the Belgians." Leopold was a steadying influence as the country modernized. His son rebuilt this palace—near the site of earlier palaces, dating back to the 10th century—by linking a row of townhouse mansions with a unifying facade (around 1870).

Leopold's great-great-great-grandnephew, King Albert II, today uses the palace as an office. (His head is on Belgium's euro coins.) Albert and his wife, Queen Paola, live in a palace north of here (near the Atomium) and on the French Riviera. If the Belgian flag (black-yellow-red) is flying from the palace, the king is somewhere in Belgium.

Albert II (born 1932) is a figurehead king, as in many

European democracies, but he serves an important function as a common bond between bickering Flemish and Walloon citizens. His son, Prince Philippe, is slated to succeed him, though Philippe—awkward and standoffish—is not as popular as his wife, Mathilde, also a Belgian native. Their daughter, Elisabeth, born in 2001, will someday become the first Belgian queen.

The bulk of the palace is off-limits to tourists except from late July through early September (see www.opt.be for the latest schedule; gardens open April-May). The adjacent **BELvue Museum** has an impressive exhibit on Belgian history and the royal family, but I'd skip the ho-hum **Coudenberg Palace** ruins (same entry for both; see page 466).

• *Return to Place Royale, then continue south along Rue de la Régence, noticing the main entrance to the Royal Museums of Fine Arts of Belgium complex (see tour on page 498). Just past the museums, on the right, you'll see a...*

❹ Sculpture Garden (Jardin de Sculpture)

This pleasant public garden features a statue by Rodin's contemporary, Aristide Maillol, a master of the female form. In *The River* (1938-1943), the moving water is personified as a woman sprawled on her side (and looking terrified, or at least stressed—the statue was originally conceived to represent a victim of war). The wave-like figure teeters on the edge of a pool of water, about to pour in. Or is she just washing her hair? Another copy of this bronze  statue sprawls near a pool in the courtyard of New York's Museum of Modern Art.

The garden looks like a great way to descend into the Sablon Quarter, but the gates at the bottom are often locked.

• *About 100 yards farther along Rue de la Régence, you reach the top of the Sablon neighborhood, dominated by the...*

❺ Notre-Dame du Sablon Church

The round, rose, stained-glass windows in the clerestory of this 14th-century Flamboyant Gothic church are nice by day, but are thrilling at night, when the church is lit from inside and glows like a lantern, enjoyed by locals at the cafés in the surrounding square.

Step inside (free, open daily 8:00-18:00). An artistically carved pulpit stands midway up the nave. The stained-glass windows in the nave (which date from the 19th and 20th centuries) are notable for their symmetry—rows of saints in Gothic niches topped by coats of arms. The glorious apse behind the altar—bathed in colorful

light from original 15th-century windows—is what Gothic is all about. The left transept has relics of Karl I, the last Habsburg emperor (1887-1922), who was deposed when Austria became a republic after World War I. Karl's Catholic devotion was legendary, and he was beatified in 2004. Many devoted people pray here, inspired by his patient suffering in exile.

Next to the altar, see a small wooden **statue of Mary** dressed in white with a lace veil. This is a copy, made after iconoclastic Protestant vandals destroyed the original. The original statue was thought to have had miraculous powers that saved the town from plagues. In 1348, when the statue was in Antwerp, it spoke to a godly woman named Beatrix, prompting her to snatch Mary, board a boat, and steal the statue away from Antwerp. (That's why the church is decorated with several images of boats, including the small **wooden boat** high up in the right transept.) When the citizens of Antwerp tried to stop Beatrix, the Mary statue froze them in their tracks.

When Beatrix and the statue arrived here, the Bruxelloise welcomed Mary with a joyous parade. Not long after, this large church was erected in her honor. Every summer, in Brussels' famous Ommegang procession, locals in tights and flamboyant costumes re-create the joyous arrival with colorful banners and large puppets. Imagine the scene as they carry Mary from here through the city streets to the parade's climax on the Grand Place.

• *We'll return to the colorful Place du grand Sablon (below the church) later in the walk. For now, head to the other side of Rue de la Régence from the church, where you'll find a leafy, fenced-off garden called the...*

❻ Place du Petit Sablon

Step into this charming little park, a pleasant refuge from the busy street and part of why this neighborhood is considered so livable. Its central fountain, a fine example of 19th-century Romanticism, honors two local nobles who were executed because they promoted tolerance during the Inquisition. Good friends, one Catholic and the other Protestant, they were beheaded on the Grand Place in 1568.

Check out the other statues. The 48 small statues atop the wrought-iron fence represent the craftsman guilds—weavers, brewers, and butchers—of 16th-century Brussels. And inside the garden, the 10 large statues represent hometown thinkers of the 16th century—a time of great intellectual accomplishments in Brussels. Gerardus Mercator (1512-1594), the Belgian mapmaker who devised a way to more accurately show the spherical Earth on a flat surface, holds a globe.

This collection of statues functions as a reminder that, even though Belgium was never a great power, Belgians have much to be proud of as a people. From here, look back at the church and enjoy its flamboyant late Gothic lines.

• We'll visit the Sablon neighborhood below the church later, but before losing elevation, let's continue along Rue de la Régence, passing on the left the Music Academy and Brussels' main synagogue—its sidewalk fortified with concrete posts to keep car bombs at a distance—and an ugly, prefab, concrete Lego-style building of the 1960s on the right, before reaching the long-scaffolded...

❼ Palace of Justice (Palais de Justice)

This domed mountain of marble sits on the edge of the Upper Town ridge, dominating the Brussels skyline. Built in wedding-cake layers of Greek columns, it's topped with a dome taller than St. Peter's in Rome, rising 340 feet. Covering more than six acres, it's the size of a baseball stadium. Extending seven floors underground, it's so big it has its own postal code.

The palace was built in the time of King Leopold II (son of Leo I, r. 1865-1909) and epitomizes the brassy, showy grandeur of his reign. Leopold became obscenely wealthy by turning Africa's Congo region—80 times the size of Belgium—into his personal colony. Whip-wielding Belgian masters forced Congolese slaves to tend lucrative rubber plantations, exploiting the new craze for car tires. Leopold spent much of this wealth expanding and beautifying the city of Brussels.

The building, (which stands on the historic site of the town gallows) serves as a Hall of Justice, where major court cases are tried. If you pop in to the lobby, you may see lawyers in black robes buzzing about.

Notice the rack of city bikes. Like many other European cities, Brussels subsidizes a public-bike system. The program, called "Villo," lets locals use bikes scattered all over town (note the map here) for a token €1 per hour (see details on page 451). You can pick up a bike in one part of town and drop it off anywhere else. But the scheme doesn't always work as well as intended: These bike racks are often empty, since this is a popular place to grab a bike for the easy ride back down to the Lower Town.

• *One of the best views of Brussels is immediately to the right of the Palace of Justice.*

❽ Viewpoint from Place Poelaert

You're standing 200 feet above the former Senne River Valley. Gazing west over the Lower Town, pan the valley from right (north) to left:

Near you is the stubby **clock tower** of the Minimen Church (which hosts lunchtime concerts in the summer). To the left of that, in the distance past a tall square skyscraper, is the lacy, white Town Hall **spire** (marking the Grand Place).

Twinkling in the far distance, six miles away, you can see one of the city's landmarks, the **Atomium.** (No doubt, someone atop it is looking back at you.) The Atomium's nine shiny steel balls form the shape of an iron molecule that's the size of the Palace of Justice behind you. Built for the 1958 World's Fair, it's now a middle-aged symbol of the dawn of the Atomic Era.

Next (closer to you) rises the **black clock tower** of the Notre-Dame de la Chapelle church, the city's oldest (from 1134, with a

tower that starts Gothic and ends Baroque). On the distant horizon, see **four boxy skyscrapers,** part of the residential sprawl of this city of over a million, which now covers 62 square miles. Breaking the horizon to the left is a **green dome,** which belongs to the Basilica of Koekelberg (fourth-biggest in the world). And finally (panning quickly to the left), you see a **black glass skyscraper** marking the Midi/Zuid/South train station, where you can catch special high-speed train lines, such as the Eurostar, to London.

At your feet lies the **Marolles neighborhood.** Once a funky, poor place where locals developed their own quirky dialogue, today it can be either seedy or colorful, depending on the time of day and your perception. The area is famous for its sprawling flea market (daily 7:00-14:00, best on weekends). Two of the streets just below you—Rue Haute/Hoogstraat and Rue Blaes/Blaesstraat—

are lined with secondhand shops. An **elevator** (free, daily 6:00-23:00) connects Place Poelaert with the Marolles neighborhood, which is worth a 10-minute detour to descend to the café-lined square. People who brake for garage sales may want to cut out of this walk early and head to the Marolles from here.

Gazing off into the distance to the far left (south), you can't quite see the suburb of **Waterloo,** 10 miles away. But try to imagine it, because it was there that the tide of European history turned. On the morning of June 18, 1815, Napoleon waited two hours for the ground to dry before sending his troops into battle. That time lag may have cost him the battle. His 72,000 soldiers could have defeated Wellington's 68,000, but the two-hour delay was just enough time for Wellington's reinforcements to arrive—45,000 Prussian troops. Napoleon had to surrender, his rule of Europe ended, and Belgium was placed under a Dutch king—until the Belgians won their independence in the 1830 revolution.

Behind you, in Place Poelaert, is a memorial to the two World Wars, both of which slashed through Belgium with deadly force.

• *Backtrack east, descending to Place du Grand Sablon by walking down Rue Ernest Allard. Passing lots of antiques shops and galleries, you'll eventually reach a square below the Notre-Dame du Sablon Church. (For a light, healthy, and characteristic meal, Le Pain Quotidien—just off the square at Rue des Sablons 11—offers a fine value with delightful seating and baked goods right out of the oven.)*

❾ Place du Grand Sablon

The Sablon neighborhood features cafés and restaurants, antiques stores, and art galleries. Every weekend, there's an antiques mar-

ket on the square. On warm summer evenings, the square sparks magic, as sophisticated locals sip apéritifs at the café tables, admiring the church's glowing stained glass. Chocolatier Wittamer (on the far side of the square, at #6) often has elaborate window displays. And at the bottom of the square is the shop of the innovative Pierre Marcolini—

who was declared the world's top chocolatier—with a tempting buffet upstairs.

• *Sloping Place du Grand Sablon funnels downhill into the pedestrian-only street called Rue de Rollebeek. With a few surviving buildings, it gives a little sense of the city before its 1695 bombardment (which leveled the center of town). It leads you past fun shops to the busy Boulevard de l'Empereur. To the right on the boulevard, just past the gas station, is the...*

⑩ Tour d'Angle

The "Corner Tower" is a rare surviving section of Brussels' medieval city wall. It stood over one of seven gates along the 2.5-mile-

long wall that enclosed one of Europe's great cities—13th-century Brussels. Notice the slash through the city here that marks where underground train lines connect the Central Station (to your right) and the South Station (to your left). Six tracks under you are kept busy with about a thousand trains a day. This ambitious bit of city infrastructure was a project started in 1902 and not finished until 1952—two occupations by Germany slowed things down.

• *Cross the street, head right, and take first left which leads downhill to a pleasant square at the T-intersection.*

⑪ Place Vieille Halle aux Blés

Do a 360-degree sweep from the center of this charming little square, circled by nice apartments. Imagine what a delight it would be to call this neighborhood home. Twenty years ago, this was a derelict slum—a good reason why Brussels was famous as a fine place to work but a lousy place to live. People were moving out, leaving the down-and-out downtown. But in 1989 Brussels became its own political region and got its own government. Since then, its policy has been to revitalize the center of town; tearing down homes to build office space is no longer allowed. Consequently, new construction is reserved for residences and people are moving into the area again. As in so many European cities, government policies are spurring the revitalization of old town centers.

• *Your walk is finished. From here, to reach the* Manneken-Pis *and the* Grand Place, *just follow the signs.*

ROYAL MUSEUMS OF FINE ARTS and MAGRITTE MUSEUM TOUR

Musées Royaux des Beaux-Arts de Belgique • Musée Magritte

This museum complex, spread throughout three large buildings, covers much of the history of Western painting. There are technically three museums here: the Museum of Ancient Art (pre-1850), the Fin de Siècle Museum (1850-1910), and—covered by a separate ticket—the Magritte Museum, which celebrates the work of the popular Belgian Surrealist painter. The collections, while enjoyable, can be overwhelming, so this chapter gives you a tour highlighting the museums' strengths: Flemish and Belgian artists. But don't limit your visit to these works—let the museums surprise you.

Orientation

Cost: €9 for Ancient Art and Fin de Siècle museums; €8 for Magritte Museum; €13 combo-ticket covers all three. All are free the first Wed of the month after 13:00.

Hours: Tue-Sun 10:00-17:00, closed Mon, last entry 30 minutes before closing. The Magritte Museum stays open Wed until 20:00.

Getting There: The main entrance, with access to all three museums, is at Rue de la Régence 3 in the Upper Town, just a five-minute walk uphill from Central Station (or take bus #38, #71, or #95; or tram #92 or #94). Bus #27 connects this area with the European Parliament and the Park of the Cinquantenaire. You'll also encounter these museums if you take my Upper Town Walk (see previous chapter).

Keep Your Magrittes Straight: Don't confuse this Magritte Museum with the much smaller René Magritte Museum, located in Magritte's former home on the outskirts of Brussels. This is clearly the place to enjoy his art.

Information: Consider the €4 audioguide for the Ancient Art Museum, the €5 videoguide for the Fin de Siècle Museum, or the €4 audioguide for the Magritte Museum. A €2.50 tour booklet, *Twenty Masterpieces of the Art of Painting: A Brief Guided Tour,* is sold in the museum shop. Ancient Art and Fin de Siècle museums: Tel. 02-508-3211, www.fine -arts-museum.be. Magritte Museum: Tel. 02-508-3333, www .musee-magritte-museum.be.

Length of This Tour: Allow one hour for the Ancient Art and Fin de Siècle museums, and another hour for the Magritte Museum.

Cuisine Art: The museums have a pricey café and a fancy brasserie on site. The Musical Instruments Museum, a block away, has a much-appreciated restaurant on its rooftop (see page 464).

The Tour Begins

This tour assumes you'll visit the Ancient Art and Fin de Siècle museums first, then the Magritte Museum.

Enter at Rue de la Régence 3 and buy your ticket. Continue into the large entrance hall and get oriented. The Museum of Ancient Art is on the second floor (in the galleries above you), reached by the staircase directly ahead. The Fin de Siècle Museum is through the doorway to the right, down several levels. The Magritte Museum is also to the right, through a passageway.

In the museum's entry hall stands an imposing statue of Belgium's big-thinking king, King Leopold II. His father, Leopold I, was put on the throne when Belgium was made an independent kingdom in 1830. But it was Leopold II who transformed the city and gave it grand institutions, like this museum. While Belgium doesn't even make the G-20 today, back in Leopold II's day, it was the second greatest industrial power per capita in the world.

Before diving in, stop first at the information desk near Leopold. This is also where you can rent an audioguide. Armed with the museum's free map, make your way through the maze, enjoying whatever you find. Along the way, look for these highlights.

Museum of Ancient Art

• *Go up to the second floor and start with the Flemish masters. Notice how the rooms on the second floor surround a central hall. The art is displayed in (roughly) chronological order, working counterclockwise around the central gallery. In the first room, look for...*

Rogier van der Weyden (c. 1399-1464)—*Portrait of Anthony of Burgundy (Portrait d' Antoine de Bourgogne)*

Anthony was known in his day as the Great Bastard, the bravest and most distinguished of the many bastards fathered by prolific Duke Philip the Good (a Renaissance prince whose sense of style impressed Florence's young Lorenzo the Magnificent, patron of the arts).

Anthony, a member of the Archers Guild, fingers the arrow like a bowstring. From his gold necklace dangles a Golden Fleece, one of Europe's more prestigious knightly honors. Wearing a black cloak, a bowl-cut hairdo, and a dark-red cap, with his pale face and hand emerging from a dark background, the man who'd been called a bastard all his life gazes to the distance, his clear, sad eyes lit with a speckle of white paint.

Van der Weyden, Brussels' official portrait painter, faithfully rendered life-size, lifelike portraits of wealthy traders, bankers, and craftsmen. Here he captures the wrinkles in Anthony's neck and the faint shadow his chin casts on his Adam's apple. Van der Weyden had also painted Philip the Good (in Bruges' Groeninge Museum—see page 402), and young Anthony's long, elegant face and full lips are a mirror image—pretty convincing DNA evidence in a paternity suit.

Capitalist Flanders in the 1400s was one of the richest, most cultured, and progressive areas in Europe, rivaling Florence and Venice.

• *Continue counterclockwise around the central gallery. As you head up the right side (in the third section), find...*

Hans Memling (c. 1430-1494)—*Martyrdom of St. Sebastian (Volets d'un Triptyque)*

Serene Sebastian is filled with arrows by a serene firing squad in a serene landscape. Sebastian, a Roman captain who'd converted to Christianity, was ordered to be shot to death. (He miraculously survived, so they clubbed him to death.)

Ready, freeze! Like a *tableau vivant* (popular with Philip the

Good's crowd), the well-dressed archers and saint freeze this moment in the martyrdom so the crowd can applaud the colorful costumes and painted cityscape backdrop.

Hans Memling, along with his former employer, Rogier van der Weyden, are called Flemish Primitives. Why "Primitive"? The term comes from the lack of 3-D realism so admired in Italy at the time (for more on Flemish Primitives, see sidebar on page 401). Sebastian's arm is tied to a branch that's not arching overhead, as it should be, but instead is behind him. An archer aims slightly behind, not at, Sebastian. The other archer strings his bow in a stilted pose. But Memling is clearly a master of detail, and the faces, beautiful textiles, and hazy landscape combine to create a meditative mood appropriate to the church altar in Bruges where this painting was once placed.

• *Next, head for the far-right corner of room 68, where paintings by Pieter Bruegel I often are displayed.*

Pieter Bruegel I, the Elder (c. 1527-1569)— *The Census at Bethlehem*

Perched at treetop level, you have a bird's-eye view over a snow-covered village near Brussels. The canals are frozen over, but life

goes on, with everyone doing something. Kids throw snowballs and sled across the ice. A crowd gathers at the inn (lower left), where a woman holds a pan to catch blood while a man slaughters a pig. Most everyone has his or her back to us or head covered, so the figures speak through poses and motions.

Into the scene rides a woman on a donkey led by a man—it's Mary and husband Joseph hoping to find a room at the inn (or at least a manger), because Mary's going into labor.

The year is 1566—the same year that Protestant extremists throughout the Low Countries vandalized Catholic churches, tearing down "idolatrous" statues and paintings of the Virgin Mary. Bruegel (more discreetly) brings Mary down to earth from her Triumphant Coronation in heaven, and places Jesus' birth in the humble here and now. The busy villagers put their heads down and work, oblivious to the future Mother of God and the wondrous birth about to take place.

Bruegel the Elder was famous for his landscapes filled with crowds of peasants in motion. His religious paintings place the miraculous in everyday settings.

In this room you'll see Bruegel's works, as well as those of his less famous sons. Pieter Brueghel II, the younger Pieter, copied his dad's style (and even some paintings, like the *Census at Bethlehem*—displayed to the left). Another son, Jan, was known as the "Velvet Brueghel" for his glossy still lifes of flower arrangements.

• *Circle counterclockwise through the rest of the Ancient Art collection, until you finally reach works by Rubens in rooms 52 and 53, including the wall-sized...*

Peter Paul Rubens (1577-1640)—
The Ascent to Calvary (La Montée au Calvaire)

Life-size figures scale this 18-foot-tall canvas on the way to Christ's Crucifixion. The scene ripples with motion, from the windblown clothes to steroid-enhanced muscles to billowing flags and a troubled sky. Christ stumbles—he might get trampled by the surging crowd. Veronica kneels to gently wipe his bloody head.

This 200-square-foot canvas was manufactured by Rubens at his studio in Antwerp. Hiring top-notch assistants, Rubens could

crank out large altarpieces for the area's Catholic churches. First, Rubens himself did a small-scale sketch in oil (like many of the studies in room 52). He would then make other sketches, highlighting individual details. His assistants would reproduce them on the large canvas, and Rubens would then add the final touches.

This work is from late in Rubens' long and very successful career. He got a second wind in his 50s, when he married 16-year-old Hélène Fourment. She was the model for Veronica, who con-

soles the faltering Christ in this painting.

• *Exit the Rubens room to the left, go into the perpendicular room 53, and look right to find...*

Jacques-Louis David (1748-1825)—
The Death of Marat (1793)

In a scene ripped from the day's headlines, Jean-Paul Marat—a well-known crusading French journalist—has been stabbed to death in his bathtub by Charlotte Corday, a conservative fanatic. Marat's life drains out of him, turning the bathwater red. With his last strength, he pens a final, patriotic, *"Vive la Révolution"* mes-

sage to his fellow patriots. Corday, a young noblewoman angered by Marat's campaign to behead the French king, was arrested and guillotined three days later.

Jacques-Louis David, one of Marat's fellow revolutionaries, set to work painting a tribute to his fallen comrade. (He signed the painting: "*À Marat*"—"To Marat.")

David makes it a secular *pietà*, with the brave writer portrayed as a martyred Christ in a classic dangling-arm pose. Still, the deathly pallor and harsh lighting pull no punches, creating in-your-face realism.

David, the official art director of the French Revolution, supervised propaganda and the costumes worn for patriotic parades. A year after finishing this painting, in 1794, his extreme brand of revolution (which included guillotining thousands of supposed enemies) was squelched by moderates, and David was jailed. He emerged later as Napoleon's court painter. When Napoleon was exiled in 1815, so was David, spending his last years in Brussels.

• *To get to the Fin de Siècle Museum, return to the ground floor and the large main entrance hall of the Museum of Ancient Art and rent the videoguide here if you like. From the entry hall a passageway leads you to the Fin de Siècle and Magritte museums. You'll pass the entrance to the Magritte Museum, then continue down into the Fin de Siècle wing (entering on level -3).*

Fin de Siècle Museum

Brussels likes to think of itself as the "capital" of Art Nouveau, and this newly remodeled space presents a convincing case. Covering the period from the mid-19th century to the early 20th century, in many ways this is Brussels' answer to the Musée d'Orsay in Paris. While it doesn't have the high-powered collection of Impressionists found at the Orsay, it does have remarkable works by Post-Impressionists, Realists, and Symbolists. It also houses the Gillion Crowet Collection—a €36 million assemblage of Art Nouveau paintings, glassware, jewelry, and furniture by the likes of Fernand Khnopff, Emile Gallé, and Victor Horta.

Don't expect to see this art in chronological order. Galleries are organized thematically, and paintings are presented in context with examples from the period's literature, opera, architecture, and photography.

This space used to house the Royal Museums' modern art collection. Unfortunately, most of its 20th-century works—including those by Paul Delvaux, Joan Miró, Salvador Dalí, Max Ernst, Yves Tanguy, and Roberto Matta—are in storage until the curators find a new place to exhibit them.

• *Go down, down, down through several levels on a route through turn-of-the-century paintings, sculpture, glassware, furniture, and even books. Keep an eye out for the following paintings; enlist the help of nearby guards if you can't find a piece.*

James Ensor (1860-1949)—*Shocked Masks* (1883)

At 22, James Ensor, an acclaimed child prodigy, proudly presented his lively Impressionist-style works to the Brussels Salon for exhibition. They were flatly rejected.

The artist withdrew from public view and, in seclusion, painted *Shocked Masks*, a dark and murky scene set in a small room of an ordinary couple wearing grotesque masks. Once again, everyone disliked this disturbing canvas and heaped more criticism on him. For the next six decades, Ensor painted the world as he saw it—full of bizarre, carnival-masked, stupid-looking crowds of cruel strangers who mock the viewer.

Georges Seurat (1859-1891)—*The Seine at Grand-Jatte* (*La Seine à la Grande-Jatte*, 1888)

Seurat paints a Sunday-in-the-park view from his favorite island in the Seine. Taking Impressionism to its extreme, he builds the scene out of small points of primary colors that blend at a distance to form objects. The bright colors capture the dazzling, sunlit atmosphere of this hazy day.

Paul Gauguin (1848-1903)—*Breton Calvary* (*Calvaire Breton*, 1889; a.k.a. *The Green Christ/Le Christ Vert*)

Paul Gauguin returned to the bold, black, coloring-book outlines of more Primitive (pre-3-D) art. The Christian statue and countryside look less like Brittany and more like primitive Tahiti, where Gauguin would soon settle.

Jean Delville (1867-1953)—
Dead Orpheus (Orphée mort, 1893)

A key figure in Belgian Symbolism, Jean Delville was heavily influenced by the paintings of Gustave Moreau and the music of Richard Wagner. Here he takes on the Greek myth of Orpheus, showing the idealized head of the legendary poet, who seems to be floating on his lyre, ready to be reborn.

Magritte Museum

Entry to the Magritte Museum is covered by a separate ticket. The €4 audioguide is essential.

This museum takes you on a chronological route (with 200 works by the Surrealist spread over several levels of the building) through René Magritte's life and art. The museum divides his life into three sections, with one floor devoted to each. In each section is a detailed timeline putting the work you'll see in a biographical and historical context. Fascinating quotes from Magritte are posted around the museum, but only in French and Dutch; pick up the English translation as you enter.

Magritte's works are perhaps best described in his own words: "My paintings are visible images which conceal nothing; they evoke mystery and, indeed, when one sees one of my pictures, one asks oneself this simple question, 'What does that mean'? It does not mean anything, because mystery means nothing either, it is unknowable." If that brainteaser titillates you, you'll love this museum.

• *From the entrance, you'll board an elevator that takes you up to level +3. (Seeing the artist's wife Georgette naked as you rise, it starts to sink in: This is not just another museum.)*

1898-1929 (Level +3)

Born to a middle-class Belgian family, René moved to Brussels at age 17 to study at the Academy, where he learned to draw meticulously and got a broad liberal arts education. In the 1920s, he eked out a living designing advertisements, posters, and sheet music, and wrote for the avant-garde *7 Arts* magazine (you'll see samples posted). Meanwhile, he dabbled in Post-Impressionism, Futurism, and Cubism, in search of his own voice.

In 1922, he married his childhood sweetheart, Georgette, who became his lifelong companion and muse. It's said that all the women he would paint (and you'll see many of them in this collection) were versions of Georgette.

Influenced by the Dada and Surrealist movements coming out of Paris (Salvador Dalí, Marcel Duchamp, Giorgio de Chirico), Magritte became intrigued with the idea of painting dreamscapes

René Magritte
(1898-1967)

René Magritte trained and worked in Brussels. Though he's world-famous now, it took decades before his peculiar brand of Surrealism caught on. He painted real objects with photographic clarity, and then jumbled them together in new and provocative ways.

Magritte had his own private reserve of symbolic images. You'll see clouds, blue sky, windows, the female torso, men in bowler hats, rocks, pipes, sleigh bells, birds, turtles, and castles arranged side by side as if the arrangement means something. He heightens the mystery by making objects unnaturally large or small. People morph into animals or inanimate objects. The juxtaposition short-circuits your brain only when you try to make sense of it. Magritte's works are at once playful and disorienting...and, at times, disturbing.

that capture an air of mystery. You'll see mysterious figures on beaches, inspired by de Chirico's similar canvases.

For Magritte, 1927 was a watershed year, when he painted his first truly Surrealist works. *The Man from the Sea* featured a man on a beach with a wood-block head, pulling a lever. At the far end of the next room, *The Secret Player* perplexed the public (then and now) with a man swinging a bat and missing a flying turtle. In this section, and throughout this floor, you can see Magritte toying with Surrealist thoughts and techniques.

Together, René and Georgette mingled in sophisticated, bohemian circles. Photos show that their creativity went beyond the canvas. Looking at Georgette pose for René's lens (as she often did for his paintbrush), it's touching to think that he had found a soul mate who seemed to truly understand and encourage his weirdness. In the same section, see the series of photos of René, Georgette, and their friends striking wacky tableaux that intentionally distort normal poses. Called *The Fidelity of the Image*, this series was knocking on the door of Magritte's next breakthrough.

He experimented with writing words on the paintings, culminating in *The Treachery of Images*. The original (from 1928-1929, in the Los Angeles County Museum of Art) is Magritte's most famous work—not for its physical appearance, but for the bold conceptual point that it made. It's a photorealistic painting of a pipe with the words (in French) "This is not a pipe." Of course it's not a pipe, Magritte always insisted—it's a *painting* of a pipe. Magritte's wordplay forces the viewer to ponder the relationship between the object and its name—between the "signified" and the "signifier," to quote the deconstructionist philosophy that Magritte's paradoxical paintings inspired. Some credit this work for planting the seeds of Postmodernism. At the end of this section you'll see a later ink-and-paper version (1952) with the message (also in French): "This continues not to be a pipe."

• *Head downstairs to...*

1930-1950 (Level +2)

After a few years in Paris, Magritte survived the Depression in Brussels by doing ad work and painting portraits of friends. (You'll see several women on his trademark Surrealist beaches.)

By the late 1930s, he'd refined his signature style: combining two arresting images to disrupt rational thought and produce an emotion of mystery. The paintings' weird titles added another layer of disruption. These were intentional nonsequiturs, which he and his Surrealist friends concocted at Sunday-night naming soirees. Perusing the paintings in here, it's fun to wonder which titles were random...and which meant something. *Forbidden Literature... The Kiss... The Unexpected Answer... God Is No Saint...*

During the World War II years—spent under Nazi occupation—Magritte used birds as a metaphor for the longing to be free *(The Companions of Fear, Treasure Island).*

In 1943, he had a brief Impressionistic period of bright colors and rough brushwork. His characteristic Georgette-inspired nude becomes Technicolor in *The Harvest.* He also took to painting tongue-in-cheek-serious "portraits" of animals *(Stroke of Luck).* Soon after, his series called *Black Magic* continued to colorize women's bodies. But he also created plenty of his distinctive paintings where the background and foreground seem to shift, with plenty of familiar motifs such as clouds and bowler hats.

In the postwar years, Magritte went through a *vache* ("cow") period, where he painted a series of comic-book-inspired paintings (including the green man with rifle-barrel nose, called *The Ellipsis).* Almost childlike, these are a dramatic departure from his normally photorealistic style.

1951-1967 (Level +1)

This floor is divided into two sections (don't overlook the easy-to-miss second one), and feels like a valedictory lap for all of the symbols and styles we've seen so far.

Like Picasso (and many other artists) nearing the end of a life of impressive output and experimentation, Magritte had a quiver full of artistic arrows to shoot at the canvas. And yet something feels rote about his final years of work—he seemed to rehash familiar territory, expressing things he'd already mastered—rather than experiment with bold new directions.

The collection culminates at his *Empire of Lights*, which shows how even well-scrubbed suburbia can possess an ominous air of mystery. Magritte loved night-sky tones. He often created several versions of the same work (which explains why there are several *Empire of Lights* canvases in the world).

By the end of his life, Magritte was well-known, especially in America. His use of everyday objects and poster-art style inspired Pop Art.

• *Exit through level -1, which has a bookshop and an appropriately perplexing 50-minute film about Magritte (plays constantly, English subtitles). Descend to level -2 to find the passageway back to the Royal Museums...and reality.*

BRUSSELS SLEEPING, EATING, NIGHTLIFE & CONNECTIONS

As the capital of Belgium—and of the European Union—Brussels is a great place to spend some time. This chapter provides suggestions for the best places to sleep and eat; tips for after-hours fun; and a rundown of the connections (from the city's three different train stations) to points throughout Belgium, the Netherlands, and beyond, as well as tips for getting to and from the city's two airports.

Sleeping in Brussels

Normal hotel prices are high in central Brussels. A popular business destination, it tends to be busiest, and most expensive, on weekdays. But if you arrive in July, August, or on a Friday or Saturday night, the city's fancy business-class hotels may rent rooms for half-price, making them your best budget bet. (Conversely, Bruges—a pleasure destination—has higher demand on weekends. If your trip is flexible, consider arranging your overnights in these two towns with these deal-finding patterns in mind.)

April, May, September, and October are very crowded in Brussels, and finding a room without a reservation can be impossible. The busiest time of year is the European Seafood Exhibition (April 22-24 in 2014, www.euroseafood.com), when the city is awash in seafood-industry employees.

You do have budget options here. The modern hostels, which rent double rooms, are especially good.

Business Hotels with Summer Rates

Brussels' fancy hotels (Db-€150-200) survive because of the business and diplomatic trade. But they're desperately empty most of

Sleep Code

(€1 = about $1.30, country code: 32)
S = Single, **D** = Double/Twin, **T** = Triple, **Q** = Quad, **b** = bathroom, **s** = shower only. Everyone speaks English and accepts credit cards. Unless otherwise noted, breakfast is included.

To help you easily sort through these listings, I've divided the accommodations into three categories, based on the price for a standard double room with bath:

$$$ Higher Priced—Most rooms €100 or more.
$$ Moderately Priced—Most rooms between €80-100.
$ Lower Priced—Most rooms €80 or less.

Prices can change without notice and don't include the city room tax; verify the hotel's current rates online or by email.

July and August (sometimes June, too) and on most weekends (Fri, Sat, and, to a lesser extent, Sun nights). During these slow times, rates can drop by a third to two-thirds. Three-star hotels in the center abound with low summer rates—you may be able to rent a double room with enough comforts to keep a diplomat happy, including a fancy breakfast, for about €70-80.

There are two ways to get these great rates: You can go through a booking website (most Brussels hotels list their rooms through www.booking.com, but you might also find deals on other sites—check www.expedia.com, www.orbitz.com, or your favorite). Or you can book direct. Because some hotels hold out until the last minute to cut their rates, prices tend to plummet as the date approaches. If waiting seems too risky, do a little homework to gauge what the demand will be when you visit: Check rates online well before your trip. If rates are only slightly discounted, demand is probably pretty strong, so you should book sooner rather than later; if rates are already deeply discounted, you might consider holding off, to see if they go even lower.

These seasonal discounts apply only to business-class hotels. Because of this, budget accommodations, which charge the same throughout the year, may go from being a good value one day (say, a Thursday in October) to a bad value the next (a Friday in October).

Near the Grand Place

$$$ Hotel Ibis off Grand Place, well-situated halfway between Central Station and the Grand Place, is the best of six Ibis locations in or near Brussels. It's a sprawling, modern hotel offering 184

Brussels Accommodations

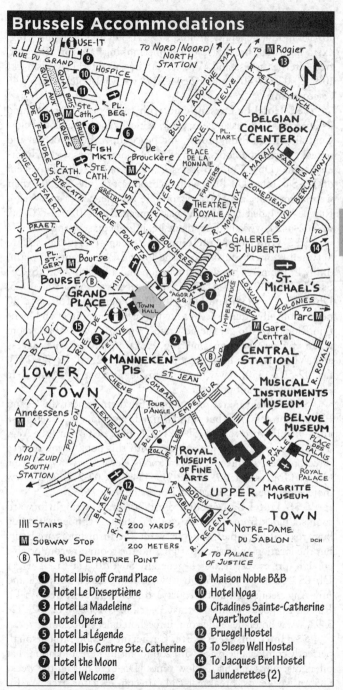

IIII Stairs

Ⓜ Subway Stop

Ⓑ Tour Bus Departure Point

① Hotel Ibis off Grand Place
② Hotel Le Dixseptième
③ Hotel La Madeleine
④ Hotel Opéra
⑤ Hotel La Légende
⑥ Hotel Ibis Centre Ste. Catherine
⑦ Hotel the Moon
⑧ Hotel Welcome

⑨ Maison Noble B&B
⑩ Hotel Noga
⑪ Citadines Sainte-Catherine Apart'hotel
⑫ Bruegel Hostel
⑬ To Sleep Well Hostel
⑭ To Jacques Brel Hostel
⑮ Launderettes (2)

BRUSSELS SLEEPING

quiet, simple, industrial-strength-yet-comfy rooms (Sb/Db-€145-169 Mon-Thu, generally around €79 Fri-Sun and daily July-Aug, extra bed-€20, breakfast-€14, non-smoking, air-con, elevator, free Internet access and Wi-Fi, Marché-aux-Herbes/Grasmarkt 100, tel. 02-514-4040, fax 02-514-5067, www.ibishotel.com, h1046 @accor.com).

$$$ **Hotel Le Dixseptième,** with rather plain rooms behind its luxurious lounges and entryway, is ideally located a block below Central Station. Prim, proper, and peaceful, with chandeliers and squeaky hardwood floors, each of its 24 rooms comes with a different theme (Db-€200, Db suites-€270, extra bed-€30, 25 percent off Fri-Sat, often Db-€100 with no breakfast in July-Aug, see their website for deals, air-con, elevator, free Internet access and Wi-Fi, Rue de la Madeleine/Magdalenasteenweg 25, tel. 02-517-1717, fax 02-502-6424, www.ledixseptieme.be, info@ledixseptieme.be).

$$$ **Hotel La Madeleine,** on the small "Agora" square between Central Station and the Grand Place, rents 56 plain, dimly lit rooms. It has a great location and a friendly staff (S-€55; Ss-€78, Sb-€108, Db-€115; bigger "executive" rooms: Sb-€125, Db-€130, Tb-€138, family Qb-€180; 20 percent off Fri-Sat, 30 percent off July-Aug—see website for deals, book direct and mention Rick Steves to get the best rates; request a quieter back room when you reserve, non-smoking, elevator, pay Internet access and Wi-Fi, Rue de la Montagne/Bergstraat 22, tel. 02-513-2973, fax 02-502-1350, www.hotel-la-madeleine.be, info@hotel-la -madeleine.be, Philippe).

$$$ **Hotel Opéra,** on a people-filled street near the Grand Place, is professional but standardized, with lots of street noise and 49 well-worn rooms (Sb-€89, Db-€119 or €89 in July-Aug, Tb-€139, Qb-€159, 10 percent less with this book if you reserve direct, request a quieter courtyard room, elevator, free Wi-Fi, Rue Grétry/Gretrystraat 53, tel. 02-219-4343, fax 02-219-1720, www .hotel-opera.be, reception@hotel-opera.be).

$$$ **Hotel La Légende** rents 26 small, straightforward rooms a block from the *Manneken-Pis* statue. Although it's on a busy road, it has a pleasant courtyard. The furnishings are basic, but the location and price are right and the rooms are comfortable enough (prices very flexible—generally Sb-€110, Db-€120, bigger Db-€5-40 extra, Tb-€155, Qb-€180, lower prices on weekends and July-Aug, request a quieter courtyard room, elevator, free Wi-Fi, Rue du Lombard/Lombardstraat 35, tel. 02-512-8290, fax 02-512-3493, www.hotellalegende.com, info@hotellalegende.com).

$$ **Hotel Ibis Centre Ste. Catherine** is a big, impersonal, perfectly comfortable place with 236 rooms in a great location that offers discounts during its slow times (Db-€150 during the week, €85 on weekends, breakfast-€14, air-con, elevator, free Wi-Fi,

Joseph Plateau street 2 at Place Ste. Catherine/Sint-Katelijneplein, tel. 02-513-7620, fax 02-514-2214, www.ibishotel.com, h1454 @accor.com).

$$ Hotel the Moon is a concrete and efficient last resort, with 17 bare-bones rooms and no public spaces. It has absolutely no character and the thin walls and doors, along with noise from the square out front, can make for a noisy night. But the location is super-convenient—just steps from the Grand Place—and it's the cheapest centrally located hotel this side of a youth hostel (Sb-€55-70, Db-€65-90, Tb-€81-110, lower prices are for slow times including July-Aug, 10 percent discount if you book direct with the latest edition of this book, ask for a quieter room in the back, stairs but no elevator, on the small "Agora" square at Rue de la Montagne/Bergstraat 4, tel. 02-508-1580, fax 02-508-1585, www.hotelthe moon.com, info@hotelthemoon.com).

In Ste. Catherine, near the Old Fish Market

The next three listings are a 10-minute walk from the intensity of the old center, near the Ste. Catherine/Sint-Katelijne Métro stop. This charming neighborhood, called "the village in Brussels," faces the canalside fish market and has many of the town's best restaurants. When you get good with the Métro, this area is a simple, two-stop ride from the Central Station and super convenient.

$$$ Hotel Welcome, run by an energetic bundle of hospitality named Michel Smeesters and his wife Sophie, offers

outrageously creative rooms, exuberantly decorated with artifacts they've picked up in their world travels. Each of the 16 rooms has a different geographic theme, from India to Japan to Bali: Take a virtual tour of the rooms on their website (Sb-€120, standard Db-€75-145, deluxe Db-€105-165, family room, discounted on weekends and with direct Rick Steves bookings in Aug, elevator, air-con, free Internet access and Wi-Fi, reasonably priced laundry service, parking-€13, free airport transfer with 2-night stay in a deluxe room, 23 Quai au Bois à Brûler/Brandhoutkaai, tel. 02-219-9546, fax 02-217-1887, www .hotelwelcome.com, info@hotelwelcome.com).

$$$ Maison Noble is a charming boutique B&B run by Matthieu and Brendon. This gay-friendly place (the well-hung art gravitates toward male nudes) has three classy, mod rooms, a gorgeous Art Nouveau/Art Deco stained-glass window over the breakfast table, and a free steam room. It's on a dull street just a block off the old fish market (D-€129, big Db-€149, 1-night stay-€20 extra,

€10 less for 4 nights or longer, €20 less mid-July-Aug, free Internet access and Wi-Fi, 10 Marcq street, tel. 02-219-2339, www.maison -noble.eu, info@maison-noble.eu).

$$$ Hotel Noga feels extremely homey, with 19 rooms, a welcoming game room, and old photos of Belgian royalty lining the hallways. It's carefully run by Frederich Faucher and his son, Mourad (Sb-€75, Db-€110, Tb-€135, Qb-€160, low rates Fri-Sat and in Aug, 5 percent discount if you pay in cash, very quiet, non-smoking, pay Internet access and Wi-Fi, garage-€15, Rue du Beguinage/Begijnhofstraat 38, tel. 02-218-6763, fax 02-218-1603, www.nogahotel.com, info@nogahotel.com).

$$$ Citadines Sainte-Catherine Apart'hotel, part of a Europe-wide chain, is a huge apartment-style hotel with modern, shipshape rooms. Choose from efficiency studios with foldout double beds or two-room apartments with a bedroom and a foldout couch in the living room. All 169 units come with a kitchen, stocked cupboards, a stereo, and everything you need to settle right in—even a dishwasher. This may be the best place if you're bringing your family and staying three to four nights (official rates: one- or two-person studio-€135, apartment for up to four people-€170, but rates very flexible—check online, much less July-Aug, 15 percent cheaper by the week, breakfast-€14, free Internet access and Wi-Fi, parking-€17, 51 Quai au Bois à Brûler/Brandhoutkaai, tel. 02-221-1411, fax 02-221-1599, www.citadines.com, stecatherine @citadines.com).

Hostels

Three classy and modern hostels—in buildings that could double as small, state-of-the-art, minimum-security prisons—are within a 10-minute walk of Central Station. Each accepts people of all ages, serves cheap and hot meals, takes credit cards, and is budget-priced. All rates include sheets, breakfast, and showers down the hall.

$ Bruegel Hostel, a fortress of cleanliness, is handiest and most comfortable, with 135 beds. Of its many rooms, 22 are bunk-bed doubles (S-€27, D-€54, beds in quads or dorms-€20, nonmembers and guests over age 26 pay €3 extra/night, open 7:00-10:00 & 14:00-1:00 in the morning, free Wi-Fi, midway between Midi/Zuid/South and Central stations, behind Chapelle church at Rue de St. Esprit/H. Geeststraat 2, tel. 02-511-0436, fax 02-512-0711, www.youthhostels.be, brussel@vjh.be).

$ Sleep Well Hostel, surrounded by high-rise parking structures, is also comfortable (bunks in 4-6-bed rooms-€23-24, Sb-€42/50, Db-€63/69, Tb-€81/95, lower price for dorm-style rooms, higher price for hotelesque rooms, non-smoking, Internet access and Wi-Fi, lockout 11:00-15:00, Rue de Damier/

Dambordstraat 23, tel. 02-218-5050, fax 02-218-1313, www.sleep well.be, info@sleepwell.be).

$ Jacques Brel Hostel, with 171 beds, is a little farther out, but it's still a reasonable walk from everything (S-€39, D-€49-54, dorm bed-€21-23, nonmembers and guests over age 26 pay €3 extra/night, no curfew, non-smoking rooms, laundry, Rue de la Sablonnière/Zavelput 30, tel. 02-218-0187, fax 02-217-2005, www .laj.be, brussels.brel@laj.be).

Eating in Brussels

For many, the obvious eating tip in Brussels is simply to enjoy the very touristy but undeniably magnificent Grand Place. My vote for northern Europe's grandest medi-
eval square is lined with hardworking eateries that serve predictable dishes to tourist crowds. Of course, you won't get the best quality or prices—but, after all, it's the Grand Place. Locals advise eating well elsewhere and enjoying a Grand Place perch for dessert or a drink. While many tourists congregate at the Rue des Bouchers, "Restaurant Row," consider a wander through the new, emerging eating zone—gay, ethnic, and trendy—past the Bourse near Place St. Géry/Sint-

Goriksplein. Compare the ambience, check posted menus, and choose your favorite.

Brussels is known for both its high-quality, French-style cuisine and for multicultural variety. Seafood—fish, eel, shrimp, and oysters—is especially well-prepared here. As in France, if you ask for the *menù* (muh-noo) at a restaurant, you won't get a list of dishes; you'll get a fixed-price meal. *Menùs,* which include three or four courses, are generally a good value if you're hungry. Ask for *la carte* (lah kart) if you want to see a printed menu and order à la carte, like the locals do. For more on Belgian cuisine, see page 354. To read local restaurant reviews, check out www.resto.be.

Mussels in Brussels

Mussels *(moules)* are available all over town. Mostly harvested from aquafarms along the North Sea, they are considered in-season from mid-July to about Easter, but are available all year. The classic Belgian method is *à la marinière,* cooked in white wine, shallots, parsley, and butter. Or, instead of wine, cooks use light Belgian beer for the stock. For a high-calorie version, try *moules à la crème,*

Brussels Restaurants

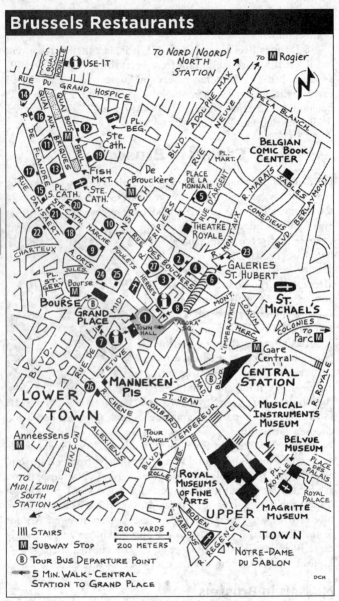

BRUSSELS EATING

USE-IT

TO NORD/NOORD/
NORTH STATION

TO M Rogier

N

QUAI DU FOIN/LILLE

RUE DU GRAND HOSPICE

RUE DE FLANDRE

QUAI AUX BRIQUES

QUAI AUX BOIS

RUE BRUL.

14

16

11

12

19

17

13

15

21

20

18

22

9

10

24

25

27

2

3

4

6

5

23

PL. BEG.

Ste. Cath.

Fish MKT.

De Brouckère

Ste. Cath.

PL. S. CATH.

Ste. Cath.

CHARTEUX

R. DANSAERT

MARCHÉ POULETS

A. ORTS

JULES

Bourse

BOURSE

PL. ST. GÉRY

BELGIAN COMIC BOOK CENTER

ADOLPHE MAX

NEUVE

RUE DE LA BLANCH.

R. DE LA BLANCH.

BLVD.

PL. MART.

RUE D'ARGENT

PLACE DE LA MONNAIE

THEATRE ROYALE

COMEDIENS

R. MARAIS

SABLE

BLVD. BERLAYMONT

R. MONTAUX

GALERIES ST. HUBERT

ST. MICHAEL'S

SPACH

RUE FRIPIERS

RUE DES BOUCHERS

HERBES

MONT.

B

GRAND PLACE

1

TOWN HALL

"AGORA" SQ.

L'IMPÉRATRICE

LOXUM

MERCI.

COLONIES TO Parc M

Gare Central

CENTRAL STATION

R. ROYALE

7

8

MANNEKEN-PIS

26

LOWER TOWN

Annéessens M

TO MIDI/ZUID/SOUTH STATION

R. CHENE

R. DE L'ÉTUVE

MIDI

ST. JEAN

LOMBARD

BLVD.

EMPEREUR

ALEXIENS

POINÇON

Tour d'Angle

ROLLE

J. LEB.

MUSICAL INSTRUMENTS MUSEUM

BELVUE MUSEUM

PL. ROYALE

PLACE DES PALAIS

ROYAL PALACE

ROYAL MUSEUMS OF FINE ARTS

MAGRITTE MUSEUM

UPPER TOWN

RÉGENCE

R. SABLONS

BODEN

NOTRE-DAME DU SABLON

DCH

|||| Stairs
M Subway Stop
B Tour Bus Departure Point
← 5 Min. Walk - Central Station to Grand Place

200 YARDS
200 METERS

Brussels Restaurants Key

1. Grand Place Dining
2. Rest. Chez Leon, Rest. Vincent & Delirium Tap House
3. Aux Armes de Bruxelles
4. Restaurant de l'Ogenblik
5. Belga Queen Brasserie
6. Arcadi Café & Le Mokafé
7. La Maison des Crêpes
8. Osteria a l'Ombra
9. AD Delhaize Grocery
10. Super GB Grocery
11. Bij den Boer
12. La Marie Joseph
13. Francois Restaurant
14. Le Royal Restaurant
15. La Villette Restaurant
16. Restaurant La Marée
17. Rest. Le Pré Salé
18. Amadeus Restaurant
19. Skylab Cocktail Bar
20. Mer du Nord/Nordzee
21. Cremerie de Linkebeek
22. Le Pain Quotidien
23. A la Mort Subite Bar
24. Le Cirio Café
25. A la Bécasse Café
26. Poechenellekelder Estaminet
27. A l'Imaige Nostre-Dame & Au Bon Vieux Temps

BRUSSELS EATING

where the stock is thickened with heavy cream.

You order by the kilo (just more than 2 pounds), which is a pretty big bucket. While restaurants don't promote these as splittable, they certainly are. Your mussels come with Belgian fries, which you probably think of as "french fries"—dip them in mayo. To accompany your mussels, try a French white wine such as Muscadet or Chablis, or a Belgian blonde ale such as Duvel or La Chouffe. When eating mussels, you can feel a little more local by nonchalantly using an empty mussel shell as a pincher to pull the meat out of other shells. It actually works quite nicely.

Dining on the Grand Place

For an atmospheric cellar or a table right on the Grand Place, **La Rose Blanche** and **L'Estaminet du Kelderke** each have the same formula, with tables outside overlooking the action. L'Estaminet du Kelderke—with its one steamy vault under the square packed with both natives and tourists—is a real Brussels fixture. It serves local specialties, including mussels (a splittable kilo bucket for €22-25; daily 12:00-24:00, no reservations taken, Grand Place 15, tel. 02-513-7344). **Brasserie L'Ommegang,** with a fancier restaurant upstairs, offers perhaps the classiest seating and best food on the square.

Rue des Bouchers ("Restaurant Row")

Brussels' restaurant streets, two blocks north of the Grand Place, are touristy and notorious for touts who aggressively suck you in and predatory servers who greedily rip you off. It's a little hard to justify dining here when far better options sit just a block or two away (see later listings). But the area is an exhilarating spectacle and is fun for at least a walk. If you are seduced into a meal here, order carefully, understand the prices thoroughly, and watch your wallet.

Restaurant Chez Leon is a touristy mussels factory, slamming out piles of good, cheap buckets since 1893. It's the original flagship branch of a chain that's now spreading throughout France. It's big and welcoming, with busy green-aproned waiters offering a "Formula Leon" for €12.90—a light meal consisting of a small bucket of mussels, fries, and a beer. They also offer a €31.30 fixed-price meal that comes with a starter, a large bucket of mussels, fries, and beer (daily 12:00-23:00, kids under 12 eat free, Rue des Bouchers/Beenhouwers 18, tel. 02-511-1415). In the family portrait of Leon's brother Honoré (hanging in the corner), the wife actually looks like a mussel.

Aux Armes de Bruxelles is a venerable restaurant that has been serving reliably good food to locals in a dressy setting for generations. This is another food factory, with white-suited waiters serving an older clientele impressed by the restaurant's reputation. You'll pay a bit more for the formality (€8-18 starters, €16-32 main dishes, €20 fixed-price lunch, €35-46 fixed-price dinner, daily 12:00-23:00, indoor seating only, Rue des Bouchers/Beenhouwers 13, tel. 02-511-5550).

Restaurant Vincent has you enter through the kitchen to enjoy their 1905-era ambience. This place is better for meat dishes than for seafood and better for wine than beer. Enjoy the engaging old tile murals of the seaside and countryside (€15-20 starters, €20-32 main dishes, daily 12:00-14:30 & 18:30-23:30, Rue des Dominicains/Predikherenstraat 8-10, tel. 02-511-2607, Michel and Jacques).

Finer Dining near Rue des Bouchers

These options, though just steps away from those listed above, are more authentic and a better value.

Restaurant de l'Ogenblik, a remarkably peaceful eddy just off the raging restaurant row, fills an early 20th-century space in the corner of an arcade. The waiters serve well-presented, near-gourmet French cuisine. This mussels-free zone has a great, split-table rack of lamb with 10 vegetables. Their sea bass with risotto and truffle oil, at €26, is a hit with return eaters. Reservations are smart (€20 first courses, €30 plates, Mon-Sat 12:00-14:30 & 19:00-24:00, closed Sun, across from Restaurant Vincent—listed earlier—at Galerie des Princes 1, tel. 02-511-6151, Yves).

Belga Queen Brasserie, a huge, trendy, dressy brasserie filling a palatial former bank building, is *the* spot for Brussels' beautiful people and visiting European diplomats. Although a little more expensive than the alternatives, their "creative Belgian cuisine" is excellent, the service is sharp, and the experience is memorable—from the fries served in silver cones, to the double-decker platters of iced shellfish (€65/person for the Belga Queen platter), to the transparent toilets stalls (which become opaque only after you nervously lock the door). The high-powered trendiness can make you feel a little gawky, but if you've got the money, this is a great splurge. Consider their €50 four-course, fixed-price meal with matching beers (€15-25 starters, €20-30 main dishes, €30-47 fixed-price meals, daily 12:00-14:30 & 19:00-24:00, call to reserve, bar open all day, Rue Fosse-aux-Loups/Wolvengracht 32, tel. 02-217-2187). The vault downstairs is a plush cigar and cocktail lounge. For just a drink or a quicker bite, you can grab a stool at the white-marble oyster bar.

More Eateries near the Grand Place

Arcadi Café is a delightful little eatery serving daily plates (€10-15), salads, and a selection of quiche-like tortes (€7.50/slice). The interior comes with a fun, circa-1900 ambience; grab a table there, on the street, or at the end of Galeries St. Hubert (daily 7:30-23:30, 1 Rue d'Arenberg/Arenbergstraat, tel. 02-511-3343).

Le Mokafé is inexpensive but feels splurgy. They dish up light café fare at the quiet end of the elegant Galeries St. Hubert, with great people-watching outdoor tables (€3-6 sandwiches, €7-11 salads, €8-10 pastas, €9-12 main dishes, daily 8:00-24:00, Galerie du Roi 9, tel. 02-511-7870).

La Maison des Crêpes, a little eatery a half-block south of the Bourse, looks underwhelming but serves delicious €8-10 crêpes (both savory and sweet varieties) and salads. It has a brown café ambience, and even though it's just a few steps away from the tourist bustle, it feels laid-back and local (good beers, fresh mint tea, sidewalk seating, daily 12:00-23:00, Rue du Midi/Zuidstraat 13, mobile 0475-957-368).

Osteria a l'Ombra, a true Italian joint, is good for a quality bowl of pasta with a glass of fine Italian wine. A block off the Grand Place, it's pricey, but the woody bistro ambience and tasty food make it a good value. If you choose a main dish (€15-18), your choice of pasta or salad is included in the price (otherwise €10-15 pasta meals). The ground-floor seating on high stools is fine, but also consider sitting upstairs (Mon-Sat 12:00-15:00 & 18:30-23:30, closed Sun, Rue des Harengs/Haringstraat 2, tel. 02-511-6710).

Cheap Eats near the Grand Place: The super-central square dubbed the "Agora" (officially Marché-aux-Herbes/Grasmarkt, just between the Grand Place and Central Station) is lined with low-end eateries, and is especially fun on sunny days.

Groceries: Two supermarkets are located about a block from the Bourse and a few blocks from the Grand Place. **AD Delhaize** is at the intersection of Anspach and Marché-aux-Poulets/Kiekenmarkt (Mon-Sat 9:00-20:00, Fri until 21:00, Sun 9:00-18:00), and **Super GB** is half a block away at Halles and Marché-aux-Poulets/Kiekenmarkt (Mon-Sat 9:00-20:00, Fri until 21:00, closed Sun). Mini-markets dot the city. Often run by Pakistani and Indian immigrants, they're pricier than supermarkets but handy and open very late.

Ste. Catherine, near the Old Fish Market

A 10-minute walk from the old center puts you in "the village within the city" area of Ste. Catherine (Métro: Ste. Catherine/Sint Katelijne). The historic fish market here has spawned a tradition of fine restaurants specializing mostly in seafood. The old fish canal survives, and if you walk around it, you'll see plenty of enticing places to eat. Make the circuit, considering these very good, yet very different, options.

Bij den Boer, a fun, noisy eatery popular with locals and tourists, has inviting tables out on the esplanade and feels like a traditional and very successful brasserie. Their specialty: fish (€14-16 starters, €22-30 main dishes, €28 four-course fixed-price meal, Mon-Sat 12:00-14:30 & 18:00-22:30, closed Sun, Quai aux Briques/Baksteenkai 60, tel. 02-512-6122).

La Marie Joseph, stylish and modern—both the food and the clientele—serves fancy fish and fries, and earns raves from the natives (€16-22 starters, €25-32 plates, Tue-Sun 12:00-15:00 & 18:30-23:00, closed Mon, no reservations taken, Quai au Bois à Brûler/Brandhoutkaai 47, tel. 02-218-0596, Sara is the fourth generation to run the place).

Francois Restaurant is a good, solid, family-run fish restaurant with fine seating indoors and on the square and a reputation for reliable quality and attentive service (€10-35 starters, €22-58 main dishes, €35-47 three-course fixed-price meal, Tue-Thu 10:30-19:00, Fri-Sat 9:00-19:00, Sun 10:00-14:00, closed Mon, Quai aux Briques/Baksteenkaai 2, tel. 02-511-6089).

Le Royal is a cool-feeling brasserie serving tasty and elegantly presented food that's worth the splurge. They offer both traditional (and well-executed) Belgian staples and modern fusion dishes— some with a hint of Asian influence. Sit in the trendy interior, or choose a sidewalk table. Reservations are smart (€8-15 starters, €20-25 main dishes, €3 sides, daily 12:00-15:00 & 18:00-23:00, Rue de Flandre/Vlaamsesteenweg 103, tel. 02-217-8500).

La Villette Restaurant ("The Slaughterhouse") is a romantic, subdued alternative, serving traditional Belgian cuisine: heavy, meaty stews, eels, *stoemp* (mashed potatoes and vegetables), and dishes with beer. The chef proudly makes the sauces from scratch, and Agata can match your order to the right beer. The restaurant has a charming red-and-white-tablecloth interior and good outdoor seating facing a small square (€15 two-course fixed-price lunch, €20-25 meals, Mon-Sat 12:00-14:30 & 18:30-22:30, closed Sun, Rue du Vieux Marché-aux-Grains/Oude Graanmarkt 3, tel. 02-512-7550).

Restaurant La Marée is a classic local scene a couple of blocks away from the trendy canalside places. A nontouristy, less trendy bistro with an older clientele, an open kitchen, and an inviting menu, it specializes in mussels and seafood—their only pretense is their insistence that it's fresh (€19-26 meals, Tue-Sat 12:00-14:00 & 18:30-22:00, closed Sun-Mon, near Rue du Marché-aux-Porcs/Varkensmarkt at Rue de Flandre/Vlaamsesteenweg 99, tel. 02-511-0040).

Restaurant Le Pré Salé is noisy and family-friendly. A Brussels fixture for its traditional local cuisine, it fills a former butcher shop with happy eaters and a busy open kitchen (big, shareable €21 pots of mussels come with a salad, €13-19 meals, Wed-Sun 12:00-14:30 & 18:30-22:30, closed Mon-Tue, a block off the fish market at Rue de Flandre/Vlaamsesteenweg 20, tel. 02-513-6545).

Amadeus Restaurant is, as its slogan brags, "*the* place for ribs." Their formula is simple: €16 gets you a plate with ribs, a baked potato, and salad—and you're welcome to go back for more. Surrounded by books, you'll feel like you're scarfing down your ribs in a circa-1940s library (long hours daily, Rue Ste. Catherine/Sint-Katelijnestraat 26, tel. 02-502-5137).

Skylab Cocktail Bar is perfect for a drink before or after dinner. It's a warm and welcoming bar with great outdoor tables right on the canal, and a casual, classy, mature ambience (Tue-Sun 15:00-2:00 in the morning, closed Mon, Quai au Bois à Brûler/Brandhoutkaai 9, tel. 02-203-0350).

Cheap, Fast, and Tasty Lunches in Ste. Catherine

Place Ste. Catherine/Sint-Katelijneplein, which branches off from the side of Ste. Catherine Church, is lined with enjoyable cafés with outdoor seating.

Mer du Nord/Nordzee is as delicious as it is inexpensive. This seafood bar—basically a grill attached to a fresh fish shop—cooks up whatever it catches and serves it on small tapas-like plates with glasses of wine to a very appreciative local crowd. Just belly up to the counter and place your order, then eat it standing at the tables. The €7 *scampi à la plancha* (grilled shrimp) is exquisite (€4-7 small dishes, Tue-Thu 11:00-17:00, Fri-Sat 11:00-18:00, Sun 11:00-20:00, closed Mon, Rue Ste. Catherine/Sint-Katelijnestraat 45, at corner with Place Ste. Catherine, tel. 02-513-1192). The similar **Poissonerie/Vishandel ABC**, across the street, has a comparable operation.

Cremerie de Linkebeek, owned by Jordan (who's part American) and Laurence, is the best place in town to shop for local Belgian cheeses—rubbed and fla-vored with beer rather than wine or alcohol. The English-speaking staff is happy to help you explore the options and choose the per-fect cheese for your picnic (they also sell baguettes, wine, and crackers—you could assemble a light meal or a snack right here).

At midday, they also sell delicious €4 baguette sandwiches to go—grab one before they sell out (Mon 9:00-15:00, Tue-Sat 9:00-18:00, closed Sun, Rue du Vieux Marché-aux-Grains/Oude Graanmarkt 4, tel. 02-512-3510).

Le Pain Quotidien ("The Daily Bread") is a popular, upscale, artisan bakery chain selling good sandwiches and other dishes in a rustic yet dignified setting. There's a handy location just below Place Ste. Catherine (Mon-Sat 7:30-19:00, Sun 7:30-18:00, Rue Antoine Dansaert/Dansaertstraat 16A, tel. 02-502-2361). Across the street is **Comocomo,** serving mediocre Basque-style tapas with an innovative twist: on a conveyor belt, sushi bar-style.

Sampling Belgian Beer with Food and Ambience

Looking for a good spot to enjoy that famous Belgian beer? Brussels is full of atmospheric cafés to savor the local brew. The eateries lining the Grand Place are touristy, but the setting—plush, old medieval guildhalls fronting all that cobbled wonder—is hard to beat. I've listed several places a few minutes' walk off the square, all with a magical, old-time feel. If you'd like something to wash down with your beer, you can generally get a cold-meat plate, an open-face sandwich, or a salad.

All varieties of Belgian beer are available, but Brussels' most distinctive beers are *lambic*-based. Look for *lambic doux, lambic blanche, gueuze* (pronounced "kurrs"), and *faro,* as well as fruit-flavored *lambics,* such as *kriek* (cherry) and *framboise* (raspberry—*frambozen* in Dutch). These beers look and taste more like a dry, somewhat bitter cider. The brewer doesn't add yeast—the beer ferments naturally from yeast found floating only in the marshy air around Brussels. For more on Belgian beer, see page 357.

A la Mort Subite, a few steps above the top end of the Galeries

St. Hubert, is a classic old bar that has retained its 1928 decor...and its loyal customers seem to go back just about as far (daily 11:00-24:00, Rue Montagne-aux-Herbes Potagères/Warmoesberg 7, tel. 02-513-1318). Named after the "sudden death" playoff that workingmen used to end their lunchtime dice games, it still has an unpretentious, working-class feel. The decor is simple, with wood tables, grimy yellow wallpaper, and some-other-era garland trim. Tiny metal plates on the walls mark spots where gas-powered flames once flickered—used by patrons to light their cigars. A typical lunch or snack here is an omelet with a salad or a *tartine* (open-face sandwich, €5) spread with *fromage blanc* (cream cheese) or pressed meat. Eat it with one of the home-brewed, *lambic*-based beers. This is a good place to try the *kriek* (cherry-flavored) beer. While their beer list is limited, they do have Chimay on tap.

At **Le Cirio,** across from the Bourse, the dark tables bear the skid marks of over a century's worth of beer steins (daily 10:00-1:00 in the morning, Rue de la Bourse/Beursstraat 18-20, tel. 02-512-1395).

A la Bécasse is lower profile than Le Cirio, with a simple wood-panel and wood-table decor that appeals to both poor students and lunching businessmen. The *lambic doux* has been served in clay jars since 1825. This place is just around the corner from Le Cirio, toward the Grand Place, hidden away at the end of a courtyard (€3-5 *tartine* sandwiches, €5-9 light meals, daily 11:00-24:00, Tabora street 11, tel. 02-511-0006).

Poechenellekelder Estaminet is a great bar with lots of real character located conveniently, if oddly, right across the street from the *Manneken-Pis.* As the word *estaminet* (tavern) indicates, it's not brewery-owned, so they have a great selection of beers. Inside tables are immersed in *Pis* kitsch and puppets. Outside tables offer some fine people-watching (Rue du Chêne/Eikstraat 5, tel. 02-511-9262).

Two tiny and extremely characteristic bars are tucked away down long entry corridors just off Rue du Marché-aux-Herbes/Grasmarkt. **A l'Imaige Nostre-Dame** (closed Sun, at #8) and **Au Bon Vieux Temps** (at #12) each treat fine beer with great reverence and seem to have extremely local clientele which you're bound to meet if you grab a stool.

Delirium Tap House is a sloppy frat party nightly with no ambience, a noisy young crowd, beer-soaked wooden floors, rock 'n' roll, and a famous variety of great Belgian beers on tap (deep in the restaurant zone not far from Chez Leon at Impasse de la Fidélité/Getrouwheidsgang 4).

Youthful Fun at Place St. Géry

The classics recommended above are famous among tourists, and understandably so. For a more trendy and youthful scene, head a few blocks west to Place St. Géry/Sint-Goriksplein. Here you'll find bar and restaurant hangouts that offer a more basic, neighborhood feel. The epicenter is at the northeast corner of the square (intersection of Pont de la Carpe/Karperbrug and Plétinckx street). Rather than recommend a particular place, I'd suggest exploring your options and choosing the menu and indoor ambience or outdoor views you like best.

Nightlife in Brussels

After dark, the **Grand Place** becomes even more magical—as day-tripping tourists are gone and the Town Hall spire is floodlit.

Pick up the free *Agenda* and *Brussels Unlimited* magazines from the TI, which list events including opera, symphony, and ballet.

At one time, Brussels had a wide range of characteristic little cinemas. These days, most Bruxelloise flock to the multi-plexes; a handy one is the **UGC** cinema on De Brouckère square (look for *v.o.* for the original version; *v.f.* means it's dubbed in French). There's also a small art-house cinema in the Galeries St. Hubert; movies here play in their original language (generally not English, as these are typically international films), with Dutch and French subtitles.

The most interesting neighborhood to explore after-hours (or any time of day) is just a few steps west of the Grand Place: **Rue du Marché-au-Charbon/Kolenmarkt** is the center of Brussels' gay scene, with many lively cafés and restaurants with outdoor seating. The trendy eateries, shops, and businesses along here change so fast, the locals can't keep track.

Across the Boulevard Anspach is **Place St. Géry,** where you'll find a raucous collection of lively bars with rollicking interiors and a sea of outdoor tables. A five-minute walk northeast is the pleas-

ant **Ste. Catherine** district, with lively local restaurants and hotels huddled around the Church of Ste. Catherine and the old fish market (and the cool and inviting Skylab Cocktail Bar, described earlier). You'll find more in-depth descriptions of both of these areas on page 458; restaurant suggestions on page 520; and hotels in the Ste. Catherine area on page 513.

Brussels Connections

By Train

Brussels has three train stations: Centraal/Central, Midi/Zuid/South, and Nord/Noord/North. Most trains stop at all three stations, but high-speed international trains serve only the Midi/Zuid/South Station. Any train ticket to any Brussels station includes a transfer to any other Brussels train station. For more details on all three stations—and tips on connecting between them—see page 447. For information on rail deals in Belgium, see page 614.

At any station, as you wait on the platform for your train, watch the track notice board that tells you which train is approaching. Trains zip in and out constantly, so a train with an open door on your train's track—three minutes before your departure time—may well be the wrong train. Anxious travelers, who think their train has arrived early, often board the wrong train on the right track.

Trains to Belgium and the Netherlands

From All Brussels Stations by Train to: Bruges (2/hour, 1

Belgian Train Lines

hour, catch InterCity train—direction: Ostende or Knokke-Blankenberge, **Antwerp** (5/hour, 40-50 minutes), **Ghent** (3/hour, 35 minutes), **Ypres/Ieper** (hourly, 1.75 hours, some change in Kortrijk).

From Brussels Centraal/Central or Midi/Zuid/South by Train to: Amsterdam (hourly, 1.75 hours to Amsterdam's Schiphol Airport, 2 hours to Amsterdam's Central Station), **Haarlem** (hourly, 2.75 hours, transfer in Rotterdam), **Delft** (hourly, 2 hours, change in Rotterdam), **The Hague** (hourly, 2 hours).

High-Speed International Trains

Catch the following special, high-speed train lines at Midi/Zuid/South Station, tracks 1-6 (described in detail on page 447). Note that these trains do not stop at the Central or North train stations. For schedules, see www.bahn.com.

From Brussels by Thalys Train: The Thalys company has a pricey monopoly on trains to **Paris** (2/hour, 1.5 hours), and runs trains to **Köln,** Germany (9/day, 1.75 hours). They also run special seasonal trains, such as to **Marseille,** France, in the summer and to the **French Alps** in the winter. From Brussels to Paris, a regular second-class Thalys ticket costs about €60-100 second class (compared to about €25 by bus; buy ticket the day before or earlier, as same-day fares are even higher). Railpass-holders need to buy a seat reservation for around €30 in second class or €41-54 in first class (first class generally includes a meal). If your railpass covers only France but not BeNeLux, it'll cost you €45-60 in second class or €65-115 in first class. Railpasses without France are not accepted on Thalys trains. Train info: Toll tel. 07-066-7788 (long wait), www.thalys.com.

By TGV Train to France: French TGV trains connect to **Paris' Charles de Gaulle Airport** (5/day, 1.25-1.75 hours, www.tgv-europe.com) and then continue on to various destinations in southern France, including Marseille, Nice, and Bordeaux. Note that since Thalys has exclusive rights for the Brussels-Paris route, TGV trains do not go to downtown Paris—to get there, you must transfer at the airport. All TGV seats are reserved, and railpass-holders pay €5-15 for a reservation (very limited availability).

By ICE Train to Germany: Germany's InterCity Express trains zip to **Köln** (3/day, 1.75 hours) and **Frankfurt** (3/day, 3 hours). Reservations are not required except for advance-ticket discounts.

To Other Places in Germany: The fastest way to most German destinations, as well as to Vienna, Austria, is to change in Köln (on the Thalys or ICE connection) or in Frankfurt (on the ICE connection).

By Eurostar to/from London: Brussels and London are 2.5 hours apart by Eurostar train (10/day). Trains to London leave from tracks 1 and 2 at Brussels' Midi/Zuid/South Station. Arrive 30 minutes early to get your ticket validated and your luggage and passport checked by British authorities (similar to airport check-in for an international flight).

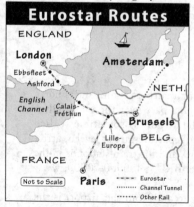

Fares are reasonable but complicated. Prices vary depending on how far ahead you reserve (up to six months out), whether you can live with restrictions, and whether you're eligible for any discounts (children, youths, seniors, and railpass-holders all qualify). Rates are lowest for round-trips. Fares can change without notice, but typically a **one-way, full-fare ticket** (with no restrictions on refundability) runs about $425 for first class and $310 for second class. Accepting more restrictions lowers the price substantially (figure $90-200 for second class, one-way), but these **cheaper rates** can sell out quickly. Railpasses qualify you for a discount on a Eurostar ticket. Those traveling with a railpass that covers Belgium, France, or Britain should look first at the **pass-holder** fare (about $90-160 for second-class, one-way Eurostar trips, sold through most agents but not through Eurostar website). See more general info at www.ricksteves.com/eurostar or buy most ticket types at www.eurostar.com (prices in pounds; Belgian tel. 02-528-2828).

More Discounts: A Thalys ticket between Brussels and Paris or a Eurostar ticket between Brussels and London can also cover a regional train connection to/from any Belgian station for a few dollars more, if you choose the "ABS option" at the time of purchase. Just show your ticket when boarding the connecting train(s) within 24 hours of the reserved Brussels arrival or departure (as long as the connecting train is not a Thalys).

All of these fast-train services offer significant price discounts, with restrictions, on tickets reserved in advance (most available 3 months ahead, Eurostar available 6 months ahead). Each company sells e-tickets through its website or through US agents such as www.raileurope.com (prices in dollars, US tel. 800-438-7245). In Europe, you can buy tickets at any major train station in any country or at any travel agency that handles train tickets (expect a booking fee).

By Bus

You can save money—but not time—by traveling by Eurolines bus from Brussels to Paris or London (Eurolines tel. 02-274-1350 in Brussels, www.eurolines.be).

From Brussels by Bus to: Paris (generally €34 one-way, €54 round-trip, about 4 hours), **London** (generally €43 one-way, €72 round-trip, about 6 hours).

By Plane

Brussels Airport

Brussels' big but well-organized main airport is nine miles north of downtown (many arriving flights pass over the giant, silver molecule-shaped Atomium). The airport is sometimes called "Zaventem," for the nearby town. Departures are at level 3, arrivals are at level 2, buses are at level 0, and the train station is in the basement at level -1 (airport code: BRU, tel. 0900-70000, www.brusselsairport.be).

The clear winner for getting to and from the airport is the **shuttle train** that runs between the airport and all three Brussels train stations (€7.60, 4/hour, 25 minutes, daily 6:00-23:00). If you're connecting the airport with Bruges, take this shuttle train and transfer at Brussels' North Station (about 1.5 hours total). For a **taxi**, figure on spending around €40 between downtown Brussels and the airport.

Thrifty Brussels Airlines flies between Brussels and several European cities, including Athens, London, Milan, Florence, Zürich, Nice, Lisbon, Barcelona, Madrid, and more (Belgian tel. 07-035-1111, www.brusselsairlines.com).

Brussels South Charleroi Airport

Discount airlines Ryanair (www.ryanair.com) and Wizz Air (www.wizzair.com) use this smaller airport, located about 30 miles from downtown Brussels in the town of Gosselies, on the outskirts of the city of Charleroi (airport code: CRL, tel. 09-020-2490, www.charleroi-airport.com).

The easiest way to connect to downtown Brussels is to take the **shuttle bus** to Brussels' Midi/Zuid/South Station (likely 2/hour, about 1 hour, runs 4:00-22:30, €13; stops right in front of airport terminal; if you're taking the bus from Brussels' South Station, look for it outside at the corner of Rue de France/Frankrijkstraat and Rue de l'Instruction/Onderwijsstraat—the bus stop is not clearly marked and can be confusing, but locals are generally happy to help, www.voyages-lelan.be). You can also take a **bus-plus-train** connection: Bus #A connects Charleroi Airport and Charleroi Station (2/hour, 18 minutes, €3 covers both bus and train), where you can take the train to all three Brussels train stations (2/hour, 40 minutes). It's costly by taxi (figure around €85-90); depending on traffic, it can take between 45 minutes and 1.5 hours to drive between downtown Brussels and Charleroi Airport.

By Cruise Ship
Zeebrugge Cruise Port

The tiny town of Zeebrugge, just 10 miles north of Bruges, has a gigantic port. From the cruise port, it's an easy tram-plus-train connection (with a little walking) to reach Brussels or Bruges.

Zeebrugge's port has two cruise berths (but no real terminal buildings or TIs): Larger ships generally use **Swedish Quay** (Zweedse Kaai), which pokes straight up into the main harbor; smaller ships use **Maritime Station** (Zeestation), across the harbor along Leopold II-Dam. From either place, you'll ride a free shuttle bus out of the port area.

From Swedish Quay, your shuttle bus drops you at the port gate. Exit the port area to the right, following the busy road with the sea on your right. Walk about 10 minutes until you reach the big church, and the Zeebrugge Kerk stop for the coastal tram (explained later).

From Maritime Station, your shuttle bus drops you off right at the Zeebrugge Strandwijk stop for the coastal tram (described next).

The coastal tram (Kusttram) zips from Zeebrugge and Blankenberge, and beyond. From either of the stops described earlier, hop on a tram going in the direction of Oostende or De Planne, and ride it to Blankenberge Station (€2, buy ticket from driver and validate in yellow machine, 2-3/hour, 14 minutes). Stepping off the tram in Blankenberge, simply cross the street to the train station, with a handy hourly train that zips to **Bruges** (€2.90, 15 minutes), then on to **Ghent** (€8.10, 50 minutes total) and **Brussels** (€15.40, 1.5 hours total)—it typically leaves at :11 past each hour.

Services: If you need an **ATM,** walk from the port to the Zeebrugge Kerk tram stop (described previously), but continue past the church and tram stop another long block to find banks flanking the street (there are also ATMs at the Blankenberge train station). The most convenient Internet access and pharmacy are in Blankenberge, near the station (get online at the library, Onderwijsstraat 17; the pharmacy is at Kerkstraat 83, which is on a pedestrian shopping street near the train station). Zeebrugge also has a pharmacy, near the beach at Brusselstraat 34.

ANTWERP

Antwerpen

Antwerp (Antwerpen in Dutch, Anvers in French) is one of Europe's great once-drab, now-reborn port cities—ranking right up there with Liverpool, Barcelona, and Gdańsk. It's the biggest city and de facto capital of Flanders, with an illustrious history, a collection of top-tier museums, and a unique urban grittiness (some might say seediness) mingling with avant-garde fashion and a youthful trendiness. Its big-city bustle is the yang to Bruges' cutesy-village yin. Once Europe's most important trading city, later the hometown of accomplished painter Peter Paul Rubens, destroyed by World War II and then reborn, and recently emerging as a European fashion capital, Antwerp is more than the sum of its parts.

In the late 15th century, as Bruges' harbor silted up, Antwerp became a major trading center and the Low Countries' top city of the Baroque period. As the Age of Exploration dawned, Portuguese and Spanish ships returning from the New World laden with exotic goods docked here in Antwerp. During Antwerp's 16th-century Golden Age, it became Europe's wealthiest city, with a population of about 100,000.

In the mid-16th century, Antwerp was pulled into the Eighty Years' War between the Dutch rebel Protestants and the ruling Spanish Catholics. In 1576, after growing impatient at not being paid by Habsburg King Philip II, Spanish troops relentlessly sacked Antwerp for three days—massacring thousands of its residents and destroying hundreds of homes. The outraged public response to this so-called "Spanish Fury" elevated Antwerp to the capital of the Dutch Revolt. (Meanwhile, the event irrevocably damaged Antwerp's trade ties with partners who wanted no business with a war zone.) But the crushing, Spanish-led Siege of Antwerp (July 1584 through August 1585) wore down the independence movement, and the city fell under Spanish/ Catholic control. More than half of the city's population fled to Amsterdam, where they restarted their businesses. Amsterdam's ensuing Golden Age was, in many ways, a direct result of talent and resources that Antwerp lost during this postwar "brain drain."

Seeking to rehabilitate its image in the aftermath of the bloody warfare, the Catholic Church invested mightily in building and decorating churches in Antwerp. A local artist named Peter Paul Rubens (1577-1640)—while arguably less talented than some of his contemporaries—found himself in the right place at the right time, and was a brilliant salesman who allied himself with the Church to win big commission after big commission. Rubens' style epitomized exactly what the Church was looking for: bold, bombastic images trumpeting the glory of God (and his Church on earth).

The treaty that ended the Eighty Years' War in 1648 imposed rigid regulations on shipping on the Scheldt River, restricting Antwerp's outlet to the North Sea. This caused the city to become more of a regional port than an international one. Antwerp's industry, led by an elite group of pro-Catholic traders, began to specialize in luxury goods—cabinets, paintings, tapestries, and so on. The city would languish as a Catholic backwater and second-rate shipping city for centuries, although its industry was kick-started by Napoleon, then by Belgian independence, and later by Belgium's colonization of the Congo. By the 20th century, Antwerp ranked as Europe's second-busiest port (just after Dutch rival Rotterdam). Damaged in both World Wars, Antwerp has recently begun to enjoy a new gentrification that's making it one of Europe's most exciting young cities.

While Brussels has become international, enlivened by the European Union headquarters and lots of immigrants, Antwerp has more of a local identity. It's an honest, what-you-see-is-what-you-get place that feels more Flemish.

Antwerpenaars (as locals are called) have a love of life. If funky urbanity is your thing, Antwerp is one of Europe's most intriguing cities. It's a great place for browsing without a sightseeing agenda. But its sights are easily on par with Brussels' and Bruges': Antwerp boasts a wide range of well-presented museums with exciting new exhibits opening all the time, interesting churches packed with great art, and fun-to-explore neighborhoods. And compared to stodgy, bureaucratic Brussels, Antwerp has a colorful personality that respects its storied past even as it embraces a bright future.

Planning Your Time

While Antwerp could easily fill a day or two, it's worth at least a few hours (as a side-trip from Brussels—less than an hour away by train—or on the way between Brussels and Amsterdam). Take the first half of my self-guided walk from the train station to the Old Town (by way of the Rubens House), tour the cathedral, ogle the Grote Markt, and pay a quick visit to other sights that intrigue you. (Historians enjoy the Museum Plantin-Moretus, art lovers savor the Rockox House, fashionistas love the ModeMuseum and nearby window-shopping, and architecture fans drool over the building housing the new Museum aan de Stroom (Museum on the River, or MAS for short). Then zip back to the train station on underground trams known as the "metro." If you have more time, Antwerp's diverse restaurant scene and lively nightlife make it worth considering for an overnight. With a different variety of quirky boutiques and cafés on each street, it's a delightful place to linger. As in most of Belgium, be aware that most Antwerp museums are closed on Mondays.

Orientation to Antwerp

Belgium's "second city" (with 490,000 people), Antwerp sits along the east bank of the Scheldt River (Schelde in Dutch). The main tourist area is fairly compact. On a quick trip, narrow your focus to these main zones: the **Old Town** along the river; the **train station area** and **Diamond Quarter** to the east, and the **Meir** shopping district between the Old Town and train station; the newly rejuvenated **Little Island** (Eilandje) zone and the red light district to the north; and, to the south, the **Sint-Andries** fashion district and, beyond that, the happening nightlife zone aptly called **'t Zuid** ("The South"). All of these areas are within about a 30-minute walk (or a quick tram or taxi ride) of one another.

Tourist Information

Antwerp's TI has two branches: in the train station (at the head of the tracks, on level 0), and right on the Grote Markt (both open Mon-Sat 9:00-17:45, Sun 9:00-16:45; tel. 03-232-0103, phone answered Mon-Fri 9:00-17:50 only; www.visitantwerp.be). Peruse their racks of fliers and pick up a free town map. The **City Card,** which covers entry to most museums and churches (plus discounts on special exhibits), could save a busy sightseer some money (€28/48 hours, sold at TI, clock starts running when you visit your first sight).

The Grote Markt TI also has a desk where you can get information and buy tickets for musical events and half-price tickets for weekend performances (possible €1 service charge—depends on event, Tue-Fri 10:00-17:45, Sat 12:00-17:00, closed Sun-Mon, half-price tickets go on sale at 12:00 Fri and Sat only).

Arrival in Antwerp

By Train: Antwerp's Central Station (Antwerpen Centraal)—with a grand century-old shell recently refurbished and expanded with a modern underground zone—is one of Europe's most impressive. It's easy to navigate, with three well-signed levels of tracks connected by escalators and elevators.

The ground floor's atrium (on level 0) is the hub of activity, where escalators funnel passengers from all three track levels. At the front of this area is the large TI, and behind that (through the passage, tucked under the stairs) are luggage lockers (€3-4, exact change only, swipe the printout when you're ready to open the locker, security cameras reassure nervous travelers). Continuing past the lockers, you emerge into the great hall, a gorgeously restored temple of travel. Here you'll find ticket windows. Exiting straight ahead out the front door puts you in the vast and somewhat seedy Koningin Astridplein, with the city's zoo on your immediate right.

To get to the Old Town and most sights, you have two basic options: You can walk (see my self-guided walk, later); or, if you're in a hurry (or the weather's bad) and you want to make a beeline to the Grote Markt, ride the **metro** (actually an underground tram line). From next to the TI, take the escalator marked *metro* to the underground tracks. Buy a ticket from the automated machines on the platform—they accept coins and bills—and take tram #3, #9, or #15 in direction: Linkeroever or Zwijndrecht. Be sure to validate your ticket in the yellow machine when you board. Get off at the Groenplaats stop for the Grote Markt and the historical center. Note: The train station's metro stop is named Diamant (for the surrounding Diamond Quarter).

Getting Around Antwerp

Sprawling Antwerp is walkable, but using the city's public-transit network saves time and sweat. For visitors, the main downtown corridor, where underground tram ("metro") lines #3, #9, and #15 connect, matters the most. The four stops you'll likely use are: Diamant (train station), Opera (at east end of Meir shopping street), Meir (at west end of Meir shopping street, a block from the Rubens House), and Groenplaats (near the cathedral and Grote Markt). A maddening lack of English and logic can make sorting out your options difficult. Tram lines heading to the Old Town from the train station are marked by an array of end stations: If you see *Linkeroever* or *Zwijndrecht*, you're OK. To return from the Old Town to the train station, look for *Merksem/Eksterlaar/Boechout*.

Transit ticket options: basic ride €1.20 (easy to buy at automated machines on the platform, or pay €2 on board), day pass-€5, three-day pass-€10, shareable 10-ride ticket-€9. Validate your ticket when you board—day passes need validation only once. Smart travelers buy their return ticket at the same time to avoid later hassles. Information: Toll tel. 070-220-200, www.delijn.be.

Tours in Antwerp

Walking Tours—The TI organizes a historical **walking tour** through town (2 hours, combining English and French, €8—or €6 if you book at least a day in advance, July-Aug daily at 14:00, Sept-June Sat-Sun only, departs from TI on Grote Markt).

Local Guide—The TI can arrange a private guide for an affordable city tour (€65/2 hours, tel. 03-338-9539, gidsenwerking @stad.antwerpen.be). One of their excellent guides, **Ariane van Duytekom,** tells Antwerp's story well, with a knack for psychoanalyzing its complicated history. If Ariane isn't available, the TI can book another good guide for you.

Self-Guided Walk

▲▲▲Welcome to Antwerp

This walk laces together Antwerp's most important districts and sights in a memorable walk from the train station, through the Old Town, and on to the harbor and the towering Museum aan Stroom (MAS). Along the way I reference several sights described in more detail later, under "Sights in Antwerp." If you'd rather not visit the town's in-your-face red light district, finish this walk at the riverfront and consider the MAS a separate sight. We'll start at the train station, not for convenience but because the station itself is a worthwhile sight.

• *Start on the level above the TI and look all around you.*

Antwerp's Train Station

The city's central train station is a work of art and a loud-and-clear comment on a confident new age. Built around the turn of the 20th

century, it's Industrial Age meets Art Nouveau, giddy with steel and glass. This eclectic mix of Historicism is a temple of time.

Below you are tracks on different levels. While the original tracks dead-ended in the station, today's express trains are required to pass through. The

bottom tracks, which tunnel under the station, let bullet trains zip right through with only a quick stop, connecting Antwerp with Paris in roughly two hours and Amsterdam in about an hour.

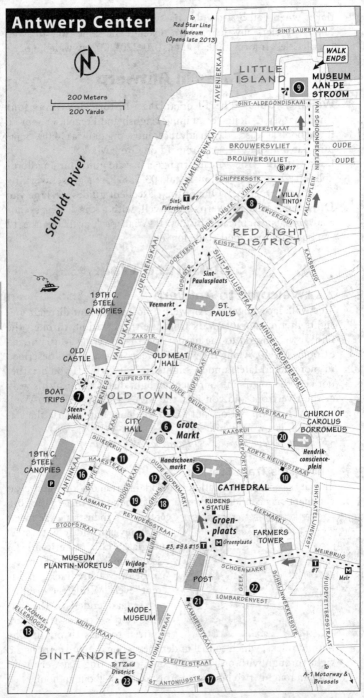

Antwerp Center

To Red Star Line Museum (Opens late 2013)

SINT LAUREIKAAI

LITTLE ISLAND

WALK ENDS

MUSEUM AAN DE STROOM ⑨

⑦

SINT-ALDEGONDISKAAI

BROUWERSTRAAT

BROUWERSVLIET

BROUWERSVLIET Ⓑ #17

OUDE

OUDE

SCHIPPERSSTR.

VILLA TINTO

Sint-Pietersvliet Ⓣ #7

⑧ VERVERSRUI

RED LIGHT DISTRICT

KEISTR.

KAASBRUG

200 Meters
200 Yards

Scheldt River

19TH C. STEEL CANOPIES

Sint-Paulusplaats

SINT-PAULUSSTRAAT

ST. PAUL'S

MINDERBROEDERSRUI

Veemarkt

OLD CASTLE

ZAKSTR.

OLD MEAT HALL

ZIRKSTRAAT

KUIPERSTR.

OLD TOWN

BOAT TRIPS ⑦

Steen-plein

CITY HALL

ZILVER Ⓘ

⑥ Grote Markt

WOLSTRAAT

CHURCH OF CAROLUS BORROMEUS

KAASRUI

KORTE KOEPOORTSTR.

⑳

Hendrik-conscience-plein

19TH C. STEEL CANOPIES

SUIKERRUI

HAARSTRAAT

⑪

Handschoen-markt

⑤

KORTE NIEUWESTR.

⑯

GR. PIETER POTSTR.

HOOGSTRAAT

OUDE KOORNMARKT

⑫

CATHEDRAL

⑩

VLASMARKT

⑲

PELGRIMSTR.

⑱

RUBENS STATUE

EIERMARKT

FARMERS TOWER

REYNDERSSTRAAT

Groenplaats Ⓜ Groenplaats

SINT-KATELIJNEVEST

STOOFSTRAAT

⑭

LEEUWEN

#3, #9 & #15 Ⓣ

SCHOENMARKT

MEIRBRUG

Ⓣ #7

Meir Ⓜ

MUSEUM PLANTIN-MORETUS

Vrijdag-markt

POST

GEEF

㉒

LOMBARDENVEST

SCHRIJNWERKERSSTR.

HUIDEVETTERSSTRAAT

KROMME-ELLEBOOGSTR.

MUNTSTRAAT

㉑

NATIONALESTRAAT

MODE-MUSEUM

KAMMENSTRAAT

⑬

SINT-ANDRIES

To 'T Zuid District & ㉓

SLEUTELSTRAAT

ST. ANTONIUSSTR. ⑰

To A-1 Motorway & Brussels

Walk

1. To Train Station & Start of Walk
2. Upper Main Drag
3. Rubens House
4. Lower Main Drag
5. Cathedral of Our Lady
6. Grote Markt
7. Riverfront
8. Red Light District
9. Old Dockyards & MAS

Hotels & Restaurants

10. Hotel Julien
11. Matelote Hotel
12. Le Patio B&B
13. Big Sleep B&B
14. Enich Anders B&B
15. Ibis Antwerpen Centrum Hotel
16. 't Katshuis Rooms
17. Pulcinella Youth Hostel
18. Pelgrimstraat Eateries
19. Lam & Yin Chinese Restaurant
20. Hendrik Conscienceplein Eateries
21. Fresh 'n Fruity Sandwich Shop
22. Hungry Henrietta
23. To t'Zuid Eateries

ANTWERP

Notice the clock towering high above the tracks. Time was important in the age of steam train travel, and the interior facade is a kind of triumphal arch crowned by the clock.

The "builder king" Leopold II was a force for modernity—you'll see his double-cursive *L* monogram and *KB* for "King of Belgium" everywhere. The station was constructed in an era when Belgium was a new colonial power, with the vast and resource-rich Congo providing a wealth of ivory and rubber.

The Royal Café, at the original track level, is first-class, yet economic and elegant...a fine place for a quiet cup of coffee or light bite.

• *Go through the door right under the ornate clock.*

Welcome to the main lobby of the train station. You're surrounded by some of the most grandiose architecture found in any train station in Europe. Note that even though we are in the Dutch-speaking part of Belgium, the mottos inscribed in the elaborate shields are all in French.

• *Exit the main lobby of the station. Facing the train ticket office, turn left. Look for the sign that reads* Keyserlei/Meir/Centrum. *From here, we'll walk basically straight ahead on the Keyserlei pedestrian mall all the way the Old Town. From the station steps, look down the pedestrian zone, past the ugly gold skyscraper, and between the twin black cupolas to the lacy spire of the cathedral in the distance. That's where you're heading.*

Upper Main Drag: Station to Rubens House

Stroll three blocks gradually downhill on the bustling, sand-colored boulevard called **De Keyserlei,** lined with chain restaurants and shops. Following European trends, this boulevard, like much of the old center, is becoming a bike-and-pedestrian zone.

The area around the train station is known as the **Diamond Quarter**—one of the world's top centers where diamonds are sold and cleaved (split into smaller pieces to prepare them for cutting). Other than casual-looking people with brief cases handcuffed to their wrists, there's little to see.

This stretch of the walk is light on actual sights but great for people- and city-watching. You'll run into the big boulevard called Frankrijklei, which marks the former course of the town wall. Continue straight across the street, then stroll between the twin grand facades that exemplify the style called Historicism. All the rage in the late 19th century, this school of architectural thought

Antwerp's Diamond Quarter

The area around the train station is known as the **Diamond Quarter**—one of the world's top centers for commerce in these gems. Although the industry is highly secretive, experts guess that four out of every five of the world's rough diamonds pass through Antwerp at some point. The diamond industry is located in the train-station neighborhood for good reason: If you're carrying millions of dollars worth of precious jewels in your briefcase through a strange city, you don't want to have to venture too far to reach a trader or diamond cutter.

Beginning in the 16th century, the diamond industry in Antwerp was dominated by Sephardic Jews from Spain, but under Catholic rule, they fled to Amsterdam. Then, in the late 19th century, Hasidic Orthodox Jews fleeing the pogroms in Russia settled here and took up the industry. In the streets around the train station, you'll likely see men wearing tall hats and black coats, with long beards and curly locks at their temples, and women with long dresses and hair covers. More recently, the diamond trade here is increasingly dominated by Indians.

The history of the diamond trade focuses on Africa, where diamond seekers dug the world's biggest manmade hole, the Kimberley Crater in South Africa. In some parts of Africa, the exploitative conditions for finding these gems haven't improved much since the early days of Belgian colonialism. A strict new diamond-certification process, introduced in Antwerp in 2000, attempts to block the sale of so-called "blood diamonds"—stones sold by rebels fighting governments in war zones in central and western Africa.

borrowed the best, most bombastic bits and pieces from past styles to wow the viewer. Now turn around and look at the towering 1960s-era skyscraper, and compare the aesthetics of the ages.

Beyond the facades, you enter a delightful pedestrians-only shopping zone. Bear left as the road curves at the statue of Anthony

van Dyck (1599-1641), a talented Antwerp artist who became the court painter for English King Charles I, and whose works now appear in many local museums. This puts you on **the Meir** (pronounced "mare"), Antwerp's showcase shopping zone, built, like the train station, in the boom times around 1900. (Meir is the name of both the street and the neighborhood.) A block later, on the left, notice the grand

Stadsfeestzaal shopping mall (with the gold niche over the door). Venture inside for a look at its astonishing interior.

Lower Main Drag—Rubens House to Cathedral

One block later, the big gap in the buildings with the fountain on your left marks the square called Wapper; detour a half-block down this square to one of the city's top sights, the **Rubens House.** This former home of Peter Paul Rubens does a fine job of introducing visitors both to the artist's works—several of which are displayed here—and to his lifestyle (for more on the museum, see page 546).

Backtrack to the Meir, where the ornate building on the left-hand corner (just after Wapper) is the **Paleis op de Meir,** a gorgeous Rococo-style palace built in 1745 by a local aristocrat who died before he could actually move in. Later, Napoleon purchased the home and decorated the upstairs in Empire Style. With Belgium independence in 1830, this became an official residence of the king of the Belgians. Around 1900, Leopold II spiffed it up even more. Finally, in 1969, the royal family donated the house to the government of Flanders, which refurbished it and opened it to the public.

But what really matters is chocolate. Step into the **Chocolate Line** shop (and notice the amazingly 3-D *grisailles*—the monochrome paintings above the doors). Here, you can see the creative work of the crazy "shock-o-latier" Dominique Persoone (€3.75 for your choice of three wacky flavors, daily until 18:30).

Continuing along the Meir, look ahead at the Art Deco, Gotham City-style **Farmers Tower** (Boerentoren, marked for its

current occupant, KBC). Completed in 1932, this was considered the first American-style skyscraper in Europe, and held the title of Europe's tallest skyscraper for 20 years. Pass the Meir metro stop, built on the cheap under the road, and a rack of city loaner bikes. Then cross the tram tracks and continue straight, bearing left on Schoenmarkt around the Farmers Tower.

After two blocks on Schoenmarkt, you come to the square called **Groenplaats,** with its handy metro stop, statue of Rubens, and the cathedral spire hovering just beyond. The high-fashion district is to your left, and the Old Town is beyond the cathedral. (If you're skipping the red light district,

you can return to this metro stop after seeing the riverfront to catch a tram back to the train station.)

• *Stroll through the square. Bear left up "Little Italy Lane"—the narrow street at the top of the square (Jan Blomstraat), passing a row of Italian restaurants—you'll pop out at Handschoenmarkt in front of the cathedral.*

Cathedral of Our Lady

Antwerp's biggest church, with its 400-foot-tall spire, dominates the Old Town. This tallest church steeple in the Low Countries marks a richly ornamented interior packed with fine artwork, including four paintings by Peter Paul Rubens (for more on the cathedral and a self-guided tour of its interior, see page 550).

• *After visiting the cathedral, head straight out from the main entrance and squeeze through the little gap at the far end of the square. Bearing right, you'll wind up in the...*

Grote Markt

Antwerp's main square is dominated by the looming tower of the cathedral at one end and the stately City Hall at the other. With a facade dating from Antwerp's Golden Age (16th century), the **City Hall** (Stadhuis) is adorned with flags from many different countries—representing the importance of international trade to the city. There's no US flag because we closed our consulate after 9/11, thinking one building per country is enough to defend. (The embassy in Brussels is famously fortified.)

The other buildings fronting the square are **guild houses,** celebrating the trade associations of each of the city's industries. Each

one is topped with a golden statue, which usually represents that guild's patron saint. Some of these are over-the-top, exaggerated rebuilt versions from the Romantic period in the 19th century. The many ground-floor cafés (especially the venerable Den Engel and

Den Bengel) are inviting places for a drink with a view. Locals say that when the outdoor terraces open up, they know summer has arrived in Antwerp.

The **fountain** in the middle of Grote Markt illustrates a gruesome story from Flemish folklore. Supposedly, a giant named Druon Antigoon collected tolls along the  Scheldt River. If someone was unable or unwilling to pay, the giant would sever their hand. His reign of terror finally ended when a brave young Roman soldier named Silvius Brabo defeated Antigoon, then cut off the giant's own hand and threw it into the river. Here we see Brabo in his wind-up, ready to toss Antigoon's blood-spouting hand. Tour guides love to explain that *hand werpen* ("to throw a hand") evolved into "Antwerpen"... though scholars prefer less glamorous alternatives: *an 't werf*, "on the wharf"; or *ando verpis*, "where land is thrown up against land" (the river has long deposited sludge along the bank here).

• *From the Grote Markt, backtrack a few steps to the left of the City Hall. Now head toward the river up the big street called Suikerrui.*

The Riverfront

Though historically important, Antwerp's waterfront is now dingy and drab. From the Grote Markt, Suikerrui street leads you to the busy riverfront street and, beyond it, a long parking lot, a tiny park, and a forgotten castle. Cross the street and stand along the river.

This now-derelict waterfront, with its priceless access to where the Scheldt River spills into the North Sea, is where the shipping settlement of Antwerp began in the Middle Ages. All that's left from those glory days is the forlorn and empty **castle** (to the right), which was once part of a city wall that fortified the heart of town. Surveying this scene, we see how Antwerp has turned its back on the river that once made it wealthy. When a train station opened across town in 1836, it pushed the city to the east. The shipping ports to the north are still busy, but most of the city is happy to ignore its river.

But occasionally, the river demands attention. Notice the concrete wall with its orange **floodgates**—long, heavy, waist-high steel doors that can roll along railroad tracks to open or close. Because the Scheldt is a tidal river, there's a huge risk of flooding—made more serious because of a rising sea level and the town center's proximity to the river.

Gloomy as it seems, the **embankment** is a popular place for

Antwerpenaars to walk, and young people enjoy hanging out along the river on warm summer evenings. Notice the 19th-century, Industrial Age-style steel canopies that line the waterfront. These formerly functioned as warehouses, but now they're used for other purposes: As you face the river, the buildings to the left are covered parking; the ones on the right shelter an impressive array of seafaring vessels (once part of the maritime museum). The fancy elevated terrace, across the little park from the castle, provides a view of the river (notice that I didn't say "good" view), and has WCs below; this is also the river's cruise-ship terminal.

Antwerp's riverfront is awaiting development. Ambitious plans would raise the seawalls to accommodate rising sea levels and turn this area into a lively people zone. (This is part of the Sigma Project, a coordinated Belgian and Dutch effort to raise seawalls everywhere in anticipation of a rising sea.)

• *From the riverfront, you have a choice: You can continue this walk through the graphic red light district (where you'll likely be flashed top and bottom by a transvestite), or you can end your walk here.*

If you are ready to return to the train station, backtrack to Groenplaats and take tram line #3, #9, or #15, direction: Merksem/ Eksterlaar/Boechout, to Diamant, the train station stop.

Or, to continue the walk, from the riverside castle, take the modest stairs over the highway barrier, cross the busy street at the crosswalk, and then climb the stairs up to a tiny view square. At the castle end of the viewpoint, look for a street sign that reads Willem Ogier Plaats, *and follow the adjoining Kuipersstraat away from the river two blocks through an affordable housing project to the Old Meat Hall (on your left).*

Red Light District

Belgium's biggest hub of legalized prostitution lacks the touristy patina of Amsterdam's...which makes it feel that much creepier. You'll see fewer rowdy "stag parties" making a racket, but lots of lonely men silently prowling the pedestrian zone. As with other red light districts, this area is not as dangerous as it might seem— the mayor actually encourages visitors to stroll here—but it's also not entirely safe either. And, as you can imagine, it feels more comfortable during the day and more lively after dark.

• *Pass the Old Meat Hall (which has nothing to do with sex workers— it now houses the Musical Instruments Museum described on page 552), and head downhill on Vleeshouwersstraat.*

You're walking through drab brick "projects"—subsidized housing built during the 1970s. These sterile rows of buildings replaced a very run-down, overpopulated, and characteristic old quarter that some residents miss—notice there are no pubs or shops along here.

• *Walk two blocks. At the square (Veemarkt), cut diagonally across the basketball court and continue up Nosestraat, passing a church...and some sex-toys shops.*

You'll wind up at the square called **Sint-Paulusplaats,** which used to be a medieval harbor, then a bustling sailors' quarter with red lights in the windows. This area, now with its share of trendy restaurants, is changing. (If you follow the tram tracks to the left, you'll come to the Sint-Pietersvliet stop, where tram #7 can take you back to the Old Town.)

• *Walk past the big anchor and over the tram tracks, up the unsigned pedestrian street (Oudemanstraat), which becomes Vingerlingstraat, and into the heart of the red light district, with its streets lined with ladies shimmying in windows.*

In the 19th century, Antwerp's red light district was known (or notorious) the world over; these days, it's a much tamer place... but still provocative, particularly so when you realize that about a third of the "girls" are men.

• *Bear right on Schippersstraat.*

Halfway down the block on the right is **Villa Tinto,** a modern-looking mall, designed by prominent artist Arne Quinze. You might call it the ultimate form-follows-function building. Considered one of Europe's most high-tech brothels, it has a system of "panic buttons" that sex workers can use to call for help if necessary, and a police station right in the middle. In Belgium, as throughout the Low Countries, prostitution is pragmatically integrated into the larger society without blushing. City leaders firmly believe that concentrating prostitution in this small neighborhood makes things safer both for the sex workers and for city residents at large. The Belgians believe that when a prostitute needs help, it's better that a policeman rather than a pimp comes to her rescue.

• *Pass through Villa Tinto (or, to skip the Villa Tinto experience, just continue on Schippersstraat), and then bear left.*

You'll pop out on a long, narrow square called **Falconplein.** This used to be dubbed "Red Square," for its Russian-dominated illegal activity (Russian mafia-style thugs selling designer knock-offs...and worse). Determined not to let this sketchy scene put a damper on this neighborhood's up-and-coming gentrification, city leaders recently cracked down, evicted the worst offenders, and spiffed up the square.

Turn left and walk across Falconplein to the big, tree-lined Brouwersvliet. Notice how wide this street is. Once a canal accommodating cargo ships that moored here to unload, it was paved over in the 19th century when the mightier docklands you're facing were constructed just beyond.

• *Cross Brouwersvliet and stroll toward the towering museum in the midst of Antwerp's old dockyards.*

Old Dockyards and MAS (Museum aan de Stroom)

Antwerp's formerly derelict and dangerous old port area has been rejuvenated and redeveloped. Built by Napoleon in the early 1800s, and filled with brick warehouses around the turn of the 20th century, this part of town became deserted in the 1950s and 1960s, when the city's shipping industry relocated to the larger ports farther north. In the mid-1980s, city leaders decided it was time to reclaim this prime real estate, and invested heavily in a systematic gentrification program. Today it's a youthful SoHo-type area, home to a tidy little yacht marina, a row of desirable condos, some trendy restaurants, and a state-of-the-art museum housed in an eye-catching tower. Perched on the Little Island next to the new museum is a towering black floating crane, kept here to keep alive the memory of ships unloading in this first Industrial-Age harbor from the early 19th century.

The new **Museum aan de Stroom** (Museum on the River), or **MAS** for short, is housed in a purpose-built, 210-foot-tall blocky tower, encased in hand-cut red stone, and speckled with silver hands (the symbol of Antwerp). Designed to resemble the spiraling stacks of goods in an old maritime warehouse, the museum emphasizes the way that Antwerp's status as a shipping center has made it a crossroads for people from around the world (for more on the museum, see page 556).

Since you've made it this far, it would be a shame not to take the escalators up 10 stories to the museum's rooftop panorama (the elevators are restricted to disabled visitors). The building itself, including the roof terrace, is free to enter (open Tue-Sun 9:30-24:00, closed Mon). Just outside the museum are a couple of small exhibits: While the diamond exhibit is remarkably unimpressive, the harbor exhibit is fascinating (free, Tue-Sun 9:30-17:30, closed Mon).

• *Your walk is over. To return to the Old Town, you could* **walk** *15-20 minutes along the river back to the riverside castle. To return to the train station by* **bus**, *backtrack to the wide Brouwersvliet, cross it, and look for the bus stop on your right. From here you can catch bus #17 (direction: UZA) to the train station. To return to the Old Town or train station by* **tram**, *continue walking on Brouwersvliet to the river, turn left, and watch for the tram tracks that loop right next to the roadway on the left. This is the terminus for tram #7 (the Sint-Pietersvliet metro stop). Hop on and get off three stops later at Meirbrug, where you can transfer to trams #3, #9, and #15.*

Sights in Antwerp

Antwerp offers visitors an eclectic array of sightseeing. If you have just one day (or less), you'll need to be selective: art, churches, history, fashion, and so on. Most of these sights are stops on the city walk described earlier. And every sight is either in the old center or within easy walking distance.

▲▲**Rubens House (Rubenshuis)**—Though the house looks untouched, after Rubens' death in 1640, his heirs sold it, and it was updated and remodeled over the years. In the 1940s, it was restored to its original condition. As you tour the place, keep in mind that it's basically a replica of where Rubens lived (for more authentic period houses, visit the home of Rubens' friend at the Rockox House Museum—see page 552, or the Museum Plantin-Moretus—see page 554). There are better places in Antwerp to see Rubens' paintings, but this exhibit offers you a unique opportunity to also learn about how he lived and the methods he employed—interesting even to people who think Peter Paul Rubens is the guy who plays Pee-Wee Herman.

Cost and Hours: €8, includes free guide-booklet in English, essential audioguide-€2, Tue-Sun 10:00-17:00, closed Mon, last entry 30 minutes before closing, Wapper 9-11, tel. 03-201-1555, www.rubenshuis.be.

Getting There: The house is between the train station and the Old Town—to walk here, follow my self-guided walk, earlier. To get here quickly, you can ride the metro to the Meir stop, then walk one long block east (back toward the train station).

❍ Self-Guided Tour: Buy your ticket at the glass pavilion in the middle of the square in front of the house, then head inside. The excellent, 1.5-hour tour provided by the audioguide explains all the details. Here are the highlights:

In the **courtyard,** you can see the original 16th-century house (on the left), the studio that Rubens added on to the complex (on the right), and the elaborate Michelangelo-flavored portico that connects them. An architect as well as a painter, Rubens designed the additions himself. The influence of his time in Italy is evident: Notice the dramatic contrast between the traditional Flemish home and the flamboyant Italian palazzo-style studio.

Now go inside the **house** and follow the one-way route through the various rooms. Many of the paintings are not by Rubens, but by artists he admired; in fact, his personal art collection was the biggest in the

Low Countries. In the dining room (with leather-tooled walls) is a rare self-portrait of Rubens in his fifties—one of only four known Rubens self-portraits. Facing him from across the room is a portrait (not by Rubens) of his second wife, Hélène Fourment. After his first wife died, Rubens married the much younger Hélène for love instead of entering into a strategic marriage with a noblewoman. Upstairs in his bedroom is a short, carved-wood bed like the one Rubens likely used—people slept sitting up in those days.

Continue into the **studio,** where Rubens and his students produced thousands of paintings. Lingering over the selection of canvases displayed here helps you understand their production process. In general, Rubens' paintings came about in one of three ways: For an important commission, he'd paint the entire work himself. More often, he'd paint an original, then have his school make many copies of it for him to sell on a wide scale (each one would get just a few personal highlights from the master...only Rubens himself could create just the perfect twinkle in an eye, or glimmer of light on that cellulite). And other times, he would simply do a rough oil sketch of what he wanted, then enlist experts in certain areas (such as flowers or portraits) to fill in the blanks. Then he'd sweep through at the end to finalize the work.

In the main hall, peruse the paintings counterclockwise, beginning with the canvases to the right as you enter. In the two early (pre-Italy) Rubens canvases of *St. Sebastian* and *Adam and Eve*, notice that the colors are subdued, and the bodies aren't as developed—lacking the rippling muscles and folds of fat that would later become Rubens' trademark.

The end of the room is flanked by twin portraits of the Spanish

monarchs of the Netherlands, **Archduke Albert** and **Infanta Isabella** (dressed in a nun's habit—after her husband died, she joined the Poor Clares, and wore this habit as a sign of mourning for the rest of her life). Rubens was this couple's official court painter, and these original Rubens works were copied in large numbers by his assistants. The monarchs' time was valuable, so Rubens worked quickly. To pose for her portrait, Isabella reportedly came to Antwerp for only one night; Rubens sketched her

ANTWERP

Peter Paul Rubens
(1577-1640)

Born in Germany in 1577, Rubens at age 12 moved with his family to Antwerp, where he was apprenticed to a local painter. Showing

great promise, Rubens went to study in Rome during his twenties, where he picked up the Italian fad of painting giant compositions on huge canvases. After eight years, in 1608, he returned to Antwerp to care for his dying mother. He married Flemish aristocrat Isabella Brant and settled down here, buying today's Rubens House in 1610, and living in it for the next 25 years. He added on to the house, turning it into a workshop that churned out painting after painting.

Rubens' work runs the gamut, from realistic portraits to lounging nudes, Greek myths to Catholic altarpieces, pious devotion to rough sex. Rubens painted anything that would raise your pulse: battles, miracles, hunts, rapes, and, especially, fleshy "Rubenesque" women with dimples on all four cheeks.

An expert of composition, Rubens could arrange a pig pile of many figures into a harmonious unit. Each painting was powered with an energy that people called his "fury of the brush." Rubens turns the wind machine on high, and scenes ripple with motion—windblown clothes, steroid-juiced muscles, billowing flags under a troubled sky.

In Rubens' work, everything is on a larger-than-life scale. Many canvases almost fill entire walls—you can see the seams

face quickly, just enough to capture her likeness, then filled in the details later.

High on the wall between the Spanish rulers is *The Annunciation*, with an Italian-inspired dynamism typical of the master.

The unfinished battle scene, *Henry IV at the Battle of Ivry*, illustrates Rubens' collaborative process. Rubens never completed this oil sketch, but you can see—at the top of the canvas—where the battle specialist has already filled in his section.

where the cloth pieces were stitched together—and approximately 2,500 canvases bear his name. How could he paint so many enormous canvases in one lifetime? He didn't. This house was an art factory, designed to mass-produce masterpieces. As was standard at the time, his assistants, students, and colleagues did much of the work: After he laid out a painting, his apprentices worked from Rubens' sketches, painting the background and filling in the minor details. Rubens orchestrated the production from a balcony, and before a painting was carried outside his tall, narrow door, he would put on the finishing touches, whipping each figure to life with a flick of his furious brush, and then signing it.

Rubens distinguished himself not necessarily with his technical ability, but as a smart businessman who knew how to provide wealthy benefactors (such as the Catholic Church) with exactly what they wanted—and he was welcomed at every royal court in Catholic Europe. In his long career, he was famous, wealthy, well-traveled, the friend of kings and princes; he was an artist, diplomat, and man about town.

During those Counter-Reformation days, when the Church was eager to win back fans after its ruthlessness in the Eighty Years' War, Rubens' flashy and fleshy Baroque style was perfect. His fascination with plus-size models, and his skill at capturing their rippling folds of fat, are the reason why we now describe certain figures as "Rubenesque." The sweet faces and ample proportions of the damsels he painted were inspired by Hélène Fourment, 37 years Rubens' junior, whom the artist married in 1630 after his first wife died. A true Renaissance man in the Baroque Age, Rubens was also an accomplished diplomat, who helped to negotiate peace between England and Spain (and was knighted by the kings of both countries in appreciation).

The Feast of St. Martin—with its bonfire in the midst of revelers—is much older. It was actually painted by a lesser-known artist and then purchased by Rubens, who added his own touches to make it his own. He'd add sparkle to the teeth and eyes, include golden hairnets, and elevate a scene by placing a few nobles among the peasants. Rubens enjoyed doing this as a fun pastime, to get a painting just right for his own collection—not to sell.

Finally is a **portrait by Anthony van Dyck.** While Rubens got the lion's share of the fame, some of his students were even more talented than he was—and Van Dyck was a verifiable genius, who prodded Rubens to become a better painter. And yet Van Dyck was just a painter...whereas Rubens was also an architect, an aristocrat, and a diplomat—a true jack-of-all-trades.

▲▲Cathedral of Our Lady (Onze-Lieve-Vrouwekathedraal)—Antwerp's biggest church has a spire that shoots 400 feet up from the middle of the Old Town, like a Gothic rocket. Its cavernous interior is packed with fine artwork, including four paintings by Peter Paul Rubens. While the Museum of Fine Arts is closed for renovation (through late 2017), you'll see these fine original canvases *in situ* (in the setting for which they were intended) here in the cathedral.

Cost and Hours: €5, Mon-Fri 10:00-17:00, Sat 10:00-15:00, Sun 13:00-16:00, Handschoenmarkt, tel. 03-213-9951, www.dekathedraal.be.

Tours: Free English tours are offered most days when guides are available—ask. The €2 audioguide is designed not to describe the church but to give meaning to the collection of paintings—mostly three-paneled works that hang in their original positions, creating a private little garden of worship space at the base of each column. Inside the church is a rack of pamphlets in English that also explain these paintings.

⊙ Self-Guided Tour: Stepping inside, notice how remarkably wide the cathedral is, with seven aisles (three on either side

of the nave). Looking up, you'll see that the Gothic design is also dramatically vertical—everything stretches upward, toward heaven. In the Middle Ages, the interior was filled with countless candles, and this was the only place to find bright light after dark. The stained-glass windows (some of them still original) colorized the light emanating from inside, drawing worshippers like moths to a flame.

The cathedral has a dynamic, troubled history—in fact, it's amazing the place has survived at all. Built over many generations in the Middle Ages (1352-1521), two tragedies befell it soon after completion: In 1533, it was scorched by fire; and in 1566, it was gutted by iconoclastic Protestants, who stripped it of its medieval decoration. (Though most of the interior was whitewashed, you can still see fragments of some very colorful murals on the underside of the vaults, where the iconoclasts couldn't reach.) After the Catholics came to power here, in 1585, they decorated the church in bubbly Baroque, including several pieces by Rubens. Each local guild had their own private altar area (at the base of each pillar), where they celebrated baptisms, weddings, and funerals—this was truly a community church.

When Napoleon's troops arrived in the late 18th century, they again emptied the church of its decorations, turned the building into a stable, and had plans to destroy it entirely before Napoleon was defeated. Once again needing to redecorate the place, church leaders bought a hodgepodge of ecclesiastical art from other churches and monasteries throughout the region, which Napoleon had also shut down.

The Baroque pulpit, carved for another church in 1713, was brought here in 1803 with a riot of birds, foliage, and cupids symbolizing the spread of the faith and the word.

The church's collection includes Rubens' big three: The *Raising of the Cross*, *The Assumption*, and *The Descent from the Cross*. In the

left transept is ***Raising of the Cross*** (1610-1611). Biblical bodybuilders strain to upright the cross, which is heavy with the swooning body of Christ. The painting is emotive, sumptuous, and almost sensual. Having just returned from eight years in Italy—where he'd studied the works of Michelangelo and Caravaggio (both of whose influence is evident here)—Rubens was eager to show off his mastery of musculature and human skin. Notice how lifelike Jesus' skin appears—a Rubens forte. The bold diagonal composition, thickly muscled bodies in motion, bright (almost garish) colors,

and illusion of movement are vintage Rubens. The painting is the inner panel of a hinged altarpiece; it was normally kept closed, and opened to reveal this scene only on special occasions—when its color and motion must have been even more striking to churchgoers unaccustomed to this sort of spectacle.

Continue farther into the church, and go into the choir area. Over the main altar is ***The Assumption*** (1626), showing the moment that the cathedral's namesake was brought up to heaven. Beneath Mary are the twelve apostles (after the Resurrection, the faithful disciple Matthias replaced Judas) and the three women who were present at her death. The role of Mary in church doctrine was one of the major dividing lines between Catholics and Protestants; whereas the Catholic Church considered her a saint to be venerated, the Protestants embraced the notion that she was an ordinary woman called to do God's work. The gauzy heroine-worship of this canvas makes it clear who finally controlled the turf here.

Circle back up into the right transept to see ***Descent from the Cross*** (1612-1614). Rubens' diagonal composition is the mirror

image of *Raising of the Cross*, the painting across the nave. It's a freeze-frame of an action-packed moment...just as workers strained to erect the cross with Christ's limp body, now they struggle to lower him from it. But at this somber moment, the subjects seem to be moving more slowly, methodically. Notice the pale pallor of Christ's dead skin—a strong contrast to the lifelike luster of the other painting. The details make the poignancy of this moment come to life: the man in the top-right corner who's holding onto the shroud with his teeth; Mary's outstretched arm, in a tender matronly effort to comfort her son even in death; and, in the lower-right section, a blood-filled bronze basin holding the crown of thorns and the nails.

The sacristy shows historic portraits of the church's 21 local bishops. In the apse, beyond the high altar, a video in a chapel shows the church in action on Easter and Christmas.

Musical Instruments Museum at the Old Meat Hall (Museum Vleeshuis)—This restored brick palace, erected to house meat during Antwerp's glory days, now houses a collection of musical instruments. The Klank van de Stad ("Sound of the City") exhibition presents two floors of instruments and old music manuscripts (don't miss the cellar). The collection is decent and well presented, but English information is limited (unless you buy a €3.50 booklet with descriptions). Even the included touchscreen audioguide is mostly in Dutch—but at least it lets you hear some of the instruments. And though the experience here can be a little underwhelming, it's fun to see the impressive brick vaults

inside; consider just ducking into the entry area for a peek (it's a fine place to use the WC, or to warm up on a cold day).

Cost and Hours: €5, Tue-Sun 10:00-17:00, closed Mon, Vleeshouwersstraat 38-40, tel. 03-233-6404, www.museum vleeshuis.be. To get here from the Grote Markt, face the City Hall and turn right up Braderijstraat, take the first left on Kuipersstraat, then look right.

▲**Rockox House Museum (Museum Rockoxhuis)**—Nicolaas Rockox (1560-1640) was a mayor of Antwerp and a friend and sponsor of Peter Paul Rubens. Today his house—buried in a residential zone a 10-minute walk northeast of the cathedral and

ANTWERP

Grote Markt—is a lovely museum.

Here you can get a truly authentic look at an aristocratic home from the period (unlike the Rubens House, which was rebuilt), while viewing impressive artwork. The house also has interesting themed exhibits (which highlight, for example, period food or clothing). Rounding out the experience is a fine furniture collection and a beautiful period garden/courtyard.

Cost and Hours: €2.50, Tue-Sun 10:00-17:00, closed Mon, Keizerstraat 10-12, tel. 03-201-9250, www.rockoxhuis.be. There is no audioguide, but the museum is well described in a free English booklet. In the small auditorium, request the 25-minute video, "Antwerp in 1600," to set the context for your visit.

Visiting the Museum: You'll make a big counterclockwise circuit on the ground floor, then stroll through the courtyard with its Renaissance-style garden.

While the walls were originally covered from floor to ceiling with paintings, these days the curator is more selective; he regularly assembles good temporary exhibits that draw from Rockox's vast personal art collection. People used art to decorate as a way of expressing themselves—their values, the people they knew, and so on—so viewing the collection lets you psychoanalyze Rockox. Highlights include an original Rubens canvas of Mary looking tenderly over Baby Jesus (modeled after Rubens' own first wife and son), and Van Dyck's study of two old men's heads. David Teniers the Younger's *Village Feast* evokes the action-packed canvases of the Brueghels (in fact, Teniers—a contemporary of Rubens—married into that prolific clan).

Though the collection is always good, it's particularly worth seeing while Antwerp's Museum of Fine Arts is closed for restoration (through late 2017); during this time, the Rockox House is displaying Rubens' *Doubting Thomas* triptych, the left panel of which features a portrait of Nicolaas Rockox (who commissioned the work for the chapel where he was ultimately entombed). It's clear that Rubens really knew this man, as the portrait truly captures his personality. Nearby are usually displayed two replicas, in which Rockox's gaze is less intense—clearly executed by a lesser artist.

Another highlight—and just plain fun to look at—is Peter Brueghel the Younger's *The Proverbs* (actually a copy of his father's earlier work), which strives to make literal more than a hundred Flemish sayings of the day. Try to find some of the examples: "armed to the teeth," "banging your head against the wall," "the die is cast," "don't cry over spilled milk," "the blind leading the blind," and dozens of others that make no sense in English ("Who knows why the geese go barefoot?").

▲▲Museum Plantin-Moretus—More interesting than it sounds, this museum about the history of the local printing industry offers an engaging look at Antwerp's 16th-century Golden Age. You'll find out how Antwerp became one of Europe's most important printing cities. Every Flemish kid comes here on a field trip to ogle the old printing presses, smartly decorated aristocratic rooms, and fine collection

of antique manuscripts. The excellent audioguide tells the whole story. You'll need at least an hour or two (and the audioguide) to really appreciate the place.

Cost and Hours: €8, audioguide-€2, Tue-Sun 10:00-17:00, closed Mon, last entry 30 minutes before closing, Vrijdagmarkt 22, tel. 03-221-1450, www.museumplantinmoretus.be.

Visiting the Museum: The museum is named for two influential Antwerp printers: Frenchman Christoffel Plantin, who began a printing business here in 1546; and his son-in-law Jan Moretus, who carried on the family business. Eventually their business became the official court printer for the Spanish monarchs of the Low Countries. This building was both the family's home and their workshop, and, since the family was wealthy enough to maintain the property, it's a remarkably well-preserved look at 16th- and 17th-century aristocratic life. The sprawling complex surrounds a pleasant garden, with wings dating from different periods. You'll follow the one-way, counterclockwise tour route through the ground floor, then head upstairs. Sprinkled throughout these rooms are ample samples of period manuscripts and maps, a Gutenberg Bible, and more.

The ground floor is devoted mostly to the printing shop, starting with the reception rooms. In the bookshop, look for the list of books forbidden by the Catholic Church—the list was printed

by, and includes books sold by, Christoffel Plantin. In the proofreaders' room, you can imagine diligent editors huddled around the shared oak desk, debating the 17th-century equivalent of whether "email" takes a hyphen. The publisher's private leather-bound office is classy. In the print shop you'll see some of the oldest printing presses in the world (c. 1600); neatly stacked in the back room are some 10 tons of lead letters, with racks of complete sets of fonts and different type sizes.

Upstairs is the residence, showing off how the upper crust lived a few centuries ago—tapestry wall hangings, high-beamed ceilings, leather-tooled walls, and so on. The 18th-century library displays a polyglot bible, with five languages on one page, printed by Christoffel Plantin. The Rubens Room is a reminder that the famous painter was an old family friend.

Nearby: The museum is on a charming square called Vrijdagmarkt, where there really is a "Friday market" each week with an auction of secondhand stuff.

Red Star Line Museum—A five-minute walk beyond the MAS (north, past the greenish skyscraper) is a brand-new exhibit that's scheduled to open in late 2013. Its "People on the Move" exhibit promises to show the "other end" of the Ellis Island experience.

During the great migration to the US and Canada between 1873 and 1935, the Red Star shipping line brought some two million emigrants to New York City, and those steamers began their journey here in Antwerp. In addition to "steerage-class" peasants, the line also transported luxury travelers and cargo. By the 1930s, many of the emigrants were Jews fleeing the Nazi regime in Germany. In these red-brick warehouses, emigrants were given humiliating health exams, had their clothes and luggage fumigated, and nervously waited while clerks processed their paperwork. Today, the same buildings are being turned into a museum documenting the experience of the people who said their final farewell to Europe right here. The exhibit traces the history of the Red Star Line and its passengers, displays artifacts from the emigrants, and shows evocative artwork depicting emigrants poignantly waiting for a steamship to whisk them off to the New World in pursuit of the American Dream.

Cost and Hours: Opening in late 2013; likely €8, Tue-Fri 10:00-17:00, Sat-Sun 10:00-18:00, closed Mon, Rijnkaai 15, tel. 03-206-0350, www.redstarline.org.

▲**ModeMuseum ("MoMu")**—The collection here, like fashion itself, is always changing...but it's also always good. Housed in the modern ModeNatie facility in the heart of the Sint-Andries fashion zone, this museum presents good rotating exhibits about fashion history or a big-name designer, with a new exhibit every six months. The building is also home to the Antwerp Fashion Academy, a library with books about fashion, a good bookshop, and—on the ground floor near the ticket desk—a gallery showcasing works by students. Everything is (no surprise) very stylishly presented. You stroll a one-floor, one-way circuit as you visit.

Cost and Hours: €8, includes English guidebook, Tue-Sun 10:00-18:00, closed Mon, last entry 30 minutes before closing, a five-minute walk south of Groenplaats at Nationalestraat 28, tel. 03-470-2770, www.momu.be.

Museum aan de Stroom (MAS—Museum on the River)— The collections of several smaller Antwerp museums—including the maritime, ethnographic, and folklore museums—have been brought together in this brand-new facility. Billed as a "museum of, for, and about the city and the world," MAS includes four permanent exhibits that emphasize connections between people by juxtaposing old items in new ways, temporary exhibits, a top-floor top-class restaurant, and a roof terrace with panoramic views. While most of the collections are underwhelming, the pre-Columbian religious art collection is truly world-class. The building's many windows offer great views over Antwerp, its sprawling harbor—one of the world's biggest, oil refineries, and beyond. The building itself and its roof terrace are free, as are several small exhibits just outside (for details, see page 545 of the self-guided walk).

Cost and Hours: €5 for permanent collection, €8 for temporary exhibits, €10 for both; free audioguide, Tue-Sun 10:00-17:00, closed Mon, a 15-minute walk north of Groenplaats at Hanzestedenplaats 1, from train station take bus #17 in direction: Rijnkaai to the Van Schoonbekeplein stop, tel. 03-338-4434, www.mas.be.

Shopping in Antwerp

As a capital of both fashion and avant-garde culture, Antwerp is a shopper's delight, with a seemingly endless array of creative little corner boutiques selling unique items, as well as outlets for big-name international designers. The large department stores are on the boulevard called **the Meir,** between the train station and the Old Town (see page 539). South of the Rubens House, streets like Leopoldstraat, Sint-Jorispoort, and Mechelsesteenweg are noted for antiques and home decor.

The **Sint-Andries** district, a few minutes' walk south of the Old Town, just to the west along Nationalestraat, is the center of the fashion scene. While it's a three-star destination for couture lovers, anybody would have fun window-shopping here. In the shops along the streets of Sint-Andries, you'll find everything from top-name international designers to funky hole-in-the-wall boutiques to vintage shops to jewelers.

Antwerp's status as a fashion mecca is a relatively recent development. In 1988, six students from the Royal Academy of Fine Arts' fashion department traveled to a London show, where they got a lot of attention. Because their Flemish names were too challenging to pronounce, the English press simply dubbed them the "Antwerp Six." Each one opened a shop in Sint-Andries, which at the time was a very poor neighborhood. They put this area on the map, other designers began to move in, and now it's one of Europe's top fashion zones. The academy is still up and running; it has a small enrollment and a strong focus on creativity (www .antwerp-fashion.be).

As you explore, you'll discover that each street has its own personality and specialties. For example, Schuttershofstraat and Hopland are where you'll find famous-label international couture, while Kammenstraat is better for young, trendy, retro-hipster fashions. For antiques, head to Kloosterstraat (to the west).

Sleeping in Antwerp

$$$ Hotel Julien, an extremely chic boutique hotel, is Antwerp's most enticing splurge. Located in a renovated 16th-century building on a drab street just outside the Old Town, its 22 rooms are a perfectly executed combination of old and new. The public areas, with high ceilings and lots of unfinished wood, feel like an art gallery (Db-€170-290 depending on size and amenities, air-con in most rooms, elevator, free Internet access and Wi-Fi, spa in basement, Korte Nieuwstraat 24, tel. 03-229-0600, www.hotel-julien .com, info@hotel-julien.com).

$$$ Matelote Hotel ("Fisherman") is a less pretentious boutique hotel, with a central location on a characteristic street deep in the Old Town. Its 10 rooms have artistic decor and some nice touches, such as mini-fridges with free soft drinks and a central music system playing Belgian classics (small "cozy comfort" Db-€80-130—usually €90-100, deluxe Db-€100-150—usually €120, breakfast-€12, free Internet access and Wi-Fi, Haarstraat 11a, tel. 03-201-8800, www.hotel-matelote.be, info@matelote.be, helpful Anton).

$$ Le Patio is the best B&B I found in Antwerp, with three comfortable, thoughtfully appointed ground-floor rooms around a little courtyard on the restaurant-lined Pelgrimstraat. The location is perfect, and the service is as sweet as Belgian chocolate (Db-€105, Tb-€130, 20 percent less for 3 nights or more, free Wi-Fi, Pelgrimstraat 8, tel. 03-232-7661, www.lepatio.be, info@lepatio .be, Nicole and Roger).

Sleep Code

(€1 = about $1.30, country code: 32)
S = Single, **D** = Double/Twin, **T** = Triple, **Q** = Quad, **b** = bathroom, **s** = shower only. Everyone speaks English. Unless otherwise noted, breakfast is included and credit cards are accepted.

To help you easily sort through these listings, I've divided the accommodations into three categories, based on the price for a standard double room with bath:

$$$ Higher Priced—Most rooms €105 or more.
$$ Moderately Priced—Most rooms between €60-105.
$ Lower Priced—Most rooms €60 or less.

Prices can change without notice and don't include the city room tax; verify the hotel's current rates online or by email.

$$ Big Sleep B&B, between the Old Town and 't Zuid, has two very mod rooms in an old warehouse, with lots of minimalist white and frosted glass—a little too transparent if privacy is a priority (Sb-€55, Db-€80, includes breakfast in your room, cash only, free Wi-Fi, Kromme-Elleboogstraat 4, mobile 0474-849-565, www.intro04.be/thebigsleep, els.hubert@skynet.be, Els Hubert).

$$ Enich Anders B&B is well-priced and nicely located above an art gallery around the corner from Vrijdagmarkt, in the heart of town. This is a great place for families, as most rooms come with lofts (Sb-€66, Db-€72, Tb-€88, Qb-€104, €5 cheaper per night with two-night stay, includes breakfast served in your own kitchenette, cash only, free Wi-Fi, tight and steep stairs, Leeuwenstraat 12, mobile 0476-998-601, www.enich-anders.be, charming Ine).

$$ Ibis Antwerpen Centrum, the cookie-cutter standby, has 150 predictable rooms sharing the big Oudevaartplaats square with the modern City Theater, just south of the Meir and the Rubens House between the train station and Old Town (Sb/Db-€92-109 depending on demand, as low as €59 in slow times if you book online 3 weeks ahead, breakfast-€14/person, air-con, elevator, free Internet access and Wi-Fi, Meistraat 39, tel. 03-231-8830, www.ibishotel.com, h1453@accor.com).

$ 't Katshuis is a rough-around-the-edges budget option, with nine sketchy but affordable rooms in two buildings right in the center of town. This last resort has some of the best-located cheap beds in town, if you don't mind sharing a WC (Ss-€35, Ds-€55, Db-€60, includes coffee but not breakfast, Grote Pieter Potstraat 18 and 19—reception at #19, mobile 0476-206-947, www.katshuis.be, katshuis@gmail.com).

$ Pulcinella Youth Hostel is Antwerp's newest and best official hostel. With 21 doubles, it offers privacy and bargain prices (bed in 4-6 person dorm-€23, Sb-€37, Db-€54, nonmembers pay €3 fee, includes breakfast, no curfew, free Wi-Fi, in the fashion district at Bogaardeplein 1, tel. 03-234-0314, www.vjh.be, antwerpen @vjh.be).

Eating in Antwerp

This trendy, youthful city is changing all the time, and the range of options is impressive. Because what's good one year is old news the next, it's risky to recommend any particular place. Instead, I suggest poking around the neighborhoods described next and choosing the menu and ambience that appeal to you the most. Exploring this evolving scene is actually enjoyable—a fun part of the Antwerp experience. Ask your hotelier for pointers.

If you're dining in the Old Town area, simply accept that anywhere you go will cater at least partly to tourists. But since Antwerp isn't overrun by visitors, these places also entertain their share of locals. For a more authentic Antwerp experience, head south to 't Zuid. And if you want the local beer, there's just one: De Koninek.

In the Old Town

Touristy restaurants with outdoor seating abound on the Grote Markt and Handschoenmarkt, the square in front of the cathedral. Choose your view and overpay for mediocre food. Better yet, venture a few blocks away to one of these neighborhoods.

Pelgrimstraat: Just a block south of the cathedral, this delightful, cobbled, traffic-free lane is still a tourist zone—but a bit more respectable than the high-profile squares. You'll find a staggering variety along here: Italian and tapas, sushi and Thai, rustic taverns and chic bars.

Keep an eye out for these (coming from the cathedral): **Pasta Hippo** has a reputation for good pasta. On the right at #4, go through the doorway to discover a series of narrow alleyways (called **Vlaeykensngang**) that twist through the middle of the block, passing a trio of well-regarded restaurants en route. Back on the main drag, on the left, is **Pelgrom,** a tavern in a cozy brick cellar that oozes atmosphere (but isn't good on a hot day). Farther down on the right is **Lollapalooza,** with a fun, eclectic menu; it comes with a charming little brick grotto across the street. Two nearby streets (Grote Pieterpotstraat and Haarstraat) are similar, but less developed and more bar-oriented.

At the end of Pelgrimstraat, **De Groote Witte Arend,** a rustic beer hall with an inviting cobbled courtyard, slams out traditional food and offers a wonderful list of Belgian beers (Reynderstraat 18, tel. 03-233-5033). The local phenomenon is the **Lam & Yin Chinese Restaurant,** with a small menu, great service, and wonderful traditional Chinese served by Hong Kong immigrants. They have two seatings (18:00 and 20:30), and you'll choose from four starters (€15 each) and five main dishes (€25 each). This is a rare place, with a Michelin star and no pretense—but you'll need to reserve well in advance to snare one of its 36 seats (Wed-Sun only, across from De Groote Witte Arend at Reyndersstraat 17, tel. 03-232-8838).

Near Hendrik Conscienceplein: The streets branching off from Hendrik Conscienceplein (about a block northeast of the cathedral), with its very Italian-feeling Baroque Jesuit church, are a charming cobbles-and-red-brick maze of alleys with intriguing little eateries. **Neuze Neuze** is a dressy and romantic place serving "classic Belgian cuisine" (which is essentially French) under old beams (€20-30 starters and main dishes, Mon-Sat 12:00-14:00 & 19:00-21:30, closed for lunch Wed and Sat and all day Sun, Wijngaardstraat 19-21, tel. 03-232-2797).

Just South and East of the Old Town

In Sint-Andries: The area called Sint-Andries, the center of the fashion district, has its share of enjoyable bars and restaurants. For a quick lunch, try **Fresh 'n Fruity,** selling good €2-5 baguette sandwiches and fresh-squeezed fruit juice (closed Sun, Kammenstraat 19, tel. 03-231-1308). **Hungry Henrietta,** tucked away in a nondescript, businesslike neighborhood just south of Groenplaats, has mod black decor and good Belgian food (€9-15 starters, €20-26 main dishes, €15 daily specials, daily 12:00-14:00 & 18:00-21:00, Lombardenvest 19, tel. 03-232-2928).

In 't Zuid

Literally "The South," this zone is Antwerp's top restaurant and nightlife zone. Frequented mostly by urbanites, this is where you'll find most of the city's hot new restaurants. Options are scattered around a several-block area, with one or two tempting eateries on each block. The long parking lot that runs parallel to the river a block inland (between Waalsekaai and Vlaamsekaai) is lined with several options.

At **Marnixplaats,** the confluence of eight streets creates a circle of corner buildings made-to-order for restaurants with outdoor seating. **Fiskebar** is done up like a fish market (as its name implies), and lists a wide range of seafood specialties on its chalkboard menu high on the wall (€7-10 starters, €15-25 main dishes, €17-20 specials, open daily, Marnixplaats 12-13, tel. 03-257-1357). **Osteria Casa Zaga** dishes up Italian food in one long room that stretches along the open kitchen (€16-18 pastas and salads, €23 main dishes, open daily, Marnixplaats 10, tel. 03-216-4616).

Antwerp Connections

From Antwerp by Train to: Brussels (5/hour, 40-50 minutes), **Ghent** (3/hour, 50-55 minutes), **Bruges** (2/hour, 1.5 hours, half change in Ghent), **Ypres/Ieper** (hourly, 2.25 hours, change in Kortrijk), **Amsterdam** (hourly, 1.25 hours), Amsterdam's **Schiphol Airport** (hourly, 1 hour), **Delft** (hourly, 1 hour, change in Rotterdam), **Paris** (about hourly direct on Thalys, 2 hours; more possible with a transfer at Brussels Midi/Zuid/South to Thalys, 2.5 hours). In Belgium, dial 050-302-424 for train information—press 4 for English, www.b-rail.be.

GHENT

Gent

Made terrifically wealthy by the textile trade, medieval Ghent was a powerhouse—for a time, it was one of the biggest cities in Europe. It erected grand churches and ornate guild houses to celebrate its resident industry. But, like its rival Bruges, eventually Ghent's fortunes fell, leaving it with a well-preserved historic nucleus surrounded by a fairly drab modern shell.

Ghent doesn't ooze with cobbles and charm, as Bruges does; this is a living, thriving city—home to Belgium's biggest university. In contrast to the manicured-but-empty back lanes of Bruges, Ghent enjoys more urban grittiness and a thriving restaurant and nightlife scene. It's also a browser's delight, with a wide range of fun and characteristic little shops and boutiques that aren't aimed squarely at the tourist crowds. Simply put, Ghent feels more real than idyllic. Visitors enjoy exploring its historic quarter, ogling the breathtaking Van Eyck altarpiece in its massive cathedral, touring its impressive art and design museums, strolling its picturesque embankments, basking in its finely decorated historic gables, and prowling its newly revitalized Patershol restaurant quarter.

Planning Your Time

Ghent is ideally located, about halfway between Brussels and Bruges. It's easy to get the gist of the town in a few hours (either toss your bag in a locker at Ghent's train station on your way between those two cities, or side-trip here from either one). With limited time, focus on the historical center: Follow my self-guided walk, tour the cathedral, and dip into any museums that intrigue you. With more time or a strong interest in art, also visit the art museums closer to the train station. Be aware that nearly all museums in Ghent are closed on Mondays (though the cathedral and other churches remain open).

If you'd like to home-base in Belgium, Ghent couldn't be more handy—just a half-hour from either Brussels or Bruges and 50 minutes from Antwerp (though be aware that most Ghent hotels are a tram ride away from the train station).

Orientation to Ghent

Although it's a mid-sized city (pop. 240,000), the tourist's Ghent is appealingly compact—you can walk from one end of the central zone to the other in about 15 minutes. Its Flemish residents call it Gent (gutturally: hhhent), while its French name is Gand (sounds like "gone").

Tourist Information

Ghent's TI is in the Fish Market (Vismijn) building next to the Castle of the Counts (daily mid-March-mid-Oct 9:30-18:30, off-season 9:30-16:30, tel. 09-266-5232, www.visitgent.be). Pick up a free town map and a pile of brochures (including a good self-guided walk).

The **Gent Museum Card,** which includes public transit and entrance to all the major museums and monuments in town, is worth the price if you'll be visiting four or more sights (€20/3 days, sold at TI, hotels, and museums).

Arrival in Ghent

By Train: Ghent's main train station, called Gent-Sint-Pieters, is about a mile and a half south of the city center. As the station is undergoing an extensive renovation (through 2020), you might find things different than described. The left-luggage desk (daily 6:15-21:30) is across the hall from the Travel Centre ticket office, and lockers are just down the same hall on the right (€3-4/day for either bag-storage option).

It's a dull 30-minute **walk** to the city center. Instead, take the **tram:** Buy a ticket from the Relay shop just inside the train station exit or at the ticket machines outside, then find the stop for tram #1 (out the front door and to the left, on the far side of the tram tracks). Board tram #1 in the direction of Wondelgem/Evergem (departs about every 10 minutes, ride into town takes 15 minutes, €1.20 if you buy the ticket in advance at a shop or automated machine, €2 from the driver; you can also get a shareable 10-ride ticket for €9). Get off at the Korenmarkt stop; continue one block straight ahead to Korenmarkt, from where you can see most of the city's landmark towers (St. Michael's Bridge, where my self-guided walk begins, is just to the left). Figure €10 for a **taxi** into town (€8.50 drop good for about 2 miles, after 18:00 the drop jumps to €11).

To reach the art museums in Citadelpark, simply exit the station straight ahead, then bear right at the end of the square (onto Koningin Astridlaan); for more details, see page 581.

By Car: Exit the E-40 expressway at the Gent Centrum exit, then follow the *P-route* (parking route) to various pay garages in town; the most central include P1 (Vrijdagmarkt) and P5 (Kouter).

Helpful Hints

Festivals: Ghent is proud of its Gentse Feesten (Ghent Festivities), which last for 10 days and begin around the city holiday of July 21. This open-air music festival features different types of music in venues around town and lots of boozing. Book hotels during this period well in advance. Other events include a jazz festival (the week before the big festival), and a film festival in mid-October.

Market Day: Sunday is the main market day in Ghent, with small markets filling squares around town: a flower market at Kouter, secondhand books along Ajuinlei, clothes and pets on Vrijdagmarkt, and more. There are also smaller markets on Fridays and Saturdays.

Laundry: A handy, unstaffed coin-op launderette is in the heart of the Patershol restaurant neighborhood... handy for multitaskers (daily 7:00-22:00, corner of Oudburg and Zwaanstraat, mobile 0475-274-686).

Tours in Ghent

Walking Tours—Guided two-hour tours of Ghent (in English and usually another language, too) depart from the TI (€8, May-Oct daily at 14:30, Sun only off-season).

Local Guide—**Toon Van den Abeele** enthusiastically shares Ghent's charms (€70/2-hour tour, book through the local guide agency at tel. 09-233-0772, www.ghentguides.be, or info@gidsenbond-gent.be).

Boat Tours—Lazy little tour boats, jammed with tourists listening to the spiel in several languages, cruise the waterways. Several companies offer essentially the same tour for the same price (€7, 50 minutes, live guides).

Self-Guided Walk

Welcome to Ghent

This walk takes in the historic center of Ghent. Begin at the bridge in the heart of town, next to the bustling Korenmarkt square.

St. Michael's Bridge (Sint-Michielsbrug)

This viewpoint offers Ghent's best 360-degree panorama. The city was founded at the confluence (the origin of the word "Ghent")

of two rivers: the Lys (Leie in Dutch) and the Scheldt (Schelde in Dutch, Escaut in French). Ghent boomed in the Middle Ages, when the wool trade made it wealthy. By the 14th century, Ghent's population was around 65,000—positively massive in an age when most of Europe was rural farmland (north of the Alps, only Paris was larger). Two-thirds of the city's population were textile workers, making Ghent arguably Europe's first industrial city. The waterway in front of you—now plied by tourist-laden boats—was the city's busy harbor. Lining the embankment on the right are several ornately decorated guild houses—meeting halls for the town's industries (such as corn traders or seamen). Straight ahead is the newly renovated Fish Market (the new home of the TI), which marks the start of the seedy-chic Patershol zone (a residential district sprinkled with great restaurants); behind that is the imposing Castle of the Counts. (We'll circle through town and end near there.)

• *Turn to the right and walk to...*

Korenmarkt

This "Corn Market" is one of many small squares throughout the city. Whereas many Belgian cities (including Brussels, Bruges, and Antwerp) have a single "Great Market" (Grote Markt), Ghent was too big for just one such square. Instead it had a smattering of smaller squares that specialized in different areas of commerce. They retain these traditional names today.

The big building on the left is the former **post office** (now the Post Plaza mall). While it seems to match the classic medieval style of old Ghent, it's much newer—Neo-Gothic dating from 1913. As

Ghent

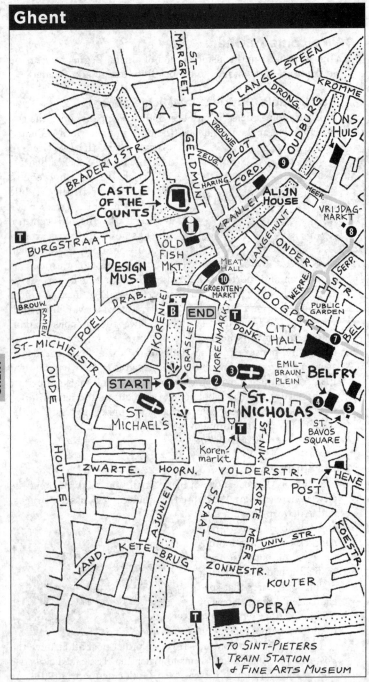

GHENT

PATERSHOL

ST-MARGRIET. STR.

LANGE STEEN
DRONG.
KROMME
OUDBURG
ONS HUIS

BRADERIJSTR.
GELDMUNT
VROUWE PLOT
ZEUG
HARING
CORD.
KRANLEI
9

CASTLE OF THE COUNTS
ALIJN HOUSE

MEER.

VRIJDAG-MARKT
8

BURGSTRAAT
T

OLD FISH MKT.
DESIGN MUS.
MEAT HALL
LANGEMUNT
ONDER-
SERP. STR.

BROUW.
RAMEN
POEL
DRAB.
KORENLEI
GRASLEI
B
END
GROENTEN-MARKT
10
KORENMARKT
T
DONK.
IL
CITY HALL
HOOGPOORT
WERRE.
PUBLIC GARDEN
7
BEL

ST-MICHIELSTR.

START **1**
2 **3**
EMIL-BRAUN-PLEIN
BELFRY
4 **5**

ST. MICHAEL'S
VELD-
T
ST-NIK.
ST. NICHOLAS
ST. BAVOS SQUARE

OUDE
HOUTLEI

Koren-markt

ZWARTE.
HOORN.
VOLDERSTR.
KORTE MEER
HENE
POST

VAND.
AJUNLEI
KETELBRUG
STRAAT
ZONNESTR.
UNIV. STR.
KOESTR.

T
OPERA

KOUTER

→ TO SINT-PIETERS TRAIN STATION & FINE ARTS MUSEUM

1. St. Michael's Bridge
2. Korenmarkt
3. St. Nicholas' Church
4. Belfry
5. St. Bavo's Square
6. Cathedral of St. Bavo
7. Hoogpoort
8. Friday Market Square & Van Artevelde Statue
9. Patershol
10. Vegetable Market

T TRAM #1
B CANAL CRUISES
↙ VIEW

200 YARDS
200 METERS

DCH

throughout Europe, the late 1800s and early 1900s were a time of powerful nationalism, when smaller minority groups (such as the Flemish) rose up against the more dominant groups (such as the French-speaking Belgians) to assert their legitimacy and worth. There was a flurry of Neo-Gothic construction, hearkening back to a time when the Flemish had more power.

Looking straight ahead (with the Corn Market on your far left), you can see the spires of Ghent's three main buildings (left to right): the Church of St. Nicholas, the Belfry (with a dragon rather than a cross on top), and St. Bavo's Cathedral. As you tour Ghent, you can play amateur archaeologist to quickly deduce the age of various buildings. Before the year 1400, when Ghent was rolling in wool money,

they built with valuable, imported gray limestone. Between 1400 and 1500, as the economy slowed, they used yellow sandstone, which was quarried nearby. And after 1500—when competition from Brussels and England, combined with very conservative guild leadership that was slow to adapt to the changing markets, caused Ghent's economy to tank—they resorted to the cheapest material: locally produced red brick. Even in a single building—such as these old churches—you can spot several centuries of construction at a glance. (People from Ghent gleefully point out that their rival, Bruges, is built mostly of brick—indicating that city's lowlier economic status in medieval times.)

• *Turn your attention to the big church at the end of the square.*

St. Nicholas' Church (Sint-Niklaaskerk)

This stout church is made mostly of gray limestone, indicating that it dates from a boom time for Ghent.

Go inside (free, daily 10:00-17:00). You can tell it was built from the back to the front, as the gray limestone transitions to the yellow sandstone. While the building itself is Gothic, the decorations inside—like most in Ghent—are much newer. As this region was at the forefront of the Protestant Reformation in the 16th century, the interior of Ghent's churches suffered at the hands of the iconoclasts—Protestants (Calvinists) who stripped Catholic churches of all adornments to unclutter their communion with God. The church was later partly redecorated by Catholics, who installed the very Baroque altar (painted wood, not marble). Iconoclasts destroyed essentially all the medieval glass in Ghent—the modern stained glass above represents the seven sacraments.

• *Exiting the church, look straight ahead and notice the stepped gable of* the **Masons' Guild House.** *This 15th-century facade was only revealed in the 1980s, when workers peeled back a more modern layer on top of it. They restored the building, added the decorations at the tops of the gables (bottom row: humans; middle row: devils; top row: angels), then added a very modern section behind it (notice the glass-and-steel structure down St.-Niklaasstraat).*

The square beyond St. Nicholas, **Emil-Braunplein,** *features a modern (and controversial) market hall with a wooden roof, an original 17th-century bell from the adjacent belfry, and the "Fountain of Kneeling Youth." The next tall building is the...*

Belfry

Although most of this tower has stood here since the 14th century, the Neo-Gothic top spire (from the gargoyles up) was added when Ghent proudly hosted a World's
Fair in 1913. The tower was originally built to house and protect the parchment record of Ghent's favored privileges, granted to the city by the Counts of Flanders in exchange for financial support. The dragon topping the spire symbolizes not the devil (as was typical in the Middle Ages), but a protector who never sleeps as it watches over the city's rights. It was also a fire watchtower, represented by the four sentries positioned at the corners. The carillon

in the tower often plays the Ghent town anthem at the top of the hour.

Visitors enjoy ascending the belfry for a view over town. It's just a couple of flights of stairs, then an elevator most of the way (€5, borrow English explanations as you enter, daily 10:00-18:00, last entry 30 minutes before closing, www.belfortgent.be). On the way, you'll pass a modest exhibit about the history of the building, including models of former spires that topped it.

The long building at the base of (and behind) the belfry is the **Cloth Hall,** which was important to this textile center.
• *The square beyond the Belfry is...*

St. Bavo's Square (Sint-Baafsplein)

This square became a symbolic battleground during the period of Flemish nationalism in the early 20th century. Previously, when Belgium gained its independence from the Netherlands in 1830, it was ruled by its Walloon (French-speaking) aristocracy, even though the Dutch speakers were in the majority. The Flemish people felt mistreated by their Francophone overlords. (It took a century after independence for Ghent's prestigious university to finally start offering classes in Dutch; to mark that day in 1930, the Walloon-aristocracy-owned electric company spitefully cut power to mourn the university's end of "enlightened" thinking.) For more on the Flemish-Walloon conflict, see "The Battle for Belgium: Flanders vs. Wallonia" on page 354.

The ornate building on the square is the **Dutch Theater** (Koninklijke Nederlandse Schouwburg, a.k.a. NT Gent), built in 1899 to provide the town's Dutch speakers a place to perform plays of their own. By embracing Dutch as a language worthy of theater, the spunky Flemish were asserting their cultural legitimacy. The golden mosaic depicts Apollo returning to Mount Parnassus, much as the Flemish felt they were coming home to their beloved language.

Circle around for a look at the far side of

the **statue** in the middle of the square. The relief on the base (facing the theater) depicts Jan Frans Willems, one of the founders of the Flemish movement. The man and woman in the statue represent the resurrection of the Dutch language here—notice the lion, a symbol of Flanders, on their flag.

As you face the theater, look to the left to see **Van Hoorebeke Chocolatier,** a producer of fine pralines. Peek in the window (or go in the shop and look through the glass floor) to see the chocolate-makers hard at work (€4/100 grams—about 7 pieces, daily 10:00-18:00, tel. 09-221-0381).

• *At the end of the square is Ghent's top sight...*

▲▲Cathedral of St. Bavo (Sint-Baafskathedraal)

The main church of Ghent, this also houses three of the city's art treasures: the exquisite *Adoration of the Mystic Lamb* altarpiece, by Jan Van Eyck and his brother, Hubert; an elaborately carved pulpit; and an altar painting by Rubens depicting the town's patron saint (and the church's namesake).

Cost and Hours: Free to enter, €4 to see original altarpiece—includes excellent audioguide, Mon-Sat 9:30-16:45, Sun 13:00-16:30, later in summer. During busy times, volunteer guides can show you around.

Ⓢ Self-Guided Tour: Step inside. This giant Gothic cathe-

dral was built over many centuries—
notice the telltale three materials: gray
stone (choir), red brick (nave), and yellow stone (tower and cathedral interior).
As in St. Nicholas' Church, all of the
decorations and stained glass date from
the 19th century (following the iconoclasm of the 16th century).

Below, I've first described the
great altarpiece, and then a plan for
visiting the church. Note that there
are two opportunities to see the altarpiece: You can view a replica in the cha-
pel that originally contained the piece (at the front-right corner
of the church) for free. Or you can pay to see the original, in a
small room in the back-left corner of the church. The locations
of both the original and the replica are explained under "Visiting
the Church," later. Before your visit, Google "closer to van eyck"
to enjoy an extremely close-up view of this playfully and lovingly
detailed masterpiece.

The Adoration of the Mystic Lamb: The highlight of the
church (and, for art lovers, of all Ghent) is Jan and Hubert Van
Eyck's *Adoration of the Mystic Lamb* altarpiece. Hubert Van Eyck
(c. 1385-1426) began the painting, but after his death, his better-
known younger brother, Jan (1395-1441), picked up the brush and
completed Hubert's vision. Finished in 1432, this altarpiece represents a monumental stride in Northern European art from medieval stiffness to Renaissance humanism, with a closely observed
attention to detail. The first work signed by Jan Van Eyck, it's also
considered one of the first works of the Flemish Primitives (char-
acterized by a precise dedication to detail, if an imperfect mastery
of perspective). The audioguide gives you 50 wonderful minutes of
narration, if you want the full experience. Over the next few years,
restoration will make sections of the altarpiece unviewable (you
can watch the restoration process at the Fine Arts Museum—see
page 582). But most of this amazing painting will always be on
display.

It's a miracle the altarpiece has survived for almost six centuries. During the wave of iconoclasm in the 16th century, the altar
was hidden in the cathedral tower. In 1934 two of its panels were
stolen—ones depicting John the Baptist and the "Just Judges." The
church was able to recover the John the Baptist panel but the Just
Judges panel never turned up (what you see here is a top-notch
copy). More than 75 years later, the theft remains Belgium's greatest unsolved mystery. Later, during World War II, the altar was on
its way to safe storage at the Vatican when it was caught up in the

GHENT

fighting and squirreled away in the French Pyrenees, then swiped by Hitler and stored in a Bavarian castle, then a salt mine, before being returned here by US forces at war's end.

The altarpiece has a dozen separate paintings on each side (front and back). On weekdays, the altarpiece was closed to show only the outside panels; it was opened up on Sundays and holidays to reveal the scenes inside. (On the replica, you can actually open and close the panels; on the original, you'll have to circle around back to see them in their open position.)

First, look at the **outside panels,** showing the Annunciation—when the archangel Gabriel comes to Mary to tell her she will bear God's child. Gabriel, holding a lily (representing purity), says to Mary, "Hail Mary, full of grace." Mary (with the Holy Spirit above her) replies, "I am the servant of the Lord." Notice that Mary's words are upside-down—intended for God above. Through the windows, we get a glimpse of medieval Ghent, and in the niche is a medieval "bathroom" (with a pitcher and basin). Below are the kneeling couple who commissioned the work for their private chapel, and statues of St. John the Baptist (holding the lamb) and St. John the Evangelist (holding the cup of poison). Above are two sibyls (pagan prophets) flanked by the Old Testament prophets Zechariah (on the left) and Micah (on the right)—all of whom prophesied the coming of Christ.

Now get the full feast-day effect of the **inside panels.** The main scene, playing out at the bottom, depicts the adoration of the

lamb (representing Jesus) at the Revelation. The scene is a big Christ-celebrating party, and everyone's here: angels, church teachers, holy virgins, Old Testament prophets (in the left-fore-ground), the 12 apostles (in the right-foreground), saints, popes, pagan writers, Jewish prophets, knights and judges (on the left panel) and pilgrims and hermits (on the right panel)... all coming to worship their savior. (The copy of the stolen panel is on the bottom left corner when the altarpiece is open.) Notice the diversity of the people assembled, wearing all different styles of clothing and headwear—from Asia, India, and the entire known world at the time. Hovering overhead is a dove (the Holy Spirit), and in the foreground is the well of life, spewing water and jewels. As in Christian tradition, the lamb at the very center is a stand-in for Christ—but it also has a special meaning here in Ghent, whose wool trade put it on the map. It's too bad that the lamb itself—which scholars suspect was later retouched by a lesser artist—isn't particularly well-depicted. He looks more like a sheep...and is that an extra right ear I see?

Above this scene are (from left to right) Mary, the resurrected Christ (or is it God himself, wearing a triple-tiara to represent the Trinity?), and John the Baptist (wearing a garment of camel hair, per biblical descriptions). On the upper outside panels are angels playing music, and a pair of famous portraits of **Adam and Eve**—which scholars believe were the first Renaissance-era nudes painted north of the Alps. The tiny, wedge-shaped panels above them tell the story of Cain and Abel.

Take a moment to simply bask in the astonishing level of detail. You can see each hair on Adam's legs (and notice the not-quite-perfectly executed, Italian-inspired perspective—with Adam's toes breaking the plane as they seem to emerge from the panel). Hymnals of the time indicated which face a singer should make when singing a particular note; today's experts can guess which notes the angels are singing from their expressions. The countryside scenes are decorated with dozens of different, identifiable species of plants and flowers, and the angels around the lamb in the lower panel have feathers from a variety of actual birds (peacocks, pigeons, and swallows). And in the amulet around the neck of the angel by Adam, you can actually see a faint reflection of the stained-glass window that decorated the chapel where this altarpiece originally stood.

Visiting the Church: Go for a counterclockwise spin around the cathedral's interior. Along the way, you'll have a chance to see both the replica and the original of the altarpiece described above.

Begin in the back-right corner of the church (to the right as you enter). Near the information desk, see the panels showing **Adam and Eve with clothes**—added to cover Van Eyck's nudes during the puritanical 19th century (1825-1896).

Along the right wall of the church, near the shop, find the chapel with a statue of **Pater Damiaan** (Father Damien, 1840-1889), a Flemish missionary who went to Hawaii to care for lepers, but after 16 years died of leprosy himself. Canonized in 2009, he's a rare saint with a connection to the United States, and an important figure both to Belgians and to Hawaiians.

Step to the center of the nave and look up at the elaborately carved, remarkable Rococo **pulpit,** representing the tree of life and the tree of knowledge. Notice the golden serpent entwined around the top of the pulpit; follow its body to find the pudgy, winged baby (a sure

sign of Rococo) prying the apple of sin from the snake's mouth. The Carrara marble statues just beneath the pulpit drive home a Counter-Reformation message: The woman on the right (with the sun on her bosom, representing the power of her faith) wakes up the winged old man on the left (representing time): It's time to wake up to the Catholic faith. The goody-two-shoes angels at the bases of the staircases offer a lesson in appropriate worship: The angel on the left watches the pulpit intently, and the one on the right points up to the pulpit while glancing scoldingly to the back of the church: Hey, you in the back row—pay attention! Up above, notice the two hard-working cupids struggling to raise the cross.

Now look all the way to the front of the church. In the distance, above the main altar, is **St. Bavo,** the beloved local saint, on his way to heaven. Walk around and up as close as you can to the altar. This seventh-century saint was once a wealthy and rambunctious young soldier, but became a born-again Christian after the death of his wife. Bavo rejected his life of materialism and became a monk, living for a time in a hollow tree. He is also the patron saint of Haarlem, the Netherlands.

In the front-right part of the church (just to the right, as you face the main altar) is the Vijdt Chapel, housing the **replica of the Van Eyck altarpiece** (described earlier). Van Eyck painted the altarpiece specifically to be displayed in this room—in fact, the light and subtle reflections in his work are designed to fit this space.

Circling around the back of the church to the left transept, you'll find another great work of art, Peter Paul Rubens' *Entrance*

of St. Bavo into the Monastery of Ghent, depicting the moment this local-boy-done-good started on his righteous course. Notice the parallel, diagonal composition: On the top, Bavo, in the red cloak (and with the face of the painter, Rubens—a rare self-portrait), kneels before the abbot. The lower group shows Bavo's estate manager distributing his belongings after he became a monk to the poor. The women on the left, representing Bavo's daughter and her servant, are modeled after Rubens'

GHENT

two wives—his older first wife, wearing the giant hat; and his much younger, more voluptuous second wife, Hélène Fourment, in the red dress. (The Flemish like to say, with a wink, "An old billy goat loves a young leaf.") Compare the very static composition of Van Eyck's altarpiece (1432) with this dynamic canvas, pregnant with motion (1624)—illustrating the contrast between staid medieval and exuberant Baroque. For more about Rubens, see page 548.

Across from this canvas is the entrance to the **crypt,** where you can see some of the building's Romanesque foundations and various chapels decorated with ecclesiastical art both old and modern. Along with tombs of bishops, you'll see faint traces of 15th-century paintings that were whitewashed over by Calvinists, then rediscovered in the 1930s.

Circling back to the entrance, you reach the chapel with the artistic highlight of Ghent: the **original** *Adoration of the Mystic Lamb* by Jan and Hubert Van Eyck (described earlier).

• *Exiting the cathedral, turn right and head down the narrow, twisty Biezekapelstraat. You'll pass the turrets and other medieval-looking features (most are from the 19th century) of the back of the Achtersikkel mansion, the home of a powerful aristocratic family. The music you might hear is provided by students rehearsing at the nearby music college. Exiting this narrow street, turn left on Nederpolder and head up to the main street of medieval Ghent...*

Hoogpoort

This "High Gate" street connects Ghent's two rivers. As you walk, notice you're on a slight hill; Ghent was founded at a high point between two rivers, which people made ample use of for trade.

Crossing Belfortstraat, you'll see the giant, eclectic, slightly run-down **City Hall** on your left. Onto the ornate Gothic core of the building, from the early 16th century, have been grafted many centuries of additions (for example, the blocky Renaissance-style section just down Belfortstraat).

Continue along Hoogpoort, observing the many facets of this one building.

At the end of the City Hall, watch (on the right) for the narrow, covered lane called Werregaren Straat. Once used to drain water away from this high ground, today it has a different purpose and an apt nickname: **Graffitistraat.** Walk down the lane, enjoying the artwork provided by the people of Ghent. This is a typically pragmatic Belgian solution to a social problem: Rather

than outlawing graffiti entirely, the police have designated this one street to give would-be artists a legal, controlled outlet for their impulses. Halfway down the lane, notice the beautiful fenced-in garden on your right. This restful, picnic-perfect space is open to the public: When you emerge from Graffitistraat, turn right on Onderstraat; on the right, at #22, you can go through the giant green door (if it's open) into this city-owned garden courtyard.

• *Roughly across the street from #22—and just before the worth-a-peek* **Flamingo's Pub***, with its avant-garde, funky-kitsch interior and Barbie chandelier—head down Serpentstraat, which is lined with some fun boutiques and colorful secondhand stores. When you pop out, turn left and you'll be in…*

Friday Market Square (Vrijdagmarkt)

These days, the primary market day is Sunday, but historically the action was on Friday, as the name indicates.

The statue in the square depicts **Jakob van Artevelde,** a clever businessman who saved the day in the 14th century, when the Hundred Years' War between France (which then controlled Ghent) and England (which provided Ghent with much-needed wool) threatened local industry. When the English

king refused to export his wool to Ghent, Van Artevelde—not an aristocrat, but an ordinary citizen—boldly negotiated directly with the king to keep Ghent neutral in the conflict and keep the wool coming in. Largely forgotten by history, Van Artevelde's memory was resurrected during the nationalism of the late 19th century, as a symbol of the Flemish people of Ghent asserting their independence from the Francophones. Today he's still celebrated by the people of Ghent, who sometimes call their city "Artevelde-Stad."

Behind the statue is the eclectic **"House of the People"** (Ons Huis), the headquarters for the region's socialist movement. Not surprisingly for a city with a long industrial heritage, Ghent is a hotbed of left-leaning politics, and the birthplace of the Belgian Labor Party. Above the door on the right, notice the rooster—crowing to wake up the workers.

Farther to the right, peek up the street called **Baudelostraat** for some particularly beautiful gables dating to the early 20th century.

• *Go down the narrow street just left of the workers' hall (Meerseniers-straat). In a block you reach a bridge. Notice the remnants of mills and industry, and the giant red cannon on the left. Several different tour-guide stories have circulated about this giant piece of artillery, but it's more fun to make up your own.*

Cross the bridge to enter the district called...

Patershol

Until recently a run-down and dangerous district, today this neighborhood is one of Ghent's trendiest. And though it's pre-dominantly residential, Patershol is also a great place for restau-

rant-hunting (see "Eating in Ghent," later).

Looking straight ahead as you cross the bridge, you'll see two particularly fine (and sym-bolism-packed) gabled **facades.** Move in for a close-up look at the red facade on the right. It features five panels showing the five senses, each one represented by an animal (taste = monkey; sight = eagle; hearing = deer; smell = dog; and touch = humans, since we have no hair on our hands). The building on the left has panels demonstrating six virtuous acts (the seventh—burying the dead—was deemed too gruesome to depict, so it's symbolized by the urn on top). The ground floor of this building houses a favor-ite old-fashioned candy shop, **Temmerman,** with some unique Ghent treats, including Wippers—toffee with sugar coating; Lieve Vrouwkens—in the shape of the Virgin Mary; and the local favor-ite, raspberry-flavored Cuperdons (Wed-Sat 11:00-18:00, closed Sun-Tue, Kraanlei 79, tel. 09-224-0041).

• *Turn left and walk along Kraanlei, passing the House of Alijn (with a tourable interior—see page 579). Continue along the embankment, curving right with the road. Pause at the next intersection.*

At the corner on the right, notice the brasserie called 't Stropkje ("The Noose"). The people of Ghent are called **"noose-wearers"** *(Stropkens).* This dates back to the time of King Charles V, who had been born here in Ghent but ruled from Spain. In 1540, he demanded a huge tribute from the people of Ghent. When they refused and revolted, he came here personally to enforce his authority. The leaders of Ghent had to beg on their knees with nooses around their necks for his forgiveness. (It worked, but only with the help of a huge payment.)

Across the street, the imposing **Castle of the Counts** is worth touring, if you have time (described later, under "Sights in Ghent").

Across the little square from the castle is the fancy arched facade of the **Old Fish Market** (Oude Vismijn, home of the TI with its racks of tourist information). Study the facade: That's Neptune on top; below him are Ghent's two rivers: Scheldt (male) and Lys (female). It's said that Ghent is the child of these two rivers.

• *Now walk back toward the 't Stropkje brasserie and turn right down Kleine Vismarkt street. Cross the bridge to one final stop.*

Vegetable Market (Groentenmarkt)

As you cross the bridge to the Vegetable Market square, look for the long white **Meat Hall** (Groot Vleeshuis) to the right. The hall

looks like it's seen better days, but it's worth a peek inside to see its impressive wooden vault (built entirely without nails, and clearly employing ship-builders' expertise). For hygienic reasons, until the 19th century, this was the only place in town allowed to sell meat. You'll see local cured ham hanging from the rafters. The shop inside sells specialty products from East Flanders (Tue-Sun 10:00-18:00, closed Mon).

Back out on the square are more snacking opportunities. Across the square from the Meat Hall is a good traditional bakery (Himschoot); next to that, a café selling delicious take-away waffles; and to the right of that, the **Tierenteyn Verlent mustard shop.** Made in the cellar, then pumped into a barrel in the back of the shop, the mustard is some of the horseradish-hottest you'll ever sample. They use no preservatives, so you'll need to refrigerate it—or use it for today's picnic (Mon-Sat 8:30-18:00, closed Sun, Groentenmarkt 3, tel. 09-225-8336, www.tierenteyn-verlent.be).

• *Head to the far end of the Meat Hall, then the building beyond it. The bridge here affords another good view of Ghent's canals. Just across the bridge and to the right is the good* **Design Museum** *(described later). Near this bridge, various companies sell 50-minute* **boat tours** *along the canals of Ghent (see "Tours in Ghent," earlier). Or you can backtrack (turn right along the river) to the* **Castle of the Counts** *or the* **House of Alijn.** *Most of what's worth seeing in Ghent is within a few steps of right here. Enjoy.*

Sights in Ghent

Most of Ghent's sights cluster in one of two areas: in the historic city center, or at a park two long blocks from the train station.

In the Historic Center

The House of Alijn (Huis van Alijn)—This museum shows how everyday Belgian lifestyles evolved over the course of the

20th century. It assembles an intriguing collection of bric-a-brac from various themes and walks of life (including an old pharmacy, grocery, and candy shop). Unfortunately, the museum administration has chosen not to include much in the way of descriptions. While their hope is to encourage visitors to experience the place on their own, potentially meaningful artifacts are rendered meaningless. This place could be fascinating with a good audioguide or regularly scheduled guided tour, but neither is available; instead you'll borrow generalized explanations in each section. It's exhibited in several buildings around a tranquil courtyard, which used to be a refuge for poor elderly people (similar to a begijnhof). The courtyard hosts an authentic Ghent pub where you can sample *jenever*, or gin *('t plumeetse)*.

Cost and Hours: €5, Tue-Sun 11:00-17:00, closed Mon, Kraanlei 65, tel. 09-269-2350, www.huisvanalijn.be.

▲**Castle of the Counts (Gravensteen)**—Built in 1180 by Philip of Alsace, this fortress was designed not to protect the peo-

ple of Ghent, but to intimidate the city's independence-minded citizens. Erected outside the city walls, it's morphed over the centuries, and was partly destroyed by an accidental explosion (when it served as a textile factory), then restored. It's impressive from the outside, but explanations and exhibits inside are pretty modest. Still, it's a fun opportunity to twist through towers and ramble over ramparts, especially if you love the TV show, *Game of Thrones*. You'll see an interesting armory collection and a reconstructed guillotine that was last used in 1861. For fans of torture museums, this one has real instruments of "persuasion" (see sidebar). One display shows how waterboarding was practiced

A Torturer's Toolbox

Travelers may think that the endless security lines at the airport are torturous—but that's child's play compared with what heretics and criminals faced in the Middle Ages. Medieval torture was used both to extract confessions and to punish the convicted prior to an execution. Torturers, who were often clergy, had a huge toolkit with which to practice their art.

One device was the rack, a bed-like instrument designed to pull the victim's limbs apart. A prisoner's arms and legs were tied to opposite ends of the machine. Then the torturer turned the crank, expanding the rack and leaving the victim with dislocated joints or even limbless.

Another nasty tool was a finger screw—a set of bars and screws that tightened to crush fingers and toes. Since finger screws were small and portable, they were a favorite of traveling medieval interrogators.

The iron maiden was a spike-filled cabinet, just tall enough to fit a standing human. It had small holes where torturers would insert sharp objects to stab prisoners, sometimes killing them. A variant was the torture chair, which was entirely covered in spikes. Victims' wrists were tied to the arms of the chair, and weights were attached to their legs and feet. Sitting in the chair usually resulted in death due to blood loss.

The wheel was a public execution device. Prisoners would be stretched over a wheel, and the executioner would break their bones with an iron hammer. They were then left to die from shock and dehydration. For less serious crimes, the prisoner was given the gift of one swift and deadly blow to the neck.

Then there was waterboarding. In medieval times jailers poured water—and often bodily fluids—down the throat of the prisoner. To avoid drowning, "suspects" might drink the liquid, which resulted in a sort of intoxication and often death. The modern variation—practiced by the Japanese during World War II, the French in Algeria, and the CIA at Guantanamo Bay—could be described as "slow-motion drowning." Interrogators covered the victim's face with cloth or some other thin material. Then they poured water over the prisoner's nose and mouth, triggering the gag reflex and a sensation that the victim is drowning.

Today, although 146 members of the United Nations have ratified an international convention outlawing torture, the organization says it remains rampant worldwide. Medieval or modern, it's a practice that won't go away, which makes Carl Jung's 20th-century observation even more relevant: "The healthy man does not torture others—generally it is the tortured who turn into torturers."

by the Inquisition (centuries before Dick Cheney endorsed its use as "a no-brainer"). There are paintings and photos that explain the history of the place, an 18-foot-deep dungeon, and great views from the tops of the towers (be prepared for lots of climbing up claustrophobic stairs). Although more explanations would help bring this somewhat empty shell to life, you do get a feel for the medieval world. Admission includes a pointless, portable "movie-guide," with corny dramatizations of actual historic events in each room—skip it.

Cost and Hours: €8, dry €1.50 guidebook tells the history of the place, daily May-Sept 10:00-18:00, Oct-April 10:00-17:00, last entry one hour before closing, tel. 09-225-9306.

▲**Design Museum**—Worth ▲▲▲ for those interested in decorative arts and design, and enjoyable to anybody, this collection cel-

ebrates the Belgian knack for design. It combines a classic old building with a creaky wood interior, with a bright-white, spacious, and glassy new hall in the center. You'll cross back and forth between these sections, seeing both old-timey rooms and exquisite pieces of Art Nouveau,

Art Deco, and contemporary design. Just explore: Everything is clearly explained in English and easy to appreciate. The temporary exhibits are well-presented and interesting. Don't miss the 18th-century dining room, with a remarkable wood-carved chandelier.

Cost and Hours: €5, Tue-Sun 10:00-18:00, closed Mon, Jan Breydelstraat 5, tel. 09-267-9999, www.designmuseumgent.be.

Near the Train Station

Two art museums—the **Fine Arts Museum and the Stedelijk Contemporary Art Museum**—cluster closer to the train station than to the historical center, which makes them ideal to visit on your way into or out of Ghent (lockers are at the station).

Getting There: To reach the museums from the train station (about a 10-minute walk), exit straight ahead to the modern sculpture in the middle of the plaza. Turn right and walk up the tree- and bike-lined Koningin Astridlaan about five minutes, then cross the road and enter Citadel Park. Walk straight ahead, then curl around the left side of the big, modern building at the center of the park; as you round the far side, the Neoclassical entrance to the Fine Arts Museum is across the small street, and the **Stedelijk Contemporary Art Museum** (with a large *S.M.A.K.* sign over the entrance) is on your right.

GHENT

▲**Fine Arts Museum (Museum voor Schone Kunsten)**—This museum offers a good, representative look at Northern European art. It's one of the most user-friendly collections of Low Countries art you'll find in Belgium, with lesser-known yet fun works by artists such as Bosch, Rubens, Van Dyck, and Magritte. As you enter, to the right (in numbered rooms) are older works, and to the left (in lettered rooms) are 19th- and 20th-century works and temporary exhibits. The €2.50 audioguide is both essential and excellent. Information sheets in English are in almost all of the rooms.

Cost and Hours: €5, Tue-Sun 10:00-18:00, closed Mon, in Citadelpark along Fernand Scribedreef street, tel. 09-240-0700, www.mskgent.be.

◑ Self-Guided Tour: Turn right from the entrance, and take a counterclockwise, chronological spin though the collection, keeping an eye out for these fine pieces.

In room 2, **Hieronymus Bosch**'s jarring *Christ Carrying the Cross* (1515-1516) features a severe-looking Jesus surrounded by gro-

tesque faces. Typical of the Middle Ages, Bosch believed that evil was ugly—and all but three faces on this canvas (forming a diagonal, from lower-left to upper-right) are hideous. The serene woman to the left of Christ is Veronica, who has just wiped his face. In the upper-right, with an ashen complexion, is the stoic good thief, flanked by a doctor and a taunting monk. Meanwhile, in the lower-right, the orange-tinged unrepentant thief sneers back at his hecklers. Nearby, Bosch's portrait of St. Jerome (c. 1505)—who was his personal patron saint—shows the holy hermit having discarded his clothes. Just above his legs, notice the owl (representing evil) sinisterly eyeing a titmouse (good). Also in this room, in **Rogier Van der Weyden**'s *The Virgin with a Carnation* (1480), the Baby Jesus makes a benediction gesture with his little hand. This painting was designed as a focal point for meditation.

Room 5 displays **Peter Paul Rubens'** altarpiece painting of *St. Francis of Assisi Receiving the Stigmata*, with Francis' brother Leo staring in amazement from below. According to Church accounts, an angel appeared to Francis in the form of a six-winged seraphim.

Room 4 is devoted to the restoration of **Jan and Hubert Van Eyck**'s *Adoration of the Mystic Lamb* altarpiece housed in the Cathedral of St. Bavo. You can watch as conservators work on one panel at a time, removing old varnish and retouching damaged sections. The €1.3 million project won't be completed until 2017.

In room 7, Rubens' student **Anthony Van Dyck** depicts the

mythological story of *Jupiter and Antiope*—a horned-and-horny god about to inseminate a sleeping woman.

Room 8 features **Pieter Brueghel the Younger**'s copy of his more famous father, Pieter Bruegel the Elder's, much-loved *Peasant Wedding in a Barn*. The elder painter trained his kids to

carry on the family business. But Brueghel the Younger was a talented painter in his own right: In his *Village Lawyer,* we see the attorney behind a desk piled with papers, as peasants bring items to barter for his services.

Circle into the modern (lettered) wing. Near the front of this section, in room B's *Portrait of Physician Ludwig Adler,* Viennese Secessionist painter **Oskar Kokoschka** uses dynamic, expressionistic brushstrokes to capture the personality, rather than a precise reproduction, of his subject.

In room F you'll find works by homegrown Belgian modernist **René Magritte.** His clever *Perspective II*—part of a larger series—wryly replaces the four subjects on Edouard Manet's famous *Balcony* with coffins. Next to him you'll find similar surrealist works by **Max Ernst** and **Paul Delvaux.** A Belgian artist who studied, worked, and taught in Brussels, Delvaux became famous for his surrealistic paintings of nude women, often wandering through weirdly lit landscapes. They cast long shadows, wandering bare-breasted among classical ruins. Beyond this room, the sculpture gallery underneath the rotunda is also worth a peek.

Stedelijk Contemporary Art Museum (Stedelijk Museum voor Actuele Kunst, a.k.a. SMAK)—This art gallery is constantly changing, both the so-called "permanent" collection and many temporary exhibits. It's worth a visit only for art lovers, and is conveniently located just across the street from the Fine Arts Museum.

Cost and Hours: €6, more for special exhibits, Tue-Sun 10:00-18:00, closed Mon, tel. 09-240-7601, www.smak.be.

▲Ghent City Museum (Stadsmuseum Gent, a.k.a. STAM)— This facility, which opened in 2010, explains the history of Ghent with all the bells and whistles you'd expect in this fashion-forward city. It's housed in a beautiful 14th-century Gothic abbey complex called Bijloke and in a modern annex. The permanent exhibit traces the city's history in high-tech treatments mixed with historic artifacts—all well explained in English. The last room on 21st-century Ghent is a techie's paradise of computers, videos, and interactive displays. Come here if you want to see what museums in the 21st century should look like.

Cost and Hours: €6, Tue-Sun 10:00-18:00, closed Mon, Godshuizenlaan 2, tel. 09-267-1400, www.stamgent.be.

Getting There: From the train station, it's about a 15-20-minute walk: Exit straight ahead, then angle left up the busy tram-tracks-lined Koning Albertlaan. After the bridge, turn right on Godshuizenlaan. Or, from the station, you could ride tram #1 to the Veergrep stop, backtrack a block to the first busy road, and turn right.

Sleeping in Ghent

A convention town, Ghent is busiest in spring (April-June) and fall (Sept-mid-Dec); things are quieter (and prices lower) in July and August, and even more so in the winter.

$$$ Chambre Plus is a three-room B&B run with an impeccable French flair for design by Mia (a cook) and Hendrik (a chocolatier, who makes chocolates in the basement). They say the "Plus" is for the personal touch they put into their B&B, and this is no exaggeration. This place, with a cozy lounge and an inviting garden, oozes class with a contemporary charm (rooms are €95 or €125; "honeymoon" cottage out back with Jacuzzi is €175, 2-night stay preferred on weekends; air-con, free Internet access and cable Internet in rooms, Hoogpoort 31, tel. 09-225-3775, www.chambre plus.be, chambreplus@telenet.be).

$$$ Hotel Harmony is a pricey, classy, four-star, family-run boutique hotel with modern style and 25 rooms ideally located on the embankment in the town center (Sb-€135-210, Db-€150-225, price varies with room size and amenities, air-con, elevator, pay Internet access and Wi-Fi, very medieval breakfast room and music room/parlor, heated outdoor pool in summer, Kraanlei 37, tel. 09-324-2680, fax 09-324-2688, www.hotel-harmony.be, info @hotel-harmony.be).

$$$ Simon Says offers two rooms over a colorful café at the far end of Patershol. You're on a small square, so there is some street noise, but you'll feel like a local taking breakfast with the natives in the downstairs café (Db-€105, Sluizeken 8, tel. 09-233-0343, www.simon-says.be, info@simon-says.be, Welshman Simon Turner).

$$ B&B King, hiding in a nondescript residential area a 10-minute walk from the main tourist zone, is a find. Charmingly run by Sarah and Dominiek, this mod B&B has two black-and-white rooms filled with artistic flair, and there's more modern art exhibited in the halls (Sb-€80, Db-€85, free Wi-Fi, Brouwersstraat 22, mobile 0489-572-909, www.bbking.be, info@bbking.be). From Drabstraat/Poelstraat, swing right onto the big street, then turn immediately right again on Ramen, then left on Brouwersstraat; it's the last house on the right.

Sleep Code

(€1 = about $1.30, country code: 32)
S = Single, **D** = Double/Twin, **T** = Triple, **Q** = Quad, **b** = bathroom,
s = shower only. Everyone speaks English. Unless otherwise
noted, breakfast is included and credit cards are accepted.

To help you easily sort through these listings, I've divided
the accommodations into three categories, based on the
price for a standard double room with bath:

$$$ Higher Priced—Most rooms €100 or more.
  $$ Moderately Priced—Most rooms between €50-100.
    $ Lower Priced—Most rooms €50 or less.

Prices can change without notice; verify the hotel's current rates online or by email. Generally B&Bs include the city
room tax in their prices while hotels do not.

$$ Erasmus Hotel, well-run by Peter, has 12 well-maintained
rooms around a creaky wooden staircase in a classic 400-year-old
building. It's on a boring street, just a short walk from the embank-
ment (Sb-€79, Db-€99, large Db-€120, prices can flex depending
on demand, no elevator, pay Wi-Fi, Poel 25, tel. 09-224-2195, fax
09-233-4241, www.erasmushotel.be, info@erasmushotel.be).

$$ Ibis Gent Centrum St-Baafs Kathedraal is a good
branch of the Europe-wide chain, offering affordable, predictable
cookie-cutter comfort in 120 rooms right next door to the cathedral (Db-€79-119—generally €82 in summer, €99 in high season,
and €109 for special events; breakfast-€14, elevator, free Internet
access and Wi-Fi, Limburgstraat 2, tel. 09-233-0000, www.ibis
hotel.com, h1455-re@accor.com).

$$ *Other B&Bs:* Other good rooms in the town center include
In's Inn (1 room, in Patershol, Db-€85, Corduwaniersstraat 11,
tel. 09-225-1705, mobile 0494-361-861, insinn@telenet.be) and
Brooderie (3 rustic, woody rooms sharing a single bathroom over
a café along the embankment in the heart of town, D-€70-75, Jan
Breydelstraat 8, tel. 09-225-0623, www.brooderie.be, brooderie
@pandora.be).

$ De Draecke, Ghent's very institutional HI youth hostel,
has 106 beds—including some private rooms—in a residential
zone a short walk from the castle (all rooms have private bath-
rooms inside, €19 for a dorm bed, Sb-€33, Db-€48, €3 extra for
nonmembers, about €2-3 extra for guests older than 26, includes
breakfast and sheets, towel rental extra, pay Internet access, free
Wi-Fi, Sint-Widostraat 11, tel. 09-233-7050, www.vjh.be, gent
@vjh.be).

Ghent Accommodations & Restaurants

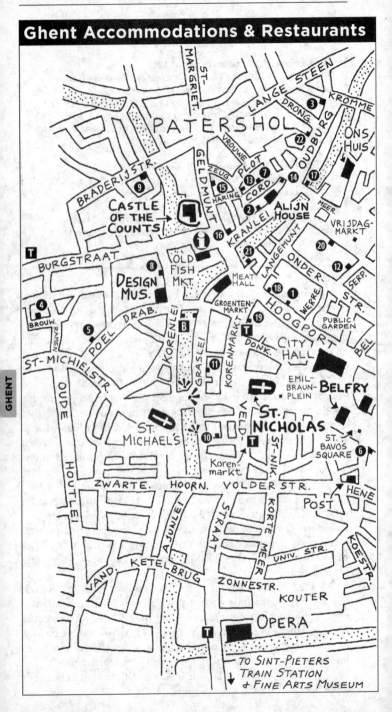

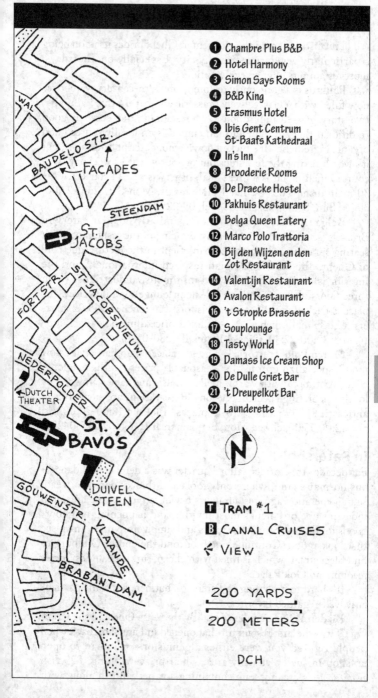

1. Chambre Plus B&B
2. Hotel Harmony
3. Simon Says Rooms
4. B&B King
5. Erasmus Hotel
6. Ibis Gent Centrum St-Baafs Kathedraal
7. In's Inn
8. Brooderie Rooms
9. De Draecke Hostel
10. Pakhuis Restaurant
11. Belga Queen Eatery
12. Marco Polo Trattoria
13. Bij den Wijzen en den Zot Restaurant
14. Valentijn Restaurant
15. Avalon Restaurant
16. 't Stropke Brasserie
17. Souplounge
18. Tasty World
19. Damass Ice Cream Shop
20. De Dulle Griet Bar
21. 't Dreupelkot Bar
22. Launderette

T TRAM #1
B CANAL CRUISES
↙ VIEW

200 YARDS
200 METERS

DCH

Eating in Ghent

All of my listings are in the city center. Ghent prides itself on being a particularly vegetarian-friendly city. Especially on Thursdays, most restaurants offer a veggie option.

Pakhuis is a gorgeously restored, late-19th-century warehouse now filled with a classy, lively brasserie and bar. In this light, airy, two-story, glassed-in birdhouse of a restaurant, they serve up good traditional Belgian food with an emphasis on locally sourced and organic ingredients. It's tucked down a nondescript brick alley, but it's worth taking the few steps out of your way (€12 weekday two-course lunch menu is a great deal, otherwise €9-14 starters, €14-30 main dishes, €25-42 fixed-price meals, Mon-Sat 12:00-23:00, closed Sun, Schuurkenstraat 4, tel. 09-223-5555).

Belga Queen, an outpost of a similarly popular eatery in Brussels (see page 519), is the most enticing of the restaurants with seating sprawling along the embankment in the picturesque core of Ghent. The food is "Belgian-inspired international," and the interior is extremely trendy and minimalist/industrialist (with three floors of seating, plus a top-floor lounge). While pricey, the place is packed with locals and visitors (€16 lunches, €15-22 starters, €21-35 main dishes, €33-42 fixed-price dinners, daily 12:00-14:30 & 19:00-22:30, Graslei 10, tel. 09-280-0100).

Marco Polo Trattoria is a good choice for Italian-style "slow food" (specializing in fish) at reasonable prices. It fills one long, cozy, tight room with warm, mellow music and tables crowded by locals celebrating special occasions. Reservations are smart (€9-14 antipasti, €14-19 pastas, €10-15 pizzas, Tue-Sun 18:00-22:00, Fri also 12:00-15:00, closed Mon, Serpentstraat 11, tel. 09-225-0420).

In Patershol

For decades this former sailors' quarter was a derelict and dangerous no-man's land, where only fools and thieves dared to tread. But a generation ago, restaurateurs began to reclaim the area, and today it's one of Ghent's most inviting and happening neighborhoods for dining. Stroll the streets and simply drop in on any place that looks good. Continue north beyond the end of Oudburg to find Sleepstraat, which is lined with cheap Turkish eateries (locals recommend Gok Palace).

It's hard to go wrong in Patershol, but here are some particularly well-regarded favorites:

Bij den Wijzen en den Zot ("By the Wise One and the Crazy One") was the first restaurant that opened in Patershol, back when people figured you were either a genius or a madman to open up shop in such a sketchy area. Their prize-winning, €23 fish *waterzooi*—a creamy soup containing a variety of fish along with potatoes and vegetables—is a hit with diners (traditional Belgian with some French, €11-15 starters, €20-30 main dishes, Tue-Sat 12:00-14:00 & 18:30-22:00, closed Sun-Mon, Hertogstraat 42, tel. 09-223-4230).

Valentijn, in the heart of the district, has a romantic, dressy interior and a no-fuss menu of classics (€20-25 main dishes, €33 meals, Mon-Wed and Fri-Sat from 18:30, closed Thu, Sun open for lunch only, Rodekoningstraat 1, tel. 09-225-0429).

Avalon, across the street from the castle, offers tasty vegetarian fare (€11-13 main dishes, €16-19 specials, daily 11:30-14:30, lunch only, Geldmuntstraat 32, tel. 09-244-3724).

't Stropke ("The Noose"), down the street from Avalon, is a brasserie with bright, woody, rustic ambience and a treehouse floor plan. They serve Belgian and French food, with Ghent specialties, such as the creamy *waterzooi* soup (€8 sandwiches served until 18:00, €10-14 starters, €16-20 main dishes, Fri-Wed 9:00-22:00, closed Thu, Kraanlei 1, tel. 09-329-8335).

Oudburg street is lined with fun, ethnic, and youthful eateries, including a good Turkish place (Ankara, at #44).

Fast and Cheap

These centrally located options are suitable for a quick lunch.

Souplounge is basic, but cheap and good. They offer four daily soups, along with salads; a bowl of soup, two rolls, and a piece of fruit runs just €4. Eat in the mod interior, or at the outdoor tables overlooking one of Ghent's most scenic stretches of canal (also €5 salads, daily 10:00-19:00, Zuivelbrugstraat 6, tel. 09-223-6203).

Tasty World serves up decent €5 veggie burgers with various toppings, plus a wide range of fresh fruit juices and salads (Mon-Sat 11:00-20:00, closed Sun, Hoogpoort 1, tel. 09-225-7407).

Damass is a popular ice cream place where you can hang out and enjoy people-watching or get a cone to stroll with (at the north end of Korenmarkt, #2-C).

Bar Scene

Two touristy bars in the center are worth considering if you want to sample a wide range of Belgian favorites: beer or gin.

De Dulle Griet, on Vrijdagmarkt, serves up 249 types of beer in a cozy, sprawling bar with beer glasses hanging from the ceiling. The local beer, Gruut, is made with no hops; instead, it's flavored with a medieval (pre-hops) mix of herbs that brewers call *gruit* (Tue-Sat 12:00-24:00, Sun 12:00-19:00, Mon 16:30-1:00 in the morning, Vrijdagmarkt 50, tel. 09-244-2455).

't Dreupelkot is a cozy little bar along the river, helmed by chain-smoking Pol, who offers a lukewarm welcome and 100 different types of Dutch and Flemish gin, or *jenever* (€2-5 shots, daily from 16:00, or from 18:00 in July-Aug, open until late, Groentenmarkt 12, tel. 09-224-2120).

Ghent Connections

From Ghent by Train to: Brussels (3/hour, 35 minutes), **Bruges** (4/hour, 30 minutes), **Antwerp** (3/hour, 50 minutes), **Ypres/Ieper** (hourly, 1.25 hours, transfer in Kortrijk), **Paris** (2/hour, 2-2.5 hours, change at Brussels Midi/Zuid/South to Thalys train), **Amsterdam** (hourly, 2.5 hours, transfer in Antwerp), **Delft** (2/hour, 2-2.5 hours, transfer in Antwerp and Rotterdam). In Belgium, dial 050-302-424 for train information—press 4 for English, www.b-rail.be.

HISTORY

Twenty Centuries in Six Pages

A.D. 1-1300—Romans and Invasions

When Rome falls (c. 400), the Low Countries shatter into a patchwork of local dukedoms that are ravaged by Viking raids. Out of this poor, agricultural, and feudal landscape emerge three self-governing urban centers—Amsterdam, Bruges, and Brussels—each in a prime location for trade. Amsterdam and Bruges sit where rivers flow into the North Sea, while Brussels hugs a main trading highway.

Sights

- Amsterdam's Dam Square
- Exhibits in Amsterdam Museum
- Haarlem's Grote Markt
- The Hague's Ri8derzaal and Binnenhof
- Bruges' original fort and church ruins
- Bruges' Basilica of the Holy Blood (1150)
- Brussels' St. Michael's Cathedral, model in the City Museum, and Tour d'Angle (tower) from city wall
- Ghent's Castle of the Counts

1300-1500—Booming Trade Towns

Bruges, the midway port between North Sea and Mediterranean trade routes, becomes one of Europe's busiest and richest cities.

When Bruges' harbor silts up in the late 15th century, trade shifts to the bustling port city of Antwerp. Amsterdam augments its beer and herring trade with budding capitalism: banking, loans, and speculation in stock and futures. Brussels sells waffles and beer to passing travelers. Politically, the Low Countries are united through marriage with the cultured empire of the Dukes of Burgundy.

Sights

- Churches: Amsterdam's Old Church (Oude Kerk) and New Church (Nieuwe Kerk), Delft's New Church (Nieuwe Kerk), Haarlem's Grote Kerk, Antwerp's Cathedral of Our Lady, and Ghent's Cathedral of St. Bavo
- Amsterdam's Waag (in the Red Light District), the Mint Tower from the original city wall, and the wooden house at Begijnhof 34

- Bruges' bell tower, the Gothic Room in the City Hall, and the Church of Our Lady
- Flemish Primitive art (Van Eyck, Memling, Van der Weyden) in Bruges' Groeninge and Memling museums, and in Brussels' Royal Museums of Fine Arts of Belgium, as well as Van Eyck's *The Adoration of the Mystic Lamb* altarpiece in Ghent's cathedral
- Brussels' Grand Place, medieval street Rue des Bouchers (Restaurant Row), and Notre-Dame du Sablon Church
- Antwerp's riverfront and Old Town

1500s—Protestants vs. Catholics, Freedom-Fighters vs. Spanish Rulers

Protestantism spreads through the Low Countries, particularly in Holland (while Belgium remains more Catholic). Thanks to other

royal marriages, the Low Countries are ruled from afar by the very Catholic Habsburg family in Spain. In 1566, angry Protestants rise up against Spain and Catholicism, vandalizing Catholic churches ("iconoclasm") and deposing Spanish governors. King Philip II of Spain sends troops to restore order and brutally punish the rebel-heretics, beginning the Eighty Years' War, also known as the Dutch War of Independence (1568-1648).

Sights

- Amsterdam's whitewashed, simply decorated, post-iconoclasm churches
- Civic Guard portraits in Amsterdam Museum
- Mementos of the Siege of Haarlem in Haarlem's Grote Kerk
- Brussels' tapestry designs

1600s—Holland's Golden Age

Holland gains its independence from the Habsburgs (officially in 1648), while Belgium languishes under Spanish rule. Amsterdam invents the global economy, as its hardy sailors ply the open seas, trading in Indonesian spices and South American sugar. Establishing colonies all over the world, they also conceive the African slave trade.

Their nautical and capitalist skills combine to make Amsterdam the world's wealthiest city.

Sights

- Amsterdam's Rijksmuseum and Haarlem's Frans Hals Museum—paintings by Rembrandt, Hals, Vermeer, and Steen
- Old townhouses and gables in Amsterdam's Jordaan neighborhood and Red Light District
- Amsterdam's Begijnhof, Royal Palace, Westerkerk, and Rembrandt's House
- Delftware porcelain
- The Hague's Mauritshuis Royal Picture Gallery—paintings by Vermeer, Rembrandt, and Rubens
- Edam's Grote Kerk
- Brussels' *Manneken-Pis*
- Lace (popularity peaks c. 1700)
- Antwerp's Rubens House, Rockox House, and Museum Plantin-Moretus

1700s—Elegant Decline

Holland and Belgium are both surpassed by the rise of superpowers France and England. Wars with those powers drain their economies and scuttle Holland's fleet. Still, they survive as bankers, small manufacturers, and craftsmen in luxury goods—but on a small scale fitting their geographical size. They hit rock bottom in 1795, when French troops occupy the Low Countries (1795-1815), and Europe's powers subsequently saddle them with a monarchy.

Islam and the Netherlands Today

The hottest hot-button issue in the Netherlands today is the culture clash between secular, multicultural Netherlands and its recent Muslim immigrants. Many Muslims arrived in the last half of the 20th century after Indonesia (a Dutch colony) gained independence. Guest workers from Turkey and Morocco—drawn by economic incentives—swelled the ranks. Today, one in ten Amsterdammers is Muslim. The Muslim cultures have not meshed seamlessly with the Netherlands' Western, secular, and liberal culture.

The Dutch are still haunted by a shameful episode concerning Muslims during the Bosnian War. In 1995, Dutch soldiers were stationed in Bosnia, charged by the UN with keeping peace during that region's troubled civil war. In July, the Dutch-protected town of Srebrenica was overrun by Bosnian Serbs. The 400 Dutch troops were outnumbered, and the UN gave them no logistical support. While Dutch soldiers huddled helplessly in their compound, the Serbs rounded up 8,000 Muslim men and boys and massacred them. In hindsight, there was little the soldiers could have done to prevent the atrocity, but it remains disturbing to the Dutch psyche. Discussions of current events still tend to mention this episode.

In spring of 2002, a charismatic Dutch politician named Pim Fortuyn campaigned for Parliament on a strong anti-immigration platform. Like many Dutch, he was socially liberal (including being openly gay, pro-feminist, pro-drug, and pro-euthanasia) but was concerned that Islam posed a threat to Dutch tolerance. On May 6, Fortuyn was gunned down in a parking lot by a mentally troubled man who disagreed with his politics (though the assassin's full motives remain unclear). Dutch people were

HISTORY

Sights

- Amsterdam's Amstelkring Museum (hidden church), Willet-Holthuysen Museum (Herengracht Canal Mansion), and Jewish Historical Museum synagogue
- Brussels' Grand Place guildhalls
- Antwerp's Paleis op de Meir (Napoleon's palace)

1800s—Dutch Revival and Belgian Independence

Though slow to join the Industrial Revolution, Holland picks up speed by century's end. A canal to the North Sea rejuvenates Amsterdam's port, railroads lace cities together, and Amsterdam hosts a World Exhibition. Meanwhile, Belgium—having been placed under a Dutch king—revolts, gains its independence (1830), and picks its own king, a German this time (Leopold I). King Leopold II claims Africa's Congo as his own private colony

stunned by the violence, the kind of thing they thought happened only in America. Fortuyn's legacy seems to be that his outspokenness broke taboos of political correctness and opened the floodgates of debate about these touchy issues.

On the morning of November 2, 2004, the great-grand-nephew of Vincent van Gogh was bicycling past Amsterdam's Oosterpark on his way to work. Theo van Gogh was a well-known filmmaker who'd recently released a controversial film about women and Islam. A Muslim Dutch citizen of Moroccan descent shot Van Gogh, then stabbed a letter into his dead body threatening to harm the film's female screenwriter as well.

Screenwriter Ayaan Hirsi Ali has become a lightning rod for Western/Muslim controversy. Born a Muslim in Somalia, she emigrated to the Netherlands, where she became a member of Parliament and an outspoken critic of Islam and its treatment of women. (She also gained notoriety for gaining her citizenship under false pretenses.) Hirsi Ali, who is under a 24-hour security watch, currently lives in the US and is a fellow at the American Enterprise Institute in Washington, DC.

Lately, Dutch politician Geert Wilders has taken up Fortuyn's mantle, advocating the banning of the Quran and an end to Muslim immigration (he's proposed that current immigrants be paid to leave). His party won 15 percent of the votes in 2010 (but lost nine seats in 2012).

Whatever happened to peaceful, tolerant, quaint old Holland? That's what the Dutch want to know. The Muslim immigration issue has forced the Dutch to confront a difficult paradox—how to be tolerant of what they perceive to be an intolerant culture.

(1885), exploiting both its natural resources (ivory, rubber) and its people to finance massive building projects in his capital, Brussels—earning him the nickname "The Builder King."

Sights

- Amsterdam's Central Station, Rijksmuseum, Stadsschouwburg theater, Concertgebouw music hall, and Magna Plaza
- Van Gogh paintings at the Van Gogh Museum
- Indonesian foods from the colonial era
- Brussels' Upper Town buildings and Parc du Cinquantenaire
- Brussels' Galeries Royales St. Hubert and BELvue Museum
- Ghent's Dutch Theater

- Antwerp's Central Station
- Chocolate

1900s-2000s—Invasions by Germans, Hippies, and Immigrants

The 20th century starts off badly, as Belgium is a major battleground in World War I, particularly in Flanders. In the 1930s, the Netherlands gets significantly bigger when it dikes off huge areas of its inland sea to create more farmland. Holland, neutral in World War I, joins Belgium in suffering a brutal occupation by the Nazis during World War II (Rotterdam is utterly destroyed). After the war, Brussels becomes the center of the budding movement toward European economic unity. In Amsterdam, postwar prosperity and a tolerant atmosphere in the 1960s and 1970s make it a global magnet for hippies... and your co-authors. In the 1970s and 1980s, Amsterdam and Brussels are flooded with immigrants from their former colonies, causing friction and bringing a degree of ethnic diversity to the population. Beginning in the 1990s, as Europe's nations unite to form the European Union, Brussels gradually becomes the de facto capital of this "United States of Europe." Facing an uncertain future today, the "Low Countries"—with much of their territory below sea level—keep a close watch on global warming with its associated bigger storms and rising seas.

ANNE FRANK
TAGEBUCH

Sights

- Amsterdam's Beurs, Tuschinski Theater, and National Monument on Dam Square
- Belgium's Flanders Fields
- Enkhuizen's Zuiderzee Museum
- Amsterdam's Anne Frank House and Dutch Resistance Museum
- Amsterdam's Heineken Brewery, rock-and-roll clubs Paradiso and Melkweg, and the new "Stopera" opera house
- Haarlem's Corrie ten Boom House
- Paintings by René Magritte in Bruges' Groeninge Museum and in Brussels' Magritte Museum
- Brussels' Atomium and European Parliament quarter
- Antwerp's Sint-Andries fashion district, ModeMuseum, "Little Island" area, and 't Zuid district
- Ghent's Design Museum

The Netherlands and Belgium— A Timeline

57 B.C. Julius Caesar invades the Low Countries, conquering local Batavian, Frisian, and Belgae tribes, beginning four centuries of Roman rule.

A.D. 406 Frankish tribes from Germany drive out the last Roman legions as Rome's Europe-wide empire collapses. Christian missionaries work to prevent the area from reverting to paganism.

c. 800 Charlemagne, born in Belgium, rules the Low Countries as part of a large northern European empire. After his death, his grandsons divide the kingdom and bicker among themselves.

c. 880-1000 Vikings rape and pillage during two centuries of raids in the Low Countries.

c. 900 The Low Countries are a patchwork of small dukedoms ruled by bishops and local counts (of Holland, Flanders, Brabant, and so on), who owe allegiance to greater kings in France, Germany, and England.

c. 1250 In Amsterdam, fishermen build a dike (dam) where the Amstel River flows into the North Sea, creating a prime trading port. Soon the town gains independence and trading privileges from the local count and bishop. Meanwhile, Bruges becomes a major weaver of textiles, and Brussels becomes a minor trading town along the Germany-Bruges highway.

c. 1300 Italian and Portuguese sailors forge a coast-hugging trade route from the Mediterranean to the North Sea, with Bruges as the final stop.

1302 In Bruges, Flemish rebels drive out French rulers at the Battle of the Golden Spurs.

1345 Amsterdam experiences the Miracle of the Host, when a flame-resistant communion wafer causes miracles and attracts pilgrims.

1384 The discovery of a process to cure herring with salt makes Amsterdam a major fish exporter (to augment its thriving beer trade).

1384 Mary of Flanders marries Duke Philip the Bold of Burgundy, turning Holland and Belgium into part of a Burgundian empire that eventually stretches from Amsterdam to Switzerland.

c. 1400 Bruges is Europe's greatest trade city, the middleman between North and South.

1432 Painter Jan Van Eyck completes *The Adoration of the Mystic Lamb* altarpiece (in Ghent's cathedral)—considered the first work of the Flemish Primitives, known for their painstakingly detailed style.

1433 Burgundy's empire peaks when Duke Philip the Good takes over the titles of the local counts. His cultured court makes the Low Countries a center of art, literature, ideas, and pageantry.

1482 Mary of Burgundy, the last heir to the Burgundian throne, falls from a horse and dies. Her possessions (including Holland and Belgium) pass to her Austrian Habsburg husband, Maximilian, and get swallowed up in his family's large Holy Roman Empire, ruled from Austria and later Spain.

1492 Columbus' voyage demonstrates the potential wealth of New World trade.

c. 1510 Bruges' harbor silts up, and business migrates to the port city of Antwerp, which becomes northern Europe's greatest trading city.

1517 The German Martin Luther's 95 theses inspire Protestantism, which becomes popular in the Low Countries (especially Holland). Later, refugees of religious persecution, including Calvinists and Anabaptists (such as the Amish and Mennonites), find a home in tolerant Amsterdam.

1519 King Charles V (1500-1558), the grandson of Mary of Burgundy and Maximilian, inherits all of his family's combined possessions. Charles rules Holland and Belgium, as well as Austria, Spain, Germany, Spain's New World colonies, and much more. A staunch Catholic, Charles battles rebellious Protestant princes.

1535 On Amsterdam's Dam Square, Anabaptist rebels are hanged, drawn, and quartered.

1540 Emperor Charles' son, Philip of Spain, invites the Inquisition to Spain.

1556 Philip II, based in Spain, succeeds his father as ruler of the Netherlands and intensifies the wars on Protestants (especially Calvinists).

1566 The "Dutch Revolt" begins when, in a wave of anti-Catholic and anti-Spanish fury, extreme Protestants storm Catholic churches, vandalizing religious objects and converting the churches to Protestant ("iconoclasm"). Philip II sends soldiers to the Low Countries to establish order and punish rebels and heretics.

1568 Holland's Protestant counts rally around William "The Silent" of Orange, demanding freedom from Spanish Habsburg rule (the Beggars' Revolt). This begins 80 years of on-again-off-again war with Spain, called...the Eighty Years' War.

1572-1573 The Spanish conquer Haarlem after a long siege, but Haarlem's brave stand inspires other towns to carry on the fight.

1576 In the "Spanish Fury," Antwerp is sacked by Spanish troops impatient at not being paid by King Philip II. This devastates the city, causes irreparable damage to its trade ties, and turns public opinion in the Low Countries against the Habsburgs. Antwerp becomes the hot spot of the Dutch revolt.

1578 Amsterdam switches sides (the Alteration), joining the Protestant independence movement. Extreme Calvinists control the city for several decades, officially outlawing Catholic services. Within a few years, Spanish troops are driven south out of Holland, and future battles take place mostly on Belgian soil.

1580 Holland and Belgium go separate ways in the war. Holland's towns and nobles form a Protestant military alliance (the United Provinces) against Catholic Spain, while Belgium remains Catholic, with Brussels as the capital of Spanish Habsburg rule.

1585 After a brutal siege, Protestant-holdout Antwerp falls to Spanish troops. In the chaos, half the population flees, leaving Antwerp a largely forgotten Catholic backwater. Many Antwerp businessmen restart their businesses in industrious Amsterdam, which gradually steps up to fill the vacuum of trade.

1588 Elizabeth I of England defeats the Spanish Armada (navy), breaking Spain's monopoly on overseas trade.

1602 The Dutch East India Company (VOC), a government-subsidized trading company, is formed, soon followed by the West India Company (1622). Together, they make Amsterdam (pop. 100,000) the center of a global trading empire, spawning the Dutch Golden Age (c. 1600-1650).

1608 Peter Paul Rubens returns to Antwerp after eight years studying painting in Italy. His brush becomes the ambassador of the Counter-Reformation aesthetic, with bombastic biblical scenes extolling the glory of God (and his Church on earth).

1609 Henry Hudson's *Half Moon,* sailing for the Dutch East India Company, departs Amsterdam in search of a western passage to the Orient. Instead, Hudson finds the island of Manhattan, which soon becomes New Amsterdam (New York, 1625).

1616 Frans Hals paints the *St. George Civic Guards* (Frans Hals Museum, Haarlem).

1620 Pilgrims from England stop in Holland on their way to America.

1631 Rembrandt moves to Amsterdam, a wealthy city of 120,000 people, including René Descartes, plus many different religious sects and a thriving Jewish Quarter.

1637 After several years of insanely lucrative trade in tulip bulbs ("tulip mania"), the market crashes.

1648 The Treaty of Munster (and the Treaty of Westphalia) officially ends the Eighty Years' War with Spain. The United Provinces (today's Netherlands) are now an independent nation.

1652-1654 Holland battles England over control of the seas. This is the first of three wars with England (also in 1665 and 1672) that sap Holland's wealth.

1672-1678 Louis XIV of France invades Holland and gets to within 15 miles of Amsterdam, but is finally stopped when the citizens open the Amstel locks and flood the city. After another draining war with France (1701-1713), England and France overtake Holland in overseas trade.

1689 Holland's William of Orange is invited by England's Parliament to replace the despot they'd deposed. He, ruling with wife Mary, becomes King William III of England.

1695 Louis XIV of France bombs and incinerates Brussels during the Nine Years' War, punishing William III for allying against him.

1776 The American Revolution inspires European democrats and worries nobles.

1787 Holland's budding democratic movement, the Patriots, is suppressed and exiled when Prussian troops invade Holland.

1789 The French Revolution begins.

1795 France, battling Europe's monarchs to keep their Revolution alive, invades and occupies Holland (establishing the "Batavian Republic," 1795-1806) and Belgium.

1806 Napoleon Bonaparte, who turned France's

Revolution into a dictatorship, proclaims his brother, Louis Napoleon, to be King of Holland (1806-1810).

1815 After Napoleon's defeat at Waterloo (near Brussels), Europe's nobles decide that the Low Countries should be a monarchy, ruled jointly by a Dutch prince, who becomes King William I. (Today's King Willem-Alexander is descended from him.)

1830 Belgium rebels against the Dutch-born king, becoming an independent constitutional monarchy under the German-born Leopold I, King of the Belgians. French-speaking aristocrats control the government, while the lower class consists mainly of Dutch-speaking Flemish peasants.

1860 The novel *Max Havelaar*, by the Dutch writer Multatuli, exposes the dark side of Holland's repressive colonial rule in Indonesia.

1876 The North Sea Canal opens after 52 years of construction, revitalizing Amsterdam's port. In the next decade, the city builds Central Station, the Rijksmuseum, and Concertgebouw, and hosts a World Exhibition (1883) that attracts three million visitors.

1885 King Leopold II of Belgium acquires Africa's Congo region as his personal realm, robbing its resources to rebuild Brussels with broad boulevards and big marble buildings (Neoclassical style).

1908 After three decades of exploiting the Congo for his personal financial gain, growing public outcry convinces King Leopold II to turn it over to the government of Belgium.

1914 In World War I, Holland remains neutral, while Belgium becomes a horrific battleground where Germany dukes it out with England and France; some of the worst fighting takes place at Flanders Fields near Ypres (Ieper).

1929 Belgian cartoonist Hergé publishes the first of nearly 50 years' worth of comics about an adventurous young reporter named Tintin, who will become beloved by all Europeans.

1932 The Dutch Zuiderzee dike is completed, turning the former arm of the North Sea into a freshwater lake (the IJsselmeer) and creating many square miles of reclaimed land.

1940-1945 Nazi Germany bombs Holland's Rotterdam and easily occupies the Netherlands and Belgium (1940). Belgium's king officially surrenders, and Holland's Queen Wilhelmina (1880-1962) flees to England. In

Amsterdam, Anne Frank and her Jewish family go into hiding in an attempt to avoid arrest by the Nazis (1942-1944). Late in the war, Belgium is the site of Germany's last-gasp offensive, the Battle of the Bulge—Hitler's attempt to divide the Allied armies and capture Antwerp (1944-1945).

1945 Holland and Belgium are liberated by Allied troops.

1949 Indonesia gains its independence from Holland.

1953 Major floods in Holland kill almost 2,000 people, prompting more dams and storm barriers (the Delta Project, 1958-1997).

1957 Belgium and the Netherlands join the EEC (Common Market)—the forerunner of today's European Union—with headquarters in Brussels.

1960 The BeNeLux economic union between Belgium, the Netherlands, and Luxembourg—first proposed in 1944—becomes fully operational. After years of protests in the Belgian Congo, Belgium grants independence to the African nation.

1967 Amsterdam is Europe's center for hippies and the youth movement.

1970 Belgium passes reforms designed to ease long-standing tensions between its Flemish and Walloon factions; the nation is divided into three semi-autonomous regions: Flanders (Dutch speaking), Wallonia (French speaking), and Brussels (bilingual).

1975 Suriname (Dutch Guyana) gains its independence from Holland, and many emigrants flock to Holland.

1992 Belgium and the Netherlands sign the Treaty of Maastricht, which creates the European Union (EU).

1993 King Albert II (b. 1934) becomes King of the Belgians.

1995 Floods in the Netherlands cause a billion dollars in damage.

2005 Dutch voters reject the adoption of a European Constitution in the first national referendum in more than 200 years.

2010 In the Belgian general election, the nationalistic Nieuw-Vlaamse Alliantie (N-VA) party—which promotes Flemish independence from Belgium—wins more votes than any other party.

2013 King Willem-Alexander (b. 1967) becomes ruler of the Netherlands.

Today You arrive in Amsterdam, Bruges, and Brussels and make your own history.

APPENDIX

Contents

Tourist Information

National tourist offices **in the US** can be a wealth of information. Before your trip, request or download any specific information you may want (such as city maps and schedules of upcoming festivals).

For the Netherlands, call 212/370-7360 or visit www.holland .com. They no longer distribute printed material; all information is now available only on the Internet. Another useful website is www.iamsterdam.com (Amsterdam Tourism Board).

For Belgium, call 212/758-8130 or go to www.visitbelgium .com. Over the phone or filling out the online form, you can request hotel and city guides; brochures for ABC lovers—antiques, beer, and chocolates; a map of Brussels; information on WWI and WWII battlefields; and a list of Jewish sights.

In the **Netherlands** or **Belgium,** the tourist information office (abbreviated **TI** in this book) is generally your best first stop in any new town (although Amsterdam's TIs are so crowded that you're better off visiting the airport TI or the TI in Haarlem).

TIs are good places to get a city map and information on public transit (including bus and train schedules), walking tours, special events, and nightlife—some even have Internet access. Many have information on the entire country or at least the region, so try to pick up maps for destinations you'll be visiting later in your trip. If you're arriving in town after the TI closes, call ahead or pick up a map in a neighboring town. Note that in the Netherlands, TIs tend to be privately run, which can color their advice; however, in Belgium, they are state-run, so they're not tainted by a drive for profits. Steer clear of the room-finding services at for-profit TIs, especially in the Netherlands (bloated prices, booking fees, and they take a sizeable cut from your host). Even if there's no "fee," you'll save yourself and your host money by going direct with the listings in this book.

Communicating

Telephones

Smart travelers use the telephone to reserve or reconfirm rooms, get tourist information, reserve restaurants, confirm tour times, or phone home. This section covers dialing instructions, phone cards, and types of phones (for more in-depth information, see www .ricksteves.com/phoning).

How to Dial

Calling from the US to Europe, or vice versa, is simple—once you break the code. The European calling chart later in this chapter will walk you through it.

Dialing Domestically in the Low Countries

The following instructions apply to dialing from a landline (such as a pay phone or your hotel-room phone) or a Dutch or Belgian mobile phone.

The Netherlands, like much of the US, uses an area-code dialing system. If you're dialing within an area code, you just dial the local number to be connected; but if you're calling outside your area code, you have to dial both the area code (which starts with a 0) and the local number. For example, the number of a recommended hotel in Haarlem is 023/532-4530. To call it within Haarlem, dial 532-4530. To call it from Amsterdam, dial 023/532-4530.

Belgium uses a direct-dial system (no area codes). To call anywhere within Belgium, you always dial a nine-digit number.

If you're dialing within the Netherlands or Belgium using your US mobile phone, you may need to dial as if it's a domestic call, or you may need to dial as if you're calling from the US (see

What Language Barrier?

People speak Dutch in Amsterdam. In Bruges, Ghent, and Antwerp they also speak Dutch—but with a Flemish accent. It's mostly French in Brussels. But you'll find almost no language barrier in the Netherlands or Belgium, as all well-educated folks, nearly all young people, and almost everyone in the tourist trade also speak English. (When asked if they speak English, the Dutch reply, *"Natuurlijk"*—"naturally.") In tourist-friendly Bruges, you also won't encounter any difficulties with English. You will meet some French-only speakers in Brussels, but it's generally a minor language barrier. Regardless, it's polite to use some Dutch or French pleasantries (see pages 633 and 635).

"Dialing Internationally," next). Try it one way, and if it doesn't work, try it the other way.

Dialing Internationally to or from the Low Countries

If you want to make an international call, follow these steps:

• Dial the international access code (00 if you're calling from Europe, 011 from the US or Canada). If you're dialing from a mobile phone, you can replace the international access code with +, which works regardless of where you're calling from. (On many mobile phones, you can insert a + by pressing and holding the 0 key.)

• Dial the country code of the country you're calling (31 for the Netherlands, 32 for Belgium, or 1 for the US or Canada).

• Dial the area code (without its initial 0) and the local number. (For specifics per country, see the European calling chart in this chapter.)

Calling from the US to the Low Countries: To call a Haarlem hotel from the US, dial 011 (the US international access code), 31 (the Netherlands' country code), 23 (Haarlem's area code without the initial 0), and then the hotel's phone number (e.g., 532-4530). To call a hotel in Bruges from the US, dial 011 (the US international access code), 32 (Belgium's country code), and then the hotel's number without its initial zero (e.g., 50-444-444).

Calling from any European country to the US: To call my office in Edmonds, Washington, from anywhere in Europe, I dial 00 (Europe's international access code), 1 (the US country code), 425 (Edmonds' area code), and 771-8303.

Mobile Phones

Traveling with a mobile phone is handy and practical. For specifics on using your smartphone to get online, see the sidebar.

Smartphones and Data Roaming

I take my smartphone to Europe, using it to make phone calls (sparingly) and send texts, but also to check email, listen to audio tours, and browse the Internet. If you're clever, you can do all this without incurring huge data-roaming fees. Here's how.

Many smartphones, such as the iPhone, Android, and BlackBerry, work in Europe (though some older Verizon iPhones don't). For voice calls and text messaging, smartphones work like any mobile phone (as described under "Roaming with Your Mobile Phone," opposite page)—unless you're connected to free Wi-Fi, in which case you can use Skype, Google Talk, or FaceTime to call for free (or at least very cheaply; see "Calling over the Internet," later).

The (potentially) *really* expensive aspect of using smartphones in Europe is not voice calls or text messages, but sky-high rates for using data: checking email, browsing the Internet, streaming videos, using certain apps, and so on. If you don't proactively adjust your settings, these charges can mount up even if you're not actually using your phone—because the phone is constantly "roaming" to update your email and such. (One tip is to switch your email settings from "push" to "fetch," so you can choose when to download your emails rather than having them automatically "pushed" over the Internet to your device.)

The best solution: Disable data roaming entirely, and use your device to access the Internet only when you find free Wi-Fi (at your hotel, for example). Then you can surf the net to your heart's content, or make free (or extremely cheap) phone calls via Skype. You can manually turn off data roaming on your phone's menu (check under the "Network" settings). For added security, you can call and ask your service provider to temporarily suspend your data account entirely for the length of your trip.

Some travelers enjoy the flexibility of getting online even when they're not on free Wi-Fi. But be careful. If you simply switch on data roaming, you'll pay exorbitant rates of about $20 per megabyte (figure around 40 cents per email downloaded, or about $3 to view a typical Web page)—much more expensive than it is back home. If you know you'll be doing some data roaming, it's far more affordable to sign up for a limited international data-roaming plan through your carrier (but be very clear on your megabyte limit to avoid inflated overage charges). In general, ask your provider in advance how to avoid unwittingly roaming your way to a huge bill.

Roaming with Your Mobile Phone: Your US mobile phone works in Europe if it's GSM-enabled, tri-band or quad-band, and on a calling plan that includes international calls. Phones from T-Mobile and AT&T, which use the same GSM technology that Europe does, are more likely to work overseas than Verizon or Sprint phones (if you're not sure, ask your service provider). Most US providers will charge you $1.29-1.99 per minute to make or receive calls while roaming internationally, and 20-50 cents to send or receive text messages. If you sign up for an international calling plan with your provider, you'll save a few dimes per minute. Though pricey, roaming on your own phone is easy and can be a cost-effective way to keep in touch—especially on a short trip or if you won't be making many calls.

Buying and Using SIM Cards in Europe: You'll pay much cheaper rates if you put a European SIM card in your mobile phone; to do this, your phone must be electronically "unlocked" (ask your provider about this, buy an unlocked phone before you leave, or get one in Europe—see "Other Mobile-Phone Options," next). Then, in Europe, you can buy a fingernail-size **SIM card,** which gives you a European phone number. SIM cards are sold at mobile-phone stores, most newsstand kiosks, and most GWK Travelex counters for €15-25 and often include at least that much prepaid domestic calling time (making the card itself almost free). On my last trip, I spent €25 for a Dutch SIM card and about 90 minutes of call time, which was plenty for a two-week trip. In the Netherlands, Lebara has an English option for its mobile-phone voicemail and website (see www.lebara.nl). In Belgium, Proximus has a similar English-language option (see www.proximus.be).

Insert the SIM card in your phone (sometimes in a slot behind the battery or on the side), and it'll work like a European mobile phone. Before purchasing a SIM card, always ask about fees for domestic and international calls, roaming charges, and how to check your credit balance and buy more time. When you're in the SIM card's home country, domestic calls average 10-20 cents per minute, and incoming calls are free. Rates are higher if you're roaming in another country, and you may pay more to call a toll number than you would dialing from a fixed line.

Other Mobile-Phone Options: Many travelers like to carry two phones: both their own US mobile phone (allowing them to stay reachable on their own phone number) and a second, unlocked European phone (which lets them do all their local calling at far cheaper rates). You could either bring two phones from home, or get one in Europe. If you have an old mobile phone sitting around, ask your provider for the "unlock code" so it can be used with European SIM cards. Or buy a cheap, basic phone before you go

European Calling Chart

Just smile and dial, using this key:
AC = Area Code, LN = Local Number.

European Country	Calling long distance within ...	Calling from the US or Canada to ...	Calling from a European country to ...
Austria	AC + LN	011 + 43 + AC (without the initial zero) + LN	00 + 43 + AC (without the initial zero) + LN
Belgium	LN	011 + 32 + LN (without initial zero)	00 + 32 + LN (without initial zero)
Bosnia-Herzegovina	AC + LN	011 + 387 + AC (without initial zero) + LN	00 + 387 + AC (without initial zero) + LN
Britain	AC + LN	011 + 44 + AC (without initial zero) + LN	00 + 44 + AC (without initial zero) + LN
Croatia	AC + LN	011 + 385 + AC (without initial zero) + LN	00 + 385 + AC (without initial zero) + LN
Czech Republic	LN	011 + 420 + LN	00 + 420 + LN
Denmark	LN	011 + 45 + LN	00 + 45 + LN
Estonia	LN	011 + 372 + LN	00 + 372 + LN
Finland	AC + LN	011 + 358 + AC (without initial zero) + LN	999 (or other 900 number) + 358 + AC (without initial zero) + LN
France	LN	011 + 33 + LN (without initial zero)	00 + 33 + LN (without initial zero)
Germany	AC + LN	011 + 49 + AC (without initial zero) + LN	00 + 49 + AC (without initial zero) + LN
Gibraltar	LN	011 + 350 + LN	00 + 350 + LN
Greece	LN	011 + 30 + LN	00 + 30 + LN
Hungary	06 + AC + LN	011 + 36 + AC + LN	00 + 36 + AC + LN
Ireland	AC + LN	011 + 353 + AC (without initial zero) + LN	00 + 353 + AC (without initial zero) + LN

European Country	Calling long distance within ...	Calling from the US or Canada to ...	Calling from a European country to ...
Italy	LN	011 + 39 + LN	00 + 39 + LN
Montenegro	AC + LN	011 + 382 + AC (without initial zero) + LN	00 + 382 + AC (without initial zero) + LN
Morocco	LN	011 + 212 + LN (without initial zero)	00 + 212 + LN (without initial zero)
Netherlands	AC + LN	011 + 31 + AC (without initial zero) + LN	00 + 31 + AC (without initial zero) + LN
Norway	LN	011 + 47 + LN	00 + 47 + LN
Poland	LN	011 + 48 + LN	00 + 48 + LN
Portugal	LN	011 + 351 + LN	00 + 351 + LN
Slovakia	AC + LN	011 + 421 + AC (without initial zero) + LN	00 + 421 + AC (without initial zero) + LN
Slovenia	AC + LN	011 + 386 + AC (without initial zero) + LN	00 + 386 + AC (without initial zero) + LN
Spain	LN	011 + 34 + LN	00 + 34 + LN
Sweden	AC + LN	011 + 46 + AC (without initial zero) + LN	00 + 46 + AC (without initial zero) + LN
Switzerland	LN	011 + 41 + LN (without initial zero)	00 + 41 + LN (without initial zero)
Turkey	AC (if there's no initial zero, add one) + LN	011 + 90 + AC (without initial zero) + LN	00 + 90 + AC (without initial zero) + LN

- The instructions above apply whether you're calling a land line or mobile phone.

- The international access code (the first numbers you dial when making an international call) is 011 if you're calling from the US or Canada. It's 00 if you're calling from virtually anywhere in Europe (except Finland, where it's 999 or another 900 number, depending on the phone service you're using).

- To call the US or Canada from Europe, dial 00, then 1 (the country code for the US and Canada), then the area code and number. In short, 00 + 1 + AC + LN = Hi, Mom!

(search your favorite online shopping site for "unlocked quad-band GSM phone").

In Europe, basic phones are sold at mobile-phone stores, at hole-in-the-wall vendors at many airports and train stations, and at phone desks within larger department stores. Phones that are "locked" to work with a single provider start around $40; "unlocked" phones (which work with any SIM card) start around $60. Regardless of how you get your phone, remember that you'll need a SIM card to make it work.

Car-rental companies and mobile-phone companies offer the option to rent a mobile phone with a European number. While this seems convenient, hidden fees (such as high per-minute charges or expensive shipping costs) can really add up—which usually makes it a bad value. One exception is Verizon's Global Travel Program, available only to Verizon customers.

Calling over the Internet

Some things that seem too good to be true...actually are true. If you're traveling with a laptop, tablet, or smartphone, you can make free calls over the Internet to another wireless device, anywhere in the world, for free. (Or you can pay a few cents to call from your computer to a telephone.) The major providers are Skype, Google Talk, and (on Apple devices) FaceTime. You can get online at a Wi-Fi hotspot and use these apps to make calls without ringing up expensive roaming charges (though call quality can be spotty on slow connections). You can make Internet calls even if you're traveling without your own mobile device: Many European Internet cafés have Skype, as well as microphones and webcams, on their terminals—just log on and chat away.

Landline Telephones

As in the US, these days most Dutch and Belgian people make the majority of their calls on mobile phones. But you'll still encounter landlines in hotel rooms and at pay phones.

Hotel-Room Phones: Calling from your hotel room phone can be great for local calls, and for international calls if you have an international phone card (described later). Otherwise, hotel-room phones can be an almost criminal rip-off for long-distance or international calls. Many hotels charge a fee for local and sometimes even "toll-free" numbers—always ask for the rates before you dial. Incoming calls are free, making this an inexpensive way for friends and family to stay in touch (provided they have a long-distance plan with good international rates—and a list of your hotels' phone numbers).

Public Pay Phones: Coin-op phones are virtually extinct in

Europe. To make calls from public phones, you'll need a prepaid phone card, described next.

Telephone Cards

There are two types of phone cards: insertable (for pay phones) and international (cheap for overseas calls and usable from any type of phone). A phone card works only in the country where you bought it, so if you have a live card at the end of your trip, give it to another traveler to use—most cards expire three to six months after the first use.

Insertable Phone Cards: These cards are a convenient way to make a call from public pay phones. Buy these cards at TIs, newsstands, and train stations. They are sold in several denominations starting at about €5. To use the card, physically insert it into a slot in the pay phone. While you can use these cards to call anywhere in the world, they're only a good deal for making quick local calls from a phone booth. Each European country has its own insertable phone card—so your Dutch card won't work in a Belgian phone. Be aware that with the prevalence of mobile phones, pay phones are becoming harder to find.

International Phone Cards: With these cards, phone calls from the Low Countries to the US can cost less than a nickel a minute. The cards can also be used to make local calls, and they work from any type of phone, including your hotel-room phone or a mobile phone with a European SIM card. To use the card, dial a toll-free access number, then enter your scratch-to-reveal PIN code.

You can buy the cards at small newsstand kiosks, electronics stores, and hole-in-the-wall Internet shops. Ask the clerk which brands have the best rates for calls to America. Buy a lower denomination in case the card is a dud. Some international phone cards work in multiple countries—if traveling to both the Netherlands and Belgium, try to buy a card that will work in both places. Some shops also sell cardless codes, printed right on the receipt.

When using an international calling card, the area code must be dialed even if you're calling across the street. If the prompts are in Dutch or French, wait to see if the announcement also follows in English. If not, experiment: Dial your code, followed by the pound sign (#), then the number, then the pound sign again, and so on, until it works. Sometimes the star (*) key is used instead of the pound sign.

US Calling Cards: These cards, such as the ones offered by AT&T, Verizon, and Sprint, are a rotten value, and are being phased out. Try any of the options outlined earlier.

Useful Phone Numbers

Emergency Needs

Police, Ambulance, or Fire (Netherlands): 112
Police (Belgium): 101 or 112
Ambulance or Fire (Belgium): 100 or 112

Embassies/Consulates in the Netherlands

US Embassies and Consulates: Amsterdam—tel. 020/575-5309 during normal office hours, otherwise in case of emergency call after-duty officer at tel. 070/310-2209 (Museumplein 19, http://amsterdam.usconsulate.gov). Online appointments are mandatory for all public services.

The Hague—tel. 070/310-2209, visits by appointment only (Lange Voorhout 102, http://netherlands.usembassy.gov).
Canadian Embassy: The Hague—tel. 070/311-1600 (Sophialaan 7, Mon-Fri 9:00-13:00 & 14:00-17:30, closed Sat-Sun; consular services Mon-Fri 9:30-13:00, closed Sat-Sun; www.canada.nl).

Embassies in Belgium

US Embassy: Brussels—tel. 02-811-4300 (Boulevard du Régent 27; phone hours are Mon-Thu 8:00-12:30, Fri 13:30-15:30; for after-hours emergencies, call 02-811-4000 and ask to be connected to the duty officer, http://belgium.usembassy.gov). Consulate is next door to embassy (Boulevard du Régent 25). Online appointments are mandatory for all public services.
Canadian Embassy: Brussels—tel. 02-741-0611 (Avenue de Tervueren 2, Mon-Fri 9:00-12:30 & 13:30-17:00, closed Sat-Sun; consulate open Mon-Fri 9:00-12:00, afternoon by appointment only, www.ambassade-canada.be).

Travel Advisories

US Department of State: Tel. 888-407-4747, from outside US tel. 1-202-501-4444, www.travel.state.gov
Canadian Department of Foreign Affairs: Canadian tel. 800-267-6788 from outside Canada tel. 1-613-996-8885, www.voyage.gc.ca
US Centers for Disease Control and Prevention: Tel. 800-CDC-INFO (800-232-4636, www.cdc.gov/travel)

Internet Access

It's useful to get online periodically while you travel—to confirm trip plans, check train or bus schedules, get weather forecasts, catch up on email, blog or post photos from your trip, or call folks back home (explained earlier, under "Calling over the Internet").

Your Mobile Device: The majority of accommodations in the Low Countries offer Wi-Fi, as do many cafés, making it easy for you to get online with your laptop, tablet, or smartphone. Access is often free, but sometimes there's a fee.

Some hotel rooms and Internet cafés have high-speed Internet jacks that you can plug into with an Ethernet cable. A cellular modem—which lets your device access the Internet over a mobile phone network—provides more extensive coverage, but is much more expensive than Wi-Fi.

Public Internet Terminals: Many accommodations offer a computer in the lobby with Internet access for guests. If you ask politely, smaller places may let you sit at their desk for a few minutes just to check your email. If your hotelier doesn't have access, ask to be directed to the nearest place to get online.

Security: Whether you're accessing the Internet with your own device or at a public terminal, using a shared network or computer comes with the potential for increased security risks. Be careful about storing personal information online, such as passport and credit-card numbers. If you're not convinced a connection is secure, avoid accessing any sites that could be vulnerable to fraud (e.g., online banking).

Mail

You can mail one package per day to yourself worth up to $200 duty-free from Europe to the US (mark it "personal purchases"). If you're sending a gift to someone, mark it "unsolicited gift." For details, visit www.cbp.gov and search for "Know Before You Go."

The Netherlands recently closed its post offices in all but the biggest cities. You can still buy stamps at any newsstand with an orange *TNT* logo. To send a package in a smaller town, ask your hotelier for assistance. Belgium has a more traditional postal system with offices throughout the country. Both postal services work fine, but for quick transatlantic delivery (in either direction), consider services such as DHL (www.dhl.com).

Transportation

By Car or Train?

Because of the short distances and excellent public transportation systems in the Low Countries, and the fact that this book covers three big cities, I recommend connecting Amsterdam, Bruges, and Brussels by train. Hourly trains connect each of these towns faster and easier than you could by driving. But for other destinations, a car could be a good alternative. In the Low Countries, cars are best for three or more traveling together (especially families with small kids), those packing heavy, and those scouring the countryside.

Trains

The easiest way to reach nearly any Dutch or Belgian destination is by train. Connections are fast and frequent. The Dutch train system—Nederlandse Spoorwegen—is usually identified by its initials NS. Because Belgium is bilingual, the rail system has a more complicated ID—NMBS/SNCB. InterCity (IC) and Fyra trains are speedy for connecting big cities, and the high-speed Thalys is the fastest (the speed comes at a price; see "Reservations for Railpass Holders," later). InterRegio (IR) and *sneltreins* connect smaller towns; *stoptreins* are pokey milk-run trains that stop at every station; and the Netherlands' misnamed "Sprinter" trains are actually slow *stoptreins*. Throughout the Netherlands and Belgium, smoking is prohibited in trains and train stations.

Schedules

To get train schedules in advance, use the German Rail (Deutsche Bahn) website, which has comprehensive schedules for almost anywhere in Europe (www.bahn.com). Or try the Dutch Rail site (www.nshighspeed.nl for international trains to Belgium and beyond, www.ns.nl for domestic trains). For a slick website that combines information on Dutch trains, buses, and trams (and even includes walking directions to get to the bus stop), visit www.9292.nl. The Belgian rail site is www.belgianrail.be. In the Netherlands dial toll tel. 0900-202-1163. In Belgium, dial 025-282-828.

To find schedules at train stations, check the yellow schedule posters, or look for TV screens listing upcoming departures. The direction of the train is identified by its final station. If you can't find your train, or are unclear on departure details, visit an information booth or enlist the help of any official-looking employee.

Buying Tickets in the Netherlands

Dutch stations are often understaffed (meaning ticket-window lines are long), or not staffed at all (using cash at ticket machines may be your only option). Your best option for avoiding the stress of hitting a long ticket-buying line (or a frantic search for a machine that takes cash) is to buy tickets a day or two in advance. You can buy tickets from a station ticket window (€0.50 extra, more for international trips, worth it if the lines are short, cash only—the agent knows where you can find an ATM), or with coins at a yellow-and-blue machine.

Ticket machines have instructions in English (press the British flag) and levy no additional fees. But they don't take US credit or debit cards unless you're at Schiphol Airport or Amsterdam Central Station and have a smart chip in your credit card. This means you'll need to pay with cash—which not every machine accepts. Examine each machine carefully. Some will have

Train Lines in the Low Countries

✈ AIRPORT

50 MILES
100 KM

See Detail Map in Day Trips Chapter →

TO HAMBURG

NORTH SEA

GRONINGEN
LEEUW.
MEPPEL

NETHERLANDS

HAARLEM
THE HAGUE
DELFT
ROTTERDAM

AMSTERDAM

TO BERLIN

DEVENTER   HENGELO

UTRECHT
GOUDA   ARNHEM

RHINE   GERMANY

Roos.
EINDHOVEN

BRUGES
OSTENDE
BUS
FLANDERS
YPRES
KORTRIJK
GHENT

ANTWERP
✈ BRUSSELS

MAAS-TRICHT

KÖLN

EUROSTAR TO LONDON

BELGIUM

AACHEN

RHINE

LIEGE

LILLE

MONS   NAMUR
WALLONIE

KOBLENZ

N

BASTOGNE

LUX.

TRIER

FRANCE

LUXEMBOURG CITY

TO PARIS

DCH

a coin slot above the upper right corner of the video screen—others won't. You can also check the bottom of the screen to see what forms of payment are accepted. To avoid confusion, check out the step-by-step instructions at the NS website under "Purchasing Tickets"; see www.ns.nl.

Types of Tickets: Round-trip tickets are always a bit cheaper than two one-way tickets, but are only issued for same-day travel (it's a small country). If you're going somewhere and back on different days, you'll need two one-way tickets. The exception: weekend return tickets, which give you the round-trip discount, but can be used on different days (valid from 19:00 Fri to 4:00 in the morning on Mon, each leg of the trip has to be taken within one day; if Fri or Mon is a holiday, validity is extended to 4:00 in the morning on Tue). While you can buy international tickets with a credit card at the www.nshighspeed.nl website, you can only

Railpasses

Prices listed are for 2014 and are subject to change. For the latest prices, details, and train schedules (and easy online ordering), see www.ricksteves.com/rail.

Benelux = Belgium, Netherlands and Luxembourg. "Saver" prices are per person for two or more people traveling together. "Youth" means under age 26. The fare for children 4–11 is half the adult individual fare or Saver fare. Kids under age 4 travel free.

BENELUX PASS

	Individual 1st Class	Individual 2nd Class	Saver 1st Class	Saver 2nd Class	Youth 2nd Class
3 days in 1 month	$331	$266	$282	$227	$174
5 days in 1 month	$452	$362	$385	$309	$237

Valid on Thalys trains within Benelux (with paid seat reservation), but not to/from Paris.

BENELUX–FRANCE PASS

	Individual 1st Class	Individual 2nd Class	Saver 1st Class	Saver 2nd Class	Youth 2nd Class
5 days in 2 months	$508	$433	$433	$369	$332
6 days in 2 months	$557	$474	$474	$413	$363
8 days in 2 months	$645	$562	$549	$492	$421
10 days in 2 months	$728	$641	$619	$558	$482

BENELUX–GERMANY PASS

	Individual 1st Class	Individual 2nd Class	Saver 1st Class	Saver 2nd Class	Youth 2nd Class
5 days in 2 months	$495	$372	$372	$301	$301
6 days in 2 months	$547	$412	$412	$329	$329
8 days in 2 months	$646	$484	$484	$389	$389
10 days in 2 months	$753	$563	$563	$450	$450

SELECTPASS

This pass covers travel in three adjacent countries, such as Benelux-Germany-Switzerland, but not including France. Please visit www.ricksteves.com/rail for four- and five-country options.

	Individual 1st Class	Saver 1st Class	Youth 2nd Class
5 days in 2 months	$528	$450	$345
6 days in 2 months	$583	$496	$381
8 days in 2 months	$688	$585	$449
10 days in 2 months	$797	$679	$520

buy a ticket on the domestic NS website if you have a Dutch bank account. While you'll see locals using an OV-Chipkaart instead of a ticket (described later), this isn't practical for visitors traveling by train unless you have...a Dutch bank account. Hmmm.

Buying Tickets in Belgium

Belgian train ticket machines only take Belgian debit cards, but you can use US credit and debit cards at ticket windows. It's also possible to purchase tickets online at www.belgianrail.be with a US credit card and print them out at home, or retrieve a hard copy at special ticket-dispensing machines at major train stations.

Ticket Deals

If you're not traveling with a railpass, consider the region's money-saving deals.

In the Netherlands, most age-based train deals are tied to the OV-Chipkaart, described later. In Belgium, youths under age 26 can get a Go Pass (€50 for 10 rides anywhere in Belgium). A similar deal is available for anyone over 26 for €76. Seniors (age 65-plus) can get a same-day round-trip ticket to anywhere in Belgium for €5.30 (weekdays: after 9:00; weekends: no restrictions except not valid on weekends in July-Aug). There are also weekend discounts for round-trips (50 percent off, valid Fri after 19:00). For more information, visit www.begianrail.be.

Bikes on Trains

If you're traveling with a bike, you'll pay extra to bring it on the train. In the Netherlands, bikes are only allowed during off-peak hours (all day on weekends, and weekdays only after 9:00) and require a "Bicycle Day Travel Card" (€6, no matter the destination). In Belgium, bikes cost €5 extra for a one-way trip, and €8 round-trip.

Railpasses

Most visits to the Netherlands and Belgium don't cover enough miles to justify a railpass, but if you're traveling beyond these countries, a railpass could save you money. For instance, good railpass options exist for those traveling between BeNeLux (Belgium, the Netherlands, and Luxembourg) and either France or Germany; Eurail Select Passes (or a Global Pass) make sense if you're touring the Netherlands and Belgium as part of a larger trip (see sidebar).

Reservations for Railpass Holders: Regional and InterCity trains do not require reservations, allowing you plenty of flexibility as you explore Benelux. Between Amsterdam-Brussels or Brussels-Köln, fast Thalys trains cost more (for point-to-point tickets) or require expensive reservations with a railpass, so I'd choose a Fyra train if going to Brussels (reservation €4-6) or an ICE train if going to Köln (reservation optional). The only direct service from Amsterdam, Brussels, or Köln to Paris is by Thalys, with reservations costing €25-60 in addition to a pass that covers BeNeLux and France. To avoid Thalys fees when heading from Bruges or Brussels to Paris, you can take a little more time and connect in Lille to a TGV with cheaper (but limited) €5-15 reservations. Note that you can buy a Thalys ticket if you don't have a railpass; you'll simply pay more for it.

Eurostar: Any pass that covers Belgium allows you a discounted ticket price on the Eurostar to/from London. (For information on the Eurostar train, see page 527.)

Buses

While you'll mostly use trains to travel in this region, a few destinations (for example, the tulip gardens of Keukenhof, the flower auction in Aalsmeer, or the Kröller-Müller Museum near Arnhem) are reachable only by bus.

Confusingly, there's no unified national bus company for the Netherlands or Belgium—various destinations are served by different companies. Arriva (www.arriva.nl) and Connexxion (www.connexxion.nl) are the main companies serving the Netherlands. The best public transit website in the Netherlands for bus schedules is www.9292.nl. In Belgium, Flanders is served largely by De Lijn (www.delijn.be), while French-speaking areas have TEC (www.infotec.be).

If you'll be in the Netherlands for more than a week and plan to ride a lot of trams and buses, it might make sense to buy an **OV-Chipkaart**—a smartcard that the locals use (see www.ov-chipkaart.nl). You can save money with the card—a €2.80 trip on the Amsterdam tram costs around €1.50 with the OV-Chipkaart—but there are drawbacks: You'll pay €7.50 to buy the card, plus whatever amount you load onto it. You can only add money at train stations and Amsterdam Metro stations—that's more waiting in line unless you have coins to stuff into a ticket machine. Any money left on the card won't be refunded at the end of your trip, and you can't return the card for a refund. If you think it's worth the hassle, ask for an "anonymous" OV-Chipkaart at bookstores, tobacco shops, or train and bus stations; it will come preloaded with €10 for travel.

Renting a Car

If you're renting a car in the Low Countries, bring your driver's license. In the Netherlands, you're also required to have an International Driving Permit—an official translation of your driver's license (sold at your local AAA office for $15 plus the cost of two passport-type photos; see www.aaa.com). While that's the letter of the law, I've often rented cars in the Netherlands without having this permit. If all goes well, you'll likely never be asked to show this permit—but it's a must if you end up dealing with the police.

Rental companies require you to be at least 21 years old and to have held your license for one year. Drivers under the age of 25 may incur a young-driver surcharge, and some rental companies do not rent to anyone 75 and over. If you're considered too young or old, look into leasing (covered later), which has less-stringent age restrictions.

Research car rentals before you go. It's cheaper to arrange most car rentals from the US. Call several companies and look online to compare rates, or arrange a rental through your home-town travel agent.

Most of the major US rental agencies (including National, Avis, Budget, Hertz, and Thrifty) have offices throughout Europe. Also consider the two major Europe-based agencies, Europcar and Sixt. It can be cheaper to use a consolidator, such as Auto Europe (www.autoeurope.com) or Europe by Car (www.ebctravel.com), which compares rates at several companies to get you the best deal. However, my readers have reported problems with consolidators, ranging from misinformation to unexpected fees; because you're going through a middleman, it can be more challenging to resolve disputes that arise with the rental agency.

Regardless of the car-rental company you choose, always read the contract carefully. The fine print can conceal a host of common add-on charges—such as one-way drop-off fees, airport surcharges, or mandatory insurance policies—that aren't included in the "total price," but can be tacked on when you pick up your car. You may need to query rental agents pointedly to find out your actual cost.

For the best deal, rent by the week with unlimited mileage. To save money on fuel, ask for a diesel car. I normally rent the smallest, least-expensive model with a stick shift (cheaper than an automatic). An automatic transmission adds about 50 percent to the car-rental cost over a manual transmission. Almost all rentals are manual by default, so if you need an automatic, you must request one in advance; be aware that these cars are usually larger models (not as maneuverable on narrow roads).

For a three-week rental, allow roughly $900 per person—based on two people sharing rental fees, gas, and insurance. For trips of this length, look into leasing; you'll save money on insurance and taxes. Be warned that international trips—say, picking up in Amsterdam and dropping off in Paris—can be expensive (it depends partly on distance).

You can sometimes get a GPS unit with your rental car or

leased vehicle for an additional fee (around $15/day; be sure it's set to English and has all the maps you need before you drive off). Or, if you have a portable GPS device at home, consider taking it with you to Europe (buy and upload European maps before your trip). GPS apps are also available for smartphones, but downloading maps on one of these apps in Europe could lead to an exorbitant data-roaming bill (for more details, see the sidebar on page 606).

Big companies have offices in most cities; ask whether they can pick you up at your hotel. Small local rental companies can be cheaper but aren't as flexible.

Compare pickup costs (downtown can be less expensive than the airport) and explore drop-off options. When selecting a location, don't trust the agency's description of "downtown" or "city center." In some cases, a "downtown" branch can be on the outskirts of the city—a long, costly taxi ride from the center. Before choosing, plug the addresses into a mapping website. You may find that the "train station" location is handier. Returning a car at a big-city train station or downtown agency can be tricky; get precise details on the car drop-off location and hours, and allow ample time to find it. Note that rental offices usually close from midday Saturday until Monday morning.

When you pick up the rental car, check it thoroughly and make sure any damage is noted on your rental agreement. Find out how your car's lights, turn signals, wipers, and fuel cap function, and know what kind of fuel the car takes. When you return the car, make sure the agent verifies its condition with you.

Car Insurance Options

When you rent a car, you are liable for a very high deductible, sometimes equal to the entire value of the car. Limit your financial risk by choosing one of these three options: Buy Collision Damage Waiver (CDW) coverage from the car-rental company, get coverage through your credit card (free, if your card automatically includes zero-deductible coverage), or buy coverage through Travel Guard.

CDW includes a very high deductible (typically $1,000-1,500). Though each rental company has its own variation, basic CDW costs $15-35 a day (figure roughly 30 percent extra) and reduces your liability, but does not eliminate it. When you pick up the car, you'll be offered the chance to "buy down" the basic deductible to zero (for an additional $10-30/day; this is sometimes called "super CDW").

If you opt for **credit-card coverage**, there's a catch. You'll technically have to decline all coverage offered by the car-rental company, which means they can place a hold on your card (which can be up to the full value of the car). In case of damage, it can be time-consuming to resolve the charges with your credit-card company. Before you decide on this option, quiz your credit-card company about how it works.

Finally, you can buy collision insurance from **Travel Guard** ($9/day plus a one-time $3 service fee covers you for up to $35,000, $250 deductible, tel. 800-826-4919, www.travelguard.com). It's valid everywhere in Europe except the Republic of Ireland, and some Italian car-rental companies refuse to honor it. Note that various states differ on which products and policies are available to their residents.

For more on car-rental insurance, see www.ricksteves.com/cdw.

Leasing

For trips of three weeks or more, consider leasing (which automatically includes zero-deductible collision and theft insurance). By technically buying and then selling back the car, you save lots of money on tax and insurance. Leasing provides you a brand-new car with unlimited mileage and a 24-hour emergency assistance program. You can lease for as little as 21 days to as long as six months. Car leases must be arranged from the US. One of many companies offering affordable lease packages is Europe by Car (US tel. 800-223-1516, www.ebctravel.com).

Driving

Road Rules: Traffic cameras are everywhere in the Netherlands and Belgium; speeding tickets for even a few kilometers over the limit are common. In both countries, kids under age 12 (or less than about 5 feet tall) must ride in an appropriate child-safety seat. Seat belts are mandatory for all, and two beers under those belts are enough to land you in jail. Be aware of other typical European road rules; for example, many countries require headlights to be turned on at all times, and it's illegal to drive while using your mobile phone without a hands-free headset. In Europe, you're not allowed to turn right on a red light, unless there is a sign or signal specifically authorizing it. Ask your car-rental company about these rules, or check the US State Department website (www.travel.state.gov, search for your country in the "Learn about your destination" box, then click on "Travel and Transportation").

Fuel: Gas (*benzine* in Dutch, *essence* in French) is expensive—about $8-9 per gallon. Diesel (*diesel or dieselolie* in Dutch, *gazole* in French) is less—about $7 per gallon—and diesel cars get better mileage, so try to rent a diesel to save money. Be sure you know what type of fuel your car takes before you fill up. Gas is most expensive on freeways and cheapest at big supermarkets. About 30 percent of the filling stations in the Netherlands are unmanned, and your US credit and debit cards may not work at self-service gas pumps. Look for stations with an attendant or be sure to carry sufficient cash in euros.

Parking: Finding a parking place can be a headache in larger cities. Ask your hotelier for ideas, and pay to park at well-patrolled lots (blue *P* signs direct you to parking lots). Parking structures usually require that you take a ticket with you and pay at a machine on your way back to the car. US credit cards may not work in these automated machines but euro coins (and sometimes bills) will.

Cheap Flights

If you're visiting other countries in Europe, a flight may save you both time and money. When comparing your options, factor in the time it takes to get to the airport and how early you'll need to arrive to check in.

The best comparison search engine for both international and intra-European flights is www.kayak.com. For inexpensive flights within Europe, try www.skyscanner.com or www.hipmunk.com. If you're not sure who flies to your destination, check its airport's website for a list of carriers.

Well-known cheapo airlines include easyJet (www.easyjet .com) and Ryanair (www.ryanair.com), along with Amsterdam-based Transavia (www.transavia.com) and Brussels Airlines (www .brusselsairlines.com).

Be aware of the potential drawbacks of flying on the cheap: nonrefundable and nonchangeable tickets, minimal or nonexistent customer service, treks to airports far outside town, and stingy baggage allowances with steep overage fees. If you're traveling with lots of luggage, a cheap flight can quickly become a bad deal. To avoid unpleasant surprises, read the small print before you book.

Resources

Resources from Rick Steves

Rick Steves' Amsterdam, Bruges & Brussels is one of many books in my series on European travel, which includes country guidebooks, city and regional guidebooks, Snapshot guides (excerpted chapters from my country guides), Pocket guides (full-color little books on big cities), and my budget-travel skills handbook, *Rick Steves' Europe Through the Back Door*. Most of my titles are available as ebooks. My phrase books—for German, French, Italian, Spanish, and Portuguese—are practical and budget-oriented. My other books include *Europe 101* (a

Begin Your Trip at www.ricksteves.com

At our travel website, you'll find a wealth of free information on European destinations, including fresh monthly news and helpful tips from thousands of fellow travelers. You'll also find my latest guidebook updates (www.ricksteves.com/update), a monthly travel e-newsletter (easy and free to sign up), my personal travel blog, and my free Rick Steves Audio Europe smartphone app (if you don't have a smartphone, you can access the same content via podcasts). You can even follow me on Facebook and Twitter.

Our **online Travel Store** offers travel bags and accessories specially designed to help you travel smarter and lighter. These include my popular carry-on bags (rolling carry-on and backpack versions), money belts, totes, toiletries kits, adapters, other accessories, and a wide selection of guidebooks, journals, planning maps, and DVDs.

Choosing the right **railpass** for your trip—amidst hundreds of options—can drive you nutty. We'll help you choose the best pass for your needs, plus give you a bunch of free extras.

Want to travel with greater efficiency and less stress? We organize **tours** with more than three dozen itineraries and 500 departures reaching the best destinations in this book... and beyond. We offer an 11-day Heart of Belgium and Holland tour and a 21-day tour of Europe that includes Amsterdam and Haarlem. You'll enjoy great guides, a fun bunch of travel partners (with small groups of generally around 24-28), and plenty of room to spread out in a big, comfy bus. You'll find European adventures to fit every vacation length. For all the details, and to get our Tour Catalog and a free Rick Steves Tour Experience DVD (filmed on location during an actual tour), visit www.ricksteves.com or call our Tour Department at 425/608-4217.

APPENDIX

crash course on art and history), *Northern European Cruise Ports* and *Mediterranean Cruise Ports* (how to make the most of your time in port), and *Travel as a Political Act* (a travelogue sprinkled with tips for bringing home a global perspective). A more complete list of my titles appears near the end of this book.

Video: My public television series, *Rick Steves' Europe*, covers European destinations in 100 shows, with two shows on the Low Countries. To watch episodes online, visit www.hulu.com; for scripts and local airtimes, see www.ricksteves.com/tv.

Audio: My weekly public radio show, *Travel with Rick Steves*, features interviews with travel experts from around the world. I've also produced free, self-guided **audio tours** of the top walks in Amsterdam. All of this audio content is available for free at Rick Steves Audio Europe, an extensive online library organized by destination. Choose whatever interests you, and download it for free via the Rick Steves Audio Europe smartphone app, www.ricksteves.com/audioeurope, iTunes, or Google Play.

Maps

The black-and-white maps in this book, drawn by Dave Hoerlein, are concise and simple. Dave, who is well-traveled in the Low Countries, has designed the maps to help you locate recommended places and get to local TIs, where you can pick up more in-depth maps of cities and regions. Consider buying a city map at any of the cities' TIs for a euro or two. Before you buy a map, look at it to make sure it has the level of detail you want. For most Belgian cities, look for Use It tourist maps, designed by locals and geared for backpackers, but loaded with insight and informative for anyone.

Other Guidebooks

If you're like most travelers, this book is all you need. But if you're heading beyond my recommended destinations, $40 for extra maps and books is money well-spent.

The following books are worthwhile, though most are not updated annually; check the publication date before you buy. Historians like the green Michelin guides and the Cadogan series; both have individual books on all three cities—Amsterdam, Bruges, and Brussels. Others go for the well-illustrated Eyewitness guides (titles include *Amsterdam; Holland;* and *Brussels/Bruges/ Ghent/Antwerp*). The Lonely Planet series (which has books on Amsterdam, the Netherlands, and Belgium & Luxembourg) is well researched and geared for a mature audience. Students and vagabonds enjoy *Let's Go: Amsterdam* (updated annually) for its coverage of hosteling, nightlife, and the student scene.

Recommended Books and Movies

To learn more about the Netherlands and Belgium past and present, check out some of these books and films.

Nonfiction

If you're interested in the WWII years in the Netherlands, read *The Diary of a Young Girl* (Anne Frank), *The Hiding Place* (Corrie ten Boom), and *A Bridge Too Far* (the story of the battle of Arnhem, by Cornelius Ryan).

Amsterdam (Mak) is an academic but engaging look at centuries of the city's history. Equally comprehensive is Simon Schama's *The Embarrassment of Riches: An Interpretation of Dutch Culture in the Golden Age*. Covering a similar time frame, *Daily Life in Rembrandt's Holland* (Zumthor) focuses more on the everyday concerns of Dutch society in the 17th century.

Tulipmania (Dash) is about the Golden Age financial craze. Holland was at the center of the spice trade back when a pinch of cinnamon was worth its weight in gold. For engaging histories of these times, try *Spice: The History of a Temptation* (Turner) and *Nathaniel's Nutmeg: Or the True and Incredible Adventures of the Spice Trader Who Changed the Course of History* (Milton).

The Undutchables: An Observation of the Netherlands, Its Culture and Its Inhabitants (White and Boucke) is an irreverent guide to modern Dutch culture. *My 'Dam Life: Three Years in Holland* (Condon) is a humorous account of adventures in a low country.

Fans of Vincent may want to consider *Dear Theo: The Autobiography of Vincent van Gogh,* edited by Irving Stone. (Stone also wrote the fictional book about Van Gogh, *Lust for Life*.)

If you're visiting Belgium and have an interest in World War I, read Barbara Tuchman's Pulitzer Prize-winning book, *The Guns of August*. For a look at contemporary Belgium, try *A Tall Man in a Low Land* (Pearson).

Fiction

Set in 17th-century Holland, Alexandre Dumas' *The Black Tulip* tells a swashbuckling story of fortunes held in the balance. *Max Havelaar: Or the Coffee Auctions of the Dutch Trading Company* is another literary classic, in which the author, Multatuli, writes of the injustices of the Dutch colonial system in Indonesia.

For more modern reads, best sellers set in Holland include *Girl in Hyacinth Blue* (Vreeland), *Girl with a Pearl Earring* (Chevalier), *Tulip Fever* (Moggach), and *Confessions of an Ugly Stepsister* (Maguire). For Belgium, consider *Resistance* (Shreve) and

The Adventures of Tintin (featuring the famous Belgian comic-book character, by Hergé).

Films

Vincent and Theo (1990) captures the relationship between the great artist and his brother. *Girl with a Pearl Earring* (2003) shows a fictionalized Vermeer in love with his servant in Delft.

The Diary of Anne Frank (1959) is a good version of Anne's story, which has been translated into film and theater many times. Paul Verhoeven's *Soldier of Orange* (1977) delves into the bleak WWII years (it's also a fine book). In *Black Book* (2006)—another Verhoeven film, which was filmed in Holland—a sexy blonde bombshell fights for the Dutch Resistance.

Set partially in the modern era, *Antonia's Line* (1995) tells the story of five generations of Dutch women. *Ocean's Twelve* (2004) has many scenes set in Amsterdam's Jordaan neighborhood. The dark and violent comedy *In Bruges* (2008) was filmed just where you'd think.

Holidays and Festivals

This list includes selected festivals in major cities, plus national holidays. Many sights and banks close on national holidays—keep this in mind when planning your itinerary. Before planning a trip around a festival, make sure you verify its dates by checking the festival's website or the national TI websites: www.holland.com and www.visitbelgium.com; www.whatsonwhen.com also lists many festival dates.

Here are some major holidays:

Jan 1	New Year's Day
Feb	Carnival (Mardi Gras)
March-May	Keukenhof flower show, Lisse, Netherlands (www.keukenhof.nl)
Easter Weekend	Good Friday through Easter Monday (April 18-21 in 2014, April 3-6 in 2015)
April	Flower Parade (April 26 in 2014, www.bloemencorso-bollenstreek.nl), Noordwijk to Haarlem, Netherlands
April 27	King's Day (Koningsdag), King Willem-Alexander's birthday, party in the streets of Amsterdam (held on April 26 in 2014)
May 1	Labor Day (some closures in Belgium)
May 4	Remembrance of WWII Dead (Dodenherdenking), Netherlands

May 5	Liberation Day (Bevrijdingsdag), Netherlands
May	Art Amsterdam—contemporary-art exhibition (May 15-20 in 2014, www.kunstrai.nl), Amsterdam
May or June	Ascension (May 29 in 2014, May 14 in 2015); Procession of the Holy Blood (takes place on Ascension day), Bruges
May or June	Pentecost (June 8 in 2014, May 24 in 2015)
Mid-June	Grachtenloop run around canals, www.grachtenloop.nl), Haarlem
June	Holland Arts Festival (concerts, theater, etc., www.hollandfestival.nl), Amsterdam
June	Amsterdam Roots Festival—Oosterpark (ethnic food, music, world culture; www.amsterdamroots.nl)
June	The Hague Festivals—three weeks of music festivals: Festival Classique, Parkpop, and The Hague jazz (www.thehaguefestivals.com)
Late June/early July	Ommegang Pageant—historic costumed parade to Grand Place (www.ommegang.be), Brussels
Mid-July	North Sea Jazz Festival (July 12-14 in 2013, www.northseajazz.nl), The Hague
July 21	Belgian Independence Day (parades, fireworks)
Early Aug	Gay Pride (Aug 2-4 in 2013, www.amsterdamgaypride.nl), Amsterdam
Early-mid-Aug	Pluk de Nacht—outdoor film festival on the site of an old harbor (www.plukdenacht.nl), Amsterdam
Aug 15	Assumption Day, Procession in Bruges
Mid-Aug	Prinsengracht canal concert on barges—music and other festivities (Aug 16-25 in 2013, www.grachtenfestival.nl), Amsterdam
Aug	Carpet of Flowers (celebrated only in even years, next in 2014, www.flowercarpet.be), Brussels
Aug	Open-air spectacle staged on the canals, held every three years, next in 2014 (Reiefeesten, www.reiefeest.be), Bruges

Late Aug	Haarlem Jazz—free jazz festival held on Grote Markt (third weekend of August, www.haarlemjazzstad.nl)
Sept (first week)	Flower parade on canals, Aalsmeer to Amsterdam
Mid-Sept	Jordaan Festival—neighborhood street party (www.jordaanfestival.nl), Amsterdam
Sept or Oct	Yom Kippur (Sept 13-14 in 2013, Oct 3-4 in 2014, Jewish holiday, some closures, including Anne Frank House and Jewish Historical Museum in Amsterdam)
Nov 1	All Saints' Day, Belgium
Nov 11	Armistice Day (banks closed), Belgium
Mid-Nov	Sinterklaas ("Santa Claus") procession, Amsterdam
Dec	"Winter Wonders" European Christmas Market (www.plaisirsdhiver.be), Brussels
Dec 5	St. Nicholas' Eve (Sinterklaasavond, when Sinterklaas and Zwarte Piet arrive), procession and presents
Dec 25	Christmas
Dec 26	"Second Day" of Christmas (Tweede Kerstdag), Netherlands

Conversions and Climate

Numbers and Stumblers

- Europeans write a few of their numbers differently than we do. 1 = 1, 4 = 4, 7 = 7.
- In Europe, dates appear as day/month/year, so Christmas is 25/12/12.
- Commas are decimal points, and decimal points are commas. A dollar and a half is 1,50, one thousand is 1.000, and there are 5.280 feet in a mile.
- When pointing, use your whole hand, palm down.
- When counting with fingers, start with your thumb. If you hold up your first finger to request one item, you'll probably get two.
- What Americans call the second floor of a building is the first floor in Europe.
- On escalators and moving sidewalks, Europeans keep the left "lane" open for passing. Keep to the right.

APPENDIX

Metric Conversions (approximate)

A kilogram is 2.2 pounds, and 1 liter is about a quart, or almost four to a gallon. A kilometer is six-tenths of a mile. I figure kilometers to miles by cutting them in half and adding back 10 percent of the original (120 km: 60 + 12 = 72 miles, 300 km: 150 + 30 = 180 miles).

1 foot = 0.3 meter	1 square yard = 0.8 square meter
1 yard = 0.9 meter	1 square mile = 2.6 square kilometers
1 mile = 1.6 kilometers	1 ounce = 28 grams
1 centimeter = 0.4 inch	1 quart = 0.95 liter
1 meter = 39.4 inches	1 kilogram = 2.2 pounds
1 kilometer = 0.62 mile	32°F = 0°C

Clothing Sizes

When shopping for clothing, use these US-to-European comparisons as general guidelines (but note that no conversion is perfect).

- Women's dresses and blouses: Add 30
  (US size 10 = European size 40)
- Men's suits and jackets: Add 10
  (US size 40 regular = European size 50)
- Men's shirts: Multiply by 2 and add about 8
  (US size 15 collar = European size 38)
- Women's shoes: Add about 30
  (US size 8 = European size 38-39)
- Men's shoes: Add 32-34
  (US size 9 = European size 41; US size 11 = European size 45)

The Low Countries' Climate

The first line is the average daily high; the second line, the average daily low; the third line, average days without rain. For more detailed weather statistics for destinations throughout the Low Countries (as well as the rest of the world), check www.world climate.com.

J	F	M	A	M	J	J	A	S	O	N	D
Amsterdam											
41°	42°	49°	55°	64°	70°	72°	71°	66°	56°	48°	41°
30°	31°	35°	40°	45°	52°	55°	55°	51°	43°	37°	33°
8	9	16	14	16	16	14	12	11	11	10	9
Brussels											
41°	44°	51°	58°	65°	71°	73°	72°	69°	60°	48°	42°
30°	32°	34°	40°	45°	53°	55°	55°	52°	45°	38°	32°
9	11	14	12	15	15	13	12	15	13	10	11

Temperature Conversion: Fahrenheit and Celsius

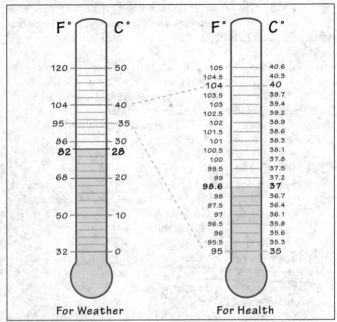

For Weather   For Health

Europe takes its temperature using the Celsius scale, while we opt for Fahrenheit. For a rough conversion from Celsius to Fahrenheit, double the number and add 30. For weather, remember that 28°C is 82°F— perfect. For health, 37°C is just right.

Packing Checklist

Whether you're traveling for five days or five weeks, here's what you'll need to bring. Pack light to enjoy the sweet freedom of true mobility. Happy travels!

- ❏ 5 shirts: long- and short-sleeve
- ❏ 1 sweater or lightweight fleece
- ❏ 2 pairs of pants
- ❏ 1 pair of shorts
- ❏ 5 pairs of underwear and socks
- ❏ 1 pair of shoes
- ❏ 1 rainproof jacket with hood
- ❏ Tie or scarf
- ❏ Sleepwear
- ❏ Swimsuit
- ❏ Money belt
- ❏ Money—your mix of:
  - ❏ Debit card
  - ❏ Credit card(s)
  - ❏ Hard cash ($20 bills)
- ❏ Documents plus photocopies:
  - ❏ Passport
  - ❏ Printout of airline eticket
  - ❏ Driver's license
  - ❏ Student ID, hostel card, etc.
  - ❏ Railpass/train reservations/ car-rental voucher
  - ❏ Insurance details
- ❏ Guidebooks and maps
- ❏ Address list for postcards
- ❏ Notepad and pen
- ❏ Journal
- ❏ Daypack
- ❏ Electronics—your choice of:
  - ❏ Camera (and related gear)
  - ❏ Mobile phone

- ❏ Portable media player (iPod or other)
- ❏ Laptop/netbook/tablet
- ❏ Ebook reader
- ❏ Headphones or earbuds
- ❏ Chargers for each of the above
- ❏ Plug adapter(s)
- ❏ Alarm clock
- ❏ Earplugs
- ❏ Toiletries kit
  - ❏ Toiletries
  - ❏ Medicines and vitamins
  - ❏ First-aid kit
  - ❏ Glasses/contacts/ sunglasses (with prescriptions)
- ❏ Sealable plastic baggies
- ❏ Laundry soap
- ❏ Clothesline
- ❏ Small towel/washcloth
- ❏ Sewing kit

If you plan to carry on your luggage, note that all liquids must be in 3.4-ounce or smaller containers and fit within a single quart-size sealable baggie. For details, see www.tsa.gov.

Hotel Reservation

To: _____   _____
                hotel   *email or fax*

From: _____   _____
                name   *email or fax*

Today's date: _____ /_____ /_____
                      day   *month*   *year*

Dear Hotel _____ ,
Please make this reservation for me:

Name: _____

Total # of people: _____   # of rooms: _____   # of nights: _____

Arriving: _____ /_____ /_____   My time of arrival (24-hr clock): _____
              day   month   year   (I will telephone if I will be late)

Departing: _____ /_____ /_____
                day   month   year

Room(s): Single____   Double ____   Twin____   Triple ____   Quad____

With: Toilet ____   Shower____   Bath ____   Sink only ____

Special needs: View____   Quiet____   Cheapest ____   Ground Floor____

Please email or fax confirmation of my reservation, along with the type of
room reserved and the price. Please also inform me of your cancellation
policy. After I hear from you, I will quickly send my credit-card information
as a deposit to hold the room. Thank you.

_____
Name

_____
Address

_____
City   *State*   *Zip Code*   *Country*

*Before hoteliers can make your reservation, they want to know the informa-
tion listed above. You can use this form as the basis for your email, or you can
photocopy this page, fill in the information, and send it as a fax (also available
online at www.ricksteves.com/reservation).*

Dutch Survival Phrases

You won't need to learn Dutch, but knowing a few phrases can help if you're traveling off the beaten path. Taking a few moments to learn the pleasantries (such as please and thank you) will improve your connections with locals even in the bigger cities. In northern Belgium, they also speak Dutch, but with a Flemish accent.

To pronounce the difficult Dutch "g" (indicated in phonetics by hhh) make a hard, guttural, clear-your-throat sound, similar to the "ch" in the Scottish word "loch."

Hello.	**Hallo.**	hol-LOH
Good day.	**Dag.**	dahhh
Good morning.	**Goeiemorgen.**	hhhoy-ah MOR-hhhen
Good afternoon.	**Goeiemiddag.**	hhhoy-ah MIT-tahk
Ma'am	**Mevrouw**	meh-frow
Sir	**Meneer**	men-ear
Yes	**Ja**	yah
No	**Nee**	nay
Please	**Alstublieft**	AHL-stoo-bleeft
Thank you.	**Dank u wel.**	dahnk yoo vehl
You're welcome.	**Graag gedaan.**	hhhrahhk hhkeh-dahn
Excuse me.	**Pardon.**	par-DOHN
Do you speak English?	**Spreekt u Engels?**	spraykt oo ENG-els
Okay.	**Oké.**	"okay"
Goodbye.	**Tot ziens.**	toht zeens
one / two	**een / twee**	ayn / t'vay
three / four	**drie / vier**	dree / feer
five / six	**vijf / zes**	fife / ses
seven / eight	**zeven / acht**	say-fen / ahkht
nine / ten	**negen / tien**	nay-hhhen / teen
What does it cost?	**Wat kost?**	vaht kost
I would like...	**Ik wil graag...**	ik vil hhhrahhhk
...a room.	**...een kamer.**	un kah-mer
...a ticket.	**...een kaart.**	un kart
...a bike.	**...een fiets.**	un feets
Where is...?	**Waar is...?**	vahr is
...the station	**...het station**	het sta-tsee-on
...the tourist info office	**...de VVV**	duh vay vay vay
left / right	**links / rechts**	links / rechts
open / closed	**open / gesloten**	"open" / hhhe-sloh-ten

In the Restaurant

Dutch speakers have an all-purpose word, alstublieft (AHL-stoo-bleeft), that means: "Please," or "Here you are," (if handing you something), or "Thanks," (if taking payment from you), or "You're welcome" (when handing you change). Here are other words that might come in handy at restaurants, particularly if you're day-tripping to small towns:

I would like...	Ik wil graag...	ik vil hhhrahhk
...a cup of coffee.	...kopje koffie.	kop-yeh "coffee"
menu	menu	muh-NOO
non-smoking	niet-roken	neet roh-ken
smoking	roken	roh-ken
with / without	met / buiten	met / bow-ten
and / or	en / of	en / of
bread	brood	broht
salad	sla	slah
cheese	kaas	kahs
meat	vlees	flays
chicken	kip	kip
fish	vis	fis
egg	ei	eye
fruit	vrucht	frucht
pastries	gebak	hhhe-bak
water	water	WAH-tuhr
beer	bier	beer
wine	wijn	wayn
coffee	koffie	"coffee"
tea	thee	tay
I am vegetarian.	Ik ben vegetarish.	ik ben vay-hhhe-tah-rish
Tasty.	Lekker.	lek-ker
Enjoy!	Smakelijk!	smak-kuh-luk
Cheers!	Proost!	prohst
The bill, please.	De rekening, alstublieft.	duh Ray-kun-ing AHL-stoo-bleeft

French Survival Phrases

When using the phonetics, try to nasalize the <u>n</u> sound.

Good day.	**Bonjour.**	bohn-zhoor
Mrs. / Mr.	**Madame / Monsieur**	mah-dahm / muhs-yur
Do you speak English?	**Parlez-vous anglais?**	par-lay-voo ahn-glay
Yes. / No.	**Oui. / Non.**	wee / nohn
I understand.	**Je comprends.**	zhuh kohn-prahn
I don't understand.	**Je ne comprends pas.**	zhuh nuh kohn-prahn pah
Please.	**S'il vous plaît.**	see voo play
Thank you.	**Merci.**	mehr-see
I'm sorry.	**Désolé.**	day-zoh-lay
Excuse me.	**Pardon.**	par-dohn
(No) problem.	**(Pas de) problème.**	(pah duh) proh-blehm
It's good.	**C'est bon.**	say bohn
Goodbye.	**Au revoir.**	oh vwahr
one / two	**un / deux**	uhn / duh
three / four	**trois / quatre**	twah / kah-truh
five / six	**cinq / six**	sank / sees
seven / eight	**sept / huit**	seht / weet
nine / ten	**neuf / dix**	nuhf / dees
How much is it?	**Combien?**	kohn-bee-an
Write it?	**Ecrivez?**	ay-kree-vay
Is it free?	**C'est gratuit?**	say grah-twee
Included?	**Inclus?**	an-klew
Where can I buy / find...?	**Où puis-je acheter / trouver...?**	oo pwee-zhuh ah-shuh-tay / troo-vay
I'd like / We'd like...	**Je voudrais / Nous voudrions...**	zhuh voo-dray / noo voo-dree-ohn
...a room.	**...une chambre.**	ewn shahn-bruh
...a ticket to ___.	**...un billet pour ___.**	uhn bee-yay poor
Is it possible?	**C'est possible?**	say poh-see-bluh
Where is...?	**Où est...?**	oo ay
...the train station	**...la gare**	lah gar
...the bus station	**...la gare routière**	lah gar root-yehr
...tourist information	**...l'office du tourisme**	loh-fees dew too-reez-muh
Where are the toilets?	**Où sont les toilettes?**	oo sohn lay twah-leht
men	**hommes**	ohm
women	**dames**	dahm
left / right	**à gauche / à droite**	ah gohsh / ah dwaht
straight	**tout droit**	too dwah
When does this open / close?	**Ça ouvre / ferme à quelle heure?**	sah oo-vruh / fehrm ah kehl ur
At what time?	**À quelle heure?**	ah kehl ur
Just a moment.	**Un moment.**	uhn moh-mahn
now / soon / later	**maintenant / bientôt / plus tard**	man-tuh-nahn / bee-an-toh / plew tar
today / tomorrow	**aujourd'hui / demain**	oh-zhoor-dwee / duh-man

In a French-speaking Restaurant

I'd like / We'd like...	**Je voudrais / Nous voudrions...**	zhuh voo-dray / noo voo-dree-oh<u>n</u>
...to reserve...	**...réserver...**	ray-zehr-vay
...a table for one / two.	**...une table pour un / deux.**	ewn tah-bluh poor uh<u>n</u> / duh
Non-smoking.	**Non fumeur.**	noh<u>n</u> few-mur
Is this seat free?	**C'est libre?**	say lee-bruh
The menu (in English), please.	**La carte (en anglais), s'il vous plaît.**	lah kart (ah<u>n</u> ah<u>n</u>-glay) see voo play
service (not) included	**service (non) compris**	sehr-vees (noh<u>n</u>) koh<u>n</u>-pree
to go	**à emporter**	ah ah<u>n</u>-por-tay
with / without	**avec / sans**	ah-vehk / sah<u>n</u>
and / or	**et / ou**	ay / oo
special of the day	**plat du jour**	plah dew zhoor
specialty of the house	**spécialité de la maison**	spay-see-ah-lee-tay duh lah may-zoh<u>n</u>
appetizers	**hors-d'oeuvre**	or-duh-vruh
first course (soup, salad)	**entrée**	ah<u>n</u>-tray
main course (meat, fish)	**plat principal**	plah pra<u>n</u>-see-pahl
bread	**pain**	pa<u>n</u>
cheese	**fromage**	froh-mahzh
sandwich	**sandwich**	sah<u>n</u>d-weech
soup	**soupe**	soop
salad	**salade**	sah-lahd
meat	**viande**	vee-ah<u>n</u>d
chicken	**poulet**	poo-lay
fish	**poisson**	pwah-soh<u>n</u>
seafood	**fruits de mer**	frwee duh mehr
fruit	**fruit**	frwee
vegetables	**légumes**	lay-gewm
dessert	**dessert**	duh-sehr
mineral water	**eau minérale**	oh mee-nay-rahl
tap water	**l'eau du robinet**	loh dew roh-bee-nay
milk	**lait**	lay
(orange) juice	**jus (d'orange)**	zhew (doh-rah<u>n</u>zh)
coffee	**café**	kah-fay
tea	**thé**	tay
wine	**vin**	va<u>n</u>
red / white	**rouge / blanc**	roozh / blah<u>n</u>
glass / bottle	**verre / bouteille**	vehr / boo-teh-ee
beer	**bière**	bee-ehr
Cheers!	**Santé!**	sah<u>n</u>-tay
More. / Another.	**Plus. / Un autre.**	plew / uh<u>n</u> oh-truh
The same.	**La même chose.**	lah mehm shohz
The bill, please.	**L'addition, s'il vous plaît.**	lah-dee-see-oh<u>n</u> see voo play
tip	**pourboire**	poor-bwar
Delicious!	**Délicieux!**	day-lee-see-uh

For more user-friendly French phrases, check out *Rick Steves' French Phrase Book and Dictionary* or *Rick Steves' French, Italian & German Phrase Book.*

INDEX

INDEX

MAP INDEX

Rick's Free Travel App

Join a Rick Steves tour

Enjoy Europe's warmest welcome... with the flexibility and friendship of a small group getting to know Rick's favorite places and people. It all starts with our free tour catalog and DVD.

Great guides, small groups, no grumps.

See more than three dozen itineraries throughout Europe

Free information and great gear to

▸ Explore Europe

Browse thousands of articles, video clips, photos and radio interviews, plus find a wealth of money-saving tips for planning your dream trip. You'll find up-to-date information on Europe's best destinations, packing smart, getting around, finding rooms, staying healthy, avoiding scams and more.

▸ Travel News

Subscribe to our free Travel News e-newsletter, and get monthly updates from Rick on what's happening in Europe!

▸ Travel Forums

Learn, ask, share—our online community of savvy travelers is a great resource for first-time travelers to Europe, as well as seasoned pros.

Rick Steves' Europe Through the Back Door, Inc.

turn your travel dreams into affordable reality

▶ Rick's Free Audio Europe™ App

The Rick Steves Audio Europe™ app brings history and art to life. Enjoy Rick's audio tours of Europe's top museums, sights and neighborhood walks—plus hundreds of tracks including travel tips and cultural insights from Rick's radio show—all organized into geographic playlists. Learn more at ricksteves.com.

▶ Great Gear from Rick's Travel Store

Pack light and right—on a budget—with Rick's custom-designed carry-on bags, wheeled bags, day packs, travel accessories, guidebooks, journals, maps and Blu-ray/DVDs of his TV shows.

130 Fourth Avenue North, PO Box 2009 • Edmonds, WA 98020 USA
Phone: (425) 771-8303 • Fax: (425) 771-0833 • ricksteves.com

Rick Steves®

www.ricksteves.com

EUROPE GUIDES

Best of Europe
Eastern Europe
Europe Through the Back Door
Mediterranean Cruise Ports
Northern European Cruise Ports

COUNTRY GUIDES

Croatia & Slovenia
England
France
Germany
Great Britain
Ireland
Italy
Portugal
Scandinavia
Spain
Switzerland

CITY & REGIONAL GUIDES

Amsterdam, Bruges & Brussels
Barcelona
Budapest
Florence & Tuscany
Greece: Athens & the Peloponnese
Istanbul
London
Paris
Prague & the Czech Republic
Provence & the French Riviera
Rome
Venice
Vienna, Salzburg & Tirol

SNAPSHOT GUIDES

Berlin
Bruges & Brussels
Copenhagen & the Best of
    Denmark
Dublin
Dubrovnik
Hill Towns of Central Italy
Italy's Cinque Terre
Krakow, Warsaw & Gdansk
Lisbon
Madrid & Toledo
Milan & the Italian Lakes District
Munich, Bavaria & Salzburg
Naples & the Amalfi Coast
Northern Ireland
Norway
Scotland
Sevilla, Granada & Southern Spain
Stockholm

POCKET GUIDES

Amsterdam
Athens
Barcelona
Florence
London
Paris
Rome
Venice

Rick Steves guidebooks are published by Avalon Travel,
a member of the Perseus Books Group.

Credits

For help with this edition, Rick and Gene relied on...

Tom Griffin, Researcher

Tom edits and researches guidebooks for Rick Steves. As a young lad, he acquired an affinity for Dutch and Belgian culture, thanks to Paul Verhoeven movies, Belgian chocolate, and his dad's war stories about the Battle of the Bulge. Tom has lived and worked in London, Paris, and Germany, and now makes his home in Seattle with his wife, Julie.

Chapter Images

The following list identifies the chapter-opening images and credits their photographers.

Location	Photographer
Netherlands full-page: Edam	Jennifer Hauseman
Amsterdam full-page:	
Amsterdam Canal	Cameron Hewitt
Haarlem full-page: Haarlem Hofje	Rick Steves
Belgium full-page: Belgium Canal	Dominic Bonuccelli
Bruges full-page: Belgium Canal	Dominic Bonuccelli
Brussels full-page: Brussels	Rick Steves

NOW AVAILABLE:
eBOOKS, DVD & BLU-RAY

TRAVEL CULTURE

Europe 101
European Christmas
Postcards from Europe
Travel as a Political Act

eBOOKS

Nearly all Rick Steves guides are available as eBooks. Check with your favorite bookseller.

RICK STEVES' EUROPE DVDs

11 New Shows 2013–2014
Austria & the Alps
Eastern Europe
England & Wales
European Christmas
European Travel Skills & Specials
France
Germany, BeNeLux & More
Greece, Turkey & Portugal
Iran
Ireland & Scotland
Italy's Cities
Italy's Countryside
Scandinavia
Spain
Travel Extras

BLU-RAY

Celtic Charms
Eastern Europe Favorites
European Christmas
Italy Through the Back Door
Mediterranean Mosaic
Surprising Cities of Europe

PHRASE BOOKS & DICTIONARIES

French
French, Italian & German
German
Italian
Portuguese
Spanish

JOURNALS

Rick Steves' Pocket Travel Journal
Rick Steves' Travel Journal

PLANNING MAPS

Britain, Ireland & London
Europe
France & Paris
Germany, Austria & Switzerland
Ireland
Italy
Spain & Portugal

Rick Steves books and DVDs are available at bookstores and through online booksellers.